JOHN DONNE AND THE METAPHYSICAL POETS

Bloom's Classic Critical Views

JOHN DONNE AND THE METAPHYSICAL POETS

Edited and with an Introduction by
Harold Bloom
Sterling Professor of the Humanities
Yale University

 BLOOM'S
LITERARY CRITICISM
An imprint of Infobase Publishing

Bloom's Classic Critical Views: John Donne and the Metaphysical Poets

Copyright © 2008 Infobase Publishing

Introduction © 2008 by Harold Bloom

Bloom's Literary Criticism
An imprint of Infobase Publishing
132 West 31st Street
New York NY 10001

Library of Congress Cataloging-in-Publication Data
John Donne and the metaphysical poets / edited and with an introduction by Harold Bloom.
    p. cm. — (Bloom's classic critical views)
  A selection of older literary criticism on John Donne.
  Includes bibliographical references and index.
  ISBN 978-1-60413-139-0 (hardcover : acid-free paper) 1. Donne, John, 1572–1631—Criticism and interpretation. I. Bloom, Harold. II. Title. III. Series.

  PR2248.J593 2008
  821'.3—dc22

                          2008008428

Contributing editor: Michael G. Cornelius
Series design by Erika K. Arroyo
Cover design by Takeshi Takahashi
Printed in the United States of America
Bang EJB 10 9 8 7 6 5 4 3 2 1

This book is printed on acid-free paper.

Contents

Series Introduction

Bloom's Classic Critical Views is a new series presenting a selection of the most important older literary criticism on the greatest authors commonly read in high school and college classes today. Unlike the Bloom's Modern Critical Views series, which for more than 20 years has provided the best contemporary criticism on great authors, Bloom's Classic Critical Views attempts to present the authors in the context of their time and to provide criticism that has proved over the years to be the most valuable to readers and writers. Selections range from contemporary reviews in popular magazines, which demonstrate how a work was received in its own era, to profound essays by some of the strongest critics in the British and American tradition, including Henry James, G.K. Chesterton, Matthew Arnold, and many more.

Some of the critical essays and extracts presented here have appeared previously in other titles edited by Harold Bloom, such as the New Moulton's Library of Literary Criticism. Other selections appear here for the first time in any book by this publisher. All were selected under Harold Bloom's guidance.

In addition, each volume in this series contains a series of essays by a contemporary expert, who comments on the most important critical selections, putting them in context and suggesting how they might be used by a student writer to influence his or her own writing. This series is intended above all for students, to help them think more deeply and write more powerfully about great writers and their works.

Introduction by Harold Bloom

1

The title of this volume is itself both a necessary misnomer and an instructive oracle of the odd processes that constitute literary history. John Donne and his disciple George Herbert both were great poets, and can be considered "metaphysical" in some of the senses given to that displaced philosophical term by the major Western literary critic, Dr. Samuel Johnson.

Andrew Marvell is as great a poet as Donne and Herbert, but remains a party-of-one, an original creator without English literary antecedents, and no affiliation to the metaphysicals. Robert Herrick, a charming poet, was a disciple of Ben Jonson, and the Sons of Ben were not metaphysicals. Richard Crashaw, though primarily the major English representative of the Catholic baroque mode (the poetry of Giambattista Marino, the sculpture of Bernini), was also a disciple of George Herbert's metaphysical devotional poetry.

Any discussion of the metaphysical poets must begin with Dr. Johnson's "Life of Cowley," the long lead-off essay in *The Lives of the Most Eminent English Poets: With Critical Observations on Their Works* (1779). Abraham Cowley is now read only by specialists and is a weak poet, whether in his vapid Pindaric odes or in his faded imitations of Donne. To the eighteenth century, he was an honored bard, though hardly in Johnson's estimate. But Johnson nodded in valuing Cowley over Donne, thus agreeing too readily with the general climate of opinion in the great critic's day.

Nevertheless Johnson's "invention" of the metaphysical poets has permanently prevailed, flowering from an ironic sentence in his "Life of Cowley":

> The metaphysical poets were men of learning, and to shew their learning was their whole endeavour; but, unluckily resolving to shew it in rhyme, instead of writing poetry, they only wrote verses, and very often such verses as stood the trial of the finger better than

of the ear; for the modulation was so imperfect, that they were only found to be verses by counting the syllables.

Johnson must mean Donne, a generation before Cowley, but who else would say of a great poet that his whole endeavor was to show his learning? What causes the strongest of critics to go so wrong? Dryden is quoted by Johnson as confessing that he falls below Donne in wit yet surpasses him in poetry. Wit is defined by Johnson "as a kind of *discordia concors*, a combination of dissimilar images or discovery of occult resemblances in things apparently unlike." That catches something of Donne; unfortunately Johnson expands this into an attack:

> The most heterogeneous ideas are yoked by violence together; nature and art are ransacked for illustrations, comparisons, and allusions; their learning instructs, and their subtilty surprises; but the reader commonly thinks his improvement dearly bought, and, though he sometimes admires, is seldom pleased.

Taste changed in the generation after Johnson, and, from Coleridge on through the entire nineteenth and twentieth centuries, readers have been pleased.

2

John Donne's popularity thus long preceded T.S. Eliot's belated discovery, which led on to the generous overvaluation by Eliotic critics such as Cleanth Brooks, Allen Tate, and R.P. Blackmur, who seemed to place Donne in Shakespeare's sublime company while joining Eliot in the denigration of Milton and all the Romantics and Victorians. Now, in the twenty-first century, balance has been restored, and I can agree happily with Ben Jonson that John Donne was the best poet in the world for *some* things.

The wonder of Donne's poetry is its unitary nature. His early libertine lyrics, in *Song and Sonnets*, display the same modes of wit and mastery of images that continue in his devotional verse, the Holy Sonnets and the great hymns. "The Ecstasy" and the "Hymn to God my God, in My Sickness" are palpably the work of the same poetic mind. Donne's wit is an instrument of discovery and an avenue always to fresh invention, as here at the close of his *A Hymn to God the Father*:

I have a sin of fear, that when I have spun
    My last thread, I shall perish on the shore;
But swear by thy self, that at my death thy son
    Shall shine as he shines now, and heretofore;
        And, having done that, thou hast done,
        I fear no more.

3

George Herbert, by common critical consent, is the most considerable devotional poet in the language. His starting point is Donne, and he converts both the erotic wit and the libertine contexts into further pathways to God. Like Donne, Herbert is immensely fecund in discovering new metaphors burgeoning out of prior ones; indeed he transcends Donne in this regard. Both are process-poets, recasting their poems even after they are under way. Here is Herbert's wonderful "Prayer (1)":

> Prayer is the Church's banquet, Angel's age,
> > God's breath in man returning to his birth,
> > The soul in paraphrase, heart in pilgrimage,
> The Christian plummet sounding heaven and earth;
> Engine against the Almighty, sinners' tower,
> > Reversed thunder, Christ-side-piercing spear,
> > The six-day's-world transposing in an hour,
> A kind of tune, which all things hear and fear;
> Softness, and peace, and joy, and love, and bliss,
> > Exalted manna, gladness of the best,
> > Heaven in ordinary, man well dressed,
> The milky way, the bird of paradise,
> > Church-bells beyond the stars heard, the soul's blood,
> > The land of spices; something understood.

This is a montage of two dozen tropes or images of prayer, but itself declines to be a prayer. Instead it dances from metaphor to metaphor until it concludes with the beautiful suggestiveness of the final three lines. An extraordinary artist, Herbert demands and rewards close reading:

> Of what strange length must that needs be,
> Which e'vn eternity excludes!
> Thus far Time heard me patiently:
> Then chafing said, This man deludes:
> > What do I here before his door?
> > He doth not crave less time, but more.

4

Andrew Marvell, an unclassifiable poet, has nothing in him of Donne or of Herbert, and I prefer him to either, not out of any distaste for metaphysical poetry, but because Marvell is an unique poet, without precursors in English. Herbert is somewhat monolithic, as even the best of exclusively devotional poets have to be. Marvell matches Donne in variety and has also a rich strangeness entirely unique to him.

Except for some satires, Marvell published very little poetry in his lifetime. Neither did Herbert, but he carefully prepared *The Temple* for posthumous publication. Like Emily Dickinson and Gerard Manley Hopkins, Marvell had little interest in auctioning his mind and art to a public.

Not even the hermetic poems of the Welsh metaphysical Henry Vaughan are as enigmatic as Marvell's pastoral meditations and lyrics. They are difficult not because of esoteric thought, as in Henry Vaughan, nor in Donnean paradoxes, but because Marvell is individualistic in the highest degree. In a very subtle way, he is a somewhat allegorical poet, but freestyle. His best poems intimate otherness, but only suggestively. There is little continuous allegory, as in the mode of Edmund Spenser.

Finally, there is the question of Marvell's tone, which has an uncanny detachment unlike any other. What tonalities do we hear in the superb lines ending my favorite poem by Marvell, "The Mower Against Gardens"?

> 'Tis all enforced, the founding and the grot,
>   While the sweet fields do lie forgot,
> Where willing Nature does to all dispense
>   A wild and fragrant innocence;
> And fauns and fairies do the meadows till
>   More by their presence than their skill.
> Their statues polished by some ancient hand,
>   May to adorn the gardens stand;
> But, howsoe're the figures do excel,
>   The Gods themselves with us do dwell.

William Empson called Damon the Mower "the clown as Death." There is something in that version of Adam, but what about the tone? My inner ear detects an ironic sense of content. Nature may be fallen, Marvell implies, but we are not. The Clown is also the Hermetic God-Man, unfallen Adam, so that "the Gods themselves with us do dwell."

5

The delightful Robert Herrick owes his perpetual audience to his *Hesperides; or the Works both Humane and Divine* rather than to his *Noble Numbers; or Pious Pieces*. *Hesperides* has many triumphs, of which the masterpiece is "Corinna's Going A-Maying." Here is the last of its five stanzas, thus maintaining my propensity, in this introduction, for emphasizing the end of poems:

> Come, let us goe, while we are in our prime;
> And take the harmlesse follie of the time.
>   We shall grow old apace, and die
>   Before we know our liberty.
>   Our life is short; and our dayes run

As fast away as does the Sunne:
And as a vapour, or a drop of raine
Once lost, can ne'r be found againe:
   So when you or I are made
   A fable, song, or fleeting shade;
   All love, all liking, all delight
   Lies drown'd with us in endless night.
Then while time serves, and we are but decaying;
Come my *Corinna*, come, let's goe a Maying.

There are few rivals to that, even in English seventeenth-century poetry. Herrick implicitly understood that love, shadowed by mortality, kindles itself into eroticism.

6

The baroque sensibility of Richard Crashaw sets him apart from other metaphysicals, though two of his volumes were written in tribute to George Herbert. metaphysical style, in Donne at his most exuberant, still is very different from the fierce extravagance of the continental baroque. Crashaw's two baroque masterpieces are his hymns celebrating the Carmelite nun Saint Teresa of Avila: "A Hymn to the Name and Honor of the Admirable Saint Teresa" and "The Flaming Heart." Here is the energetic conclusion of the latter:

O though undaunted daughter of desires!
By all thy dower of *Lights & Fires*;
By all the eagle in thee, all the dove;
By all thy lives & deaths of love;
By thy large draughts of intellectual day,
And by thy thirsts of love more large than they;
By all thy brim-fill'd Bowls of fierce desire
By the last Morning's draught of liquid fire;
By the full kingdom of that final kiss
That seiz'd thy parting Soul, & seal'd thee his;
By all the heavens thou hast in him
(Fair sister of the *Seraphim*!)
By all of *Him* we have in *Thee*;
Leave nothing of my *Self* in me,
Let me so read thy life, that I
Unto all life of mine may die.

As an intellectual and spiritual fireworks display, this is memorable and transcendent, a baroque ascension into the sublime. Reading Teresa's autobiography, Crashaw merges himself both with her and with God.

❖

JOHN DONNE

❖

BIOGRAPHY

JOHN DONNE
(1572–1631)

❖

John Donne was born in London in 1572. His father was a prosperous merchant; his mother (the daughter of the epigrammatist John Heywood) was a devout Catholic whose family had suffered religious persecution and exile. Donne matriculated from Oxford in 1584, and although he did not receive a degree, the university would later award him an honorary MA. Donne also trained as a lawyer—his entrance in 1591 to Thavies Inn was followed by admittance to Lincoln's in 1592—and some critics have remarked upon the traces of legal training evident in the conceits and tight reasoning of his verse. Donne appears to have remained at Lincoln's until 1596, when he joined the English expedition to Cadiz. On his return to England in 1597, he spent several years in the service of Sir Thomas Egerton, staying with Egerton while he entered Parliament as the Member for Brackley. One of the decisive turning points of his life occurred in December 1601, when he secretly married Ann More, Lady Egerton's niece. The confession of his marriage to his father-in-law in February 1602 resulted in imprisonment and dismissal from Egerton's service. His marriage was subsequently to cause Donne so much difficulty that he would write in a letter to his wife in 1602, "John Donne, Ann Donne, Un-done."

Donne was unsuccessful in his application for employment in the Queen's household, and for secretaryships in Ireland and with the Virginia Company. In 1614, he served as Member of Parliament for Taunton and sat on several select committees; he was, however, still unable to find state employment. In 1615, he took orders in the Church of England, a step which had been urged on him by the Dean of Gloucester eight years before. From this time on, he served in various ecclesiastical functions: as Royal Chaplain, rector and vicar of several parishes, Reader in Divinity at Lincoln's Inn, and as a Justice in the Court of Delegates. The crowning achievement of his career came in 1621, when he was elected Dean of St. Paul's. He preached widely, both at Court and abroad, and his sermons were received with acclaim and published in 1622, 1625, and 1626. He was a strong candidate for a bishopric in 1630, but fell seriously ill late that year. He died in 1631 and is buried in St. Paul's. Although he is best known today for his poems, few of them were published in his lifetime: the First and Second Anniversaries came out in 1612, as did "Break of Day," and "Elegy upon Prince Henry" was published the following year. The first collected edition of the poetry appeared in 1633.

❖

PERSONAL

❖

Inscription on a Monument

JOHANNES DONNE,
  Sac. Theol. Profess.
  Poet Varia Studia, Quibus Ab Annis
  Tenerrimis Fideliter, Nee Infeliciter
      Incubuit;
Instinctu Et Impulsu Sp. Sancti, Monitu
      Et Hortatu
Regis Jacobi, Ordines Sacros Amplexus,
Anno Sui Jesu, MDCXIV. Et Suae Ætatis
          XLII.
  Decanatu Hujus Ecclesiae Indutus,
    XXVII. Novembris, MDCXXI
    Exutus Morte Ultimo Die Martii,
      MDCXXXI.
    Hie Licet In Occiduo Cinere, Aspicit Eum
      Cujus Nomen Est Oriens.

—Inscription

Henry King "To the Memory of My Ever Desired Friend Doctor Donne" (1631)

A former Bishop of Chicester, Henry King (1592–1669) was a noted churchman and author of his day. A close friend of Donne's and executor of his estate, King's elegy on Donne's death is often considered amongst the finest of his works.

To have liv'd eminent, in a degree
Beyond our lofti'st flights, that is, like Thee
Or t' have had too much merit, is not safe;
For such excesses find no Epitaph.
At common graves we have Poetic eyes
Can melt themselves in easy Elegies.
But at Thine, Poem, or Inscription
(Rich soul of wit, and language) we have none.
Indeed, a silence does that tomb befit, Where is no Herald left to blazon it.

—Henry King, "To the Memory of My Ever
Desired Friend Doctor Donne," c. 1631

Izaak Walton (1639)

John Donne was once Izaak Walton's (1593–1683) pastor at St. Dunstan's in addition to being a close friend. Walton considered himself a "Convert" of Donne, who was clearly an important influence on both his spiritual and literary life. Walton wrote the first biography of Donne, published in 1640 and revised in 1658.

He was of stature moderately tall; of a straight and equally-proportioned body, to which all his words and actions gave an unexpressible addition of comeliness. The melancholy and pleasant humour were in him so contempered, that each gave advantage to the other, and made his company one of the delights of mankind. His fancy was unimitably high, equalled only by his great wit; both being made useful by a commanding judgment. His aspect was cheerful, and such as gave a silent testimony of a clear knowing soul, and of a conscience at peace with itself. His melting eye shewed that he had a soft heart, full of noble compassion; of too brave a soul to offer injuries, and too much a Christian not to pardon them in others. He was by nature highly passionate, but more apt to reluct at the excesses of it. A great lover of the offices of humanity, and of so merciful a spirit, that he never beheld the miseries of mankind without pity and relief.

—Izaak Walton,
The Life of Dr. John Donne, 1639

Sir Richard Baker (1641)

Sir Richard Baker (1568–1645) was an author and occasional member of the British parliament. He is most know for his work *Chronicle of the Kings of England from the Time of the Romans' Government unto the Death of King James*, which he completed while incarcerated in Fleet debtor's prison.

Mr. John Dunne, who leaving Oxford, lived at the Innes of Court, not dissolute, but very neat; a great Visitor of Ladies, a great frequenter of Playes, a great writer of conceited Verses; until such times as King James taking notice of the pregnancy of his Wit, was a means that he betook him to the study of Divinity, and thereupon proceeding Doctor, was made Dean of Pauls; and became so rare a Preacher, that he was not only commended, but even admired by all who heard him.

—Sir Richard Baker,
A Chronicle of the Kings of England, 1641

JOHN HACKET (1693)

John Hacket (1592–1670) was a renowned English churchman, formerly Bishop of both Lichfield and Coventry. He wrote several works, most noted of which are the comedy *Loiola* and the biography, published posthumously, that is excerpted below.

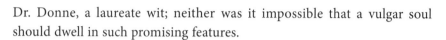

Dr. Donne, a laureate wit; neither was it impossible that a vulgar soul should dwell in such promising features.

—John Hacket, *Life of Archbishop Williams,*
1693, par. 74

THOMAS CAMPBELL (1819)

An important and influential poet and writer of the latter portion of the Romantic period, Thomas Campbell (1777–1844) was most known for his biographies and his humanist work, *The Pleasures of Hope.*

The life of Donne is more interesting than his poetry.

—Thomas Campbell,
Specimens of the British Poets, 1819

ANNA BROWNELL JAMESON (1829)

Famed as an art historian, travel writer, and feminist pioneer, Anna Brownell Jameson (1794–1860) wrote the popular, two-volume work *The Loves of the Poets,* which explored the lives of the women who were loved and celebrated by great poets throughout time.

Dr. Donne, once so celebrated as a writer, now so neglected, is more interesting for his matrimonial history, and for one little poem addressed to his wife, than for all his learned, metaphysical, and theological productions.

—Anna Brownell Jameson,
The Loves of the Poets, 1829, vol. 2, p. 94

William Minto "John Donne" (1880)

William Minto (1845–1893) was a Scottish critic and scholar, a professor at the University of Aberdeen, and author of the respected *Characteristics of English Poets from Chaucer to Shirley*.

The knowledge of Donne's immense learning, the subtlety and capacity of his intellect, the intense depth and wide scope of his thought, the charm of his conversation, the sadness of his life, gave a vivid meaning and interest to his poems, circulated among his acquaintances, which at this distance of time we cannot reach without a certain effort of imagination. Dr. Donne is one of the most interesting personalities among our men of letters. The superficial facts of his life are so incongruous as to be an irresistible provocation to inquiry. What are we to make of the fact that the founder of a licentious school of erotic poetry, a man acknowledged to be the greatest wit in a licentious Court, with an early bias in matters of religion towards Roman Catholicism, entered the Church of England when he was past middle age and is now numbered among its greatest divines? Was he a convert like St. Augustine, or an indifferent worldling like Talleyrand? Superficial appearances are rather in favour of the latter supposition.

—William Minto, "John Donne,"
The Nineteenth Century, 1880, p. 849

J.B. Lightfoot (1895)

Joseph Barber Lightfoot (1828–1889) was an English churchman and bishop of Durham. A noted scholar of theology, Lightfoot published over a dozen well-respected books, most of which deal with biblical subject matter.

Against the wall of the south choir aisle in the Cathedral of St. Paul is a monument which very few of the thousands who visit the church daily observe, or have an opportunity of observing, but which, once seen, is not easily forgotten. It is the long, gaunt, upright figure of a man, wrapped close in a shroud, which is knotted at the head and feet, and leaves only the face exposed—a face wan, worn, almost ghastly, with eyes closed as in death. This figure is executed in white marble, and stands on an urn of the same, as if it had just arisen therefrom. The whole is placed in a black niche, which, by its contrast, enhances the death-like paleness of the shrouded figure. Above the canopy is an inscription recording that the man whose effigy stands beneath, though his ashes are mingled with western dust, looks towards Him whose name is the Orient. It was not such a memorial as Donne's surviving friends might think suitable to commemorate the deceased, but it was the very monument which Donne himself designed as a true emblem of his past life and his future hopes.

—J.B. Lightfoot,
Historical Essays, 1895, pp. 221–223

Augustus Jessopp (1897)

A noted English author and archaeologist, Augustus Jessopp (1823–1914) was, like Donne, a churchman and rector, and often acted as chaplain in ordinary to King Edward VII.

His graceful person, vivacity of conversation, and many accomplishments secured for him the *entree* at the houses of the nobility and a recognised position among the celebrities of Queen Elizabeth's court. He was conspicuous as a young man of fortune who spent his money freely, and mixed on equal terms with the courtiers, and probably had the character of being richer than he was. The young man, among his other gifts, had the great advantage of being able to do with very little sleep. He could read all night and be gay and wakeful and alert all day. He threw himself into the amusements and frivolities of the court with all the glee of youth, but never so as to interfere with his duties. The favourite of fortune, he was too the favourite of the fortunate—the envy of some, he was the darling of more. Those of his contemporaries who knew him intimately speak of him at all times as if there was none like him; the charm of his person and manners were irresistible. He must have had much love to give, or he could never had so much bestowed upon him.

—Augustus Jessopp, *John Donne,
Sometime Dean of St. Paul's*, 1897, pp. 13, 18

Edmund Gosse (1899)

Edmund Gosse (1849–1928) was a prolific and important "man of letters" from the late Victorian Era through the first quarter of the twentieth

century. Though also a poet and author of prose, Gosse was most
revered as a literary critic, penning a wide scope of literary criticism
and biography on such seemingly disparate figures as Algernon Charles
Swinburne, Henrik Ibsen, William Congreve, Robert Browning, and, of
course, John Donne.

History presents us with no instance of a man of letters more obviously
led up to by the experience and character of his ancestors than was John
Donne. As we have him revealed to us, he is what a genealogist might
wish him to be. Every salient feature in his mind and temperament is
foreshadowed by the general trend of his family, or by the idiosyncrasy
of some individual member of it . . . The greatest preacher of his age
. . . No one, in the history of English literature, as it seems to me, is
so difficult to realise, so impossible to measure, in the vast curves of his
extraordinary and contradictory features. Of his life, of his experiences,
of his opinions, we know more now than it has been vouchsafed to us to
know of any other of the great Elizabethan and Jacobean galaxy of writers,
and yet how little we fathom his contradictions, how little we can account for
his impulses and his limitations. Even those of us who have for years made
his least adventures the subject of close and eager investigation must admit
at last that he eludes us. He was not the crystal-hearted saint that Walton
adored and exalted. He was not the crafty and redoubtable courtier whom
the recusants suspected. He was not the prophet of the intricacies of fleshly
feeling whom the young poets looked up to and worshipped. He was none of
these, or all of these, or more. What was he? It is impossible to say, for, with
all his superficial expansion, his secret died with him. We are tempted to
declare that of all great men he is the one of whom least is essentially known.
Is not this, perhaps, the secret of his perennial fascination?

—Edmund Gosse, The Life and Letters of John Donne,
1899, vol. 1, pp. 3, 11, vol. 2, p. 290

SERMONS

The following six excerpts specifically examine aspects of Donne's sermon
writing, offering both criticism and praise, and any reader interested in
Donne's homilies will find these comments particularly useful.

Izaak Walton (1639)

A preacher in earnest; weeping sometimes for his auditory, sometimes with them; always preaching to himself, like an angel from a cloud, but in none; carrying some, as St. Paul was, to heaven in holy raptures; and enticing others by a sacred art and courtship to amend their lives: here picturing a Vice so as to make it ugly to those that practised it; and a Virtue so as to make it beloved, even by those who loved it not; and all this with a most particular grace and an unexpressible addition of comeliness.

—Izaak Walton, *The Life of Dr. John Donne*, 1639

Henry Hallam (1837–39)

Henry Hallam (1777–1859) was a prominent nineteenth-century literary historian and scholar. Often viewed as a philosopher or moralist, Hallam penned several well-regarded works, including one on the constitutional history of England.

The sermons of Donne have sometimes been praised in late times. They are undoubtedly the productions of a very ingenious and a very learned man; and two folio volumes by such a person may be expected to supply favorable specimens. In their general character, they will not appear, I think, much worthy of being rescued from oblivion. The subtilty of Donne, and his fondness for such inconclusive reasoning as a subtle disputant is apt to fall into, runs through all of these sermons at which I have looked. His learning he seems to have perverted in order to cull every impertinence of the fathers and schoolmen, their remote analogies, their strained allegories, their technical distinctions; and to these he has added much of a similar kind from his own fanciful understanding.

—Henry Hallam, *Introduction to the Literature of Europe*, 1837–39, pt. 3, ch. 2, par. 70

Edwin P. Whipple (1859–68)

Edwin Percy Whipple (1819–1886) was a prominent American essayist and critic, one of the foremost authors on literary works of the nineteenth century.

Donne's published sermons are in form nearly as grotesque as his poems, though they are characterized by profounder qualities of heart and mind. It was his misfortune to know thoroughly the works of fourteen hundred writers, most of them necessarily worthless; and he could not help displaying his erudition in his discourses. Of what is now called taste he was absolutely destitute. His sermons are a curious mosaic of quaintness, quotation, wisdom, puerility, subtilty, and ecstasy. The pedant and the seer possess him by turns, and in reading no other divine are our transitions from yawning to rapture so swift and unexpected. He has passages of transcendent merit, passages which evince a spiritual vision so piercing, and a feeling of divine things so intense, that for the time we seem to be communing with a religious genius of the most exalted and exalting order; but soon he involves us in a maze of quotations and references, and our minds are hustled by what Hallam calls "the rabble of bad authors" that this saint and sage has always at his skirts, even when he ascends to the highest heaven of contemplation.

—Edwin P. Whipple, *The Literature of the Age of Elizabeth*, 1859–68, p. 237

Anne C. Lynch Botta (1860)

An American poet and critic of modest achievement, Anne C. Lynch Botta (1815–1891) was more renowned for hosting a famous literary salon, first in Providence, Rhode Island, and then later in New York City. At these weekly salons, prominent writers of the day shared new and emerging works with eager audiences. Edgar Allen Poe, Horace Greeley, and Catharine Sedgwick are amongst the writers who appeared in Botta's drawing room.

The sermons of Donne, while they are superior in style, are sometimes fantastic, like his poetry, but they are never coarse, and they derive a touching interest from his history.

—Anne C. Lynch Botta, *Hand-Book of Universal Literature*, 1860, p. 476

William Minto (1872–80)

In Donne's sermons, an intellectual epicure not too fastidious to read sermons will find a delicious feast. Whether these sermons can be taken as patterns by the modern preacher is another affair. It will not be contended that any congregation is equal to the effort of following his subtleties. In short, as exercises in abstract subtlety, fanciful ingenuity, and scholarship, the sermons are admirable. Judged by the first rule of popular exposition, the style is bad—a bewildering maze to the ordinary reader, much more to the ordinary hearer.

—William Minto, *Manual of
English Prose Literature,* 1872–80, p. 253

AUGUSTUS JESSOPP (1888)

During this year, 1622, Donne's first printed sermon appeared. It was delivered at Paul's Cross on 15 Sept. to an enormous congregation, in obedience to the king's commands, who had just issued his "Directions to Preachers," and had made choice of the dean of St. Paul's to explain his reasons for issuing the injunctions. The sermon was at once printed; copies of the original edition are rarely met with. Two months later Donne preached his glorious sermon before the Virginian Company. Donne's sermon struck a note in full sympathy with the larger views and nobler aims of the minority. His sermon may be truly described as the first missionary sermon printed in the English language. The original edition was at once absorbed. The same is true of every other sermon printed during Donne's lifetime; in their original shape they are extremely scarce. The truth is that as a preacher at this time Donne stood almost alone. Andrewes's preaching days were over (he died in September 1626), Hall never carried with him the conviction of being much more than a consummate gladiator, and was rarely heard in London; of the rest there was hardly one who was not either ponderously learned like Sanderson, or a mere performer like the rank and file of rhetoricians who came up to London to air their eloquences at Paul's Cross. The result was that Donne's popularity was always on the increase, he rose to every occasion, and surprised his friends, as Walton tells us, by the growth of his genius and earnestness even to the end.

—Augustus Jessopp,
Dictionary of National Biography,
1888, vol. 15, p. 229

❖

GENERAL

❖

JOHN DONNE (1614)

One thing more I must tell you; but so softly, that I am loth to hear myself: and so softly, that if that good lady were in the room, with you and this letter, she might not hear. It is, that I am brought to a necessity of printing my poems, and addressing them to my Lord Chamberlain. This I mean to do forthwith: not for much public view, but at mine own cost, a few copies. I apprehend some incongruities in the resolution; and I know what I shall suffer from many interpretations; but I am at an end, of much considering that; and, if I were as startling in that kind, as I ever was, yet in this particular, I am under an unescapable necessity, as I shall let you perceive when I see you. By this occasion I am made a rhapsodist of mine own rags, and that cost me more diligence, to seek them, than it did to make them. This made me ask to borrow that old book of you, which it will be too late to see, for that use, when I see you; for I must do this as a valediction to the world, before I take orders. But this is it, I am to ask you: whether you ever made any such use of the letter in verse, *a notre comtesse chez vous,* as that I may not put it in, amongst the rest to persons of that rank; for I desire it very much, that something should bear her name in the book, and I would be just to my written words to my Lord Harrington to write nothing after that. I pray tell me as soon as you can, if I be at liberty to insert that: for if you have by any occasion applied any pieces to it, I see not, that it will be discerned, when it appears in the whole piece. Though this be a little matter, I would be sorry not to have an account of it, within as little after New Year's-tide, as you could.

—John Donne, letter to Sir Henry Goodyere,
Dec. 20, 1614, *The Works of John Donne,*
ed. Henry Alford, vol. 6, 1839, p. 367

BEN JONSON
"TO JOHN DONNE" (1616)

Ben Jonson (1572?–1637) was one of the most prominent authors of his time, a renowned dramatist and poet. A contemporary and colleague of Donne's, Jonson was a great admirer of the poet, often praising him in his works, though, as is typical of Jonson, some of his praise was also tempered by criticism as well.

Donne, the delight of Phoebus and each Muse,
Who, to thy one, all other brains refuse;
Whose every work of thy most early wit
Came forth example, and remains so yet;
Longer a-knowing than most wits do live,
And which no affection praise enough can give!
To it, thy language, letters, arts, best life,
Which might with half mankind maintain a strife;
All which I meant to praise, and yet I would;
But leave, because I cannot as I should!

—Ben Jonson, "To John Donne," 1616

WILLIAM DRUMMOND (1619)

William Drummond of Hawthornden (1585–1649) was a sublime Scottish poet and the unofficial poet laureate of Edinburgh in his day. Today he is most remembered for publishing a series of notes and observations based on conversations with Ben Jonson, whose views on Donne, both praising and critical, Drummond repeats below. In another letter, Drummond is also credited with being the first critic to write of a group of metaphysical writers.

That Done's Anniversarie was profane and full of blasphemies: that he told Mr. Done, if it had been written of the Virgin Marie it had been something; to which he answered, that he described the Idea of a Woman, and not as she was. That Done, for not keeping of accent, deserved hanging . . . He esteemeth John Done the first poet in the world in some things: his verses of the "Lost Chaine" he heth by heart; and that passage of the "Calme," *That dust and feathers doe not stirr, all was so quiet.* Affirmeth Done to have written all his best pieces ere he was 25 years old.

—William Drummond,
Notes on Ben Jonson's Conversations, 1619

THOMAS CAREW "AN ELEGIE UPON THE DEATH OF DOCTOR DONNE" (1631)

Thomas Carew (1594 or 1595–1640) was one of the more successful and well-known poets of the court of King Charles I. Today he is remembered as belonging to the Cavalier style of poetry, along with Sir John Suckling, Richard Lovelace, and others. Carew's deservedly famous elegy on the death of Donne, excerpted below, has often been considered one of the most perceptive appraisals of the great metaphysical poet's work dating from his own time.

The Muses' garden, with pedantic weeds
O'erspread, was purg'd by thee, the lazie seeds
Of servile imitation throwne away,
And fresh invention planted; thou didst pay
The debts of our penurious banquerout age:
. . .whatsoever wrong
By ours was done the Greek or Latin tongue,
Thou hast redeem'd, and opened as a mine
Of rich and pregnant fancie . . .
. . . to the awe of thy imperious wit
Our troublesome language bends, made only fit,
With her tough thick-rib'd hoopes, to gird about
Thy gyant fancy.

> —Thomas Carew, "An Elegie upon the Death of
> Doctor Donne," *Works*, c. 1631, ed. Hazlitt, pp. 93–94

George Daniel
"A Vindication of Poesy" (1647)

George Daniel (1616–1657) was a poet best known for his work "The Robin." As many of his contemporaries did, Daniel responded to Donne's work in poetic form, a sure sign of Donne's significance to his fellow writers.

. . . all the softnesses,
The Shadow, Light, the Air, and Life, of Love;
The Sharpness of all Wit; ev'n bitterness
Makes Satire Sweet; all wit did God improve,
'Twas flamed in him, 'Twas but warm upon
His Embers; He was more; and it is Donne.

> —George Daniel, "A Vindication of Poesy," 1647

JOHN DRYDEN
"ESSAY ON SATIRE" (1692)

The greatest playwright and satirist of his day, John Dryden (1631–1700) ranks as foremost among the generation of English writers that succeeded Donne and his contemporaries. Though clearly an admirer of Donne's body of work, Dryden's criticism of the poet helped usher in an era where some of Donne's writing fell from the highest lofts of artistic favor. Though not present in the excerpt below, Dryden was the first critic to use the term "metaphysic" when writing about Donne.

Would not Donne's satires, which abound with so much wit, appear more charming, if he had taken care of his words, and of his numbers? But he followed Horace so very close, that of necessity he must fall with him; and I may safely say it of this present age, that if we are not so great wits as Donne, yet, certainly, we are better poets.

—John Dryden, "Essay on Satire," *Works,*
1692, vol. 13, eds. Scott, Saintsbury, p. 109

NATHAN DRAKE (1798)

Nathan Drake (1766–1836) was an English physician and literary scholar most noted for his comprehensive, two-volume work on William Shakespeare.

If it be true that the purport of poetry should be to please, no author has written with such utter neglect of the rule. It is scarce possible for a human ear to endure the dissonance and discord of his couplets, and even when his thoughts are clothed in the melody of Pope, they appear to me hardly worth the decoration.

—Nathan Drake, *Literary Hours,* 1798, no. 28

HENRY KIRKE WHITE
"MELANCHOLY HOURS" (1806)

Henry Kirke White (1785–1806) gained some fame as a young poet whose natural genius for poesy was hailed by numerous prominent men of his day, including Robert Southey and George Gordon, Lord Byron. Having died young, White's second collection—where the below excerpt can be found—was published posthumously in 1807.

Donne had not music enough to render his broken rhyming couplets sufferable, and neither his wit, nor his pointed satire, were sufficient to rescue him from that neglect which his uncouth and rugged versification speedily superinduced.

—Henry Kirke White, "Melancholy Hours,"
Remains, 1807, vol. 2, ed. Southey

SAMUEL TAYLOR COLERIDGE (1818)

One of the most significant authors and critics of his time, Samuel Taylor Coleridge (1772–1834) is perhaps most well-known today for his epic poems "Kubla Khan" and "Rime of the Ancient Mariner."

Since Dryden, the metre of our poets leads to the sense: in our elder and more genuine bards, the sense, including the passion, leads to the metre. Read even Donne's satires as he meant them to be read, and as the sense and passion demand, and you will find in the lines a manly harmony.

—Samuel Taylor Coleridge,
Notes on Beaumont and Fletcher,
1818, ed. Ashe, p. 427

ROBERT SOUTHEY (1807)

Renowned as one of the famous Lake Poets, whose ranks also included Coleridge and William Wordsworth, Robert Southey (1774–1843) served as poet laureate of England for thirty years. An important critic and man of letters, Southey's criticism of Donne, especially when compared and contrasted to the other excerpts presented here from his contemporaries Coleridge, Campbell, and Hallam, demonstrates the inconstant opinion with which Donne was regarded in the early part of the nineteenth century.

Nothing could have made Donne a poet, unless as great a change had been worked in the internal structure of his ears, as was wrought in elongating those of Midas.

—Robert Southey, *Specimens of the Later English Poets,* 1807, vol. 1, p. xx iv

Thomas Campbell (1819)

Donne was the "best good-natured man, with the worst natured Muse." A romantic and uxorious lover, he addresses the object of his real tenderness with ideas that outrage decorum. He begins his own epithalamium with most indelicate invocation to his bride. His ruggedness and whim are almost proverbially known. Yet there is a beauty of thought which at intervals rises from his chaotic imagination, like the form of Venus smiling on the waters.

—Thomas Campbell, *An* Essay *on English Poetry,* 1819

Henry Hallam (1837–39)

Donne is the most inharmonious of our versifiers, if he can be said to have deserved such a name by lines too rugged to seem metre. Of his earlier poems, many are very licentious; the later are chiefly devout. Few are good for much; the conceits have not even the merit of being intelligible: it would perhaps be difficult to select three passages that we should care to read again.

—Henry Hallam, *Introduction to the Literature of Europe,* 1837–39, pt. 3, ch. 5, para. 39

Elizabeth Barrett Browning (1842–63)

The most renowned woman poet of the nineteenth century, Elizabeth Barrett Browning (1806–1861) is famous today for her "Sonnets from the Portuguese" and her romantic marriage to fellow poet Robert Browning. Though she mainly published her own poetry, Barrett Browning was also a respected critic of other poets' work.

Having a dumb angel, and knowing more noble poetry than he articulates.

—Elizabeth Barrett Browning,
The Book of Poets, 1842–63, vol. 2, p. 50

HARTLEY COLERIDGE "DONNE" (1849)

The son of Samuel Taylor Coleridge, Hartley Coleridge (1796–1849) was a minor writer who never lived up to the promise and expectations his father placed upon him. Coleridge was more known for his literary journalism and criticism, placing essays and poems in several popular magazines of the day and publishing one biographical work in his lifetime.

Of stubborn thoughts a garland thought to twine;
To his fair Maid brough cabalistic posies,
And sung quaint ditties of metempsychosis;
"Twists iron pokers into true love-knots,"
Coining hard words, not found in polyglots.

—Hartley Coleridge, "Donne," *Sketches of the English Poets, Poems,* 1849, vol. 2, p. 295

EDWIN P. WHIPPLE (1859–68)

With vast learning, with subtile and penetrating intellect, with a fancy singularly fruitful and ingenious, he still contrived to disconnect, more or less, his learning from what was worth learning, his intellect from what was reasonable, his fancy from what was beautiful. His poems, or rather his metrical problems, are obscure in thought, rugged in versification, and full of conceits which are intended to surprise rather than to please; but they still exhibit a power of intellect, both analytical and analogical, competent at once to separate the minutest and connect the remotest ideas. This power, while it might not have given his poems grace, sweetness, freshness, and melody, would still, if properly directed, have made them valuable for their thoughts; but in the case of Donne it is perverted to the production of what is *bizarre* or unnatural, and his muse is thus as hostile to use as to beauty. The intention is, not to idealize what is true, but to display the writer's skill and wit in giving a show of reason to what is false. The effect of this on the moral character of Donne was pernicious. A subtile intellectual scepticism, which weakened will, divorced thought from action and literature from life, and made existence a puzzle and a dream, resulted from this perversion of his intellect. He found that he could wittily justify what was vicious as well as what was unnatural; and his amatory poems, accordingly, are characterized by a cold, hard, labored, intellectualized sensuality, worse than the worst impurity of his contemporaries, because it has no excuse of passion for its violations of decency.

—Edwin P. Whipple, *The Literature of
the Age of Elizabeth,* 1859–68, p. 231

GEORGE GILFILLAN (1860)

George Gilfillan (1813–1878) was a revered Scottish clergyman and author, writing popular biographies of Robert Burns and Sir Walter Scott and numerous other important texts. Gilfillan collected and edited volumes of the work of dozens of prominent writers, including contemporaries of Donne like George Herbert, Richard Crashaw, and John Milton. As evidenced below, his opinion of Donne—written in his characteristic, at times grandiloquent, style—was decidedly mixed.

Donne, altogether, gives us the impression of a great genius ruined by a false system. He is a charioteer run away with by his own pampered steeds. He begins generally well, but long ere the close, quibbles, conceits, and the temptation of shewing off recondite learning, prove too strong for him, and he who commenced following a serene star, ends pursuing a will-o'-wisp into a bottomless morass. Compare, for instance, the ingenious nonsense which abounds in the middle and the close of his "Progress of the Soul" with the dark, but magnificent stanzas which are the first in the poem. In no writings in the language is there more spilt treasure—a more lavish loss of beautiful, original, and striking things than in the poems of Donne.

—George Gilfillan, *Specimens with Memoirs
of the Less-Known British Poets,* 1860, vol. 1, p. 203

GEORGE L. CRAIK (1861)

George Little Craik (1798–1866) was a Scottish historian and literary scholar.

On a superficial inspection, Donne's verses look like so many riddles. They seem to be written upon the principle of making the meaning as difficult to be found out as possible,—of using all the resources of language, not to express thought, but to conceal it. Nothing is said in a direct, natural manner; conceit follows conceit without intermission; the most remote analogies, the most farfetched images, the most unexpected turns, one after another, surprise and often puzzle the understanding; while things of the most opposite kinds—the harsh and the harmonious, the graceful and the grotesque, the grave and the gay, the pious and the profane—meet and mingle in the strangest of dances. But, running through all this bewilderment, a deeper insight detects not only a vein of the most exuberant wit, but often the sunniest and most delicate fancy, and the truest tenderness and depth of feeling.

—George L. Craik, A *Compendious History of English Literature and of the English Language*, 1861, vol. 1, p. 579

RICHARD CHENEVIX TRENCH (1868)

Richard Chenevix Trench (1807–1886) was an Irish poet and churchman who eventually became Archbishop of Dublin. Sometimes considered a poetic follower of Wordsworth's, Trench also contributed to the study of English linguistics.

There is indeed much in Donne, in the unfolding of his moral and spiritual life, which often reminds us of St. Augustine. I do not mean that, noteworthy as on many accounts he was, and in the language of Carew, one of his contemporaries,

A king who ruled as he thought fit
The universal monarchy of wit.

he at all approached in intellectual or spiritual stature to the great Doctor of the Western Church. But still there was in Donne the same tumultuous youth, the same final deliverance from them; and then the same passionate and personal grasp of the central truths of Christianity, linking itself as this did with all that he had suffered, and all that he had sinned, and all through which by God's grace he had victoriously struggled.

—Richard Chenevix Trench, A *Household Book of English Poetry*, 1868, p. 403

H.A. TAINE (1871)

A French literary critic and historian, Hippolyte Adolphe Taine (1828–1893) was the author of numerous important works, including his four-volume *History of English Literature*, which he penned in 1864 and was translated into English in 1871. Taine was an important literary theorist and is often credited as the architect of literary historicism.

A pungent satirist, of terrible crudeness, a powerful poet, of a precise and intense imagination, who still preserves something of the energy and thrill of the original inspiration. But he deliberately abuses all these gifts, and succeeds with great difficulty in concocting a piece of nonsense. Twenty times while reading him we rub our brow, and ask with astonishment, how a man could so have tormented and contorted himself, strained his style, refined on his refinement, hit upon such absurd comparisons?

> —H.A. Taine, *History of English Literature*,
> 1871, vol. 1, tr. Van Laun, bk. 2, ch. 1, pp. 203–04

ROBERT CHAMBERS (1876)

A noted Scottish publisher and author, Robert Chambers (1802–1871) was the author of dozens of works, including the *Cyclopaedia of English Literature*, which he first completed in 1840 and which was subsequently revised. He is often best remembered today as the author of *Vestiges of the Natural History of Creation*, released anonymously in 1844, which presented a somewhat radical and highly controversial view of evolution.

His reputation as a poet, great in his own day, low during the latter part of the seventeenth and the whole of the eighteenth centuries, has latterly revived. In its days of abasement, critics spoke of his harsh and rugged versification, and his leaving nature for conceit. It seems to be now acknowledged that, amidst much bad taste, there is much real poetry, and that of a high order, in Donne.

> —Robert Chambers, *Cyclopaedia of
> English Literature*, 1876, ed. Carruthers

Robert Browning (1878)

One of the most important Victorian poets, Robert Browning (1812–1889) professed his admiration for Donne in his 1878 collection *La Saisiaz: The Two Poets of Croisic.*

Better and truer verse none ever wrote
Than thou, revered and magisterial Donne!

—Robert Browning,
The Two Poets of Croisic, 1878

Alfred Welsh (1882)

An American literary scholar and author, Alfred Welsh (1849–1889) spent most of his career in the English Department at the Ohio State University. Welsh, unlike many of his contemporaries, who were beginning to rediscover admiration for Donne (as Chambers expresses above,) reflected the views of critics of the previous century, who found much to criticize in the poet's work.

We find little to admire, and nothing to love. We see that farfetched similes, extravagant metaphors, are not here occasional blemishes, but the substance. He should have given us simple images, simply expressed; for he loved and suffered much: but fashion was stronger than nature.

—Alfred Welsh, *Development of English Literature and Language,* 1882, vol. 1, p. 413

Francis T. Palgrave (1889)

Francis Turner Palgrave (1824–1897) was an oft controversial Victorian critic of both art and literature. Though Palgrave was an occasional poet and prose author, he is best remembered for his criticisms, which were widely respected in his day.

Donne's poems were first collected in 1633: they cover an extraordinary range in subject, and are throughout marked with a strange originality almost equally fascinating and repellent. It is possible that his familiarity with Italian and Spanish literatures, both at that time deeply coloured by fantastic and far-fetched thought, may have in some degree influenced him in that direction. His poems were probably written mainly during youth. There is a strange solemn passionate earnestness about them, a quality which underlies the fanciful "conceits" of all his work.

—Francis T. Palgrave, The Treasury of
Sacred Song, 1889, note, p. 333

EDMUND GOSSE (1894)

In him the Jacobean spirit, as opposed to the Elizabethan, is paramount. His were the first poems which protested, in their form alike and their tendency, against the pastoral sweetness of the Spenserians. Something new in English literature begins in Donne, something which proceeded, under his potent influence, to colour poetry for nearly a hundred years. The exact mode in which that influence was immediately distributed is unknown to us, or very dimly perceived. To know more about it is one of the great desiderata of literary history. The imitation of Donne's style begins so early, and becomes so general, that several critics have taken for granted that there must have been editions of his writings which have disappeared. . . . The style of Donne, like a very odd perfume, was found to cling to every one who touched it, and we observe the remarkable phenomenon of poems which had not passed through a printer's hands exercising the influence of a body of accepted classical work. In estimating the poetry of the Jacobean age, therefore, there is no writer who demands more careful study than this enigmatical and subterranean master, this veiled Isis whose utterances outweigh the oracles of all the visible gods..

—Edmund Gosse, The Jacobean Poets,
1894, pp. 47–48

EDWARD DOWDEN (1895)

An Irish poet and scholar, Edward Dowden (1843–1913) was a professor of English literature at Trinity College in Dublin for over forty years. He published extensively on French and English authors, including full-length works on William Shakespeare, Michel de Montaigne, Edmund Spenser, and Percy Bysshe Shelley.

After he had taken holy orders Donne seldom threw his passions into verse; even his "Divine Poems" are, with few exceptions, of early date; the poet in

Donne did not cease to exist, but his ardour, his imagination, his delight in what is strange and wonderful, his tenderness, his tears, his smiles, his erudition, his intellectual ingenuities, were all placed at the service of one whose desire was that he might die in the pulpit, or if not die, that he might take his death in the pulpit, a desire which was in fact fulfilled. . . . Donne as a poet is certainly difficult of access. . . . He sometimes wrote best, or thought he wrote best, when his themes were wholly of the imagination. Still it is evident that Donne, the student, the recluse, the speculator on recondite problems, was also a man who adventured in pursuit of violent delights which had violent ends. . . . In whatever sunny garden, and at whatever banquet Donne sits, he discerns in air the dark Scythesman of that great picture attributed to Orcagna. An entire section of his poetry is assigned to death.

—Edward Dowden, *New Studies in Literature,*
1895, pp. 90–91, 107–17

Felix E. Schelling "Introduction" (1895)

Felix Emmanuel Schelling (1858–1945) was an American educator and literary scholar. In the essay below, taken from an introductory essay to a collection of Elizabethan poetry, Schelling describes what he calls the "positive originality" and "negative originality" of Donne's work. Donne's "positive originality" manifests in Donne's poetic insight, which Schelling writes "the power which, proceeding by means of the clash of ideas familiar with ideas remote, flashes light and meaning into what has hitherto appeared mere commonplace." Donne's "negative originality" is found in the uniqueness of his lyrics and work; Schelling argues that Donne was "by far the most independent lyrical metrist of this age" and that unlike many of his contemporaries, Donne was not highly shaped by the prevailing influence of Renaissance Italian poetry.

Schelling also compares Donne to several of his contemporaries, including George Daniel, Fulke Greville, and especially Ben Jonson. Schelling bristles at the notion, often debated in his time, that Jonson may have originated the metaphysical school of poetry; Schelling clearly places this mantle onto Donne's shoulders, arguing that, excepting Shakespeare, no one "has done so much to develop intellectualized emotion in the Elizabethan lyric as John Donne." Any individual carefully studying Donne's work may find Schelling's essay particularly interesting, and applying Schelling's concepts of positive and negative originality to

not only Donne but also Jonson and the other poets Schelling mentions
below may prove a fruitful endeavor in further understanding Donne's
unique place amongst Renaissance poets.

—⁓⁓— —⁓⁓— —⁓⁓—

The most important poetical influence of this decade (1590–1600) is that
of that grave and marvelous man, Dr. John Donne. I would respectfully
invite the attention of those who still persist with Dr. Johnson in regarding
this great poet as the founder of a certain "Metaphysical School of Poetry,"[1]
a man all but contemporary with Cowley, and a writer harsh, obscure,
and incomprehensible in his diction, first to an examination of facts
which are within the reach of all, and, secondly, to an honest study of
his works. Ben Jonson told Drummond[2] that "Donne's best poems were
written before he was twenty-five years old," *i.e.,* before 1598, and Francis
Davison, apparently when collecting material for his *Poetical Rhapsody*
in 1600, includes in a memorandum of "M.S. S. to get," certain poems of
Donne.[3] The Carews, Crashaws, and Cowleys begin at least thirty years
later, and, be their imitations of Donne's characteristics what they may,
Donne himself is an Elizabethan in the strictest possible acceptation of
that term, and far in fact as in time from the representative of a degenerate
and false taste. It is somewhat disconcerting to find an author whom, like
Savage Landor in our own century, the critic cannot glibly classify as the
founder of a school or the product of a perfectly obvious series of literary
influences. Donne is a man of this difficult type. For, just as Shakespeare
touched life and man at all points, and, absorbing the light of his time,
gave it forth a hundredfold, so Donne, withdrawn almost wholly from the
influences affecting his contemporaries, shone and glowed with a strange
light all his own.

Few lyrical poets have ever rivaled Donne in contemporary popularity.
Mr. Edmund Gosse has recently given a reason for this, which seems worthy
of attention, while by no means explaining everything. "Donne was, I would
venture to suggest, by far the most modern and contemporaneous of the
writers of his time. . . . He arrived at an excess of actuality of style, and it
was because he struck them as so novel, and so completely in touch with
his age, that his immediate coevals were so much fascinated with him."[4]
A much bequoted passage of the *Conversations with Drummond* informs
us that Ben Jonson "esteemeth Donne the first poet in the world in some
things."[5] An analysis of these "some things," which space here forbids, will,
I think, show them to depend, to a large degree, upon that deeper element

of the modern lyric, poetic insight; the power which, proceeding by means of the clash of ideas familiar with ideas remote, flashes light and meaning into what has hitherto appeared mere commonplace. This, mainly, though with much else, is the positive originality of Donne. A quality no less remarkable is to be found in what may be called his negative originality, by which I mean that trait which caused Donne absolutely to give over the current mannerisms of his time; to write neither in the usual Italian manner, nor in borrowed lyrical forms; indeed, to be at times wantonly careless of mere expression, and, above all, to throw away every trace of the conventional classic imagery and mannerisms which infected and conventionalized the poetry of so many of his contemporaries. It seems to me that no one, excepting Shakespeare, with Sidney, Greville, and Jonson in lesser measure, has done so much to develop intellectualized emotion in the Elizabethan lyric as John Donne. But Donne is the last poet to demand a proselyting zeal of his devotees, and all those who have learned to love his witching personality will agree to the charming sentiment of his faithful adorer, Izaak Walton, when he says: "Though I must omit to mention divers persons, friends of Sir Henry Wotton; yet I must not omit to mention of a love that was there begun betwixt him and Dr. Donne, sometime Dean of Saint Paul's; a man of whose abilities I shall forbear to say anything, because he who is of this nation, and pretends to learning or ingenuity, and is ignorant of Dr. Donne, deserves not to know him."[6]

But in the great age of Elizabeth, miracles were not the monopoly of the immortals. Strenuous Titans, such as those that wrought poetical cosmos out of the chaos of *Barons Wars* or *Civil Wars,* out of disquisitions on statecraft and ponderous imitations of Senecan rhetoric, could also work dainty marvels in song. The lyrics of that most interesting and "difficult" of poets, Fulke Greville, have already been noticed, and are the more remarkable in their frequent grace of fancy, uncommon wit, originality, and real music of expression in that they are the sister products of the obscure and intricate musings and the often eccentric didacticism of *Mustapha* and *Alaham.* Of Daniel, a conscientious artist as he was a sensible theorist in verse, we might expect less masterly restraint; whilst Donne displayed the daring of an individualism that enabled him, while his poems were yet in manuscript, to exercise upon his contemporaries the effect of an accepted classic.

The story of Shakespeare's gradual enfranchisement from the trammels of imitation and the adherence to ephemeral rules of art has been often told, and is as true of his work, considered metrically, as from any other point of view. With increasing grasp of mind came increasing power and abandon in style and versification; and this applies to the incidental lyrics of his plays (as far as the data enables us to judge), as it applies to the sweep and cadence of his blank verse.[7]

On the other hand, Jonson, despite his unusual versatility in the invention and practice of new and successful lyrical forms, displays the conservative temper throughout, in avoiding mixed meters, stanzas of irregular structure or of differing lengths, and in such small matters as his careful indication of elision where the syllable exceeds the strict number demanded by the verse-scheme. Many of Jonson's utterances, too, attest his detestation of license (e.g., "that Donne, for not keeping of accent, deserved hanging"); his esteem of the formal element in literature (e.g., "that Shakespeare wanted art"); or his dislike to innovation.[8] Towards the close of his life, Jonson grew increasingly fond of the decasyllabic rimed couplet, the meter which was to become the maid of all work in the next generation. This meter it was that he defended in theory against the heresies of Campion and Daniel,[9] and it was in this meter that he wrote, at times with a regularity of accent and antithetical form that reminds us of the great hand of Dryden in the next age.[10] Jonson's tightening of the reins of regularity in the couplet and in lyric forms—in which latter, despite his inspiration, Herrick followed his master with loving observance of the law—is greatly in contrast with the course of dramatic blank verse, which, beginning in the legitimate freedom of Shakespeare, descended, through the looseness of Fletcher and Mas-singer, to the license of Davenant and Crowne.

By far the most independent lyrical metrist of this age was John Donne, who has been, it seems to me, quite as much misunderstood on this side as on the side of his eccentricities of thought and expression. In a recent chapter on Donne, in several other respects far from satisfactory, Mr. Edmund Gosse has treated this particular topic very justly. Speaking of Donne's "system of prosody," he says: "The terms 'irregular,' 'unintelligible' and 'viciously rugged,' are commonly used in describing it, and it seems even to be supposed by some critics that Donne did not know how to scan. This last supposition may be rejected at once; what there was to know about poetry was known to Donne. But it seems certain that he intentionally introduced a revolution into English versification. It was doubtless a rebellion against the smooth and somewhat nervous iambic flow of Spenser and the earliest contemporaries of Shakespeare, that Donne invented his violent mode of breaking up the line into quick and slow beats." Mr. Gosse finds this innovation the result of a desire for "new and more varied effects," adding: "The iambic rimed line of Donne has audacities such as are permitted to his blank verse by Milton, and although the felicities are rare in the older poet instead of being almost incessant, as in the later, Donne at his best is not less melodious than Milton."[11] We need not be detained by the query, whether it was not the strange personality of the poet rather than any unusual desire for "new and more varied effects" which produced a result so unusual. It is certain, that for inventive variety, fitness, and success, the lyrical stanzas of Donne are surpassed by scarcely any Elizabethan poet. In short, Donne seems to have applied to the lyric the freedom of the best dramatic verse of his age, and stood as the exponent of novelty and individualism in form precisely as Jonson stood for classic conservatism.

We have thus seen how in form as well as in thought the governing influence upon the English Elizabethan lyric was the influence of Italy, the Italy of the Renaissance; how, organically considered, there was a steady advance towards greater variety of measure and inventiveness in stanzaic form, and a general growth of taste in such matters as alliteration, the distribution of pauses, and the management of rime. As might be expected, the analogies of certain forms of verse to certain forms of thought were far less rigidly preserved in the English literature of this day than in that of Italy; and there is scarcely a form of English verse, of which it can be said that it was restricted to a given species of poetry. Spenser less completely than Sidney is the exponent of the Italianate school of poetry in England; for in Sidney is to be found not only its pastoral presentation, but the sonnet sequence and the madrigal, both long to remain the favorite utterance of contemporary lyrists. But even if Sidney was the representative of the Italianate school, the lyric took almost at once in his hands, and in those of Spenser and Shakespeare, the characteristics of a genuine vernacular utterance which it afterwards maintained, adapting itself in the minutiae of style and versification as in the character of thought and theme. The Italian influence, although completely assimilated especially among dramatists like Dekker, Fletcher, and Beaumont, and in Browne and the later poetry of Drayton, still continued dominant in poets such as Davison, Drummond, and the writers of madrigals; but failed, as the classic influence too failed, to reach Donne. It was here that the new classic influence arose with Ben Jonson, an assimilated classicism—as far as possible removed from the imitative classicism of Harvey and Spenser in the days of the Areopagus; and it was this spirit that came finally to prevail—not that of Donne which substituted one kind of radicalism for another;—it was this spirit of conservative nicety of style and regularity of versification that led on through Herrick and Sandys to the classicism of Dryden and Pope.

Notes

1. Lives *of the English Poets,* ed. Tauchnitz, 1,11.
2. *Conversations,* Shakespeare Society, p. 8.
3. *Poetical Rhapsody,* ed. Nicolas, p. xlv.
4. Edmund Gosse, *The Jacobean Poets,* 1894, p. 64.

Conversations, as above, p. 8.

6. *Life of Wotton, Lives,* etc., Amer. ed., 1846, p. 136.
7. There is a wide step in versification between *Silvia* or the Song from the *Merchant of Venice,* and the free cadenced songs of the *Tempest.*
8. See *Jonson's Conversations, Sh. Soc. Pub.,* p. 3.
9. See, especially, the opening passage of the *Conversations* concerning his Epic, "all in couplets, for he detesteth all other rimes. Said he had written a Discourse of Poesie, both against Campion and Daniel,where he proves couplets to be the bravest sort of verse, especially when they are broken like hexameters," i.e., exhibit a strong medial caesura.
10. See, especially, the later epistles and occasional verses, such as the *Epigrams* to the Lord Treasurer of England, *To my Muse,* etc.
11. *The Jacobean Poets,* p. 61 f.

—Felix E. Schelling, from "Introduction,"
A Book of Elizabethan Lyrics, 1895, pp. xxi–lxix

OSWALD CRAWFURD (1896)

Oswald Crawfurd (1834–1909) was an English novelist, poet, and travel writer. He is best known for his travel writings on Portugal and his novels *The World We Live In* and *Sylvia Arden.*

"The Will of John Donne" is probably the wittiest and the bitterest lyric in our language. Donne's love passages and their record in verse were over before the author was of age. His wit then turned into metaphysical sermon-writing and theological polemics, and his bitterness into a despairing austerity.

—Oswald Crawfurd, *Lyrical Verse from
Elizabeth to Victoria,* 1896, p. 426

J.B. Lightfoot
"Donne, the Poet-Preacher" (1896)

In the essay below, Lightfoot writes eloquently of Donne's passions and ability as a preacher, declaring that in his published sermons, "There is throughout an energy, a glow, an impetuosity, a force as of a torrent, which must have swept his hearers onward despite themselves." Lightfoot provides a contextual understanding of how Donne approached composing his sermons, and likewise suggests how contemporary readers and critics should approach these works as well: "Donne's sermons are not faultless models of pulpit oratory. From this point of view they cannot be studied as the sermons of the great French preachers may be studied . . . even here he is elevated above himself and his time by his subject. There is still far too much of that conceit of language, of that subtlety of association, of that 'sport with ideas,' which has been condemned in his verse compositions . . . [yet] we marvel at the profusion of learning, the richness of ideas and imagery, the abundance in all kinds . . . [he] speaks directly to our time, because he speaks to all times." Any student examining Donne's sermonic writings is well advised to begin with this essay, which not only highlights the few flaws Lightfoot finds in Donne's oratorical works but which also, and much more effectively, unabashedly demonstrates the longstanding admiration with which critics and scholars have viewed these same works.

As a layman he had been notably a poet; as a clergyman he was before all things a preacher. He had remarkable gifts as an orator, and he used them well. Henceforward preaching was the main business of his life. After he had preached a sermon, "he never gave his eyes rest," we are told, "till he had chosen out a new text, and that night cast his sermon into a form, and his text into divisions, and the next day he took himself to consult the fathers, and so commit his meditations to his memory, which was excellent."[1] On the Saturday he gave himself an entire holiday, so as to refresh body and mind, "that he might be enabled to do the work of the day following not faintly, but with courage and cheerfulness." When first ordained he shunned preaching before town congregations. He would retire to some country church with a single friend, and so try his wings. His first sermon was preached in the quiet village of Paddington. But his fame grew rapidly; and he soon took his rank as the most powerful preacher of his day in the English Church. Others envied him and murmured, says an admirer, that, having been called to the vineyard late in the day, he received his penny with the first.[2]

More than a hundred and fifty of his sermons are published. Some of them were preached at Lincoln's Inn, where he held the Lectureship; others at St. Dunstan's-in-the-West, of which church he was vicar; others at Whitehall, in his turn as Royal Chaplain, or before the Court on special occasions; others, and these the most numerous, at St. Paul's. Of this last class a few were delivered at the Cross, by special appointment, but the majority within the Cathedral, when year after year, according to the rule which is still in force at St. Paul's, he preached as Dean at the great festivals of the Church—Christmas and Easter and Whitsunday—or when he expounded the Psalms assigned to his prebendal stall, or on various incidental occasions.

An eminent successor of Donne, the late Dean Milman, finds it difficult to "imagine, when he surveys the massy folios of Donne's sermons—each sermon spreads out over many pages—a vast congregation in the Cathedral or at Paul's Cross listening not only with patience, but with absorbed interest, with unflagging attention, even with delight and rapture, to those interminable disquisitions." "It is astonishing to us," he adds, "that he should hold a London congregation enthralled, unwearied, unsatiated."

And yet I do not think that the secret of his domination is far to seek.
        Fervet immensusque ruit.

There is throughout an energy, a glow, an impetuosity, a force as of a torrent, which must have swept his hearers onward despite themselves. This rapidity of movement is his characteristic feature. There are faults in abundance, but there is no flagging from beginning to end. Even the least manageable subjects yield to his untiring energy. Thus he occupies himself largely with the minute interpretation of scriptural passages. This exegesis is very difficult of treatment before a large and miscellaneous congregation. But with Donne it is always interesting. It may be subtle, wire-drawn, fanciful at times, but it is keen, eager, lively, never pedantic or dull. So, again, his sermons abound in quotations from the fathers; and this burden of patristic reference would have crushed any common man. But here the quotations are epigrammatic in themselves; they are tersely rendered, they are vigorously applied, and the reader is never wearied by them. Donne is, I think, the most animated of the great Anglican preachers.

I select two or three examples out of hundreds which might be chosen, as exhibiting this eagerness of style, lit up by the genius of a poet, and heated by the zeal of an evangelist. Hear this, for instance:

"God's house is the house of prayer. It is His court of requests. There he receives petitions; there He gives orders upon them. And you come to God in His house as though you came to keep Him company, to sit down and talk with Him half an hour; or you come as ambassadors, covered in His presence, as though ye came from as great a prince as He. You meet below, and there make your bargains for biting, for devouring usury, and then you come up hither to prayers, and so make God your broker. You rob and spoil and eat His people as bread by extortion and bribery, and deceitful weights and measures, and deluding oaths in buying and selling, and then come hither, and so make God your receiver, and His house a den of thieves. . . . As if the Son of God were but the son of some lord that had been your schoolfellow in your youth, and so you continue a boldness to him ever after; so because you have been brought up with Christ from your cradle, and catechised in His name, His name becomes reverend unto you; and *sanctum et terribile*, holy and reverend, holy and terrible, should His name be."[4] . . .

Listen to such words as I have read; and to complete the effect summon up in imagination the appearance and manner of the preacher. Recall him as he is seen in the portrait attributed to Vandyck—the keen, importuning "melting eye,"[5] the thin, worn features, the poetic cast of expression, half pensive, half gracious. Add to this the sweet tones of his voice and the "speaking action,"[6] which is described by eye-witnesses as more eloquent than the words of others, and you will cease to wonder at the thraldom in which he held his audience. "A preacher in earnest," writes Walton, "weeping sometimes *for* his auditory, sometimes *with* them; always preaching to himself; like an angel *from* a cloud but *in* none; carrying some, as St. Paul was, to heaven in holy raptures and enticing others by a sacred art and courtship to amend their lives; here picturing a vice so as to make it ugly to those who practised it, and a virtue so as to make it beloved even by those that loved it not."[7] Indeed we cannot doubt that he himself was alive to that feeling which he ascribes to the "blessed fathers" when preaching, "a holy delight to be heard and to be heard with delight."[8]

Donne's sermons are not faultless models of pulpit oratory. From this point of view they cannot be studied as the sermons of the great French preachers may be studied. Under the circumstances this was almost an impossibility. Preaching his hour's sermon once or twice weekly, he had not time to arrange and rearrange, to prune, to polish, to elaborate. As it is, we marvel at the profusion of learning, the richness of ideas and imagery, the abundance in all kinds, poured out by a preacher who thus lived, as it were, from hand to mouth.

Moreover, the taste of the age for fantastic imagery, for subtle disquisition, for affectations of language and of thought, exercised a fascination over him. Yet even here he is elevated above himself and his time by his subject. There is still far too much of that conceit of language, of that subtlety of association, of that "sport with ideas," which has been condemned in his verse compositions; but, compared with his poems, his sermons are freedom and simplicity itself. And, whenever his theme rises, he rises too; and then in the giant strength of an earnest conviction he bursts these green withers which a fantastic age has bound about him, as the thread of tow snaps at the touch of fire. Nothing can be more direct or more real than his eager impetuous eloquence, when he speaks of God, of redemption, of heaven, of the sinfulness of human sin, of the bountifulness of Divine Love.

At such moments he is quite the most modern of our older Anglican divines. He speaks directly to our time, because he speaks to all times. If it be the special aim of the preacher to convince of sin and of righteousness and of judgment, then Donne deserves to be reckoned the first of our classic preachers. We may find elsewhere more skilful arrangement, more careful oratory, more accurate exegesis, more profuse illustration; but here is the light which flashes and the fire which burns.

Donne's learning was enormous; and yet his sermons probably owe more to his knowledge of men than to his knowledge of books. The penitent is too apt to shrink into the recluse. Donne never yielded to this temptation. He himself thus rebukes the mistaken extravagance of penitence: "When men have lived long from God, they never think they come near enough to Him, except they go beyond Him."[9] No contrition was more intense than his; but he did not think to prove its reality by cutting himself off from the former interests and associations of his life. He had been a man of the world before; and he did not cease to be a man in the world now. "Beloved"—he says this term "beloved" is his favourite mode of address—"Beloved, salvation itself being so often presented to us in the names of glory and of joy, we cannot think that the way to that glory is a sordid life affected here, an obscure, a beggarly, a negligent abandoning of all ways of preferment or riches or estimation in this world, for the glory of heaven shines down, in those beams hither. As God loves a cheerful giver, so He loves a cheerful taker that takes hold of His mercies and His comforts with a cheerful heart."[10] This healthy, vigorous good sense is the more admirable in Donne, because it is wedded to an intense and passionate devotion.

I wish that time would allow me to multiply examples of his lively imagination flashing out in practical maxims and lighting up the common things of life; as, for instance, where he pictures the general sense of insecurity on the death of Elizabeth: "Every one of you in the city were running up and down like ants with their eggs bigger than themselves, every man with his bags, to seek where to hide them safely."[11] Or where he enforces the necessity of watchfulness against minor temptations: "As men that rob houses thrust in a child at the window, and he opens greater doors for them, so lesser sins make way for greater."[12] Or when he describes the little effect of preaching on the heartless listener: "He hears but the logic or the rhetoric or the ethic or the poetry of the sermon, but the sermon of the sermon he hears not."[13] Of such pithy sayings Donne's sermons are an inexhaustible storehouse, in which I would gladly linger; but I must hasten on to speak of one other feature before drawing to a close. Irony is a powerful instrument in the preacher's hands, if he knows how to wield it; otherwise it were better left alone. The irony of Donne is piercing. Hear the withering scorn which he pours on those who think to condone sinful living by a posthumous bequest: "We hide our sins in His house by hypocrisy all our lives, and we hide them at our deaths, perchance, with an hospital. And truly we had need do so; when we have impoverished God in His children by our extortions, and wounded Him and lamed Him in them by our oppressions, we had need to provide God an hospital."[14] Or hear this again, on the criticism of sermons: "Because God calls preaching foolishness, you take God at His word and think preaching a thing under you. Hence it is that you take so much liberty in censuring and comparing preacher and preacher."[15] And lastly, observe the profound pathos and awe which are veiled under the apparent recklessness of these daring words: "At how cheap a price was Christ tumbled up and down in this world! It does almost take off our pious scorn of the low price at which Judas sold Him, to consider that His Father sold Him to the world for nothing."[16]

For preaching Donne lived; and in preaching he died. He rose from a sick-bed and came to London to take his customary sermon at Whitehall on the first Friday in Lent. Those who saw him in the pulpit, says Walton quaintly, must "have asked that question in Ezekiel, 'Do these bones live?'" The sermon was felt to be the swan's dying strain. Death was written in his wan and wasted features, and spoke through his faint and hollow voice.

The subject was in harmony with the circumstances. He took as his text[17] the passage in the Psalms, "Unto God the Lord belong the issues of death." His hearers said at the time that "Dr. Donne had preached his own funeral sermon."

The sermon was published. It betrays in part a diminution of his wonted fire and animation. We seem to see the preacher struggling painfully with his malady. But yet it is remarkable. The theme and the circumstances alike invest it with a peculiar solemnity; and there are flashes of the poet-preacher still.

"This whole world," he says, "is but a universal churchyard, but one common grave: and the life and motion that the greatest persons have in it is but as the shaking of buried bodies in their graves by an earthquake."[18]

"The worm is spread under thee, and the worm covers thee. *There* is the mats and carpet that lie under, and *there* is the state and the canopy that hangs over the greatest of the sons of men."[19]

"The tree lies as it falls, it is true, but yet it is not the last stroke that fells the tree, nor the last word nor the last gasp that qualifies the man."[20]

Hear now the closing words, and you will not be at a loss to conceive the profound impression which they must have left on his hearers, as the dying utterance of a dying man:

"There we leave you in that blessed dependency, to hang upon Him that hangs upon the Cross. There bathe in His tears, there suck at His wounds, and lie down in peace in His grave, till He vouchsafes you a resurrection and an ascension into that kingdom which He hath purchased for you with the inestimable price of His incorruptible blood. Amen."

Amen it was. He had prayed that he might die in the pulpit, or (if not this) that he might die of the pulpit; and his prayer was granted. From this sickness he never recovered; the effort hastened his dissolution; and, after lingering on a few weeks, he died on the last day of March 1631. This study of Donne as a preacher will be fitly closed with the last stanza from his poem entitled, "Hymn to God, my God, in my sickness," which sums up the broad lesson of his life and teaching:

So in His purple wrapped, receive me, Lord;
By these His thorns give me His other crown;
And as to others' souls I preached Thy Word,
Be this my text, my sermon to mine own:
Therefore, that He may raise, the Lord throws down.[21]

Notes
1. Walton's *Life,* p. 119.
2. Elegy by Mr. R. B., attached to *Poems* by John Donne (1669), p. 393.
3. *Annals of St. Paul's Cathedral,* p. 328.
4. *Works,* vol. iii. p. 217 sq.

5. Walton's *Life,* p. 150.

6. Elegy by Mr. Mayne, attached to *Poems* by John Donne (1669), p. 387.

7. *Life,* p. 69.

8. *Works,* vol. i. p. 98.

9. *Works,* vol. ii. p. 31.

10. *Works,* vol. ii. p. 142.

11. Ibid. vol. vi. p. 137.

12. Ibid. vol. ii. p. 556.

13. Ibid. vol. i. p. 72.

14. Ibid. vol. ii. p. 555.

15. Ibid. vol. ii. p. 219.

16. Ibid. vol. i. p. 61.

17. *Life,* p. 135 sq.

18. *Works,* vol. vi. p. 283.

19. Ibid. p. 288.

20. Ibid. p. 290.

21. *Poems,* vol. ii. p. 340.

—J.B. Lightfoot, "Donne, the Poet-Preacher,"
Historical Essays, 1896, pp. 232–45

Frederic Ives Carpenter
"Introduction" (1897)

Frederic Ives Carpenter (1861–1925) was an American literary scholar and long-time faculty member at the University of Chicago.

Donne is a thoroughly original spirit and a great innovator; he is thoughtful, indirect, and strange; he nurses his fancies, lives with them, and broods over them so much that they are still modern in all their distinction and ardour, in spite of the strangeness of their apparel—a strangeness no greater perhaps than that of some modern poets, like Browning, as the apparel of their verse will appear two hundred years hence. Ingenuity, allusiveness, the evocation of remote images and of analogies that startle the mind into a more than half acquiescence, phantoms of deep thoughts, and emotions half-sophisticated and wholly intense: these things mark the poetry of Donne. His lyric is original and taking, but it lacks simple thoughts; it does not sing. It is ascetic and sometimes austere; the sense of sin, the staple of contemporary tragedy, enters the lyric with Donne. He is all for terseness and meaning; and his versification accords with his thought and is equally elliptical.

—Frederic Ives Carpenter, "Introduction,"
to *English Lyric Poetry, 1500–1700,* 1897, p. lviii

DAVID HANNAY (1898)

An English journalist and author, David Hannay (1853–1934) was mostly known for his biographies and newspaper work.

⸻⸻⸻

One of the most enigmatical and debated, alternately one of the most attractive and most repellent, figures in English literature.

—David Hannay, *The Later Renaissance,* 1898, p. 220

LESLIE STEPHEN "JOHN DONNE" (1899)

Leslie Stephen (1832–1904) was the father to famed author Virginia Woolf and the first editor of *The Dictionary of National Biography.* Though long overshadowed by his famous progeny, Stephen was a prolific author and critic whose agnostic ideals shine through his analysis of Donne.

⸻⸻⸻

In one way he has partly become obsolete because he belonged so completely to the dying epoch. The scholasticism in which his mind was steeped was to become hateful and then contemptible to the rising philosophy; the literature which he had assimilated went to the dust-heaps; preachers condescended to drop their doctorial robes; downright common-sense came in with Tillotson and South in the next generation; and not only the learning but the congenial habit of thought became unintelligible. Donne's poetical creed went the same way, and if Pope and Parnell perceived that there was some genuine ore in his verses and tried to beat it into the coinage of their own day, they only spoilt it in trying to polish it. But on the other side, Donne's depth of feeling, whether tortured into short lyrics or expanding into voluble rhetoric, has a charm which perhaps gains a new charm from modern sentimentalists. His morbid or "neurotic" constitution has a real affinity for latter-day pessimists. If they talk philosophy where he had to be content with scholastic theology the substance is pretty much the same. He has the characteristic love for getting pungency at any price; for dwelling upon the horrible till we cannot say whether it attracts or repels him; and can love the "intense" and supersublimated as much as if he were skilled in all the latest aesthetic canons.

—Leslie Stephen, "John Donne,"
The National Review, 1899, p. 613

ARTHUR SYMONS "JOHN DONNE" (1899)

A British playwright, poet, translator, and critic, Arthur Symons (1865–1945) was as much of a "Renaissance man" as he paints Donne to be in the portrait excerpted below. He published numerous volumes of his poetry and essays, and was also praised for his editorial work on volumes by Shakespeare and Ernest Dowson.

Was the mind of the dialectician, of the intellectual adventurer; he is a poet almost by accident, or at least for reasons with which art in the abstract has but little to do. He writes verse, first of all, because he has observed keenly, and because it pleases the pride of his intellect to satirise the pretensions of humanity. Then it is the flesh which speaks in his verse, the curiosity of woman, which he has explored in the same spirit of adventure; then passion, making a slave of him for love's sake, and turning at last to the slave's hatred; finally, religion, taken up with the same intellectual interest, the same subtle indifference, and, in its turn, passing also into passionate reality. A few poems are inspired in him by what he has seen in remote countries; some are marriage songs and funeral elegies, written for friendship or for money. But he writes nothing "out of his own head," as we say; nothing lightly, or, it would seem, easily; nothing for the song's sake. He speaks, in a letter, of "descending to print anything in verse"; and it is certain that he was never completely absorbed by his own poetry, or at all careful to measure his achievements against those of others. He took his own poems very seriously, he worked upon them with the whole force of his intellect; but to himself, even before he became a divine, he was something more than a poet. Poetry was but one means of expressing the many-sided activity of his mind and temperament. Prose was another, preaching another; travel and contact with great events and persons scarcely less important to him, in the building up of himself.

—Arthur Symons, "John Donne,"
Fortnightly Review, 1899, p. 735

REUBEN POST HALLECK (1900)

Reuben Post Halleck (1859–1936) was a scholar and writer most known for his excellent companion works, *History of English Literature* and *History of American Literture.*

———— ———— ————

John Donne is of interest to the student of literature chiefly because of the influence which he exerted on the poetry of the age. His verse teems with forced comparisons and analogies between things remarkable for their dissimilarity. An obscure likeness and a worthless conceit were as important to him as was the problem of existence to Hamlet.

—Reuben Post Halleck, *History of English Literature,* 1900, p. 186

JOHN W. HALES "JOHN DONNE" (1903)

John Wesley Hales (1836–1914) was a prominent scholar best known for his work on Renaissance poet Edmund Spenser. In the piece below, though Hales professes himself an admirer of Donne's, the author rails against the metaphysical school of poetry, arguing that Donne's poetic gifts were "perversely directed," and that the metaphysics represent a "certain bad taste of [the] day." Hales's main issue with the metaphysical school is "what may be called its fantasticality, its quaint wit, elaborate ingenuity, far-fetched allusiveness." This was the most prominent criticism leveled against Donne in the nineteenth century (and, indeed, prior to that time) and Hales demonstrates the continuing authority of the argument in the early twentieth century. Paradoxically, Hales assails the fact that Donne's reputation has suffered because of this idea: "Donne's contemporary reputation as a poet, and still more as a preacher, was immense; and a glance at his works would suffice to show that he did not deserve the contempt with which he was subsequently treated." Nonetheless, Hales reproduces the argument himself, demonstrating that the chief complaint against the metaphysical poets is the very nature of metaphysical poetry itself.

———— ———— ————

Donne's contemporary reputation as a poet, and still more as a preacher, was immense; and a glance at his works would suffice to show that he did not deserve the contempt with which he was subsequently treated. But yet his chief interest is that he was the principal founder of a school which especially expressed and represented a certain bad taste of his day. Of his genius there can be no question; but it was perversely directed. One may almost invert Jonson's famous panegyric on Shakespeare, and say that Donne was not for all time but for an age.

To this school Dr. Johnson has given the title of the Metaphysical; and for this title there is something to be said. 'Donne,' says Dryden, 'affects the metaphysics not only in his Satires, but in his amorous verses where Nature only should reign, and perplexes the minds of the fair sex with nice speculations of philosophy when he should engage their hearts and entertain them with the softnesses of love.' Thus he often ponders over the mystery of love, and is exercised by subtle questions as to its nature, origin, endurance. But a yet more notable distinction of this school than its philosophising, shallow or deep, is what may be called its fantasticality, its quaint wit, elaborate ingenuity, far-fetched allusiveness; and it might better be called the Ingenious, or Fantastic School. Various and out-of-the-way information and learning is a necessary qualification for membership. Donne in one of his letters speaks of his 'embracing the worst voluptuousness, an hydroptic immoderate desire of human learning and languages.' Eminence is attained by using such stores in the way to be least expected. The thing to be illustrated becomes of secondary importance by the side of the illustration. The more unlikely and surprising and preposterous this is, the greater the success. This is wit of a kind. From one point of view, wit, as Dr. Johnson says, 'may be considered as a kind of *discordia concors;* a combination of dissimilar images or discovery of occult resemblances in things apparently unlike. Of wit thus defined they [Donne and his followers] have more than enough. The most heterogeneous ideas are yoked by violence together; nature and art are ransacked for illustrations, comparisons, and allusions; their learning instructs, and their subtility surprises; but the reader commonly thinks his improvement dearly bought, and though he sometimes admires is seldom pleased.'

And so in the following curious passage from Donne's Dedication of certain poems to Lord Craven it should be observed how 'wit' and 'poetry' are made to correspond: 'Amongst all the monsters this unlucky age has teemed with, I find none so prodigious as the poets of these late times [this is very much what Donne's own critics must say], wherein men, as if they would level undertakings too as well as estates, acknowledging no inequality of parts and judgments, pretend as indifferently to the chair of wit as to the pulpit, and conceive themselves no less inspired with the spirit of poetry than with that of religion.' Dryden styles Donne 'the greatest wit though not the best poet of our nation.'

The taste which this school represents marks other literatures besides our own at this time. It was 'in the air' of that age; and so was not originated by Donne. But it was he who in England first gave it full expression—who was its first vigorous and effective and devoted spokesman. And this secures him a conspicuous position in the history of our literature when we remember how prevalent was the fashion of 'conceits' during the first half of the seventeenth century, and that amongst those who followed it more or less are to be mentioned, to say nothing of the earlier poems of Milton and Waller and Dryden, Suckling, Denham, Herbert, Crashaw, Cleveland, Cowley.

This misspent learning, this excessive ingenuity, this laborious wit seriously mars almost the whole of Donne's work. For the most part we look on it with amazement rather than with pleasure. It reminds us rather of a 'pyrotechnic display,' with its unexpected flashes and explosions, than of a sure and constant light (compare the *Valediction* given in our selections). We weary of such unmitigated cleverness—such ceaseless straining after novelty and surprise. We long for something simply thought, and simply said.

His natural gifts were certainly great. He possesses a real energy and fervour. He loved, and he suffered much, and he writes with a passion which is perceptible through all his artificialities. Such a poem as *The Will* is evidence of the astonishing rapidity and brightness of his fancy.

He also claims notice as one of our earliest formal satirists. Though not published till much later, there is proof that some at least of his satires were written three or four years before those of Hall. Two of them (ii. and iv.) were reproduced—'versified'—in the last century by Pope, acting on a suggestion by Dryden; No. iii. was similarly treated by Parnell. In these versions, along with the roughness of the metre, disappears much of the general vigour; and it should be remembered that the metrical roughness was no result of incapacity, but was designed. Thus the charge of metrical uncouthness so often brought against Donne on the ground of his satires is altogether mistaken. How fluently and smoothly he could write if he pleased, is attested over and over again by his lyrical pieces.

—John W. Hales, "John Donne," *The English Poets,*
ed. Thomas Humphrey Ward, 1903, vol. l, pp. 558–60

❖

WORKS

❖

And now dost laugh and triumph on this bough.
Little think'st thou
That it will freeze anon, and that I shall
To-morrow find thee fall'n, or not at all.

This simple and delicate description is only introduced as a foundation for
an elaborate metaphysical conceit as a parallel to it, in the next stanza.

Little think'st thou (poor heart
That labour'st yet to nestle thee,
And think'st by hovering here to get a part
In a forbidden or forbidding tree,
And hop'st her stiffness by long siege to bow:)
Little think'st thou,
That thou to-morrow, ere the sun doth wake,
Must with this sun and me a journey take.

This is but a lame and impotent conclusion from so delightful a beginning.
He thus notices the circumstance of his wearing his late wife's hair about
his arm, in a little poem which is called the Funeral.

Whoever comes to shroud me, do not harm
Nor question much
That subtle wreath of hair, about mine arm;
The mystery, the sign you must not touch.

The scholastic reason he gives quite dissolves the charm of tender and
touching grace in the sentiment itself—

For 'tis my outward soul,
Viceroy to that, which unto heaven being gone,
Will leave this to control,
And keep these limbs, her provinces, from
    dissolution.

Again, the following lines, the title of which is Love's Deity, are highly
characteristic of this author's manner, in which the thoughts are inlaid in
a costly but imperfect mosaic-work.

I long to talk with some old lover's ghost,
Who died before the God of Love was born:
I cannot think that he, who then lov'd most,
Sunk so low, as to love one which did scorn.

WILLIAM HAZLITT "ON COWLEY, BUTLER, SUCKLING, ETC." (1819)

One of the greatest English literary critics of the nineteenth centur
William Hazlitt (1778–1830) also wrote on art, politics, and history.
renowned intellect and essayist, Hazlitt comments below on Donne
satirical works, stating that in his satires, Donne strove to demonstrat
"disagreeable truths in as disagreeable a way as possible, or to conve
a pleasing and affecting thought (of which there are many to be foun
in his other writings) by the harshest means, and with the most painf
effort." Ultimately Hazlitt concludes that he does not admire Donne
satires as much as his other works for this reason; they are too fille
with contempt and dogma for Hazlitt's liking, who seemingly preferre
a lighter, defter approach to satire. Hazlitt's critique of Donne's satir
reflect those made by critics of his other works, and those studyin
Donne's body of work may find it suggestive to compare Hazlitt
criticisms to others presented in this collection.

Donne, who was considerably before Cowley, is without his fanc
was more recondite in his logic, and in his descriptions. He is hen
particularly in his satires, to tell disagreeable truths in as disagreeable
as possible, or to convey a pleasing and affecting thought (of which the
many to be found in his other writings) by the harshest means, an
the most painful effort. His Muse suffers continual pangs and throe
thoughts are delivered by the Caesarean operation. The sentiments, pro
and tender as they often are, are stifled in the expression; and 'h
pantingly forth,' are "buried quick again' under the ruins and rubb
analytical distinctions. It is like poetry waking from a trance: with
bent idly on the outward world, and half-forgotten feelings cro
about the heart; with vivid impressions, dim notions, and disjointed
The following may serve as instances of beautiful or impassioned refle
losing themselves in obscure and difficult applications. He has som
to a Blossom, which begin thus:

> Little think'st thou, poor flow'r,
> Whom I have watched six or seven days,
> And seen thy birth, and seen what every hour
> Gave to thy growth, thee to this height to raise,

But since this God produc'd a destiny,
And that vice-nature, custom, lets it be;
I must love her that loves not me.

The stanza in the Epithalamion on a Count Palatine of the Rhine, has been often quoted against him, and is an almost irresistible illustration of the extravagances to which this kind of writing, which turns upon a pivot of words and possible allusions, is liable. Speaking of the bride and bridegroom he says, by way of serious compliment—

Here lies a she-Sun, and a he-Moon there,
She gives the best light to his sphere;
Or each is both and all, and so
They unto one another nothing owe.

His love-verses and epistles to his friends give the most favourable idea of Donne. His satires are too clerical. He shews, if I may so speak, too much disgust, and, at the same time, too much contempt for vice. His dogmatical invectives hardly redeem the nauseousness of his descriptions, and compromise the imagination of his readers more than they assist their reason. The satirist does not write with the same authority as the divine, and should use his poetical privileges more sparingly. 'To the pure all things are pure,' is a maxim which a man like Dr. Donne may be justified in applying to himself; but he might have recollected that it could not be construed to extend to the generality of his readers, *without benefit of clergy.*

—William Hazlitt, from "On Cowley, Butler, Suckling, etc.,"
Lectures on the English Comic Writers, 1819,
The Collected Works of William Hazlitt, eds.
A.R. Walker and Arnold Gower, 1903, vol. 8, pp. 51–53

UNSIGNED (1823)

The unsigned piece below, published in an early nineteenth-century literary magazine, is quite critical of Donne, suggesting that, "In pieces that can be read with unmingled pleasure, and admired as perfect wholes, the poetry of Donne is almost entirely deficient. Almost every beauty we meet with, goes hand in hand with some striking deformity, of one kind or another; and the effect of this is, at first, so completely *irritating* to the imagination, as well as to the taste, that, after we have experienced it a few times, we hastily determine to be without the one, rather than purchase it at the price of the other." Though the author considers Donne learned and in possession of a strong wit, he dislikes the poet's "fantastical imagination" (a criticism shared by Hazlitt and Lightfoot in above excerpted texts) and suggests that Donne lacks sensitivity and taste. In fact, the author generally criticizes the entire school of metaphysical poetry, writing that the metaphysical poets "had little simplicity of feeling, and still less of taste. They did not know the real and intrinsic value of any object, whether moral or physical; but only in what manner it might be connected with any other object, so as to be made subservient to their particular views at the moment." The author does, however, find little gems in Donne's works to admire, phrases, lines and passages that are not encumbered by the poet's numerous "faults," and in sharing those particular moments in Donne's poesy with the reader, the author is perhaps initiating a larger conversation about the merit of individual pieces of work in Donne, though students studying the author will more likely find this author's criticisms a more useful springboard in constructing their own arguments about Donne.

Theobald, in his egregious preface to Shakspeare, calls Donne's Poems "nothing but a continued heap of riddles."—We shall presently shew that he knew as little about Donne as he himself has shewn that he knew about Shakspeare. If *he* could have written such "riddles," or even expounded them, Pope might have put him into the *Dunciad* in vain.

Donne was contemporary with Shakspeare, and was not unworthy to be so. He may fairly be placed, in point of talent, at the head of the minor poets of that day. Imbued, to saturation, with all the learning of his age—with a most active and piercing intellect—an imagination, if not grasping and comprehensive, most subtle and far-darting—a fancy rich, vivid, picturesque, and, at the same time, highly *fantastical,*—if we may so apply the term—a mode of expression singularly terse, simple, and condensed—an exquisite ear for the melody of versification—and a wit, admirable as well for its caustic severity as its playful quickness; all he wanted to make him an accomplished poet of the second order was, sensibility and taste: and both of these he possessed in a certain degree; but neither in a sufficient degree to keep them from yielding to the circumstances in which he was placed. His sensibility was by nature strong, but sluggish and deep-seated. It required to be roused and awakened by the imagination, before it would act; and this process seldom failed to communicate to the action which it created, an appearance of affectation (for it was nothing more than the appearance), which is more destructive to the effect of sentimental poetry than any thing else. We do not mind the images and illustrations of a sentiment being recondite and far-fetched; and, indeed, this has frequently a good effect; but if the sentiment itself has any appearance of being so, we doubt the truth of it immediately; and if we doubt its truth, we are disposed to give it any reception rather than a sympathetic one. The scholastic habits of Donne's intellect also, without weakening his sensibility, contributed greatly to deform and denaturalize its outward manifestations. It was not the fashion of his time for a scholar and a poet to express himself as other people would; for if he had done so, what advantage would he or the world have derived from his poetry or his scholarship? Accordingly, however intense a feeling might be, or however noble a thought, it was to be heightened and illustrated, in the expression of it, by clustering about it a host of images and associations (congruous or not, as it might happen), which memory or imagination, assisted by the most quick-eyed wit, or the most subtle ingenuity, could in any way contrive to link to it: thus pressing the original thought or sentiment to death, and hiding even the form of it, beneath a profusion of superfluous dress. This was the crying fault of all the minor poets of the Elizabethan age; and of Donne more than of any other: though *his* thoughts and feelings would, generally speaking, bear this treatment better than those of any of his rivals in the same class. These persons never acted avowedly, (though they sometimes did unconsciously) on the principle that an idea or a sentiment may be poetical *per se;* for they had no notion whatever of the fact. They considered that *man* was the creator of poetry, not Nature; and that any thing might be made poetical, by connecting it, in a certain manner, with something else. A thought or a feeling was, to them, not a thing *to express,* but a theme to write *variations* upon—a nucleus, about which other thoughts and feelings were to be made to crystallize. A star was not bright to *their* eyes till it had been set in a constellation; a rose was not sweet till it had been gathered into a bouquet, and its hue and odour contrasted and blended with a thousand others. In fact, they had little simplicity of feeling, and still less of taste. They did not know the real and intrinsic value of any object, whether moral or physical; but only in what manner it might be connected with any other object, so as to be made subservient to their particular views at the moment. They saw at once how far it was available *to them,* but nothing whatever of the impression it was calculated to make for itself.

We are speaking, now, of a particular class or school of poets of that day; for they differed as much from all others, and were as much allied by a general resemblance of style among themselves, as the Delia Cruscan school in our own day. Indeed, in some particulars, there is no slight resemblance between the two styles; inasmuch, as both are purely artificial, and are dependent for their effect on a particular *manner* of treating their subject: at least, their intended effect is dependent on this—for the school to which Donne belongs often delights us in the highest degree, not in consequence of this manner, but in spite of it. There is also this other grand difference in favour of the latter,—that, whereas the Delia Cruscans tried to make things poetical by means of *words* alone, *they* did it by means of thoughts and images;—the one considered poetry to consist in a certain mode of expression; the other, in a certain mode of seeing, thinking, and feeling. This is nearly all the difference between them; but this is a vast difference indeed: for the one supposes the necessity of, and in fact uses, a vast fund of thoughts and images; while the other can execute all its purposes nearly as well without any of these. In short, the one kind of writing requires very considerable talent to produce it, and its results are very often highly poetical; whereas the other requires no talent at all, and can in no case produce poetry, but very frequently covers and conceals it where it is.

But it is not at present our intention to go into a general discussion of that particular school of poetry to which Donne belongs; but merely to bring to light some of the exquisite beauties which have hitherto lain concealed from the present age, among the learned as well as unlearned lumber which he has so unaccountably mixed up with them. We say unaccountably—for it is impossible to give a reasonable account of any poetical theory, the perpetual results of which are the most pure and perfect beauties of every kind—of thought, of sentiment, of imagery, of expression, and of versification—lying in immediate contact with the basest deformities, equally of every kind; each given forth alternately in almost equal proportions, and in the most unconscious manner on the part of the writer as to either being entitled to the preference; and indeed without one's being able to discover that he saw any difference between them, even in kind.

Before doing this, however, it may be well to let the reader know what was thought of Donne in his own day, lest he should suppose that we are introducing him to a person little known at that time, or lightly valued.

If a prophet has little honour in his own time and country, the same can seldom be said of a poet; though *he*, too, is in some sort a prophet. The day in which Donne lived was the most poetical the world ever knew, and yet there can be little doubt, from the evidence of the fugitive literature of the time, that Donne was, upon the whole, more highly esteemed than any other of his contemporaries. We do not, however, mean to attribute all his fame to his published poetry. He was undoubtedly a very extraordinary person in many other respects. He possessed vast knowledge and erudition, and was highly distinguished for the eloquence of his public preaching. But the greater part of the admiration bestowed on him, was avowedly directed to the poetical writings.

It is remarkable that the writer, of whom this could be said by persons of repute, (whether truly or not is no matter) in an age which produced Shakspeare and the elder dramatists—besides Spenser, Syndey, Herbert, Raleigh, and a host of minor names—should so long have remained unknown in an after age, one of the distinguishing boasts of which is, that it has revived a knowledge of, and a love for its great predecessor, at the same time that it has almost rivalled it.

In pieces that can be read with unmingled pleasure, and admired as perfect wholes, the poetry of Donne is almost entirely deficient. This may serve, in some degree, to account for the total neglect which has so long attended him. Almost every beauty we meet with, goes hand in hand with some striking deformity, of one kind or another; and the effect of this is, at first, so completely *irritating* to the imagination, as well as to the taste, that, after we have experienced it a few times, we hastily determine to be without the one, rather than purchase it at the price of the other. But the reader who is disposed, by these remarks, and the extracts that will accompany them, to a perusal of the whole of this poet's works, may be assured that this unpleasant effect will very soon wear off, and he will soon find great amusement and great exercise for his *thinking* faculties, (if nothing else) even in the objectionable parts of Donne; for he is always, when indulging in his very worst vein, filled to overflowing with thoughts, and materials for engendering thought.

The following short pieces are beautiful exceptions to the remark made just above, as to the mixed character of this poet's writings. The first is a farewell from a lover to his mistress, on leaving her for a time. For clearness and smoothness of construction, and a passionate sweetness and softness in the music of the versification, it might have been written in the present day, and may satisfy the ear of the most fastidious of modern readers; and for thought, sentiment, and imagery, it might *not* have been written in the present day;—for, much as we hold in honour our living poets, we doubt if any one among them is capable of it. In fact, it is one of those pieces which immediately strike us as being purely and exclusively attributable to the writer of them—which satisfy us, that, *but for him,* we never could have become possessed of them—which bear a mark that we cannot very well expound, even to ourselves, but which we know no one could have placed on them but him; and this, by-the-bye, is one of the most unequivocal criterions of a true poet. Perhaps the piece itself will explain better what we mean, than any thing we could say of it.

As virtuous men pass mildly away

The simile of the compasses, notwithstanding its quaintness, is more perfect in its kind, and more beautiful, than any thing we are acquainted with. Perhaps the above is the only poem we could extract, that is not disfigured by *any* of the characteristic faults of Donne. Several of them have, however, very few. The following is one of these. It has an air of serious gaiety about it, as if it had been composed in the very bosom of bliss. The versification too, is perfect. It is called, "The Good-Morrow."

I wonder by my troth, what thou and I
Did till we lov'd

The following, though not entirely without the faults of his style, is exceedingly graceful and elegant:

THE DREAM
Dear love, for nothing less than thee
What follows is extremely solemn and fine, and scarcely at all
    disfigured by the author's characteristic faults:

THE APPARITION
When by thy scorn, O murderess, I am dead

The next specimens that we shall give of this singular writer will be taken from among those of his poems which unite, in a nearly equal proportion, his characteristic faults and beauties; and which may be considered as scarcely less worthy of attention than the foregoing, partly on account of that very union of opposite qualities, but chiefly on account of their remarkable fullness of thought and imagery; in which, indeed, his very worst pieces abound to overflowing.

Notwithstanding the extravagance, as well as the ingenuity, which characterize the two following pieces, there is an air of sincerity about them, which renders their general effect impressive, and even solemn; to say nothing of their individual beauties, both of thought and expression.

THE ANNIVERSARY
All kings, and all their favourites

LOVE'S GROWTH
I scarce believe my love to be so pure

The reader will not fail to observe the occasional obscurities which arise out of the extreme condensation of expression in the foregoing pieces, and in most of those which follow. These passages may always be unravelled by a little attention, and they seldom fail to repay the trouble bestowed upon them. But they must be regarded as unequivocal faults nevertheless.

The following is, doubtless, "high-fantastical," in the last degree; but it is fine notwithstanding, and an evidence of something more than mere ingenuity.

Let me pour forth

The feelings which dictated such poetry as this, (for it is poetry, and nothing but real feelings *could* dictate it,) must have pierced deeper than the surface of both the heart and the imagination. In fact, they wanted nothing but to have been excited under more favourable circumstances, to have made them well-springs of the richest poetry uttering itself in the rarest words.

For clearness of expression, melody of versification, and a certain wayward simplicity of thought peculiarly appropriate to such compositions as these, the most successful of our modern lyrists might envy the following trifle:

THE MESSAGE
Send home my long stray'd eyes to me

Perhaps the two short pieces which follow, include all the characteristics of Donne's style—beauties as well as faults.

A LECTURE [UPON THE SHADOW]
Stand still, and I will read to thee

THE EXPIRATION
So, so,—break off this last lamenting kiss

The following piece, entitled "The Funeral," is fantastical and far-fetched to be sure; but it is very fine nevertheless. The comparison of the nerves and the braid of hair, and anticipating similar effects from each, could never have entered the thoughts of any one but Donne; still less could any one have made it *tell* as he has done. The piece is altogether an admirable and most interesting example of his style.

Whoever comes to shroud me, do not harm

As a specimen of Donne's infinite fullness of meaning, take a little poem, called "The Will"; almost every line of which would furnish matter for a whole treatise in modern times.

Before I sigh my last gasp, let me breathe

The following (particularly the first stanza) seems to us to express even more than it is intended to express; which is very rarely the case with the productions of this writer. The love expressed by it is a love for the passion excited, rather than for the object exciting it; it is a love that lives by *"chewing the cud* of sweet and bitter fancy," rather than by hungering after fresh food—that broods, like the stock dove, over its own voice, and listens for no other—that is all sufficient to itself, and (like virtue) its own reward.

I never stooped as low as they

What follows is in a different style, and it offers a singular specimen of the perverse ingenuity with which Donne sometimes bandies a thought about (like a shuttle-cock) from one hand to the other, only to let it fall to the ground at last.

THE PROHIBITION
Take heed of loving me

The following, in common with many other whole pieces and detached thoughts of this writer, has been imitated by other love-poets in proportion as it has not been read.

SONG
Go and catch a falling star

The following is to the same purpose, but more imbued with the writer's subtlety of thought and far-fetched ingenuity of illustration.

WOMAN'S CONSTANCY
Now thou hast loved me one whole day

The whole of the foregoing extracts are taken from the first department of Donne's poetry—the Love-verses. The only others that we shall choose from these, will be a few specimens of the truth and beauty that are frequently to be met with in Donne, in the shape of detached thoughts, images, &c. Nothing was every more exquisitely felt or expressed, than this opening stanza of a little poem, entitled "The Blossom."

Little thinkest thou, poor flower

The admirer of Wordsworth's style of language and versification will see, at once, that it is, at its best, nothing more than a *return* to this.

How beautiful is the following bit of description!
    When I behold a stream, which from the spring
    Doth with doubtful melodious murmuring,
    Or in a speechless slumber calmly ride
    Her wedded channel's bosom, and there chide,
    And bend her brows, and swell, if any bough
Do but stoop down to kiss her utmost brow, &c.

The following is exquisite in its way. It is part of an epithalamion.

    —and night is come; and yet we see
    Formalities retarding thee.
    What mean these ladies, which (as though
    They were to take a clock to pieces) go
    So nicely about the bride?
    A bride, before a good-night could be said,
    Should vanish from her cloathes into her bed,
    As souls from bodies steal, and are not spy'd.

The simile of the clock is an example (not an offensive one) of Donne's peculiar mode of illustration. He scarcely writes a stanza without some ingenious simile of this kind.

The two first lines of the following are very solemn and far-thoughted. There is nothing of the kind in poetry superior to them. I add the lines which succeed them, merely to shew the manner in which the thought is applied.

    I long to talk with some old lover's ghost
    Who died before the God of Love was born

Of Donne's other poems, the Funeral Elegies, Epistles, Satires, and what he calls his "Divine Poems," particularly the last named, we have little to say in the way of general praise, and but few extracts to offer. We shall, however, notice and illustrate each class briefly, in order that the reader may have a fair impression of the whole body of this writer's poetical works.

The Epistles of Donne we like less than any of his other poems, always excepting the religious ones. Not that they are without his usual proportion of subtle thinking, felicitous illustration, and skilful versification; but they are disfigured by more than his usual obscurity—by a harshness of style, that is to be found in few of his other poems, except the satires—by an extravagance of hyperbole in the way of compliment, that often amounts to the ridiculous—and by an evident want of sincerity, that is worse than all. To whomever they are addressed, all are couched in the same style of expression, and reach the same pitch of praise. Every one of his correspondents is, without exception, "wisest, virtuousest, discreetest, best." It is as if his letters had been composed at leisure, and kept ready *cut and dried* till wanted.

Though it will not exactly bear quotation, perhaps the most poetical, as well as the most characteristic of the Epistles is the imaginary one (the only one of that description) from Sappho to Philaenis.

The following is finely thought and happily expressed. It is part of an Epistle to Sir Henry Wotton.

> Be then thine own home, and in thyself dwell;
> Inn anywhere, continuance maketh hell.
> And seeing the snail, which everywhere doth roam,
> Carrying his own house still, still is at home,
> Follow (for he is easy paced) this snail,
> Be thine own palace, or the world's thy goal.
> And in the world's sea, do not like cork sleep
> Upon the water's face; nor in the deep
> Sink like a lead without a line: but as
> Fishes glide, leaving no print where they pass,
> Nor making sound, so closely thy course go,
> Let men dispute, whether thou breathe, or no.

We can afford no other extract from the Epistles, although many most curious ones might be found; but pass on to the Funeral Elegies. All Donne's poems, even his best, with one or two exceptions, are laboured in the highest degree; and the Funeral Elegies are still more so than any of the others. They have all the faults of his style, and this one above all. Still they abound in passages of great force, depth, and beauty; but none of them will bear extracting entire—at least, none which are properly included in this class. But there is one poem printed among these, which we shall extract the greater portion of, and which the reader will find to be written in a somewhat different style from that of almost all the others that we have quoted. There is a solemn and sincere earnestness about it, which will cause it to be read with great interest, even by those who may not be capable of appreciating, in detail, the rich and pompous flow of the verse, and the fine harmony of its music; the elegant simplicity of the language; and the extreme beauty of some of the thoughts and images.

The poem seems to have been addressed to his mistress, on the occasion of his taking leave of her, after her having offered to attend him on his journey in the disguise of a page. It is headed strangely enough.

ELEGY ON HIS MISTRESS
By our first strange and fatal interview

It only remains to speak of Donne's Satires; for his Divine Poems must be left to speak for themselves. General readers are probably acquainted with Donne chiefly as a writer of satires; and, in this character, they know him only through the medium of Pope; which is equivalent to knowing Homer only through the same medium. The brilliant and refined modern attempted to give his readers an idea of Donne, by changing his roughness into smoothness, and polishing down his force into point. In fact, he altered Donne into Pope—which was a mere impertinence. Each is admirable in his way—quite enough so to make it impossible to change either, with advantage, into a likeness of any other.

Donne's Satires are as rough and rugged as the unhewn stones that have just been blasted from their native quarry; and they must have come upon the readers at whom they were levelled, with the force and effect of the same stones flung from the hand of a giant. The following detached character is the only specimen we have left ourselves room to give of them. It strikes us as being nearly the perfection of this kind of writing.

Therefore I suffered this; towards me did run
A thing more strange than on Nile's slime the sun
E'er bred, or all which into Noah's Ark came:
A thing, which would have posed Adam to name:
Stranger than seven antiquaries' studies,
Than Afric's monsters, Guiana's rarities,
Stranger than strangers; one, who for a Dane,
In the Danes' Massacre had sure been slain,
If he had lived then; and without help dies,
When next the 'prentices 'gainst strangers rise.
One, whom the watch at noon lets scarce go by,
One, to whom, the examining Justice sure would cry,

'Sir, by your priesthood tell me what you are.'
His clothes were strange, though coarse; and black, though bare;
Sleeveless his jerkin was, and it had been
Velvet, but 'twas now (so much ground was seen)
Become tufftaffaty; and our children shall
See it plain rash awhile, then naught at all.
This thing hath travelled, and saith, speaks all tongues
And only knoweth what to all states belongs,
Made of th' accents, and best phrase of all these,
He speaks one language; if strange meats displease,
Art can deceive, or hunger force my taste,
But pedant's motley tongue, soldier's bombast,
Mountebank's drugtongue, nor the terms of law
Are strong enough perparatives, to draw
Me to bear this, yet I must be content
With his tongue: in his tongue, called compliment:
. . .
He names me, and comes to me; I whisper, 'God!
How have I sinned, that thy wrath's furious rod,
This fellow, chooseth me?' He sayeth,
'Sir, I love your judgement; whom do you prefer,
For the best linguist?' And I sillily
Said, that I thought Calepine's Dictionary;
'Nay but of men, most sweet Sir'. Beza then,
Some Jesuits, and two reverend men
Of our two Academies, I named. There
He stopped me, and said; 'Nay, your Apostles were
Good pretty linguists, and so Panurge was;
Yet a poor gentleman, all these may pass
By travail.' Then, as if he would have sold
His tongue, he praised it, and such wonders told
That I was fain to say, 'If you had lived, Sir,
Time enough to have been interpreter
To Babel's bricklayers, sure the Tower had stood.'
He adds, 'If of Court life you knew the good,
You would leave loneness.' I said, 'Not alone
My loneness is; but Spartan's fashion,
To teach by painting drunkards, doth not last
Now; Aretine's pictures have made few chaste;

No more can princes' Courts, though there be few
Better pictures of vice, teach me virtue';
He, like to a high stretched lute string squeaked, 'O Sir,
'Tis sweet to talk of kings.' 'At Westminster,'
Said I, 'the man that keeps the Abbey tombs,
And for his price doth with whoever comes,
Of all our Harrys, and our Edwards talk,
From king to king and all their kin can walk:
Your ears shall hear naught, but kings; your eyes meet
Kings only; The way to it, is King Street.'
He smacked, and cried, 'He's base, mechanic, coarse,
So are all your Englishmen in their discourse.
Are not your Frenchmen neat?' 'Mine? as you see,
I have but one Frenchman, look, he follows me.'
'Certes they are neatly clothed. I of this mind am,
Your only wearing is your grogaram.'
'Not so Sir, I have more.' Under this pitch
He would not fly; I chaffed him; but as itch
Scratched into smart, and as blunt iron ground
Into an edge, hurts worse: so, I (fool) found,
Crossing hurt me; to fit my sullenness,
He to another key his style doth dress,
And asks, 'What news?' I tell him of new plays.
He takes my hand, and as a still, which stays
A semi-breve 'twixt each drop, he niggardly,
As loth to enrich me, so tells many a lie,
More than ten Holinsheds, or Halls, or Stows,
Of trivial household trash he knows; he knows
When the Queen frowned, or smiled, and he knows what
A subtle statesman may gather of that;
He knows who loves; whom; and who by poison
Hastes to an office's reversion;
He knows who hath sold his land, and now doth beg
A licence, old iron, boots, shoes, and egg-
Shells to transport; shortly boys shall not play
At span-counter, or blow-point, but they pay
Toll to some courtier; and wiser than all us,
He knows what lady is not painted; thus

We had intended to close this paper with a few examples of the most glaring faults of Donne's style; but the reader will probably think that we have made better use of our space. We have endeavoured to describe those faults, and the causes of them; and not a few of them—or of those parts which should perhaps be regarded as *characteristics,* rather than absolute faults—will be found among the extracts now given. Those who wish for more may find them in almost every page of the writer's works. They may find the most far-fetched and fantastical allusions and illustrations brought to bear upon the thought or feeling in question, sometimes by the most quick-eyed and subtle ingenuity, but oftener in a manner altogether forced and arbitrary; turns of thought that are utterly at variance with the sentiment and with each other; philosophical and scholastic differences and distinctions, that no sentiment could have suggested, and that nothing but *searching for* could have found; and, above all, paradoxical plays of words, antitheses of thought and expression, and purposed involutions of phrase, that nothing but the most painful attention can untwist. All this they may find, and more. But, in the midst of all, they not only may, but must find an unceasing activity and an overflowing fullness of mind, which seem never to fail or flag, and which would more than half redeem the worst faults (of mere style) that could be allied to them.

—Unsigned, *Retrospective Review,*
1823, pp. 31–35

HENRY ALFORD "LIFE OF DR. DONNE" (1839)

One of Donne's most renowned editors, Henry Alford (1810–1871) was a celebrated English literary and theological scholar and author in his own right. A longtime dean at Canterbury, Alford was also a prominent photographer, poet, and translator, and his four-volume *New Testament in Greek* changed the way in which scholars examined biblical text. The text below is from Alford's edition of Donne's works. In it Alford labels Donne "a wit in an age of wit." The laudatory piece acts as an introduction to Donne's sermons, pieces that Alford suggests are "arrangements are often artificial and fanciful; but always easily retained, and instructive to the Scripture student" and that Alford hopes will become "standard volumes in the English Divinity Library." Alford also offers interesting discussions of Donne's rediscovery in the nineteenth century and how the term "metaphysical" came to be applied to Donne's works in the first place.

As a preacher he was most highly valued by his illustrious contemporaries. It was an age of flattery; but the encomiums which I have collected below[1] will bear with them the evidence of genuineness and real feeling. His royal master, no mean judge of ability, except in his own case, first foresaw his eminence in preaching, and ever afterwards valued himself on that discernment.

Donne is a rare instance of powers first tried, and then consecrated. Having studied, not by compulsion, but by choice, the whole body of divinity, and matured his judgment on controverted points, in the fulness of age and mental strength he commenced his clerical labours. Hence we never find in him poverty of thought, but are rather sensible (as generally in reading the most eminent of human writings, and always in the Scriptures) that the store has been but sparingly dealt out, and that much more remained, if he would have said it. Having shone as a wit in an age of wit, and an age when wit was not confined to ludicrous associations, but extended to a higher skill of point and antithesis, and cunning interweaving of choice words, he gained his hearers by flattering their discernment; and served up to the English Solomon and his court, dark sentences, which, in these days, when we have levelled our diction for convenience, and use language as a mere machine, require some thoughtful unravelling before their meaning is detected. That he should have gained among the moderns the reputation of obscurity is no wonder; for, on the one hand, the language of one age will always be strange to those who live in, and are entirely of, another of a totally different character; and again, this intricacy of words frequently accompanies subtle trains of thoughts and argument, which it requires some exertion to follow. But it must be remembered that obscurity is a subjective term, that is, having its place in the estimation of him who judges, and not necessarily in the language judged of; and is therefore never to be imputed to an author without personal examination of his writings. And I am satisfied that such an examination of the sermons of Donne would result in his being cleared from this charge. A man is obscure, either from his thoughts being confused and ill-arranged; or from his language being inadequate to express his meaning; or because he affects obscurity. Neither of these three was the fault of Donne. Precision and definiteness of thought, and studied arrangement of the steps of an argument, are to be found in all his sermons; and it is always more evident what he is proving, than whether his premises legitimately belong to that conclusion. "Whereunto all this tendeth" is a note which never need be placed in his margin, as far as the immediate subject is concerned. Again, his power over the English language, one rarely surpassed in its capabilities of ministering to

thought, was only equalled by one or two of his great contemporaries. And
the affectation of obscurity, (the resource of weakness and ignorance, and
the greatest of crimes in a literary, much more in an ecclesiastical writer,)
can hardly be laid to the charge of one so single-hearted in his zeal, and so
far above such a meanness, both from his learning and genius. His faults in
this matter are the faults of his time, somewhat increased by a mind naturally
fond of subtilty and laborious thought. And even the real difficulties of his
style will soon give way and become familiar to the reader, who is capable of
discovering and appreciating the treasures which it contains.

But it is not in diction, or genius, or power of thought, that we must look
for the crowning excellence of these Sermons. We find in them, what we feel
to be wanting in most of the great preachers of that and the succeeding age,
a distinct and clear exposition of the doctrines of redemption, as declared
in the Scriptures, and believed by the Church in England. This too is
set forth, without any dread of that poisonous maxim, "the further from
Rome, the nearer the truth;" to the working of which we owe most of the
dissent from, and the ignorance in, the present English church. That these
remarks are not to be taken without exception; that Donne does fall, upon
comparatively minor points, into very many puerilities and superstitions;
that the implicit following of the Fathers is, in divinity, his besetting fault,
and often interferes with his lucid declarations of the truth, no impartial
reader of his sermons can deny.[2] Still when all these have been amply allowed
for—all the obnoxious or trifling passages struck out—I think every reader
will be equally convinced, that there is left unimpaired a genuine body of
orthodox divinity (in the best sense of the words) not to be found, perhaps,
in any other English theologian.

In his expositions of Scripture he follows chiefly the close and verbal
method of the day: which though it frequently leads him to make too much
of an indifferent word, never allows the passing over of an important one;
and the want of which is, perhaps, more to be regretted in modern divinity,
than its use despised in ancient. His arrangements are often artificial and
fanciful; but always easily retained, and instructive to the Scripture student.
It has been observed of him, that he has the faculty of making whatever
he touches upon to appear important. It should, perhaps, rather have been
said, that he resolves all minor matters into more important ones, and by
constantly fixing the attention of his hearer on the great objects of Christian
faith, and bringing every doctrine and opinion to bear upon them in
greater or less degree, invests every subject with a dignity which does not
belong to it, considered apart.

In illustration by simile or allusion, Donne shows the true marks of great genius. The reader of the following Sermons will find sentences and passages which he will be surprised he never before had read, and will think of ever after. In depth and grandeur these far surpass (in my judgment) the strings of beautiful expressions to be found in Jeremy Taylor; they are the recreations of a loftier mind; and while Taylor's similes are exquisite in their melody of sound, and happy in external description, Donne enters into the inner soul of art, and gives his reader more satisfactory and permanent delight.[3] Sir Thomas Browne is, perhaps, the writer whose style will be most forcibly recalled to the mind of the reader by many parts of these Sermons; but here again Donne has immeasurably the advantage. While the one is ever guessing at truth, the other is pouring it forth from the fulness of his heart. While the one in his personal confessions keeps aloof and pities mankind, the other is of them, and feels with them.

Donne's epistolary writings are models in their kind. Laboured compliments, and studied antitheses have seldom been so ably or pleasingly strung together; or playfulness and earnest, pathos and humour, more happily blended.

His poems were mostly written in his youth; his satires, according to one of the panegyrics on him, before he was twenty. It has been remarked, that the juvenile poems of truly great men are generally distinguished by laborious condensation of thought; and the remark is amply borne out in this instance. This labour of compression on his part has tended to make his lines harsh and unpleasing; and the corresponding effort required on the reader's part to follow him, renders most persons insensible to his real merits. That he had and could turn to account a fine musical ear, is amply proved by some of his remaining pieces.[4] Why Dr. Johnson should have called him a metaphysical poet, is difficult to conceive. What "wittily associating the most discordant images" has to do with metaphysics is not very clear; and Johnson, perhaps, little thought that the title which he was giving to one of the most apparently laboured of poets, belonged of all others to his immortal contemporary, who is recorded "never to have blotted a line" A greater man that Dr. Johnson, even Dryden, has said in his dedication of Juvenal to the Earl of Dorset, that Donne "affects the metaphysics;" probably meaning no more than that scholastic learning and divinity are constantly to be found showing themselves in his poems.

The personal character of Donne is generally represented to us to have undergone a great change, between his youth and the time when he entered holy orders. This representation is countenanced by the uniform tenor of deep penitence with which he speaks in his Sermons of his former life; and by the licentiousness of some of his poetical pieces. It would be wrong, however, to infer moral depravity solely from the latter circumstance, as this strain was in keeping with the prevalent taste of the times; and the object addressed in the Love-poems of the day, and the circumstances introduced, were often both equally imaginary. That his manners were the manners of the court and the society in which he lived, is the most reasonable and the most charitable sentence; and the reader who values what is truly valuable, will rather consider the holiness and purity of his more mature years, than any reproach which report or his writings may have fixed on his youth; and with the charity which "rejoiceth not in iniquity, but rejoiceth in the truth," will look rather on these Sermons and Devotions, in which he has built himself and the church a lasting memorial, than on the few scattered leaves, which betray after all, perhaps, no more than simplicity and fearlessness of natural disposition; and that he snowed what others have concealed. Mankind are always more apt to judge mildly of one whose heart is open; and to sympathise where confidence is given. And we find, I think, that those writers with whose lives, and trials, and changes of opinion we are acquainted, and who speak to us not from the forbidding height of apathy, but as men giving and requiring sympathy, have always stood, other things being equal, highest in the public esteem. With no writer is this more the case than with Donne. Every Sermon is the voice of the same man; in every solemn appeal, every serious direction for self-searching and reflection, we see the footsteps of the same Providence, whose ways having been manifested to the preacher in his own experience, are by him imparted to the hearer. Egotism is a word which has obtained a bad name; but it must not be forgotten that it has a good sense; and that in this sense every truly great man is an egotist. For it is by intimate moral and critical acquaintance with himself that he becomes powerful over the thoughts and feelings of our kind in general; and, as the greatest of public speakers says in his Funeral Oration, That the praises of others are only tolerable up to a point of excellence, which the hearer thinks he could have equalled[5], so it may be generally said of the productions of the greatest minds, that they are most valued, and take most hold of the universal heart of mankind, when the man uttering them is shown to have been what all might have been, and to have felt what all have felt.[6]

I own I have indulged a hope, that these Sermons will become standard volumes in the English Divinity Library. For myself, what I have acquired from them has been invaluable; and I can only wish that they may give as much instruction and delight to the reader, as I have received in editing them.

Notes

1. Walton, a frequent hearer of Donne, thus characterises his preaching:—
"A preacher in earnest, weeping sometimes for his auditory, sometimes
with them; always preaching to himself like an angel from a cloud, but
in none; carrying some, as St. Paul was, to heaven in holy raptures, and
enticing others by a sacred art and courtship to amend their lives; here
picturing a vice so as to make it ugly to those that practised it; and a virtue,
so as to make it beloved even by those that loved it not; and all this with a
most particular grace and an inexpressible addition of comeliness."—
Life of Donne. Ed. Zouch.

Mr. Chudleigh, one of the contributors of Elegies on Donne's death, has
the following lines:—

He kept his love, but not his object. Wit
He did not banish, but transplanted it;
Taught it both time and place, and brought it home
To piety, which it doth best become.
For say, had ever pleasure such a dress?
Have you seen crimes so shaped, or loveliness
Such as his lips did clothe religion in?
Had not reproof a beauty passing sin?
                    —Id. ibid.

In a Latin Poem, by Darnelly, the following description of his
eloquence occurs:—

vidi

Audivi, et stupui, quoties orator in aede
Paulina stetit, et nura gravitate levantes
Corda oculosque viros tenuit: dum Nestoris ille
Fudit verba; omni quanto mage dulcia melle!
Nunc habet attonitos, pandit mysteria plebi
Non concessa prius, nondum intellecta; revolvunt
Mirantes, tacitique arrectis auribus astant.
Mutatis mox ille modo formaque loquendi
Tristia pertractat; fatumque, et flebile mortis
Tempus, et in cineres redeunt quod corpora primos.
Turn gemitum cunctos dare, tune lugere videres,
Forsitan a lacrimis aliquis non temperat, atque
Ex oculis largum stillat rorem.

In an Elegy by Mr. R. B.—

Methinks I see him in the pulpit standing.
Not ears, nor eyes, but all men's hearts commanding,
When we that heard him, to ourselves did feign
Golden Chrysostom was alive again;
And never were we wearied, till we saw
His hour (and but an hour) to end did draw.

In another by Mr. Mayne of Christ Church:—

Thou with thy words could'st charm thine audience,
That at thy sermons, ear was all our sense;
Yet have I seen thee in the pulpit stand,
Where we might take notes, from thy look, and hand;
And from thy speaking action bear away
More sermon, than some teachers use to say.
Such was thy carriage, and thy gesture such,
As could divide the heart, and conscience touch.
Thy motion did confute, and we might see
An error vanquished by delivery.
Not like our sons of zeal, who to reform
Their hearers, fiercely at the pulpit storm,
And beat the cushion into worse estate
Than if they did conclude it reprobate,
Who can out-pray the glass, then lay about
Till all predestination be run out;
And from the point such tedious uses draw,
Their repetitions would make Gospel, law.
No, in such temper would thy sermons flow,
So well did doctrine, and thy language show,
And had that holy fear, as, hearing thee,
The court would mend, and a good Christian be.

2. I have selected a few passages which may enable the reader shortly to
exemplify the above remarks:—

For an exposition of the doctrine of redemption free and universal,
by the assumption of the human nature by Christ, see vol. I., p. 566,
line 36.

On the Church, and the Scripture, see vol. I., p. 418,1. 33; vol. IV.,
p. 176, 1. 20.

On the Sacraments—Baptism, see vol. I., p. 583, 1. 12. Baptism
and the Lord's Supper, see the whole of Ser. 78, vol. IV., p. 414.

The sacrificial nature of the Lord's Supper, vol. VI., p. 39,1. 21, seq.

The real presence, in ditto, vol. V., p. 327,1. 13-22; vol. I., p. 479,
1. 5-10.

Prayer for the dead entered into, Ser. 77, vol. III.

His judgment of the Roman Church, Ser. 99, vol. IV., p. 295, 1. 4.

Confession to the priest, Ser. 66, vol. V., p. 563, 1. 22, seq.

Estimation of the fathers by the Roman Church, vol. III., p. 309, 1.
18, seq.

Prayer to saints; vol. III., p. 320, 1. 7.

For an instance of puerility and superstition, see vol. I., p. 456,
1. 12.

3. I have subjoined one or two specimens as a foretaste to the reader.
Speaking of eternity, he says:—"A day that hath no *pridie*, nor
postridie; yesterday doth not usher it in, nor to-morrow shall not
drive it out. Methusalem, with all his hundreds of years, was but a
mushroom of a night's growth, to this day; all the four monarchies,
with all their thousands of years, and all the powerful kings, and all the
beautiful queens of this world, were but as a bed of flowers, some gathered
at six, some at seven, some at eight, all in one morning, in respect of this
day." Vol. m., p. 326.

"Our flesh, though glorified, cannot make us see God better, nor
clearer, than the soul above hath done, all the time, from our death to our
resurrection. But as an indulgent father, or a tender mother, when they
go to see the king in any solemnity, or any other thing of observation and
curiosity, delights to carry their child, which is flesh of their flesh, and
bone of their bone, with them, and though the child cannot comprehend
it as well as they, they are as glad that the child sees it, as that they see it
themselves;—such a gladness shall my soul have, that this flesh (which
she will no longer call her prison, nor her tempter, but her friend, her
companion, her wife), that this flesh, that is, I, in the re-union and
redintegration of both parts, shall see God: for then one principal clause
in her rejoicing, and acclamation, shall be, that this flesh is her flesh; in *my
flesh shall I see God*." Vol. iv., p. 239.

"O what a Leviathan is sin, how vast, how immense a body! and then what
a spawner, how numerous! Between these two, the denying of sins which we
have done, and the bragging of sins which we have not done, what a space,
what a compass is there, for millions of millions of sins!" Vol. iv., p. 370.

4. See especially the piece, "Come live with me and be my love;" that written to his wife on parting from her to go into France, (vol. vi., p. 554,) and the opening of his Epithalamion on the marriage of the Princess Elizabeth.

5. Thucydides, book n., chap. 35.

6. It may be interesting to the reader to know that the marble figure of Donne in his shroud, which formed part of his monument in old St. Paul's, is the only relic which has been preserved whole from the ravages of the fire, and is now to be seen in the crypt.

—Henry Alford, from "Life of Dr. Donne,"
The Works of John Donne, 1839, vol. 1,
pp. xvii–xxvi

UNSIGNED (1846)

The following excerpt, from an anonymous mid-nineteenth-century magazine, deigns to "name and illustrate some of [Donne's] peculiarities" as a poet. The author suggests that the first of Donne's flaws is that his versification "is about the very ruggedest that ever has been written." The author adds that any text from Donne would prove this point, and a later fault of the poet's the author of the article points out is the "average flow" of his verse, noting that, though there are exceptions, most of Donne's works lack "a tolerable smoothness of versification."

The third "peculiarity" faults Donne's wit: "Another quality, equally against his popularity, is his profundity of thought, and the constant attention which is therefore required in order to understand him." This has always been a common criticism of Donne, and remained so until T. S. Eliot reintroduced this aspect of the poet in a more favorable light in the early twentieth century.

The fourth flaw concerns Donne's love poems, which the author below suggests "seem rather to be inspired by a *love of love,* than by any very powerful passion for the object of whom they chiefly discourse." Though the text does provide an example of Donne's love poetry that goes beyond this flaw, the author generally disapproves of this portion of Donne's oeuvre. Lastly, the author suggests that much of Donne's remaining work, anything below what he labels Donne's "second class," is troubled by an "inexplicable, incommunicable *aura.*" This aura relates both to Donne's unsettled versification as well as his at-times impenetrable wit. Ultimately, the claims presented in the essay below reflect much of the criticism Donne's work faced in both the eighteenth and the nineteenth centuries, and are often echoed in the other excerpts presented in this collection.

—◦◦◦— —◦◦◦— —◦◦◦—

For every individual reader of the poems of John Donne, there have probably been a hundred readers of the exquisite "Life" of him, by Izaak Walton. Unprefaced by this "Life," no edition of Donne's poems ought ever to have appeared. Not only is the memoir itself in every respect worthy of its subject— executed *con amore*—coming, paragraph after paragraph, like a succession of "meadow-gales in spring," over the heart of the habitual wanderer in the arid wastes of modern biographical literature; touching the souls of men with a tender sorrow for the noble days gone by—a sorrow which hardly subsides at thought of the nobler, but far different days to come; not only has it all these and many similar merits, but it moreover supplies a commentary upon the writings of our poet which could ill have been dispensed with. To the fact that "his father was masculinely and lineally descended from a very ancient family in Wales," and that "by his mother he was descended of the family of the famous and learned Sir Thomas More, some time Lord Chancellor of England," we may trace the lofty self-possession which breathes through all his writings, and which, in literature as in manners, is almost invariably the result of lofty extraction. In the circumstances, that although "his friends were of the Romish persuasion," young Donne would not receive their, or any creed implicitly; but "about the nineteenth year of his age, he being then unresolved what religion to adhere to, and considering how much it concerned his soul to choose the most orthodox, did therefore (though his youth and health promised him a long life), to rectify all scruples that might concern that, presently lay aside all study of the law, and of all other sciences that might give him a denomination, and began seriously to survey and consider the body of divinity, as it was controverted betwixt the Reformed and the Roman Church," we find an explanation of the peculiar vent of thought and imagination which characterizes all his writings, but particularly the first, namely the "Satires," and "Funeral Elegies." In his deep and various acquaintance with the physical, mathematical, and metaphysical sciences, as they then existed, we discover the origin of many of his far-fetched, and often painfully-ingenious illustrations. In his travels and his troubles, we find him undergoing the true poet-education, an experimental knowledge of men and sorrows. Finally, in his latterly blameless and holy life, we behold his defence against those who might otherwise have been inclined to infer, from the wonderful subtlety of his religion, an absence of a great sincerity in its pursuit.

Though too often neglected, it is one of the first duties of the critic, in his estimation of the merits and demerits of a literary production, to point out, as far as may be in his power, what of those merits and demerits belong to the author, and what to the time he wrote in. An endeavour to do this in a general manner shall be our first step in criticizing the poems of Donne.

His death occurred in 1631, when he was 58 years old. Shakespeare died in 1616. Therefore English intellect was at its height in the age Donne wrote. Mental philosophy was profounder and purer than it had ever been before; but it was occasionally wronged by an attempt to wed it with physical science: a marriage of which the times forbade the bans, because the latter was as yet unripe. Philosophy being profound and pure, so was religion; and in the midst of a vigorous and flourishing philosophy, and of a true religion, what could poetry be but vigorous, flourishing, and true?

Religion, also, in various ways, enhanced the poetic liberty of the time: especially it extinguished that false shame which Romanism had attached to the contemplation of the sexual relations. The purity of these relations had been for long ages lied away by the enforcement, as *a permanent doctrine,* of what St. Paul had advised merely as *"good for the present distress,"* (I Cor. vii. 26) caused by the persecutions in his day. But the Reformation had arisen, and commanded, that what God had declared to be clean, no man should call common. The command had been received with an obedience which had not, in Donne's time, been deadened or destroyed by the poisonous taint of Romanism, which yet lurked in the doctrine, and afterwards developed itself in the life-blood of the new era. The consequence was, that the sphere of nature was yet widened to the rejoicing poet, who now revered true chastity all the more that he was no longer obliged to bow down to the really unchaste mockeries of her "unblemished form," which had been set up for his worship by the harlot, Rome.

Again, a true philosophy gave birth to powers of the subtlest perception; which it did by inducing a faith in those powers. A good, perhaps the best, test of the subtlety of a poet's perception, is his appreciation of the female character; which, presenting, as it does, an endless series of contradictions to the understanding, thus declares itself to be the subject of a wholly different tribunal. Poets, whose powers of perception have fallen short of the highest, have made endless unavailing attempts to *solve* the character of woman. The subtle singers of Donne's time knew that they might as well endeavour to solve an irrational equation, or to express, in terminated decimals, a "surd quantity." But they knew that a comprehension of her character was no indispensable qualification for depicting it; and accordingly, and *therefore,* they have depicted it, as no poets had ever done before, or have done since.

In Donne's day, the faith in instinctive immediate perception was not a thing merely to talk about and admire, or to act upon within due and decent limitation, as it is with our living poets; it was a thing to possess and act upon unconsciously, and without limits imposed by the logical faculty, or by the hyperbole-hating decencies of flat conventionality. Our modern carpet-poets tread their way upon hyperbole as nicely as they would do over ice of an uncertain strength, dreading every moment to be drowned by ridicule, or sucked into some bottomless abyss, by an "Edinburgh" or "Quarterly" "Attack." Not so in Shakespeare's time:—

> Tempests themselves, high seas, and howling
> winds,
> The gutter'd rocks, and congregated sands,—
> Traitors ensteep'd to clog the guiltless keel,
> As having sense of beauty, did omit
> Their mortal natures, letting go safely by
> The divine Desdemona.

So much then, for the qualities of the period; qualities which Donne, as a poet, must necessarily participate in, and represent. We now proceed to name and illustrate some of his peculiarities. To begin with censure, and to prepare our readers for the quotations we shall make, let us state our conviction, that Donne's ordinary *versification* is about the very ruggedest that ever has been written. We shall not extract any particular lines to prove this assertion, since we shall make few quotations which will *not* prove it. This defect will always prevent Donne from becoming popular: fit and few will be his audience as long as poetry is read.

Another quality, equally against his popularity, is his profundity of thought, and the constant attention which is therefore required in order to understand him. Though his poems may be read once through, as a kind of disagreeable duty, by the professed student of English literature, they will be pored over, again and again, as true poetry should be, only by the most faithful and disciplined lovers of the muse. With these latter, however, Donne will always be a peculiar favourite. By them his poems will be valued as lumps of precious golden ore, touched, here and there, with specks of richest gold, and almost everywhere productive of the shining treasure, when submitted to the operation of affectionate reflection. By such readers even his worst versification will be pardoned, since no sacrifice of meaning is ever made to it,—it thus becoming so much more palatable to the truly cultivated taste than the expensive melody of some modern versifiers.

Donne's poems seem to divide themselves naturally into three classes:— I. His early "Songs and Sonnets" and "Elegies," chiefly love-poems, and his "Epithalamions." II. His "Satires," "Letters," and "Funeral Elegies." III. His "Divine Poems." We will notice the contents of each class in its order.

The love-poems seem rather to be inspired by a *love of love,* than by any very powerful passion for the object of whom they chiefly discourse. Most lovers love their object because they confound her with their ideal of excellence. Donne seems ever aware that his is the mere suggestion of that ideal which he truly loves. His love is a lofty and passionate, but voluntary, contemplation, deriving its nourishment mainly from the intellect, and not a fiery atmosphere, in which he lives and moves always, and whether he will or no.

On the whole, this class of his poems is greatly inferior to the second order. It is much more deformed by the intrusion of "conceits" and its general lack of spontaneous feeling is compensated by no general profundity of thought. Here and there, however, we find gems of admirable and various lustre, though no one, of any magnitude, without defect. We give the following noble poem entire. It is, perhaps, the most perfect thing of its length in Donne's whole volume. Its versification is generally good, and, sometimes, exquisite.

> As virtuous men pass mildly away,
>   And whisper to their souls, to go,
> Whilst some of their sad friends do say,
>   The breath goes now, and some say, no:
> So let us melt, and make no noise,
>   No tear-floods, nor sigh-tempests move,
> 'Twere profanation of our joys
>   To tell the laity our love.
> Moving of th'earth brings harms and fears,
>   Men reckon what it did and meant,
> But trepidation of the spheres,
>   Though greater far, is innocent.
> Dull sublunary lovers' love
>   (Whose soul is sense) cannot admit

Absence, because it doth remove
    Those things which elemented it.
But we by a love, so much refined,
    That our selves know not what it is,
Inter-assured of the mind,
    Care less, eyes, lips, and hands to miss.
Our two souls therefore, which are one,
    Though I must go, endure not yet
A breach, but an expansion,
    Like gold to aery thinness beat.
If they be two, they are two so
    As stiff twin compasses are two,
Thy soul the fixed foot, makes no show
    To move, but doth, if th'other do.
And though it in the centre sit,
    Yet when the other far doth roam,
It leans, and hearkens after it,
    And grows erect, as that comes home.
Such wilt thou be to me, who must
    Like th' other foot, obliquely run;
Thy firmness makes my circle just,
    And makes me end, where I begun.

Old Izaak Walton mentions this poem in his "Life,"—"a copy of verses given by Mr. Donne to his wife at the time he then parted from her (to spend some months in France). And I beg leave to tell, that I have heard some critics, learned both in languages and poetry, say, that none of the Greek or Latin poets did ever equal them."

The above is the only entire poem, and indeed the only considerable passage of continuous beauty in the love-poems. There are indeed little exquisite touches without number, starting up here and there, like violets in the rough, and, as yet, leafless woods. Of these we will give only as many as we think may be sufficient to sharpen the appetite of the lover of poetry, and send him to their source for more.

Unfortunately, (or shall we say, fortunately?) the best thing in a true poet is that which it is impossible to convey any fit notion of, by a few and limited extracts. "Every great poet has, in a measure, to create the taste by which he is to be enjoyed." (Wordsworth) The divine *aura* that breathes about his works, is not to be found by the chance reader in any particular passage or poem. This only reveals itself to the loving student of the Muses, and departs from him who departs from them, or endeavours to a-muse himself by carelessly attending to their songs. The longest and most famous of these "Epithalamions," has scarcely a quotable passage. Its whole merit lies in this inexplicable, incommunicable *aura*.

The "Elegies," which we have classed with the early poems, and "Epithalamions," form rather, indeed, a link between these and the second class. We give the following passage, which seems to illustrate our assertion, combining, as it does, the fantastic beauty of the former, the maturer thought of the latter, and the faults of both.

Donne's "Satires,"—to speak of which we now come— are, to our mind, the best in the English language. A satirist should never get into a passion with that which he is satirizing, and call names, as Dryden and Pope do; it is totally inconsistent with the dignity of the judicial position he assumes. To be sure, a lofty indignation may sometimes be allowed, but only on great occasions, and not against such petty-larceny practices and people as are, for the most part, the objects of satire. This was fully felt by the gentlemanly Donne, who, in his satires, resorts more often to the simple and the crushing strength of truth, than to the "cat-o'-nine-tails" of invective. We quote largely from Satire III.; it is upon the adoption of a religion—a subject which, as we have seen, had engaged our author's deepest thoughts.

Throughout all our former quotations, there was a tolerable smoothness of versification: sometimes there was the sweetest music; but they were, in this, exceptions to the rule. The above passage is a good specimen of the average flow of Donne's verses. But who, that, loving best of course the marriage of sound and meaning, would not yet prefer climbing, with Donne, these crags, where all the air is fresh and wholesome, to gliding with Thomas Moore, over flats, from beneath the rank verdure of which arises malaria and invisible disease?

Pope took it upon himself to "improve" some of Donne's satires; and he did it, but in much the same style as the sailor who, having obtained a curiosity in the form of the weapon of a sword-fish, "improved" it by scraping off, and rubbing down, all the protuberances by which it was distinguishable from any other bone. Fortunately, however, in most editions of Pope's writings, the original crudities are printed side by side with the polished improvement upon them; as sometimes we see, up-hung in triumph at the doors of writing-masters, pairs of documents to some such effect as this:—I. "This is my handwriting before taking lessons of Mr. Pope. Signed. John Donne." II. "This is my handwriting after taking lessons of Mr.

Pope. Signed. John Donne." Let us, however, give specimens of those so-different handwritings. The theme is the appearance of a reduced courtier.

    I. This is Donne, before being improved by Pope:—
                      T'wards me did run
A thing more strange than on Nile's slime the sun
E'er bred, or all which into Noah's ark came;
A thing which would have posed Adam to name:
Stranger than seven antiquaries' studies,
Than Afric monsters, Guiana's rarities,
Stranger than strangers: one who for a Dane
In the Dane's massacre had sure been slain,
If he had lived then; and without help dies,
When next the 'prentices 'gainst strangers rise;
One, whom the watch at noon scarce lets go by—
One, to whom th' examining justice sure would cry,
"Sir, by your priesthood, tell me what you are!"

    II. This is Donne, after being improved by Pope:—
                      Behold! there came
A thing which Adam had been posed to name;
Noah had refused it lodging in his ark,
Where all the race of reptiles might embark:
A verier monster than on Afric's shore
The sun e'er got, or slimy Nilus bore;
Or Sloan or Woodward's wondrous shelves
    contain,—
Nay, all that lying travellers can feign.
The watch would scarcely let him pass at noon,
At night would swear him dropp'd out of the moon;
One whom the mob, when next we find or make
A popish plot, shall for a Jesuit take;
And the wise justice, starting from his chair,
Cry, "By your priesthood, tell me what you are!"

Oh, wonderful Mr. Pope! powerful to knock off such excrescences as,
        Stranger than seven antiquaries' studies.
and, "Stranger than strangers"; powerful to introduce such improvements as,
        Nay, all that lying travellers can feign!

We had marked many more passages for quotation from the "Satires," but we must, for want of space, hurry on, skipping the "Letters," which are crowded with gems of purest ray serene, and give a sweet word or two from the "Funeral Elegies," which contain more wisdom and poetry in the same space, than almost anything out of Shakespeare. We will take only one of the Elegies and string some of its gems together without remark,—

> Her pure and eloquent soul
> Spoke in her cheeks, and so distinctly wrought,
> That one might almost say, her body thought.
> They who did labour Babel's tower to erect,
> Might have consider'd that, for that effect,
> All His whole solid earth would not allow
> Nor furnish forth materials enow;
> And that his centre, to raise such a place,
> Was far too little to have been the base;
> No more affords this world foundation
> To erect true joy.
>   In all she did
> Some figure of the golden times was hid.
> She is in Heaven; whither who doth not strive
> The more because she's there, he doth not know
> That accidental joys in Heaven do grow.
> (Speaking of closing the eyes of the dead)
> O, they confess much in the world amiss,
> Who dare not trust a dead man's eyes with that,
> Which they from God and angels cover not.

The "Divine Poems" are, for the most part, very poor, compared to these "Elegies"; but here, as everywhere, splendid thoughts and splendid words abound. One instance or two is all we can give. Here is a description of Leviathan in the style of Milton, who made him "swim the ocean stream."

> At every stroke his brazen fins do take,
> More circles in the broken sea they make
> Than cannons voices, when the air they tear;
> His ribs are pillars and his high-arch'd roof
> Of bark that blunts best steel, is thunder-proof.
> To his soul—
> O make thyself with holy mourning black,
> And red with blushing as thou art with sin.
> Of a repentant sinner,—

Tears in his eyes quench the amazing light. With these extracts we conclude, hoping that we shall have introduced many of our readers to hundreds more like them, by having sent them to the volume out of which we have copied.

—Unsigned, *Lowe's Edinburgh Magazine*,
1846, pp. 228–236

JOHN ALFRED LANGFORD
"AN EVENING WITH DONNE" (1850)

The English scholar, critic, and journalist John Alfred Langford (1823–1903) writes below of the great religious poets spawned by England, and proposes that "old, antiquated, and venerable Donne" ranks high amongst them. After providing a brief biography of Donne, Langford writes of that chief characteristic of the metaphysical poets that all nineteenth-century critics commented upon: their wit. Langford, however, unlike many of his contemporaries, seemed to relish the puzzling opportunities the wit of Donne and his ilk presented to him: "Forsaking the pure and genial naturalness of the Elizabethan poets, they seek by strange and farfetched allusions, similes, and figures, to clothe a simple thought in party-coloured garments; and to offer it to the reader in as many varied aspects as the most violent twistings and torturings of this brave English language would allow. Extremely learned, in whatever was considered learning in their day, they ransacked all their store in the search for refined, *recherche,* and difficult analogies. Physics, metaphysics, scholastic literature, were made to bear tribute to their love of 'the blue-eyed maid' chimera." Langford thus becomes one of the most ardent defenders of the metaphysical voice in his era, and students examining this aspect of Donne's work will surely find his argument an impassioned counterpoint to many of the others presented in this text.

Among the many glories of English literature, not the least is her possession of so long a list of truly religious poets. In this, the highest order of poetry, we have names unsurpassed by those of any nation, or of any time. Setting aside the matchless glory of Milton, we have the quaint song of the pious old George Herbert; the epigrammatic force of the "Night Thoughts" of Young; the genial, warm-hearted homeliness of the strains of Cowper; the childlike lyrics of the ever-loved Watts; the smooth, stream-like flow of

Montgomery; the soul-raising thought of the nature-loving Wordsworth; and not to mention others of high and lofty fame, whose works the world will not willingly let die, we have him with whom we propose to spend the present evening—the old, antiquated, and venerable Donne.

Dr. Johnson has offered some very curious reasons why religious poetry has not been successful in attaining a very high state of excellence. We venture to opine that in this respect the Doctor has committed himself, by giving a verdict which posterity will not confirm. We could select from our religious writers passages unequalled, in all that constitutes high poetry, by any equal number of passages from the greatest bards who have not especially devoted their talents to religion, such as Byron and Shelley, for instance. It is curious to think that the Doctor should fall into such a mistake; and it is still more curious to think of the numbers who have since re-echoed the opinion, considering that all the facts are against them. Why, the greatest of every land, and of every faith, are the religious ones, whether we look at the sublime old Hebrew bards, with "the fires of Sinai, and the thunders of the Lord!" or at the poets of classic Greece, or at their numerous successors, who have drawn their inspiration from the Christian faith, the fact is the same. Well has a modern poet said,

> The high and holy works, mid lesser lays,
> Stand up like churches among village cots:
> And it is joy to think that in every age,
> However much the world was wrong therein,
> The greatest works of mind or hand have been
> Done unto God. So may they ever be!
> It shows the strength of wish we have to be great,
> And the sublime humility of might.
>   —Festus.

But now to Donne. He was born in London in the year 1573. His parents were of the Roman Catholic faith, but their son, convinced of the truth of Protestantism, early declared himself a proselyte to the doctrines of the Reformation. He studied, and successfully, at both the Universities, and became, as one of the critics well observes, "completely *saturated* with the learning of his times." His works are rather voluminous, filling six goodly sized volumes, and consist of satires, ejaculations, occasional poems, elegies, and devotional pieces.

There is a class of poets known as the metaphysical. Of these Donne is perhaps the first in point of time, though some give "rare old Ben," the precedence. Their chief characteristic is their intellectualism. Forsaking the pure and genial naturalness of the Elizabethan poets, they seek by strange and farfetched allusions, similes, and figures, to clothe a simple thought in party-coloured garments; and to offer it to the reader in as many varied aspects as the most violent twistings and torturings of this brave English language would allow. Extremely learned, in whatever was considered learning in their day, they ransacked all their store in the search for refined, *recherche,* and difficult analogies. Physics, metaphysics, scholastic literature, were made to bear tribute to their love of "the blue-eyed maid" chimera. "The metaphysical poets," says Dr. Johnson, "were men of learning; and to show their whole endeavour, but, unluckily, resolving to show it in rhyme, instead of writing poetry, they only wrote verses, and very often such verses as stood the trial of the finger better than of the ear, for the modulation was so imperfect, that they were only found to be verses by counting the syllables." Such is sure to be the case, when men sit down to put thoughts into verse, instead of waiting till the divine afflatus compels them to utter their feelings, which necessarily take the form of song; as different a thing from verse as light is from darkness. Goethe has well said in one of those world-famous *Xenien* of his,

> What many sing and say,
> Must still by us be borne!
> Ye worthy—great and small—
> Tired you sing yourselves and lorn;
> And yet let no one tune his lay
> Except for what he has to say.

But of these poets, if we except Cowley, Donne holds the highest place. He had much wit, in which gift Dryden confesses himself and his contemporaries to be inferior. He had, as we have seen, a vast erudition, some fancy and elegance, together with strong piety. These combined must surely make a poet of no ordinary power. His satires are strong, vigorous, and masculine. Compared with Pope his verses would certainly want smoothness, but Pope himself would have been a much greater poet, had he possessed some of the wholesome roughness, and known that amidst a profusion of sweets that a bitter is often welcome and good. It is true that Donne is very capricious about the place of accent; but few readers would have to count the fingers to tell whether it were verse or no. Certain we are, if much of his writing be not verse, there is much of it that is poetry. Take the following lines on the "Last Night of the Year":—

This twilight of two years, not past nor next,
    Some emblem is of me, or I of this,
Who meteor-like, of stuff and form perplext,
    Whose what and where in disputation is,
    If I should call me anything, should miss.
I sum the years and me, and find me not,
    Debtor to th' old, nor creditor to th' new.
That cannot say, my thanks I have forgot,
    Nor trust I this with hopes, and yet scarce
       true
    This bravery is, since these times showed me
    you.

The critic we have quoted above as saying that Donne was saturated with all the learning of his times, also says of him "That he was endowed with a most active and piercing intellect—an imagination, if not grasping and comprehensive, most subtle and far-darting—a fancy rich, vivid, and picturesque—and a wit admirable as well for its caustic severity as for its playful quickness." This is particularly applicable to his satires, which are the precursors of Dryden and Pope's. It would be useless to select from these, as it is but by examination of them as a whole that their force, their truthfulness, and their caustic severity and playful quickness can be felt. To take a passage from any at all adapted to the limits of this paper, in order to show their quality, would be about as wise as the man who having a house to sell, carried a brick with him as a specimen. We may say of them, what can be said of but few satires, that they possess more than a temporary interest, and may be read with profit and advantage at the present time.

The following piece illustrates pretty well the best and worst qualities of Donne.

As virtuous men pass mildly away,
    And whisper to their souls, to go,
Whilst some of their sad friends do say,
    The breath goes now, and some say, no:
So let us melt, and make no noise,
    No tear-floods, nor sigh-tempests move,
 profanation of our joys
    To tell the laity our love.
Moving of th' earth brings harms and fears,
    Men reckon what it did and meant,

But trepidation of the spheres,
    Though greater far, is innocent.
Dull sublunary lovers' love
    (Whose soul is sense) cannot admit
Absence, because it doth remove
    Those things which elemented it.
But we by a love, so much refined,
    That our selves know not what it is,
Inter-assured of the mind,
    Care less, eyes, lips, and hands to miss.
Our two souls therefore, which are one,
    Though I must go, endure not yet
A breach, but an expansion,
    Like gold to aery thinness beat.
If they be two, they are two so
    As stiff twin compasses are two,
Thy soul the fixed foot, makes no show
    To move, but doth, if th'other do.
And though it in the centre sit,
    Yet when the other far doth roam,
It leans, and hearkens after it,
    And grows erect, as that comes home.
Such wilt thou be to me, who must
    Like th' other foot, obliquely run;
Thy firmness makes my circle just,
    And makes me end, where I begun.

A strange analogy this; but yet not so absurd as at first reading it may appear. It is true it may need reading over more than once clearly to seize its hidden meaning; but what then, shall we turn aside from every one "who does not wear his heart upon his sleeve for daws to peck at"?

One more extract, and we bid our poet good night. It is on the littleness of temporal existence, compared with the great, solemn eternity beyond. The lines are quaint, but their spirit fine.

Think in how poor a prison thou didst lie
After, enabled but to suck and cry.
Think, when 'twas grown to most, 'twas a poor inn,
A province packed up in two yards of skin,
And that usurped or threatened with the rage

Of sicknesses, or their true mother, age.
But think that death hath now enfranchised thee,
Thou hast thy expansion now, and liberty;
Think that a rusty piece, discharged, is flown
In pieces, and the bullet is his own,
And freely flies; this to thy soul allow,
Think thy shell broke, think thy soul hatched but
now.

—John Alfred Langford, from
"An Evening with Donne," *The Working
Man's Friend*, December 1850, pp. 18–21

George MacDonald "Dr. Donne: His Mode and Style" (1868–69)

George MacDonald (1824–1905) was a Scottish author and minister. Most famous for his fairy tales and fantasy novels, MacDonald inspired the works of such authors as W. H. Auden, J.R.R. Tolkien, and Madeline L'Engle. In the piece below, MacDonald, like many of his contemporaries, praises Donne for his intellect and wit but chastises the poetical qualities of the man, echoing earlier complaints that Donne's poesy is rugged and his rhythm "is often as bad as it can be to be called rhythm at all." Anyone studying Donne's works will find MacDonald's close readings particularly useful, especially his explorations of Donne's "Hymn to God, my God, in my Sickness" and "A Hymn to God the Father." MacDonald also examines, to a lesser degree, "A Hymn to Christ," three of the Holy Sonnets (including the famous "Death, be not proud . . .,") and a fragment of the "Resurrection."

He (Donne) is represented by Dr. Johnson as one of the chief examples of that school of poets called by himself the *metaphysical,* an epithet which, as a definition, is almost false. True it is that Donne and his followers were always ready to deal with metaphysical subjects, but it was from their mode, and not their subjects, that Dr. Johnson classed them. What this mode was we shall see presently, for I shall be justified in setting forth its strangeness, even absurdity, by the fact that Dr. Donne was the dear friend of George Herbert, and had much to do with the formation of his poetic habits. Just twenty years older than Herbert, and the valued and intimate friend of his mother, Donne was in precisely that relation of age and circumstance to influence the other in the highest degree.

The central thought of Dr. Donne is nearly sure to be just: the subordinate thoughts by means of which he unfolds it are often grotesque, and so wildly associated as to remind one of the lawlessness of a dream, wherein mere suggestion without choice or fitness rules the sequence. As some of the writers of whom I have last spoken would play with words, Dr. Donne would sport with ideas, and with the visual images or embodiments of them. Certainly in his case much knowledge reveals itself in the association of his ideas, and great facility in the management and utterance of them. True likewise, he says nothing unrelated to the main idea of the poem; but not the less certainly does the whole resemble the speech of a child of active imagination, to whom judgment as to the character of his suggestions is impossible, his taste being equally gratified with a lovely image and a brilliant absurdity: a butterfly and a shining potsherd are to him similarly desirable. Whatever wild thing starts from the thicket of thought, all is worthy game to the hunting intellect of Dr. Donne, and is followed without question of tone, keeping, or harmony. In his play with words, Sir Philip Sidney kept good heed that even that should serve the end in view; in his play with ideas, Dr. John Donne, so far from serving the end, sometimes obscures it almost hopelessly: the hart escapes while he follows the squirrels and weasels and bats. It is not surprising that, their author being so inartistic with regard to their object, his verses themselves should be harsh and unmusical beyond the worst that one would imagine fit to be called verse. He enjoys the unenviable distinction of having no rival in ruggedness of metric movement and associated sounds. This is clearly the result of indifference; an indifference, however, which grows very strange to us when we find that he *can* write a lovely verse and even an exquisite stanza.

Greatly for its own sake, partly for the sake of illustration, I quote a poem containing at once his best and his worst, the result being such an incongruity that we wonder whether it might not be called his best *and* his worst, because we cannot determine which. He calls it *Hymn to God, my God, in my Sickness.* The first stanza is worthy of George Herbert in his best mood.

> Since I am coming to that holy room,
>> Where with the choir of saints for evermore
> I shall be made thy music, as I come
>> I tune the instrument here at the door,
> And what I must do then, think here before.

To recognize its beauty, leaving aside the depth and truth of the phrase, "Where I shall be made thy music," we must recall the custom of those days to send out for "a noise of musicians." Hence he imagines that he has been summoned as one of a band already gone in to play before the king of "The High Countries:" he is now at the door, where he is listening to catch the tone, that he may have his instrument tuned and ready before he enters. But with what a jar the next stanza breaks on heart, mind, and ear!

> Whilst my physicians by their love are grown
>   Cosmographers, and I their map, who lie
> Flat on this bed, that by them may be shown
>   That this is my south-west discovery,
> *Per fretum febris*—by these straits to die;—

Here, in the midst of comparing himself to a map, and his physicians to cosmographers consulting the map, he changes without warning into a navigator whom they are trying to follow upon the map as he passes through certain straits—namely, those of the fever—towards his south-west discovery, Death. Grotesque as this is, the absurdity deepens in the end of the next stanza by a return to the former idea. He is alternately a map and a man sailing on the map of himself. But the first half of the stanza is lovely: my reader must remember that the region of the West was at that time the Land of Promise to England.

> I joy that in these straits I see my West;
>   For though those currents yield return to
>   none,
> What shall my West hurt me? As west and east
>   In all flat maps (and I am one) are one,
>   So death doth touch the resurrection.

It is hardly worth while, except for the strangeness of the phenomenon, to spend any time in elucidating this. Once more a map, he is that of the two hemispheres, in which the east of the one touches the west of the other. Could anything be much more unmusical than the line, "In all flat maps (and I am one) are one"? But the next stanza is worse.

> Is the Pacific sea my home? Or are
>   The eastern riches? Is Jerusalem?
> Anvan, and Magellan, and Gibraltar?
>   All straits, and none but straits are ways to
>   them,
>   Whether where Japhet dwelt, or Cham, or
>   Sem.

The meaning of the stanza is this: there is no earthly home: all these places are only straits that lead home, just as they themselves cannot be reached but through straits. Let my reader now forget all but the first stanza, and take it along with the following, the last two:

We think that Paradise and Calvary,
    Christ's cross and Adam's tree, stood in one
      place:
Look, Lord, and find both Adams met in me;
    As the first Adam's sweat surrounds my face,
    May the last Adam's blood my soul embrace.
So, in his purple wrapped, receive me, Lord;
    By these his thorns give me his other crown;
And as to others' souls I preached thy word,
    Be this my text, my sermon to mine own:
    Therefore, that he may raise, the Lord throws down.

Surely these are very fine, especially the middle verse of the former and the first verse of the latter stanza. The three stanzas together make us lovingly regret that Dr. Donne should have ridden his Pegasus over quarry and housetop, instead of teaching him his paces.

The next I quote is artistic throughout. Perhaps the fact, of which we are informed by Izaak Walton, "that he caused it to be set to a grave and solemn tune, and to be often sung to the organ by the choristers of St. Paul's church in his own hearing, especially at the evening service," may have something to do with its degree of perfection. There is no sign of his usual haste about it. It is even elaborately rhymed after Norman fashion, the rhymes in each stanza being consonant with the rhymes in every stanza.

A HYMN TO GOD THE FATHER
Wilt thou forgive that sin where I begun,
    Which was my sin, though it were done before?
Wilt thou forgive that sin, through which I run,
    And do run still, though still I do deplore?—
      When thou hast done, thou hast not done;
      For I have more.
Wilt thou forgive that sin which I have won
    Others to sin, and made my sins their door?
Wilt thou forgive that sin which I did shun
    A year or two, but wallowed in a score?—
When thou hast done, thou hast not done;

> For I have more.
> I have a sin of fear, that when I've spun
>   My last thread, I shall perish on the shore;
> But swear by thyself, that at my death thy Son
>   Shall shine, as he shines now and heretofore;
>   And having done that, thou hast done:
>   I fear no more.

In those days even a pun might be a serious thing: witness the play in the last stanza on the words *son* and *sun*—not a mere pun, for the Son of the Father is the Sun of Righteousness: he is Life *and* Light.

What the Doctor himself says concerning the hymn, appears to me not only interesting but of practical value. He "did occasionally say to a friend, 'The words of this hymn have restored to me the same thoughts of joy that possessed my soul in my sickness, when I composed it.'" What a help it would be to many, if in their more gloomy times they would but recall the visions of truth they had, and were assured of, in better moments!

Here is a somewhat strange hymn, which yet possesses, rightly understood, a real grandeur:

A HYMN TO CHRIST
At the Author's last going into Germany.[1]
In what torn ship soever I embark,
That ship shall be my emblem of thy ark;
What sea soever swallow me, that flood
Shall be to me an emblem of thy blood.
Though thou with clouds of anger do disguise
Thy face, yet through that mask I know those eyes,
    Which, though they turn away sometimes—
        They never will despise.
I sacrifice this island unto thee,
And all whom I love here and who love me:
When I have put this flood 'twixt them and me,
Put thou thy blood betwixt my sins and thee.
As the tree's sap doth seek the root below
In winter, in my winter[2] now I go
    Where none but thee, the eternal root
        Of true love, I may know.
Nor thou, nor thy religion, dost control
The amorousness of an harmonious soul;

But thou wouldst have that love thyself: as thou
Art jealous, Lord, so I am jealous now.
Thou lov'st not, till from loving more thou free
My soul: who ever gives, takes liberty:
    Oh, if thou car'st not whom I love,
      Alas, thou lov'st not me!
Seal then this bill of my divorce to all
On whom those fainter beams of love did fall;
Marry those loves, which in youth scattered be
On face, wit, hopes, (false mistresses), to thee.
Churches are best for prayer that have least light:
To see God only, I go out of sight;
    And, to 'scape stormy days, I choose
      An everlasting night.

To do justice to this poem, the reader must take some trouble to enter into the poet's mood.

It is in a measure distressing that, while I grant with all my heart the claim of his "Muse's white sincerity," the taste in—I do not say *of*—some of his best poems should be such that I will not present them.

Out of twenty-three *Holy Sonnets*, every one of which, I should almost say, possesses something remarkable, I choose three. Rhymed after the true Petrarchian fashion, their rhythm is often as bad as it can be to be called rhythm at all. Yet these are very fine.

Thou hast made me, and shall thy work decay?
    Repair me now, for now mine end doth haste;
    I run to death, and death meets me as fast,
And all my pleasures are like yesterday.
I dare not move my dim eyes any way,
    Despair behind, and death before doth cast
    Such terror; and my feeble flesh doth waste
By sin in it, which it towards hell doth weigh.
Only thou art above, and when towards thee
    By thy leave I can look, I rise again;
But our old subtle foe so tempteth me,
    That not one hour myself I can sustain:
Thy grace may wing me to prevent his art,
And thou like adamant draw mine iron heart.

———

If faithful souls be alike glorified
  As angels, then my father's soul doth see,
  And adds this even to full felicity,
That valiantly I hell's wide mouth o'erstride:
But if our minds to these souls be descried
  By circumstances and by signs that be
  Apparent in us—not immediately—
How shall my mind's white truth by them be tried?
  They see idolatrous lovers weep and mourn,
And, style blasphemous, conjurors to call
On Jesu's name, and pharisaical
  Dissemblers feign devotion. Then turn,
O pensive soul, to God; for he knows best
Thy grief, for he put it into my breast.

––––––––

Death, be not proud, though some have called thee
  Mighty and dreadful, for thou art not so;
  For those whom thou think'st thou dost
   overthrow,
Die not, poor Death; nor yet canst thou kill me.
From rest and sleep, which but thy picture be,
  Much pleasure, then from thee much more
   must flow;
  And soonest our best men with thee do go,
Rest of their bones, and soul's delivery!
  Thou'rt slave to fate, chance, kings, and
   desperate men,
And dost with poison, war, and sickness dwell;
And poppy or charms can make us sleep as well,
  And better than thy stroke. Why swell'st thou
   then?
One short sleep past, we wake eternally,
And death shall be no more: Death, thou shalt die.

In a poem called *The Cross,* full of fantastic conceits, we find the following remarkable lines, embodying the profoundest truth.

As perchance carvers do not faces make,
But that away, which hid them there, do take:
Let crosses so take what hid Christ in thee,
And be his image, or not his, but he.

One more, and we shall take our leave of Dr. Donne. It is called a fragment; but it seems to me complete. It will serve as a specimen of his best and at the same time of his most characteristic mode of presenting fine thoughts grotesquely attired.

RESURRECTION
>Sleep, sleep, old sun; thou canst not have
>>re-past
As yet the wound thou took'st on Friday last.
Sleep then, and rest: the world may bear thy stay;
A better sun rose before thee to-day;
Who, not content to enlighten all that dwell
On the earth's face as thou, enlightened hell,
And made the dark fires languish in that vale,
As at thy presence here our fires grow pale;
Whose body, having walked on earth and now
Hastening to heaven, would, that he might allow
Himself unto all stations and fill all,
For these three days become a mineral.
He was all gold when he lay down, but rose
All tincture; and doth not alone dispose
Leaden and iron wills to good, but is
Of power to make even sinful flesh like his.
Had one of those, whose credulous piety
Thought that a soul one might discern and see
Go from a body, at this sepulchre been,
And issuing from the sheet this body seen,
He would have justly thought this body a soul,
If not of any man, yet of the whole.

What a strange mode of saying that he is our head, the captain of our salvation, the perfect humanity in which our life is hid! Yet it has its dignity. When one has got over the oddity of these last six lines, the figure contained in them shows itself almost grand.

As an individual specimen of the grotesque form holding a fine sense, regard for a moment the words,

>He was all gold when he lay down, but rose
>All tincture;

which means, that, entirely good when he died, he was something yet greater when he rose, for he had gained the power of making others good: the *tincture* intended here was a substance whose touch would turn the basest metal into gold.

Through his poems are scattered many fine passages; but not even his large influence on the better poets who followed is sufficient to justify our listening to him longer now.

Notes

1. He was sent by James I. to assist an embassy to the Elector Palatine, who had married his daughter Elizabeth.
2. He has lately lost his wife, for whom he had a rare love.

> —George MacDonald, from "Dr. Donne:
> His Mode and Style," *England's Antiphon*,
> 1868–69, pp. 114–24

EDMUND GOSSE "JOHN DONNE" (1894)

In the essay below, part of a larger work on Jacobean poets, Gosse begins by classifying Donne's work into seven distinct categories. The first are the satires, which Gosse suggests are "brilliant and picturesque beyond any of their particular compeers," though they still suffer from the flaws that suffuse all Elizabethan satire. After pausing to examine the poem "The Progress of the Soul" (or "Poema Satyricon"), Gosse next classifies Donne's epistles, or poems structured as letters, which includes a brief but useful discussion of "Letter to the Countess of Huntingdon." Gosse does not generally admire Donne's epistles, writing that the "epistles are stuffed hard with thoughts, but poetry is rarely to be found in them; the style is not lucid, the construction is desperately parenthetical."

Next for Gosse are the Epithalamia, the marriage-songs. Gosse considers these works inspired by Edmund Spenser, and labels them "elegant and glowing." Fourth are the Elegies, a grouping of Donne's secular works that Gosse believes are often marred by "inconceivable offences against good taste." Gosse finds Donne's fifth category of work, his funeral elegies or requiems, almost as curious as the Epithalamia, though "lovely sudden bursts of pure poetry are more frequent in the 'Funeral Elegies' than in any section of Donne's poetry which we have mentioned."

The sixth classification of Donne's work includes the Holy Sonnets, which includes a closer examination of Holy Sonnet 17, "Since she whom I loved hath paid her last debt." The final classification is that which Gosse finds most interesting—Donne's amatory lyrics. Gosse suggests these works are "personal, confidential, and vivid; the stamp of life is on them."

After he classifies Donne's work, Gosse defends the poet's meter. Rejecting earlier critical claims that Donne's work is rugged and lacks versification, Gosse writes that Donne "intentionally introduced a revolution into English versification. It was doubtless as a rebellion against the smooth and somewhat nerveless iambic flow of Spenser and the earliest contemporaries of Shakespeare, that Donne invented his violent mode of breaking up the line into quick and slow beats." Though Gosse still considers Donne's scansion "violent," he does defend it, noting that far from being an almost accidental poet, Donne's harsh versification was the conscious act of a poet at the height of his intellectual gifts, an experiment that, while not always successful, is certainly worthy, in Gosse's mind, of admiration and serious consideration.

—⌇⌇⌇— —⌇⌇⌇— —⌇⌇⌇—

The poems of Donne were not published until after his death. The first edition, the quarto of 1633, is very inaccurate and ill-arranged; the octavos of 1635 and 1639 are much fuller and more exact. Donne, however, still lacks a competent editor. We have no direct knowledge of the poet's own wish as to the arrangement of his poems, nor any safe conjecture as to the date of more than a few pieces. The best lyrics, however, appear to belong to the first decade of James I.'s reign, if they are not even of earlier composition. There seems to be no doubt that the *Satires,* an imperfect manuscript of which bears the date 1593, are wholly Elizabethan. These are seven in number, and belong to the same general category as those of Hall, Lodge, and Guilpin. Neither in date nor in style do they belong to the period treated of in this volume, and it is therefore not necessary to dwell on them at great length here. They are brilliant and picturesque beyond any of their particular compeers, even beyond the best of Hall's satires. But they have the terrible faults which marked all our Elizabethan satirists, a crabbed violence alike of manner and matter, a fierce voluble conventionality, a tortured and often absolutely licentious and erroneous conception of the use of language. The fourth is, doubtless, the best written, and may be taken as the best essay in this class of poetry existing in English literature before the middle-life of Dryden; its attraction for Pope is well known.

"The Progress of the Soul," as named by its author "Poema Satyricon," takes its natural place after the satires, but is conjectured to have been written not earlier than 1610. De Quincey, with unwonted warmth, declared that "massy diamonds compose the very substance of this poem, thoughts and descriptions which have the fervent and gloomy sublimity of Ezekiel or /Eschylus." It is written in a variant of the Spenserian stanza, and is a hyperbolical history of the development of the human soul, extended to more than five hundred lines, and not ended, but abruptly closed. It is one of the most difficult of Donne's writings, and started a kind of psychologi- cal poetry of which, as the century progressed, many more examples were seen, none, perhaps, of a wholly felicitous character. It has the poet's characteristics, however, to the full. The verse marches with a virile tread, the epithets are daring, the thoughts always curious and occasionally sublime, the imagination odd and scholastic, with recurring gleams of passion.

Here is a fragment of this strange production—

Into an embryon fish our soul is thrown,
And in due time thrown out again, and grown
To such vastness, as if, unmanacled
From Greece, Morea were, and that, by some
Earthquake unrooted, loose Morea swum,
Or seas from Afric's body had severed
And torn the hopeful promontory's head;
This fish would seem these, and, when all hopes fail,
A great ship overset, or without sail
    Hulling, might (when this was a whelp) be like
      this whale.
At every stroke his brazen fins do take
More circles in the broken sea they make
Then cannons' voices, when the air they tear;
His ribs are pillars, and his high-arch'd roof,
Of bark that blunts best steel, is thunder-proof;
Swim in him, swallow'd dolphins, without fear,
And feel no sides, as if his vast womb were
Some inland sea, and ever as he went
He spouted rivers up, as if he meant
    To join our seas with seas above the
      firmament.
. . .

Now drinks he up seas, and he eats up flocks;
He jostles islands and he shakes firm rocks;
Now in a roomful house this soul doth float,
And like a prince she sends her faculties
To all her limbs, distant as provinces.

The Sun hath twenty times both crab and goat
Parched, since first launch'd forth this living boat;
'Tis greatest now and to destruction
Nearest; there's no pause at perfection,
    Greatness a period hath, but hath no station.

Far less extraordinary are the Epistles, which form a large section of Donne's poetical works. All through life he was wont to address letters, chiefly in the heroic couplet, to the most intimate of his friends. These epistles are conceived in a lighter vein than his other writings, and have less of his characteristic vehemence. The earliest, however, "The Storm," which he addressed from the Azores, possesses his Elizabethan mannerism; it is crudely picturesque and licentious, essentially un-poetical. "The Calm," which is the parallel piece, is far better, and partly deserves Ben Jonson's high commendation of it to Drummond. The epistle to Sir Henry Goodyer is noticeable for the dignified and stately manner in which the four-line stanza, afterwards adopted by Gray for his *Elegy*, is employed; this poem is exceedingly like the early pieces written by Dryden some fifty years later. The school of the Restoration is plainly foreshadowed in it.

Many of these epistles are stuffed hard with thoughts, but poetry is rarely to be found in them; the style is not lucid, the construction is desperately parenthetical. It is not often that the weary reader is rewarded by such a polished piece of versification as is presented by this passage about love in the "Letter to the Countess of Huntingdon."

It is not love that sueth, or doth contend;
Love either conquers, or but meets a friend.
Man's better part consists of purer fire,
And finds itself allowed, ere it desire.
Love is wise here, keeps home, gives reason sway,
And journeys not till it find summer-way.
A weather-beaten lover, but once known,
Is sport for every girl to practise on.
Who strives, through woman's scorns, woman to
    know,
Is lost, and seeks his shadow to outgo;
It must be sickness, after one disdain,
Though he be called aloud, to look again;
Let others sin and grieve; one cunning slight
Shall freeze my love to crystal in a night.

I can love first, and, if I win, love still,
And cannot be removed, unless she will;
It is her fault if I unsure remain;
She only can untie, I bind again;
The honesties of love with ease I do,
But am no porter for a tedious woe.

Most of these epistles are New Year's greetings, and many are addressed
to the noble and devout ladies with whom he held spiritual converse in
advancing years. The poet superbly aggrandizes the moral qualities of these
women, paying to their souls the court that younger and flightier cavaliers
reserved for the physical beauty of their daughters.

The Epithalamia of Donne form that section of his work in which, alone,
he seems to follow in due succession after Spenser. These marriage-songs
are elegant and glowing, though not without the harshness which Donne
could not for any length of time forego. That composed for the wedding of
Frederick Count Palatine and the Lady Elizabeth, in 1613, is perhaps the
most popular of all Donne's writings, and opens with a delicious vivacity.

Hail, Bishop Valentine, whose day this is!
All the air is thy diocese,
And all the chirping choristers
And other birds are thy parishioners;
Thou marryest every year
The lyric lark and the grave whispering dove,
The sparrow that neglects his life for love,
The household bird with the red stomacher;
Thou mak'st the blackbird speed as soon
As doth the goldfinch or the halcyon;
The husband cock looks out, and straight is sped,
And meets his wife, which brings her feather-bed.
This day more cheerfully than ever shine,—
This day, which might enflame thyself, old
Valentine.

The ode within the rather stiff setting of the Allophanes and Idios
eclogue is scarcely less felicitous.

The miscellaneous secular poems of Donne are generically classed under
the heading of "Elegies." We have here some of the most extraordinary
aberrations of fancy, some of the wildest contrasts of character and style,

to be observed in literature. They are mainly Ovidian or Tibullan studies of the progress of the passion of love, written by one who proclaims himself an ardent, but no longer an illusioned lover,—hot, still, but violent and scandalous. The youth of the author is disclosed in them, but it is not the callous youth of first inexperience. He is already a past master in the subtle sophistry of love, and knows by rote "the mystic language of the eye and hand." Weary with the beauty of spring and summer, he has learned to find fascination in an autumnal face. The voluptuous character of these elegies has scandalized successive critics. Several of them, to be plain, were indeed too outspoken for the poet's own, or for any decent age. Throughout it is seldom so much what the unbridled lover says, as his utter intemperance in saying it, that surprises, especially in one who, by the time the poems were given to the public, had come to be regarded as the holiest of men. Even saints, however, were coarse in the age of James, and the most beautiful of all Donne's elegies, the exquisite "Refusal to Allow His Young Wife to Accompany Him Abroad as a Page," which belongs to his mature life and treats of a very creditable passion, is marred by almost inconceivable offences against good taste.

Another section of Donne's poems is composed of funeral elegies or requiems, in which he allowed the sombre part of his fancy to run riot. In these curious entombments we read nothing that seems personal or pathetic, but much about "the magnetic force" of the deceased, her spiritual anatomy, and her soul's "meridians and parallels." Amid these pedantries, we light now and then upon extraordinary bursts of poetic observation, as when the eminence of the spirit of Mistress Drury reminds the poet of a vision, seen years before in sailing past the Canaries, and he cries out—

Doth not a Teneriffe or higher hill,
Rise so high like a rock, that one might think
The floating moon would shipwreck there, and sink,

or as when one of his trances comes upon him, and he sighs—

when thou know'st this,
Thou know'st how wan a ghost this our world is.

These lovely sudden bursts of pure poetry are more frequent in the "Funeral Elegies" than in any section of Donne's poetry which we have mentioned, and approach those, to be presently noted, in the Lyrics. The spirit of this strange writer loved to dwell on the majestic and gorgeous aspects of death, to wave his torch within the charnel-house and to show that its walls are set with jewels.

This may be taken as an example of his obscure mortuary imagination—

As men of China, after an age's stay,
Do take up porcelain where they buried clay,
So at this grave, her limbeck (which refines
The diamonds, rubies, sapphires, pearls and mines
Of which this flesh was), her soul shall inspire
Flesh of such stuff, as God, when his last fire
Annuls this world, to recompense it, shall
Make and name them the elixir of this All.
They say, the sea, when it gains, loseth too,
If carnal Death (the younger brother) do
Usurp the body; our soul, which subject is
To the elder Death, by sin, is freed by this;
They perish both, when they attempt the just,
For graves our trophies are, and both death's dust.

The presence of the emblems of mortality rouses Donne to an unusual intellectual ecstasy. The latest of these elegies is dated 1625, and shows that the poet retained his art in this kind of writing to the very end of his career, adding polish to his style, without any perceptible falling off in power.

A large number of "Holy Sonnets," which Izaak Walton thought had perished, were published in 1669, and several remain still unprinted. They are more properly quatorzains than sonnets, more correct in form than the usual English sonnet of the age—for the octett is properly arranged and rhymed—but closing in the sestett with a couplet. These sonnets are very interesting from the light they throw on Donne's prolonged sympathy with the Roman Church, over which his biographers have been wont to slur. All these "Holy Sonnets" probably belong to 1617, or the period immediately following the death of Donne's wife. In the light of certain examples in the possession of the present writer, which have not yet appeared in print, they seem to confirm Walton's remark that though Donne inquired early in life into the differences between Protestantism and Catholicism, yet that he lived until the death of his wife without religion.

A pathetic sonnet from the Westmoreland manuscript, here printed for the first time, shows the effect of that bereavement upon him—

Since she whom I loved hath paid her last debt,
    To Nature, and to hers and my good is dead,
    And her soul early into heaven vanished.—

Wholly on heavenly things my mind is set.
Here the admiring her my mind did whet
    To seek thee, God; so streams do show their
      head,
    But tho' I have found thee, and thou my thirst
      has fed,
A holy thirsty dropsy melts me yet.
But why should I beg more love, when as thou
    Does woo my soul for hers, off'ring all thine:
And dost not only fear lest I allow
    My love to Saints and Angels, things divine,
But in thy tender jealousy dost doubt
Lest this World, Flesh, yea Devil put thee out?

The sonnet on the Blessed Virgin Mary, however, has probably been attributed to Donne by error; the more likely name of Constable has been suggested as that of its author.

In his other divine poems, also, the Roman element is often very strong, and the theology of a cast which is far removed from that of Puritanism. In the very curious piece called "The Cross," he seems to confess to the use of a material crucifix, and in "A Litany" he distinctly recommends prayer to the Virgin Mary,

That she-cherubim which unlocked Paradise.

All these are matters which must be left to the future biographers of Donne, but which are worthy of their closest attention in developing the intricate anomalies of his character.

We have now, by a process of exhaustion, arrived at what is the most interesting of the sections of Donne's poetry, his amatory lyrics. These are about seventy in number, and so far as the scanty evidence can be depended upon, belong to various periods from his twentieth to his thirty-fifth year. The series, as we now hold it, begins with the gross and offensive piece of extravagance called, "The Flea," but is followed by "The Good-Morrow," which strikes a very different note. As a rule, these poems are extremely personal, confidential, and vivid; the stamp of life is on them. None the less, while confessing with extraordinary frankness and clearness the passion of the writer, they are so reserved in detail, so immersed and engulphed in secrecy, that no definite conjecture can be hazarded as to the person, or persons, or the class of persons, to whom they were addressed. One or two were evidently inspired by Donne's wife, others most emphatically were not, and in their lawless, though not gross, sensuality, remind us of the still more outspoken "Elegies." In spite of the alembicated verbiage, the tortuousness and artificiality of the thought, sincerity burns in every stanza, and the most exquisite images lie side by side with monstrous conceits and ugly pedantries.

A peculiarity of the lyrics is that scarcely two of the seventy are written in the same verse-form. Donne evidently laid himself out to invent elaborate and farfetched metres. He was imitated in this down to the Restoration, when all metrical effects tended to merge in the heroic couplet. But of the innumerable form-inventions of Donne and of his disciples scarcely one has been adopted into the language, although more than one, by their elegance and melody, deserve to be resumed.

This exemplifies one of the prettiest of his stanza-forms—

> If thou be'st born to strange sights,
>   Things invisible to see,
> Ride ten thousand days and nights,
>   Till age snow white hairs on thee;
> Thou, when thou return'st, wilt tell me
> All strange wonders that befell thee,
>   And swear
>   Nowhere
> Lives a woman true and fair.
> If thou find'st one, let me know;
>   Such a pilgrimage were sweet.
> Yet do not,—I would not go
>   Though at next door we might meet,
> Though she were true when you met her,
> And last till you write your letter,
>   Yet she
>   Will be
> False, ere I come, with two or three.

It now remains to examine this body of poetry in general terms, and, first of all, it is necessary to make some remarks with regard to Donne's whole system of prosody. The terms "irregular," "unintelligible," and "viciously rugged," are commonly used in describing it, and it seems even to be supposed by some critics that Donne did not know how to scan. This last supposition may be rejected at once; what there was to know about poetry was known to Donne. But it seems certain that he intentionally introduced a revolution into English versification. It was doubtless as a rebellion against the smooth and somewhat nerveless iambic flow of Spenser and the earliest contemporaries of Shakespeare, that Donne invented his violent mode of breaking up the line into quick and slow beats. The best critic of his own generation, Ben Jonson, hated the innovation, and told Drummond "that Donne, for not keeping of accent, deserved hanging." It is difficult to stem a current of censure which has set without intermission since the very days of Donne itself, but I may be permitted to point out what I imagine was the poet's own view of the matter.

He found, as I have said, the verse of his youth, say of 1590, exceedingly mellifluous, sinuous, and inclining to flaccidity. A five-syllabled iambic line of Spenser or of Daniel trots along with the gentlest amble of inevitable shorts and longs. It seems to have vexed the ear of Donne by its tendency to feebleness, and it doubtless appeared to him that the very gifted writers who immediately preceded him had carried the softness of it as far as it would go. He desired new and more varied effects. To see what he aimed at doing, we have, I believe, to turn to what has been attempted in our own time, by Mr. Robert Bridges, in some of his early experiments, and by the Symbolists in France. The iambic rhymed line of Donne has audacities such as are permitted to his blank verse by Milton, and although the felicities are rare in the older poet, instead of being almost incessant, as in the later, Donne at his best is not less melodious than Milton. When he writes—

Blasted with sighs and surrounded with tears,

we must not dismiss this as not being iambic verse at all, nor,— much less,—attempt to read it—

Blasted with sighs, and surrounded with tears,

but recognize in it the poet's attempt to identify the beat of his verse with his bewildered and dejected condition, reading it somewhat in this notation:—

Blasted | with sighs || and surrounded | with tears.

The violence of Donne's transposition of accent is most curiously to be observed in his earliest satires, and in some of his later poems is almost entirely absent. Doubtless his theory became modified with advancing years. No poet is more difficult to read aloud. Such a passage as the following may excusably defy a novice:

No token of worth but Queen's man and fine
Living barrels of beef and flagons of wine.
I shook like a spied spy. Preachers which are
Seas of wit and arts, you can then dare
Drown the sins of this place, for, for me,
Which am but a scant brook, it enough shall be
To wash the stains away.

But treat the five-foot verse not as a fixed and unalterable sequence of cadences, but as a norm around which a musician weaves his variations, and the riddle is soon read—

No token | of worth | but Queen's | man | and fine
Living | barrels of | beef and | flagons of | wine.
I shook | like a spied | spy. | Preachers | which are
Seas | of wit | and arts, | you can then | dare D
rown | the sins | of this place, | for, | for me,
Which am | but a scant | brook, | it enough | shall be
To wash | the stains | away.

The poetry of Donne possesses in no small degree that "unusual and indefinable witchery" which Dr. Jessopp has noted as characteristic of the man himself. But our enjoyment of it is marred by the violence of the writer, by his want of what seems to us to be good taste, and by a quality which has been overlooked by those who have written about him, but which seems to provide the key to the mystery of his position. Donne was, I would venture to suggest, by far the most modern and contemporaneous of the writers of his time. He rejected all the classical tags and imagery of the Elizabethans, he borrowed nothing from French or Italian tradition. He arrived at an excess of actuality in style, and it was because he struck them as so novel that his immediate coevals were so much fascinated with him. His poems are full of images taken from the life and habits of the time. Where earlier poets had summoned the myths of Greece to adorn their verse, Donne weaves in, instead, the false zoology, the crude physics and philosophy, of his own fermenting epoch. The poem called "Love's Exchange," is worthy of careful examination in this respect. Each stanza is crowded with conceits, each one of which is taken from the practical or professional life of the moment in which the poet wrote. This extreme modernness, however, is one potent source of our lack of sympathy with the poetry so inspired. In the long run, it is the broader suggestion, the wider if more conventional range of classic imagery, which may hope to hold without fatigue the interest of successive generations.

For us the charm of Donne continues to rest in his occasional felicities, his burst of melodious passion. If his song were not so tantalizingly fragmentary, we should call him the unqestioned nightingale of the Jacobean choir. No other poet of that time, few poets of any time, have equalled the concentrated passion, the delicate, long-drawn musical effects, the bold and ecstatic rapture of Donne at his best. In such a poem as "The Dream," he realizes the very paroxysm of amatory song. In his own generation, no one approached the purity of his cascades of ringing monosyllables, his

For God's sake, hold your tongue and let me love,

or,

I long to talk with some old lover's ghost
Who died before the God of Love was born,

or,

Oh more than moon,
Draw not thy seas to drown me in thy sphere.

or,

A bracelet of bright hair about the bone.

In these and similar passages, of which a not very slender florilegium might be gathered from his voluminous productions, Donne reminds us that Ben Jonson esteemed him "the first poet in the world in some things." But this quality of passionate music is not the only one discernible, nor often to be discerned. The more obvious characteristic was summed up by Coleridge in a droll quatrain—

With Donne, whose Muse on dromedary trots,
Wreathe iron pokers into true-love-knots;
Rhyme's sturdy cripple, Fancy's maze and clue,
Wit's forge and fire-blast, Meaning's press and screw.

In the use of these ingenuities, which it was once the fashion to call "metaphysical," Donne shows an amazing pertinacity. He is never daunted by the feeling that his wit is exercised "on subjects where we have no right to expect it," and where it is impossible for us to relish it. He pushes on with relentless logic,—sometimes, indeed, past chains of images that are lovely and appropriate;

but, oftener, through briars and lianas that rend his garments and trip up his feet. He is not affected by the ruggedness of his road, nor by our unwillingness to follow him. He stumbles doggedly on until he has reached his singular goal. In all this intellectual obstinacy he has a certain kinship to Browning, but his obscurity is more dense. It is to be hoped that the contemporary maligned him who reported Donne to have written one of his elegies in an intentional obscureness, but that he delighted in putting his readers out of their depth can scarcely be doubted. It is against this lurid background, which in itself and unrelieved would possess a very slight attraction to modern readers, that the electrical flashes of Donne's lyrical intuition make their appearance, almost blinding us by their brilliancy, and fading into the dark tissue of conceits before we have time to appreciate them.

The prominence here given to Donne will be challenged by no one who considers what his influence was on the poetical taste of the time. It is true that among his immediate contemporaries the following of Spenser did not absolutely cease at once. But if a study on the poets of Charles I. were to succeed the present volume, the name of Donne would have to be constantly prominent. On almost everything nondramatic published in the succeeding generation, from Crashaw to Davenant, from Carew to Cowley, the stamp of Donne is set. Dryden owed not a little to him, although, as time went on, he purged himself more and more fully of the taint of metaphysical conceit. So late as 1692, in the preface to *Eleanora*, Dryden still held up Donne as "the greatest wit, though not the best poet of our nation." His poems were among the few non-dramatic works of the Jacobean period which continued to be read and reprinted in the age of Anne, and Pope both borrowed from and imitated Donne.

So far as we trace this far-sweeping influence exercised on the poets of a hundred years, we have difficulty in applauding its effects. The empassioned sincerity, the intuitions, the clarion note of Donne were individual to himself and could not be transmitted. It was far otherwise with the jargon of "metaphysical" wit, the trick of strained and inappropriate imagery. These could be adopted by almost any clever person, and were, in fact, employed with fluent effect by people in whom the poetical quality was of the slightest. Writers like Mildmay Fane, Earl of Westmoreland, or like Owen Feltham (in his verse), show what it was that Donne's seed produced when it fell upon stony ground.

—Edmund Gosse, "John Donne,"
The Jacobean Poets, 1894, pp. 51–67

GEORGE SAINTSBURY "INTRODUCTION" (1896)

For the piece below, Saintsbury relies at first on a theme of duality he believes somewhat defines Donne as a writer: "Always in him are the two conflicting forces of intense enjoyment of the present, and intense feeling of the contrast of the present with the future. He has at once the transcendentalism which saves sensuality and the passion which saves mysticism. Indeed the two currents run so full and strong in him, they clash and churn their waves so boisterously, that this is of itself sufficient to account for the obscurity, the extravagance, the undue quaintness which have been charged against him." This duality, Saintsbury argues, is marked by a transition in Donne's life that is reflected in a transition in his writings. The first part of his writings, chronologically speaking, are the secular works, which belongs to the first period in his life; the second part, the sacred works and prose, belongs to a second period accompanied by a spiritual awakening. Saintsbury puts it thusly: "the greater part of the verse is animated by what may be called a spiritualized worldliness and sensuality, the whole of the prose by a spiritualism which has left worldliness far behind." Saintsbury punningly refers to this as a "Renaissance" within Donne, a transition shared by other writers, but one that is key, Saintsbury suggests, to understanding Donne.

While the above cataloguing of Donne's work is based on chronology and biography, critically speaking, Saintsbury places Donne's works into three categories: the satires; the elegies and amatory poems; and the sacred work (plus other miscellaneous texts). Much of the rest of the excerpted material focuses on the satires; this proves eminently useful, as Saintsbury's examination of the satires in general proves one of the most thorough studies in this text. Saintsbury begins by probing their metrical structure, claiming that while unmusical, they reflect only the freeform nature of Renaissance poetry in and of itself. He then looks at specific passages in some of the satires. Saintsbury next examines some of Donne's other works, but students will no doubt find his examinations of the satires and his explanation of Donne's duality the most illuminating and useful section of the text.

There is hardly any, perhaps indeed there is not any, English author on whom it is so hard to keep the just mixture of personal appreciation and critical measure as it is on John Donne. It is almost necessary that those who do not like him should not like him at all; should be scarcely able to see how any decent and intelligent human creature can like him. It is almost as necessary that those who do like him should either like him so much as to speak unadvisedly with their lips, or else curb and restrain the expression of their love for fear that it should seem on that side idolatry. But these are not the only dangers. Donne is eminently of that kind which lends itself to sham liking, to coterie worship, to a false enthusiasm; and here is another weapon in the hands of the infidels, and another stumbling-block for the feet of the true believers. Yet there is always something stimulating in a subject of this kind, and a sort of temptation to attempt it.

To write anything about Donne's life, after Walton, is an attempt which should make even hardened *écrivailleurs* and *écrivassiers* nervous. That the good Izaak knew his subject and its atmosphere thoroughly; that he wrote but a very few years after Donne's own death; and that he was a writer of distinct charm, are discouraging things, but not the most discouraging. It is perhaps only those who after being familiar for years with Donne's poems, of which Walton says very little, make subsequent acquaintance with Walton's presentment of the man, who can appreciate the full awkwardness of the situation. It is the worst possible case of *pereant qui ante nos*. The human Donne whom Walton depicts is so exactly the poetical Donne whom we knew, that the effect is uncanny. Generally, or at least very frequently, we find the poet other than his form of verse: here we find him quite astoundingly akin to it.

. . .(T)here is a strange, though by no means unexampled, division between the two periods of his life and the two classes of his work. Roughly speaking, almost the whole of at least the secular verse belongs to the first division of the life, almost the whole of the prose to the second. Again, by far the greater part of the verse is animated by what may be called a spiritualized worldliness and sensuality, the whole of the prose by a spiritualism which has left worldliness far behind. The conjunction is, I say, not unknown: it was specially prevalent in the age of Donne's birth and early life. It has even passed into something of a commonplace in reference to that Renaissance of which, as it slowly passed from south to north, Donne was one of the latest and yet one of the most perfect exponents. The strange story which Brantome tells of Margaret of Navarre summoning a lover to the church under whose flags his mistress lay buried, and talking with him of her, shows, a generation before Donne's birth, the influence which in his day had made its way across the narrow seas as it had earlier across the Alps, and had at each crossing gathered gloom and force if it had lost lightness and colour. Always in him are the two conflicting forces of intense enjoyment of the present, and intense feeling of the contrast of the present with the future. He has at once the transcendentalism which saves sensuality and the passion which saves mysticism. Indeed the two currents run so full and strong in him, they clash and churn their waves so boisterously, that this is of itself sufficient to account for the obscurity, the extravagance, the undue quaintness which have been charged against him. He was "of the first order of poets"; but he was not of the first amongst the first. Only Dante perhaps among these greatest of all had such a conflict and ebullition of feeling to express. For, as far as we can judge, in Shakespeare, even in the Sonnets, the poetical power mastered to some extent at the very first the rough material of the poetic instinct, and prepared before expression the things to be expressed. In Dante we can trace something of the presence of slag and dross in the ore; and even in Dante we can perhaps trace faintly also the difficulty of smelting it. Donne, being a lesser poet than Dante, shows it everywhere. It is seldom that even for a few lines, seldomer that for a few stanzas, the power of the furnace is equal to the volumes of ore and fuel that are thrust into it. But the fire is always there—over-tasked, over-mastered for a time, but never choked or extinguished; and ever and anon from gaps in the smouldering mass there breaks forth such a sudden flow of pure molten metal, such a flower of incandescence, as not even in the very greatest poets of all can be ever surpassed or often rivalled.

For critical, and indeed for general purposes, the poetical works of Donne may be divided into three parts, separated from each other by a considerable difference of character and, in one case at least, of time. These are the Satires, which are beyond all doubt very early; the Elegies and other amatory poems, most of which are certainly, and all probably, early likewise; and the Divine and Miscellaneous Poems, some of which may not be late, but most of which certainly are. All three divisions have certain characteristics in common; but the best of these characteristics, and some which are not common to the three, belong to the second and third only.

It was the opinion of the late seventeenth and of the whole of the eighteenth century that Donne, though a clever man, had no ear. Chalmers, a very industrious student, and not such a bad critic, says so in so many words; Johnson undoubtedly thought so; Pope demonstrated his belief by his fresh "tagging" of the Satires. They all to some extent no doubt really believed what they said; their ears had fallen deaf to that particular concord. But they all also no doubt founded their belief to a certain extent on certain words of Dryden's which did not exactly import or comport what Mr. Pope and the rest took them to mean. Dryden had the knack, a knack of great value to a critic, but sometimes productive of sore misguiding to a critic's readers—of adjusting his comments solely to one point of view, to a single scheme in metric and other things. Now, from the point of view of the scheme which both his authority and his example made popular, Donne *was* rather formless. But nearly all the eighteenth-century critics and criticasters concentrated their attention on the Satires; and in the Satires Donne certainly takes singular liberties, no matter what scheme be preferred. It is now, I believe, pretty well admitted by all competent judges that the astonishing roughness of the Satirists of the late sixteenth century was not due to any general ignoring of the principles of melodious English verse, but to a deliberate intention arising from the same sort of imperfect erudition which had in other ways so much effect on the men of the Renaissance generally. Satiric verse among the ancients allowed itself, and even went out of its way to take, licences which no poet in other styles would have dreamt of taking. The Horace of the impeccable odes writes such a hideous hexameter as—

Non ego, namque parabilem amo Venerem facilemque,

and one of the Roman satirists who was then very popular, Persius, though he could rise to splendid style on occasion, is habitually as harsh, as obscure, and as wooden as a Latin poet well can be. It is not probable, it is certain, that Donne and the rest imitated these licences of malice prepense.

But it must be remembered that at the time when they assumed this greater licence, the normal structure of English verse was anything but fixed. Horace had in his contemporaries, Persius and Juvenal had still more in their forerunners, examples of versification than which Mr. Pope himself could do nothing more "correct"; and their licences could therefore be kept within measure, and still be licentious enough to suit any preconceived idea of the ungirt character of the Satiric muse. In Donne's time the very precisians took a good deal of licence: the very Virgils and even Ovids were not apt to concern themselves very greatly about a short vowel before s with a consonant, or a trisyllable at the end of a pentameter. If therefore you meant to show that you were *sans gene*, you had to make demonstrations of the most unequivocal character. Even with all this explanation and allowance it may still seem probable that Donne's Satires never received any formal preparation for the press, and are in the state of rough copy. Without this allowance, which the eighteenth century either did not care or did not know how to give, it is not surprising that they should have seemed mere monstrosities.

The satiric pieces in which these peculiarities are chiefly shown, which attracted the attention of Pope, and which, through his recension, became known to a much larger number of persons than the work of any other

Elizabethan Satirist, have the least share of Donne's poetical interest. But they display to the full his manly strength and shrewd sense, and they are especially noticeable in one point. They exhibit much less of that extravagant exaggeration of contemporary vice and folly which makes one of their chief contemporaries, Marston's *Scourge of Villainy*, almost an absurd thing, while it is by no means absent from Hall's *Virgidemiarum*. We cannot indeed suppose that Donne's satire was wholly and entirely sincere, but a good deal in it clearly was. Thus his handling of the perennial subjects of satire is far more fresh, serious, and direct than is usual with Satirists, and it was no doubt this judicious and direct quality which commended it to Pope. Moreover, these poems abound in fine touches. The Captain in the first Satire—

> Bright parcel-gilt with forty dead men's pay—
> the ingenious evildoers in the second—
> > > for whose sinful sake,
> Schoolmen new tenements in hell must make—

the charming touch at once so literary and so natural in the fifth—

> > so controverted lands
> 'Scape, like Angelica, the striver's hands,

are only a few of the jewels five words long that might be produced as specimens. But it is not here that we find the true Donne: it was not this province of the universal monarchy of wit that he ruled with the most unshackled sway. The provinces that he did so rule were quite other: strange frontier regions; uttermost isles where sensuality, philosophy, and devotion meet, or where separately dwelling they rejoice or mourn over the conquests of each other. I am not so sure of the *Progress of the Soul* as some writers have been—interesting as it is, and curious as is the comparison with Prior's *Alma*, which it of necessity suggests, and probably suggested. As a whole it seems to me uncertain in aim, unaccomplished in execution. But what things there are in it! What a line is—

> Great Destiny, the Commissary of God!

What a lift and sweep in the fifth stanza—

> To my six lustres almost now outwore!

What a thought that—

> This soul, to whom Luther and Mahomet were
> Prisons of flesh!

And the same miraculous pregnancy of thought and expression runs through the whole, even though it seems never to have found full and complete delivery in artistic form. How far this curious piece is connected with the still more famous 'Anniversaries,' in which so different a stage of "progress" is reached, and which ostensibly connect themselves with the life and death of Mrs. Elizabeth Drury, is a question which it would be tedious to argue out in any case, and impossible to argue out here. But the successive stages of the 'Anatomy of the World' present us with the most marvellous poetical exposition of a certain kind of devotional thought yet given. It is indeed possible that the union of the sensual, intellectual, poetical, and religious temperaments is not so very rare; but it is very rarely voiceful. That it existed in Donne's pre-eminently, and that it found voice in him as it never has done before or since, no one who knows his life and works can doubt. That the greatest of this singular group of poems is the 'Second Anniversary,' will hardly, I think, be contested. Here is the famous passage—

> Her pure and eloquent blood
> Spoke in her cheeks and so distinctly wrought,
> That one might almost say her body thought—

which has been constantly quoted, praised, and imitated. Here, earlier, is what I should choose if I undertook the perilous task of singling out the finest line in English sacred poetry—

> so long

> As till God's great *Venite* change the song—a *Dies Iras* and a *Venite* itself combined in ten English syllables. Here is that most vivid and original of Donne's many prose and verse meditations on death, as—

> A groom
> That brings a taper to the outward room.

Here too is the singular undernote of "she'" repeated constantly in different places of the verse, with the effect of a sort of musical accompaniment or refrain, which Dryden (a great student of Donne) afterwards imitated on the note "you" in *Astrcea Recluse,* and the *Coronation.* But these, and many other separate verbal or musical beauties, perhaps yield to the wonder of the strange, dreamy atmosphere of moonlight thought and feeling which is shed over the whole piece. Nowhere is Donne, one of the most full-blooded and yet one of the least earthly of English poets, quite so unearthly.

The Elegies, perhaps better known than any of his poems, contain the least of this unearthliness. The famous 'Refusal to Allow His Young Wife to Accompany Him as His Page,' though a very charming poem, is, I think, one of the few pieces of his which have been praised enough, if not even a little overpraised. As a matter of taste it seems to me indeed more open to exception than the equally famous and much more "fie-fied" 'To His Mistress Going to Bed,' a piece of frank naturalism redeemed from coarseness by passion and poetic completeness. The Elegies again are the most varied of the divisions of Donne's works, and contain next to the Satires his liveliest touches, such as—

The grim, eight-foot-high, iron-bound,
     serving-man,
That oft names God in oaths, and only than

or as the stroke—

Lank as an unthrift's purse.

In Epithalamia Donne was good, but not consummate, falling far short of his master, Spenser, in this branch. No part of his work was more famous in his own day than his 'Epistles' which are headed by the 'Storm' and 'Calm,' that so did please Ben Jonson. But in these and other pieces of the same division, the misplaced ingenuity which is the staple of the general indictment against Donne, appears, to my taste, less excusably than anywhere else. Great passion of love, of grief, of philosophic meditation, of religious awe, had the power to master the fantastic hippogriff of Donne's imagination, and make it wholly serviceable; but in his less intense works it was rather unmanageable. Yet there are very fine things here also; especially in the Epistle to Sir Henry Goodyere, and those to Lucy Countess of Bedford, and Elizabeth Countess of Huntingdon. The best of the 'Funeral Elegies' are those of Mrs. Boulstred. In the Divine Poems there is nothing so really divine as the astonishing verse from the 'Second Anniversary' quoted above. It must always however seem odd that such a poet as Donne should have taken the trouble to tag the Lamentations of Jeremiah into verse, which is sometimes much more lamentable in form than even in matter. The epigram as to Le Franc de Pompignan's French version, and its connection, by dint of Jeremiah's prophetic power, with the fact of his having lamented, might almost, if any Englishman had had the wit to think of it, have been applied a century earlier to parts of this of Donne. The 'Litany' is far better, though it naturally suggests Herrick's masterpiece in divine song-writing; and even the 'Jeremiah' ought not perhaps to be indiscriminately disapproved. The opening stanzas especially have a fine melancholy clang not unknown, I think, as a model to Mr. Swinburne. But to my fancy no division of Donne's poems—the 'Second Anniversary' always excepted—shows him in his quiddity and essence as do the Lyrics. Some of these are to a certain extent doubtful. One of the very finest of the whole, 'Absence, hear thou my protestation,' with its unapproached fourth stanza, appeared first in Davison's *Poetical Rhapsody* unsigned. But all the best authorities agree (and for my part I would almost go to the stake on it) that the piece is Donne's. In those which are undoubtedly genuine the peculiar quality of Donne flames through and perfumes the dusky air which is his native atmosphere in a way which, though I do not suppose that the French poet had ever heard of Donne, has always seemed to me the true antitype and fulfilment by anticipation of Baudelaire's

> Encensoir oublie qui fume
> En silence a travers la nuit.

Everybody knows the

> Bracelet of bright hair about the bone

of the late discovered skeleton, identifying the lover: everybody the perfect fancy and phrase of the exordium—

> I long to talk with some old lover's ghost
> Who died before the god of Love was born.

But similar touches are almost everywhere. The enshrining once for all in the simplest words of a universal thought—

> I wonder by my troth what thou and I Did till we loved?

The selection of single adjectives to do the duty of a whole train of surplusage—

> Where can we find two better hemispheres
> Without *sharp* north, without *declining* west?—

meet us, and tell us what we have to expect in all but the earliest. In comparison with these things, such a poem as 'Go and catch a falling star,' delightful as it is, is perhaps only a delightful quaintness, and 'The Indifferent' only a pleasant quip consummately turned. In these perversities Donne is but playing *tours de force*. His natural and genuine work re-appears in such poems as 'Canonizations', or as 'The Legacy'. It is the fashion sometimes, and that not always with the worst critics, to dismiss this kind of heroic rapture as an agreeable but conscious exaggeration, partly betrayed and partly condoned by flouting-pieces like those just mentioned. The gloss does not do the critic's knowledge of human nature or his honesty in acknowledging his knowledge much credit. Both moods and both expressions are true; but the rapture is the truer. No one who sees in these mere literary or fashionable exercises, can ever appreciate such an *aubade* as 'Stay, O Sweet, and Do Not Rise', or such a midnight piece as 'The Dream', with its never-to-be-forgotten couplet—

> I must confess, it could not choose but be
> Profane to think thee anything but thee.

If there is less quintessence in 'The Message', for all its beauty, it is only because no one can stay long at the point of rapture which characterizes Donne at his most characteristic, and the relaxation is natural—as natural as is the pretty fancy about St. Lucy—

> Who but seven hours herself unmasks—

the day under her invocation being in the depths of December. But the passionate mood, or that of mystical reflection, soon returns, and in the one Donne shall sing with another of the wondrous phrases where simplicity and perfection meet—

> So to engraft our hands as yet
>   Was all our means to make us one,
> And pictures in our eyes to get
>   Was all our propagation.
> Or in the other dwell on the hope of buried lovers—
> To make their souls at the last busy day,
> Meet at this grave, and make a little stay.

I am not without some apprehension that I shall be judged to have fallen a victim to my own distinction, drawn at the beginning of this paper, and shown myself an unreasonable lover of this astonishing poet. Yet I think I could make good my appeal in any competent critical court. For in Donne's case the yea-nay fashion of censorship which is necessary and desirable in the case of others is quite superfluous. His faults are so gross, so open, so palpable, that they hardly require the usual amount of critical comment and condemnation. But this very peculiarity of theirs constantly obscures his beauties even to not unfit readers. They open him; they are shocked, or bored, or irritated, or puzzled by his occasional nastiness (for he is now and then simply and inexcusably nasty), his frequent involution and eccentricity, his not quite rare indulgence in extravagances which go near to silliness; and so they lose the extraordinary beauties which lie beyond or among these faults. It is true that, as was said above, there are those, and many of them, who can never and will never like Donne. No one who thinks *Don Quixote* a merely funny book, no one who sees in Aristophanes a dirty-minded fellow with a knack of Greek versification, no one who thinks it impossible not to wish that Shakespeare had not written the Sonnets, no one who wonders what on earth Giordano Bruno meant by *Gli eroici Furori,* need trouble himself even to attempt to like Donne. "He will never *have done* with that attempt," as our Dean himself would have unblushingly observed, for he was never weary of punning on his name.

But for those who have experienced, or who at least understand, the ups-and-downs, the ins-and-outs of human temperament, the alternations not merely of passion and satiety, but of passion and laughter, of passion and melancholy reflection, of passion earthly enough and spiritual rapture almost heavenly, there is no poet and hardly any writer like Donne. They may even be tempted to see in the strangely mixed and flawed character of his style, an index and reflection of the variety and the rapid changes of his thought and feeling. To the praise of the highest poetical art he cannot indeed lay claim. He is of course entitled to the benefit of the pleas that it is uncertain whether he ever prepared definitely for the press a single poetical work of his; that it is certain that his age regarded his youth with too much disapproval to bestow any critical care on his youthful poems. But it may be retorted that no one with the finest sense of poetry as an art, could have left things so formless as he has left, that it would have been intolerable pain and grief to any such till he had got them, even in MS., into shape. The retort is valid. But if Donne cannot receive the praise due to the accomplished poetical artist, he has that not perhaps higher but certainly rarer, of the inspired poetical creator. No study could have bettered—I hardly know whether any study could have produced—such touches as the best of those which have been quoted, and as many which perforce have been left out. And no study could have given him the idiosyncrasy which he has. *Nos passions,* says Bossuet, *ont quelque chose d'infini.* To express infinity no doubt is a contradiction in terms. But no poet has gone nearer to the hinting and adumbration of this infinite quality of passion, and of the relapses and reactions from passion, than the author of 'The Second Anniversary' and 'The Dream,' of 'The Relique' and 'The Ecstasy.'

—George Saintsbury, from "Introduction,"
Poems of John Donne, ed. E.K. Chambers, 1896,
vol. 1, pp. xi–xxxiii

EDMUND GOSSE (1899)

Gosse responds to much of the conventional nineteenth-century thought on Donne, both directly and indirectly, in the critical study below. Gosse approaches Donne as a biographer, and thus examines how changes in Donne's life conditions and beliefs alter his works (a process mimicked by Courthope, below). As Gosse puts it: "the careful study of Donne, when the first obscure crust is broken, reveals a condition of mind and even a sequence of events so personal, that we hardly dare to take our legitimate advantage from it." Gosse's approach to Donne's work has been more commonly applied to writers like Andrew Marvell, who espouse an overt politicism in their poems. Gosse's method here is a bit more personal, and thus a bit more tenuous; nonetheless, his findings are both illuminating on Donne and his work and suggestive of further areas of thought and research for individuals studying the works of the first metaphysical poet.

Gosse begins his analysis by suggesting that Donne's early life was, unsurprisingly for a youth, frivolous and carefree, and that his work reflects this: "In these early days his experiences are all sensation and superficial emotion. He wanders wherever his desires attract him, rifles all blossoms for their honey, boasts—in the manner of impudent youth—his detachment from all chains of duty or reflection." Gosse examines this construct in several of Donne's early works, including his famous pieces "The Sun Rising," "The Flea," and "The Legacy." Gosse then suggests that Donne begins to transition out of his young adulthood and into a more mature phase of thought and writing: "He had been pursuing with frenzy an illusive chimera of pleasure. But in spite of all his impudent protests, the strong heart of John Donne could not be satisfied by these ephemeral captures. His passions were now dominant and his blood imperious." These "passions" caused a growth in what Gosse calls Donne's "ethical ambition," his desire to examine philosophical and poetic concepts from a more earnest and intellectual perspective. This passage in Donne's life coincided with a move to the Azores and a secret affair; Donne's return from the islands and rejection of the affair implies to Gosse another transition for the author, one chronicled amongst Donne's "Elegies." Gosse writes that Donne's work becomes infused with "hatred and enforced resignation," and argues that the poem "The Apparition" is the best example of this period in Donne's life: "as he tosses between sleep and waking, the horror of his situation, the vileness of the woman he has loved, and the whole squalor of the outworn liaison come upon him and overwhelm him. The fierce passion in this brief lyric, a 'hate-poem' of the very first class, is closely akin to those flashes of lurid light in which the contemporary tragedians excelled, 'steeping us,' as Charles Lamb says, 'in agonies infernal.' "

As Courthope will likewise indicate below, Donne's marriage marks another transitory period in his life and work, which Gosse examines through the piece "Epithalamion made at Lincoln's Inn." This leads Gosse into a close examination of Donne's divine poems, a period of the author's life that reflected a movement towards intellectualizing his own work. This, Gosse asserts, is where metaphysics comes into Donne's writing: "That is to say, the more metaphysical pieces are the outcome of the years when religious inquiry formed one of his prominent studies, but when no exclusive call had summoned him to the ministry." Though Gosse admires the wit of Donne's early work in this genre, he finds the pieces "frigid" and cold—to Gosse, a work like "The Litany" is "burdened with ingenuity." Still, Gosse believes that Donne does begin to hone this aspect of his craft, until a particular "richer gloom" inhabits some of his better sacred works.

Gosse then moves into examining how Donne influenced his successors. He first begins by exploring Donne's own Italian influences before lamenting that Donne himself had a significant impact on the poetry of his day: "In examining the remarkable wide and deep, though almost entirely malign, influence of Donne upon the poetry of this country, it is necessary first of all to dwell on the complete intellectual isolation of his youth and middle age." Partly because Donne was not interested in the poetic fashions of his day, and partly because of his inconsistent meter (though Gosse does defend Donne's versification, he seems to suggest that it should not be copied—his study of "Twickenham Garden" in this section of the essay is the best examination of this particular work in the entire collection). Eventually, Gosse concludes that it was Donne's intellectualism that attracted young poets to attempt to imitate him; to them, Donne represented a new tradition in poetry. Still, Gosse laments these imitations, suggesting that none managed to replicate the genius of the original.

Ultimately, Gosse concludes that Donne and his genius were a particular product of their time, best understood in their own day. Gosse writes of Donne: "His writings, like his actions, were faulty, violent, a little morbid even, and abnormal." Still, he admires him greatly, and in his work below, does address and redress the most prominent criticisms leveled against Donne in the nineteenth century, and his arguments should prove of enormous use to anyone still studying Donne today.

When we come to consider the relation of the early poetry of Donne to that which was being produced elsewhere in England, so abundantly, during the closing years of the sixteenth century, we shall have to dwell on its curious divergence from all the established literary traditions of the time. Among these traditions, that of taking an imaginary episode in love and embroidering fancies upon it was one of the most accepted. In the more favourable instances of a pretended revelation of amatory adventure in verse, such as the *Idea* of Drayton in 1593 and 1594, or the *Amoretti* of Spenser in 1595, it is almost impossible for the most ingenious reader to build on the shadowy and nebulous basis any superstructure of conjectural biography. At first sight it may seem that Donne offers the same intangibility; but there is this difference, that, after twenty readings, the story indicated by Spenser or Drayton in his sonnets continues as vague as ever, whereas the careful study of Donne, when the first obscure crust is broken, reveals a condition of mind and even a sequence of events so personal, that we hardly dare to take our legitimate advantage from it.

We read Donne, however, to little purpose if we do not perceive that he was, above all things, sincere. His writings, like his actions, were faulty, violent, a little morbid even, and abnormal. He was not, and did not attempt to be, an average man. But actions and writings alike, in their strangeness, their aloofness, were unadulterated by a tinge of affectation. Donne was Elizabethan in his absolute straightforwardness of character; it was left to his Caroline disciples to introduce into a mode of expression founded upon his a trick of pastiche, an alloy of literary pretence. Donne, in turbid and violent language—for, with all his genius, he lacked the last ornament of a perfect style, lucidity—expressed what he himself perceived, suffered, and desired. If, therefore, we can but comprehend what Donne is saying, and realise what his character is, if we can but appreciate the curious alternations of cautious reserve and bold confession in which he indulges, if we can but discover how to stand on his own level, there is hardly a piece of his genuine verse which, cryptic though it may seem, cannot be prevailed upon to deliver up some secret of his life and character.

The dangers of such a conjectural reconstruction of biography are obvious, yet I believe that in few cases in literary history is that method more legitimate than here. When Donne speaks of his personal experience, there is something so convincing in his accent, poignant and rude at once, that it is impossible not to believe it the accurate record of a genuine emotional event. I am not unaware that, in 1625, writing to Sir Robert Ker, he said, "You know my uttermost [in verse] when it was best, and even then I did best when I had least truth for my subjects." By truth he means here what, in the evolution of his taste, he had come to regard as an excess of realism; and beyond question, what he here describes as his "best" were those pieces of metaphysical extravagance, where he had "least truth for his subjects," but embroidered conceit after conceit upon a false or trivial first idea. The Second Elegy, with its extravagant ingenuity about the elements of a fair face, the "anagram" of beauty, is a capital example of what we now have come to detest as thoroughly bad art, but of what particularly dazzled the followers of Donne, and laid the foundation of his excessive fame as a wit. These are what Donne regarded with complacency as his "best," but to us they are little else than grotesque, the symptoms of a malady of the mind.

Very different, however, from these chains of "enormous and disgusting hyperboles," as Dr. Johnson called them, are the numerous poems in which Donne, retaining of course the tortured manner natural to him, recounted the adventures of his body and his soul. In their consideration of these poems the biographers of Donne, misled by an amiable fallacy, have not chosen to give their true weight and meaning to words about the scope of which there can be no honest question. Walton, in his exquisite portrait of his friend, has nothing at all to say of the stormy and profane youth which led up to that holy maturity of faith and unction. He chose to ignore or to forget anything which might seem to dim the sacred lustre of the exemplary Dean of St. Paul's. Yet even Walton admitted that Donne "was by nature highly passionate," and doubtless he was well aware that below the sanctity of his age lay a youth scored with frailty and the injuries of instinct. Later biographers have had less excuse for attempting to conceal those tenebrous and fiery evidences, which but add a more splendid majesty to the career rising out of them into peace and light. To pretend that Donne was a saint in his youth is to nullify the very process of divine grace in the evolution of a complex soul, in the reduction of a magnificent rebel to a still more brilliant and powerful servant.

In (the) earliest series of his poems we find him a mere butterfly of the court, ostentatiously flitting from flower to flower, indulging his curiosity and his sensuousness wherever satisfaction is offered to him. "Women's Constancy" is the complete expression of his unattached condition of mind and body. In "Love's Usury," with the impertinence of the successful gallant, he promises to turn monogamous when he is old. In these early days his experiences are all sensation and superficial emotion. He wanders wherever his desires attract him, rifles all blossoms for their honey, boasts—in the manner of impudent youth—his detachment from all chains of duty or reflection. He is the ideal light o' love; he will pluck the rose wherever he finds it, and he is confident that for the wise youth who knows how to nip the flower discreetly there can be no thorns. The tone of these earliest lyrics is one of sceptical, even contemptuous, arrogance. In "A Fever" the mistress of the moment is ill, but it only amuses the lover. The malady is an excuse for a *feu de joie* of conceits; she may die of it, for all he really cares. In these foppish, heartless lyrics Donne is most interesting when most frankly sensual. "The Good Morrow" is the perfectly contented and serene record of an illicit, and doubtless of an ephemeral, adventure. "The Sun Rising," perhaps the strongest of the early lyrics, gives no evidence of soul, but is a fine hymn of sturdy, virile satisfaction. What could be more spirited, in its boyish way, than the opening stanza—

> Busy old fool, unruly Sun,
>   Why dost thou thus,
> Thro' windows and thro' curtains, call on us?
> Must to thy motions lovers' seasons run?
>   Saucy pedantic wretch, go chide
>   Late schoolboys and sour prentices;
> Go tell court-huntsmen that the king will ride,
>   Call country ants to harvest offices;
> Love, all alike, no season knows nor clime,[1]
> Nor hours, days, months, which are the rags of time.

From a young lover in this mood we need not be scandalised to receive such a poem as "The Flea," that extremely clever piece of impudent ribaldry, nor expect a deeper sense of the dignity of womanhood than is found in "The Indifferent," that uproarious claim to absolute freedom in love. Here Donne reminds us of a very different poet, of the nomadic Verlaine, with his "Es tu brune ou es tu blonde?—Je ne sais!" In "The Legacy," more seriously, and with an intuition of deeper feeling, Donne playfully upbraids his heart for its own too-flagrant infidelities. When he rips up his bosom to send his heart to the woman of the moment he is alarmed at first to find none there, and he suffers his first shudder, his earliest movement of conscience, in this instant, when the threatened impotency of genuine feeling suddenly chills the light tumult of his love. But in another moment he recovers his composure: all is not lost—

> Yet I found something like a heart,
> But colours it, and corners had;
> It was not good, it was not bad,
> It was entire to none, and few had part;
> As good as could be made by art
> It seemed, and therefore for our loss be sad.
> I meant to send that heart instead of mine,
> But O! no man could hold it, for 'twas thine.

Serious for a moment, with a presage of better things, the mood has changed before the stanza was over, and the lash of satire at feminine frailty leaps out. Of this arrogance of juvenile cynicism the mandrake song remains the most poetical expression—

> If thou be'st born to strange sights,
>   Things invisible to see,
> Ride ten thousand days and nights
>   Till age snow white hairs on thee,
> Thou, when thou return'st, wilt tell me
> All strange wonders that befell thee,
>   And swear
>   Nowhere
> Lives a woman true and fair.
> If thou find'st one, let me know;
>   Such a pilgrimage were sweet.
> Yet do not, I would not go,
>   Though at next door we might meet.
> Tho' she were true when you met her,
> And last till you write your letter,
>   Yet she
>   Will be
> False, ere I come, to two or three.

... His life since manhood had been haunted by all the phantoms of infidelity. He had been pursuing with frenzy an illusive chimera of pleasure. But in spite of all his impudent protests, the strong heart of John Donne could not be satisfied by these ephemeral captures. His passions were now dominant and his blood imperious. The instinct that drives vehement young men to acts of madness was violent in him. He had been looking around him for an adventure, for some liaison which could give him the measure of his own vital intensity. If the moralists will allow us to say so, his ethical ambition had risen a grade, from the pursuit of woman as a *speqes* to the selection of one who should present herself to his imagination as a symbol of the Feminine. We must remember, to comprehend the conditions depicted in the "Songs and Sonnets" and the "Elegies," that we have to do with no simple pastoral swain, but with one of the most headstrong and ingenious intellects of the century, now, for the time being, concentrating itself on the evolution of its own *vita sexualis*. And we must remember, too, that it was from these agonies and errors, bleeding as from rods with the wounds of passion, that Donne rose slowly to those spiritual heights in which he so glorified the grace of God.

But to such a nature, so roused even in the storm of illicit passion, there was but a short space for complete satisfaction. At first the crushing of "joy's grape," as Keats puts it, excluded every other sentiment, and Donne composed—we dare not allow ourselves to overlook the fact—some of the most sensual poetry written in the history of English literature by any poet of eminence. It was, perhaps, needful that he should go off to the Islands, since the liaison was carried on in the first instance with astonishing effrontery. The husband was a deformed man, and was stationary all day in a basket-chair. This gave the lovers confidence, but the lady, as Donne tells her in one of the later denunciatory pieces, was dull in speech and unready in mind. Their secret meetings, stolen correspondence, and artificial language were, no doubt, thoroughly after Donne's own ingenious heart, but they distracted and alarmed the lady. With singular complacency, alluding to her original want of cleverness, he says that he has "refined her into a blissful paradise." "The Apparition" shows that Donne did too well his work of awakening those slumbering faculties which the roughness and jealousy of her husband had crushed so long. On this subject the Seventh Elegy throws a curious light.

But when he returned from the Azores, and took up once more those vows of constancy which had been sealed during his absence by stealthy means—"we can love by letters still, and gifts"—there seems evidence of a

change in the poet's sentiments. By a perverse ingenuity very characteristic
of him, he reversed the process which had made the easy seduction of the
lady grateful to his vanity, and in that very fact, no longer flattering to him,
he sees a proof of her lack of stability and value. He discovers her to be less
youthful than he thought her, and, in the reflex of his passion, her autumnal
sensuality exasperates him. She overdoes the mysteries of their meetings,
the alphabet of flowers, the secret messengers, the elaborate and needless
subterfuges. The Thirteenth Elegy is, doubtless, the expression of this turn
of the tide. She is still his "dove-like friend," still in profuse and burning
couplets his love rages when he thinks upon her. Yet he upbraids the passion
which he cannot resist, and even the lady he still worships—

> Was't not enough that thou didst hazard us
> To paths in love so dark and dangerous,
> And those so ambush'd round with household spies,
> And over all thy husband's towering eyes?

He begins to feel the horror and the ridicule of the intimate feast under
the light of the family candlesticks, where the afflicted and jealous husband,
daring not to complain openly in words, yet

> Swollen and pamper'd with great fare,
> Sits down and snorts, caged in his basket-chair.

The poet's first revolt is a refusal to meet in the lady's own house—

> Now I see many dangers; for it is
> His realm, his castle, and his diocese.

As yet, Donne still exults in the betrayal, but the Nemesis of his sin is
falling upon him. They must part, make fewer meetings, run less risk;
"she must go, and I must mourn." He permits the symptoms of a growing
lassitude in himself to be perceived; there follow angry words, and those
recriminations that are so surely the death of love. The Third Elegy marks a
sense of her declining devotion to him, and characteristically, although he
cools to her, his pride is exquisitely wounded at her becoming less ardent to
him. In a note of mingled mockery and trepidation he recommends to her
an "apostasy" that may confirm her love, and in a brilliant flash of caprice
informs her that

> Change is the nursery
> Of music, joy, life and eternity.

Does she take him at his word, or does he mistake her timorous withdrawal for the heart's act of treason? We cannot tell, but the sources of his forbidden joy are poisoned, and jealousy stings him at last to vehement and gross attack. There are no hate-poems in the language finer of their kind, filled with a stronger wind of vindictive passion, than those which now close this incident.

To distribute these lyrics according to the order of their composition would be preposterous. They possess a close similarity of style; they were probably written at short intervals, all possibly in the summer of 1597. "The Curse" is an expression of the angry lover's first rage; but he comforts himself that his mistress has been extremely discreet and secret, and that the open ridicule of defeat may be spared him. "The Message" breathes the same egotistical spirit, and denounces the forced fashions and false passions which have fooled him and destroyed him. He perversely parodies Marlowe's beautiful pastoral song to satirise those hands and eyes that, as he believes, have been his ruin—

> Let others freeze with angling reeds,
> And cut their legs with shells and weeds,
> Or treach'rously poor fish beset,
> With strangling snare or windowy net.
>
> Let coarse bold hands from slimy nest
> The bedded fish in banks out-wrest;
> Or curious traitors, sleeve-silk flies,
> Bewitch poor fishes' wandering eyes.

With all his rage, he feels himself still drawn to the false one, with agonising threads of desire; and "Love's Deity," with the enchanting melody of its opening couplet, gives expression to his torture—

> I long to talk with some old lover's ghost,
>   Who died before the God of Love was born;
> I cannot think that he who, then, loved most,
>   Sunk so low as to love one which did scorn.
> But since this God produced a destiny,
> And that vice-nature, custom, lets it be,
> I must love her that loves not me.

Here the note is as the note of Catullus—

> Odi et amo. Quare id faciam fortasse requiris.
>   Nescio, sed fieri sentio et excrucior.

To this period also we may assign the passionate wilfulness of "The Prohibition"—

> Take heed of loving me;
> At least remember, I forbade it thee.
> Not that I shall repair my unthrifty waste
>   Of breath and blood upon thy sighs and tears,
> By being to me then what to me thou wast;
>   But so great joy our life at once outwears.
> Then, lest that love by my dearth frustrate be,
> If thou love me,—take heed of loving me.

"The Will" carries us on a further step to acrid scorn and contemptuous satire. He will die, smitten by great Love, to whom, however, he prays for a moment's respite, that he may make some legacies. His codicils are burning ironies; he gives—

> My tongue to Fame; to ambassadors mine ears;
>   To women—or the sea—my tears.

Jealousy has now taken possession of him. He fancies that his mistress has had twenty lovers before him, that she entertains younger lovers now. In the midst of the boisterous cynicism of this poem there are touches which we like to note—

> My constancy I to the planets give;
> My truth to them who at the court do live;
> Mine ingenuity and openness
> To Jesuits; to buffoons my pensiveness;
> My silence to any, who abroad have been;
>   My money to a Capuchin;

and this—

> To him for whom the passing-bell next tolls,
> I give my physic-books; my written rolls
> Of moral counsels I to Bedlam give;
> My brazen medals unto them which live
> In want of bread; to them which pass among
>   All foreigners, my English tongue.

Much more serious, indeed of a noble and resigned melancholy, is "The Funeral," in which he announces that he is "Love's martyr," and, by an image which had impressed his fancy so much that he repeats it in several poems, announces that when they come to enshroud his body, they will find

> That subtle wreath of hair, which crowns my arm,
> The mystery, the sign you must not touch,

all that remains to him now of one loved so passionately and proved to be so false. Since she will now have none of him, he will at least bury some of her, and at the Last Day, when the bodies stir, his arm will be seen to wave with "a bracelet of bright hair about the bone."

But all these poems of hatred and enforced resignation pale before "The Apparition," in which, as he tosses between sleep and waking, the horror of his situation, the vileness of the woman he has loved, and the whole squalor of the outworn liaison come upon him and overwhelm him. The fierce passion in this brief lyric, a "hate-poem" of the very first class, is closely akin to those flashes of lurid light in which the contemporary tragedians excelled, "steeping us," as Charles Lamb says, "in agonies infernal." Such error, however, as Donne had indulged in could be washed out in no less bitter waters. "The Apparition" is brief, and must be read complete to produce the terrific effect of its reluctant malediction—

> When by thy scorn, O murderess, I am dead,
>   And that thou think'st thee free
>   From all solicitation from me,
> Then shall my ghost come to thy bed,
> And thee, feign'd vestal, in worse arms shall see;
> Then thy sick taper will begin to wink,
> And he, whose thou art then, being tired before,
> Will, if thou stir, or pinch to wake him, think
>   Thou call'st for more,
>   And, in false sleep, will from thee shrink:
> And then, poor aspen wretch, neglected thou,
> Bathed in a cold quicksilver sweat wilt lie
>   A verier ghost than I.
> What I will say, I will not tell thee now.
> Lest that preserve thee; and since my love is spent,
> I'd rather thou should'st painfully repent,
> Than by my threatenings rest still innocent.

This is the culmination of the incident, the flames of hatred now quickly subsiding into a heap of the ashes of indifference and satiety. This exhausted cynicism is interpreted by "Love's Alchemy," where the poet protests that all women are alike vile, and the elixir of happiness an imposture not to be discovered by any alchemist who "glorifies his pregnant pot," only to be fooled and disenchanted. So, also, in a most curious ode, the "Nocturnal upon St. Lucy's Day," amid fireworks of conceit, he calls his mistress dead, and protests that his hatred has grown calm at last. So this volcanic passion sinks back into its crater at length, leaving this series of astonishing poems to illustrate it, poems which, as Donne himself says, are "as itself. When he grew supine once more, he reflected, rather splenetically, on his want of common prudence in this revelation of the adventures of the soul. As he said to Rowland Woodward, he had shown these "love-song weeds and satiric thorns" to too many of his friends to be able to quench the incident in oblivion, and too many copies of them had been made by his private admirers to preclude their circulation.

Donne, in his own words, had "stained" his soul's "first white," but his conduct from this time forth seems to have given no scandal. One or two love-passages appear to have ruffled the tenour of the wave of life which was carrying him towards the bourne of matrimony. He sees and is the sudden victim of beauty again and again.

His sensitive heart is ingenious in self-torture, and to what extremities it still can fling him we read in "The Blossom." The lady of the moment has left him a week ago, and in three weeks more he is to meet her in London. In subtle, modulated verse his heart taunts and plagues him, for he no longer knows what he desires nor what he is. His previous adventures have made him cautious, even sceptical, and he will not frankly give way to this sweet, insidious hope. He apostrophises his own trembling heart, which knows not whether to bide with him or to follow the new and desired mistress—

> Well then, stay here; but know,
> When thou hast stay'd and done thy most,
> A naked thinking heart, that makes no show,
> Is to a woman but a kind of ghost;
> How shall she know my heart?

To the same vague category of emotions which faintly stirred the poet between his great criminal liaison and his ultimate betrothal, I am inclined also to attribute, on internal and structural evidence, the Tenth Elegy, as well as, perhaps, the extremely fantastic lyric called "The Ecstasy," with its obsession on the word "violet"; this had, unquestionably, at the time of its composition an illuminating meaning which time has completely obscured. A few of the Epistles, too, may belong to this early period, and one of the most important of these, the second to Sir Henry Wotton, I am able for the first time to date. This poem is given in the Westmoreland MS., in my possession, with the heading, "To Mr. H. W. 20 July 1598. At Court." But the majority of the Letters in Verse, and probably all the Divine Poems, belong to a period subsequent to the poet's marriage.

To any date earlier than that of his own marriage may be assigned a poem which holds a somewhat unique position in the rolls of Donne's undoubted writings. In the "Epithalamion made at Lincoln's Inn" he drops his accustomed manner and closely imitates the imagery, the prosody, and the tone of Spenser. His own peculiar individuality lies below the rich Spenserian embroidery, and the result has a mellifluous glow which we could wish to see more frequent in Donne. The occasion of this stately, sensuous ode is uncertain; all we know is that the bridegroom was one who was a member of the Inn, and not an assiduous one, for he combined "study" with "play" in it. So impersonal is the poem, so made to order, that we know not whether to indulge a guess that the nuptials of Christopher Brooke form its theme. If it were suggested that Donne's own secret marriage was here celebrated, we should be unable to reject the idea on any internal evidence. In this class of Elizabethan poem the best of men permitted themselves so fescennine a liberty, that it is difficult to give a specimen to modern readers; this stanza, however, represents the poem not unfairly—

> Daughters of London, you which be
> Our golden mines and furnish'd treasury,
> You which are angels, yet still bring with you
> Thousands of angels on your marriage days,
> Help with your presence, and devise to praise
> These rites, which also unto you grow due;
> Conceitedly dress her, and be assign'd
> By you fit place for every flower and jewel;
> Make her for love fit fuel,
> As gay as Flora and as rich as Ind;
> So may she, fair and rich, in nothing lame,
> To-day put on perfection and a woman's name.

The pun about "angels"—the divine ministrants and the earthly coin—was a favourite one with Donne. In the Eleventh Elegy he plays upon it until we lose all patience with so much self-satisfied ingenuity—

Angels, which heaven commanded to provide
All things to me, and be my faithful guide,
To gain new friends, to appease great enemies,
To comfort my soul, when I lie or rise;

or—

Twelve righteous *angels,* which as yet
No leaven of vile solder did admit;

or—

Pity these *angels* yet; their dignities
Pass Virtues, Powers, and Principalities.

The extravagance might be pardoned once, but its recurrence is more and more intolerable. Yet it was precisely this dross and slag of his genius which endeared Donne as a poet to his immediate followers . . .

Divine Poems

The Divine Poems of Donne offer considerable difficulty to his biographer. A few of them already are, or can approximately be, dated, but the majority are subject to conjecture founded upon internal evidence. They are of two orders; there are hymns and spiritual poems of Donne's which, however rugged their form, breathe a fervid spirit of faith and a genuine humility. In others the intellectual element outweighs the religious. These verses are rather extremely ingenious exercises in metrical theology than bursts of impulsive piety. It may be broadly suggested that the latter belong to the second, and the former to the third or final, division of Donne's career. That is to say, the more metaphysical pieces are the outcome of the years when religious inquiry formed one of his prominent studies, but when no exclusive call had summoned him to the ministry. In form all the sacred poetry of Donne suffers from his determination to introduce Spanish effects into English prosody, and Spanish ingenuities into the expression of English thought. If Donne's early hymns and litanies do not move us, it is largely due to the fact that they did not move himself. They are frigid, they are stiffened with legal and medical phraseology, the heart of a sinner saved does not beat beneath their "cross and correct concupiscence of wit."

An excess of ingenuity is peculiarly fatal to the unction of religious poetry. Unless it is spontaneous, unless it palpitates with ecstasy or moans with aspiration, unless it is the outpouring of a contrite spirit, it leaves upon the listener a sense of painful artificiality. The dogmatic verses of Donne do not escape from this disability. We admit their cleverness, and are sure that it is misplaced. The solemn mystery of Christ's three days' sojourn in the tomb is not, for instance, illuminated

> when Donne speaks of Him as one
> Whose body, having walk'd on earth, and now
> Hasting to heaven, would—that He might allow
> Himself unto all stations and fill all—
> For those three days become a mineral.
> He was all gold when He lay down, but rose
> All tincture, and doth not alone dispose
> Leaden and iron wills to good, but is
> Of power to make e'en sinful flesh like His.

Here Donne's intellectual arrogance stood him in evil stead. He would not continue and intensify the tradition of such gentle Catholic singers of the Elizabethan age as Southwell and Constable; the hymns of Wither he had probably never seen, and would have despised; he shows not the slightest sign of having read the noblest religious poem written between the Vision of *Piers Plowman* and *Paradise Lost,* that *Christ's Victory and Triumph* which Giles Fletcher published just when Donne was moving into Drury House in 1610. He had doubtless read, without advantage to his style, Sylvester's popular version of the *Divine Weeks and Works.* But he disdained all that was purely English. His sympathy with Elizabethan verse, good or bad, was a negative quality, and we can scarcely trace that he allowed himself to be even conscious of the existence of Spenser or Shakespeare. Among his English contemporaries he admired but one poet, Ben Jonson, and to him he was attracted by the very qualities which we now recognise as being anti-Elizabethan. Hence, in the history of literature, the sacred poetry of Donne is interesting mainly for its resolute independence of all existing English types, and for its effect in starting a new and efficient school of religious verse in which many of the disciples far exceeded the master. Donne prophesied, while those poets were not born or were but children, of George Herbert, of Crashaw, of the Vaughans, of Herrick in the *Noble Numbers,* of Cowley in the *Davideis;* and when we come to consider his posthumous glory we shall have to return to his crabbed and litigious early sacred poetry.

Of Donne's spiritual poems the most important, if we omit the two cycles of "Holy Sonnets," which belong to a later period, is that which he called "A Litany." He composed it in his bed, during his tedious illness at

Mitcham in 1609, and he sent it to Sir Henry Goodyer with a learned note on the Litaneia, or public form of chanted prayer to God, and on its use in the Primitive Church. His own specimen is composed in a curious measure of his invention, in grave lines with an odd singing break in the middle of each stanza, an artifice from which, it is only fair to say, he rarely extracts so much charm as we might reasonably expect. The "Litany" is burdened with ingenuity. From a dogmatic point of view it shows Donne still imperfectly divorced from the tenets of Rome. He still proclaims the efficacy of the Virgin Mary's prayers to God the Father for souls on earth. Donne, who was much occupied at this time with the principle of martyrdom, dedicates these stanzas to the martyrs and confessors—

> And since Thou so desirously
> Didst long to die, that long before thou could'st
>   And long since Thou no more could'st die,
> Thou in thy scatter'd mystic body would'st
>   In Abel die; and ever since
>   In Thine; let their blood come
> To beg for us a discreet patience
> Of death, or of worse life; for O, to some
> Not to be martyrs is a martyrdom.
>   Therefore with thee triumpheth there
> A virgin squadron of white confessors,
>   Whose bloods betroth'd, not married, were,
> Tender'd, not taken, by those ravishers.
>   They know, and pray that we may know,
>   In every Christian
> Hourly tempestuous persecutions grow;
> Temptations martyr us alive; a man
> Is to himself a Diocletian.

The ingenious darkness of Donne's poetical expression never went further or achieved a richer gloom than it does in some of his Sacred Poems. The "Litany" is certainly not for use by the poor of the flock. The intellectual dangers so strangely petitioned against in the following stanza do not certainly afflict many humble-minded Christians, although they were real enough to Donne—

> That learning, Thine ambassador,
> From Thine allegiance we never tempt;

That beauty, paradise's flower,—

For physic made,—from poison be exempt;

That wit—born apt high good to do—

By dwelling lazily

On Nature's nothing be not nothing too;
That our affections kill us not, nor die;
Hear us, weak echoes, O Thou Ear and Eye.

One more stanza may be given from this highly metaphysical poem, in which a considerable flower of beauty is choked by the weeds of pedantry and misplaced intelligence—

From being anxious, or secure,
Dead clods of sadness, or light squibs of mirth,
From thinking that great courts immure
All, or no happiness, or that this earth
Is only for our prison fram'd;
Or that Thou'rt covetous
To them whom Thou lovest, or that they are maim'd
From reaching this world's sweet who seek Thee
thus,
With all Thy might, Good Lord, deliver us.

A poem which we can exactly date is that written for Good Friday 1613. Donne had been staying at Polesworth, in Warwickshire, with Sir Henry Goodyer, and he set forth on horseback to visit Magdalen Herbert and her son, Sir Edward, at Montgomery Castle. Six years earlier he had sent to this beloved lady "holy hymns and sonnets," of which but one survives, the quatorzain beginning—

Her of your name, whose fair inheritance
Bethina was, and jointure Magdalo.

He now, looking forward to the joys of high spiritual converse with these elected friends, sends to him whom he leaves at Polesworth a meditation on the day. He is more direct and less tortured than usual—

I am carried towards the west,
This day, when my soul's form bows to the East;
There I should see a Sun by rising set,
And by that setting endless day beget;
But that Christ on His cross did rise and fall,

Sin had eternally benighted all.
Yet dare I almost be glad, I do not see
That spectacle of too much weight for me;
Who sees God's face, that is self-life, must die,—
What a death were it then to see God die!

That is impressive, and comparatively simple; but a spasm of his disease of
style catches him, and he proceeds—

It made His own lieutenant, Nature, shrink,
It made His footstool crack, and the sun wink.
Could I behold those hands, which span the poles
And tune all spheres at once, pierced with those holes?
Could I behold that endless height, which is
Zenith to us and our antipodes,
Humbled below us?

Nothing could be more odious; yet, such was the taste of the day that, no
doubt, when he read these verses that evening in Montgomery Castle, the
noble Herberts were not merely astonished, but charmed and edified.

We may confidently attribute "The Cross" to the Mitcham period. It
shows Donne still more indignant at the obstinacy of political recusants
than convinced with regard to the dogmas which separate Rome from the
Reformed Churches. He writes here precisely as any fervent Italian or
Spanish monk might do—

From me no pulpit, nor misgrounded law,
Nor scandal taken, shall this cross withdraw,

and he rejoices to see its emblem in every manifestation of natural
force—

Look down, thou spiest out crosses in small things;
Look up, thou seest birds rais'd on cross'd wings;
All the globe's frame, and spheres, is nothing else
But the meridian's crossing parallels.

In composing these early sacred poems, although he was at the very time
fighting with Morton for the Anglicans, he could not but look back to Rome
as the real arbiter, and he had no warmer excuse to make for his odes and
litanies than that the Roman Church herself need not call them defective.

It is to be observed that the early and amatory writings of Donne
contain no single example of the sonnet, and that with the exception of

one or two unimportant epistles in the quatorzain form, all his work in this class is to be found among his divine poems. He disdained the softness and vagueness of the Petrarchists, and had no ambition to compete with Drayton or Daniel in their addresses to a dimly-outlined Idea or Delia. The form he ultimately adopted for his sonnets is neither purely Italian, nor purely Elizabethan. He had not Milton's courage in recurring to the splendid fulness of the sonnet of Petrarch, but he eschewed the laxity of the English writers of his age; and though we have to regret that he adopted the final couplet, his octett is of perfect arrangement, and boasts but two rhymes. It is strange that he did not perceive how much his sonnets lose in grandeur by this concession to triviality in the sestett. It is part, however, of Donne's irremediable imperfection as an artist, that he has produced much noble poetry in his divine sonnets, and yet not one sonnet that can be considered faultless.

The style of this section of his poetry is extremely characteristic of himself and of certain exotic influences of his time. When he was in Italy, he must have been familiar with Tansillo and Molza, the polished Petrarchists of the age, who celebrated love and religion with an equal refinement. But he is not more touched by their manner of writing than by that of Spenser. Underneath the graceful accomplishment of the Cinque Cento, however, there ran hidden the vehement stream of speculative philosophic style, rugged and bold, and it was this which attracted Donne. With Galileo we know that he had a close sympathy. Did he dip with curiosity into the forbidden writings of Galileo's fellow-martyr, Giordano Bruno? We know not; yet here at least was an Italian with whom Donne had not a little fellowship in the construction of his mind. He had still more with that of a Dominican monk who was more exactly his contemporary, and of whose misfortunes he cannot fail to have heard. The Sonnets of Campanella have more kinship with "La Corona" and the Ecclesiastical Sonnets of Donne than with any other English writings. Yet neither poet can well have read the work of the other, and it is even a stretch of probability to hope that Donne may have seen the obscure volume of Campanula's poems which the German, Tobias Adami, published in 1622. The similarity is accidental, and is founded upon a certain double sympathy with the obscurity and with the heterodoxy of the strange Italian pantheists of the age. Had Donne been born south of the Alps, his work might probably have taken a less tormented form than it actually adopted, but his body would almost certainly have been tortured with Campanella's, if by a happy fate it escaped the stake with Vanini's.

The Influence of Donne

In examining the remarkable wide and deep, though almost entirely malign, influence of Donne upon the poetry of this country, it is necessary first of all to dwell on the complete intellectual isolation of his youth and middle age. The Elizabethan poets were, as a rule, a sociable and sympathetic body of men. They acted and interacted upon one another with vivacity; they met at frequent intervals to encourage themselves in the art they exercised and to read each other's verses. The habit which sprang up of contributing strings of complimentary effusions to accompany the published efforts of a friend was symptomatic of the gregarious tendency of the age. So, even, were the fierce feuds and noisy, rather than envenomed, encounters which periodically thrilled the poetic world. It was not hatred, so much, or even jealousy, which inspired these famous battles, as the inevitability that in a society, the atoms of which hustled about so rapidly in the immediate neighbourhood of the rest, collisions should occasionally occur. In the last years of Elizabeth and the first years of James, London swarmed with poets and poeticules, and each of these was, more or less, in personal relation with the others.

Herein lies the first peculiarity of Donne. After the juvenile concession to the taste of the hour, implied in his *Satires* of 1593 and onward, he gave no further hostages to the fashion. Nor do we find that he paid any attention to the leaders of literature whom it was inevitable that he should meet at Court or in the taverns. At no period even of his youth does he seem to have been impressed by the fame of his English compeers, to have felt admiration or even curiosity in their work. One is left with the impression that Donne would not have turned to see Edmund Spenser go by, nor have passed into an inner room at the Mermaid to listen to the talk of Shakespeare. His was the scornful indifference of the innovator, the temperament of the man born to inaugurate a new order of taste . . .

It is a curious fact that Jonson alone, of those who in the first half of the seventeenth century discussed the characteristics of Donne's style, commented on the peculiarities of his metre. This would seem to have filled even his fondest disciples with horror, and it is much to be doubted whether they understood the principle upon which he worked. On this point, successive critics have agreed in finding Donne an unpardonable sinner. It seems even to be supposed by some writers that the curious condition of his early verse is due to ignorance, and that Donne did not know how to scan. As to this, I can but repeat, what I have said before,[2] that what there was to know about prosody was, we may be sure, perfectly known by Donne.

But it is evident that he intentionally essayed to introduce a revolution into English versification. One of the main objections he took to the verse of his youth was that it was so mellifluous, sinuous, and soft. A five-syllabled iambic line of Spenser or of Daniel trots along with the gentlest amble of inevitable shorts and longs. Donne thought that the line should be broken up into successive quick and slow beats. The conventional line vexed his ear with its insipidity, and it doubtless appeared to him that his great predecessors had never completely shaken off a timidity and monotony which had come down to them from Surrey and Gascoigne. It is possible that he wished to improve on the rhymed verse of Spenser, as Shakespeare had improved on the blank verse of Sackville.

The curious ruggedness of the *Satires* and *Elegies* becomes comprehensible only when we adopt some such theory I have suggested. Part of Donne's iconoclasm consisted in his scorn of the flaccid beat of the verse of the sonneteers. He desired greatly to develop the orchestral possibilities of English verse, and I have remarked that the irregular lyrics of Mr. Robert Bridges and the endless experiments of the Symbolists in France are likely to be far more fruitful to us in trying to understand Donne's object, than any conventional repetition of the accepted rules of prosody. The iambic rhymed line of Donne has audacities such as are permitted to his blank verse by Milton; and although the felicities are rare in the older poet, instead of being almost incessant as in the younger, Donne at his best is not less melodious than Milton. One of his most famous traps for the ear, is the opening line of "Twickenham Garden," which the ordinary reader is ever tempted to dismiss as not being iambic verse at all. We have to recognise in it the poet's attempt to identify the beat of his verse with his bewildered and dejected state, reading it somewhat in this notation:—

Blasted | with sighs || and | surrounded | with tears.

It is almost certain that this intrepid shifting about at will of the accent is a symptom of youth in the poem, that we can almost, that is to say, approximately, date any given piece of his by the degree in which this prosodical violence is sustained.[3] After middle-life, Donne dropped the experiment more and more completely, having found, no doubt, that his closest friends were by no means certain to comprehend what he meant by the rapid changes of the instrument; nor, in reading to themselves, could produce the effect which he had intended. These variations of cadence, then, must be looked upon as a peculiarity not essential to Donne's style, nor persistent in it, but as a studied eccentricity of his youth. At his very best, as in

> I long to talk with some lover's ghost,
> Who died before the God of Love was born,

Or as in

> A naked, thinking heart, that makes no show,
> Is to a woman but a kind of ghost,

there is no trace of this not keeping of accent, which puzzled and enraged Ben Jonson.

His conscious isolation, no doubt, made Donne hesitate to press his poetry upon his own generation. He found its flavour, the strong herbal perfume of it, not agreeable in the nostrils of the latest Elizabethans. Neither the verse, nor the imagination, nor the attitude of soul were what people in 1600 were ready to welcome, or even to apprehend. We can imagine Donne rather wistfully saying—

> Ho io appreso quel che, s'io ridico,
> A molti fia savor di forte agrume,[4]

and this may have been a main reason why he refrained from publication. He kept his rosemary and his marjoram, his rough odorous herbs, to himself.

What these young poets (who emulated Donne between 1620 and 1650) saw in Donne, and what attracted them so passionately to him, was the concentration of his intellectual personality. He broke through the tradition; he began as if poetry had never been written before; he, as Carew says—

> open'd us a mine
> Of rich and pregnant fancy.

He banished the gods and goddesses from his verse, not a Roundhead fiercer than he in his scorn of "those old idols." He wiped away "the wrong" which the English language in its neo-pagan raptures had "done the Greek or Latin tongue." His gigantic fancy put such a strain upon the resources of the English language, that its "tough, thick-ribb'd hoops" almost burst beneath the pressure. The earlier Elizabethan writers had been "libertines in poetry"; Donne recalled them to law and order. This is how Carew describes the extraordinary emotion caused by the first reading of Donne's poems—

>   the flame
> Of thy brave soul, that shot such heat and light
> As burned our earth and made our darkness bright,
> Committed holy rapes upon the will,

> Did through the eye the melting heart distil,
> And the deep knowledge of dark truths did teach.

Once again, Donne has

> open'd us a mine
> Of rich and pregnant fancy, drawn a line
> Of masculine expression. . .
> Thou shalt yield no precedence, but of time,—

that is to say, the ancient poets have no advantage of originality over thee, save the purely accidental one of having been born in an earlier age.

When we turn to Donne's poems, but in particular to his lyrics, and endeavour to find out what it was which excited these raptures of appreciation, we are at first unable to accept the seventeenth-century point of vision. Nothing is more difficult than to be certain that we value in the old poets what their contemporaries valued. Those pieces of Shakespeare which are on every tongue to-day, and excite our unbounded admiration, are not alluded to by any of his contemporaries. We have no evidence that a single friend of Milton saw what we all see in the central part of "L'Allegro" or in "At a Solemn Music." What contemporary criticism found in Herrick was "a pretty flowery and pastoral gale of fancy, in a vernal prospect of some hill, cave, rock, or fountain." We ask ourselves, in despair, what can the people who wrote such words have seen in "Gather the Rosebuds While Ye May," or in "Bid Me to Live"? In the same way, we have the greatest difficulty in constraining ourselves to regard Donne's verse from the point of view and in the light of its early, enthusiastic readers of 1620.

Perhaps we cannot do better than read over again an entirely typical poem, written towards the middle of his career, and illustrating, without extravagance, the very peculiarities which Donne's disciples admired. For this purpose, "Twickenham Garden" may serve as well as any:—

> Blasted with sighs, and surrounded with tears,
>   Hither I come to seek the spring.
> And at mine eyes, and at mine ears,
>   Receive such balms as else cure every thing.
>   But O! self-traitor, I do bring
> The spider Love, which transubstantiates all,
> And can convert manna to gall;
> And that this place may thoroughly be thought
> True paradise, I have the serpent brought.

'Twere wholesomer for me that winter did
    Benight the glory of this place,
And that a grave frost did forbid
    These trees to laugh and mock me to my face;
    But that I may not this disgrace
Endure, nor yet leave loving, Love, let me
Some senseless piece of this place be;
Make me a mandrake, so I may grow here,

Or a stone fountain weeping out my year.
Hither with crystal phials, lovers, come,
    And take my tears, which are love's wine,
And try your mistress' tears at home,
    For all are false, that taste not just like mine.
    Alas! hearts do not in eyes shine,
Nor can you more judge woman's thoughts by tears
Than, by her shadow, what she wears.
O perverse sex, where none is true but she
Who's therefore true, because her truth kills me.

If we compare this with an analogous piece of ordinary Elizabethan or early Jacobean poetry, we observe, first of all, that it is tightly packed with thought. As to the value of the thought, opinions may differ, but of the subtlety, the variety, and the abundance of mental movement in this piece there can be no question. The Elizabethan poet had held a mirror up to nature; Donne (the illustration is almost his own) shivered the glass, and preserved a reflection from every several fragment. This redundancy of intellectual suggestion was one of Donne's principal innovations.

In the second place, we notice an absence of all conventional or historical ornament. There is no mention here of "cruel Amaryllis," or "great Pan," or "the wanton shears of Destiny." A rigid adherence to topics and to objects familiar to the non-poetical reader of the moment is strictly observed. This, as I suppose, was another of the main sources of Donne's fascination; he was, in a totally new and unprecedented sense, a realist. In this he revolted with success against all the procedure of the Renaissance, and is, in his turbid and unskilful way, the forerunner of modern Naturalism in English poetry. This is an aspect of his influence which has been strangely overlooked, and, no doubt, for this reason, that what was realistic in the reign of James I. seems utterly old-fangled and antiquarian in that of Victoria; so that the poetry of Donne, instead of striking us—as it did his contemporaries—as amazingly fresh and new in its illustrations, strikes us as unspeakably moth-eaten and decrepid. In this poem of "Twickenham Hill" there is even an innovation in naming, topographically, a place by its existing, modern name; and this prepares us for all the allusions to habits, superstitions, rites, occasions of the moment which occur to the rapid brain of the author.

If the poems of Donne are examined, we shall find that it is only on the rarest occasions that he draws his imagery from mythology or romantic history. He has no interest in Greek or Latin legend. He neither translates nor paraphrases the poets of antiquity. For the conventional elements of beauty, as it was understood in that age, for roses, that is to say, and shepherds, lutes, zephyrs, "Thetis' crystal floods," and "flower-enamelled meadows," Donne has a perfect contempt. He endeavours to extract intellectual beauty from purely subjective sources, by the concentration of intensity and passion upon modern thought. Accordingly, he draws his illustrations, not from asphodel or from the moon, but from the humdrum professional employments of his own age, from chemistry, medicine, law, mechanics, astrology, religious ritual, daily human business of every sort. The decency of reticence between lovers reminds him of a sacerdotal mystery, and he cries—

> 'Twere profanation of our joys
>   To tell the laity our love.

Love is a spider dropped into the luscious chalice of life and "transubstantiating" it to poison. The sun is no more Phoebus, or the golden-haired son of Hyperion, but a pedantic lackey, whose duty is to "tell court-huntsmen that the king will ride." If the poet abuses his mistress for her want of faith, he does it in the language of an attorney, and his curses are "annexed in schedules" to the document. A woman's tear, on which her lover's tear falls, is like a round ball, on which a skilled workman paints the countries of the world.

From the days of Dr. Johnson downwards, the nature of these images has been not a little misunderstood. They have two characteristics, which have been unduly identified—they are sometimes realistic, and they are sometimes inappropriate. To us to-day they are almost all grotesque, because they are fetched from a scheme of things now utterly obsolete; but we must endeavour to recollect that such phrases as—

> no chemic yet the elixir got
> But glorifies his pregnant pot,

> If by the way to him befall
> Some odoriferous thing, or medicinal,

or,

> As he that sees a star fall, runs apace,
> And finds a jelly in the place,

phrases which now call for a commentary, and disturb our appreciation of the poet's fancy, were references to the science or half-science of the Jacobean age as modern and "topical" as allusions to the Rontgen rays would be today.

. . . We must, at length, give to Donne such credit as is due to complete originality in working out and forcing upon English taste a style in which affectation and wilful obscurity took a part so prominent that by ordinary readers no other qualities are nowadays perceived.

Notes

1. If, as I think likely, this was written about 1595, the "clime" was probably France, and "the king" Henry IV, a mighty hunter, our ally, and very popular in England. But there is no need to press a poet to this extremity of exact allusion.
2. *The Jacobean Poets,* 1894, pp. 60-63; from which a few lines are here reproduced.
3. In the interesting notes scribbled in 1811 by Coleridge, in Lamb's copy of Donne's *Poems,* S.T.C. remarks on the judicious use Donne makes of the anapaest in iambic measures where he wishes, in the eagerness of haste, to confirm or to exaggerate emotion. This valuable copy is now in the possession of Mr. W. H. Arnold, of New York.
4. *Paradiso,* xvii. 116, 117.

—Edmund Gosse, from *The Life and Letters*
of John Donne, 1899, vol. I, pp. 61–77,
263–69, vol. II, p. 329–44, *The Lyrical Poems*

W.J. Courthope "The School of Metaphysical Wit: John Donne" (1903)

English author and literary scholar William John Courthope (1842–1917) was one of the most prominent historians of English verse in his day. In the piece below, Courthope states that "the essence of Donne's wit is abstraction," which results in a type of "paradoxical logic, the same subtlety of thought and imagery," and it is this notion that truly informs Courthope's view of Donne. Courthope begins his piece by agreeing with the thesis Gosse illustrates in the excerpt above, namely, that "character of Donne's poetry reflects very exactly the changes in his life and opinions." He further classifies this notion: "Most of his compositions in verse are said to have been written while he was still a young man. To this class belong his *Satires*, his *Songs and Sonnets*, his *Elegies*, and *The Progress of the Soul*. A graver and more philosophic period follows, in which were produced most of the *Verse Epistles*, his *Epicedes and Obsequies*, and *The Anatomy of the World*; while the *Divine Poems* and the paraphrase of the *Lamentations of Jeremiah* are the work of the time when he was about to be, or had been, ordained." This classification is useful in not only understanding Courthope's thesis, but also in further elucidating Gosse's work above as well.

Courthope believes that a "mixture of strong religious instinct and philosophic scepticism" is the cornerstone of Donne's writing. However, as Donne matures, this "philosophic scepticism" becomes more contemplative. This switch is illustrated by Donne's piece *The Progress of the Soul*, a piece Courthope discusses in useful detail. Also early in his life, Courthope suggests that Donne was "at this stage a sceptic in religion, so was he a revolutionist in love." Donne's love poetry, he writes, was "To him love, in its infinite variety and inconsistency, represented the principle of perpetual flux in Nature. At the same time, his imagination was stimulated by the multitude of paradoxes and metaphors which were suggested to him by the varying aspects of the passion." He examines this concept in Donne's work *Cours d'Amours*, another useful explication for any student studying that same work.

There is a measurable shift in Donne's work once he is wed, and "in the poems written after his marriage in 1601 we find a complete change of sentiment and style." Courthope traces this change through *The Anatomy of the World*, a poem written on the death of one Elizabeth Drury. Long a heavily criticized work, Courthope argues, as Donne himself did, that "an elaborate exposition of Donne's philosophy of life. The girl stood to Donne, for his poetical purpose, in the same relation as Beatrice stood to Dante in the *Vita Nuova* and the *Divine Comedy*, being the incarnate symbol of the spiritual perfection—the Idea of Woman, as he put it to Ben Jonson—which he sought to express." Courthope's section on this poem is the best represented in this text, and any student studying this particular work will no doubt find Courthope's ideas helpful.

Courthope next discusses Donne's divine poems as he continues examining how Donne's maturation in thought and experience affects his work. Ultimately, Courthope suggests that Donne should not be remembered as one of the truly great poets of all time, but "to those who see in poetry a mirror of the national life, and who desire to amplify and enrich their own imagination by a sympathetic study of the spiritual existence of their ancestors, the work of Donne will always be profoundly interesting. No more lively or characteristic representative can be found of the thought of an age when the traditions of the ancient faith met in full encounter with the forces of the new philosophy." Donne's own growth as a poet thus mirrors, to some extent, the growth of the nation as well, and Courthope seems to suggest that a careful study of Donne will reveal as much of the time he lived in as the methods he used to create his works themselves.

——— ——— ———

Beyond the sphere of theological allegory, in which the traditions of the schools were still preserved, lay the region of pure thought; and here the contradiction between mediaeval and modern ideas furnished ample materials for the exercise of "wit." Assailed at once by the forces of the new faith, the new science, and the growing spirit of civic liberty, the ancient fabric of Catholicism and Feudalism fell more and more into ruin, but the innovating philosophy was yet far from having established a system of order and authority. The reasoning of Copernicus and Galileo shook men's belief in the truth of the Ptolemaic astronomy: the discoveries of Columbus extended their ideas of the terrestrial globe: the study of Greek and Hebrew literature in the original disturbed the symmetrical methods of scholastic logic: the investigations of the Arabian chemists produced havoc in the realm of encyclopaedic science. Still, the old learning had rooted itself too firmly in the convictions of society to be easily abandoned, and the first effect of the collision between the opposing principles was to propagate a feeling of philosophic doubt. In the sphere of reason a new kind of Pyrrhonism sprang up, which expressed itself in Montaigne's motto, *Que sqay je?* and this disposition of mind naturally exerted another kind of influence on the men of creative imagination. In active life the confusion of the times was the opportunity of the buccaneer and the soldier of fortune, who hoped to advance themselves by their swords; and like these, many poets, in their ideal representations of Nature, seized upon the rich materials of the old and ruined philosophy to decorate the structures which they built out of their lawless fancy. On such foundations rose the school of metaphysical wit, of which the earliest and most remarkable example is furnished in the poetry of John Donne . . .

The character of Donne's poetry reflects very exactly the changes in his life and opinions. Most of his compositions in verse are said to have been written while he was still a young man. To this class belong his *Satires,* his *Songs and Sonnets,* his *Elegies,* and *The Progress of the Soul.* A graver and more philosophic period follows, in which were produced most of the *Verse Epistles,* his *Epicedes and Obsequies,* and *The Anatomy of the World;* while the *Divine Poems* and the paraphrase of the *Lamentations of Jeremiah* are the work of the time when he was about to be, or had been, ordained.

Ben Jonson said to Drummond, speaking of *The Progress of the Soul:* "Of this he (Donne) never wrote but one sheet, and now, since he was made Doctor, repenteth highly, and seeketh to destroy all his poems." The thing is probable enough. Donne was educated as a Roman Catholic. His love-poems are those of a man who has assimilated, with thorough appreciation, all the learning and intellectual methods of the schoolmen—their fine distinctions, their subtle refinement, their metaphysical renderings of the text of Scripture. We know that, at some uncertain date, he abandoned the Roman Catholic faith, but his scholastic education had grounded in his mind a doctrine which, to the close of his life, continued to lie at the root of all his convictions, and to give form and colour to his poetical style, namely, the belief in the indestructible character of the soul. He constantly alludes to the old theory of the schoolmen respecting the triple nature of the soul, as in the lines:—

We first have souls of growth and sense; and those,
When our last soul, our soul immortal, came,
Were swallowed into it, and have no name.[1]

In the middle period of his life, when his opinions were becoming more settled and religious, he writes of this individual soul:—

Our soul, whose country's heaven, and God her
     father,
          Into this world, corruption's sink, is sent;
Yet so much in her travel she doth gather,
          That she returns home wiser than she went.[2]

This mixture of strong religious instinct and philosophic scepticism appears in its simplest form in his third *Satire,* which we know to have been among the earliest of his works. What interest is there, the poet asks, which can compare with religion? Why, then, are men prepared to risk their lives for the smallest material stake—money, adventure, honour—while at the same time they give no thought to their spiritual foes—the world, the flesh, and the devil?—

> Flesh itself's death; and joys which flesh can taste
> Thou lovest; and thy fair goodly soul, which doth
> Give this flesh power to taste joy, thou dost loathe.

But then he goes on: "Seek true religion, O where?" Some, he says, seek her in the ancient, decayed authority of Rome; others in the sullen Protestantism of Geneva; some put up with Eras-tianism; others abhor all forms of religion, just because all cannot be good; others, on the contrary, think all are equally good. He concludes:—

> Doubt wisely; in strange way
> To stand inquiring right, is not to stray;
> To sleep or run wrong is. On a huge hill,
> Cragged and steep, Truth stands, and he that will
> Reach her, about must and about must go,
> And what th' hill's suddenness resists win so.
> Yet strive so, that before age, death's twilight,
> Thy soul rest, for none can work in that night.

On this principle he himself seems to have proceeded. Certain it is that, in his poem called *The Progress of the Soul,* he had reached a stage of contemplative scepticism. To this composition, which bears the following title and date: "Infinitati sacrum, 16 August 1601. Metempsychosis. Poema Satyricon," is prefixed a highly characteristic epistle, in which the author says:—

> I forbid no reprehender, but him that like the Trent Council forbids not books but authors, damning whatever such a name hath or shall write. None writes so ill, that he gives not something exemplary to follow or fly. Now when I begin this book I have no purpose to come into any man's debt; how my stock will hold out I know not; perchance waste, perchance increase in use. If I do borrow anything of antiquity, besides that I make account that I pay it with as much and as good, you shall still find me to acknowledge it, and to thank not only him that hath digged out treasure for me, but that hath lighted me a candle to the place, all

which I will bid you remember (for I will have no such readers as I can teach) is, that the Pythagorean doctrine doth not only carry one soul from man to man, nor man to beast, but indifferently to plants also; and therefore you must not grudge to find the same soul in an Emperor, in a Posthorse, and in a Macaron, since no unreadiness in the soul, but an indisposition in the organs, works this.

In the poem itself Donne feigns that the soul, which moves all things—plants and beasts, as well as men—entered into the world by the plucking of an apple from the Tree of Life. The subtle and searching analysis of the poet's imagination may be illustrated by the following stanza:—

> For the great soul which here amongst us now
> Doth dwell, and moves that hand, and tongue, and
> > brow,
> Which, as the moon the sea, moves us; to hear
> Whose story with long patience you will long,
> —For 'tis the crown and last strain of my song—
> This soul to whom Luther and Mahomet were
> Prisons of flesh; this soul which oft did tear
> And mend the wracks of th' Empire, and late Rome,
> And lived when every great change did come,
> > Had first in Paradise a low but fatal room.

By the woman eating the apple, corruption passed by transmission through the whole race of mankind; and Donne's "wit" settles on each detail of the metaphysical conception, thus:—

> Prince of the orchard, fair as dawning morn,
> Fenced with the law, and ripe as soon as born,
> That apple grew, which this soul did enlive,
> Till the then climbing serpent, that now creeps
> For that offence, for which all mankind weeps,
> Took it, and to her whom the first man did wive
> —Whom and her race only forbiddings drive—
> He gave it, she to her husband; both did eat:
> So perished the eaters and the meat;
> > And we—for treason taints the blood—thence
> > > die and sweat.
> Man all at once was thus by woman slain,

And one by one we're here slain o'er again
By them. The mother poisoned the well-head,
The daughters here corrupt us, rivulets;
No smallness scapes, no greatness breaks their nets;
She thrust us out, and by them we are led
Astray, from turning to whence we are fled.
Were prisoners judges, 'twould seem rigorous:
She sinned, we bear; part of our pain is thus
    To love them whose fault to this painful love
      yoked us.
So fast in us did this corruption grow,
That now we dare ask why we should be so.
Would God—disputes the curious rebel—make
A law, and would not have it kept? Or can
His creature's will cross His? Of every man
For one will God (and be just) vengeance take?
Who sinned? 'twas not forbidden to the snake,
Nor her, who was not then made; nor is't writ
That Adam cropp'd, or knew, the apple; yet
    The worm, and he, and she, and we endure
      for it.

The apple once plucked, the soul flies from the Tree through the aperture, and enters successively into a plant (the mandrake), the egg of a bird (sparrow, symbol of lechery), a fish, a sea-osprey, a whale, a mouse, an elephant, a wolf, an ape, and a woman. All these are described, with various allegorical and satirical reflections by the way upon the manners and morals of mankind, especially at Court. The poem has no conclusion. Ben Jonson told Drummond: "The conceit of Done's transformation or Metempsychosis was that he sought the soul of that apple which Eve pulled, and thereafter made it the soul of a bitch, then of a she-wolf, and so of a woman: his general purpose was to have brought in all the bodies of the heretics from the soul of Cain, and at last left it in the body of Calvin." Though this description of the poem is inaccurate in detail, it may well be that Donne originally designed some satiric stroke against Calvin; for his conclusion is steeped in the merest Pyrrhonism:—

Whoe'er thou beest that read'st this sullen writ,
Which just so much courts thee as thou dost it,
Let me arrest thy thoughts; wonder with me,

Why ploughing, building, ruling, and the rest
Or most of these arts, whence our lives are blest,
By cursed Cain's race invented be,
And blest Seth vex'd us with astronomy.
There's nothing simply good or ill alone;
Of every quality Comparison
The only measure is, and judge, Opinion.

Here we have plainly the utterance of a sceptic in religion, who, having thrown off the forms of authoritative belief, indulges his imagination with a reconstruction of the ruins of Pythagorean and Rabbinical philosophy. Many allusions to natural history and theological dogma are scattered through Donne's Songs *and Sonnets,* and all are couched in the same reckless spirit.

And as Donne was at this stage a sceptic in religion, so was he a revolutionist in love. We have seen that, for many centuries, the law of chivalrous love had been rigorously defined. The Provengal poets and the female presidents of the *Cours dAmours* had revised and extended the ancient canons of the art as expounded by Ovid; and, while they tacitly recognised the physical basis of the passion, they disguised it by the elaborate character of the imaginative superstructure they raised upon it. In the delicacy of their observation, the nicety of their distinctions, and the keenness of their logic, they rivalled the theological science of the schoolmen; and by allying the phenomena of love with the loftier virtues of constancy, patience, loyalty, and self-surrender, they so spiritualised the former that, under the *regime* of chivalry—to use the words of Burke,— "vice itself lost half its evil by losing all its grossness."[3]

This fine Platonic edifice is ruthlessly demolished in the poetry of Donne. To him love, in its infinite variety and inconsistency, represented the principle of perpetual flux in Nature. At the same time, his imagination was stimulated by the multitude of paradoxes and metaphors which were suggested to him by the varying aspects of the passion. He pushed to extremes the scholastic analysis and conventional symbolism of the Provencals; but he applied them within the sphere of vulgar *bourgeois* intrigue, as may be inferred from the following characteristic lines:—

Nature's lay idiot, I taught thee to love,
And in that sophistry, O! thou dost prove
Too subtle; fool, thou didst not understand
The mystic language of the eye nor hand;

Nor couldst thou judge the difference of the air
Of sighs, and say, "This lies, this sounds despair";
Nor by th' eye's water cast a malady,
Desperately hot, or changing feverously.
I had not taught thee then the alphabet
Of flowers, how they, devisefully being set
And bound up, might, with speechless secrecy,
Deliver errands mutely and mutually.
Remember since all thy words used to be
To every suitor, "Ay, if my friends agree";
Since household charms thy husband's name to
    teach,
Were all the love-tricks that thy wit could reach;
And since an hour's discourse could scarce have
    made
An answer in thee, and that ill-arrayed
In broken proverbs and short sentences.[4]

The law of love in the *Cours d'Amours* required unfailing constancy in both lovers: in the philosophy of Donne this law is contrary to Nature, and is therefore heresy:—

Venus heard me sigh this song,
And by love's sweetest part, variety, she swore
She heard not this till now; it should be so no more.
She went, examined, and returned ere long,
And said, "Alas! some two or three
Poor heretics in love there be,
Which think to 'stablish dangerous constancy.
But I have told them, 'Since you will be true,
You shall be true to them who're false to you.'"[5]

Over and over again he insists on the essential falsehood and fickleness of women. He asks, for instance, "where lives a woman true and fair," and proceeds:—

If thou find'st one let me know;
    Such a pilgrimage were sweet.
Yet do not, I would not go,
    Though at next door we might meet.
Though she were true when you met her,

And last till you write your letter,
>> Yet she
>> Will be
False, ere I come, to two or three.[6]

This is the spirit of Ariosto's story of Giocondo. But Donne goes further, and cynically erects this observed habit of fickleness into a rule for constant, but discriminating, change:—

By Nature, which gave it, this liberty
Thou lovest, but O! canst thou love it and me?
Likeness glues love; and if that thou so do,
To make us like and love, must I change too?
More than thy hate I hate it; rather let me
Allow her change, then change as oft as she;
And so not teach, but force, my opinion
To love not any one, nor every one.
To live in one land is captivity,
To run all countries a wild roguery.
Waters stink soon, if in one place they bide,
And in that vast sea are more putrified;
But when they kiss one bank, and leaving this
Never look back, but the next bank do kiss,
There are they purest; change is the nursery
Of music, joy, life, and eternity.[7]

From this spirit of cynical lawlessness he was perhaps reclaimed by genuine love. To his wife he seems to have been devotedly attached, and in the poems written after his marriage in 1601 we find a complete change of sentiment and style. The old underlying conviction of the indestructible nature of the soul and of the corruption of the material world remains, but it is now made the starting-point for a graver philosophy of conduct. The *Verse Letters* written to the Countesses of Bedford, Huntingdon, and Salisbury, though all are couched in a vein of metaphysical compliment, are decorous in tone; in *The Anatomy of the World* Donne seems to have intended to embody his serious thoughts about the meaning and duties of human life. Whether there was any real ground for the hyperbolical praise with which he exalts the memory of Elizabeth Drury, we have no means of knowing. It is said, indeed, that she was betrothed to Henry, Prince of Wales; but Ben Jonson probably expressed a general opinion when he said to Drummond that "Done's 'Anniversarie' was profane and full of blasphemies: that he told Mr. Done, if it had been written of the Virgin Marie it had been something; to which he answered that it described the Idea of a Woman, and not as she was."

Viewed literally, *The Anatomy of the World* fully deserves the sentence passed upon it by Jonson. The poet asserts that after the death of Elizabeth Drury the whole mortal universe lost its vitality; that nothing but the shadow of life remained in it; that the disorder in the constitution of things, the decay and weakness of mankind, and the failure of the influence of the heavenly bodies, are all due to her removal from the earthly sphere. It is no wonder that such absurdities should have provoked matter-of-fact criticism. They are, however, not of the essence of the composition. "I hear from England," writes Donne in Paris to a correspondent with the initials Sir G. F. "of many censures of my book of Mrs. Drury; if any of these censures do but pardon me my descent in printing anything in verse (which if they do they are more charitable than myself; for I do not pardon myself, but confess that I did it against my conscience, that is against my own opinion, that I should not have done so), I doubt not that they will soon give over that other part of the indictment, which is that I have said so much; for nobody can imagine that I, who never saw her, could have purpose in that, than that when I had received so very good testimony of her worthiness, and was gone down to print verses, it became me to say, not what I was sure was just truth, but the best that I could conceive; for that would have been a new weakness in me to have praised anybody in printed verse, that had not been capable of the best verse that I could give."

The true character of *The Anatomy of the World* is indicated in the respective titles of the two Anniversaries. That of the first runs: "Wherein, *by occasion of the untimely death of Mistress Elizabeth Drury,* the frailty and decay of this whole world is represented." The subject of the second is defined thus: "Wherein, *by occasion of the religious death of Mistress Elizabeth Drury,* the incommodities of the soul in this life, and her exaltation in the next, are contemplated." In other words, the early death and religious character of Elizabeth Drury are merely the text justifying an elaborate exposition of Donne's philosophy of life. The girl stood to Donne, for his poetical purpose, in the same relation as Beatrice stood to Dante in the *Vita Nuova* and the *Divine Comedy,* being the incarnate symbol of the spiritual perfection—the Idea of Woman, as he put it to Ben Jonson—which he sought to express. When he says that her death was the cause of all the imperfections of the material world, he intended, in the first place, to pay a hyperbolical compliment to the daughter of his patron, and in the second, to express the theological doctrine of the corruption of Nature after the fall of man from his original state of perfection.

On the whole, it seems to me probable that the publication of *The Anatomy of the World* was part of a deliberate literary design on Donne's part. His affected depreciation of verse-writing is not to be taken seriously. His views of life were changing with his years: he was anxious for either secular or sacred employment: he regretted the evidences of a dissipated past which existed in his youthful poems: he hoped to attain the object of his ambition by giving public proof of the present gravity of his mind, and by securing the special favour of the most influential patrons of literature, such as the famous ladies of the Court, to whom so many of his *Verse Letters* are addressed. He writes to a correspondent in 1614: "This made me ask to borrow that old book" (i.e. an MS. collection of his poems), "which it will be too late to see, for that use, when I see you: for I must do this as a valediction to the world before I take orders. But this it is I am to ask of you: whether you ever made any such use of the letter in verse *a nostre comtesse chez vous,* as that I may put it in among the rest to persons of rank; for I desire it very much that something should bear her name in the book, and I would be just to my written words to my Lord Harrington, to write nothing after that." To Lady Bedford herself he writes, in a *Verse Letter,* perhaps the one above referred to:—

So whether my hymns you admit or choose,
In me you've hallowed a pagan muse,
And denizened a stranger who, mistaught
By blamers of the times they've marred, hath sought
Virtues in corners, which now bravely do
Shine in the world's best part, or all it,—you.

As to the poems being a "valediction to the world," Donne kept his promise. His letter to Sir H. Goodyere was written within a year of his taking orders, and henceforth all his publications in prose and verse were of a religious and theological cast. The last period of his poetical genius contains the *Divine Poems,* comprising meditations on the various mysteries of the Christian faith, a version of Tremellius' *Lamentations of Jeremiah,* written after the death of his much-loved wife, and other religious topics. As John Chudleigh, one of his panegyrists, said in the edition of his poems published after his death in 1650:—

Long since this task of tears from you was due,
Long since, O poets, he did die to you,
Or left you dead, when wit and he took flight
On divine wings, and soared out of your sight.

In close friendship with George Herbert and other divines of the period, he helped during the remainder of his life to swell the volume of Anglican ascetic thought which, under the direction of Laud, formed, in the reign of Charles I., the counterbalancing force to the movement of iconoclastic Puritanism.

But though his view of life and his object in art were thus completely altered, his poetical method remained consistently the same. As his admirer, Chudleigh, again remarks:—

He kept his loves, but not his objects: Wit
He did not banish, but transplanted it;
Taught it his place and use, and brought it home
To piety which it doth best become;
He showed us how for sins we ought to sigh,
And how to sing Christ's epithalamy.

How just this criticism is may be seen from Donne's *Hymn to Christ at the Author's last going into Germany:*—

Nor Thou, nor Thy religion, dost control
The amorousness of an harmonious soul;
But Thou wouldst have that love Thyself; as Thou
Art jealous, Lord, so am I jealous now;
Thou lovest not, till from loving more Thou free
My soul; whoever gives takes liberty; Oh, if Thou carest not whom I
　　love, Alas! Thou lovest not me.
Seal then this bill of my divorce to all
On whom those fainter beams of love did fall;
Marry those loves, which in youth scattered be
On fame, wit, hopes—false mistresses—to Thee.
Churches are best for prayer that have least light;
To see God only I go out of sight;
　　And to escape stormy days, I choose
　　An everlasting night.

Here we have precisely the same kind of paradoxical logic, the same subtlety of thought and imagery, as we find in the *Elegy on Change,* and though the imagination is now fixed on an unchangeable object, it plays round it precisely in the same way. The essence of Donne's wit is abstraction. Whether he is writing on the theme of sacred or profane love, his method lies in separating the perceptions of the soul from the entanglements of sense, and after isolating a thought, a passion, or a quality, in the world of pure ideas, to make it visible to the fancy by means of metaphorical images and scholastic allusions. The most characteristic specimens of his wit are to be found in his *Songs and Sonnets*, where he is dealing with the metaphysics of love, for here his imagination is at liberty to move whithersoever it chooses; and the extraordinary ingenuity with which he masters and reduces to epigrammatic form the most minute distinctions of thought, as well as the facility with which he combines contrary ideas and images, are well exemplified in a poem called *The Primrose Hill:*—

> Upon this Primrose Hill,
>   Where, if heaven would distill
> A shower of rain, each several drop might go
> To his own primrose, and grow manna so;
> And where their form and their infinity
>   Make a terrestrial galaxy,
>   As the small stars do in the sky,
> I walk to find a true-love, and I see
> That 'tis not a mere woman that is she,
> But must or more or less than woman be.[8]
>   Yet know I not which flower
>   I wish, a six or four:
> For should my true love less than woman be,
> She were scarce anything; and then should she
> Be more than woman, she would get above
>   All thought of sex, and think to move
>   My heart to study her, and not to love.
> Both these were monsters; since there must reside
> Falsehood in woman, I could more abide
> She were by art than nature falsified.
>   Live, primrose, then, and thrive
>   With thy true number five;
> And, woman, whom this flower doth represent,
> With this mysterious number be content;
> Ten is the farthest number; if half ten

> Belongs unto each woman, then
> Each woman may take half us men:
> Or—if this will not serve their turn—since all
> Numbers are odd or even, and they fall
> First into five, women may take us all.[9]

But for the purposes of great and true art the flight of metaphysical wit soon reveals the limitations of its powers. Sceptic as he was, Donne never formed any organic idea of Nature as a whole, and his sole aim, as a poet, was to associate the isolated details of his accumulations of learning with paradoxes and conceits, which are of no permanent value. For example, he was acquainted with the Copernican theory, but he is only interested in it as far as it helps to supply him with a poetical illustration:—

> As new philosophy arrests the sun,
> And bids the passive earth about it run,
> So we have dulled our mind; it hath no ends,
> Only the body's busy, and pretends.[10]

The theory that the earth was gradually approaching the sun suggests to him the following reflection:—

> If the world's age and death be argued well
>   By the sun's fall, which now towards earth
>   doth bend,
> Then we might fear that virtue, since she fell
>   So low as woman, should be near her end.

But he at once corrects this conclusion into an extravagant compliment:—

> But she's not stooped but raised; exiled by men,
>   She fled to heaven, that's heavenly things,
>   that's you. [11]

The general scepticism, produced in his mind by the collision between the new philosophy and the old theology, is forcibly expressed in his first Anniversary:-—

> The new philosophy calls all in doubt;
> The element of fire is quite put out;
> The sun is lost, and th' earth, and no man's wit
> Can well direct him where to look for it.
> And freely men confess that the world's spent,

When in the planets and the firmament
They seek so many new; they see that this
Is crumbled out again to his atomies.
'Tis all in pieces, all coherence gone,
All just supply and all relation.
Prince, subject, father, son, are things forgot,
For every man alone thinks he hath got
To be a phoenix, and that there can be
None of that kind of which he is, but he.[12]

The conclusion at which he finally arrived was the one to which all such souls, who have in them the element of religion, must be brought:—

In this low form, poor soul, what wilt thou do?
When wilt thou shake off this pedantry
Of being taught by sense and fantasy?
Thou look'st through spectacles; small things seem
    great
Below; but up into thy watch-tower get,
And see all things despoiled of fallacies;
Thou shalt not peep through lattices of eyes,
Nor hear through labyrinths of ears, nor learn
By circuit or collections to discern.
In heaven thou straight know'st all concerning it,
And what concerns it not shalt straight forget.

But before he arrives at this intelligible goal, his soul, wandering through an infinite maze of metaphysical ideas, has made shift to embody its transitory perceptions in the forms of poetical art; and, while he is engaged in a business which he acknowledges to be vain, he delights in involving himself and his readers in inextricable labyrinths of paradox. One of his favourite ideas is that Love is Death, and this thought he divides and subdivides by means of an endless variety of images. Thus he finds an opportunity of associating it with the reflections aroused by the shortest day, sacred to St. Lucy. All Nature, he says, seems to have shrivelled into nothing:—

The world's whole sap is sunk;
The general balm th' hydroptic earth hath drunk,
Whither, as to the bed's feet, life is shrunk,
Dead and interr'd; yet all these seem to laugh,
Compared to me, who am their epitaph.

He then calls on all lovers to come and study him as a "very dead thing,"

> For whom Love wrought new alchemy;
>> For his art did express
> A quintessence even from nothingness,
> From dull privations, and lean emptiness;
> He ruin'd me, and I am rebegot
> Of absence, darkness, death—things which are not.

He goes on to intensify the idea of annihilation, by saying that he is "the grave of all that's nothing"; that he is

> Of the first nothing the elixir grown;
> nay, he is something less than nothing:
>> If I an ordinary nothing were,
>> As shadow, a light and body must be here,
>> But I am none. [13]

In a poem called *The Paradox* he indulges in still more intricate logic on the same subject:—

> No lover saith I love, nor any other
>> Can judge a perfect lover;
> He thinks that else none can nor will agree
>> That any loves but he:
> I cannot say I loved, for who can say
>> He was killed yesterday?
> Love with excess of heat, more young than old,
>> Death kills with too much cold.
> We die but once, and who loved best did die,
>> He that saith twice did lie;
> For though he seem to move and stir awhile,
>> He doth the sense beguile.
> Such life is like the light which bideth yet,
>> When the life's light is set,
> Or like the heat which fire in solid matter
>> Leaves behind two hours after.
> Once I loved and died; and am now become
>> Mine epitaph and tomb;
> Here dead men speak their last, and so do I;
>> Love slain, lo! here I lie.

This perpetual endeavour to push poetical conception beyond the limits of sense and Nature produced its necessary effect on the character of Donne's metrical expression. When he seeks to embody a comparatively simple and natural thought, he can write with admirable harmony, as in the following lines, describing love in the Golden Age:—

What pretty innocence in those days moved!
Man ignorantly walked by her he loved;
Both sigh'd and interchang'd a speaking eye;
Both trembled and were sick; both knew not why.
That natural fearfulness, that struck man dumb,
Might well—those times considered—man become.
As all discoverers, whose first essay
Finds but the place, after, the nearest way,
So passion is to woman's love, about,
Nay, farther off, than when we first set out.
It is not love that sueth or doth contend;
Love either conquers or but meets a friend;
Man's better part consists of purer fire,
And finds itself allowed ere it desire.[14]

Here, too, is an excellent compliment in a *Verse Letter* to the Countess of Salisbury, grounded on the idea that chivalrous love is a liberal education:—

So, though I'm born without those eyes to live,
Which Fortune, who hath none herself, doth give,
Which are fit means to see bright courts and you,
Yet, may I see you thus, as now I do:
I shall by that all goodness have discern'd,
And, though I burn my library, be learn'd.

His whole philosophy of life, in his early days, is condensed in the following couplet:—

Be then thine own home, and in thyself dwell;
Inn anywhere: continuance maketh hell.[15]

And he is most vivid in the presentation of abstract ideas, as in the famous lines:—

Her pure and eloquent blood
Spoke in her cheeks, and so distinctly wrought
That one might almost say her body thought.[16]

The abrupt and forcible openings of his poems often strike a key-note of thought which promises completeness of treatment, but his metaphysical wit and his love of endless distinctions generally cause the composition to end nowhere. He begins a poem called Love's *Deity* thus:—

> I long to talk with some old lover's ghost,
>   Who died before the God of Love was born.

The object of the discourse is to be the mystery why love should be forced from one lover where there is no return from the other. This is a subject of universal interest, and the poet, on the assumption that Love, after being made into a deity, has abused his power, conducts a striking thought, by means of an appropriate image, to an intelligible conclusion:—

> O were we wakened by this tyranny
> To ungod this child again, it could not be
>   I should love her who loves not me.

But such straightforward logic would not have suited the super-subtle character of Donne's intellect; and he proceeds to invert his reasoning, and to close his poem with a stanza of pure paradox, leaving the mind without that sense of repose which art requires:—

> Rebel and atheist, why murmur I,
>   As though I felt the worst that love could do?
> Love may make me leave loving, or might try
>   A deeper plague, to make her love me too;
> Which, since she loves before, I'm loth to see.
> Falsehood is worse than hate; and that must be,
>   If she whom I love should love me.

Where he thinks simply the reader perceives that his thoughts are really common enough. He begins a *Verse Letter* to Sir H. Goodyere on his favourite subject of the necessity of change:—

> Who makes the last a pattern for next year,
>   Turns no new leaf, but still the same thing
>   reads;
> Seen things he sees again, heard things doth hear,
>   And makes his life but like a pair of beads.

This has the simplicity and directness of Sir John Davies in his Nosce
Teipsum. But we soon come to a quatrain in which the poet is anxious to
show his wit:—

> To be a stranger hath that benefit,
>   We can beginnings, but not habits choke.
> Go—whither? hence. You get, if you forget;
>   New faults, till they prescribe to us, are
>   smoke.

We certainly do *not* get anything by the mere negative act of forgetting; and
nobody could gather from the last line that the meaning was, "new faults,
till they become our masters, are *merely* smoke." Eagerness for novelty and
paradox leads the poet to obscurity of expression; and the reader is justly
incensed when he finds that the labour required to arrive at the meaning,
hidden behind involved syntax and unmeasured verse, has been expended
in vain. Ben Jonson does not express this feeling too strongly when he says,
"That Done for not keeping of accent deserved hanging." It is superfluous to
justify this verdict by examples. The reader, in the numerous extracts I have
given from Donne's poems, will have observed for himself how deliberately he
seeks to attract attention to the extravagance of his thought, by the difficulty
of his grammatical constructions, and by the dislocation of his accents.

All these things must be taken into account in deciding the place to be
assigned to this acute and powerful intellect in the history of English poetry.
Donne's qualities were essentially those of his age. His influence on his
contemporaries and on the generation that succeeded him was great. They
had all been educated under the same scholastic conditions as himself; they
were all in touch with his theological starting-point, and set a value on the
subtlety of his metaphysical distinctions. In Dryden's time, when the prestige
of "wit," still represented by the genius of Cowley, was weakening before
the poetical school which aimed first at correctness of expression, men
continued to speak with reverence of Donne's genius. But as the philosophy
of Bacon, Newton, and Locke gradually established itself, the traditions
of the schoolmen fell into discredit, so that, in the days of Johnson and
Burke, the practice of the metaphysical wits had come to be regarded in
the light of an obsolete curiosity. The revival of mediaeval sentiment, which
has coloured English taste during the last three generations, has naturally
awakened fresh interest in the poems of Donne, and there is perhaps in our

own day a tendency to exaggerate his merits. "If Donne," writes a learned and judicious critic, "cannot receive the praise due to the accomplished poetical artist, he has that not perhaps higher, but certainly rarer, of the inspired poetical creator."[17] Poetical creation implies that organic conception of Nature, and that insight into universal human emotions, which make the classical poets of the world—Homer and Dante, and Chaucer and Milton; and to this universality of thought, as I have endeavoured to show, Donne has no claim. Nor can he be reckoned among the poets who, by their sense of harmony and proportion, have helped to carry forward the refinement of our language from one social stage to another. The praise which Johnson bestows upon his learning adds little to his fame, for the science contained in his verse is mostly derived from those encyclopaedic sources of knowledge which, even in his own time, were being recognised as the fountains of "Vulgar Error." On the other hand, to those who see in poetry a mirror of the national life, and who desire to amplify and enrich their own imagination by a sympathetic study of the spiritual existence of their ancestors, the work of Donne will always be profoundly interesting. No more lively or characteristic representative can be found of the thought of an age when the traditions of the ancient faith met in full encounter with the forces of the new philosophy. The shock of that collision is far from having spent its effect, even in our own day; and he who examines historically the movements of imagination will find in Donne's subtle analysis and refined paradoxes much that helps to throw light on the contradictions of human nature.

Notes

1. *Verse Letter* to the Countess of Bedford.
2. *Verse Letter* to Sir H. Goodyere.
3. *Reflections on the French Revolution.*
4. Elegy vii.
5. *The Indifferent.*
6. Song, "Go and catch a falling star."
7. Elegy iii.
8. The conceit of the poem turns on the two facts that the normally constituted primrose has five segments in its corolla, and that the token of true love among the country folk of Donne's time was the exceptional primrose, with either four or six segments.
9. The argument in this stanza is drawn from the science of numbers. Five being half of ten, the farthest number (i.e. the first double number, and the basis of

the whole metric system), women may claim to represent half of what is in human nature; or, if this be not enough for their ambition, then (numbers being either odd or even, and falling first into five, i.e. 2 + 3) since five is woman's number, women may have the whole of human nature given over to them.

10. *Verse Letter* to Countess of Bedford.
11. *Verse Letter* to Countess of Huntingdon.
12. *Anatomy of the World,* first Anniversary, 205-218.
13. A *Nocturnal upon St. Lucy's Day.*
14. *Verse Letter* to the Countess of Huntingdon.
15. *Verse Letter* to Sir H. Wotton.
16. *Anatomy of the World,* second Anniversary, 244-246.
17. Professor Saintsbury, Preface to Poems of John Donne. Edited by E. K. Chambers.

—W.J. Courthope, from "The School of Metaphysical Wit: John Donne," *A History of English Poetry,* 1903, vol. 3, pp. 147–168

❖

ANDREW MARVELL

❖

◈

BIOGRAPHY

◈

ANDREW MARVELL
(1621–1678)

❖

Andrew Marvell was born on March 31, 1621, near Hull, in Yorkshire. His father, a clergyman with Calvinist leanings, was Master of the Aknshouse at Hull. Marvell was educated at the Hull Grammar School and Trinity College, Cambridge, from which he graduated with a B.A. in 1639. After his mother's death in 1638 and his father's in 1640, Marvell left England to travel on the Continent. Little is known of the ten years that followed; he was abroad from 1642 to 1646, possibly as a tutor in France.

In 1650 he became tutor to Lord Fairfax's daughter, and it was about Fairfax's home that he wrote one of his best-known poems, "Upon Appkton House." Marvell remained at Nun Appleton for two years, and it is from that period that much of his lyric poetry seems to date.

While his sympathies appear to have been with the Royalists during his years with Fairfax, who was himself in exile because of his monarchist leanings, Marvell later came to admire Cromwell. The admiration was mutual, and in 1653 Marvell became tutor to William Dutton, a ward of Cromwell's. In 1657 he was appointed assistant to John Thurloe, Secretary of State, a position for which Milton had recommended him in 1652. He became the Member of Parliament for Hull in 1659 and served in that capacity, apart from a brief interruption, until his death. Milton's championing of Marvell was repaid in kind in 1660, when Marvell defended him against charges of regicide. From 1662 until his death Marvell published various satires, including *The Reheersall Transpros'd* in two parts in 1672 and 1673. He died on August 16, 1678, in London and is buried at St. Giles-in-the-Fields. His *Miscellaneous Poems,* containing most of his poems, was purportedly published by his housekeeper, claiming to be his widow, in 1681; it appears, however, that Marvell never married.

❖

PERSONAL

❖

John Norton "Letter to Reverend Marvell" (1640)

The notation above refers to a famous letter written to Marvell by a local clergyman, Reverend John Norton (fl. 1640), from the parish of Welton. The letter inquires about Marvell's own flirtation with Catholicism in his college days and queries how Marvell's family managed to sway him away from the faith. The actual text presented below is from Thomas Cooke's 1726 commentary on the same subject.

He had not been long there (at Cambridge), before his Studys were interrupted by this remarkable Accident. Some *Jesuits*, with whom he was then conversant, seeing in him a Genius beyond his Years, thought of Nothing less than gaining a Proselyte. And doubtless their Hopes extended farther. They knew, if that Point was once obtained, he might in Time be a great Instrument towards carrying on their Cause. They used all the Arguments they could to seduce him away, which at last they did. After some Months his Father found him in a Bookseller's Shop in London and prevailed with him to return to the College.

—John Norton, letter to Reverend Marvell,
c. January 1640

John Milton (1652/3)

One of the greatest English authors of all time, John Milton (1608–1674) penned the seminal work *Paradise Lost*. Milton was a contemporary and friend of Marvell's and, in the letter below, recommends him for the position of assistant to the secretary of state.

My Lord,
But that it would be an interruption to the publick, wherein your studies are perpetually imployd, I should now & then venture to supply this my enforced absence with a line or two, though it were my onely busines, & that would be noe slight one, to make my due acknowledgments of your many favours; which I both doe at this time & ever shall; & have this farder which I thought my parte to let you know of, that there will be with you to morrow upon some occasion of busines a Gentleman whose name is Mr. Marvile; a man whom both by report, & the converse I have had with him, of singular desert for the

State to make use of; who alsoe offers himselfe, if there be any imployment for him. His father was the Minister of Hull & he hath spent foure yeares abroad in Holland, France, Italy, & Spaine, to very good purpose, as I beleeve, & the gaineing of those 4 languages; besides he is a scholler & well read in the latin & Greeke authors, & noe doubt of an approved conversation; for he corn's now lately out of the house of the Lord Fairefax who was Generall, where he was intrusted to give some instructions in the Languages to the Lady his Daughter. If upon the death of Mr. Wakerley the Councell shall thinke that I shall need any assistant in the performance of my place (though for my part I find noe encumberance of that which belongs to me, except it be in point of attendance at Conferences with Ambassadors, which I must confesse, in my Condition I am not fit for) it would be hard for them to find a Man soe fit every way for that purpose as this Gentleman, one who I beleeve in a short time would be able to doe them as good service as Mr. Ascan.

—John Milton, letter to Lord Bradshaw,
February 21, 1652/3

John Aubrey
"Andrew Marvell" (1669–96)

An English historian and writer, John Aubrey (1626–1697) gained much renown for his short biographical works entitled *Brief Lives*, whose section on Marvell is excerpted below.

He was of middling stature, pretty strong sett, roundish faced, cherry cheek't, hazell eie, browne haire. He was in his conversation very modest, and of very few words: and though he loved wine he would never drinke hard in company, and was wont to say that, he would not play the goodfellow in any man's company in whose hands he would not trust his life. He had not a generall acquaintance.

In the time of Oliver the Protector he was Latin Secretarie. He was a great master of the Latin tongue; an excellent poet in Latin or English: for Latin verses there was no man could come into competition with him.

I remember I have heard him say that the Earle of Rochester was the only man in England that had the true veine of Satyre.

His native towne of Hull loved him so well that they elected him for their representative in Parliament, and gave him an honourable pension to maintaine him.

He kept bottles of wine at his lodgeing, and many times he would drinke liberally by himselfe to refresh his spirits, and exalt his Muse. (I remember I have been told that the learned Goclenius (an High-German) was wont to keep bottells of good Rhenish-wine in his studie, and, when his spirits wasted, he would drinke a good Rummer of it.)

Obiit Londini, Aug. 18. 1678; and is buried in St. Giles church in-the-fields about the middle of the south aisle. Some suspect that he was poysoned by the Jesuites, but I cannot be positive.

—John Aubrey, "Andrew Marvell,"
Brief Lives, 1669–96

RICHARD MORTON (1692)

Richard Morton (1637–1698) was a prominent physician and doctor to the king. He penned two well-received medical volumes, *Phthisiologica* in 1689 and *Pyretologia* in 1692. In the excerpt below Morton talks about the death of Marvell, which he feels was brought about through the treating physician's incompetence and quackery.

The way having been made ready after this fashion, at the beginning of the next fit [the fourth, that is, of tertian ague] a great febrifuge was administered, that is to say, a draught of Venice treacle, etc. By the doctor's orders the patient was covered up close with blankets, or rather buried under them; and composed himself to sleep and sweat, in order to escape the cold shivers that ordinarily accompany the onset of the ague-fit. Seized with the profoundest sleep and sweating profusely, in the short space of twenty-four hours after the last fit he died comatose *[Apopleptice]*. Thus the patient died who, had a single ounce of Peruvian bark been properly administered, might easily have escaped, in twenty four hours, from the jaws of death and the grave. This is what I, burning with anger, informed the doctor when he told me this story without any sense of shame.

—Richard Morton, *Pyretologia,* 1692

SAMUEL PARKER (1727)

Samuel Parker (1640–1688) was an English writer and theologian who served as Bishop of Oxford. Parker advocated state control of religious

affairs, which caused a public argument with Marvell, as evidenced by
the account below.

Amongst these lewd Revilers, the lewdest was one whose name was *Marvel.*
As he had liv'd in all manner of wickedness from his youth, so being of a
singular impudence and petulancy of nature, he exercised the province of a
Satyrist . . . Being abandon'd by his father, and expell'd the University, . . . A
vagabond, ragged, hungry Poetaster, . . . At length, by the interest of *Milton,*
to whom he was somewhat agreeable for his ill-natur'd wit, he was made
Undersecretary to *Cromwell's* Secretary. . . . But the King being restor'd, this
wretched man falling into his former poverty, did, for the sake of a livelihood,
procure himself to be chosen Member of Parliament for a Borough, in
which his father had exercis'd the office of a Presbyterian teacher. . . . In
all Parliaments he was an enemy to the King's affairs. . . . But out of the
House, when he could do it with impunity, he vented Himself with the
greater bitterness, and daily spewed infamous libels out of his filthy mouth
against the King himself. . . . But this *Bustuarius,* or fencer, never fought
with more fury, than near his own grave, in a book written a little before his
death, to which he gave this title, *An Account of the Growth of Popery, and
Arbitrary Government in England.*

—Samuel Parker, *History of His Own Time,* 1727

❖

GENERAL

❖

CHARLES CHURCHILL "THE AUTHOR" (1763)

Charles Churchill (1731–1764) was an English writer most famous for his satirical work *The Rosciad*, which harshly criticized the most noteworthy actors of the day. Churchill's other satirical poems attacked members of Parliament and fellow authors.

—⁓⁓— —⁓⁓— —⁓⁓—

Is this the Land, where, in those worst of times, The hardy Poet rais'd his honest rimes To dread rebuke, and bade controulment speak In guilty blushes on the villain's cheek, Bade Pow'r turn pale, kept mighty rogues in awe, And made them fear the Muse, who fear'd not Law?

—Charles Churchill, "The Author," 1763

JAMES GRANGER (1769–1824)

James Granger (1723–1776) was a prominent English biographer and collector.

—⁓⁓— —⁓⁓— —⁓⁓—

His pen was always properly directed, and had some effect upon such as were under no check or restraint from any laws human or divine. He hated corruption more than he dreaded poverty; and was so far from being venal, that he could not be bribed by the king into silence, when he scarce knew how to procure a dinner. His satires give us a higher idea of his patriotism, parts, and learning, than of his skill as a poet.

—James Granger, *Biographical History of England*, 1769–1824

JOHN AIKIN (1799–1815)

John Aikin (1747–1822) was an English doctor who, upon his retirement, devoted himself entirely to writing and became a prominent man of letters. His six volume *Evenings at Home*, completed before his retirement in 1795, was translated into over a dozen languages.

—⁓⁓— —⁓⁓— —⁓⁓—

By his writings Marvell obtained the character of the wittiest man of his time, and doubtless was of great service to the cause he espoused, which had in general been defended rather by serious argument than by ridicule. He occasionally threw out a number of poetical effusions of the humorous and satirical kind, in which he did not spare majesty itself. These are careless and loose in their composition, and frequently pass the bounds of decorum; but they were well calculated for effect as party pieces, and became very popular. He exercised his wit still more copiously in prose. In 1672, Dr. Sam. Parker, afterwards bishop of Oxford, a flaming and intolerant high churchman, published a work of bishop Bramhall's, to which he added a preface of his own, maintaining the most extravagant positions concerning the rights of sovereigns over the consciences of their subjects. This piece Marvell attacked in the same year in a work which he entitled *The Rehearsal Transprosed*. With a profusion of witty sarcasm, it contains much solid argument, and may be reckoned one of the ablest exposures of the maxims of religious tyranny. Parker wrote an answer, to which Marvell replied; and the reverend champion did not choose to carry the controversy further.

—John Aikin, *General Biography; or Lives of the Most Eminent Persons*, 1799–1815

WILLIAM LISLE BOWLES "INTRODUCTION" (1806)

William Lisle Bowles (1762–1850) was an English poet who gained more fame as a literary critic. He advocated certain principles of poetic interpretation that eventually became widely accepted and ushered in a new era of literary criticism.

Marvell abounds with conceits and false thoughts, but some of the descriptive touches are picturesque and beautiful. His description of a gently rising eminence is more picturesque, although not so elegantly and justly expressed, as the same subject is in Denham. . . . Sometimes Marvell observes little circumstances of rural nature with the eye and feeling of a true poet:

> Then as I careless on the bed
> Of gelid strawberries do tread,
> And through the hazels thick, espy,
> The hatching throstle's shining eye.

The last circumstance is new, highly poetical, and could only have been described by one who was a real lover of nature, and a witness of her beauties in her most solitary retirement. It is the observation of such *circumstances* which can alone form an accurate descriptive rural poet. In this province of his art Pope therefore must evidently fail, as he could not describe what his physical infirmities prevented his observing. For the same reason Johnson, as a critic, was not a proper judge of this sort of poetry.

—William Lisle Bowles, "Introduction,"
The Works of Alexander Pope, Esq., 1806

THOMAS CAMPBELL (1819)

The humour and eloquence of Marvell's prose tracts were admired and probably imitated by Swift. In playful exuberance of figure he sometimes resembles Burke. For consistency of principles, it is not so easy to find his parallel. His few poetical pieces betray some adherence to the school of conceit, but there is much in it that comes from the heart warm, pure, and affectionate.

—Thomas Campbell, *Specimens of
the British Poets*, 1819

HENRY ROGERS "ANDREW MARVELL" (1844)

Essayist Henry Rogers (1806–1877) was a Congregationalist minister and professor of English literature at University College in London. More known for his theological writing, Rogers also edited an edition of Marvell's work. The majority of Rogers' piece below focuses on an examination of Marvell's wit, in both how that characteristic manifested itself in Marvell's work and in how Marvell's wit affected his reception as a satirist. Rogers writes: "The characteristic attribute of Marvell's genius was unquestionably wit, in all the varieties of which—brief sententious sarcasm, fierce invective, light raillery, grave irony, and broad laughing humour—he seems to have been by nature almost equally fitted to excel." As a satirist and humor writer, Marvell has few equals. "His *forte* . . . appears to be a grave ironical banter, which he often pursues at such a length that there seems no limit to his fertility of invention. In his endless accumulation of ludicrous images and allusions, the untiring exhaustive ridicule with which he will play upon the same topics, he is unique." Yet what especially defines Marvell's humor for Rogers is its lack of malice. Marvell's satire is gentler than that of Donne, for example, and for Rogers, this elevates Marvell's abilities above many of his contemporaries and successors. Though Rogers laments that Marvell's wit is occasionally coarse, "often amounting to buffoonery," its lack of pretense and rancor overcomes the occasional vulgarity that Rogers spies amongst Marvell's work.

Rogers' consideration of Marvell's satirical works is perhaps the most informative aspect of Rogers' essay, as no other essay in this collection so extensively reflects on Marvell's satirical abilities. Comparing what Rogers has written about Marvell as a satirist to what other critics in this text have written about Donne, for example, might make for an interesting contrast. Still, Rogers is quick to point out that wit was not the only one of Marvell's assets: "But he who supposes Marvell to have been nothing but a wit, simply on account of the predominance of that quality, will do him injustice." Rogers labels and describes what he feels are Marvell's other fine qualities as a poet: "His judgment was remarkably clear and sound, his logic by no means contemptible, his sagacity in practical matters great, his talents for business apparently of the first order, and his industry indefatigable." Rogers does lament that Marvell's work was given over to lengthy conceits and "quaint" artifice and that his style was markedly uneven, complaints commonly leveled against most of the metaphysical poets in the nineteenth century. Despite this truism, though, Rogers' appraisal of Marvell's finer qualities is a somewhat unique approach to the subject. He concludes by arguing that Marvell's "moral worth" far exceeds his literary and intellectual achievements, a worth that is perhaps reflected in the geniality of Marvell's satire and humor. Rogers' take on Marvell as satirist and author is thus worth examining, as it proffers both very similar and very differing arguments from many of his critical peers.

<hr />

The characteristic attribute of Marvell's genius was unquestionably wit, in all the varieties of which—brief sententious sarcasm, fierce invective, light raillery, grave irony, and broad laughing humour—he seems to have been by nature almost equally fitted to excel. To say that he *has* equally excelled in all would be untrue, though striking examples of each might easily be selected from his writings. The activity with which his mind suggests ludicrous images and analogies is astonishing; he often absolutely startles us by the remoteness and oddity of the sources from which they are supplied, and by the unexpected ingenuity and felicity of his repartees.

His *forte*, however, appears to be a grave ironical banter, which he often pursues at such a length that there seems no limit to his fertility of invention. In his endless accumulation of ludicrous images and allusions, the untiring exhaustive ridicule with which he will play upon the same topics, he is unique; yet this peculiarity not seldom leads him to drain the generous wine even to the dregs—to spoil a series of felicitous ralleries by some far-fetched conceit or unpardonable extravagance.

But though Marvell was so great a master of wit, and especially of that caustic species which is appropriate to satirists, we will venture to say that he was singularly free from many of the faults which distinguish that irritable brotherhood. Unsparing and merciless as his ridicule is, contemptuous and ludicrous as are the lights in which he exhibits his opponent; nay, further, though is invectives are not only often terribly severe, but (in compliance with the spirit of the age) often grossly coarse and personal, it is still impossible to detect a single particle of malignity. His general tone is that of broad laughing banter, or of the most cutting invective; but he appears equally devoid of malevolence in both. In the one, he seems amusing himself with opponents too contemptible to move his anger; in the other, to lay on with the stern imperturbable gravity of one who is performing the unpleasant but necessary functions of a public executioner. This freedom from the usual faults of satirists may be traced to several causes; partly to the *bonhommie* which, with all his talents for satire, was a peculiar characteristic of the man, and which rendered him as little disposed to take offence, and as placable when it was offered, as any man of his time; partly to the integrity of his nature, which, while it prompted him to champion any cause in which justice had been outraged or innocence wronged, effectually preserved from the wanton exercise of his wit for the gratification of malevolence; partly, perhaps principally, to the fact, that both the above qualities restricted him to encounters in which he had personally no concern. If he carried a keen sword, it was a most peaceable and gentlemanly weapon; it never left the scabbard except on the highest provocation, and even then, only on behalf of others, His magnanimity, self-control, and good temper, restrained him from avenging any insult offered to himself; his chivalrous love of justice instantly roused all the lion within him on behalf of the injured and oppressed. It is perhaps well for Marvell's fame that his quarrels were not personal: had they been so, it is hardly probable that such powers of sarcasm and irony should have been so little associated with bitterness of temper.

This freedom from malignity is highly honourable to him. In too many cases it must be confessed that wit has been sadly dissociated from amiability and generosity. It is true, indeed, that there is no necessary connexion between that quality of mind and the malevolent passions, as numberless illustrious examples sufficiently prove. But where wit is conjoined with malevolence, the latter more effectually displays itself; and even where there is originally no such conjunction, wit is almost always combined with that constitutional irritability of genius which is so readily gratifies, and which, by gratifying, it transforms into something worse. Half the tendencies of our nature pass into habits only from the facilities which encourage their development. We will venture to say, that there is not a tithe of the quarrels in the world that there used to be when all men were accustomed to wear arms; and we may rest assured, that many a waspish temper has become so, principally from being in possession of the weapon of satire. Not seldom, too, it must with sorrow be admitted, the most exquisite sense of the ridiculous has been strangely combined with a morbid, gloomy, saturnine temperament, which looks on all things with a jaundiced imagination, and surveys human infirmities and foibles with feelings not more remote from those of compassionate benevolence than of good-humoured mirth. Happy when, as in the case of Cowper, the influence of a benign heart and unfeigned humility, prevents this tendency from degenerating into universal malevolence. There are few things more shockingly incongruous than the ghastly union of wit and misanthropy. Wit should be ever of open brow, joyous, and frank-hearted. Even the severest satire may be delicious reading, when penned with the *bonhommie* of Horace, or of Addison, or the equanimity of Plato, or of Pascal. Without pretending these immortal writers, we firmly believe he had as much kindly feeling as any of them. Unhappily the two by no means go together; there may be the utmost refinement without a particle of good-nature; and a great deal of goodnature without any refinement. It were easy to name writers, who with the most exquisite grace of diction can as little disguise the malice of their nature, as Marvell, with all his coarseness, can make us doubt his benevolence. Through the veil of their language (of beautiful texture, but too transparent) we see chagrin poorly simulating mirth; anger struggling to appear contempt, and failing; scorn writhing itself into an aspect of ironical courtesy, but with grim distortion in the attempt; and sarcasms urged by the impulses which, under different circumstances, and in another country, would have prompted to the use of the stiletto.

It is impossible, indeed, not to regret the coarseness, often amounting to buffoonery, of Marvell's wit; though, from the consideration just urged, we regard it with the more forbearance. Other palliations have been adverted to, derived from the character of his adversaries, the haste with which he wrote, and the spirit of the age. The last is the strongest. The tomahawk and the scalping-knife were not yet discreditable weapons, or thrown aside as fit only for savage warfare; and it is even probable, that many of the things which we should regard as gross insults would then pass as pardonable jests. It is difficult for us, of course, to imagine that callousness which scarcely regards any thing as an insult but what is enforced by the *argumentum baculinum*. Between the feelings of our forefathers and our own, there seems to have been as great a difference as between those of the farmer and the clergyman, so ludicrously described by Cowper, in his 'Yearly Distress':

> O, why are farmers made so coarse,
> Or clergy made so fine?
> A kick that scarce would move a horse,
> May kill a sound divine.

The haste with which Marvell wrote must also be pleaded as an excuse for the inequalities of his works. It was not the age in which authors elaborated and polished with care, or submitted with a good grace to the *lima labor;* and if it had been, Marvell allowed himself no leisure for the task. The second part of the *Rehearsal,* for example, was published in the same year in which Parker's *Reproof* appeared. We must profess our belief, that no small portion of his writings stand in great need of this apology. Exhibiting, as they do, amazing vigour and fertility, the wit is by no means always of the first order.

We must not quit the subject of his wit, without presenting the reader with some few of his pleasantries; premising that they form but a very small part of those which we had marked in the perusal of his works; and that, whatever their merit, it were easy to find others far superior to them, if we could afford space for long citations.

Ironically bewailing the calamitous effects of printing, our author exclaims—'O Printing! how hast thou disturbed the peace of mankind? Lead, when moulded into bullets, is not so mortal as when founded into letters. There was a mistake, sure, in the story of Cadmus; and the serpents' teeth which he sowed, were nothing else but the letters which he invented.' Parker having declared, in relation to some object of his scurrility, that he had written, 'not to impair his esteem,' but 'to correct his scribbling humour;' Marvell says—'Our author is as courteous as lightning; and can melt the sword without ever hurting the scabbard.' After alleging that his opponent often has a byplay of malignity even when bestowing commendations, he remarks—'The author's end was only railing. He could never have induced himself to praise one man but in order to rail on another. He never oils his hone but that he may whet his razor, and that not to shave but to cut men's throats.' On Parker's absurd and bombastic exaggeration of the merits

and achievements of Bishop Bramhall, Marvell wittily says— 'Any worthy
man may pass through the world unquestioned and safe, with a moderate
recommendation; but when he is thus set off and bedaubed with rhetoric,
and embroidered so thick that you cannot discern the ground, it awakens
naturally (and not altogether unjustly) interest, curiosity, and envy. For all
men pretend a share in reputation, and love not to see it engrossed and
monopolized; and are subject to enquire (as of great estates suddenly got)
whether he came by all this honestly, or *of what credit the person is that tells
the story?* And the same hath happened as to this bishop … Men seeing
him furbished up in so martial accoutrements, like another Odo, Bishop
of Baieux, and having never before heard of his prowess, begin to reflect
what giants he defeated, and what damsels he rescued … After all our
author's bombast, when we have searched all over, we find ourselves bilked
in our expectation; and he hath created the Bishop, like a St. Christopher
in the Popish churches, as big as ten porters, and yet only employed to
sweat under the burden of an infant.' Of the paroxysms of rage with which
Parker refers to one of his adversaries, whom he distinguishes by his initials,
Marvell says—'As oft as he does but name those two first letters, he is, like
the island of Fayal, on fire in threescore and ten places;' and affirms; 'that
if he were of that fellow's diet here about town, that epicurizes on burning
coals, drinks healths in scalding brimstone, scranches the glasses for his
dessert, and draws his breath through glowing tobacco-pipes, he could
not show more flame than he always does upon that subject.' Parker, in a
passage of unequalled absurdity, having represented Geneva as on the south
side of the lake Leman, Marvell ingeniously represents the blunder as the
subject of discussion in a private company, where various droll solutions
are proposed, and where he, with exquisite irony, pretends to take Parker's
part. 'I,' says Marvell, 'that was still on the doubtful and excusing part, said,
that to give the right situation of a town, it was necessary first to know in
what position the gentleman's head then was when he made his observation,
and that might cause a great diversity—as much as this came to.' Having
charged his adversary with needlessly obtruding upon the world some
petty matters which concerned only himself, from an exaggerated idea of
is own importance, Marvell drolly says—'When a man is once possessed
with this fanatic kind of spirit, he imagines if a shoulder do but itch that
the world has galled it with leaning on it so long, and therefore he wisely
shrugs to remove the globe to the other. If he chance but to sneeze, he
salutes himself, and courteously prays that the foundations of the earth be
not shaken. And even so the author of the *Ecclesiastical Polity,* ever since

he crept up to be but the weathercock of a steeple, trembles and creaks at every puff of wind that blows him about, as if the Church of England were falling, and the state tottered.' After ludicrously describing the effect of the first part of the *Rehearsal* in exacerbating all his opponent's evil passions, he remarks—'He seems not to fit at present for the archdeacon's seat, as to take his place below in the church amongst the *energumeni.*' Parker had charged him with a sort of plagiarism for having quoted so many passages out of his book. On this Marvell observes—'It has, I believe, indeed angered him, as it has been no small trouble to me; but how can I help it? I wish he would be pleased to teach me an art (for, if any man in the world, he hath it) to answer a book without turning over the leaves, or without citing passages. In the mean time, if to transcribe so much out of him must render a man, as he therefore styles me, a "scandalous plagiary," I must plead guilty; but by the same law, whoever shall either be witness or prosecutor in behalf of the King, for treasonable words, may be indicted for a highwayman.' Parker having viewed some extravaganza of Marvell's riotous wit as if worthy of serious comment, the latter says—'Whereas I only threw it out like an empty cask to amuse him, knowing that I had a whale to deal with, and lest he should overset me; he runs away with it as a very serious business, and so moyles himself with tumbling and tossing it, that he is in danger of melting his spermaceti. A cork, I see, will serve without a hook; and, instead of a harping-iron, this grave and ponderous creature may, like eels, be taken and pulled up only with bobbing.' After exposing in a strain of uncommon eloquence the wickedness and folly of suspending the peace of the nation on so frivolous a matter as 'ceremonial,' he says 'For a prince to adventure all upon such a cause, is like Duke Charles of Burgundy, who fought three battles for an imposition upon sheep-skins;' and 'for a clergyman to offer at persecution upon this ceremonial account, is (as is related of one of the Popes) to justify his indignation for his peacock, by the example of God's anger for eating the forbidden fruit.' He justifies his severity towards Parker in a very ludicrous way—'No man needs letters of marque against one that is an open pirate of other men's credit. I remember within our own time one Simons, who robbed always on the bricolle—that is to say, never interrupted the *passengers,* but still set upon the *thieves themselves,* after, like Sir John Falstaff, they were gorged with a booty; and by this way—so ingenious that it was scarce criminal—he lived secure and unmolested all his days, with the reputation of a judge rather than of a highwayman.' The sentences we have cited are all taken from the *Rehearsal.* We had marked many more from his 'Divine in Mode,' and other writings, but have no space for them.

But he who supposes Marvell to have been nothing but a wit, simply on account of the predominance of that quality, will do him injustice. It is the common lot of such men, in whom some one faculty is found on a great scale, to fail of part of the admiration due to other endowments; possessed in more moderate degree, indeed, but still in a degree far from ordinary. We are subject to the same illusion in gazing on mountain scenery. Fixing our eye on some solitary peak, which towers far above the rest, the groups of surrounding hills look positively diminutive, though they may, in fact, be all of great magnitude.

This illusion is further fostered by another circumstance in the case of great wits. As the object of wit is to amuse, the owl-like gravity of thousands of common readers, would decide that wit and wisdom must dwell apart, and that the humorous writer must necessarily be a trifling one. For similar reasons, they look with sage suspicion on every signal display, either of fancy or passion; think a splendid illustration nothing but the ambuscade of a fallacy, and strong emotion as tantamount to a confession of unsound judgment. As Archbishop Whately has well remarked, such men having been warned that 'ridicule is not the test of truth,' and that 'wisdom and wit are not the same thing, distrust every thing that can possibly be regarded as witty; not having judgment to perceive the combination, when it occurs, of wit and sound reasoning. The ivy wreath completely conceals from their view the point of the *thyrsus.*'

The fact is, that all Marvell's endowments were on a large scale, though his wit greatly predominated. His judgment was remarkably clear and sound, his logic by no means contemptible, his sagacity in practical matters great, his talents for business apparently of the first order, and his industry indefatigable. His wit, would, if sufficiently cultivated, have made him a poet considerably above mediocrity: though chiefly alive to the ludicrous, he was by no means insensible to the beautiful. We cannot, indeed, bestow all the praise on his Poems which some of his critics have assigned them. They are very plentifully disfigured by the conceits and quaintnesses of the age, and as frequently want grace of expression and harmony of numbers. Of the compositions which Captain Thompsons's indiscriminate admiration would fain have affiliated to his Muse, the two best are proved—one not to be his, and the other of doubtful origin. The former, beginning—

When Israel, freed from Pharoah's hand,

is a well-known composition of Dr. Watts; the other, the ballad of 'William and Margaret,' is of dubious authorship. Though probably of earlier date than the age of Mallet, its reputed author—the reasons which Captain Thompson gives for assigning it to Marvell, are altogether unsatisfactory. Still, there are unquestionably many of his genuine poems which indicate a rich, though ill-cultivated fancy; and in some few stanzas there is no little grace of expression. The little piece on the Pilgrim Fathers, entitled the 'Emigrants,' the fanciful 'Dialogue between Body and Soul,' the 'Dialogue between the Resolved Soul and Created Pleasure,' and the 'Coronet,' all contain lines of much elegance and sweetness. It is in his satirical poems, that, as might be expected from the character of his mind, his fancy appears most vigorous; though these are largely disfigured by the characteristic defects of the age, and many, it must be confessed, are entirely without merit. With two or three lines from his ludicrous satire on Holland, we cannot refrain from amusing the reader. Some of the strokes of humour are irresistibly ridiculous:

> Holland, that scarce deserves the name of land,
> As but the off-scouring of the British sand;
> And so much earth as was contributed
> By English pilots when they heav'd the lead;
> Or what by th' ocean's slow alluvion fell,
> Of shipwreck'd cockle and the muscle-shell;
> This indigested vomit of the sea
> Fell to the Dutch by just propriety.
> Glad then, as miners who have found the ore,
> They, with mad labour fish'd the land to shore;
> And dived as desperately for each piece
> Of earth, as if it had been of ambergris;
> Collecting anxiously small loads of clay,
> Less than what building swallows bear away;
> For as with pigmies, who best kills the crane,
> Among the hungry he that treasures grain,
> Among the blind the one-eyed blinkard reigns,
> So rules among the drowned be that drains,
> Not who first see the rising sun commands:
> But who could first discern the rising lands.
> Who best could know to pump an earth so leak,
> Him they their lord, and country's father, speak.

His Latin poems are amongst his best. The composition often shows no contemptible skill in that language; and here and there the diction and versification are such as would not have absolutely disgraced his great coadjutor, Milton. In all the higher poetic qualities, there can of course be no comparison between them.

With such a mind we as we have ascribed to him—and we think his works fully justify what we have said—with such aptitudes for business, soundness of judgment, powers of reasoning, and readiness of sarcasm, one might have anticipated that he would have taken some rank as an orator. Nature, it is certain, had bestowed upon him some of the most important intellectual endowments of one. It is true, indeed, that with his principles and opinions he would have found himself strangely embarrassed in addressing any parliament in the days of Charles II., and stood but a moderate chance of obtaining a candid hearing. But we have no proof that he ever made the trial. His parliamentary career in this respect resembled that of a much greater man—Addison, who, with wit even superior to his own, and with much more elegance, if not more strength of mind, failed signally as a speaker.

Marvell's learning must have been very extensive. His education was superior; and, as we have seen from the testimony of Milton, his industry had made him master, during his long sojourn on the Continent, of several continental languages. It is certain also, that he continued to be a student all his days; his works bear ample evidence of his wide and miscellaneous reading. He appears to have been well versed in most branches of literature, though he makes no pedantic display of erudition, and in this respect is favourably distinguished from many of his contemporaries; yet he cites his authors with the familiarity of a thorough scholar. In the department of history he appears to have been particularly well read; and derives his witty illustrations from such remote and obscure sources, that Parker did not hesitate to avow his belief that he had sometimes drawn on his invention for them. In his Reply, Marvell justifes himself in all the alleged instances, and takes occasion to show that his opponent's learning is as hollow as all his other pretensions.

The style of Marvell is very unequal. Though often rude and unpolished, it abounds in negligent felicities, presents us with frequent specimens of vigorous idiomatic English, and now and then attains no mean degree of elegance. It bears the stamp of the revolution which was then passing on the language; it is a medium between the involved and periodic structure so common during the former half of the century, and which is ill adapted to a language possessing so few infections as ours, and that simplicity and harmony which were not fully attained till the age of Addison. There is a very large infusion of short sentences, and the structure in general is as unlike that of his great colleague's prose as can be imaged. Many of Marvell's pages flow with so much ease and grace, as to be not unworthy of a later period. To that great revolution in style to which we have just alluded, he must in no slight degree have contributed; for, little as his works are known or read now, the most noted of them were once universally popular, and perused with pleasure, as Burnet testifies, by every body, 'from the king to the tradesman.'

Numerous examples show, that it is almost impossible for even the rarest talents to confer permanent popularity on books which turn on topics of temporary interest, however absorbing at the time. If Pascal's transcendant genius has been unable to rescue even the *Lettres Provinciates* from partial oblivion, it is not to be expected that Marvell should have done more for the *Rehearsal Transprosed*. Swift, it is true, about half a century later, has been pleased, while expressing this opinion, to make an exception in favour of Marvell. 'There is indeed,' says he, 'an exception, when any great genius thinks it worth his while to expose a foolish piece; so we still read Marvell's answer to Parker with pleasure, though the book it answers be sunk long ago.' But this statement is scarcely applicable now. It is true that the 'Rehearsal' is occasionally read by the curious; but it is by the resolutely curious alone.

Yet assuredly he has not lived in vain who has successfully endeavoured to abate the nuisances of his own time, or to put down some insolent abettor of vice and corruption. Nor is it possible in a world like this, in which there is such continuity of causes and effects—where one generation transmits its good and its evil to the next, and the consequences of each revolution in principles, opinions, or tastes, are propagated along the whole line of humanity—to estimate either the degree or perpetuity of the benefits conferred by the complete success of works even of transient interest. By modifying the age in which he lives, a man may indirectly modify the character of many generations to come. His works may be forgotten while their effects survive.

Marvell's history affords a signal instance of the benefits which may be derived from well-directed satire. There are cases in which it may be a valuable auxiliary to decency, virtue, and religion, where argument and persuasion both fail. Many, indeed, doubt both the legitimacy of the weapon itself, and the success with which it can be employed. But facts are against them. To hope that it can ever supply the place of religion as a radical cure for vice or immorality, would be chimerical; but there are many pernicious customs, violations of propriety, ridiculous, yet tolerated, follies, which religion can scarcely touch without endangering her dignity. To assail them is one of the most legitimate offices of satire; nor have we the slightest doubt that the 'Spectator' did more to abate many of the prevailing follies and pernicious customs of the age, than a thousand homilies. This, however, may be admitted, and yet it may be said that it does not reach the case of Marvell and Parker. Society, it may be argued, will bear the exposure of its own evils with great equanimity, and perhaps profit by it—no individual being pointed at, and each being left to digest his own lesson, under the pleasant conviction that it was designed principally for his neighbours. As corporations will perpetrate actions of which each individual member would be ashamed; so corporations will listen to charges which every individual member would regard as insults. But no man, it is said, is likely to be reclaimed from error or vice by being made the object of merciless ridicule. All this we believe most true. But then it is not to be forgotten, that it may not be the satirist's object to reclaim the individual—he may have little hope of that; it may be for the sake of those whom he maligns and injures. When the exorcist takes Satan in hand, it is not because he is an Origenist, and 'believes in the conversion of the devil,' but in pity to the supposed victims of his malignity. It is much the same when a man like Marvell undertakes to satirize a man like Parker. Even such a man may be abashed and confounded, though he cannot be reclaimed; and if so, the satirist gains his object, and society gets the benefit. Experience fully shows us that there are many men who will be restrained by ridicule long after they are lost to virtue, and that they are accessible to shame when they are utterly inaccessible to argument.

This was just the good that Marvell effected. He made Parker, it is true, more furious; but he diverted, if he could not turn the tide of popular feeling; and thus prevented mischief. Parker, and others like him, were doing all they could to inflame angry passions, to revive the most extravagant pretensions of tyranny, and to preach up another crusade against the Nonconformists. Marvell's books were a conductor to the dangerous fluid; if there was any explosion at all, it was an explosion of merriment. 'He had all the laughers on his side,' says Burnet. In Charles II.'s reign, there were few who belonged to any other class; and then, as now, men found it impossible to laugh and be angry at the same time. It is our firm belief, that Marvell did more to humble Parker, and neutralize the influence of his party, by the *Rehearsal Transprosed*, than he could have done by writing half a dozen folios of polemical divinity; just as Pascal did more to unmask the Jesuits and damage their cause by his *Provincial Letters*, than had been effected by all the efforts of all their other opponents put together.

But admirable as were Marvell's intellectual endowments, it is his moral worth, after all, which constitutes his principal claim on the admiration of posterity, and which sheds a redeeming lustre on one of the darkest pages of the English annals. Inflexible integrity was the basis of it—integrity by which he has not unworthily earned the glorious name of the 'British Aristides.' With talents and acquirements which might have justified him in aspiring to almost any office, if he could have disburdened himself of his conscience; with wit which, in that frivolous age, was a surer passport to fame than any amount either of intellect or virtue, and which, as we have seen, mollified even the monarch himself in spite of his prejudices; Marvell preferred poverty and independence to riches and servility. He had learned the lesson, practised by few in that age, of being content with little—so that he preserved his conscience. He could be poor, but he could not be mean; could starve, but could not cringe. By economizing in the articles of pride and ambition, he could afford to keep what their votaries were compelled to retrench, the necessaries, or rather the luxuries, of integrity and a good conscience. Neither menaces, nor caresses, nor bribes, nor poverty, nor distress, could induce him to abandon his integrity; or even to take an office in which it might be tempted or endangered. He only who has arrived at this pitch of magnanimity, has an adequate security for his public virtue. He who cannot subsist upon a little; who has not learned to be content with such things as he has, and even to be content with almost nothing; who has not learned to familiarize his thoughts to poverty, much more readily than he can familiarize them to dishonour, is not yet free from peril. Andrew Marvell, as his whole course proves, had done this. But we shall not do full justice to his public integrity, if we do not bear in mind the corruption of the age in which he lived; the manifold apostasies amidst which he retained his conscience; and the effect which such wide-spread profligacy must have had in making thousands almost sceptical as to whether there were such a thing as public virtue at all. Such a relaxation in the code of speculative morals, is one of the worst results of general profligacy in practice. But Andrew Marvell was not to be deluded; and amidst corruption perfectly unparalleled, he still continued untainted. We are accustomed to hear of his virtue as a truly Roman virtue, and so it was; but it was something more. Only the best pages of Roman history can supply a parallel: there was no Cincinnatus in those ages of her shame which alone can be compared with those of Charles II. It were easier to find a Cincinnatus during the era of the English Commonwealth, than an Andrew Marvell in the age of Commodus.

The integrity and patriotism which distingusihed him in his relations to the Court, also marked all his public conduct. He was evidently most scrupulously honest and faithful in the discharge of his duty to his constituents; and, as we have seen almost punctilious in guarding against any thing which could tarnish his fair fame, or defile his conscience. On reviewing the whole of his public conduct, we may well say that he attained his wish, expressed in the lines which he has written in imitation of a chorus in the *Thyestes* of Seneca:

Climb at court for me that will—
Tottering favour's pinnacle;
All I seek is to lie still.
Settled in some secret nest,
In calm leisure let me rest,
And far off the public stage,
Pass away my silent age.
Thus, when without noise, unknown,
I have lived out all my span,
I shall die without a groan,
An old honest countryman.

He seems to have been as amiable in his private as he was estimable in his public character. So far as any documents throw light upon the subject, the same integrity appears to have belonged to both. He is described as of a very reserved and quiet temper; but, like Addison, (whom in this respect as in some few others he resembled,) exceedingly facetious and lively amongst his intimate friends. His disinterested championship of others, is no less a proof of his sympathy with the oppressed than of his abhorrence of oppression; and many pleasing traits of amiability occur in his private correspondence, as well as in his writings. On the whole, we think that Marvell's epitaph, strong as the terms of panegyric are, records little more than the truth; and that it was not in the vain spirit of boasting, but in the honest consciousness of virtue and integrity, and that he himself concludes a letter to one of his correspondents in the words—

Disce, puer, virtutem ex me, verumque laborem;
Fortunam ex aliis.

—Henry Rogers, from "Andrew Marvell"
Edinburgh Review, January 1844, pp. 90–104

Mary Russell Mitford (1851)

An English poet and playwright, Mary Russell Mitford's (1787–1855) most prominent claim to fame is as the author of a series of sketches under the title of *Our Village*, which proved enormously popular. Her *Recollections of a Literary Life* was an informal series of observations on some of her favorite books and authors.

His poems possess many of the finest elements of popularity; a rich profusion of fancy which almost dazzles the mind as bright colours dazzle the eye; an earnestness and heartiness which do not always,—do not often belong to these flowery fancies, but which when found in their company add to them inexpressible vitality and savor; and a frequent felicity of phrase, which, when once read, fixes itself in the memory, and *will* not be forgotten. (. . .) His mind was a bright garden, such a garden as he has described so finely, and that a few gaudy weeds should mingle with the healthier plants does but serve to prove the fertility of the soil.

—Mary Russell Mitford, *Recollections of a
Literary Life*, 1851, pp. 532–33

Alexander B. Grosart
"Memorial—Introduction" (1872)

Alexander Bulloch Grosart (1827–1899) was a Presbyterian minister and scholar of Puritan history and biography. He also edited and reprinted numerous volumes of the works of Elizabethan and Jacobean authors, including Marvell.

Fundamentally, the Poetry of Marvell is genuine as a bird's singing, or the singing of the brook on its gleaming way under the leafage. There is the breath and fragrance of inviolate Nature in every page of the *Poems of the Country* and *Poems of Imagination and Love*, and in *Poems of Friendship* and *State Poems* such thinking and aspiration as were worthy of their greatest themes; and I am here remembering, and wish it to be remembered, that John Milton and Oliver Cromwell and Blake are celebrated by him.

—Alexander B. Grosart, "Memorial—Introduction"
to *The Complete Poems of Andrew Marvell*,
1872, p. lxvi

Edmund K. Chambers (1892)

Sir Edmund Kerchever Chambers (1866–1954) was an English literary scholar whose four-volume work on Elizabethan theater, published in 1923, remained the authority on the subject for decades. In the piece below, Chambers favorably compares Marvell to John Milton, the great English poet and author of *Paradise Lost*: "their poetic temper is one: it is the music of Puritanism,—the Puritanism of Spenser and Sidney, not uncultivated, not ungracious, not unsensuous even, but always with the same dominant note in it, of moral strength and moral purity." Chambers then discusses Marvell's love poems, including the famous "Mower" works, before briefly examining the poems "Upon Appleton House" and "On a Drop of Dew." Any student of Marvell will certainly appreciate the comparison to Milton, as well as Chambers' enthusiastic reception of the poet's works in general.

Marvell holds a unique place in the seventeenth century. He stands at the parting of the ways, between the extravagancies of the lyrical Jacobeans on the one hand, and the new formalism initiated by Waller on the other. He is not unaffected by either influence. The modish handling of the decasyllable couplet is very marked here and there. You have it, for instance, in the poem on Blake:

> Bold Stayner leads; this fleet's designed by fate
> To give him laurel, as the last did plate.

And elsewhere, of course, he has conceits which cry aloud in their flagrancy. But his real affinities are with a greater than Waller or Suckling. Milton in those days "was like a star, and dwelt apart"; but of all who "called him friend," Marvell is the one who can claim the most of spiritual kinship. The very circumstances of their lives are curiously similar. Each left poetry for statecraft and polemic: for Milton the flowering time came late; for Marvell, never. And their poetic temper is one: it is the music of Puritanism,—the Puritanism of Spenser and Sidney, not uncultivated, not ungracious, not unsensuous even, but always with the same dominant note in it, of moral strength and moral purity. Marvell is a Puritan; but his spirit has not entered the prison-house, nor had the key turned on it there. He is a poet still, such as there have been few in any age. The lyric gift of Herrick he has not, nor Donne's incomparable subtlety and intensity of emotion; but for imaginative power, for decent melody, for that self-restraint of phrase which is the fair half of art, he must certainly hold high rank among his fellows. The clear sign of this self-restraint is his mastery over the octosyllable couplet, metre which in less skilful hands so readily becomes diffuse and wearisome.

Marvell writes love poems, but he is not essentially a love poet. He sings beautifully to Juliana and Chlora, but they themselves are only accidents in his song. His real passion—a most uncommon one in the seventeenth century—is for nature, exactly as we moderns mean nature, the great spiritual influence which deepens and widens life for us. How should the intoxication of meadow, and woodland, and garden, be better expressed than in these two lines—

> Stumbling on melons, as I pass,
> Insnared with flowers, I fall on grass.

unless indeed it be here—

> I am the mower Damon, known
> Through all the meadows I have mown,
> On me the morn her dew distils
> Before her darling daffodils;
> And if at noon my toil me heat,
> The sun himself licks off my sweat;
> While, going home, the evening sweet
> In cowslip water bathes my feet.

These mower-idylls, never found in the anthologies, are among the most characteristic of Marvell's shorter poems. I cannot forbear to quote two stanzas from "The Mower to the Glowworms":

> Ye living lamps, by whose dear light
>   The nightingale doth sit so late,
> And studying all the summer night,
>   Her matchless songs doth meditate.
> Ye country cornets, that portend
>   Nor war, nor prince's funeral
> Shining unto no higher end
>   Than to presage the grass's fall.

Observe how Marvell makes of the nightingale a conscious artist, a winged *dira*. Elsewhere he speaks of her as sitting among the "squatted thorns," in order "to sing the trials of her voice."

I must needs see in Marvell something of a nature philosophy strangely anticipative of George Meredith. For the one, as for the other, complete absorption in nature, the unreserved abandonment of self to the skyey influences, is the really true and sanative wisdom. Marvell describes his soul, freed of the body's vesture, perched like a bird upon the garden boughs—

> Annihiliting all that's made
> To a green thought in a greed shade.

The same idea is to be found in the lines "Upon Appleton House," a poem which will repay careful study from all who wish to get at the secret of Marvell's genius. It shows him at his best—and at his worst, in the protracted conceit, whereby a garden, its flowers and its bees, are likened to a fort with a garrison. And here I am minded to enter a plea against the indiscriminate condemnation of conceits in poetry. After all, a conceit is only an analogy, a comparison, a revealing of poetic imagination. Often it illumines, and where it fails it is not because it is a conceit, but because it is a bad conceit; because the thing compared is not beautiful in itself, or because the comparison is not flashed upon you, but worked out with such tedious elaboration as to be "merely fantastical." Many of Marvell's conceits are, in effect, bad; the well-known poem, "On a Drop of Dew," redeemed though it is by the last line and a half, affords a terrible example. But others are shining successes. Here is one, set in a haunting melody, as of Browning:

> Gentler times for love are meant:
> > Who for parting pleasures strain,
> > Gather roses in the rain,
> Wet themselves and spoil their scent.

Next to green fields, Marvel is perhaps happiest in treating of death. His is the mixed mode of the Christian scholar, not all unpaganised, a lover or heaven, but a lover of the earthly life too. There is the epitaph on a nameless lady, with its splendid close:

> Modest as a morn, as mid-day bright,
> Gentle as evening, cool as night:
> 'Tis true: but all too weakly said;
> 'Twas more significant. She's dead.

There is an outburst on the death of the poet's hero, the greater Portector:

> O human glory vain! O Death! O wings!
> O worthless world! O transitory things!

And to crown all, there are these lines, which remind me, for their felicities, their quaintness, and the organ-note in them, of the *Hydriotaphia:*

> But at my back I always hear
> Time's winged chariot hurrying near.
> And yonder all before us lie
> Deserts of vast eternity.
> Thy beauty shall no more be found,
> Nor, in thy marble vault, shall sound
> My echoing song; then worms shall try
> Thy long-preserved virginity,
> And your quaint honor turn to dust
> And into ashes all my lust:
> The grave's a fine and private place,
> But none, I think, do there embrace.

I have left myself no room to speak of the Satires. They are not a subject to dwell upon with pleasure. One sees that they were inevitable, that a man of Marvell's strenuous moral fibre, in all the corruption of the Restoration court, could not but break forth into savage invective; yet one regrets them, as one regrets the *Defensio* and *Eikonoklastes.*

—Edmund K. Chambers, *Academy,*
Sept. 17, 1892, pp. 230–31

FRANCIS TURNER PALGRAVE
(1896)

One of the most original poets of the Stuart period, the new tentative features of the age in poetry, again, are clearly marked. The lyrical work belonging to his early life has often passages of imaginative quality, equally strong and delicate. If we exclude Milton, no one of that time touches sweeter or nobler lyrical notes; but he is singularly unequal; he flies high, but is not long on the wing. The characteristic Elizabethan smoothness of unbroken melody was now failing; the fanciful style of Donne, the seventeenth century *concetti,* seized on Marvell too strongly, and replaced in him the earlier mythological landscape characteristic of the Renaissance.

—Francis Turner Palgrave,
Landscape in Poetry, 1896, p. 154

ALICE MEYNELL "ANDREW MARVELL" (1897)

Alice Thompson Meynell (1847–1922) was an English writer and suffragist. Though she started out as a poet, after converting to Roman Catholicism, Meynell's work focused more on theological themes. It is no surprise, then, that a Puritan writer like Marvell caught her critical eye. In the excerpt below, Meynell, like Chambers before her, favorably compares Marvell to Milton. However, most of the piece focuses on Marvell's "wild civility," which Meynell suggests is best demonstrated in Marvell's garden lyrics: "For it is only in those well-known poems, 'The Garden', translated from his own Latin, and 'The Nymph Complaining for the Death of Her Fawn', in that less familiar piece 'The Mower against Gardens', in 'The Picture of T.C. in a Prospect of Flowers', with a few very brief passages in the course of duller verses, that Marvell comes into veritable possession of his own more interior powers." Any student focusing on nature imagery in Marvell or more specifically on his garden lyrics will appreciate Meynell's work, which includes a substantial examination of the famous poem "Upon Appleton House."

———

'He earned the glorious name,' says a biographer of Andrew Marvell (editing an issue of that poet's works, which certainly has its faults), 'of the British Aristides.' The portly dullness of the mind that could make such a phrase, and, having made, award it, is not, in fairness, to affect a reader's thought of Marvell himself nor even of his time. Under correction, I should think that the award was not made in his own age; he did but live on the eye of the day that cumbered its mouth with phrases of such foolish burden and made literature stiff with them. He, doubtless, has moments of mediocre pomp, but even then it is Milton that he touches, and not anything more common; and he surely never even heard a threat of the pass that the English tongue should come to but a little later on.

Andrew Marvell's political rectitude, it is true, seems to have been of a robustious kind; but his poetry, at its rare best, has a 'wild civility', which might puzzle the triumph of him, whoever he was, who made a success of this phrase of the 'British Aristides'. Nay, it is difficult not to think that Marvell too, who was 'of middling stature, roundish-faced, cherry-cheeked', a healthy and active rather than a spiritual Aristides, might himself have been somewhat taken by surprise at the encounters of so subtle a muse. He, as a garden-poet, expected the accustomed Muse to lurk about the fountain-heads, within the caves, and by the walks and the statues of the gods, keeping the tryst of a seventeenth-century convention in which there were certainly no surprises. And for fear of the commonplaces of those visits Marvell sometimes outdoes the whole company of garden-poets in the difficult labours of the fancy. The reader treads with him a 'maze' most resolutely intricate, and is more than once obliged to turn back having been too much puzzled on the way to a small, visible, plain, and obvious goal of thought.

And yet this poet two or three times did meet a Muse he had hardly looked for among the trodden paths; a spiritual creature had been waiting behind a laurel or an apple tree. You find him coming away from such a divine ambush a wilder and a simpler man. All his garden had been made ready for poetry, and poetry was indeed there, but in unexpected hiding and in a strange form, looking rather like a fugitive, shy of the poet who was conscious of having her rules by heart, yet sweetly willing to be seen, for all her haste.

For it is only in those well-known poems, 'The Garden', translated from his own Latin, and 'The Nymph Complaining for the Death of Her Fawn', in that less familiar piece 'The Mower against Gardens', in 'The Picture of T.C. in a Prospect of Flowers', with a few very brief passages in the course of duller verses, that Marvell comes into veritable possession of his own more interior powers—at least in the series of his garden lyrics. The political poems, needless to say, have an excellence of a different character and a higher degree. They have so much authentic dignity that 'the glorious name of the British Aristides' really seems duller when it is conferred as the earnings of the 'Horatian Ode upon Cromwell's Return from Ireland' than when it inappropriately clings to Andrew Marvell, cherry-cheeked, caught in the tendrils of his vines and melons. He shall be, therefore, the British Aristides in those moments of midsummer solitude; at least, the heavy phrase shall then have the smile it never sought.

Marvell can be tedious in these gardens—tedious with every ingenuity, refinement, and assiduity of invention. When he intends to flatter the owner of the *Hill and Grove at Billborow,* he is most deliberately silly, not as the eighteenth century was silly, but with a peculiar innocence. Unconsciousness there was not, assuredly; but the aritificial phrases of Marvell had never been used by a Philistine; the artifices are freshly absurd, the cowardice before the plain face of commonplace is not vulgar, there is an evident simple pleasure in the successful evasion of simplicity, and all the anxiety of the poet comes to a happy issue before our eyes. He commends the Billborow hill because 'the stiffest compass could not strike' a more symmetrical and equal semi-circle than its form presents, and he rebukes the absent mountains because they deform the earth and affright the heavens. This hill, he says, with a little better fancy, only 'strives to raise the plain'. Lord Fairfax of the soil are dedicated, and whose own merit they illustrate, is then said to be admirable for the modesty whereby, having a hill, he has also a clump of trees on the top, wherein to sequester the honours of eminence. It is not too much to say that the whole of this poem is untouched by poetry.

So is almost that equally ingenious piece, 'Appleton House', addressed to the same friend. It chanced that Appleton House was small, and out of this plain little fact the British Aristides contrives to turn a sedulous series of compliments with fair success and with a most guileless face. What natural humility in the householder who builds in proportion to his body, and is contented like the tortoise and the bird! Further on, however, it appears that the admired house had been a convent, and that to the dispossessed nuns was due the praise of proportion; they do not get it, in any form, from Marvell. A pretty passage follows, on the wasting of gardens, and a lament over the passing away of some earlier England. . . . But nothing here is of the really fine quality of 'The Picture of T.C', or 'The Garden', or 'The Nymph Complaining for the Death of Her Fawn'.

In these three the presence of a furtive irony of the gentlest kind is the sure sign that they came of the visitings of the unlooked-for muse aforesaid. Marvell rallies his own 'Nymph', rallies his own soul for her clapping of silver wings in the solitude of summer trees; and more sweetly does he pretend to offer to the little girl 'T.C the prophetic homage of the habitual poets. . . .

The noble phrase of the 'Horatian Ode' is not recovered again high or low throughout Marvell's book, if we except one single splendid and surpassing passage from 'The Definition of Love'. The hopeless lover speaks:

Magnanimous despair alone
Could show me so divine a thing.

'To his Coy Mistress' is the only piece, not already named, altogether fine enough for an anthology. The Satires are, of course, out of reach for their inordinate length. The celebrated Satire on Holland certainly makes the utmost of the fun to be easily found in the physical facts of the country whose people 'with mad labour fished the land to shore'. The Satire on *Flecknoe* makes the utmost of another joke we know of—that of famine. Flecknoe, it will be remembered, was a poet, and poor; but the joke of his bad verses was hardly needed, so fine does Marvell find that of his hunger. Perhaps there is no age of English satire that does not give forth the sound of that laughter unknown to savages—that craven laughter.

—Alice Meynell, "Andrew Marvell,"
Pall Mall Gazette, July 14, 1897

◈

WORKS

◈

Edgar Allan Poe
"Old English Poetry" (1845)

One of the best-known American authors of the nineteenth century, Edgar Allen Poe (1809–1849) is famous today for his gruesome and macabre poems and short stories, including "The Raven," "The Black Cat," and "The Tell-Tale Heart." A true man of letters, Poe below explicates the Marvell poem "Maiden lamenting for her Fawn." Unsurprisingly, Poe is captivated by the poem's more haunting features, including the "air of lamentation" that he believes pervades the works. Poe admires very much the tone of the piece, in that it captures what he calls a great "vigor" as well as an emotional, if perhaps more languorous, delicacy.

———

We copy a portion of Marvell's "Maiden lamenting for her Fawn"—which we prefer not only as a specimen of the elder poets, but in itself as a beautiful poem abounding in pathos, exquisitely delicate imagination and truthfulness, to anything of its species:

> It is a wondrous thing how fleet
> 'T was on those little silver feet,
> With what a pretty skipping grace
> It oft would challenge me the race,
> And when 't had left me far away,
> 'T would stay, and run again, and stay;
> For it was nimbler much than hinds,
> And trod as if on the four winds.
> I have a garden of my own,
> But so with roses overgrown,
> And lilies that you would it guess
> To be a little wilderness;
> And all the spring-time of the year
> It only loved to be there.
> Among the beds of lilies I
> Have sought it oft where it should lie,
> Yet could not till itself would rise
> Find it, although before mine eyes.
> For in the flaxen lilies shade,
> It like a bank of lilies laid;
> Upon the roses it would feed
> Until its lips even seemed to bleed,

And then to me 't would boldly trip,
And print those roses on my lip,
But all its chief delight was still
With roses thus itself to fill,
And its pure virgin limbs to fold
In whitest sheets of lilies cold.
Had it lived long it would have been
Lilies without, roses within.

How truthful an air of lamentation hangs here upon every syllable! It pervades all. It comes over the sweet melody of the words—over the gentleness and grace which we fancy in the little maiden herself—even over the half-playful, half-petulant air with which she lingers on the beauties and good qualities of her favorite—like the cool shadow of a summer cloud over a bed of lilies and violets, "and all sweet flowers." The whole is redolent with poetry of a very lofty order. Every line is an idea—conveying either the beauty and playfulness of the fawn, or the artlessness of the maiden, or her love, or her admiration, or her grief, or the fragrance and warmth and *appropriateness* of the little nest-like bed of lilies and roses which the fawn devoured as it lay upon them, and could scarcely be distinguished from them by the once happy little damsel who went to seek her pet with an arch and rosy smile on her face. Consider the great variety of truthful and delicate thought in the few lines we have quoted—the *wonder* of the maiden at the fleetness of her favorite—the "little silver feet"—the fawn challenging his mistress to a race with "a pretty skipping grace," running on before, and then, with head turned back, awaiting her approach only to fly from it again—can we not distinctly perceive all these things? How exceedingly vigorous, too, is the line,

And trod as if on the four winds!—

a vigor fully apparent only when we keep in mind the artless character of the speaker and the four feet of the favorite—one for each wind. Then consider the garden of "my own," so over grown—entangled—with roses and lilies, as to be "a little wilderness"—the fawn, loving to be there, and there "only"— the maiden seeking it "where it *should* lie"—and not being able to distinguish it from the flowers until "itself would rise"—the lying among the lilies "like a bank of lilies"—the loving to "fill itself with roses,"

And its pure virgin limbs to fold
In whitest sheets of lilies cold,

and these things being its "chief" delights—and then the pre-eminent beauty and naturalness of the concluding lines— whose very hyperbole only renders them more true to nature when we consider the innocence, the artlessness, the enthusiasm, the passionate grief, and more passionate admiration of the bereaved child—

> Had it lived long, it would have been
> Lilies without—roses within.

> —Edgar Allan Poe, "Old English Poetry"
> (1845), *Complete Works*, ed. James A.
> Harrison, vol. 12, pp. 143–46

LEIGH HUNT (1846)

A prolific author of the Romantic movement, Leigh Hunt (1784–1859) is best known today for *The Story of Rimini* as well as several smaller works. In the excerpt below Hunt contrasts the more lyrical works of Marvell, including "Bermuda" and "Nymph lamenting the loss of her Faun" (the same piece Poe is commenting upon, above,) with the satirical poems about the Stuart family of rulers. Hunt also indicates he does not blame Marvell for his political leanings at all, rather believing him to be a "true patriot" who believed in the state over politics.

Andrew Marvel, a thoughtful and graceful poet, a masterly prose-writer and controversialist, a wit of the first water, and, above all, an incorruptible patriot, is thought to have had no mean hand in putting an end to the dynasty of the Stuarts. His wit helped to render them ridiculous, and his integrity added weight to the sting. The enmity, indeed, of such a man was in itself a reproach to them; for Marvel, though bred on the Puritan side, was no Puritan himself, nor a foe to any kind of reasonable and respectable government. He had served Cromwell with his friend Milton, as Latin Secretary, but would have aided Charles the Second as willingly, in his place in Parliament, had the king been an honest man instead of a pensioner of France. The story of his refusing a *carte blanche* from the king's treasurer, and then sending out to borrow a guinea, would be too well known to need allusion to it in a book like the present, if it did not contain a specimen of a sort of practical wit.

Marvel being pressed by the royal emissary to state what would satisfy his expectations, and finding that there was no other mode of persuading him that he had none, called in his servant to testify to his dining three days in succession upon one piece of mutton.

Even the wise and refined Marvel, however, was not free from the coarseness of his age; and hence I find the same provoking difficulty as in the case of his predecessors, with regard to extracts from the poetical portion of his satire. With the prose I should not have been at a loss. But the moment these wits of old time began rhyming, they seem to have thought themselves bound to give the same after-dinner license to their fancy, as when they were called upon for a song. To read the noble ode on "Cromwell," in which such a generous compliment is paid to Charles the First,—the devout and beautiful one entitled "Bermuda," and the sweet overflowing fancies put into the mouth of the "Nymph lamenting the loss of her Faun,"—and then to follow up their perusal with some, nay most of the lampoons that were so formidable to Charles and his brother, you would hardly think it possible for the same man to have written both, if examples were not too numerous to the contrary. Fortunately for the reputation of Marvel's wit, with those who chose to become acquainted with it, he wrote a great deal better in prose than in verse, and the prose does not take the license of the verse.

—Leigh Hunt, *Wit and Humour,* 1846

JAMES RUSSELL LOWELL "DRYDEN" (1868)

An important American literary critic, James Russell Lowell (1819–1891) was also a noted poet and abolitionist. Below, Lowell comments on Marvell's "Horation Ode."

Marvell's "Horation Ode," the most truly classic in our language, is worthy of its theme. The same poet's Elegy, in parts noble, and everywhere humanly tender, is worth more than all Carlyle's biography as a witness to the gentler qualities of the hero, and of the deep affection that stalwart nature could inspire in hearts of truly masculine temper.

—James Russell Lowell, "Dryden" (1868),
Among My Books, 1870, p. 19

JOHN ORMSBY "ANDREW MARVELL" (1869)

John Ormsby (1829–1895) was a renowned translator of works into English. His 1885 translation of Miguel de Cervantes' *Don Quixote de la*

Mancha was considered the best of its time. In the piece below, Ormsby is concerned with Marvell's reception as a poet, which he traces through both Marvell's publishing history and his reputation in his own day. Ormsby's detailed description of the first editions of Marvell's work is unmatched anywhere else in this collection, and his discussion of works more recently attributed to Marvell provides a fascinating glimpse into how old, sometimes anonymous or rediscovered works are often ascribed (or, perhaps more commonly, unascribed) to a known writer. Ormsby then suggests that Marvell lacked for a more popular reputation in his own day because he himself did not court fame, either through publishing or public oration; Ormsby also argues that the "undeniable coarseness of some of his political satires" likewise did not help Marvell's reputation, as the author was careful to first circulate these works anonymously to avoid any political ramifications.

Ormsby then moves into an examination of Marvell's literary influences, suggesting that Donne was Marvell's greatest inspiration. Ormsby sees nothing particularly significant about this fact, suggesting that Donne was merely the popular writer during Marvell's years at university. Ormsby extends this reasoning to suggest that Donne and his followers were not out to create a new school or style of poetry when they began to write. Rather, they were motivated by "a desire of being distinguished for wit and fancy at a time when wit and fancy were especially held in honour; a nervous dread of being thought trite, unoriginal, and commonplace, if they should be found treading in the footsteps of others; and a sort of suspicion that the legitimate fields of imagination were already worked out, and that now nothing was left to the poet but to fall back upon ingenuity." Ormsby concludes his piece by examining in useful detail several of Marvell's more famous pieces, including "Nymph Complaining for the Death of Her Fawn," "Bermudas," "To His Coy Mistress," "Ametas and Thestylis Making Hay-ropes," "To a Fair Singer," and "A Character of Holland." Students working on Marvell will find these mini-explications particularly useful, as many of these poems remain amongst Marvell's most admired works today.

When Marvell's name occurs in any work on English literature or any collection of old English poetry, the mention is generally followed by the remark that as a poet he has not received full justice. In his lifetime he does not appear to have ranked as a poet at all, but that was because he himself laid no claim to the rank. The only productions of his in verse that appeared in print during his life were three or four commendatory pieces prefixed to works of friends after the friendly fashion of the time, and some political satires which were necessarily anonymous and unacknowledged. If with posterity he has not held his due place among the minor poets of his time, one cause, undoubtedly, is that he already occupies, in another character, a higher position in the eyes of the world. The "mind's eye" is so far like that of the body, that it finds a difficulty in seeing at once more than one side of any object, and having settled itself to one point of view, it is slow to take up any other. It was Marvell's fate to stand out before the eyes of succeeding generations as an example of purity and integrity in a corrupt age, and the brightness of his virtues has in some degree outshone the lustre of his genius. Had he been less brilliant as a patriot, he would have been more conspicuous as a poet.

It would be unjust, however, to represent Marvell as an altogether neglected poet. Up to the present time five editions of his poems have appeared, a number which implies a greater posthumous popularity than any of his contemporaries obtained—Milton, Butler, and Dryden excepted. The first, dated 1681, three years after his death, is clearly a mere bookseller's speculation, published without the authority or sanction of his family or friends, and without the editorial supervision of any one in any way qualified by acquaintance with the author or with his works. The surreptitious character of the collection is shown by the impudent address to the "ingenious reader," pretending to come from one "Mary Marvell," who certifies that the contents are printed according to the exact copies in the handwriting of her "late dear husband," found after his death among his other papers. Marvell was never married; and Cooke, the editor of the next edition of his works, gives us to understand that his papers were sold by the woman in whose house he lodged. The volume is a thin folio of 126 pages, which,—at least in every copy we have seen,—are made by an ingenious fault in the pagination to appear 140 in number. It is, however, fairly printed, and is embellished with a portrait somewhat in the manner of Faithorne, though without the finish characteristic of his work. Marvell's violent satires on the court and the court-party are, of course, excluded. Eight years afterwards, when the revolution was an accomplished fact, these, which up to that time had circulated only in manuscript, or else in clandestine printed tracts, came out with the author's name attached in that curious collection, the Poems on *Affairs of State*, so necessary to every one who wishes to study the history, politics, manners, or scandals of the reigns of the two last Stuarts. In 1726 Curll published a very neat duodecimo edition in two parts: the first containing very nearly the contents of the folio; the second, the political satires, some pieces of Latin and Greek verse, and a selection from Marvell's letters. This was edited, with some care, by Thomas Cooke, who claims to have corrected the errors of the folio, and to have been careful to exclude some pieces which there, and also in the *Poems on Affairs of State,* have been wrongly attributed to the author. He has, however, reproduced everything in the folio except a dozen Latin verses on the Louvre, and every one of the pieces ascribed to Marvell in the State *Poems,* two of which are certainly not by his hand. The two we refer to are *Oceana and Britannia,* and *Hodge's Vision from the Monument,* both of which contain allusions to events that occurred after Marvell's death, especially events in connection with the so-called Popish plot, the execution of Coleman, Wakeman's trial, and the browbeating of the witnesses by Scroggs and Jones. The plot was disclosed on the 12th of August, 1678, and Marvell died four days afterwards, its first victim in the opinon of many at the time; for the suddenness of his death, and the absence of any perceptible cause, were held to be conclusive evidence of poison. The suspicion had no foundation in fact, but at such a time it was not unnatural. Marvell was a marked man as a foremost champion of Protestantism, and an uncompromising enemy of the Popish party which had, or was supposed to have, its hopes set upon the Duke of York; and no name was more likely than his to hold a high place on a roll of obnoxious Protestants to be removed on the earliest opportunity—a document the existence of which was firmly believed in by a large majority. The satires in question belong so nearly to Marvell's time, and, though wanting in the wit, pungency, and earnestness which mark all his writings of the same sort, bear such a general resemblance to his pieces in style and manner, that the error is, perhaps, somewhat excusable. It deserves notice, however, as it is one which has been repeated in every subsequent edition. In 1772, Davies, the friend of Johnson and Boswell, published an exact reprint of Cooke's edition and in 1776 Captain Edward Thompson produced his edition of the works of Marvell in prose and verse in three imposing-looking quarto volumes. This is, in some respects, the most valuable, in others the most worthless of all. Captain Thompson's only qualification for the task he undertook was an enthusiastic admiration for the personal character of his author. His zeal was abundant; it would be more correct to say superabundant; but in judgment, literary taste, and a comprehension of the duties of an editor he was entirely deficient. He had the assistance of a collection of documents previously made with a view to a complete edition of Marvell's works, among which was a manuscript book partly in Marvell's handwriting, containing, with other pieces, the well-known version of the 19th Psalm,—

The spacious firmament on high;

that of the 114th Psalm—

When Israel freed from Pharaoh's hand;

the hymn beginning with

When all thy mercies, O my God,
My rising soul surveys;

and also the ballad of *William and Margaret.* It is not made to appear that
these pieces were in Marvell's writing, but the discovery of them in a book
which was once in Marvell's possession and contained pieces in his writing,
was, to Captain Thompson's mind, full and sufficient proof that they were
his productions. As the claim thus set up has been recently reasserted, at
least as regards the first-mentioned piece, by an authority so well qualified
to give an opinion on literary questions as the *Athenceum,* it is necessary
to state the case somewhat at length. We need scarcely remind the reader
that the three first pieces of poetry appeared originally in the *Spectator,* and
that the second of them was, a few years later, acknowledged and published
as his own by Dr. Watts. Now it is incredible that a man of Dr. Watts's
character, a man too so scrupulous in acknowledging the most trifling
obligations to other writers, could have purloined an entire poem in so
barefaced a manner. The other two have been always attributed to Addison.
They belong to a series of "pieces of divine poetry," to use the *Spectator's*
favourite description, which appeared from time to time in the Saturday
numbers written by Addison. We have the *Spectator's* word for it that they
are all by the same author. "I shall never," he says in No. 461, "publish verse
on that day (Saturday) but what was written by the same hand." Therefore, if
we are to believe both Captain Thompson and the *Spectator,* not only these
two but also the version of the 23rd Psalm, in No. 441

The Lord my pasture shall prepare,
And lead me with a Shepherd's care;

and the verses in Nos. 489 and 513, beginning with

How are thy servants blest, O Lord!

and—

When rising from the bed of death—

are all the productions of Marvell. This is an attempt to prove too much. It in effect charges Addison, or the *Spectator,* with appropriating, not a fugitive piece, but a collection of pieces by an author of whom something at least must have been known to those who had obtained access to his writings. The *Athenceum* considers that the language of Addison in the essays in which these pieces are introduced favours the idea that he was not their author. We confess to holding an entirely opposite opinion: that the manner in which Addison introduced these pieces would be, to call it by the very mildest term, disingenuous, if he himself were not the author of them. That he was the author, however, we have, apart from probabilities and internal evidence, the statement of Pope. "He had," says Pope, as reported in *Spence's Anecdotes,* "a design of translating all the Psalms for the use of churches. Five or six of them that he did translate were published in the *Spectators.*" Two only of the five can be strictly called translations; but it is, of course, to these five pieces that Pope alludes. As regards the ballad of *William and Margaret* the case is simpler. It made its first appearance in print in 1724, in Aaron Hill's *Plain Dealer,* and also in the collection called *The Hive,* and was afterwards owned and printed by Mallet among his poems, with some slight alterations, and the explanation that it had been suggested to him by the fragment of the old ballad quoted in Fletcher's *Knight of the Burning Pestle.* Plagiarism has, as Dr. Johnson says, "been boldly charged but never proved" against Mallet in this matter; but, whoever the writer may have been, to any one conversant with old poetry it will be plain that he was a writer of the eighteenth and not of the seventeenth century. The same may be said of another ballad in *The Hive* collection, *The Despairing Shepherd,* which is also claimed for Marvell by Captain Thompson; and indeed, notwithstanding the opinion of the *Athenaeum,* we think the poems printed in the *Spectator* bear unmistakably the stamp of the same age. It is necessary to go into these particulars because the claims set up for Marvell must stand or fall together. In vulgar parlance they "row in the same boat," and if one sinks all sink. Against those claims there is the improbability of three men, Addison, Watts, and Mallet, all lighting upon the same mine of unpublished manuscript, and each pilfering and publishing as his own what suited him best. As we said before, Captain Thompson effectually disproves his case by attempting to prove too much. There is also the improbability of all of these pieces escaping the notice of a reasonably painstaking editor like Cooke, who was, besides, in communication with and assisted by members and friends of Marvell's family. All these poems

had been already many times printed and published at the time when
Cooke's edition appeared, and it is, to say the least, extremely unlikely that
persons interested in Marvell's name, and in posession of evidence to prove
his title to them, should have allowed them to pass unchallenged. From
the account, too, which Captain Thompson gives of the manuscript book in
which he found these pieces, it would seem that its existence and contents
could scarcely have been unknown to Cooke. Captain Thompson had it
from Mr. Raikes, who had it from Mr. Nettleton, who was the son of
Marvell's niece, and Marvell's two nieces are specially thanked by Cooke for
having furnished him with manuscripts and materials for his memoir and
edition. Against all this we have nothing but the personal conviction of an
uncritical sea-captain. There is nothing to show that the book was anything
more than a kind of poetical album, originally, it is possible, the property
of Marvell, but into which successive possessors copied such pieces as struck
their taste or fancy.

To Captain Thompson, however, we owe the addition of three pieces
undoubtedly Marvell's, which were probably considered too eulogistic of
Cromwell and the Commonwealth to be inserted in the edition of 1681: the
poem on Cromwell's Government—the genuineness of which is vouched
for by Marvell's old enemy. Bishop Parker,—that on the "Death of His late
Highness the Protector," and the "Horatian Ode upon Cromwell's Return
from Ireland," in which occur those noble lines on the death of Charles I.
so often quoted. Upon these, and the collection of Marvell's prose tracts
and letters, the merits of this edition rest, for the editor took no pains to
correct the errors or supply the deficiencies of his predecessors, and merely
flung together, without any attempt at order, method, or examination, all
the materials he could lay his hands upon.

The last edition we have to mention is one published in Boston (U.S.)
in 1857, a very elegant reprint of that of Cooke, supplemented by the
additional poems given by Captain Thompson.

It will be seen, from this statement of the case, that Marvell has not been
treated with that utter neglect which the expressions made use of by some of
his admirers would seem to imply. None of his contemporaries except those
we have named,—neither Cowley nor Waller nor Denham, so famous in
their own day, and still so conspicuous on the roll of English poets,—have
in modern times received so much attention from editors or publishers.
They, however, in a manner discounted their fame. They secured great
popularity while they lived, and left extant a sufficient number of editions
of their works to supply the demands of posterity for a considerable period.

Still, though not overlooked, Marvell cannot be said to have been generally recognized as one of the poets until the present century. That Dr. Johnson should have not thought him worthy of a place beside men whose lives and works are so ardently desired as those of Stepney, King, Duke, Yalden, Sprat, and Smith, is not indeed surprising. Marvell's earlier poetry is not of a kind at all likely to find favour in the eyes of a critic of Johnson's mould, and in manner as well as in matter, his political pieces are not well calculated to conciliate a Jacobite, high churchman, and strict moralist. He who could not forgive Milton could scarcely be expected to acknowledge Marvell. But it is not a little strange that his poetry should have been so generally excluded from the various collections and miscellanies of the last century, and his name so seldom mentioned by any of its writers. When Churchill alludes to him, it is of his "spotless virtue" he speaks; and Mason,—as far as we remember, the only one who seems aware of the fact that he was a poet,—commends him for deserting poetry for politics.

Another impediment to Marvell's fame as a poet is the undeniable coarseness of some of his political satires. His works come to us weighted with matter in the highest degree offensive to modern taste. This, however, was not the fault of the man but of the age he lived in, and it is one from which few of the writers of his time are free. For a satirist, indeed, it was scarcely possible to avoid it. Disregard of decency in conduct was the crying evil of the time; and in such cases the homoeopathic principle of *similia similibus curantur* has always been the one that has been acted upon. Party warfare, too, in those days was a rough struggle untempered by the courtesies and amenities which have been by degrees introduced into the strategy of modern politics. It was rather a *melee* fought out with any weapons that came to hand, than an organized and systematic contest waged at long range with arms of precision, and between large bodies of combatants. The periodical press was then barely in its infancy, and for attack and defence men had to trust rather to individual efforts than to the co-operation of numbers. For Marvell, besides, there is an excuse which cannot be pleaded for most of the other satirists of his day. His satires were intended for use simply, not for show. Dryden, like a skilled artificer, prided himself on the artistic finish of the weapon he forged: but Marvell plucked a cudgel from the nearest hedgerow, careless if it became fuel after it had served his purpose. It was meant to hurt, and it hurt all the more for those rough knots and excrescences so unsightly in our eyes. . . .

As a poet he is generally classed among the poets of Charles the Second's reign; but in reality he belongs to an earlier age, and has nothing whatever in common with Waller, Sedley, Dorset, or Rochester. He is, in fact, no more one of the Restoration poets than Milton. His true place is with the men of the preceding period,—with Herrick, Habingdon, Suckling, Lovelace, and Wither, to each of whom occasional resemblances may be traced in his poetry. But the poet that influenced him most, probably, was Donne. When Marvell was a student at Cambridge the influence of Donne's poetry was at its height, and it acted in the same way as the influence of Spenser in the preceding generation, of Cowley some thirty years later, and of Byron and Tennyson in modern times. Donne was the accepted poet with the young men, the orchestra-leader from whom they took their time and tone, and whose style, consciously or unconsciously, they assimilated. Marvell's earliest poem is an illustration of this. His satire on "Flecknoe, an English Priest at Rome," might easily pass for one of Donne's, so thoroughly has he caught not only the manner and rugged vigorous versification of Donne's satires, but also his very turns of thought, and the passion for elaborate conceits, recondite analogies, and out-of-the-way similitudes with which his poetry is so strongly imbued.

Few of the poets of the time of Charles I. and the Commonwealth escaped the infection of this, the metaphysical school of poetry, as Dryden somewhat awkwardly called it, which Donne is generally accused of having founded. In truth, neither he in England, nor Marini in Italy, nor Gongora in Spain, can be properly said to have founded a school. They were simply the most prominent masters of a certain style or method of writing, which came into fashion from causes independent of the example or teaching of any man, and affected prose as well as poetry. Its essential characteristic may be described as wit run to seed, or rather, perhaps, an unnatural growth of wit produced by the very richness and high cultivation of the literature of the period; for in each case the phenomenon made its appearance in, or immediately after, a period eminently rich in literature, that of Shakspeare, of Tasso, or of Cervantes and Lope de Vega. Metaphysical poets, Marinisti, or Conceptistas, all wrote under the same inspiration—a desire of being distinguished for wit and fancy at a time when wit and fancy were especially held in honour; a nervous dread of being thought trite, unoriginal, and commonplace, if they should be found treading in the footsteps of others; and a sort of suspicion that the legitimate fields of imagination were already worked out, and that now nothing was left to the poet but to fall back upon ingenuity. Traces of the prevailing fashion are to be met with frequently in Marvell's poems; and that they are not more abundant is probably owing to the fact that he wrote simply to please himself, "for his own hand," and not with any ambition of one day claiming a place among the poets. But in this respect there is a difference between his earlier and later verses. For instance, his "Nymph complaining for the Death of her Fawn," written, it would seem, before the close of the civil war, graceful, simple, and tender as the lines are, is not free from those *tours de force* of fancy which disfigure so much of the poetry of that day. Even the lowest, the mere verbal form of this forced wit, breaks out, e.g.:

> But Sylvio soon had me beguiled.
> This waxed tame; while he grew wild,
> And, quite regardless of my smart,
> Left me his *fawn,* but took his *heart.*

On the other hand, the poem on the "Bermudas," produced, we may fairly presume, several years later, when Marvell was in daily communication with John Oxenbridge,—one of those very exiles to the Bermudas whose feelings the poem is supposed to express,—is as direct, natural, and unaffected as a poem of Wordsworth's could be. Both of these pieces have been of late frequently printed in collections of old poetry and works on English literature, especially the last, which a critic whose taste and judgment no one will dispute, has called "a gem of melody, picturesqueness, and sentiment, nearly without a flaw." They are therefore, probably, too familiar already to the majority of our readers to justify quotation here, however tempting they may be as specimens of Marvell at his best; and we shall take, instead, a few illustrations from less-known poems. In the verses addressed "To his Coy Mistress," the extravagant fancy, that in the graver sort of poetry is a blemish, becomes an ornament, employed as it is to push a kind of *argumentum ad absurdum* to the farthest possible limits, and its effect is heightened by the exquisite assumption of gravity in the opening lines,—

> Had we but world enough and time,
> This coyness, lady, were no crime.
> We would sit down, and think which way
> To walk, and pass our long love's day.
> Thou by the Indian Ganges' side
> Should'st rubies find: I by the tide
> Of Humber would complain. I would
> Love you ten years before the flood:
> And you should, if you please, refuse

Till the conversion of the Jews.
My vegetable love should grow
Vaster than empires, and more slow.
An hundred years should go to praise
Thine eyes, and on thy forehead gaze:
Two hundred to adore each breast;
But thirty thousand to the rest.
An age at least to every part,—
And the last age should show your heart.
For, lady, you deserve this state:
Nor would I love at lower rate.
　　　But at my back I always hear
Time's winged chariot hurrying near:
And yonder all before us lie
Deserts of vast eternity.

The conclusion, therefore, is to the same effect as Herrick's advice, "Then be not coy, but use your time."

　　　Now, therefore, while the youthful hue
Sits on thy skin like morning dew,
Let us roll at our strength and all
Our sweetness up into one ball,
And tear our pleasures with rough strife
Thorough the iron gates of life.
Thus, though we cannot make our sun
Stand still, yet we will make him run.

The little poem of which we have here quoted the greater part is characteristic of Marvell in many ways, but more especially of that peculiarity of his which has been before alluded to, his trick—if anything so obviously natural and spontaneous can be called a trick—of passing suddenly from a light, bantering, trivial tone, to one of deep feeling, and even, as in the instance just quoted, of solemnity. Nothing in Suckling, or Carew, or any other of the poets to whom love-making in verse was a pastime, is more gay, folatre, careless, and at the same time, profoundly obsequious, than the first part; but lightly and playfully as the subject is treated, it suggests thoughts that lead to a graver and more impassioned strain. A few pages further on we find a poem which is in truth only a conceit expanded into a poem, but which in its very flimsiness shows a rare lightness of hand, and neatness of execution. It is a sort of miniature idyll cast in, the amoebean form, and entitled "Ametas and Thestylis making Hay-ropes."

Ametas: Think'st thou that this love can stand,
                Whilst thou still dost say me nay?
            Love unpaid does soon disband:
                Love binds love, as hay binds hay.
Thestylis: Thinks't thou that this rope would twine,
                If we both should turn one way?
            Where both parties so combine,
                Neither love will twist nor hay.
Ametas: Thus you vain excuses find,
                Which yourself and us delay;
            And love ties a woman's mind
                Looser than with ropes of hay.
Thestylis: What you cannot constant hope
                Must be taken as you may.
Ametas: Then let's both lay by our rope,
                And go kiss within the hay.

Nothing could be more designedly trifling than this, and yet what a finished elegance there is about it. It is not the highest art, perhaps, but there is a certain antique grace in the workmanship that reminds one, somehow, of a cameo or an old engraved gem. Charles Lamb, with his own peculiar felicity of expression, has hit off the precise phrase when he speaks of "a witty delicacy," as the prevailing quality in Marvell's poetry. If he did sin, as it must be confessed he did occasionally, in forcing wit beyond its legitimate bounds, he made amends for the offence by the graceful turn he gave to a conceit. To take an instance from the lines "To a Fair Singer": poets have again and again tasked their ingenuity to compliment ladies who are fortunate enough to add skill in music to their other charms, but we doubt if it has been ever done with greater elegance than here:

I could have fled from one but singly fair;
    My disentangled soul itself might save,
Breaking the curled trammels of her hair;
    But how should I avoid to be her slave,
Whose subtle art invisibly can wreathe
My fetters of the very air I breathe?

The taste for subtleties, ingenuities, and prettinesses, which here and there breaks out in Marvell's verse, is, however, his only artificiality. He had, what was very rare among his contemporaries, a genuine love and reverence for nature. Most of the poets of his day seem to treat nature in a somewhat patronizing spirit, as a good sort of institution, deserving of support, especially from poets, as being useful for supplying illustrations, comparisons, and descriptions available for poetic purposes. They, we suspect, regarded it very much as the cook does the shrubbery, from which he gets the holly and laurel leaves to garnish his dishes. Marvell is one of the few men of that time who appear to have delighted in nature for its own sake, and not merely for its capabilities in the way of furnishing ideas. He enjoyed it thoroughly and thankfully, and in the poems written during his residence with Lord Fairfax at Nun-Appleton, he shows a keen sense of pleasure in natural beauty and scenery, and, what was even rarer in those days, close observation and study of nature. The longest, that upon Appleton House, for an adequate specimen of which we have not sufficient space, is an ample proof of this, and from beginning to end "breathes"—to use a phrase of Washington Irving's—"the very soul of a rural voluptuary." One of his most graceful little poems, evidently belonging to this time, is a protest against the artificial gardening then coming into fashion, of which he says:

'Tis all enforced; the fountain and the grot,
    While the sweet fields do lie forgot:
Where willing nature does to all dispense
    A wild and fragrant innocence:
And fauns and fairies do the meadows till,
    More by their presence than their skill.
Their statues polished by some ancient hand,
    May to adorn the gardens stand:
But, howsoe'er the figures do excel,
    The Gods themselves do with us dwell.

The specimens we have quoted are rather one-sided, exhibiting Marvell's poetry only in its lighter and more elegant phase. In justice to his powers, we must give a few lines as an example of his graver and loftier verse. The following passage is from the conclusion of his poem "Upon the Death of his late Highness the Lord Protector"

Not much unlike the sacred oak which shoots
To heaven its branches, and through earth its roots,

Whose spacious boughs are hung with trophies
   round,
And honour'd wreaths have oft the victor crown'd;
When angry Jove darts lightning through the air
At mortals' sins, nor his own plant will spare,
It groans, and bruises all below, that stood
So many years the shelter of the wood,
The tree, erewhile foreshorten'd to our view,
When fall'n shows taller yet than as it grew.
So shall his praise to after times increase,
When truth shall be allowed and faction cease,
And his own shadows with him fall; the eye
Detracts from objects than itself more high;
But when Death takes them from that envied state,
Seeing how little, we confess how great.

There is one more point to be considered in connection with Marvell's
place among the minor poets of the seventeenth century. To Butler is
generally given the credit of having turned the extravagance of idea peculiar
to the so-called metaphysical school of poetry to good purpose, by enlisting it
in the service of burlesque, as he did in *Hudibras.* But Marvell has a certain
claim to a share of the credit, such as it is. His delightful vagary in verse
called "A Character of Holland" was written, as the latter portion clearly
shows, at the time of the great burst of national exultation at the victory
obtained by Blake, supported by Dean and Monk, over the Dutch under
Van Tromp, off Portland, in February, 1653, and, therefore, probably some
time before *Hudibras,* the first part of which did not appear till 1663. But to
whichever the merit of priority may belong, Marvell certainly struck the
same note as Butler, and if not with the same success, at least with sufficient
success to give him a high place among the poets of wit and humour. To take,
for example, his description of the genesis of Holland:

Glad then, as miners who have found the ore,
They, with mad labour, fished the land to shore;
And div'd as desperately for each piece
Of earth, as if 't had been of ambergris;
Collecting anxiously small loads of clay,
Less than what building swallows bear away;
Or than those pills which sordid beetles roll,
Transfusing into them their dunghill soul.

How they did rivet, with gigantic piles,
Thorough the centre their new catched miles;
And to the stake a struggling country bound,
Where barking waves still bait the forced ground;
Building their watery Babel far more high
To reach the sea, than those to scale the sky.

Here, as in Butler's happiest passages, we have the ludicrous exaggerations chasing each other like waves, and each as it rises seeming to overtop the absurdity of its predecessor.

Marvell's poetry cannot rank with the very highest in our language, but it unquestionably has high and varied qualities. It makes little pretension to depth or sublimity, but it abounds in wit and humour, true feeling, melody, and a certain scholarly elegance and delicate fancy. The late Mr. Tupling, the most erudite of London bibliopoles, used to add to the description of a copy of Marvell's poems in one of his quaint annotated catalogues of old books, "Few know how great the poetry here is." "Great" is not exactly the word; but it is at least genuine.

—John Ormsby, from "Andrew Marvell,"
Comhill Magazine, July 1869, pp. 21–40

EDWARD FITZGERALD (1872)

Edward Marlborough FitzGerald (1809–1883) was the first English translator of *The Rubaiyat of Omar Khayyam*. In the brief excerpt below FitzGerald comments on two of the most famous phrases from two of Marvell's most cherished works, "Appleton House" and "To His Coy Mistress."

By way of flourishing my Eyes, I have been looking into Andrew Marvell, an old favourite of mine—who led the way for Dryden in Verse, and Swift in Prose, and was a much better fellow than the last, at any rate.

Two of his lines in the Poem on "Appleton House," with its Gardens, Grounds, etc., run:

But most the *Hewel's* wonders are
Who here has the Holtseltster's care.

The "Hewel" being evidently the Woodpecker, who, by tapping the Trees, etc., does the work of one who measures and gauges Timber; here, rightly or wrongly, called "Holtseltster." "Holt" one knows: but what is "'seltster"? I do not find either this word or "Hewel" in Bailey or Halliwell. But "Hewel" may be a form of "Yaffil," which I read in some Paper that Tennyson had used for the Woodpecker in his Last Tournament.

This reminded me that Tennyson once said to me—some thirty years ago, or more—in talking of Marvell's "Coy Mistress," where it breaks in—

But at my back I always hear
Time's winged Chariot hurrying near, etc.

"*That* strikes me as Sublime—I can hardly tell why." Of course, this partly depends on its place in the Poem.

—Edward FitzGerald, Letter to
W.A. Wright, January 20, 1872

Goldwin Smith "Andrew Marvell" (1880)

An English historian and journalist, Goldwin Smith (1823–1910) became a prominent anti-slavery voice advocating for the Union position in England during the American Civil War. Mostly known as a political writer, Smith also penned texts on English history and literature. As a literary critic, Smith found much to admire and much to censure in Marvell. The excerpt below focuses briefly on several works—including "The Garden" and "The Bermudas"—but perhaps its most useful examinaiton is that on the "Horation Ode on Cromwell's Return from Ireland," a piece Smith calls "one of the noblest [odes] in the English language."

As a poet Marvell is very unequal. He has depth of feeling, descriptive power, melody; his study of the classics could not fail to teach him form; sometimes we find in him an airy and tender grace which remind us of the lighter manner of Milton: but art with him was only an occasional recreation, not a regular pursuit; he is often slovenly, sometimes intolerably diffuse, especially when he is seduced by the facility of the octosyllabic couplet. He was also eminently afflicted with the gift of 'wit' or ingenuity, much prized in his day. His conceits vie with those of Donne or Cowley. He is capable of saying of the Halcyon:—

The viscous air where'er she fly
Follows and sucks her azure dye;

The jellying stream compacts below,
If it might fix her shadow so.

And of Maria—

Maria such and so doth hush
The world and through the evening rush.
No new-born comet such a train
Draws through the sky nor star new-slain.
For straight those giddy rockets fail
Which from the putrid earth exhale,
But by her flames in heaven tried
Nature is wholly vitrified.

'The Garden' is an English version of a poem written in Latin by Marvell himself. It may have gained by being cast originally in a classical mould, which would repel prolixity and extravagant conceits. In it Marvell has been said to approach Shelley: assuredly he shows a depth of poetic feeling wonderful in a political gladiator. The thoughts that dwell in 'a green shade' have never been more charmingly expressed.

'A Drop of Dew', like 'The Garden', was composed first in Latin. It is a conceit, but a pretty conceit, gracefully as well as ingeniously worked out, and forms a good example of the contrast between the philosophic poetry of those days, a play of intellectual fancy, and its more spiritual and emotional counterpart in our own time. The concluding lines, with their stroke of 'wit' about the manna are a sad fall.

'The Bermudas' was no doubt suggested by the history of the Oxenbridges. It is the 'holy and cheerful note' of a little band of exiles for conscience sake wafted by Providence in their 'small boat' to a home in a land of beauty.

'Young Love' is well known, and its merits speak for themselves. It is marred by the intrusion in the third and fourth stanzas of the fiercer and coarser passion.

The 'Horatian Ode on Cromwell's Return from Ireland' cannot be positively proved to be the work of Marvell. Yet we can hardly doubt that he was its author. The point of view and the sentiment, combining admiration of Cromwell with respect and pity for Charles, are exactly his: the classical form would be natural to him; and so would the philosophical conceit which disfigures the eleventh stanza. The epithet *indefatigable* applied to Cromwell recurs in a poem which is undoubtedly his; and so does the emphatic expression of belief that the hero could have been happier in private life, and that he sacrificed himself to the State in taking the supreme command. The compression and severity of style are not characteristic of Marvell; but they would be imposed on him in this case by his model. If the ode is really his, to take it from him would be to do him great wrong. It is one of the noblest in the English language, and worthily presents the figures and events of the great tragedy as they would impress themselves on the mind of an ideal spectator, at once feeling and dispassionate. The spirit of Revolution is described with a touch in the lines

Though Justice against Fate complain
And plead the ancient rights in vain
    (But those do hold or break
      As men are strong or weak).

Better than anything else in our language this poem gives an idea of a grand Horatian measure, as well as of the diction and spirit of an Horatian ode.

Of the lines 'On Milton's *Paradise Lost*' some are vigorous; but they are chiefly interesting from having been written by one who had anxiously watched Milton's genius at work.

Marvell's amatory poems are cold; probably he was passionless. His pastorals are in the false classical style, and of little value. 'Clorinda and Damon' is about the best of them, and about the best of that is

Near this a fountain's liquid bell
Tinkles within the concave shell.

The Satires in their day were much admired and feared: they are now for the most part unreadable. The subjects of satire as a rule are ephemeral; but a great satirist like Juvenal or Dryden preserves his flies in the amber of his general sentiment. In Marvell's satires there is no amber: they are mere heaps of dead flies. Honest indignation against iniquity and lewdness in high places no doubt is there; but so are the meanness of Restoration politics and the dirtiness of Restoration thought. The curious may look at 'The Character of Holland,' the jokes in which are as good or as bad as ever, though the cannon of Monk and De Ruyter have ceased to roar; and in 'Britannia and Raleigh' the passage of which giving ironical advice to Charles II is a specimen of the banter which was deemed Marvell's peculiar gift, and in which Swift and Junius were his pupils.

Like Milton, Marvell wrote a number of Latin poems. One of them had the honour of being ascribed to Milton.

—Goldwin Smith, "Andrew Marvell,"
The English Poets, ed. Thomas Humphry Ward,
1880, vol. 2, pp. 382–84

EDMUND GOSSE "THE REACTION" (1885)

In the piece below, Gosse waxes poetically over Marvell and his works. He begins by tracing Marvell's inspiration to his stay at Nunappleton, the house that inspired his famous "Upon Appleton House" and other works. Gosse suggests that the place "made a lyrical poet" of Marvell, a broad declaration of the house's importance to Marvell's work. Perhaps more useful to students of the poet is Gosse's lengthy and astute comparison of Marvell to his fellow metaphysical poet John Donne. Gosse explores some of the conceits and stylistics that the two poets share, arguing, "Marvell is the last of the school of Donne, and in several respects he comes nearer to the master than any of his precursors." This discussion includes a useful examination of Marvell's "The Garden," which Gosse suggests originated a poetic style that highlights "a personal sympathy with nature, and particularly with vegetation, which was quite a novel thing, and which found no second exponent until Wordsworth came forward with his still wider and more philosophical commerce with the inanimate world."

I have . . . to present the greatest and the most interesting of the poets who wrote during the Commonwealth in opposition to Waller and his followers. The name of Andrew Marvell is illustrious wherever political purity is valued, wherever intellectual liberty is defended. To dwell upon the qualities of a character so candid, and upon the virtues of so single-minded a patriot, may seem out of place in a disquisition on the rise of classical poetry in England, but this patriot, this exquisite citizen, was a poet also, and a poet worthy of his civic reputation. Nor was there anything inconsistent in the fact that a man whose hands were pure in an age of universal corruption, and who put the interests of the people first when public virtue had scarcely been discovered, should be a romantic idealist when he came to put his innermost thoughts down in metre. Marvell is nothing if not consistent, and we find the same brain and heart engaged with rustic visions at Nunappleton and with the anger of statecraft at Westminster. . . .

The world is seldom told at what stray and occasional moments, how hurriedly, and again how seldom, a poet's inspiration flows. It may well be that the music lies frozen at a young man's heart until some peculiar condition in his circumstances, a chain of emotions called forth by some peaceful and novel situation, melts it into sudden poetry. In a few months, perhaps, the conditions change, the mind is released from its tension, and he has written in that short time most of what is to introduce him to posterity as a poet. In ages of general political disorder, and of civic and personal insecurity, this must particularly be the case. We know for how long a time the muse of Milton was silenced by public and private anxieties, and we should be ignorant of one great section of his genius, of his romantic and melodious power in lyrical writing, if it had not been for his retirement at Horton. What Horton was to Milton, Nunappleton was to Marvell, it made a lyrical poet of him.

This series of verses was carefully preserved by his widow, and given to the world, with other of his pieces, in a small folio, in 1681. A fine copy of this rare book is one of the most dainty and desirable of all English publications from the Restoration to the end of the century. It is not quite complete, and notably the celebrated Horatian Ode on Oliver Cromwell is not included in it,—Mrs Marvell did not trouble herself with any poems but those which she possessed in her husband's handwriting,—but it is still the most luxurious shape in which Marvell's poems can be read. The Nunappleton pieces are strewed over it without any attempt at arrangement, and the one which holds the key to the rest is printed last. This is a long poem in praise of the house, written in eight-line stanzas of octo-syllabic verse, and extending to nearly eight hundred lines. Any student who wishes to understand Marvell must read this long and difficult piece with care. He will soon see that he has to deal with what Dr. Johnson called a "metaphysical," and what I have ventured to call a "Marinist" poet of the most extreme order.

Marvell is the last of the school of Donne, and in several respects he comes nearer to the master than any of his precursors. Certain conceits of Donne's, for instance that one about the lover and the pair of compasses, are often quoted as examples of a monstrous class. We get to think of Donne as exclusively the forger of tawdry false jewellery such as this, "rime's sturdy cripple," as Coleridge ingeniously calls him. But Donne was also the writer of lines and passages that speak so directly to the heart and to the senses that those who have come under their spell feel a sort of shyness in quoting them; they are so personal that to discuss them seems an indiscretion. Something of the same odd reserve seems due in the reader of some of Shakespeare's *Sonnets,* of some of Coleridge's shorter poems. I cannot, myself, bear to hear poetry of this intimate kind analyzed or even touched by unsympathetic people. This is a feeling which may not be praiseworthy in the student, but it is a proof of extraordinary felicity, mingled with sincerity, in the style of the writer so discussed or touched. There can be no doubt that Donne possesses this quality, denied perhaps to all his scholars, until revealed again, in a certain measure, in Marvell. The note, however, is not so sharply struck in him as in Donne; there is more suavity and grace. The conceits are perhaps as wild. Here is one:

> Love wisely had of long foreseen
>   That he must once grow old,
> And therefore stored a magazine,
>   To save him from the cold.
> He kept the several cells replete
>   With nitre thrice refined,
> The naphtha's and the sulphur's heat,
>   And all that burns the mind.

This terrible magazine, which is fortified by a double gate, and which would have enflamed the whole of nature if one spark had fallen into it, turns out to be—the heart of Celia. Again, whole stanzas in the Nunappleton poem are taken up with a description of the garden as a military camp, through which the bee beats his drum, while the flowers are soldiers, who fire off volleys of perfume, and stand at parade, under their various colours, in stately regiments all day long:

> But when the vigilant patrol
> Of stars walks round about the pole,
> Their leaves that to their stalks are curled,
> Seem to their staves the ensigns furled.
> Then in some flower's beloved hut
> Each bee as sentinel is shut,
> And sleeps so too, but if once stirr'd
> She runs you thro' or asks the word.

This is pretty and harmless, but perhaps just because it errs so gently against the canons of style, we ask ourselves how so seriously-minded a man as Marvell could run on in such a childish way. There is a good deal in Marvell that is of this species of wit, graceful and coloured, but almost infantile. Waller and Denham had taught English people to outgrow these childish toys of fancy, and if there had been nothing more than this in Marvell, we should not be regarding him as a serious element in the reaction. But there is a great deal more, and allowing the conceits to be taken for granted, we may inquire into the character of what is best in his lyrics.

In the long Nunappleton poem, then, and in that celebrated piece which is printed now in most collections of English poetry, "The Garden," we find a personal sympathy with nature, and particularly with vegetation, which was quite a novel thing, and which found no second exponent until Wordsworth came forward with his still wider and more philosophical commerce with the inanimate world. For flowers, trees, and grasses, Marvell expresses a sort of personal passion. They stand between him and humanity, they are to him "forms more real than living man." He calls upon the woodlands of Nunappleton to save him from the noisy world:

> Bind me, ye woodbines, in your twines,
> Curl me about, ye gadding vines,
> And oh! so close your circles lace
> That I may never leave this place.

Again he says:

> How safe, methinks, and strong, behind
> These trees have I encamped my mind,

and he repeats this sentiment of the security of natural solitude again and again. His style, when he can put his conceits behind him, is extremly sharp and delicate, with a distinction of phrase that is quite unknown to most of his contemporaries. To praise "The Garden" or "Bermudas" would be an impertinence; but I think few readers know what charming and unique poetry lies hid in the series of poems in which Marvell writes as a Mower, with a fantastical regret for the flowers and grasses that he cuts down. He says:

> I am the mower Damon, known
> Through all the meadows I have mown,
> On me the morn her dew distils
> Before her darling daffodils.

He declares a profound passion for a possible Juliana, but it is really the wood-moths gleaming on the bark, the vigilant heron in its nest at the top of the ash-tree, the garish eye of the new-hatched throstle staring through the hazels, that hold his poetical affections. He is the last of the English romantic poets for several generations, and no one of them all, early or late, has regarded nature with a quicker or more loving attention than he. He is an alien indeed among the men of periwigs and ruffles.

—Edmund Gosse, from "The Reaction,"
From Shakespeare to Pope, 1885, pp. 211–21

A.C. BENSON "ANDREW MARVELL" (1892)

Arthur Christopher Benson (1862–1925) was a prominent English educator, poet, and critic. Brother to novelist E.F. Benson, A.C. Benson is best remembered today as the author of the patriotic tune, "Land of Hope and Glory." In his lifetime, however, he was a renowned academic and literary scholar, who taught at Eton College and was Master of Magdalene College of Cambridge University. Benson begins the essay below by examining the role Marvell's public life and politics played in his work before moving on to examine how Marvell's time at Nunappleton House also impacted his writing. Benson sees the influence of Nunappleton at work in Marvell's famous "Mower" poems, for example, and Benson's examination of these works is the most thorough in this entire text. This leads Benson into a discussion of Marvell's imagery in general, using several of his nature works as guides. Benson writes, "Marvell's imagery is sometimes at fault," especially when Marvell relies on literary conceit. Benson declares that the strength of Marvell's style is his "unexpectedness," and when he relies on more common seventeenth-century conceits, he fails to be unexpected.

According to Benson, it is in Marvell's nature poetry that most of his fame lies. As a pastoral poet, Benson finds Marvell remarkably "modern," and notes that all of these poems have "a strain of originality." Though Benson faults the occasional "monotony" of his subject (Benson laments that Marvell often repeats subjects and the way in which he describes said subject) these are the faults "of a young man trying his wings." Despite the prominence of Marvell's pastoral work, however, Benson seems more enthralled with the works he labels the panegyrics, and chief amongst these works in Marvell's Horation ode on Cromwell's return from Ireland: "It [the poem] has force with grace, originality with charm, in almost every stanza." This particular poem was one of the most remarked upon for Marvell in the nineteenth century, and it is thus no surprise that Benson is impressed by the piece as well.

Benson is less impressed with Marvell's satires, labeling them a "humiliating epoch" and Marvell "a satirist of the coarsest kind. His pages are crowded with filthy pictures and revolting images; the leaves cannot be turned over so quickly but some lewd epithet or vile realism prints itself on the eye. His apologists have said that it is nothing but the overflowing indignation of a noble mind when confronted with the hideous vices of a corrupt court and nation; that this deep-seated wrath is but an indication of the fervid idealistic nature of the man; that the generous fire that warmed in the poems, consumed in the satires; that the true moralist does not condone but condemn." Benson's views on Marvell's satires are shared by many of his fellow critics in this text; yet students will likely find Benson's more positive remonstrations of the "Mower" works and his "panegyric" texts the most useful sections in Benson's piece.

Few poets are of sufficiently tough and impenetrable fibre to be able with impunity to mix with public affairs. Even though the spring of their inspiration be like the fountain in the garden of grace, "drawn from the brain of the purple mountain that stands in the distance yonder," that stream is apt to become sullied at the very source by the envious contact of the world. Poets conscious of their vocation have generally striven sedulously, by sequestering their lives somewhat austerely from the current of affairs, to cultivate the tranquillity and freshness on which the purity of their utterance depends. If it be hard to hear sermons and remain a Christian, it is harder to mix much with men and remain an idealist. And if this be true of commerce in its various forms, law, medicine, and even education, it seems to be still more fatally true of politics. Of course the temptation of politics to a philosophical mind is very great. To be at the centre of the machine, to be able perhaps to translate a high thought into a practical measure; to be able to make some closer reconciliation between law and morality, as the vertical sun draws the shadow nearer to the feet,—all this to a generous mind has an attraction almost supreme.

And yet the strain is so great that few survive it. Sophocles was more than once elected general, and is reported to have kept his colleagues in good humour by the charm of his conversation through a short but disagreeable campaign. Dante was an ardent and uncompromising revolutionary. Goethe and Lamartine were statesmen. Among our own poets, the lives of Spenser and Addison might perhaps be quoted as fairly successful compromises; but of the poets of the first rank Milton is the only one who deliberately abandoned poetry for half a lifetime, that he might take an active part in public life.

It is perhaps to Milton's example, and probably to his advice, that we owe the loss of a great English poet. It seems to have been, if not at Milton's instigation, at any rate by his direct aid, that Andrew Marvell was introduced to public life. The acquaintance began at Rome; but Marvell was introduced into Milton's intimate society, as his assistant secretary, at a most impressionable age. He had written poetry, dealing like "L'Allegro" and "Il Penseroso" mainly with country

subjects, and was inclined no doubt to hang on the words of the older poet as
on an oracle of light and truth. We can imagine him piecing out his aspirations
and day-dreams, while the poet of sterner stuff, yet of all men least insensible
to the delights of congenial society, points out to him the more excellent way,
bidding him to abjure Amaryllis for a time. He has style, despatches will give
it precision; knowledge of men and life will confirm and mature his mind; the
true poet must win a stubborn virility if he is to gain the world. The younger
and more delicate mind complies; and we lose a great poet, Milton gains an
assistant secretary, and the age a somewhat gross satirist.

At a time like this, when with a sense of sadness we can point to more
than one indifferent politician who might have been a capable writer, and so
very many indifferent writers who could have been spared to swell the ranks
of politicians, we may well take the lesson of Andrew Marvell to heart.

The passion for the country which breathes through his earlier poems,
the free air which ruffles the page, the summer languors, the formal garden
seen through the casements of the cool house, the close scrutiny of
woodland sounds, such as the harsh laughter of the woodpecker, the shrill
insistence of the grasshopper's dry note, the luscious content of the drowsy,
croaking frogs, the musical sweep of the scythe through the falling swathe;
all these are the work of no town-bred scholar like Milton, whose country
poems are rather visions seen through the eyes of other poets, or written as
a man might transcribe the vague and inaccurate emotions of a landscape
drawn by some old uncertain hand and dimmed by smoke and time. Of
course Milton's "Il Penseroso" and "L'Allegro" have far more value even as
country poems than hundreds of more literal transcripts. From a literary
point of view indeed the juxtapositions of half a dozen epithets alone would
prove the genius of the writer. But there are no sharp outlines; the scholar
pauses in his walk to peer across the watered flat, or raises his eyes from his
book to see the quiver of leaves upon the sunlit wall; he notes an effect it
may be; but his images do not come like treasures lavished from a secret
storehouse of memory.

With Andrew Marvell it is different, though we will show by instances
that even his observation was sometimes at fault. Where or when this
passion came to him we cannot tell; whether in the great walled garden at
the back of the old school-house at Hull, where his boyish years were spent;
at Cambridge, where the oozy streams lapped and green fens crawled almost
into the heart of the town, where snipe were shot and wild-duck snared on the
site of some of its now populous streets; at Meldreth perhaps, where doubtless
some antique kindred lingered at the old manor-house that still bears his

patronymic, "the Marvells." Wherever it was,—and such tastes are rarely formed in later years—the delicate observation of the minute philosopher, side by side with the art of intimate expression, grew and bloomed.

We see a trace of that learning nature, the trailing dependence of the uneasy will of which we have already spoken, in a story of his early years. The keen-eyed boy, with his fresh colour and waving brown hair, was thrown on the tumultuous world of Cambridge, it seems, before he was thirteen years of age; a strange medley no doubt,—its rough publicity alone saving it, as with a dash of healthy freshness, from the effeminacy and sentimentalism apt to breed in more sheltered societies. The details of the story vary; but the boy certainly fell into the hands of Jesuits, who finally induced him to abscond to one of their retreats in London, where over a bookseller's shop, after a long and weary search, his father found him and persuaded him to return. Laborious Dr. Grosart has extracted from the Hull Records a most curious letter relating to this incident, in which a man whose son has been inveigled away in similar circumstances, asks for advice from Andrew Marvell's father.

Such an escapade belongs to a mind that must have been ardent and daring beyond its fellows; but it also shows a somewhat shifting foundation, an imagination easily dazzled, and a pliability of will that cost us, we may believe, a poet. After Cambridge came some years of travel, which afforded material for some of his poems, such as the satire on Holland, of which the cleverness is still apparent, though its elaborate coarseness and pedantic humour make it poor pasture to feed the mind upon.

But the period to which we owe almost all the true gold among his poems, is the two years which he spent at Nunappleton House, 1650–1652, as tutor to the daughter of the great Lord Fairfax, the little Lady Mary Fairfax, then twelve years old. Marvell was at this time twenty-nine; and that exquisite relation which may exist between a grown man, pure in heart, and a young girl, when disparity of fortune and circumstance forbids all thought of marriage, seems to have been the mainspring of his song. Such a relation is half tenderness which dissembles its passion, and half worship which laughs itself away in easy phrases. The lyric "Young Love," which indubitably though not confessedly refers to Mary Fairfax, is one of the sweetest poems of pure feeling in the language.

> Common beauties stay fifteen;
>   Such as yours should swifter move,
> Whose fair blossoms are too green
>   Yet for lust, but not for love.

Love as much the snowy lamb,
 Or the wanton kid, doth prize
As the lusty bull or ram,
 For his morning sacrifice.
Now then love me; Time may take
 Thee before thy time away;
Of this need we'll virtue make,
 And learn love before we may.

It is delightful in this connection to think of the signet-ring with the device of a fawn,—which he used in early life and may still be seen on his papers,—as a gift of his little pupil, earned doubtless by his poem on the Dying Fawn, which is certainly an episode of Lady Mary's childhood.

In this group of early poems, which are worth all the rest of Marvell's work put together, several strains predominate. In the first place there is a close observation of Nature, even a grotesque transcription, with which we are too often accustomed only to credit later writers. For instance, in "Damon the Mower" he writes:

The grasshopper its pipe gives o'er,
And hamstringed frogs can dance no more;
But in the brook the green frog wades,
And grasshoppers seek out the shades.

The second line of this we take to refer to the condition to which frogs are sometimes reduced in a season of extreme drought, when the pools are dry. Marvell must have seen a frog with his thighs drawn and contracted from lack of moisture making his way slowly through the grass in search of a refreshing swamp; this is certainly minute observation, as the phenomenon is a rare one. Again, such a delicate couplet as,

And through the hazels thick espy
The hatching throstle's shining eye,

is not the work of a scholar who walks a country road, but of a man who will push his way into the copses in early spring, and has watched with delight the timorous eye and the upturned beak of the thrush sunk in her nest. Or again, speaking of the dwindled summer stream running so perilously clear after weeks of drought that the fish are languid:

The stupid fishes hand, as plain
As flies in crystal overta'en,

Or of the hayfield roughly mown, into which the herd has been turned to graze:

And what below the scythe increast,
Is pinched yet nearer by the beast.

The mower's work, begun and ended with the dews, in all its charming monotony, seems to have had a peculiar attraction for Marvell; he recurs to it in more than one poem.

I am the mower Damon, known
Through all the meadows I have mown:
On me the morn her dew distils
Before her darling daffodils.

And again, of the mowers,

Who seem like Israelites to be
Walking on foot through a green sea,
To them the grassy deeps divide
And crowd a lane to either side.

The aspects of the country on which he dwells with deepest pleasure—and here lies the charm—are not those of Nature in her sublimer or more elated moods, but the gentler and more pastoral elements, that are apt to pass unnoticed at the time by all but the true lovers of the quiet country side, and crowd in upon the mind when surfeited by the wilder glories of peak and precipice, or where tropical luxuriance side by side with tropical aridity blinds and depresses the sense, with the feeling that made Browning cry from Florence,

Oh, to be in England, now that April's there! Marvell's lines, "On the Hill and Grove at Billborow," are an instance of this; there is a certain fantastic craving after antithesis and strangeness, it is true, but the spirit underlies the lines. The poem however must be read in its entirety to gain the exact impression.

Again, for simple felicity, what could be more airily drawn than the following from "The Garden"?—

Here at the fountain's sliding foot,
Or at some fruit-tree's mossy root,
Casting the body's vest aside,
My soul into the boughs doth glide,
There like a bird it sits and sings,
Then whets and claps its silver wings.

Or this, from the Song to celebrate the marriage of Lord Fauconberg and the Lady Mary Cromwell, of the undisturbed dead of night?—

> The astrologer's own eyes are set,
> And even wolves the sheep forget;
> Only this shepherd, late and soon,
> Upon this hill outwakes the moon.
> Hark! how he sings with sad delight
> Through the clear and silent night.

Other poems, such as the "Ode on the Drop of Dew" and the "Nymph Complaining for the Death of her Fawn," too long to be quoted here, are penetrated with the same essence.

At the same time it must be confessed that Marvell's imagery is sometimes at fault—it would be strange if it were not so; he falls now and then, the wonder is how rarely, to a mere literary conceit. Thus the mower Damon sees himself reflected in his scythe; the fawn feeds on roses till its lip "seems to bleed," not with a possibly lurking thorn, but with the hue of its pasturage. With Hobbinol and Tomalin for the names of swain and nymph unreality is apt to grow. When the garden is compared to a fortress and its scents to a salvo of artillery—

> Well shot, ye firemen! O how sweet
> And round your equal fires do meet—

and,

> Then in some flower's beloved hut
> Each bee as sentinel is shut,
> And sleeps so, too—but if once stirred,
> She runs you through, nor asks the word—

here, in spite of a certain curious felicity, we are in the region of false tradition and rococo expression. The poem of "Eyes and Tears," again (so whimsically admired by Archbishop Trench), is little more than a string of conceits; and when in "Mourning" we hear that

> She courts herself in amorous rain,
> Herself both Danae and the shower;

when we are introduced to Indian divers who plunge in the tears and can find no bottom, we think of Macaulay's "Tears of Sensibility," and Crashaw's fearful lines on the Magdalene's eyes—

Two walking baths, two weeping motions,
Portable and compendious oceans.

Nevertheless Marvell's poems are singularly free as a rule from this strain of affectation. He has none of the morbidity that often passes for refinement. The free air, the wood-paths, the full heat of the summer sun—this is his scenery; we are not brought into contact with the bones beneath the rose-bush, the splintered sun-dial, and the stagnant pool. His pulses throb with ardent life, and have none of the "inexplicable faintness" of a deathlier school. What would not Crashaw have had to say of the "Nuns of Appleton" if he had been so unfortunate as to have lighted on them? But Marvell writes:

Our orient breaths perfumed are
With incense of incessant prayer,
And holy water of our tears
Most strangely our complexion clears;
Not tears of Grief, but such as those
With which calm Pleasure overflows.

And passing by a sweet and natural transition to his little pupil, the young Recluse of Nunappleton—

I see the angels, in a crown,
On you the lilies showering down,
And, round about you, glory breaks,
That something more than human speaks

The poems contain within themselves the germ of the later growth of satire in the shape of caustic touches of humour, as well as a certain austere philosophy that is apt to peer behind the superficial veil of circumstance, yet without dreary introspection. There is a "Dialogue between Soul and Body," which deals with the duality of human nature which has been the despair of all philosophers and the painful axiom of all religious teachers. Marvell makes the Soul say;

Constrained not only to endure
Diseases, but what's worse, the cure,
And ready oft the port to gain,
Am shipwrecked into health again.

In the same connection in "The Coronet," an allegory of theIdeal and the Real, he says:

Alas! I find the serpent old,
Twining in his speckled breast,
About the flowers disguised doth fold,
With wreaths of fame and interest.

Much of Marvell's philosophy however has not the same vitality, born of personal struggle and discomfiture, but is a mere echo of stoical and pagan views of life and its vanities drawn from Horace and Seneca, who seem to have been his favourite authors. Such a sentiment as the following, from "Appleton House"—

But he, superfluously spread,
Demands more room alive than dead;
What need of all this marble crust,
To impart the wanton mole of dust?—

and from "The Coy Mistress"—

The grave's a fine and private place,
But none, methinks, do there embrace—

are mere pagan commonplaces, however daintily expressed.

But there is a poem, an idyll in the form of a dialogue between Clorinda and Damon, which seems to contain an original philosophical motive. Idylls in the strict sense of the word are not remarkable for including a moral; or if they do include one it may be said that it is generally bad, and is apt to defend the enjoyment of an hour against the conscience of centuries; but in "Clorinda and Damon," the woman is the tempter, and Damon is obdurate. She invites him to her cave, and describes its pleasures.

Clo.: A fountain's liquid bell
Tinkles within the concave shell.
Da.: Might a soul bathe there and be clean,
Or slake its drought?
Clo.: What is't you mean?
Da.: Clorinda, pastures, caves, and springs,
These once had been enticing things.
Clo: And what late change?—
Da.. The other day
Pan met me.
Clo.: What did great Pan say?
Da.: Words that transcend poor shepherds' skill.

This poem seems a distinct attempt to make of the sickly furniture of the idyll a vehicle for the teaching of religious truth. Is it fanciful to read in it a poetical rendering of the doctrine of conversion, the change that may come to a careless and sensuous nature by being suddenly brought face to face with the Divine light? It might even refer to some religious experience of Marvell's own: Milton's "mighty Pan," typifying the Redeemer, is in all probability the original.

The work then on which Marvell's fame chiefly subsists—with the exception of one poem which belongs to a different class, and will be discussed later, the Horatian Ode—may be said to belong to the regions of nature and feeling, and to have anticipated in a remarkable degree the minute observation of natural phenomena characteristic of a modern school, even to a certain straining after unusual, almost bizarre effects. The writers of that date, indeed, as Green points out, seem to have become suddenly and unaccountably modern, a fact which we are apt to overlook owing to the frigid reaction of the school of Pope. Whatever the faults of Marvell's poems may be, and they are patent to all, they have a strain of originality. He does not seem to imitate, he does not even follow the lines of other poets; never,—except in a scattered instance or two, where there is a faint echo of Milton,—does he recall or suggest that he has a master.

At the same time the lyrics are so short and slight that any criticism upon them is apt to take the form of a wish that the same hand had written more, and grown old in his art. There is a monotony, for instance, about their subjects, like the song of a bird, recurring again and again to the same phrase; there is an uncertainty, an incompleteness not so much of expression as of arrangement, a tendency to diverge and digress in an unconcerned and vagabond fashion. There are stanzas, even long passages, which a lover of proportion such as Gray (who excised one of the most beautiful stanzas of the Elegy because it made too long a parenthesis) would never have spared. It is the work of a young man trying his wings, and though perhaps not flying quite directly and professionally to his end, reveling in the new-found powers with a delicious ecstasy which excuses what is vague and prolix; especially when over all is shed that subtle, precious quality which makes a sketch from one hand so unutterably more interesting than a finished picture from another,—which will arrest with a few commonplace phrases, lightly touched by certain players, the attention which has wandered throughout a whole sonata.

The strength of Marvell's style lies in its unexpectedness. You are arrested by what has been well called a "pre-destined" epithet, not a mere otiose addition, but a word which turns a noun into a picture; the "hook-shouldered" hill "to abrupter greatness thrust," "the sugar's uncorrupting oil," "the vigilant patrol of stars," "the squatted thorns," "the oranges like golden lamps in a green night," "the garden's fragrant innocence,"— these are but a few random instances of a tendency that meets you in every poem. Marvell had in fact the qualities of a consummate artist, and only needed to repress his luxuriance and to confine his expansiveness. In his own words,

> Height with a certain grace doth bend,
> But low things clownishly ascend.

Before passing on to discuss the satires I may be allowed to say a few words on a class of poems largely represented in Marvell's works, which may be generally called Panegyric.

Quite alone among these—indeed, it can be classed with no other poem in the language—stands the Horatian Ode on Cromwell's return from Ireland. Mr. Lowell said of it that as a testimony to Cromwell's character it was worth more than all Carlyle's biographies; he might without exaggeration have said as much of its literary qualities. It has force with grace, originality with charm, in almost every stanza. Perhaps the first quality that would strike a reader of it for the first time is its quaintness; but further study creates no reaction against this in the mind—the usual sequel to poems which depend on quaintness for effect. But when Mr. Lowell goes on to say that the poem shows the difference between grief that thinks of its object and grief that thinks of its rhymes (referring to Dryden), he is not so happy. The pre-eminent quality of the poem is its art; and its singular charm is the fact that it succeeds, in spite of being artificial, in moving and touching the springs of feeling in an extraordinary degree. It is a unique piece in the collection, the one instance where Marvell's undoubted genius burned steadily through a whole poem. Here he flies *penna metuente solvi*. It is in completeness more than in quality that it is superior to all his other work, but in quality too it has that lurking divinity that cannot be analysed or imitated.

> Tis madness to resist or blame
> The force of angry heaven's flame,
>   And if we would speak true,
>   Much to the man is due
> Who from his private gardens, where
> He lived reserved and austere,
>   (As though his highest plot
>   To plant the bergamot,)

Could by industrious valour climb
To ruin the great work of Time,
  And cast the kingdoms old
  Into another mould.

This is the apotheosis of tyrants; it is the bloom of republicanism just flowering into despotism. But the Ode is no party utterance; the often-quoted lines on the death of Charles, in their grave yet passionate dignity, might have been written by the most ardent of Royalists, and have often done service on their side. But, indeed, the whole Ode is above party, and looks clearly into the heart and motives of man. It moves from end to end with the solemn beat of its singular metre, its majestic cadences, without self-consciousness or sentiment, austere, but not frigid.

Marvell's other panegyrics are but little known, though the awkward and ugly lines on Milton have passed into anthologies, owing to their magnificent exordium, "When I beheld the poet blind yet old." But no one can pretend that such lines as these are anything but prosaic and ridiculous to the last degree—

Thou hast not missed one thought that could be fit,
And all that was improper dost omit;
At once delight and horror on us seize,
Thou sing'st with so much gravity and ease—

though the unfortunate alteration in the meaning of the word *improper* makes them now seem even more ridiculous than they are. The poems on the "First Anniversary of the Government of the Lord Protector," on the "Death of the Lord Protector," and on "Richard Cromwell," are melancholy reading though they have some sonorous lines.

And as the angel of our Commonweal
Troubling the waters, yearly mak'st them heal,

may pass as an epigram. But that a man of penetrating judgment and independence of opinion should descend to a vein of odious genealogical compliment, and speak of the succeeding of

Rainbow to storm, Richard to Oliver,

and add that

A Cromwell in an hour a prince will grow,

by way of apology for the obvious deficiencies of his new Protector, makes us very melancholy indeed. Flattery is of course a slough in which many poets have wallowed; and a little grovelling was held to be even more commendable in poets in that earlier age; but we see the pinion beginning to droop, and the bright eye growing sickly and dull. Milton's poisonous advice is already at work.

But we must pass through a more humiliating epoch still. The poet of spicy gardens and sequestered fields seen through the haze of dawn is gone, not like the Scholar Gipsy to the high lonely wood or the deserted lasher, but has stepped down to jostle with the foulest and most venal of mankind. He becomes a satirist, and a satirist of the coarsest kind. His pages are crowded with filthy pictures and revolting images; the leaves cannot be turned over so quickly but some lewd epithet or vile realism prints itself on the eye. His apologists have said that it is nothing but the overflowing indignation of a noble mind when confronted with the hideous vices of a corrupt court and nation; that this deep-seated wrath is but an indication of the fervid idealistic nature of the man; that the generous fire that warmed in the poems, consumed in the satires; that the true moralist does not condone but condemn. To this we would answer that it is just conceivable that a satirist may be primarily occupied by an immense moral indignation, and no doubt that indignation must bear a certain part in all satires; but it is not the attitude of a hopeful or generous soul. The satirist is after all only destructive; he has not learned the lesson that the only cure for old vices is new enthusiasms. Nor if a satirist is betrayed into the grossest and most unnecessary realism can we acquit him entirely of all enjoyment of his subject. It is impossible to treat of vice in the intimate and detailed manner in which Marvell treats of it without having, if no practical acquaintance with your subject, at least a considerable conventional acquaintance with it, and a large literary knowledge of the handling of similar topics; and when one critic goes so far as to call Marvell an essentially pure-minded man, or words to that effect, we think he would find a contradiction on almost every page of the satires.

They were undoubtedly popular. Charles II. was greatly amused by them; and their reputation lasted as late as Swift, who spoke of Marvell's genius as pre-eminently indicated by the fact that though the controversies were forgotten, the satires still held the mind. He started with a natural equipment. That he was humorous his earlier poems show, as when for instance he makes Daphne say to Chloe:

> Rather I away will pine
>   In a manly stubbornness,
>   Than be fatted up express,
> For the cannibal to dine.

And he shows, too, in his earlier poems, much of the weightier and more dignified art of statement that makes the true satirist's work often read better in quotations than entire; as for instance—

Wilt thou all the glory have,
       That war or peace commend?
Half the world shall be thy slave,
       The other half thy friend.

But belonging as they do to the period of melancholy decadence of Marvell's art, we are not inclined to go at any length into the question of the satires. We see genius struggling like Laocoon in the grasp of a power whose virulence he did not measure, and to whom sooner or later the increasing languor must yield. Of course there are notable passages scattered throughout them. In "Last Instructions to a Painter," the passage beginning, "Paint last the king, and a dead shade of night," where Charles II. sees in a vision the shapes of Charles I. and Henry VIII. threatening him with the consequences of unsympathetic despotism and the pursuit of sensual passion, has a tragic horror and dignity of a peculiar kind; and the following specimen from "The Character of Holland" gives on the whole a good specimen of the strength and weakness of the author:

Holland, that scarce deserves the name of land,
As but the off-scouring of the British sand,
And so much earth as was contributed
By English pilots when they heaved the lead,
Or what by the Ocean's slow alluvion fell
Of shipwrecked cockle and the mussel-shell,
This undigested vomit of the sea,
Fell to the Dutch by just propriety.

Clever beyond question; every couplet is an undeniable epigram, lucid, well-digested, elaborate; pointed, yet finikin withal,—it is easy to find a string of epithets for it. But to what purpose is this waste? To see this felicity spent on such slight and intemperate work is bitterness itself; such writing has, it must be confessed, every qualification for pleasing except the power to please.

Of the remainder of Marvell's life, there is little more to be said. He was private tutor at Eton to a Master Dutton, a relative of Cromwell's, and wrote a delightful letter about him to the Protector; but the serious business of his later life was Parliament. Of his political consistency we cannot form a high idea. He seems, as we should expect him to have been, a Royalist at heart and by sympathy all along; "Tis God-like good," he wrote, "to save a falling king." Yet he was not ashamed to accept Cromwell as the angel of the Commonweal, and to write in fulsome praise of Protector Richard; and his bond of union with the extreme Puritans was his intense hatred of prelacy and bishops which is constantly coming up. In "The Loyal Scot" he writes:

> The friendly loadstone has not more combined,
> Than Bishops cramped the commerce of mankind.

And in "The Bermudas" he classes the fury of the elements with "Prelates' rage" as the natural enemies of the human race. Such was not the intermeddling in affairs that Milton had recommended. To fiddle, while Rome burnt, upon the almost divine attributes of her successive rulers, this was not the austere storage of song which Milton himself practised.

Andrew Marvell was for many years member for Hull, with his expenses paid by the Corporation. His immense, minute, and elaborate correspondence with his constituents, in which he gave an exact account of the progress of public business, remains to do him credit as a sagacious and conscientious man. But it cannot be certainly imputed to any higher motive than to stand well with his employers. He was provided with the means of livelihood, he was in a position of trust and dignity, and he may well be excused for wishing to retain it. In spite of certain mysterious absences on the Continent, and a long period during which he absented himself from the House in the suite of an embassy to Russia, he preserved the confidence of his constituents for eighteen years, and died at his post. He spoke but little in the House, and his reported speeches add but little to his reputation. One curious incident is related in the Journals. In going to his place he stumbled over Sir Philip Harcourt's foot, and an interchange of blows in a humorous and friendly fashion with hand and hat, took place. At the close of the sitting the Speaker animadverted on this, Marvell being absent; and a brief debate took place the next day on the subject, Marvell speaking with some warmth of the Speaker's grave interference with what appears to have been nothing more than a piece of childish horse-play. "What passed (said Mr. Marvell) was through great acquaintance and familiarity between us. He never gave him an affront nor intended him any. But the Speaker cast a severe reflection upon him yesterday when he was out of the House, and he hopes that as the Speaker keeps us in order, he will keep himself in order for the future."

For one thing Marvell deserves high credit; in a corrupt age, he kept his hands clean, refusing even when hard pressed for money a gift of £1000 proffered him by Danby, the Lord-Treasurer, "in his garret," as a kind of retainer on the royal side. In Hartley Coleridge's life of Marvell this is told in a silly, theatrical way, unworthy and not even characteristic of the man. "Marvell," he says, "looking at the paper (an order on the Treasury which had been slipped into his hand) calls after the Treasurer, 'My lord, I request another moment.' They went up again to the garret; and Jack the servant-boy was called. 'Jack, child, what had I for dinner yesterday?' 'Don't you remember, sir? You had the little shoulder of mutton that you ordered me to bring from a woman in the market.' 'Very right, child. What have I for dinner to-day?' 'Don't you know, sir, that you bid me lay by the blade-bone to broil?' ''Tis so; very right, child; go away.' 'My lord, do you hear that? Andrew Marvell's dinner is provided. There's your piece of paper; I want it not. I know the sort of kindness you intended. I live here to serve my constituents; the Ministry may seek men for their purpose,—I am not one.' " But with the exception of perhaps the concluding words, there is no reason to think the story authentic, though the fact is unquestioned.

Over Prince Rupert, Marvell seems to have had a great influence, so much so that, when the Prince spoke in public, it was commonly said: "He has been with his tutor."

Marvell died suddenly in 1678, not without suspicion of poisoning; but it seems to have been rather due to the treatment he underwent at the hands of an old-fashioned practitioner, who had a prejudice against the use of Peruvian bark which would probably have saved Marvell's life. Upon his death a widow starts into existence, Mary Marvell by name, so unexpectedly and with such a total absence of previous allusion, that it has been doubted whether her marriage was not all a fiction. But Dr. Grosart points out that she would never have administered his estate had there been any reason to doubt the validity of her claims; and it was under her auspices that the Poems were first given to the world a few years after his death, in a folio which is now a rare and coveted book.

Of his Prose Works it is needful to say but little; they may be characterised as prose satires for the most part, or political pamphlets, "The Rehearsal Transposed" and "The Divine in Mode" are peculiarly distasteful examples of a kind of controversy then much in vogue. They are answers to publications, and to the ordinary reader contrive to be elaborate without being artistic, personal without being humorous, and digressive without being entertaining; in short, they combine the characteristics of tedium, dulness, and scurrility to a perfectly phenomenal degree. As compared with the poems themselves, the prose works fill many volumes; and any reader of ordinary perseverance has ample opportunities of convincing himself of Andrew Marvell's powers of expression, his high-spirited beginning, the delicate ideals, the sequestered ambitions of his youth, and their lamentable decline.

It is a perilous investment to aspire to be a poet,— *periculosce plenum opus aleaz.* If you succeed, to have the world, present and to come, at your feet, to win the reluctant admiration even of the Philistine; to snuff the incense of adoration on the one hand, and on the other to feel yourself a member of the choir invisible, the sweet and solemn company of poets; to own within yourself the ministry of hope and height. And one step below success, to be laughed at or softly pitied as the dreamer of ineffectual dreams, the strummer of impotent music; to be despised alike by the successful and the unsuccessful; the world if you win,—worse than nothing if you fail.

> Mediocribus esse poetis
> Non di, non homines, non concessere columns.

There is no such thing as respectable mediocrity among poets. Be supreme or contemptible.

And yet we cannot but grieve when we see a poet over whose feet the stream has flowed, turn back from the brink and make the great denial; whether from the secret consciousness of aridity, the drying of the fount of song, or from the imperious temptations of the busy, ordinary world we cannot say. Somehow we have lost our poet. It seems that,

> Just for a handful of silver he left us,
> Just for a ribbon to stick in his coat.

And the singer of an April mood, who might have bloomed year after year in young and ardent hearts, is buried in the dust of politics, in the valley of dead bones.

—A.C. Benson, "Andrew Marvell,"
1892, *Essays,* 1896, pp. 68–95

H.C. Beeching "The Lyrical Poems of Andrew Marvell" (1901)

Henry Charles Beeching (1859–1919) was a well-known English cler-gyman and scholar. Beeching begins the piece below by examining

Marvell's reception in the centuries after his death, especially focusing on the various editions of Marvell's work and important anthologies that contained his pieces. Beeching traces the rise in Marvell's popularity from the early 1700s through the end of the Vicotrian Era in excellent detail, and any student exploring Marvell's reception in the eras after his death will find Beeching's work here particularly helpful.

Beeching then examines Marvell's two main literary influences: "But a word may first be said about the poet's models. He had two; we might call them his good and bad angels. They were John Milton, whose volume of lyrics appeared in 1645, and John Donne, whose poems were not printed during his lifetime, but were widely circulated in manuscript." Beeching considers Donne the "bad angel" because of the faults that most nineteenth-century critics ascribed to the founder of the metaphysical school: "Donne, one of the most remarkable among seventeenth-century Englishmen of genius, had one of the greatest poetical virtues and two of the greatest poetical vices. His virtue was passion, intensity; his vices were a too cavalier indifference to accent, and a love of quaint and extravagant conceits. Marvell is the pupil of his intensity, and to a certain degree of his extravagance." Fortunately, according to Beeching, Marvell "was saved from his careless writing by the study of Milton." Students examining Marvell's literary predecessors would do well to take note of what Beeching writes here. Beeching suggests that the "best example of Marvell's work in the manner of Donne is the lyric entitled 'The Fair Singer,'" while Milton's influence can be seen in works including "First Anniversary" and "The Garden." Students may wish to examine these pieces for themselves to see whether they agree or disagree with Beeching's assessment of both Marvell's literary influences and their quality.

Beeching then labels the finer traits Marvell demonstrates in his lyrical poems. The first of these is his "extraordinary terseness." The second is Marvell's exquisite use of all of his senses in describing images in his works. The third is his humor. The fourth is his "witty delicacy," a term originally coined by Charles Lamb, which describes what Beeching calls Marvell's "delicate invention." The fifth quality is the one Beeching calls Marvell's "gusto," the great joy with which he wrote: "He wrote, we are sure, for his own pleasure quite as much as for ours." The sixth and last is Marvell's sense of artistry, "with an artist's love of making experiments. Perhaps he never attained perfect facility, but he is never amateurish."

Beeching also partitions Marvell's lyrical poems into three distinct subdivisions. The first of these includes his love poetry, and chief amongst these poems is "To His Coy Mistress," about which Beeching writes, "It could never be the most popular of Marvell's poems, but for sheer power I should be disposed to rank it higher than anything he ever wrote." The second subdivision includes Marvell's religious works; though Beeching discusses several pieces in this section, his longest discussion is saved for the poem "On a Drop of Dew." The third subdivision, and according to Beeching the finest, includes Marvell's pastoral works. Beeching believes that Marvell is the greatest English pastoral poet to his day (save for Shakespeare,) and notes that Marvell's depictions of "ordinary country scenes" are "full of observation." In this section, Beeching explicates Marvell's famous poems "The Garden" and "Bermudas," both eminently useful discussions for anyone writing on either of those works. Beeching also describes a fourth subdivision of Marvell's work, the patriotic poems, but explains that these are not part of the lyrical subset of Marvell's oeuvre. Students writing on Marvell should find much rich meat in both Beeching's subdivisions of Marvell's lyric poems and his six traits of Marvell's writing, and perhaps may use either as a jumping off point in their own examination of the poet's larger body of work.

Any one who wished to defend the thesis that our own generation, however it may fall below its predecessors in outstanding poetical genius, is markedly their superior in poetical taste, might find matter for his argument in the recent rise into fame of the lyrical verse of Marvell. It may be interesting to trace the progress of this growth of appreciation. In 1681, three years after Marvell's death, a well printed folio was brought out by his widow containing all his poetry that existed in manuscript, except the political pieces, which, as the Stuarts were still upon the throne, could not be published with safety. Of this book no second edition was called for. In 1726 a literary hack, one Thomas Cooke, who translated Hesiod, and for attacking Pope was rewarded with immortality:

> From these the world will judge of men and books,
> Not from the Burnets, Oldmixons, and Cookes,

issued an edition of Marvell's poems including the political satires, and rests Marvell's fame almost exclusively on political grounds. "My design," he says, "in this is to draw a pattern for all freeborn *Englishmen*, in the life of a worthy Patriot, whose every Action has truely merited to him, with *Aristides*, the surname of the *Just*." How little capable Cooke was of appreciating any of the distinctive qualities of Marvell's verse may be judged from the poems he singles out for special praise. "If we have any which may be properly said to come finished from his Hands, they are these, "On Milton's Paradise Lost," "On Blood's Stealing the Crown," and "A Dialogue between Two Horses."

Just fifty years after Cooke's pretty little edition, there appeared another in three great quarto volumes by an editor as little competent to appreciate Marvell's peculiar charm as his predecessor; though he, like Cooke, was a poet in his way. This was Edward Thompson, a captain in the Royal Navy, who was interested in the fame of Marvell, from being himself a native of Hull, and also on the political side, from his friendship with Wilkes. Thompson puts on his title-page some lines from his namesake of *The Seasons*, "Hail, Independence, Hail," &c; and dedicates his volumes to the Mayor and Aldermen of Hull as the "Friends of Liberty and England"; professing that his labour was undertaken to show his esteem for "a person who had been a general friend to mankind, a public one to his country, and a partial and strenuous one to the town of Hull." Thompson's gifts as a critic may be estimated from his assigning to Marvell not only Addison's hymn, "The Spacious Firmament on High," which at least is in Marvell's metre, if not in his manner, but also Mallet's "William and Margaret," a poem that could not have been written before Allan Ramsay's publications had revived interest in the old Scots ballads. Thompson had found these poems with others in a manuscript book, some part of which he declared to be in Marvell's handwriting; and of this fact he would have been a very competent judge from his familiarity with the many letters of Marvell written to his constituents at Hull, which he printed in his edition. From this invaluable autograph he set up his text. "Afterwards, as rare things will, it vanished." But it restored to the world the poem by which Marvell is generally known, "An Horatian Ode upon Cromwell's Return from Ireland." I must not speak here about Captain Thompson, but I may perhaps be allowed to say I have come to regard his volumes with much more interest since reading in the *Comhill Magazine* for May 1868 some extracts from a manuscript journal of his kept in the year 1783-5. The only entry there precisely bearing on our subject is the following, under date 1784, "A nephew of Emma's [his mistress] was named by me Andrew Marvell; when he comes to reason, the name may inspire him to be virtuous." This would show, if more evidence were needed, that it was mainly on the political side that Marvell interested the Captain. His own poetical effusions were chiefly squibs and epigrams, and what he well called "Meretricious Miscellanies." The list of subscribers to Thompson's volumes tells the same tale. It includes the Duke of G——, the Marquis of Granby, the Earl of Shelburne and other Whig peers, the Lord Mayor of London (Sawbridge), and a dozen Members of Parliament, among them

Burke, and such stalwarts as Wilkes and Oliver. It includes, more remarkably, the notorious Rigby, who was said by the wits to have bequeathed by his will "near half a million of public money." Learning is represented by that stout republican, Thomas Hollis, and by Daines Barrington the antiquary and naturalist, and correspondent of White of Selborne, who, according to Charles Lamb, was so much the friend of gardens that he paid the gardener at the Temple twenty shillings to poison the sparrows. But literature has only a few names. There is the Rev. Prebendary Mason, his friend the eccentric Dr. Glynn, who once wrote a prize poem, Mrs. Macaulay, and Mr. William Woty. Samuel Johnson, LL.D., is conspicuous by absence. The theatre (for Captain Thompson was himself something of a playwright) contributes David Garrick, Esq., Samuel Foote, Esq., and Mr. Colman; and among other personal friends of the editor is the notorious John Stevenson Hall, better known as Hall Stevenson. This worthy and the Duke of Cumberland (Henry Augustus), who heads the list, may have been attracted by the indelicacy of the satires, hardly by anything else.

Eleven years after Thompson's edition of Marvell, appeared that very interesting book, ominous of the dawn of a new era, *Select Beauties of Ancient English Poetry*, by Henry Headley, A.B., an enthusiastic young clergyman with genuine taste for the seventeenth-century poets. He revived the memory of Drayton and Daniel, whom he praises with discrimination, quoting from the former the now famous sonnet, "Since there's no help, come let us kiss and part"; and he has a good word to say for Drummond, Browne, Carew and Crashaw; but Marvell is not mentioned. Four years later, however, Marvell makes his appearance in George Ellis's *Specimens of the Early English Poets*, where he is spoken of as "an accomplished man who, though *principally* distinguished by his inflexible patriotism, was generally and justly admired for his learning, his acuteness in controversial writing, his wit, *and* his poetical talents." Ellis represents him by extracts from "Daphnis and Chloe," and "Young Love," which is much as if the author of the "Ancient Mariner" and "Kubla Khan" should be represented by the song "If I had but two little wings." I do not recall any reference to Marvell in Coleridge; and Wordsworth quotes him only as a patriot:

The later Sidney, Marvell, Harrington,
Young Vane, and others who called Milton friend.

It was Charles Lamb who made the discovery of Marvell's merit as a lyrical poet. In his essay upon the Old Benchers of the Inner Temple, printed in the *London Magazine* for September 1821, he quotes, *apropos* of the Temple sun-dial, four stanzas from "The Garden," and says of them that they "are full, as all his serious poetry was, of a witty delicacy." The phrase has become classical, as it deserves. The most popular anthology of the last half of the century has been Mr. Palgrave's *Golden Treasury of Songs and Lyrics,* and this shows, in its later editions, a curious and interesting growth in appreciation of Marvell. When the first edition appeared, in 1861, it contained three poems of his, "The Horatian Ode," "The Garden," and "The Bermudas." In 1883 there was added an extract from "The Nymph complaining for the Death of her Fawn," with a note saying "Perhaps no poem in this collection is more delicately fancied, more exquisitely finished"; and in 1891 room was found for "The Picture of Little T. C. in a Prospect of Flowers." With five poems in so small and picked a collection, Marvell's popular reputation as a lyric poet may be reckoned to have culminated.

Marvell was born in 1621, the son of a celebrated preacher who was also master of the Grammar School of Hull, where the boy was educated. He proceeded to Cambridge, took his degree, and then travelled in Holland, France, Italy, and Spain. When he returned to England he was engaged by Lord Fairfax as tutor to his daughter Mary, and it is to the time that he spent in retirement in Fairfax's house at Nun Appleton in Yorkshire, perhaps from 1650 to 1653, that we owe the best of his lyrical works. Before this he had written one or two things in rhymed couplets, a preface to Lovelace's *Lucasta* a copy of verses on Lord Hastings' death, full of wit, and with lines here and there that haunt the memory, like—

Go stand between the morning and the flowers;

and in 1650 was composed the Horatian Ode; but whether any of the lyrics in octosyllables are of an earlier date than these cannot be determined. It will be best, then, to waive all question of chronological precedence, and look at the poems in groups according to their subject. But a word may first be said about the poet's models. He had two; we might call them his good and bad angels. They were John Milton, whose volume of lyrics appeared in 1645, and John Donne, whose poems were not printed during his lifetime, but were widely circulated in manuscript. Donne, one of the most remarkable among seventeenth-century Englishmen of genius, had one of the greatest poetical virtues and two of the greatest poetical vices. His virtue was passion, intensity; his vices were a too cavalier indifference to accent, and a love of quaint and extravagant conceits. Marvell is the pupil of his intensity, and to a certain degree of his extravagance; but he was saved from his careless writing by the study of Milton. The best example of Marvell's work in the manner of Donne is the lyric entitled "The Fair Singer." The breathless haste of the rhythm, and the absence of any pause except at the end of the lines, are studied after that master; so is the ingenuity of the idea. The first line of the poem, "To make a final conquest of all me," is Donne pure and simple. But even in this poem there is a regularity of measure which betrays the influence of the other school, that of Ben Jonson and Milton:

> I could have fled from one but singly fair;
>   My disentangled soul itself might save,
> Breaking the curled trammels of her hair;
>   But how should I avoid to be her slave
> Whose subtle art invisibly can wreathe
>   My fetters of the very air I breathe!

Of the fantastic and forced images that Marvell copied from Donne it will suffice to offer a single example. In the "Dialogue between the Soul and the Body" he makes the body say:

> O who shall me deliver whole
> From bonds of this tyrannic soul,
> Which stretched upright impales me so
> That mine own precipice I go!

The poem called "Eyes and Tears," which is full of the same sort of thing, is, I suspect, an exercise, the inspiration of which may be traced to the appearance of Crashaw's poem of "The Weeper" in his volume of 1646. As a rule, Marvell's humour saved him from the worst banalities of this school; as a rule, also, he keeps his fantastic *tours de force* for semi-humorous passages, and often uses these, by way of contrast, to heighten the outburst of passion that follows. Thus, in the poem "Upon Appleton House," he compares Fairfax's garden to a fort:

> See how the flowers, as at parade,
> Under their colours stand displayed;
> Each regiment in order grows,
> That of the tulip, pink, and rose.
> But when the vigilant patrol
> Of stars walks round about the pole,
> The leaves that to the stalks are curled
> Seem to their staves the ensigns furled.
> Then in some flower's beloved hut,

Each bee, as sentinel, is shut,
And sleeps so too; but if once stirred,
She runs you through, nor asks the word.

And then, while the reader is still smiling, he finds himself in the midst of a passionate apostrophe to England:

Oh, thou, that dear and happy isle,
The garden of the world erewhile,
Thou Paradise of the four seas
Which Heaven planted us to please;
But, to exclude the world, did guard
With watery, if not flaming, sword,—
What luckless apple did we taste
To make us mortal, and thee waste?

The influence of Milton may be traced in the fine sense of form generally, and, in particular, in the use of the octosyllabic couplet. Occasionally we seem to hear an echo of Milton's airy grace, as in the couplet:

Near this a fountain's liquid bell
Tinkles within the concave shell.

But this is only occasional. Marvell is much more rigid in his rhythms than Milton, and he never attained to Milton's simplicity. That he had read him with care is evident; and there are a few direct reminiscences in the "First Anniversary," such as the phrase "beaked promontories," and the lines—

the dragon's tail
Swindges the volumes of its horrid flail,

and

Unto the kingdom blest of peace and love.

A more interesting reminiscence is the line in "The Garden"—

Waves in its plumes the various light,

which is certainly an echo of the difficult line in "II Penseroso,"

Waves at his wings in aery stream,

though it throws no light upon its interpretation. But too much must not be made of these imitations. After all, Milton was Milton, and Marvell was

Marvell; and what survives to charm us in Marvell is what he gives us of his own. Let me briefly summarise some of the elements in this charm.

The first quality to strike a reader who takes up Marvell's book is his extraordinary terseness. Look, for example, at the poem with which the only good modern edition, that of Mr. G. A. Aitken, opens, "Appleton House." The poet wishes to praise the house for not being too big, like most country-houses of the time, and this is how he does it:

> Within this sober frame expect
> Work of no foreign architect,
> That unto caves the quarries drew,
> And forests did to pastures hew.

If this were "transprosed," it would have to run something as follows: "Our boasted Italian architects make houses so huge that by drawing the stone for them they hollow out quarries into caves, and cut down whole forests for timber so that they become pastures." As a part of the same skill it is remarkable in how few strokes he can paint a picture. In this same poem, describing a copse, he says:

> Dark all without it knits;
> within it opens passable and thin,

which gives exactly the difference of impression from without and upon entering. A second notable quality in Marvell's verse is its sensuousness, its wide and deep enjoyment of the world of sense. "The Garden," which everybody knows, may stand as the best example of this quality—

> Stumbling on melons as I pass
> Ensnared with flowers, I fall on grass.

Marvell is the laureate of grass, and of greenery. A third excellent quality is his humour, to which I have already referred, sometimes showing itself as intellectual wit, or as irony or sarcasm. Still keeping to "Appleton House," one may notice the ingenuity of the suggestion of Fairfax's generosity—

> A stately frontispiece of poor
> Adorns without the open door,

or the deprecation of over-large houses:

> What need of all this marble crust
> To impark the wanton mole of dust;

That thinks by breadth the world to unite,
Tho' the first builders failed in height.

Once or twice the humour runs to coarseness when it allies itself with the
bitter Puritanism of the time, as in the picture of the nuns defending their
house:

Some to the breach against their foes
Their wooden saints in vain oppose;
Another bolder stands at push,
With their old holy-water brush.

But most characteristic of all the qualities of Marvell's verse is what
Lamb well spoke of as his "witty delicacy"—his delicate invention. The
shining and unapproachable instances of this delicacy are "The Nymph
complaining for the death of her Fawn" and "The picture of little T.C." The
former of these pieces is often hyperbolic in fancy, but the hyperbole fits the
pastoral remoteness of the setting; the second needs not even this apology.
It is a masterpiece in a *genre* where masterpieces are rare, though attempts
are not infrequent. Prior, Waller, and Sedley have tried the theme with a
certain success, but their pieces lack the romantic note. "The Picture of
Little T.C." has this to perfection; it has not a weak line in it, and moves
through its five stanzas, each more exquisite than the last, to its admirably
mock-serious close:

Meantime, whilst every verdant thing
Itself does at thy beauty charm,
Reform the errors of the spring;
Make that the tulips may have share
Of sweetness, seeing they are fair;
And roses of their thorns disarm;
      But most procure
That violets may a longer age endure.
But O, young beauty of the woods,
Whom Nature courts with fruit and flowers,
Gather the flowers, but spare the buds;
Lest Flora, angry at thy crime
To kill her infants in their prime,
Do quickly make the example yours;
      And ere we see,
Nip in the blossom all our hopes and thee.

One other quality of Marvell's lyrical writing remains to be noticed, which is somewhat difficult to fix with a name, unless we call it *gusto*. We imagine him smiling to himself as he writes, smiling at his own fancies, or his own sensuousness, or happy turns. He wrote, we are sure, for his own pleasure quite as much as for ours. I remember the remark being made to me that "The Bermudas," for a religious poem, went pretty far in the way of self-indulgence. And so it does. Lastly, it cannot fail to be noted that Marvell was an artist, with an artist's love of making experiments. Perhaps he never attained perfect facility, but he is never amateurish.

Among the various groups into which lyrical poetry divides itself, the least satisfactory is that whose theme is love. Marvell's love-poetry has, with the exception of one piece, as little passion as Cowley's, while it is as full of conceits. "The Unfortunate Lover" is probably the worst love-poem ever written by a man of genius. "The Definition of Love" is merely a study after Donne's "Valediction." Cleverer and more original, and somewhat more successful, is "The Gallery." The two opposite sides of one long picture-gallery into which the chambers of his heart have been thrown by breaking down partitions are supposed to be covered with portraits of his lady. On the one side she is drawn in such characters as Aurora and Venus; on the other as an enchanter and a murderess.

Marvell was the friend of Milton, and one conjectures that, like his respected friend, he also may have had theories as to the true relation of these sexes which interfered with the spontaneous expression of feeling. There is, nevertheless, one poem in which passion is allowed to take its most natural path, although even in it one feels that the poet is expressing the passion of the human race rather than his own individual feeling; and the passion being, as often in Marvell, masked and heightened by his wit, the effect is singularly striking; indeed, as a love-poem "To his Coy Mistress" is unique. It could never be the most popular of Marvell's poems, but for sheer power I should be disposed to rank it higher than anything he ever wrote. He begins with hyperbolical protestations to his mistress of the slow and solemn state with which their wooing should be conducted, if only time and space were their servants and not their masters.

> Had we but world enough and time,
> This coyness, lady, were no crime.
> We would sit down and think which way
> To walk, and pass our long love's day.
> Thou by the Indian Ganges' side

Should'st rubies find: I by the tide
Of Humber would complain.
I would Love you ten years before the flood,
And you should, if you please, refuse
Till the conversion of the Jews.

Each beauty also of face and feature should have its special and age-long praise—

But at my back 1 always hear
Time's winged chariot hurrying near;
And yonder all before us lie Deserts of vast eternity . . .
The grave's a fine and private place,
But none I think do there embrace.

A second division of Marvell's lyric poetry has for its subject religion. The most curious of the religious poems are the pastorals "Clorinda and Damon," and "Thyrsis and Dorinda." Despite their obvious artificiality I must confess that these poems give me pleasure, perhaps because religious poetry is apt to be shapeless, and these, in point of form, are admirable. It is matter for regret that in the first of the two Marvell should have made the nymph sensual and the swain pious; but the friend of Milton, as I have already suggested, probably shared his low views of the female sex. And then the conversion of the lady is sudden and leaves something to desire in its motive. In "Thyrsis and Dorinda" the two young things talk together so sweetly of Elysium that they drink opium in order to lose no time in getting there. More genuine in feeling, and more religious in the ordinary sense of the word, are two dialogues: one between the "Resolved Soul and Created Pleasure," the other between "Soul and Body." The form of the first is noteworthy. The octosyllabic stanzas are alternately unshortened and shortened, the Soul speaking in serious iambics and Pkasure in dancing trochees; and the allurements of sense rise in a well-conceived scale from mere softness through art up to the pleasures of knowledge. The dialogue between Soul and Body is a brilliant duel, each party accusing the other of his proper woes; and except for the one terrible line I quoted above, the poem is an excellent piece of writing. But religious passion sounds a higher and less artificial strain in a pair of odes, trie one "On a Drop of Dew," in which the soul is compared to the dewdrop upon a leaf, which reflects heaven and is reluctant to coalesce with its environment; the other called "The Coronet," an apology for religious poetry on the ground that because it admits art it leaves room for the artist's pride. "The Coronet" is interesting as a study in Herbert's manner, and contains one line of exquisite modesty:

Through every garden, every mead,
I gather flowers (my fruits are only flowers).

But the ode "On a Drop of Dew" is by far the finer. The ideas are evolved after the manner of Donne, but the rhythm is slower and more contemplative:

See, how the orient dew,
Shed from the bosom of the morn
    Into the blowing roses,
(Yet careless of its mansion new
For the clear region where 'twas born,)
    Round in itself incloses;
And in its little globe's extent
Frames, as it can, its native element;
How it the purple flower does slight,
    Scarce touching where it lies;
    But, gazing back upon the skies,
Shines with a mournful light
    (Like its own tear),
Because so long divided from the sphere.
Restless it rolls and unsecure,
Trembling lest it grow impure,
Till the warm sun pity its pain
And to the skies exhale it back again.
    So the soul, that drop, that ray
    Of the clear fountain of eternal day,
(Could it within the human flower be seen)
    Remembering still its former height
Shuns the sweet leaves and blossoms green,
    And recollecting its own light
    Does, in its pure and circling thoughts, express
The greater heaven in an heaven less.
        In how coy a figure wound
            Every way it turns away,
        So the world excluding round
            Yet receiving in the day.

A third and final division of Marvell's lyrics would comprise his poems upon nature; and here we have Marvell at his best, because here he lets his passion inspire him. Except in Shakespeare, who includes "all thoughts, all passions, all desires" we have but little passion for nature between Chaucer and Marvell; but in Marvell the love for natural beauty is not short of passion. Of course his love is not for wild nature—a feeling which only dates from Gray and Wordsworth—but for the ordinary country scenes:

Fragrant gardens, shady woods,
Deep meadows and transparent floods;

and for these he brings the eye of a genuine lover and, what is more, of a patient observer. The lines upon "Appleton House" are full of observation. He speaks of the "shining eye" of the "hatching throstle," and has a fine imaginative description of the woodpecker:

He walks still upright from the root
Measuring the timber with his foot,
And all the way, to keep it clean,
Doth from the bark the wood-moths glean;
He with his beak examines well
Which fit to stand and which to fell;
The good he numbers up and hacks
As if he marked them with the axe;
But where he, tinkling with his beak,
Does find the hollow oak to speak,
That for his building he designs
And through the tainted sides he mines.

In his poem called "The Garden" Marvell has sung a palinode that for richness of phrasing in its sheer sensuous love of garden delights is perhaps unmatchable. At the same time the most devout lover of gardens must agree with Marvell that even in a garden the pleasures of the mind are greater than those of the sense. The poet's thought, as he lies in the shade, can create a garden for himself far more splendid and also imperishable; as indeed, in this poem, it has done:

Meanwhile the mind from pleasure less
Withdraws into its happiness;
The mind, that ocean where each kind
Does straight its own resemblance find;

Yet it creates, transcending these,
Far other worlds and other seas,
Annihilating all that's made,
To a green thought in a green shade.
Here at the fountain's sliding foot,
Or at some fruit-tree's mossy root,
Casting the body's vest aside
My soul into the boughs does glide:
There like a bird it sits and sings,
Then whets and combs its silver wings,
And, till prepared for further flight,
Waves in its plumes the various light.

Next to "The Garden" as a descriptive poem must rank the "Bermudas." Marvell's "Bermudas" are not "still vexed" like Shakespeare's but an earthly Paradise. His interest in these islands arose from meeting at Eton, while he was there as tutor to a ward of Cromwell's, a certain John Oxenbridge, who had been one of the exiles thither for conscience sake. The poem is built upon the same plan as "The Garden"; first, the sensuous delights are described as no one but Marvell could describe them:

He hangs in shades the orange bright
Like golden lamps in a green night,
And does in the pomegranate close
Jewels more rich than Ormuz shows;
He makes the figs our mouths to meet
And throws the melons at our feet
But apples [i.e., pine-apples] plants of such a price
No tree could ever bear them twice.

And then he passes on, though in this case it must be allowed with much less effect, to the spiritual advantages of the place. We may note in passing that Mr. Palgrave in his "Golden Treasury" has taken the extraordinary liberty of altering the arrangement of some of the early lines, perhaps through not understanding their construction as they stand. In the folio and all the early editions the lines run as follows:

What should we do but sing His praise
That led us through the watery maze,
Unto an isle so long unknown
And yet far kinder than our own?

Where He the huge sea-monsters wracks
That lift the deep upon their backs,
He lands *us* on a grassy stage
Safe from the storms and prelates' rage.

Mr. Palgrave prints lines 5 and 6 before lines 3 and 4, thereby breaking up the arrangement of the line into quatrains, apparently not seeing that "where" is equivalent to "whereas," and that the safety of the exiles is contrasted with the wrecking of the sea-monsters. But to have introduced Marvell's verse to so wide a public should atone to the poet's *manes* for such an injury; especially as the Puck which sits ever upon the pen of commentators has already avenged it by making Mr. Palgrave append to the poem the following note: "Emigrants supposed to be driven *towards America* by the government of Charles I." There is no hint in the poem that the "small boat" was bringing the emigrants across the Atlantic, or that they were describing the newly-discovered islands by the gift of prophecy.

Of the patriotic verse, which in its own way is full of interest, it is impossible to speak in this paper; except of the one poem which can claim to be a lyric, the "Horatian ode upon Cromwell's return from Ireland." As was said above, this ode was first published in Captain Thomson's edition, and so must take its stand as Marvell's only by the weight of internal evidence. But that evidence is conspicuous in every line. The poem runs on in a somewhat meandering and self-indulgent course, like all Marvell's longer poems. But many details are recognisably in Marvell's vein. The stroke of cleverness about King Charles's head being as lucky as that which was found when they were digging the foundations of Rome, and the fun he pokes at the Scotch and Irish are certainly Marvell. So is the view taken that Cromwell made a great sacrifice in renouncing a private life, which we get also in Marvell's prose; so is the touch about Cromwell's garden:

> where
> He lived reserved and austere,
> (As if his highest plot
> To plant the bergamot.)

So also is the remarkable detachment from political prejudice, of which the verses prefixed to the cavalier poet Lovelace's *Lucasta,* about the same date, afford another instance, a detachment that would have been impossible for the author of "Lycidas." Even now, in an age which boasts of its tolerant spirit, it gives one a shock to remember that the stanzas about Charles, which present the very image of the cavalier saint and martyr, come in a poem to the honour and glory of the man to whom he owed his death:

> He nothing common did, or mean
> Upon that memorable scene,
>> But with his keener eye
>> The axe's edge did try;
> Nor called the gods with vulgar spite
> To vindicate his helpless right;
>> But bowed his comely head
>> Down, as upon a bed.

These two stanzas are now the only part of the ode that is remembered, and with justice; for the rest of the poem, although in form and spirit it is Horatian, yet it has little of the *curiosa felicitas* of Horace's diction to make it memorable. But in these two stanzas the diction has attained to the happiness of consummated simplicity. They recall the two stanzas at the close of the fifth ode in the third book in which Horace draws a picture of the martyred Regulus:

> Atque sciebat, quae sibi barbarus
> Tortor pararet: non aliter tamen
>> Dimovit obstantes propinquos,
>>> Et populum reditus morantem,
> Quam si clientum longa negotia
> Dijudicata lite relinqueret,
>> Tendens Venafranos in agros
>> Aut Lacedaemonium Tarentum.

—H.C. Beeching, "The Lyrical Poems of Andrew Marvell," *National Review,* July 1901, pp. 747–55

❖

GEORGE HERBERT

❖

❖

BIOGRAPHY

❖

GEORGE HERBERT
(1593–1633)

❖

George Herbert, devotional poet and miscellaneous writer, was born at Montgomery Castle, on the Welsh border. A member of a noble family, George Herbert was the brother of Edward Herbert, first Baron Herbert of Cherbury, and the son of Magdalen Herbert, a friend and patron of John Donne. Educated at Westminster School, Herbert acquired a reputation for being a brilliant scholar. He was elected a member of Trinity College, Cambridge, in 1614, a reader in rhetoric in 1618, and public orator of the University, from 1620 to 1627. Although serving in 1624 and 1625 as M.P. for Montgomery, Herbert relinquished his ambitions for a secular career after the death of his royal patron James I. Ordained a deacon in 1625, Herbert resigned from his Public Oratorship in 1628. His mother died in 1627. He became an ordained priest in 1630. Until his death in 1633, Herbert lived and worked as a rural parish priest at Bemerton in Wiltshire, with Jane Danvers, whom he had married in 1629.

George Herbert is most widely known for his devotional poems, which are largely influenced by the metaphysical school of John Donne. His earliest known poems consist of two sonnets, sent to his mother on New Year's Day, in 1610. In these, the young Herbert declares that the subject of verse should concern the poet's love of God, rather than of woman. This theme of complete religious devotion was to preoccupy Herbert throughout his life, as manifested in his works, which are exclusively devotional.

It is believed that Herbert wrote the majority of his extant poems at Bemerton, as well as revising earlier poems, writing a prose treatise on the duties of a country priest, *A Priest to the Temple, or the Country Parson* (published 1652), a translation of Luigi Cornaro's *Treatise on Temperance* (published 1558), and annotations of Juan de Valdes' *Considerations* (published Italian translation, 1550). As Herbert had a reputation during his lifetime, some of his poems doubtless circulated in manuscript form. Before he died, Herbert sent a manuscript of his collected verses to Nicholas

Ferrar, leader of a religious community at Little Gidding, with the request that Ferrar either burn or publish them. Ferrar published the volume under the title *The Temple: Sacred Poems and Private Ejaculations* (1633). Immensely popular in the seventeenth century, Herbert's poems combine metaphysical conceits, precise craftsmanship (with as much attention to the visual impression of his poems), with what appears to be a profound religious sincerity.

❖

PERSONAL

❖

EDWARD, LORD HERBERT
OF CHERBURY (1643)

Edward Herbert, the first Baron Herbert of Cherbury (1583–1648), was an English soldier and diplomat who gained some renown as a philosopher and first English proponent of deism. Edward Herbert was also brother to George. Like his more famous brother, Edward Herbert tried his hand at poetry, and has been labelled by critics as an imitator of Donne, but his works were generally considered inferior to his more famous sibling's work.

My brother George was so excellent a scholar, that he was made the public orator of the University in Cambridge; some of whose English works are extant; which, though they be rare in their kind, yet are far short of expressing those perfections he had in the Greek and Latin tongue, and all divine and human literature; his life was most holy and exemplary; insomuch, that about Salisbury, where he lived, beneficed for many years, he was little less than sainted. He was not exempt from passion and choler, being infirmities to which all our race is subject, but that excepted, without reproach in his action.

> —Edward, Lord Herbert of Cherbury,
> *The Autobiography of Edward Lord Herbert
> of Cherbury*, 1643, ed. Lee, rev. ed. 1906, pp. 11–13

THOMAS FULLER (1662)

The English theological historian Thomas Fuller (1608–1661) was also a renowned clergyman and orator, famous for his sermons and his wit.

So pious his life, that, as he was a copy of primitive, he might be a pattern of Sanctity to posterity. To testifie his independency on all others, he never mentioned the name of Jesus Christ, but with this addition, "My Master." Next God the Word, he loved the Word of God; being heard often to protest, "That he would not part with one leaf thereof for the whole world."

> —Thomas Fuller, *The Worthies of England*,
> 1662, vol. 2, ed. Nichols, p. 601

JOHN AUBREY (1669–96)

He was buryed (according to his owne desire) with the singing service for the buriall of dead, by the singing men of Sarum. Fr(ancis) Sambroke (attorney) then assisted as a chorister boy; my uncle, Thomas Danvers, was at the funerall. Vide in the Register booke at the office when he dyed, for the parish register is lost. Memorandum: in the chancell are many apt sentences of the Scripture. When he was first maried he lived a yeare or better at Dantesey house. H. Allen, of Dantesey, was well acquainted with him, who has told me that he had a very good hand on the lute, and that he sett his own lyricks or sacred poems. Tis an honour to the place, to have had the heavenly and ingeniose contemplation of this good man, who was pious even to prophesie; e.g.

> Religion now on tip-toe stands,
> Ready to goe to the American strands.

> —John Aubrey, *Brief Lives*, 1669–96,
> vol. 1, ed. Clark, pp. 309–10

IZAAK WALTON (1670)

He was for his person of a stature inclining towards tallness; his body was very straight, and so far from being cumbered with too much flesh, that he was lean to an extremity. His aspect was cheerful, and his speech and motion did both declare him a gentleman; for they were all so meek and obliging, that they purchased love and respect from all that knew him. Brought most of his parishioners, and many gentlemen in the neighbourhood, constantly to make a part of his congregation twice a day: and some of the meaner sort of his parish did so love and reverence Mr. Herbert, that they would let their plough rest when Mr. Herbert's Saint's-bell rung to prayers, that they might also offer their devotions to God with him; and would then return back to their plough. And his most holy life was such, that it begot such reverence to God, and to him, that they thought themselves the happier, when they carried Mr. Herbert's blessing back with them to their labour. Thus powerful was his reason and example to persuade others to a practical piety and devotion.

> —Izaak Walton, *The Life of*
> *Mr. George Herbert*, 1670

CHARLES COTTON "TO MY OLD, AND MOST WORTHY FRIEND MR. IZAAK WALTON" (1670)

An English poet and translator best known for rendering the works of Michel de Montaigne into English, Charles Cotton (1630–1687) was also well-known for his burlesque works, which often overshadowed his other, more serious poems. Cotton made the acquaintance of scholar and critic Izaak Walton in 1655, and the two became lifelong friends and frequently corresponded about the literary masters of the time, as the excerpt below indicates.

⸺⁓⸺ ⸺⁓⸺ ⸺⁓⸺

. . .*Herbert:* he, whose education, Manners, and parts, by high applauses blown, Was deeply tainted with Ambition; And fitted for a Court, made that his aim: At last, without regard to Birth or Name, For a poor Country-Cure, does all disclaim. Where, with a soul compos'd of Harmonies, Like a sweet Swan, he warbles, as he dies His makers praise, and, his own obsequies.

—Charles Cotton, "To My Old, and Most
Worthy Friend Mr. Izaac Walton,"
The Life of Mr. George Herbert, 1670, p. 10

JOHN DUNTON (1694)

John Dunton (1659–1733) was a well-known bookseller and occasional author most known in his day for his Whig writings. The *Athenian Mercury*, which is excerpted below, was a weekly publication that Dunton published and wrote for.

⸺⁓⸺ ⸺⁓⸺ ⸺⁓⸺

Mr. *Herbert's* Reputation is so firmly and so justly establish'd among all Persons of *Piety* and *Ingenuity,* his Sense so good, and most of his Poetry so fine, that those who Censure him will be in more danger of having their Judgments question'd, than such as with good reason Admire him. Nor can the Time he writ in, when Poetry was not near so refin'd as 'tis now, be justly objected against him, so as to make his Works of small or no Value, any more than the *oddness* or *flatness* of some Expressions and Phrases, since something of these are to be found in all other Compositions that have yet appear'd in our Language; and besides this, they were probably many of em made to Tunes,

Mr. *Herbert* being so great a Musitian, which every one knows will often weaken the Sense. For *The Synagogue,* all know 'tis none of his, tho' there are many fine Thoughts, and not a few good Lines in't, carrying all thro' in an Air and Spirit of great *Sense, Piety* and *Devotion,* much more Valuable than all the foolish Wit that has so often directed the World at so dear a Rate.

—John Dunton, *Athenian Mercury,* January 6, 1694

John Reynolds "To the Memory of the Divine Mr. Herbert" (1725)

The English theologian John Reynolds (1667–1727) was well-known in his day for his Christian writings. The piece below, originally published as *Death's Vision,* is part of a larger moral work that examines death. Written in Herbert's style, the work was said to be written at the request of John Locke, the famous English philosopher. In the excerpt below, Reynolds imagines Herbert as the greatest bard Christianity has ever known, suggesting that his words make excellent proselytizing tools: 'Tis *Herbert's* charms must chase (whate'er he boasts) / The fiends and idols from poetic coasts."

Seraphic Singer! where's the fire
That did these lines and lays inspire?
B'ing dropt from heav'n, it scorn'd to dwell
Long upon earth, and near to hell!
The heart it purg'd, it did consume,
Exhal'd the sacrifice in fume,
And with it mounted, as of old
The angel, in the smoke enroll'd;
Return'd in haste, like thine own *Star,*
Pleas'd with its prize, to native sphere.
But blest perfume, that here I find,
The sacrifice has left behind!
Strange! how each fellow-saint's surpris'd
To see himself anatomiz'd!
The *Sion's* mourner breathes thy strains.
Sighs thee, and in thy notes complains;
Amaz'd, and yet refresh'd to see

His wounds, drawn to the life, in thee!
The warrior, just resolv'd to quit
The field, and all the toils of it.
Returns with vigour, will renew
The fight, with victory in view;
He stabbs his foes, and conquers harms.
With spear, and nails, and *Herbert's* arms.
The racer, almost out of breath,
Marching through shades and vale of death,
Recruits, when he to thee is come.
And sighs for heav'n, and sings thy *Home;*
The tempted soul, whose thoughts are whirl'd.
About th' inchantments of the world.
Can o'er the snares and scandals skip.
Born up by *Frailty,* and the *Quip;*
The victor has reward paid down,
  Has earnest here of life and crown;
  The conscious priest is well releas'd
  Of pain and fear, in *Aaron* drest;
  The preaching envoy can proclaim
  His pleasure in his *Master's* name;
  A name, that like the grace in him,
  Sends life and ease to ev'ry limb;
  Rich magazine of health! where's found
  Specific balm for ev'ry wound!
Hail rev'rend bard! hail thou, th' elected shrine
Of the great Sp'rit, and Shecinah divine!
Who may speak thee! or aim at thy renown.
In lines less venerable than thy own!
Silent we must admire! upon no head
Has, since thy flight, been half thy unction shed.
What wit and grace thy lyric strains command!
Hail, great apostle of the muses land!
Scarce can I pardon the great *Cowley's* claim,
He seems t' usurp the glories of thy fame;
'Tis *Herbert's* charms must chase (whate'er he boasts)
The fiends and idols from poetic coasts;
The *Mistress,* the *Anacreontic* lays,
More demons will, and more disorders raise,

Than his fam'd hero's lyre, in modern play,
Or tun'd by Cowley's self, I fear, can lay;
'Tis *Herbert's* notes must uninchant the ear,
Make the deaf adder, and th' old serpent hear.
      Soon had religion, with a gracious smile,
Vouchsaf'd to visit this selected isle;
The *British* emp'ror first her liv'ry wore.
And sacred cross with *Roman* eagles bore;
The sev'ral states, at last, her empire own,
And swear allegiance to her rightful throne;
Only the muses lands abjure her sway.
They heathen still, and unconverted lay.
Loth was the prince of darkness to resign
Such fertiliz'd dominions, and so fine,
Herbert arose! and sounds the trumpet there.
He makes the muses land the seat of war.
The forts he takes, the squadrons does pursue.
And with rich spoils erects a *Temple* too;
A structure, that shall roofs of gold survive.
Shall *Solomonic* and *Mosaic* work out-live,
Shall stay to see the universal fire.
And only, with the temple of the world, expire.
      Strange, the late bard should his devotion rear
At *Synagogue,* when, lo! the *Temple's* near!
Such sacrilege it were of old, t' espouse
The wandring tent, before the wondrous house;
The house, in which a southern queen might be
A sacrifice to art and ecstasie.
Poor poets thus ingeniously can prove
Their sacred zeal misguided as their love!
      Go forth, saint-bard! exert thy conqu'ring hand!
Set up thy Temple through the muses land!
Down with the stage, its wanton scenes cashier,
And all the demons wont to revel there!
Great *Pan* must dy, his oracles be dumb,
Where'er thy temple and its flames shall come;
Convert the Muses, teach them how to be
Ambitious of the *Graces* companie;
Purge *Helicon,* and make *Parnassus* still

To send his vicious streams to *Sion's* hill!
Thence banish all th' unhallow'd, tuneful men,
From *Homer,* down to the phantastic Ben!
Baptize the future poets, and infuse
A sacred flame in all belov'd by muse!
Teach them the efforts of great *Shiloh's* love,
The anthems, and the melodies above!
Tell them what matter, and what theam's in store,
For sacred past'ral, and divine amour;
Shiloh himself would condescend so low,
To be a shepherd, and a bridegroom too.
What myst'ries in church militant there to,
Teach them to look, and soar, and sing like thee.
Here poesy's high birth, and glory shine,
'Tis here, that it, like other grace, we see
From glory differs only in degree!
     Whilst to thy temple proselytes repair,
And offer, and inflame devotion there.
Whilst, on its pillars deep inscrib'd, thy name
Stands consecrated to immortal fame,
Do thou enjoy the rich resolves of *Love,*
The pleasures, the society above!
No more thou'lt tune thy lute unto a strain
That may with thee all day complain;
No more shall sense of ill, and *Griefs* of time
Distune thy viol, and disturb thy rhyme;
No more shall *Sion's* wrongs and sorrows sharp,
Upon the willows hang thy trembling harp;
The wish'd-for sight, the dear perfection's gain'd
The *Longing,* and the *Search,* have now obtain'd;
On Sion's mount, join thou the blisful throng,
That here were skill'd in sacred love and song;
Consort with *Heman, Asaph,* and the rest,
Akin to thee, in Temple-service blest;
Who all rejoyce thy lov'd access to see,
And ply their harps, no doubt, to welcome thee;
Music and Love triumph! and *Herbert's* lyre,
Serenely sounds amidst th' harmonious quire!
There still, on *Love* in his own person, gaze,

Drink in the beams flow from his radiant face,
Still to thy harp chant forth th' immortal verse
Does *Love's* exploits in foreign land rehearse,
Move him to hasten his return below,
That church, now mil'tant, may triumphant grow,
And all thy pros'lyte-bands may mount, and see
The Temple there, and all the scenes of joy, with thee.

—John Reynolds, "To the Memory of
the Divine Mr. Herbert," A *View of Death*,
1725, pp. 110–18

S. Margaret Fuller
"The Two Herberts" (1846)

Sarah Margaret Fuller (1810–1850) was an American suffragist and journalist. In the piece below, Fuller imagines a dialogue between George
Herbert and his older brother Edward, Lord Herbert, a sometimes poet
whose style was more closely aligned to John Donne than his own
brother. In the excerpt, Fuller presents each brother's philosophies on
theology and faith; in Fuller's estimation, Lord Herbert, the first significant proponent of deism in England, differed greatly from his more
traditional brother in matters of God and the church. Their conversation,
though, is highly cordial:

> *Lord H;* I hear your sweet words with the more pleasure, George, that I
> had supposed you were now too much of the churchman to value the
> fruits of my thought.
>
> *George* H: God forbid that I should ever cease to reverence the mind
> that was, to my own, so truly that of an elder brother! I do lament that
> you will not accept the banner of my Master, and drink at what I have
> found the fountain of pure wisdom.

Thus while George Herbert laments that his brother does not share the
same beliefs as he, the two continue to learn from one another:

> *Lord H:* You speak wisely, George, and, let me add, religiously. Were all
> churchmen as tolerant, I had never assailed the basis of their belief.
> Did they not insist and urge upon us their way as the one only way,
> not for them alone, but for all, none would wish to put stumbling-
> blocks before their feet.

George H: Nay, my brother, do not misunderstand me. None, more than I, can think there is but one way to arrive finally at truth.

Ultimately, Fuller's dialogue represents her imagined views of each writer's religious principles and convictions based on his respective works; eventually, the two find common ground between them. Anyone writing on Herbert's religious convictions may find Fuller's work illuminating, though its fanciful style makes it difficult to cite with conviction.

The following sketch is meant merely to mark some prominent features in the minds of the two Herberts, under a form less elaborate and more reverent than that of criticism.

A mind of penetrating and creative power could not find a better subject for a masterly picture. The two figures stand as representatives of natural religion, and of that of the Son of Man, of the life of the philosophical man of the world, and the secluded, contemplative, though beneficent existence.

The present slight effort is not made with a view to the great and dramatic results so possible to the plan. It is intended chiefly as a setting to the Latin poems of Lord Herbert, which are known to few,—a year ago, seemingly, were so to none in this part of the world. The only desire in translating them has been to do so literally, as any paraphrase, or addition of words impairs their profound meaning. It is hoped that, even in their present repulsive garb, without rhyme or rhythm, stripped, too, of the majestic Roman mantle, the greatness of the thoughts, and the large lines of spiritual experience, will attract readers, who will not find time misspent in reading them many times.

George Herbert's heavenly strain is better, though far from generally, known.

There has been no attempt really to represent these persons speaking their own dialect, or in their own individual manners. The writer loves too well to hope to imitate the sprightly, fresh, and varied style of Lord Herbert, or the quaintness and keen sweets of his brother's. Neither have accessories been given, such as might easily have been taken from their works. But the thoughts imputed to them they might have spoken, only in better and more concise terms, and the facts— are facts. So let this be gently received with the rest of the modern tapestries. We can no longer weave them of the precious materials princes once furnished, but we can give, in our way, some notion of the original design.

It was an afternoon of one of the longest summer days. The sun had showered down his amplest bounties, the earth put on her richest garment to receive them. The clear heavens seemed to open themselves to the desire of mortals; the day had been long enough and bright enough to satisfy an immortal.

In a green lane leading from the town of Salisbury, in England, the noble stranger was reclining beneath a tree. His eye was bent in the direction of the town, as if upon some figure approaching or receding; but its inward turned expression showed that he was, in fact, no longer looking, but lost in thought.

"Happiness!" thus said his musing mind, "it would seem at such hours and in such places as if it not merely hovered over the earth, a poetic presence to animate our pulses and give us courage for what must be, but sometimes alighted. Such fulness of expression pervades these fields, these trees, that it excites, not rapture, but a blissful sense of peace. Yet, even were this permanent in the secluded lot, would I accept it in exchange for the bitter sweet of a wider, freer life? I could not if I would; yet, methinks, I would not if I could. But here comes George, I will argue the point with him."

"Let us not return at once," said Lord Herbert. "I had already waited for you long, and have seen all the beauties of the parsonage and church."

"Not many, I think, in the eyes of such a critic," said George, as they seated themselves in the spot his brother had before chosen for the extent and loveliness of prospect.

"Enough to make me envious of you, if I had not early seen enough to be envious of none. Indeed, I know not if such a feeling can gain admittance to your little paradise, for I never heard such love and reverence expressed as by your people for you."

George looked upon his brother with a pleased and open sweetness. Lord Herbert continued, with a little hesitation—"To tell the truth, I wondered a little at the boundless affection they declared. Our mother has long and often told me of your pure and beneficent life, and I know what you have done for this place and people, but, as I remember, you were of a choleric temper."

"And am so still!"

"Well, and do you not sometimes, by flashes of that, lose all you may have gained?"

"It does not often now," he replied, "find open way. My Master has been very good to me in suggestions of restraining prayer, which come into my mind at the hour of temptation."

Lord H: Why do you not say, rather, that your own discerning mind and maturer will show you more and more the folly and wrong of such outbreaks.

George H: Because that would not be saying all that I think. At such times I feel a higher power interposed, as much as I see that yonder tree is distinct from myself. Shall I repeat to you some poor verses in which I have told, by means of various likenesses, in an imperfect fashion, how it is with me in this matter?

Lord H: Do so! I shall hear them gladly; for I, like you, though with less time and learning to perfect it, love the deliberate composition of the closet, and believe we can better understand one another by thoughts expressed so, than in the more glowing but hasty words of the moment.

George H:

Prayer—the church's banquet; angel's age;
    God's breath in man returning to his birth;
The soul in paraphrase; heart in pilgrimage;
    The Christian plummet, sounding heaven
        and earth.
Engine against th' Almighty; sinner's tower;
    Reversed thunder; Christ's side-piercing spear;
The six-days' world transposing in an hour;
    A kind of tune, which all things hear and fear.
Softness, and peace, and joy, and love, and bliss;
    Exalted manna; gladness of the best;
Heaven in ordinary; man well drest;
    The milky way; the bird of paradise;
Church bells beyond the stars heard; the soul's blood;
The land of spices; something understood.

Lord H: (who has listened attentively, after a moment's thought.)—There is something in the spirit of your lines which pleases me, and, in general, I know not that I should differ; yet you have expressed yourself nearest to mine own knowledge and feeling, where you have left more room to consider our prayers as aspirations, rather than the gifts of grace; as—

"Heart in pilgrimage;"
"A kind of tune, which all things hear and fear.[1]"
"Something understood."

In your likenesses, you sometimes appear to quibble in a way unworthy the subject.

George H: It is the nature of some minds, brother, to play with what they love best. Yours is of a grander and severer cast; it can only grasp and survey steadily what interests it. My walk is different, and I have always admired you in yours without expecting to keep pace with you.

Lord H: I hear your sweet words with the more pleasure, George, that I had supposed you were now too much of the churchman to value the fruits of my thought.

George H: God forbid that I should ever cease to reverence the mind that was, to my own, so truly that of an elder brother! I do lament that you will not accept the banner of my Master, and drink at what I have found the fountain of pure wisdom. But as I would not blot from the book of life the prophets and priests that came before Him, nor those antique sages who knew all

That Reason hath from Nature borrowed,
Or of itself, like a good housewife spun,
In laws and policy: what the stars conspire:
What willing Nature speaks; what, freed by fire:
Both th' old discoveries, and the new found seas:
The stock and surplus, cause and history,—

As I cannot resign and disparage these, because they have not what I conceive to be the pearl of all knowledge, how could I you?

Lord H: You speak wisely, George, and, let me add, religiously. Were all churchmen as tolerant, I had never assailed the basis of their belief. Did they not insist and urge upon us their way as the one only way, not for them alone, but for all, none would wish to put stumbling-blocks before their feet.

George H: Nay, my brother, do not misunderstand me. None, more than I, can think there is but one way to arrive finally at truth.

Lord H: I do not misunderstand you; but, feeling that you are one who accept what you do from love of the best, and not from fear of the worst, I am as much inclined to tolerate your conclusions as you to tolerate mine.

George H: I do not consider yours as conclusions, but only as steps to such. The progress of the mind should be from natural to revealed religion, as there must be a sky for the sun to give light through its expanse.

Lord H: The sky is—nothing!

George H: Except room for a sun, and such there is in you. Of your own need of such, did you not give convincing proof, when you prayed for a revelation to direct whether you should publish a book against revelation?

Lord H: You borrow that objection from the crowd, George; but I wonder you have not looked into the matter more deeply. Is there any thing inconsistent with disbelief in a partial plan of salvation for the nations, which, by its necessarily limited working, excludes the majority of men up to our day, with belief that each individual soul, wherever born, however nurtured, may receive immediate response, in an earnest hour, from the source of truth.

George H: But you believed the customary order of nature to be deranged in your behalf. What miraculous record does more?

Lord H: It was at the expense of none other. A spirit asked, a spirit answered, and its voice was thunder; but, in this, there was nothing special, nothing partial wrought in my behalf, more than if I had arrived at the same conclusion by a process of reasoning.

George H: I cannot but think, that if your mind were allowed, by the nature of your life, its free force to search, it would survey the subject in a different way, and draw inferences more legitimate from a comparison of its own experience with the gospel.

Lord H: My brother does not think the mind is free to act in courts and camps. To me it seems that the mind takes its own course everywhere, and that, if men cannot have outward, they can always mental seclusion. None is so profoundly lonely, none so in need of constant self-support, as he who, living in the crowd, thinks an inch aside from, or in advance of it. The hermitage of such an one is still and cold; its silence unbroken to a degree of which these beautiful and fragrant solitudes give no hint. These sunny sights and sounds, promoting reverie rather than thought, are scarce more favourable to a great advance in the intellect, than the distractions of the busy street. Beside, we need the assaults of other minds to quicken our powers, so easily hushed to sleep, and call it peace. The mind takes a bias too easily, and does not examine whether from tradition or a native growth intended by the heavens.

George H: But you are no common man. You shine, you charm, you win, and the world presses too eagerly on you to leave many hours for meditation.

Lord H: It is a common error to believe that the most prosperous men love the world best. It may be hardest for them to leave it, because they have been made effeminate and slothful by want of that exercise which difficulty brings. But this is not the case with me; for, while the common boons of life's game have been too easily attained, to hold high value in my eyes, the goal which my secret mind, from earliest infancy, prescribed, has been high enough to task all my energies. Every year has helped to make that, and that alone, of value in my eyes; and did I believe that life, in scenes like this, would lead me to it more speedily than in my accustomed broader way, I would seek it to-morrow—nay, to-day. But is it worthy of a man to make him a cell, in which alone he can worship? Give me rather the always open temple of the universe! To me, it seems that the only course for a man is that pointed out by birth and fortune. Let him take that and pursue it with clear eyes and head erect, secure that it must point at last to those truths which are central to us, wherever we stand; and if my road, leading through the busy crowd of men, amid the clang and bustle of conflicting interests and passions, detain me longer than would the still path through the groves, the chosen haunt of contemplation, yet I incline to think that progress so, though slower, is surer. Owing no safety, no clearness to my position, but so far as it is attained to mine own effort, encountering what temptations, doubts and lures may beset a man, what I do possess is more surely mine, and less a prey to contingencies. It is a well-tempered wine that has been carried over many seas, and escaped many shipwrecks.

George H: I can the less gainsay you, my lord and brother, that your course would have been mine could I have chosen.

Lord H: Yes; I remember thy verse:—

Whereas my birth and spirits rather took
The way that takes the town;
Thou didst betray me to a lingering book,
And wrap me in a gown.

It was not my fault, George, that it so chanced.

George H: I have long learnt to feel that it noway chanced; that thus, and no other, was it well for me. But how I view these matters you are, or may be well aware, through a little book I have writ . . .

Have you never faltered till you felt the need of a friend? strong in this clear vision, have you never sighed for a more homefelt assurance to your faith? steady in your demand of what the soul requires, have you never known fear lest you want purity to receive the boon if granted?

Lord H: I do not count those weak moments, George; they are not my true life.

George H: It suffices that you know them, for, in time, I doubt not that every conviction which a human being needs, to be reconciled to the Parent of all, will be granted to a nature so ample, so open, and so aspiring.

Let me answer in a strain which bespeaks my heart as truly, if not as nobly as yours answers to your great mind,—

> My joy, my life, my crown!
>   My heart was meaning all the day
>   Somewhat it fain would say;
> And still it runneth, muttering, up and down,
> With only this—*my joy, my life, my crown.*
>   Yet slight not these few words;
>   If truly said, they may take part
>   Among the best in art.
> The fineness which a hymn or psalm affords,
> Is, when the soul unto the lines accords.
>   He who craves all the mind
>   And all the soul, and strength and time;
>   If the words only rhyme,
> Justly complains, that somewhat is behind
> To make his verse or write a hymn in kind.
>   Whereas, if the heart be moved,
>   Although the verse be somewhat scant,
>   God doth supply the want—
> As when the heart says, sighing to be approved,
> "Oh, could I love!" and stops; God writeth, *loved.*

Lord H: I cannot say to you truly that my mind replies to this, although I discern a beauty in it. You will say I lack humility to understand yours.

George H: I will say nothing, but leave you to time and the care of a greater than I. We have exchanged our verse, let us now change our subject too, and walk homeward; for I trust you, this night, intend to make my roof happy in your presence, and the sun is sinking.

Lord H: Yes, you know I am there to be introduced to my new sister, whom I hope to love, and win from her a sisterly regard in turn.

George H: You, none can fail to regard; and for her, even as you love me, you must her, for we are one.

Lord H: (smiling)—Indeed; two years wed, and say that.

George H: Will your lordship doubt it? From your muse I took my first lesson.

> With a look, it seem'd denied
>   All earthly powers but hers, yet so

As if to her breath he did owe
    This borrow'd life, he thus replied—
    And shall our love, so far beyond
        That low and dying appetite,
And which so chaste desires unite,
        Not hold in an eternal bond?
    O no, belov'd! I am most sure
        Those virtuous habits we acquire,
As being with the soul entire,
        Must with it evermore endure.
    Else should our souls in vain elect;
        And vainer yet were heaven's laws
When to an everlasting cause
    They gave a perishing effect.

Lord H: (sighing) You recall a happy season, when my thoughts were as delicate of hue, and of as heavenly a perfume as the flowers of May.

George H: Have those flowers borne no fruit?

Lord H: My experience of the world and men had made me believe that they did not indeed bloom in vain, but that the fruit would be ripened in some future sphere of our existence. What my own marriage was you know,—a family arrangement made for me in my childhood. Such obligations as such a marriage could imply, I have fulfilled, and it has not failed to bring me some benefits of good-will and esteem, and far more, in the happiness of being a parent. But my observation of the ties formed, by those whose choice was left free, has not taught me that a higher happiness than mine was the destined portion of men. They are too immature to form permanent relations; all that they do seems experiment, and mostly fails for the present. Thus I had postponed all hopes except of fleeting joys or ideal pictures. Will you tell me that you are possessed already of so much more?

George H: I am indeed united in a bond, whose reality I cannot doubt, with one whose thoughts, affections, and objects every way correspond with mine, and in whose life I see a purpose so pure that, if we are ever separated, the fault must be mine. I believe God, in his exceeding grace, gave us to one another, for we met almost at a glance, without doubt before, jar or repentance after, the vow which bound our lives together.

Lord H: Then there is indeed one circumstance of your lot I could wish to share with you. (After some moments' silence on both sides)—They told me at the house, that, with all your engagements, you go twice a-week to Salisbury. How is that? How can you leave your business and your happy home, so much and often?

George H: I go to hear the music; the great solemn church music. This is, at once, the luxury and the necessity of my life. I know not how it is with others, but, with me, there is a frequent drooping of the wings, a smouldering of the inward fires, a languor, almost a loathing of corporeal existence. Of this visible diurnal sphere I am, by turns, the master, the interpreter, and the victim; an ever burning lamp, to warm again the embers of the altar; a skiff, that cannot be becalmed, to bear me again on the ocean of hope; an elixir, that fills the dullest fibre with ethereal energy; such, music is to me. It stands in relation to speech, even to the speech of poets, as the angelic choir, who, in their subtler being, may inform the space around us, unseen but felt, do to men, even to prophetic men. It answers to the soul's presage, and, in its fluent life, embodies all I yet know how to desire. As all the thoughts and hopes of human souls are blended by the organ to a stream of prayer and praise, I tune at it my separate breast, and return to my little home, cheered and ready for my day's work, as the lark does to her nest after her morning visit to the sun.

Lord H: The ancients held that the spheres made music to those who had risen into a state which enabled them to hear it. Pythagoras, who prepared different kinds of melody to guide and expand the differing natures of his pupils, needed himself to hear none on instruments made by human art, for the universal harmony which comprehends all these was audible to him. Man feels in all his higher moments, the need of traversing a subtler element, of a winged existence. Artists have recognised wings as the symbol of the state next above ours; but they have not been able so to attach them to the forms of gods and angels as to make them agree with the anatomy of the human frame. Perhaps music gives this instruction, and supplies the deficiency. Although I see that I do not feel it as habitually or as profoundly as you do, I have experienced such impressions from it.

George H: That is truly what I mean. It introduces me into that winged nature, and not as by way of supplement, but of inevitable transition. All that has budded in me, bursts into bloom, under this influence. As I sit in our noble cathedral, in itself one of the holiest thoughts ever embodied by the power of man, the great tides of song come rushing through its aisles; they pervade all the space, and my soul within it, perfuming me like incense, bearing me on like the wind, and on and on to regions of unutterable joy, and freedom, and certainty. As their triumph rises, I rise with them, and learn to comprehend by living them, till at last a calm rapture seizes me, and holds me poised. The same life you have attained in your description of the celestial choirs. It is the music of the soul, when centred in the will of God, thrilled by the love, expanded by the energy, with which it is fulfilled through all the ranges of active life. From such hours, I return through these green lanes, to hear the same tones from the slightest flower, to long for a life of purity and praise, such as is manifested by the flowers.

At this moment they reached the door, and there paused to look back. George Herbert bent upon the scene a half-abstracted look, yet which had a celestial tearfulness in it, a pensiveness beyond joy. His brother looked on *him,* and, beneath that fading twilight, it seemed to him a farewell look. It was so. Soon George Herbert soared into the purer state, for which his soul had long been ready, though not impatient.

The brothers met no more; but they had enjoyed together one hour of true friendship, when mind drew near to mind by the light of faith, and heart mingled with heart in the atmosphere of Divine love. It was a great boon to be granted two mortals.

—S. Margaret Fuller, from "The Two Herberts,"
Papers on Art and Literature, 1846, pp. 15–34

Alexander Grosart
"George Herbert" (1873)

What was said of the late venerable Dr. John Brown, of Edinburgh, that "his face was a sermon for Christ," holds of the thought-lined, burdened-eyed, translucent as if transfigured face of Herbert. There is a noble "ivory palace" for the meek and holy soul there; brow steep rather than wide; lips tremulous as with music; nose pronounced as Richard Baxter's; cheeks worn and thin; hair full and flowing as in younger days: altogether a face which one could scarcely pass without note—all the more that there are lines in it which inevitably suggest that if George Herbert mellowed into the sweet lovingness and gentleness of John "whom Jesus loved," it was of grace, and through masterdom of a naturally lofty, fiery spirit. After all, these are the men of God who leave the deepest mark on their generation.

—Alexander Grosart, "George Herbert,"
Leisure Hour, 1873, p. 455

Donald G. Mitchell (1890)

The American scholar, educator, and critic Donald G. Mitchell (1822–1908) was a prominent and prolific literary and cultural critic of the nineteenth century.

He was buried at Bemerton, where a new church has been built in his honor. It may be found on the high-road leading west from Salisbury, and only a mile and a half away; and at Wilton—the carpet town—which is only a fifteen minutes' walk beyond, may be found that gorgeous church, built not long ago by another son of the Pembroke stock (the late Lord Herbert of Lea), who perhaps may have had in mind the churchly honors due to his poetic kinsman; and yet all the marbles which are lavished upon this Wilton shrine are poorer, and will sooner fade than the mosaic of verse built into *The Temple* of George Herbert.

—Donald G. Mitchell, *English Lands, Letters, and Kings from Elizabeth to Anne*, 1890, p. 119

William Holden Hutton (1895)

The English clergyman and scholar William Holden Hutton (1860–1930) was a fellow and tutor at St. John Baptist College at Oxford and examining chaplain to the bishop of Rochester.

At Bemerton he lived, as he wrote, the ideal life of "A Priest to the Temple." While his simple sermons and his life of goodness won his people to a good life, he was writing poems which should catch the hearts of the next generation and enlist men's sentiment and sympathy in the restoration of the Church. Herbert's life was itself the noblest of his poems, and while it had the beauty of his verses it had their quaintnesses as well. Those exquisite lines of his, so characteristic of his age and his style, give a picture suggestive of his own character:

Sweet day, so cool, so calm, so bright,
The bridal of the earth and sky.

—William Holden Hutton, *Social England*, 1895, vol. 4, ed. Traill, p. 34.

GENERAL

ROBERT CODRINGTON
"ON HERBERT'S POEM" (1638)

Robert Codrington (1602?–1665) was a Puritan bookmaker, translator, and author.

——◊◊◊—— ——◊◊◊—— ——◊◊◊——

View a true Poet, whose bare lines
Include more goodnesse then some shrines.
Wee'le canonize him, and what er
Befalls, style him heauens Chorister.
No Muse inspird his quill, the three
Graces, faith, Hope, and Charitie
Inflamd that breast, whose heat farre higher . . .

—Robert Codrington,
"On Herbert's Poem," 1638

HENRY VAUGHAN "PREFACE" (1650)

Metaphysical poet Henry Vaughan (1622–1695) was one of George Herbert's great admirers and called himself the "least" of Herbert's disciples. Vaughan credited Herbert with his own conversion and was certainly the major influence on his work.

——◊◊◊—— ——◊◊◊—— ——◊◊◊——

The first, that with an effectual success attempted a diversion of this foul and overflowing stream, was the blessed man, Mr. George Herbert, whose holy life and verse gained many pious converts—of whom I am the least—and gave the first check to a most flourishing and admired wit of his time.

—Henry Vaughan, "Preface,"
Silex Scintillans, 1650

IZAAK WALTON "THE LIFE OF
MR. GEORGE HERBERT" (1670)

The piece below comes from Walton's famous seventeenth-century biography of John Donne, Sir Henry Wotton, Richard Hooker, George Herbert, and Dr. Robert Sanderson, which traces the life of each man from birth and childhood through their education and later years. Of Herbert, Walton writes that he lived a life of virtue and holiness: "a life

so full of charity, humility, and all Christian virtues" that the piece practically canonizes the man. Though one could argue that Walton's account
is perhaps too laudatory for a critical biography, the piece not only
demonstrates the great respect accorded to Herbert in his own time, but
also demonstrates the near saint-like quality many of Herbert's admirers
ascribed to him.

⎯⟋⟍⟋⎯   ⎯⟋⟍⟋⎯   ⎯⟋⟍⟋⎯

George Herbert spent much of his childhood in a sweet content under the
eye and care of his prudent Mother, and the tuition of a Chaplain, or tutor to
him and two of his brothers, in her own family,—for she was then a widow,—
where he continued till about the age of twelve years; and being at that time
well instructed in the rules of Grammar, he was not long after commended
to the care of Dr. Neale, who was then Dean of Westminster; and by him to
the care of Mr. Ireland, who was then Chief Master of that School; where the
beauties of his pretty behaviour and wit shined and became so eminent and
lovely in this his innocent age, that he seemed to be marked out for piety, and
to become the care of Heaven, and of a particular good angel to guard and
guide him. And thus he continued in that School, till he came to be perfect in
the learned languages, and especially in the Greek tongue, in which he after
proved an excellent critic.

About the age of fifteen—he being then a King's Scholar—he
was elected out of that School for Trinity College in Cambridge, to
which place he was transplanted about the year 1608; and his prudent
Mother, well knowing that he might easily lose or lessen that virtue and
innocence, which her advice and example had planted in his mind, did
therefore procure the generous and liberal Dr. Nevil, who was then Dean of
Canterbury, and Master of that College, to take him into his particular care,
and provide him a Tutor; which he did most gladly undertake, for he knew
the excellencies of his mother, and how to value such a friendship.

And in Cambridge we may find our George Herbert's behaviour to be such,
that we may conclude he consecrated the first-fruits of his early age to virtue,
and a serious study of learning. And that he did so, this following Letter and
Sonnet, which were, in the first year of his going to Cambridge, sent his dear
Mother for a New-year's gift, may appear to be some testimony.

—"But I fear the heat of my late ague hath dried up those springs, by
which scholars say the Muses use to take up their habitations. However, I
need not their help to reprove the vanity of those many love-poems, that
are daily writ, and consecrated to Venus; nor to bewail that so few are writ,

that look towards God and Heaven. For my own part, my meaning— dear Mother—is, in these Sonnets, to declare my resolution to be, that my poor abilities in Poetry, shall be all and ever consecrated to God's glory: and I beg you to receive this as one testimony."

> My God, where is that ancient heat towards thee,
> > Wherewith whole shoals of Martyrs once did
> > > burn,
> > Besides their other flames? Doth Poetry
> Wear Venus' livery? only serve her turn?
> Why are not Sonnets made of thee? and lays
> > Upon thine altar burnt? Cannot thy love
> > Heighten a spirit to sound out thy praise
> As well as any she? Cannot thy Dove
> Outstrip their Cupid easily in flight?
> > Or, since thy ways are deep, and still the same,
> > Will not a verse run smooth that bears thy name?
> Why doth that fire, which by the power and might
> > Each breast does feel, no braver fuel choose
> > Than that, which one day, worms may chance
> > > refuse?
> Sure, Lord, there is enough in thee to dry
> > Oceans of ink; for as the Deluge did
> > Cover the Earth, so doth thy Majesty;
> Each cloud distils thy praise, and doth forbid
> Poets to turn it to another use.
> > Roses and lilies speak Thee; and to make
> > A pair of cheeks of them, is thy abuse.
> Why should I women's eyes for crystal take?
> Such poor invention burns in their low mind
> > Whose fire is wild, and doth not upward go
> > To praise, and on thee, Lord, some ink bestow.
> Open the bones, and you shall nothing find
> > In the best face but filth; when, Lord, in Thee
> > The beauty lies, in the discovery.

This was his resolution at the sending this letter to his dear Mother, about which time he was in the seventeenth year of his age; and as he grew older, so he grew in learning, and more and more in favour both with God and man; insomuch that, in this morning of that short day of his life, he seemed to be marked out for virtue, and to become the care of Heaven; for God still kept his soul in so holy a frame, that he may and ought to be a pattern of virtue to all posterity, and especially to his brethren of the Clergy, of which the Reader may expect a more exact account in what will follow.

I need not declare that he was a strict student, because, that he was so, there will be many testimonies in the future part of his life. I shall therefore only tell, that he was made Bachelor of Arts in the year 1611; Major Fellow of the College, March 15th, 1615: and, that in that year he was also made Master of Arts, he being then in the 22d year of his age; during all which time, all, or the greatest diversion from his study, was the practice of Music, in which he became a great master; and of which he would say, "That it did relieve his drooping spirits, compose his distracted thoughts, and raised his weary soul so far above earth, that it gave him an earnest of the joys of Heaven, before he possessed them." And it may be noted, that from his first entrance into the College, the generous Dr. Nevil was a cherisher of his studies, and such a lover of his person, his behaviour, and the excellent endowments of his mind, that he took him often into his own company; by which he confirmed his native gentleness: and if during his time he expressed any error, it was, that he kept himself too much retired, and at too great a distance with all his inferiors; and his clothes seemed to prove, that he put too great a value on his parts and parentage . . .

I may not omit to tell, that he had often designed to leave the University, and decline all study, which he thought did impair his health; for he had a body apt to a consumption, and to fevers, and other infirmities, which he judged were increased by his studies; for he would often say, "He had too thoughtful a wit; a wit like a penknife in too narrow a sheath, too sharp for his body." But his Mother would by no means allow him to leave the University, or to travel; and though he inclined very much to both, yet he would by no means satisfy his own desires at so dear a rate, as to prove an undutiful son to so affectionate a Mother; but did always submit to her wisdom. And what I have now said may partly appear in a copy of verses in his printed poems; 'tis one of those that bear the title of Affliction; and it appears to be a pious reflection on God's providence, and some passages of his life, in which he says,

> Whereas my birth and spirit rather took
>   The way that takes the town;
> Thou didst betray me to a lingering book,
>   And wrapt me in a gown:

I was entangled in a world of strife,
Before I had the power to change my life.
Yet, for I threaten'd oft the siege to raise,
    Not simpering all mine age;
Thou often didst with academic praise
    Melt and dissolve my rage;
I took the sweeten'd pill, till I came where
I could not go away, nor persevere.
Yet, lest perchance I should too happy be
    In my unhappiness,
Turning my purge to food, thou throwest me
    Into more sicknesses.
Thus doth thy power cross-bias me, not making
Thine own gifts good, yet me from my ways taking.
Now I am here, what thou wilt do with me
    None of my books will show.
I read, and sigh, and I wish I were a tree,
    For then sure I should grow
To fruit or shade, at least some bird would trust
Her household with me, and I would be just.
Yet, though thou troublest me, I must be meek,
   In weakness must be stout,
Well, I will change my service, and go seek
    Some other master out;
Ah, my dear God! though I am clean forgot,
Let me not love thee, if I love thee not.

In this time of Mr. Herbert's attendance and expectation of some good occasion to remove from Cambridge to Court, God, in whom there is an unseen chain of causes, did in a short time put an end to the lives of two of his most obliging and most powerful friends, Lodowick Duke of Richmond, and James Marquis of Hamilton; and not long after him King James died also, and with them, all Mr. Herbert's Court-hopes: so that he presently betook himself to a retreat from London, to a friend in Kent, where he lived very privately, and was such a lover of solitariness, as was judged to impair his health, more than his study had done. In this time of retirement, he had many conflicts with himself, whether he should return to the painted pleasures of a Court-life, or betake himself to a study of Divinity, and enter into Sacred Orders, to which his dear mother had often persuaded him. These were such conflicts, as they only can know, that have endured them; for ambitious desires, and the outward glory of this world, are not easily laid aside: but at last God inclined him to put on a resolution to serve at his altar.

He did, at his return to London, acquaint a Court-friend with his resolution to enter into Sacred Orders, who persuaded him to alter it, as too mean an employment, and too much below his birth, and the excellent abilities and endowments of his mind. To whom he replied, "It hath been formerly judged that the domestic servants of the King of Heaven should be of the noblest families on earth. And though the iniquity of the late times have made clergymen meanly valued, and the sacred name of priest contemptible; yet I will labour to make it honourable, by consecrating all my learning, and all my poor abilities to advance the glory of that God that gave them; knowing that I can never do too much for him, that hath done so much for me, as to make me a Christian. And I will labour to be like my Saviour, by making humility lovely in the eyes of all men, and by following the merciful and meek example of my dear Jesus."

This was then his resolution; and the God of constancy, who intended him for a great example of virtue, continued him in it, for within that year he was made Deacon, but the day when, or by whom, I cannot learn; but that he was about that time made Deacon, is most certain; for I find by the Records of Lincoln, that he was made Prebend of Layton Ecclesia, in the diocese of Lincoln, July 15th, 1626, and that this Prebend was given him by John, then Lord Bishop of that See. And now he had a fit occasion to shew that piety and bounty that was derived from his generous mother, and his other memorable ancestors, and the occasion was this . . . .

I have now brought him to the Parsonage of Bemerton, and to the thirty-sixth year of his age, and must stop here, and bespeak the Reader to prepare for an almost incredible story, of the great sanctity of the short remainder of his holy life; a life so full of charity, humility, and all Christian virtues, that it deserves the eloquence of St. Chrysostom to commend and declare it: a life: that if it were related by a pen like his, there would then be no need for this age to look back into times past for the examples of primitive piety: for they might be all found in the life of George Herbert. But now, alas! who is fit to undertake it? I confess I am not; and am not pleased with myself that I must; and profess myself amazed, when I consider how few of the Clergy lived like him then, and how many live so unlike him now. But it becomes not me to censure: my design is rather to assure the Reader, that I have used very great diligence to inform myself, that I might inform him of the truth of what follows; and though I cannot adorn it with eloquence, yet I will do it with sincerity.

When at his induction he was shut into Bemerton Church, being left there alone to toll the bell,—as the Law requires him,—he staid so much longer than an ordinary time, before he returned to those friends that staid expecting him at the Church-door, that his friend Mr. Woodnot looked in at the Church-window, and saw him lie prostrate on the ground before the Altar; at which time and place—as he after told Mr. Woodnot— he set some rules to himself, for the future manage of his life; and then and there made a vow to labour to keep them.

And the same night that he had his induction, he said to Mr. Woodnot, "I now look back upon my aspiring thoughts, and think myself more happy than if I had attained what then I so ambitiously thirsted for. And I now can behold the Court with an impartial eye, and see plainly that it is made up of fraud and titles, and flattery, and many other such empty, imaginary, painted pleasures; pleasures that are so empty, as not to satisfy when they are enjoyed. But in God, and his service, is a fulness of all joy and pleasure, and no satiety. And I will now use all my endeavours to bring my relations and dependents to a love and reliance on Him, who never fails those that trust him. But above all, I will be sure to live well, because the virtuous life of a Clergyman is the most powerful eloquence to persuade all that see it to reverence and love, and at least to desire to live like him. And this I will do, because I know we live in an age that hath more need of good examples than precepts. And I beseech that God, who hath honoured me so much as to call me to serve him at his altar, that as by his special grace he hath put into my heart these good desires and resolutions; so he will, by his assisting grace, give me ghostly strength to bring the same to good effect. And I beseech him, that my humble and charitable life may so win upon others, as to bring glory to my Jesus, whom I have this day taken to be my Master and Governor; and I am so proud of his service, that I will always observe, and obey, and do his will; and always call him Jesus my Master; and I will always contemn my birth, or any title or dignity that can be conferred upon me, when I shall compare them with my title of being a Priest, and serving at the Altar of Jesus my Master."

And that he did so, may appear in many parts of his book of Sacred Poems: especially in that which he calls "The Odour." In which he seems to rejoice in the thoughts of that word Jesus, and say, that the adding these words, my Master, to it, and the often repetition of them, seemed to perfume his mind, and leave an oriental fragrance in his very breath. And for his unforced choice to serve at God's altar, he seems in another place of his poems, "The Pearl," (Matth. xiii. 45, 46.) to rejoice and say—"He knew the ways of learning; knew what nature does willingly, and what, when it is forced by fire; knew the ways of honour, and when glory inclines the soul to noble expressions: knew the Court; knew the ways of pleasure, of love, of wit, of music, and upon what terms he declined all these for the service of his Master Jesus;" and then concludes, saying,

> That, through these labyrinths, not my grovelling wit,
> But thy silk twist, let down from Heaven to
>   me,
> Did both conduct, and teach me, how by it
>   To climb to thee.

The third day after he was made Rector of Bemerton, and had changed his sword and silk clothes into a canonical coat, he returned so habited with his friend Mr. Woodnot to Bainton; and immediately after he had seen and saluted his wife, he said to her—"You are now a Minister's wife, and must now so far forget your father's house, as not to claim a precedence of any of your parishioners; for you are to know, that a Priest's wife can challenge no precedence or place, but that which she purchases by her obliging humility; and I am sure, places so purchased do best become them. And let me tell you, that I am so good a Herald, as to assure you that this is truth." And she was so meek a wife, as to assure him, "it was no vexing news to her, and that he should see her observe it with a cheerful willingness." And, indeed, her unforced humility, that humility that was in her so original, as to be born with her, made her so happy as to do so; and her doing so begot her an unfeigned love, and a serviceable respect from all that conversed with her; and this love followed her in all places, as inseparably as shadows follow substances in sunshine.

It was not many days before he returned back to Bemerton, to view the Church, and repair the Chancel: and indeed to rebuild almost three parts of his house, which was fallen down, or decayed by reason of his predecessor's living at a better Parsonage-house; namely, at Minal, sixteen or twenty miles from this place. At which time of Mr. Herbert's coming alone to Bemerton, there came to him a poor old woman, with an intent to acquaint him with her necessitous condition, as also with some troubles of her mind: but after she had spoke some few words to him, she was surprised with a fear, and that begot a shortness of breath, so that her spirits and speech failed her; which he perceiving, did so compassionate her, and was so humble, that he took her by the hand, and said, "Speak, good mother; be not afraid to speak to me; for I am a man that will hear you with patience; and will relieve your necessities too, if I be able: and this I will do willingly; and therefore, mother, be not afraid to acquaint me with what you desire." After which comfortable speech, he again took her by the hand, made her sit down by him, and understanding she was of his parish, he told her "He would be acquainted with her, and take her into his care." And having with patience heard and understood her wants,—and it is some relief for a poor body to be but heard with patience,—he, like a Christian Clergyman, comforted her by his meek behaviour and counsel; but because that cost him nothing, he relieved her with money too, and so sent her home with a cheerful heart, praising God, and praying for him. Thus worthy, and—like David's blessed man—thus lowly, was Mr. George Herbert in his own eyes, and thus lovely in the eyes of others.

At his return that night to his wife at Bainton, he gave her an account of the passages betwixt him and the poor woman; with which she was so affected, that she went next day to Salisbury, and there bought a pair of blankets, and sent them as a token of her love to the poor woman: and with them a message, "That she would see and be acquainted with her, when her house was built at Bemerton."

The texts for all his future sermons—which God knows, were not many—were constantly taken out of the Gospel for the day; and he did as constantly declare why the Church did appoint that portion of Scripture to be that day read; and in what manner the Collect for every Sunday does refer to the Gospel, or to the Epistle then read to them; and, that they might pray with understanding, he did usually take occasion to explain, not only the Collect for every particular Sunday, but the reasons of all the other Collects and Responses in our Church-service; and made it appear to them, that the whole service of the Church was a reasonable, and therefore an acceptable sacrifice to God: as namely, that we begin with "Confession of ourselves to be vile, miserable sinners;" and that we begin so, because, till we have confessed ourselves to be such, we are not capable of that mercy which we acknowledge we need, and pray for: but having, in the prayer of our Lord, begged pardon for those sins which we have confessed; and hoping, that as the Priest hath declared our absolution, so by our public confession, and real repentance, we have obtained that pardon; then we dare and do proceed to beg of the Lord, "to open our lips, that our mouth may shew forth his praise;" for till then we are neither able nor worthy to praise him. But this being supposed, we are then fit to say, "Glory be to the Father, and to the Son, and to the Holy Ghost;" and fit to proceed to a further service of our God, in the Collects, and Psalms, and Lauds, that follow in the service.

And as to these Psalms and Lauds, he proceeded to inform them why they were so often, and some of them daily, repeated in our Church-service; namely, the Psalms every month, because they be an historical and thankful repetition of mercies past, and such a composition of prayers and praises, as ought to be repeated often, and publicly; for with such sacrifice God is honoured and well-pleased. This for the Psalms.

And for the Hymns and Lauds appointed to be daily repeated or sung after the first and second Lessons are read to the congregation; he proceeded to inform them, that it was most reasonable, after they have heard the will and goodness of God declared or preached by the Priest in his reading the two chapters, that it was then a seasonable duty to rise up, and express their gratitude to Almighty God, for those his mercies to them, and to all mankind; and then to say with the Blessed Virgin, "that their souls do magnify the Lord, and that their spirits do also rejoice in God their Saviour:" and that it was their duty also to rejoice with Simeon in his song, and say with him, "That their eyes have" also "seen their salvation;" for they have seen that salvation which was but prophesied till his time: and he then broke out into those expressions of joy that he did see it; but they live to see it daily in the history of it, and therefore ought daily to rejoice, and daily to offer up their sacrifices of praise to their God, for that particular mercy. A service, which is now the constant employment of that Blessed Virgin and Simeon, and all those blessed Saints that are possessed of Heaven: and where they are at this time interchangeably and constantly singing, "Holy, holy, holy, Lord God; glory be to God on high, and on earth peace." And he taught them, that to do this was an acceptable service to God, because the Prophet David says in his Psalms, "He that praiseth the Lord honoureth him."

He made them to understand how happy they be that are freed from the incumbrances of that law which our forefathers groaned under: namely, from the legal sacrifices, and from the many ceremonies of the Levitical law; freed from Circumcision, and from the strict observation of the Jewish Sabbath, and the like. And he made them know, that having received so many and so great blessings, by being born since the days of our Saviour, it must be an acceptable sacrifice to Almighty God, for them to acknowledge those blessings daily, and stand up and worship, and say as Zacharias did, "Blessed be the Lord God of Israel, for he hath—in our days—visited and redeemed his people; and—he hath in our days—remembered, and shewed that mercy, which by the mouth of the Prophets, he promised to our forefathers; and this he hath done according to his holy covenant made with them." And he made them to understand that we live to see and enjoy the benefit of it, in his Birth, in his Life, his Passion, his Resurrection, and Ascension into Heaven, where he now sits sensible of all our temptations and infirmities; and where he is at this present time making intercession for us, to his and our Father: and therefore they ought daily to express their public gratulations, and say daily with Zacharias, "Blessed be the Lord God of Israel, that hath thus visited and thus redeemed his people."—These were some of the reasons, by which Mr. Herbert instructed his congregation for the use of the Psalms and Hymns appointed to be daily sung or said in the Church-service.

He informed them also, when the Priest did pray only for the congregation, and not for himself; and when they did only pray for him; as namely, after the repetition of the Creed before he proceeds to pray the Lord's Prayer, or any of the appointed Collects, the Priest is directed to kneel down, and pray for them, saying, "The Lord be with you;" and when they pray for him, saying, "And with thy spirit;" and then they join together in the following Collects: and he assured them, that when there is such mutual love, and such joint prayers offered for each other, then the holy Angels look down from Heaven, and are ready to carry such charitable desires to God Almighty, and he as ready to receive them; and that a Christian congregation calling thus upon God with one heart, and one voice, and in one reverent and humble posture, looks as beautifully as Jerusalem, that is at peace with itself.

He instructed them also why the prayer of our Lord was prayed often in every full service of the Church; namely, at the conclusion of the several parts of that service; and prayed then, not only because it was composed and commanded by our Jesus that made it, but as a perfect pattern for our less perfect forms of prayer, and therefore fittest to sum up and conclude all our imperfect petitions.

He instructed them also, that as by the second Commandment we are required not to bow down, or worship an idol, or false God; so, by the contrary rule, we are to bow down and kneel, or stand up and worship the true God. And he instructed them why the Church required the congregation to stand up at the repetition of the Creeds; namely, because they thereby declare both their obedience to the Church, and an assent to that faith into which they had been baptized. And he taught them, that in that shorter Creed or Doxology, so often repeated daily, they also stood up to testify their belief to be, that "the God that they trusted in was one God, and three persons; the Father, the Son and the Holy Ghost; to whom they and the Priest gave glory." And because there had been heretics that had denied some of those three persons to be God, therefore the congregation stood up and honoured him, by confessing and saying, "It was so in the beginning, is now so, and shall ever be so world without end." And all gave their assent to this belief, by standing up and saying, Amen.

He instructed them also what benefit they had by the Church's appointing the celebration of holidays and the excellent use of them, namely, that they were set apart for particular commemorations of particular mercies received from Almighty God; and—as reverend Mr. Hooker says—to be the landmarks to distinguish times; for by them we are taught to take notice how time passes by us, and that we ought not to let the years pass without a celebration of praise for those mercies which those days give us occasion to remember, and therefore they were to note that the year is appointed to begin the 25th day of March; a day in which we commemorate the Angel's appearing to the Blessed Virgin, with the joyful tidings that "she should conceive and bear a son, that should be the Redeemer of mankind." And she did so forty weeks after this joyful salutation; namely, at our Christmas; a day in which we commemorate his Birth with joy and praise; and that eight days after this happy birth we celebrate his Circumcision; namely in that which we call New-year's day. And that, upon that day which we call Twelfth-day, we commemorate the manifestation of the unsearchable riches of Jesus to the Gentiles: and that that day we also celebrate the memory of his goodness in sending a star to guide the three Wise Men from the East to Bethlehem, that they might there worship, and present him with their oblations of gold, frankincense, and myrrh. And he—Mr. Herbert— instructed them, that Jesus was forty days after his birth presented by his blessed Mother in the Temple; namely, on that day which we call, "The Purification of the Blessed Virgin, Saint Mary." And he instructed them, that by the Lent-fast we imitate and commemorate our Saviour's humiliation in fasting forty days; and that we ought to endeavour to be like him in purity: and that on Good Friday we commemorate and condole his Crucifixion; and at Easter commemorate his glorious Resurrection. And he taught them, that after Jesus ^ad manifested himself to his Disciples to be "that Christ that was crucified, dead and buried;" and by his appearing and conversing with his Disciples for the space of forty days after his Resurrection, he then, and not till then, ascended into Heaven in the sight of those Disciples; namely, on that day which we call the Ascension, or Holy Thursday. And that we then celebrate the performance of the promise which he made to his Disciples at or before his Ascension; namely, "that though he left them, yet he would send them the Holy Ghost to be their Comforter;" and that he did so on that day which the Church calls Whitsunday.—Thus the Church keeps an historical and circular commemoration of times, as they pass by us; of such times as ought to incline us to occasional praises, for the particular blessings which we do, or might receive, by those holy commemorations.

He made them know also why the Church hath appointed Ember-weeks; and to know the reasons why the Commandments, and the Epistles and Gospels, were to be read at the Altar, or Communion Table: why the Priest was to pray the Litany kneeling; and why to pray some Collects standing: and he gave them many other observations, fit for his plain congregation, but not fit for me now to mention; for I must set limits to my pen, and not make that a treatise, which I intended to be a much shorter account than I have made it: but I have done, when I have told the Reader, that he was constant in catechising every Sunday in the afternoon, and that his catechising was after his Second Lesson, and in the pulpit; and that he never exceeded his half hour, and was always so happy as to have an obedient and a full congregation.

And to this I must add, that if he were at any time too zealous in his Sermons, it was in reproving the indecencies of the people's behaviour in the time of divine service; and of those Ministers that huddle up the Church-prayers, without a visible reverence and affection; namely, such as seemed to say the Lord's prayer, or a Collect, in a breath. But for himself, his custom was, to stop betwixt every Collect, and give the people time to consider what they had prayed, and to force their desires affectionately to God, before he engaged them into new petitions.

And by this account of his diligence to make his parishioners understand what they prayed, and why they praised and adored their Creator, I hope I shall the more easily obtain the Reader's belief to the following account of Mr. Herbert's own practice; which was to appear constantly with his wife and three nieces—the daughters of a deceased sister—and his whole family, twice every day at the Church-prayers, in the Chapel, which does almost join to his Parsonage-house. And for the time of his appearing, it was strictly at the canonical hours of ten and four: and then and there he lifted up pure and charitable hands to God in the midst of the congregation. And he would joy to have spent that time in that place, where the honour of his Master Jesus dwelleth; and there, by that inward devotion which he testified constantly by an humble behaviour and visible adoration, he, like Joshua, brought not only "his own household thus to serve the Lord;" but brought most of his parishioners, and many gentlemen in the neighbourhood, constantly to make a part of his congregation twice a day: and some of the meaner sort of his parish did so love and reverence Mr. Herbert, that they would let their plough rest when Mr. Herbert's Saint's-bell rung to prayers, that they might also offer their devotions to God with him; and would then return back to their plough. And his most holy life was such, that it begot such reverence to God, and to him, that they thought themselves the happier, when they carried Mr. Herbert's blessing back with them to their labour. Thus powerful was his reason and example to persuade others to a practical piety and devotion. . . .

In this time of his decay, he was often visited and prayed for by all the Clergy that lived near to him, especially by his friends the Bishop and Prebends of the Cathedral Church in Salisbury; but by none more devoutly than his wife, his three nieces,—then a part of his family,—and Mr. Woodnot, who were the sad witnesses of his daily decay; to whom he would often speak to this purpose: "I now look back upon the pleasures of my life past, and see the content I have taken in beauty, in wit, in music, and pleasant conversation, are now all past by me like a dream, or as a shadow that returns not, and are now all become dead to me, or 1 to them; and I see, that as my father and generation hath done before me, so I also shall now suddenly (with Job) make my bed also in the dark; and I praise God I am prepared for it; and I praise him that I am not to learn patience now I stand in such need of it; and that I have practised mortification, and endeavoured to die daily, that I might not die eternally; and my hope is, that I shall shortly leave this valley of tears, and be free from all fevers and pain; and, which will be a more happy condition, I shall be free from sin, and all the temptations and anxieties that attend it: and this being past, I shall dwell in the New Jerusalem; dwell there with men made perfect; dwell where these eyes shall see my Master and Saviour Jesus; and with him see my dear Mother, and all my relations and friends. But I must die, or not come to that happy place. And this is my content, that I am going daily towards it: and that every day which I have lived, hath taken a part of my appointed time from me; and that I shall live the less time, for having lived this and the day past." These, and the like expressions, which he uttered often, may be said to be his enjoyment of Heaven before he enjoyed it. The Sunday before his death, he rose suddenly from his bed or couch, called for one of his instruments, took it into his hand and said,

My God, my God,
> My music shall find thee,
>> And every string
> Shall have his attribute to sing.

And having tuned it, he played and sung

>> The Sundays of man's life,
> Threaded together on time's string,
> Make bracelets to adorn the wife
> Of the eternal glorious King:
> On Sundays Heaven's door stands ope;
> Blessings are plentiful and rife,
>> More plentiful than hope.

Thus he sung on earth such Hymns and Anthems, as the Angels, and he, and Mr. Farrer, now sing in Heaven.

Thus he continued meditating, and praying, and rejoicing, till the day of his death; and on that day said to Mr. Woodnot, "My dear friend, I am sorry I have nothing to present to my merciful God but sin and misery; but the first is pardoned, and a few hours will now put a period to the latter; for I shall suddenly go hence, and be no more seen." Upon which expression Mr. Woodnot took occasion to remember him of the re-edifying Layton Church, and his many acts of mercy. To which he made answer, saying, "They be good works, if they be sprinkled with the blood of Christ, and not otherwise." After this discourse he became more restless, and his soul seemed to be weary of her earthly tabernacle: and this uneasiness became so visible, that his wife, his three nieces, and Mr. Woodnot, stood constantly about his bed, beholding him with sorrow, and an unwillingness to lose the sight of him, whom they could not hope to see much longer. As they stood thus beholding him, his wife observed him to breathe faintly, and with much trouble, and observed him to fall into a sudden agony; which so surprised her, that she fell into a sudden passion, and required of him to know how he did. To which his answer was, "that he had passed a conflict with his last enemy, and had overcome him by the merits of his Master Jesus." After which answer, he looked up, and saw his wife and nieces weeping to an extremity, and charged them, if they loved him to withdraw into the next room, and there pray every one alone for him; for nothing but their lamentations could make his death uncomfortable. To which request their sighs and tears would not suffer them to make any reply; but they yielded him a sad obedience, leaving only with him Mr. Woodnot and Mr. Bostock. Immediately after they had left him, he said to Mr. Bostock, "Pray, Sir, open that door, then look into that cabinet, in which you may easily find my last Will, and give it into my hand:" which being done, Mr. Herbert delivered it into the hand of Mr. Woodnot, and said, "My old friend, I here deliver you my last Will, in which you will find that I have made you my sole Executor for the good of my wife and nieces; and I desire you to shew kindness to them, as they shall need it: I do not desire you to be just; for I know you will be so for your own sake; but I charge you, by the religion of our friendship, to be careful of them." And having obtained Mr. Woodnot's promise to be so, he said, "I am now ready to die." After which words, he said, "Lord, forsake me not now my strength faileth me: but grant me mercy for the merits of my Jesus. And now, Lord— Lord, now receive my soul." And with those words he breathed forth his divine soul, without any apparent disturbance, Mr. Woodnot and Mr. Bostock attending his last breath, and closing his eyes.

Thus he lived and thus he died, like a Saint, unspotted of the world, full of alms-deeds, full of humility, and all the examples of a virtuous life; which I cannot conclude better, than with this borrowed observation:

—All must to their cold graves:
But the religious actions of the just
Smell sweet in death, and blossom in the dust.

Mr. George Herbert's have done so to this, and will doubtless do so to succeeding generations.—I have but this to say more of him; that if Andrew Melvin died before him, then George Herbert died without an enemy, I wish—if God shall be so pleased—that I may be so happy as to die like him.

—Izaak Walton, from "The Life of Mr. George
Herbert," 1670, *The Lives of Dr. John Donne,*
Sir Henry Wotton, Richard Hooker, George Herbert,
and Dr. Robert Sanderson, 1860, pp. 257–308

RICHARD BAXTER
"PREFATORY ADDRESS" (1681)

Richard Baxter (1615–91) was a Puritan Church leader and theologian. The author of numerous works, his most famous was *The Saints' Everlasting Rest* (1650).

But I must confess, after all, that, next the Scripture Poems, there are none so savoury to me as Mr. George Herbert's and Mr. George Sandys'. I know that Cowley and others far exceed Herbert in wit and accurate composure; but as Seneca takes with me above all his contemporaries, because he speaketh things by words, feelingly and seriously, like a man that is past jest; so Herbert speaks to God like one that really believeth a God, and whose business in the world is most with God. Heart-work and Heaven-work make up his books.

—Richard Baxter, "Prefatory Address,"
Poetical Fragments, 1681

Unsigned "Preface" (1697)

The anonymous excerpt below speaks to Herbert's importance as a religious writer. The author uses the common descriptor "divine" to describe Herbert's works, suggesting not only the quality of the poet's oeuvre but its important connection to spirituality and the religious beliefs of the day. The author's discourse on Herbert's work as hymns and musical renderings are useful for students interested in both music and its place in the late seventeenth-century English Church.

Mr. Herbert's *Poems* have met with so general and deserv'd Acceptance, that they have undergone Eleven Impressions near Twenty Years ago: He hath obtain'd by way of Eminency, the Name of Our *Divine Poet,* and his Verses have been frequently quoted in Sermons and other Discourses; yet, I fear, few of them have been Sung since his Death, the Tunes not being at the Command of ordinary Readers.

This attempt therefore, (such as it is) is to bring so many of them as I well could, which I judg'd suited to the Capacity and Devotion of Private Christians, into the *Common Metre* to be Sung in their Closets or Families . . .

How much more fit is Herbert's *Temple* to be set to the Lute, than Cowley's *Mistress.* It is hard that no one can be taught Musick, but in such wanton Songs as fill the Hearts of many Learners with Lust and Vanity all their Days. Why should it be thought a greater Prophaning of Spiritual Songs to use them in a Musick-Scool, than it is of the New Testament, to teach Children to spell; yet what Christian would not rather have his Child taught to read in a Bible than in a Play-Book? Especially, when they who learn Musick are generally more apt to receive Impressions from the Matter of the

Song, than Children are from the Books in which they first learn to Spell. My attempt hath been easie, only to alter the measures of some Hymns, keeping strictly to the Sence of the Author; But how noble an undertaking were it, if any one could and would rescue the high flights, and lofty strains found in the most Celebrated Poets, from their sacrilegious Applications to *Carnal Love,* and restore them to the *Divine* Love! When the Devil drew off the Nations from the True God, He caus'd the same Institutions with which God was honoured, to be used in the Idol Service, *Temple, Priests, Sacrifices,* &c. and amongst the rest *Psalmody:* And it is strange, that when we have so long been emerg'd out of Heathenism, that such a Remnant of it should be amongst us, wherein the most devotional Part of Religion doth consist.

Almost all Phrases and Expressions of Worship due only to God, are continu'd in these artificial Composures in the Heathenish use of them even from the *inspirations* that they invoke in their beginning, to the *Raptures, Flames, Adorations, &c.* That they pretend to in the Progress: Nor are these meer empty Names with them, but their Hearts are more fervently carried out in the musical use of them, than they would be if their Knees were bow'd to *Baal* and *Astaroth:* Few Holy Souls are more affected with the Praises of a Redeemer, than they are of the wanton Object that they profess to adore. Oh for some to write *Parodies,* by which Name I find one Poem in *Herbert* call'd, which begins, *Souls Joy, where art thou gone,* and was, I doubt not, a light Love-song turn'd into a Spiritual Hymn. Parodia, *Est quum alterius Poetae Versus in aliud Argumentum transferuntur.* I do not find it hath been made a Matter of scruple to turn the Temples built for Idols into Churches: And as to this Case, it is to be consider'd that the Musick and Poetry was an excellent Gift of God, which ought to have been us'd for Him; and that their high strains of Love, Joy, &c. Suit none but the adorable Saviour; and all their most warm and affecting Expressions are stollen from the Churches Adoration of Christ; and who can doubt but the Church may take her own, where-ever she finds it, whether in an Idolatrous Mass-Book or Pro-phane Love-song? It was a noble Resolution of him that said,

I'll Consecrate my Magdalene to Thee

The *Eyes, Mouth, Hair,* which had been abus'd to Lust and Vanity were us'd to *Wash, Kiss, Wipe* the feet of a Saviour: May Man and Angels Praise him for ever and ever! Amen.

—Unsigned, "Preface," *Select Hymns,*
Taken out of Mr. Herbert's Temple, 1697

HENRY HEADLEY (1787)

Henry Headley (1765–1788) published a volume of his own poetry in addition to a well-received two volume collection of classic poetry, an excerpt of which is reprinted below.

⟨⟩

A writer of the same class, though infinitely inferior to both Quarles and Crashaw. His poetry is a compound of enthusiasm without sublimity, and conceit without either ingenuity or imagination ... When a man is once reduced to the impartial test of time,—when partiality, friendship, fashion, and party, have withdrawn their influence,—our surprise is frequently excited by past subjects of admiration that now cease to strike. He who takes up the poems of Herbert would little suspect that he had been public orator of an university, and a favourite of his sovereign; that he had received flattery and praise from Donne and from Bacon; and that the biographers of the day had enrolled his name among the first names of his country.

—Henry Headley, *Select Beauties*
of Ancient Poetry, 1787

HENRY NEELE (1827)

Henry Neele (1798–1828) was an English poet who first began publishing at the age of sixteen. His *Lectures on English Poetry* published a series of addresses that he began giving at the age of twenty.

⟨⟩

His beauties of thought and diction are so overloaded with farfetched conceits and quaintnesses; low, and vulgar, and even indelicate imagery; and a pertinacious appropriation of Scripture language and figure, in situations where they make a most unseemly exhibition, that there is now very little probability of his ever regaining the popularity which he has lost. That there was much, however, of the real Poetical temperament in the composition of his mind, the following lines, although not free from his characteristic blemishes, will abundantly prove: Sweet Day! so cool, so calm, so bright.

—Henry Neele, *Lectures*
on English Poetry, 1827

RALPH WALDO EMERSON (1835)

The famous American Transcendental author and thinker Ralph Waldo Emerson (1803–82) became one of the most celebrated minds in the United States in the nineteenth century, and his essays are still read by students worldwide. In addition to being a philosopher, Emerson was a scholar and man of letters, and it is no surprise that a man who thought deeply upon spiritual and intellectual issues would be attracted to a writer like Herbert. Emerson writes that Herbert is "a striking example of the power of exalted thought to melt and bend language to its fit expression." Though Emerson acknowledges that Herbert's work seems a little out of date to nineteenth-century readers, offering the same criticisms that many of Emerson's contemporaries applied to Donne and other metaphysical poets, Emerson praises Herbert for his diction, his sentiments, and especially the feeling of "moral sublime" that pervades the author's work. Ultimately, Emerson writes that "Herbert's Poems are the breathings of a devout soul reading the riddle of the world with a poet's eye but with a saint's affections," a beautiful description of Herbert's divine work.

Another poet in that age was George Herbert, the author of *The Temple*, a little book of Divine songs and poems which ought to be on the shelf of every lover of religion and poetry. It is a book which is apt to repel the reader on his first acquaintance. It is written in the quaint epigrammatic style which was for a short time in vogue in England, a style chiefly marked by the elaborate decomposition to which every object is subjected. The writer is not content with the obvious properties of natural objects but delights in discovering abstruser relations between them and the subject of his thought. This both by Cowley and Donne is pushed to affectation. By Herbert it is used with greater temperance and to such excellent ends that it is easily forgiven if indeed it do not come to be loved.

It has been justly said of Herbert that if his thought is often recondite and far fetched yet the language is always simple and chaste. I should cite Herbert as a striking example of the power of exalted thought to melt and bend language to its fit expression. Language is an organ on which men play with unequal skill and each man with different skill at different hours. The man who stammers when he is afraid or when he is indifferent, will be fluent when he is angry, and eloquent when his intellect is active. Some writers are of that frigid temperament that their sentences always seem to be made with grammar and dictionary. To such the easy structure of prose is laborious, and metre and rhyme, and especially any difficult metre is an insurmountable bar to the expression of their meaning. Of these Byron says,

> Prose poets like blank verse
> Good workmen never quarrel with their tools. (*Don Juan,* I, 201)

Those on the contrary who were born to write, have a self-enkindling power of thought which never knows this obstruction but find words so rapidly that they seem coeval with the thought. And in general according to the elevation of the soul will be the power over language and lively thoughts will break out into spritely verse. No metre so difficult but will be tractable so that you only raise the temperature of the thought.

'For my part,' says Montaigne, 'I hold and Socrates is positive in it, that whoever has in his mind a lively and clear imagination, he will express it well enough in one kind or another and though he were dumb by signs.'

Every reader is struck in George Herbert with the inimitable felicity of the diction. The thought has so much heat as actually to fuse the words, so that language is wholly flexible in his hands, and his rhyme never stops the progress of the sense . . .

What Herbert most excels in is in exciting that feeling which we call the moral sublime. The highest affections are touched by his muse. I know nothing finer than the turn with which his poem on affliction concludes. After complaining to his maker as if too much suffering had been put upon him he threatens that he will quit God's service for the world's:

> Well, I will change the service and go seek
>   Some other master out
> Ah, my dear God, though I be clean forgot
> Let me not love thee if I love thee not.
>   (*Affliction (I),* 11. 63-6)

Herbert's Poems are the breathings of a devout soul reading the riddle of the world with a poet's eye but with a saint's affections. Here poetry is turned to its noblest use. The sentiments are so exalted, the thought so wise, the piety so sincere that we cannot read this book without joy that our nature is capable of such emotions and criticism is silent in the exercise of higher faculties.

It is pleasant to reflect that a book that seemed formed for the devotion of angels, attained, immediately on its publication, great popularity. Isaac

Walton informs us that 20,000 copies had been sold before 1670, within forty years. After being neglected for a long period several new editions of it have appeared in England and one recently in America.

—Ralph Waldo Emerson, Lecture on Ben Jonson,
Herrick, Herbert, Walton, delivered December 31,
1835, *The Early Lectures of Ralph Waldo Emerson,*
1959, vol. 1, eds. Wicher, Spiller, pp. 349–53

John Ruskin (1845)

The famed English art and literary critic John Ruskin (1819–1900) was also an author and social critic. Below, Ruskin compares Herbert with John Bunyan, author of the seminal Puritan work *Pilgrim's Progress.* Compared to Bunyan's dull and pessimistic prose, Ruskin finds Herbert's poetry "full of faith & love."

Now the imagination of George Herbert is just as vigourous [as Bunyan's] and his communings with God as immediate, but they are the imagination & the communings of a well bridled & disciplined mind, and therefore though he feels himself to have sold Christ over & over again for definite pieces of silver, for pleasures or promises of this world, he repents and does penance for such actual sin—he does not plague himself about a singing in his ears. There is as much difference between the writings & feelings of the two men as between the high bred, keen, severe, thoughtful countenance of the one—and the fat, vacant, vulgar, boy's *face* of the other. Both are equally Christians, equally taught of God, but taught through different channels, Herbert through his brains, Bunyan through his liver . . .

I have been more and more struck on rethinking and rereading with the singular differences between Bunyan & Herbert. Bunyan humble & contrite enough, but always dwelling painfully & exclusively on the relations of the deity to his own little self—not contemplating God as the God of all the earth, nor loving him as such, nor so occupied with the consideration of his attributes as to forget himself in an extended gratitude, but always looking to his own interests & his own state—loving or fearing or doubting, just as *he* happened to fancy God was dealing with him. Herbert on the contrary, full of faith & love, regardless of himself, outpouring his affection in all circumstances & at all times, and never *fearing,* though often weeping. Hear him speaking of such changes of feeling as Bunyan complains of:

Whether I fly with angels, fall with dust,
Thy hands made both, & I am there.
Thy power & love, my love & trust
Make one place everywhere,
(The Temper (I), 11. 25–8)

Vide the three last lovely stanzas of The Temper. I think Bunyan's a most dangerous book, in many ways—first because to people who do not allow for his ignorance, low birth, & sinful & idle youth, the workings of his diseased mind would give a most false impression of God's dealings— secondly because it encourages in ill taught religious people, such idle, fanciful, selfish, profitless modes of employing the mind as not only bring discredit on religion generally, but give rise to all sorts of schisms, heresies, insanities and animosities—and again, because to people of a turn of mind like mine, but who have [no] less stability of opinion, it would at once suggest the idea of all religion being nothing more than a particular phase of indigestion coupled with a good imagination & bad conscience.

> —John Ruskin, Letters to His Mother,
> April 13 and 20, 1845, Ruskin in Italy:
> Letters to His Parents 1845, 1872, ed.
> Shapiro, pp. 17–18

ROBERT ARIS WILLMOTT
"INTRODUCTION" (1854)

Robert Aris Wilmott (1809–63) was a scholar and literary historian who collected and edited the poems of Robert Burns in addition to those of Herbert.

Even the friendly taste of Mr. Keble was offended by the constant flutter of his fancy, forever hovering round and round the theme. But this was a peculiarity which the most gifted writers admired. Dryden openly avowed that nothing appeared more beautiful to him than the imagery in Cowley, which some readers condemned. It must, at least, be said, in praise of this creative playfulness, that it is a quality of the intellect singularly sprightly and buoyant; it ranges over a boundless landscape, pierces into every corner, and by the light of its own fire—to adopt a phrase of Temple—discovers a thousand little bodies, or images in the world, unseen by common eyes, and only manifested by the rays of that poetic sun.

—Robert Aris Willmott, "Introduction,"
The Works of George Herbert, 1854

GEORGE L. CRAIK (1861)

Herbert was an intimate friend of Donne, and no doubt a great admirer of his poetry but his own has been to a great extent preserved from the imitation of Donne's peculiar style, into which it might in other circumstances have fallen, in all probability by its having been composed with little effort or elaboration, and chiefly to relieve and amuse his own mind by the melodious expression of his favorite fancies and contemplations. His quaintness lies in his thoughts rather than in their expression, which is in general sufficiently simple and luminous.

—George L. Craik, *A Compendious History*
of English Literature and of the
English Language, 1861, vol. 2, p. 19

JOHN NICHOL "INTRODUCTION" (1863)

John Nichol (1833–1894) was a Scottish literary scholar and professor of English literature at a university in Glasgow. Nichol was an important editor of Herbert's, and the piece below is from his introduction to a collection of the poet's works. In the excerpt, Nichol writes that despite "an almost indefinite variety of theme and measure ... [Herbert's work] is pervaded by a unity of thought and purpose which justifies the single name." Nichol correctly identifies the author's constant muse as the English church, calling his poems "Church music crystallized." Nichol also indicates that Herbert's work is not situated in "the first class of poetry," and suggests that it is the poet's "want of condensation, which has led the poet into frequent repetition of the same ideas under slightly altered phraseology. Sometimes, even within the limits of the same poem, he turns a thought over till we are tired of it; and to read through his book continuously is no easy task. It has been said correctly that Herbert has more genius than taste." Nichol's observations reflect the prevailing, dominant contemporary critical thought on Herbert, that he is a poet with much to admire but whose style and subject is often repetitive, and anyone writing on Herbert's works would do well to note the Victorian roots of these contemporary ideas.

———— ———— ————

The collection of poems entitled *The Temple,* which, with the prose treatise, "A Country Parson," "The Church Militant," and a few minor verses in English and Latin, completes the list of our author's works, embraces an almost indefinite variety of theme and measure, from the slender notes of the flute to the full tones of the organ bass; yet it is pervaded by a unity of thought and purpose which justifies the single name. Those poems are a series of hymns and meditations within the walls of an English church. They are Church music crystallised. There is a speciality about them which continually recalls the circumstances of the writer. *The Temple,* as Coleridge remarked, will always be read with fullest appreciation by those who share the poet's devotion to the Dear Mother whose praises he has undertaken to celebrate. The verses on "Easter" and "Lent," on "Baptism" and "Communion," on "Church Monuments" and "Music," seem most directly to address the worshippers in that flock of which he was so good a shepherd, whose affections are entwined around his Church, who love to linger on the associations of her festivals, the rubrics of her creed, and the formularies of her service—to feel themselves under the shadow of the old cathedrals—to draw allegories from the fantasies of their fretted stone—to watch the light flicker through the painted glass on marble tombs, and listen to the anthems throbbing through the choir. Yet there is in the author and in his work catholicity enough to give his volume a universal interest, and make his prayer and praise a fit expression of Christian faith under all varieties of form. The defects of the book—those which remove it, as a whole, from the first class of poetry—are those which are peculiar to the writer and his Church and time; its excellences, which raise it to the front of the second rank result from an exercise of those qualities which Herbert shares with all great religious poets. Those defects are serious, and have emboldened depreciatory critics to say that the author of *The Temple* has been handed down to us more by his life than his work. Foremost among them is a want of condensation, which has led the poet into frequent repetition of the same ideas under slightly altered phraseology. Sometimes, even within the limits of the same poem, he turns a thought over till we are tired of it; and to read through his book continuously is no easy task. It has been said correctly that Herbert has more genius than taste; and his deficiency in the latter quality, combined with a grotesque vein of allegory which belonged to the time, has not unfrequently, as in the verse entitled "Jesu," led the most reverent of men into conceits which seem to approach irreverence. The extremes of levity and pious word-worship meet now and then in a devout pun. There are many instances in which we cannot help complaining that too much is made of little things, as in a pre-Raphaelite picture the whole effect is apt to be sacrificed to microscopic detail; so that we think of *The Temple* rather in connexion with the mosaic-work of Wilton Chapel, than the neighbouring and more stately grandeur of the severe majestic Salisbury. Herbert is prone, by his own admission, to overlay his matter with far-fetched, and sometimes incongruous imagery.

The best poems in the volume, as "The Church Porch," "The Agony," "Sin," "Faith," "Love," "The Temper," "Employments," "Church Music," "Sunday," "The World," "Lent," "Virtue," "The Pearl," "Man," "Mortification," "The British Church," "The Quip," "The Size," and many more, in themselves make up a treasury of sacred song whose price is beyond rubies. They are more like modern psalms than any other poems we know. Like those older and grander voices, they, too, have their place by the wayside of the Christian life—rousing, warning; cheering, comforting, sorrowing and rejoicing with us as we go. Like church windows they have a double aspect; we may look in through them from without on the writer's heart, and see him as a priest and man struggling like ourselves with doubts and fears, but with "a face not fearing light," and a will well bent to do his Master's work; we may look out through them from within on the world as seen with the poet's eye—a fair round world of light and shade, overarched by clouds and stars.

Herbert's poem on "Man" is his masterpiece. The most philosophic as well as the most comprehensive of his writings, it stands by itself, and has enlisted the admiration even of those furthest removed from him in creed, and cast, and time. Embodying his recognition of the mysterious relationship of the chief of created beings to his Creator and to the universe, it seems to anticipate centuries of discovery. The faculty which can range from heaven to earth, from earth to heaven, discerns the hidden links by which the world is woven together, and poetry prophesies what science proves. In the microcosm of man—

> East and west touch,—the poles do kiss,
> > And parallels meet.
> > > ("The Search," 11. 43-4)

Man, with Herbert, is everything, "a tree," "a beast, yet is, is, or should be more;" he is

all symmetry,
Full of proportions, one limb to another.
And all to all the world besides.
("Man," 11, 13-15)

This, which was the prayer and effort of his life, was surely in full measure granted to George Herbert. Nothing arrests us more than his perfect honesty. There is no writing for effect in his pages; as we turn them we feel ourselves in the presence of a man speaking out of the fulness of his heart and carried away into a higher air by the sustaining power of his own incessant aspirations.

Herbert can scarcely be called a lesser Milton. His Gothic temple has nothing of the classic grace and grandeur of the hand that reared the great dome of our English Epic on smooth pillars of everlasting verse. He breathes rather the spirit of the author of the *Olney Hymns,* but Herbert's was a more cheerful faith than Cowper's and the brightness of God's countenance seemed ever to shine upon him as he went on his way singing to the gates of the celestial city

—John Nichol, from "Introduction,"
The Poetical Works of George Herbert,
1863, pp. vi–vii, xix–xxvi

George MacDonald (1886)

Here comes a poet indeed! and how am I to show him due honour? With his book humbly, doubtfully offered, with the ashes of the poems of his youth fluttering in the wind of his priestly garments, he crosses the threshold. Or rather, for I had forgotten the symbol of my book, let us all go from our chapel to the choir, and humbly ask him to sing that he may make us worthy of his song. In George Herbert there is poetry enough and to spare: it is the household bread of his being. With a conscience tender as a child's, almost diseased in its tenderness, and a heart loving as a woman's, his intellect is none the less powerful. Its movements are as the sword-play of an alert, poised, well-knit, strong-wristed fencer with the rapier, in which the skill impresses one more than the force, while without the force the skill would be valueless, even hurtful, to its possessor. There is a graceful humour with it occasionally, even in his most serious poems adding much to their charm.

—George MacDonald, *England's Antiphon,*
1886, pp. 174–76

John S. Hart (1872)

John Seely Hart (1810–1877) was a prominent American educator and textbook author.

———ᴠᴠᴠ— ———ᴠᴠᴠ— ———ᴠᴠᴠ—

Although later generations have moderated the lavish praise bestowed upon Herbert by his contemporaries, the final judgment seems strongly in favor of the poet's claims to lasting recognition. His poems are at times overloaded with conceits and quaint imagery—the great fault of that age—but this cannot destroy the vein of true, devotional poetry running through them all.

> —John S. Hart, *A Manual of*
> *English Literature,* 1872, p. 76

Alexander B. Grosart
"George Herbert" (1873)

The place of George Herbert among the sacred poets of England may be safely pronounced as secure as that of the greatest of his contemporaries. By this we do not at all mean to claim for him such quality or quantity of genius as belongs to these "greatest;" nor indeed would we even put him on a level with Henry Vaughan the Silurist, or Richard Crashaw. But we do mean that his fame is as true and catholic, and covetable and imperishable, as that of any. We could as soon conceive of the skylark's singing dying out of our love, or the daisy of the "grene grasse" ceasing to be "a thing of beauty," as of the verse-Temple built fully two centuries and a half ago being now suffered to go to ruin or to take stain. Myriads treasure in their heart of hearts the poems of George Herbert who know little and do not care to know more of the mighty sons of song.

> —Alexander B. Grosart, "George Herbert,"
> *Leisure Hour,* 1873, vol. 22, p. 325

Ralph Waldo Emerson
"Preface" (1875)

Herbert is the psalmist dear to all who love religious poetry with exquisite refinement of thought. So much piety was never married to so much wit. Herbert identifies himself with Jewish genius, as Michael Angelo did when carving or painting prophets and patriarchs, not merely old men in robes and beards, but with the sanctity and the character of the Pentateuch and the prophecy conspicuous in them. His wit and his piety are genuine, and are sure to make a lifelong friend of a good reader.

—Ralph Waldo Emerson, "Preface,"
Parnassus, 1875, p. vi

WENTWORTH WEBSTER (1882)

Author and scholar Wentworth Webster (1828–1907) was best known for a book of Basque legends.

It is to another literature that we must look for much that is peculiar to George Herbert; and this will not only account for many of his faults, but will explain by what side of his character this scholar and gentleman was attracted to country life, and could find contentment in the talk and ways of villagers. The writings to which we allude are those of the moralists of the silver age or later, pagans of the decline, or, at best, but demi-Christians, whose works seem to us so trite and dull, but on which our forefathers, unspoiled by excitement, and not yet exigent in literary style, ruminated with a quiet delight such as we seldom feel. It is from the writings of these authors in many cases that they formed the proverbs which they esteemed as the highest axioms of practical wisdom, and which George Herbert has treasured so fondly in his "Jacula Prudentum."

—Wentworth Webster,
The Academy, 1882, p. 22

GEORGE SAINTSBURY (1887)

In the excerpt below, Saintsbury suggests that Herbert is a populist writer, earning a better reputation with readers than with critics because his work is "never beyond the reach of any tolerably intelligent understanding." Saintsbury is speaking to a common complaint about metaphysical poetry, that the poems are often too intellectual or, as some critics have contended, too dense, to be easily understood. Saintsbury argues that both Herbert's style and his sacred subject matter make him more accessible than his fellow metaphysical writers.

It may be confessed without shame and without innuendo that Herbert has been on the whole a greater favourite with readers than with critics, and the reason is obvious. He is not prodigal of the finest strokes of poetry. To take only his own contemporaries, and undoubtedly pupils, his gentle moralising and devotion are tame and cold beside the burning glow of Crashaw, commonplace and popular beside the intellectual subtlety and, now and then, the inspired touch of Vaughan. But he never drops into the flatness and the extravagance of both these writers, and his beauties, assuredly not mean in themselves, and very constantly present, are both in kind and in arrangement admirably suited to the average comprehension. He is quaint and conceited; but his quaintnesses and conceits are never beyond the reach of any tolerably intelligent understanding. He is devout, but his devotion does not transgress into the more fantastic regions of piety. He is a mystic, but of the more exoteric school of mysticism. Thus he is among sacred poets very much (though relatively he occupies a higher place) what the late Mr. Longfellow was among profane poets. He expresses common needs, common thoughts, the everyday emotions of the Christian, just sublimated sufficiently to make them attractive. The fashion and his own taste gave him a pleasing quaintness, which his good sense kept from being ever obscure or offensive or extravagant.

—George Saintsbury, *A History of
Elizabethan Literature,* 1887, p. 372

J. HOWARD B. MASTERMAN (1897)

Herbert's imagery shows much overelaboration, after the manner of Donne, who had been a close friend of his mother, and of his own youth: but his verses are free from the dulness of most of Vaughan's poems and the extravagance of many of Crashaw's. He is the poet of a meditative and sober piety that is catholic alike in the wideness of its appeal and in its love of symbol and imagery.

—J. Howard B. Masterman,
The Age of Milton, 1897, p. 108

LOUISE IMOGEN GUINEY
"HENRY VAUGHAN" (1894)

Louise Imogen Guiney (1861–1920) was an American poet and essayist who edited editions of the work of Matthew Arnold, amongst others.

Below, Guiney is writing on Henry Vaughan, who was a poetic disciple
of Herbert's.

Vaughan's intellectual debt to Herbert revolves itself into somewhat less
than nothing; for in following him with zeal to the Missionary College of
the Muses, he lost rather than gained, and he is altogether delightful and
persuasive only where he is altogether himself. Nevertheless, a certain spirit
of conformity and filial piety towards Herbert has betrayed Vaughan into
frequent and flagrant imitations.

—Louise Imogen Guiney, "Henry Vaughan,"
A Little English Gallery, 1894, p. 95

Edmund Gosse (1897)

Herbert has an extraordinary tenderness, and it is his singular privilege to
have been able to clothe the common aspirations, fears, and needs of the
religious mind in language more truly poetical than any other Englishman.
He is often extravagant, but rarely dull or flat; his greatest fault lay in an
excessive pseudo-psychological ingenuity, which was a snare to all these
lyrists, and in a tasteless delight in metrical innovations, often as ugly as
they were unprecedented. He sank to writing in the shape of wings and
pillars and altars. On this side, in spite of the beauty of their isolated songs
and passages, the general decadence of the age was apparent in the lyrical
writers. There was no principle of poetic style recognised, and when the
spasm of creative passion was over, the dullest mechanism seemed good
enough to be adopted.

—Edmund Gosse, A *Short History of
Modern English Literature,* 1897, p. 147.

❖

WORKS

❖

George Herbert
"To Mr. Duncan" (1632)

Sir, I pray deliver this little book to my dear brother Farrer, and tell him, he shall find in it a picture of the many spiritual conflicts that have passed betwixt God and my soul, before I could subject mine to the will of Jesus my Master: in whose service I have now found perfect freedom. Desire him to read it; and then, if he can think it may turn to the advantage of any dejected poor soul: let it be made public; if not let him burn it; for I and it are less than the least of God's mercies.

—George Herbert, "To Mr. Duncan,"
The Life of George Herbert, 1632

Nicholas Farrer "Preface" (1633)

Nicholar Farrer (1592-1637), or Ferrar as it is more commonly spelled today, was Herbert's first editor and publisher. In his own right, Farrer was an ordained deacon in the Anglican church and an important churchman, businessman, and scholar of his day. Herbert, on his deathbed, sent Farrer the manuscript of *The Temple*, and instructed that if it could "turn to the advantage of any dejected poor soul" then it should be published; otherwise, Herbert wrote, let his work be destroyed. Farrer recognized the quality of Herbert's manuscript and did publish it, and the book went through at least thirteen printings over the next fifty years. The piece below is Farrer's preface of Herbert's book, which describes the work as "inspired by a diviner breath then flows from *Helicon*" and proffers a brief but servicable biography of the poet as well.

The dedication of this work having been made by the Authour to the *Divine Majestie* onely, how should we now presume to interest any mortall man in the patronage of it? Much lesse think we it meet to seek the recommendation of the Muses, for that which himself was confident to have been inspired by a diviner breath then flows from *Helicon*. The world therefore shall receive it in that naked simplicitie, with which he left it, without any addition either of support or ornament, more than is included in it self. We leave it free and unforestalled to every mans judgement, and to the benefit that he shall finde by perusall. Onely for the clearing of some passages, we have thought it not unfit to make the common Reader privie to some few particularities of the condition and disposition of the Person.

Being nobly born, and as eminently endued with gifts of the minde, and having by industrie and happy education perfected them to that great height of excellencie, whereof his fellowship of Trinitie Colledge in Cambridge, and his Orator-ship in the Universitie, together with that knowledge which the Kings Court had taken of him, could make relation farre above ordinarie. Quitting both his deserts and all the opportunities that he had for wordly prefermen, he betook himself to the Sanctuarie and Temple of God, choosing rather to serve at Gods Altar, then to seek the honour of State-employments. As for those inward enforcements to this course (for outward there was none) which many of these ensuing verses bear witnesse of, they detract not from the freedome, but adde to the honour of this resolution in him. As God had enabled him, so he accounted him meet not onely to be called, but to be compelled to this service: Wherein his faithfull discharge was such, as may make him justly a companion to the primitive Saints, and a pattern or more for the age he lived in.

To testifie his independencie upon all others, and to quicken his diligence in this kinde, he used in his ordinarie speech, when he made mention of the blessed name of our Lord and Saviour Jesus Christ, to adde, My *Master*.

Next God, he loved that which God himself hath magnified above all things, that is, his Word: so as he hath been heard to make solemne protestation, that he would not part with one leaf thereof for the whole world, if it were offered him in exchange.

His obedience and conformitie to the Church and the discipline thereof was singularly remarkable. Though he abounded in private devotions, yet went he every morning and evening with his familie to the Church; and by his example, exhortations, and encouragements drew the greater part of his parishioners to accompanie him dayly in the publick celebration of Divine Service.

As for worldly matters, his love and esteem to them was so little, as no man can more ambitiously seek, then he did earnestly endeavour the resignation of an Ecclesiasticall dignitie, which he was possessour of. But God permitted not the accomplishment of this desire, having ordained him his instrument for reedifying of the Church belonging thereunto, that had layen ruinated almost twenty yeares. The reparation whereof, having been uneffectually attempted by publick collections, was in the end by his own and some few others private freewill-offerings successfully effected. With the remembrance whereof, as of an especiall good work, when a friend went about to comfort him on his death-bed, he made answer, *It is a good work, if it be sprinkled with the bloud of Christ*: otherwise then in this respect he could finde nothing to glorie or comfort himself with, neither in this, nor in any other thing.

And these are but a few of many that might be said, which we have chosen to premise as a glance to some parts of the ensuing book, and for an example to the Reader. We conclude all with his own Motto, with which he used to conclude all things that might seem to tend any way to his own honour;
Lesse then the least of Gods mercies.

—Nicholas Farrer, "Preface,"
The Temple, 1633

John Polwhele "On Mr. Herberts Devine Poeme *The Church*" (1633)

John Polwhele (before 1623–after 1662) was an English poet and the first known person to pen a response to *The Temple*. Though little is known about him, Polwhele was associated with Lincoln's Inn, a place where barristers are called before the bar, and may have been father to the playwright Elizabeth Polwhele, one of the first English women to have works produced on the stage. This John Polwhele may also have been a royalist member of the Long Parliament from 1640–1644 who was born in 1606.

Haile Sacred Architect
　　Thou doest a glorious Temple raise
　　　　stil ecchoinge his praise.
who taught thy genius thus to florish it
with curious gravings of a Peircinge witt.
　　　　Statelye thy Pillers bee,
　　Westwards the Crosse, the Quier, and
　　　　thine Alter Eastward stande,
　　where Is most Catholique Conformitie
with out a nose-twange spoylinge harmonic
　　　　Resolve to Sinne noe more,
　　　from hence a penitent sigh, and groane
　　　　cann flintye heartes unstone;
and blowe them to their happye porte heaven's
　　doore,
where Herberts Angell's flowen awaye before.

—John Polwhele, "On Mr. Herberts
Devine Poeme *The Church*," c. 1633

Izaak Walton (1639)

A book, in which by declaring his own spiritual conflicts, he hath comforted and raised many a dejected and discomposed soul, and charmed them into sweet and quiet thoughts: a book, by the frequent reading whereof, and the assistance of that Spirit that seemed to inspire the Author, the Reader may attain habits of Peace and Piety, and all the gifts of the Holy Ghost and Heaven: and may, by still reading, still keep those sacred fires burning upon the altar of so pure a heart, as shall free it from the anxieties of this world, and keep it fixed upon things that are above.

—Izaak Walton, *Life of Dr. John Donne,*
1639, p. 37

Christopher Harvey
"The Synogague" (1640)

Christopher Harvey (1597–1663) was an Anglican clergyman and a poetic disciple and imitator of Herbert.

What Church is this? Christs Church. Who builds it?
Mr. *George Herbert.* Who assisted it?
Many assisted: who, I may not say,
So much contention might arise that way.
If I say Grace gave all, Wit straight doth thwart,
And sayes all that is there is mine: but Art
Denies and sayes ther's nothing there but's mine:
Nor can I easily the right define.
Divide: say, Grace the matter gave, and Wit
Did polish it, Art measured and made fit
Each severall piece, and fram'd it all together.
No, by no means: this may not please them neither.
None's well contented with a part alone,
When each doth challenge all to be his owne:
The matter, the expressions, and the measures,
Are eqyally Arts, Wits, and Graces treasures.
Then he that would impartially discusse
This doubtfull question, must answer thus:
In building of this temple Mr. *Herbert*

Is equally all Grace, all Wit, all Art.
>   *Roman* and *Grecian* Muses all give way:
>   One *English* Poem darkens all your day.

>   —Christopher Harvey,
>   "The Synagogue," 1640

RICHARD CRASHAW "ON MR. G. HERBERT'S BOOKE INTITULED *THE TEMPLE*" (1646)

Like Herbert, Richard Crashaw (c. 1613–1649) was a fellow metaphysical poet and "divine." As evidenced below, Crashaw was very influenced by Herbert, and today Crashaw is considered one of the finest poets of the metaphysical school.

Know you faire, on what you looke;
Divinest love lyes in this booke:
Expecting fire from your eyes,
To kindle this his sacrifice.
When your hands unty these strings,
Thinke you have an Angell by th' wings.
One that gladly will bee nigh,
To wait upon each morning sigh.
To flutter in the balmy aire,
Of your well perfumed prayer.
These white plumes of his heele lend you,
Which every day to heaven will send you:
To take acquaintance of the spheare,
And all the smooth faced kindred there.
And though *Herbert's* name doe owe
These devotions, fairest; know
That while I lay them on the shrine
Of your white hand, they are mine.

>   —Richard Crashaw, "On Mr. G.
>   Herbert's Booke intituled *The Temple*,"
>   *Steps to the Temple,* 1646

George Daniel "An Ode upon the Incomparable Liricke Poesie written by Mr. George Herbert; entitled *The Temple*" (1648)

In the piece below, Daniel praises Herbert's famous work *The Temple* in poetic form, a not uncommon response by writers when responding to works they particularly admire.

Lord! yet how dull am I?
   When I would flye!
Up to the Region, of thy Glories where
   Onlie true formes appeare;
My long brail'd Pineons, (clumsye, and unapt)
     I cannot Spread;
   I am all dullnes; I was Shap't
Only to flutter, in the lower Shrubbs
   Of Earth-borne-follies. Out alas!
     When I would treade
A higher Step, ten thousand, thousand Rubbs
     Prevent my Pace.
This Glorious Larke; with humble Honour, I
     Admire and praise;
     But when I raise
My Selfe, I fall asham'd, to see him flye:
The Royall Prophet, in his Extasie,
     First trod this path;
Hee followes neare; (I will not Say, how nigh)
   In flight, as well as faith.
Let me asham'd creepe backe into my Shell;
   And humbly Listen to his Layes:
Tis prejudice, what I intended Praise;
As where they fall soe Lowe, all Words are Still.
   Our Untun'd Liricks, onlie fitt
     To Sing, our Selfe-borne-Cares,
   Dare not, of Him. Or had wee Witt,
     Where might wee find out Ears
Worthy his Character? if wee may bring

Our Accent to his Name?
This Stand, of Lirick's, Hee the utmost Fame
Has gain'd; and now they vaile, to heare Him Sing
Horace in voice; and Casimire in winge.

—George Daniel, "An Ode upon the
Incomparable Liricke Poesie written by
Mr. George Herbert; entituled: *The Temple*"
(1648), *The Selected Poems of George Daniel of
Beswick 1616–1657*, 1959, ed. Stroup, pp. 66–67

James Duport "In Divimun Poema (Cui Titulus Templum) Georgii Herberti" (1676)

James Duport (1606–1679) is most known as an English classical scholar, though he did write numerous short subject poems, which were collected in his *Horae subsecivae* or *Stromata*. An admirer of Herbert, Duport, as Polwhele, Harvey, Crashaw, and Daniel had before him, praised the divine writer's work in his own laudatory poem.

If zeal and genius, Piety and wit in like
    Pre-em'nence in one Book have ever joined,
'Tis, Herbert, this of thine: thou'st borne off every prize,
    Who melody so sweet canst sanctify.
No Lyre sang sacred hymns so graciously as thine,
    Save David's only—his, or none's.
What profit, then, to bid my Muses hither come
    To lessen thy great Songs with measures slight?
For I in vain should try to sing such lofty praise,
    Or in thy *Temple's* feet my measures write,
Unless thy holy Dove's own wing provide my pen,
    Or coal from off thine altar touch my lips;
Unless, in fine, my heart should feel those holy flames
    Through which I too might have that sacred vein.
Permit me then thy proper phrases to return
    And mine own gardens water from thy fount.
For better, god-like Poet, I cannot praise thy work
    Than thou the Noble Royal Book didst laud:
'Why mention "Vatican" and "Bodleian", O friend?

One single book a library is to us'.
For my part this I'll add: to me no other Book,
    God's Word apart, so sacred is or good.
Since, then, on earth no Hymn is so divine, nor like
    And equal to thy *Temple* any Song,
This yet remains for thee: in heaven eternal poems
    To sound, and verses fit for angels' Choirs.

—James Duport, "In Divinum Poema
(Cui Titulus Templum) Georgii Herberti,"
Musae subsecivae, sev Poetica Stromata,
1676, pp. 357–58

DANIEL BAKER "ON MR. GEORGE HERBERT'S SACRED POEMS, CALLED, *THE TEMPLE*" (1697)

A poet in the style of Herbert, Daniel Baker (1653/4–1723) published two collections of his work, *The Book of Job* and *Poems Upon Several Occasions*. The poem below comes from the second collection. In the piece, Baker praises Herbert for rescuing poetry from the "Pagans," a likely reference to the fondness for Greek and Roman work and poetical allusions in the seventeenth century; thus Baker's work contrasts interestingly with John Reynolds' piece, which takes a very different perspective on Herbert's relationship to earlier poetical works.

I.

    So long had Poetry possessed been
        By Pagans, that a Right in her they claim'd,
        Pleaded Prescription for their Sin,
And Laws they made, and Arguments they fram'd,
Nor thought it Wit, if God therein was nam'd:
The true GOD; for of false ones they had store,
    Whom Devils we may better call,
    And ev'ry thing they deifi'd,
And to a Stone, Arise and help they cri'd.
    And Woman-kind they fell before;
Ev'n Woman-kind, which caus'd at first their Fall,
Were almost the sole Subject of their Pen,
And the chief Deities ador'd by fond and sottish Men.

II.

     Herbert at last arose,
   Herbert inspir'd with holy Zeal,
Their Arguments he solv'd, their Laws he did repeal,
   And Spight of all th'enraged Foes
That with their utmost Malice did oppose,
He rescu'd the poor Captive, Poetry,
Whole her vile Masters had before decreed
All her immortal Spirit to employ
   In painting out the Lip or Eye
Of some fantastick Dame, whose Pride Incentives did not need.
This mighty *Herbert* could not brook;
It griev'd his pious Soul to see
    The best and noblest Gift,
    That God to Man has left,
Abus'd to serve vile Lust, and sordid Flattery:
So, glorious Arms in her Defence he took;
And when with great Success he'd set her free,
He rais'd her fancy on a stronger Wing,
Taught her of God above, and Things Divine to sing.

III.

Th' infernal Powers that held her fast before
   And great Advantage of their Pris'ner made,
   And drove of Souls a gainful Trade,
Began to mutiny and roar.
So when *Demetrius* and his Partners[1] view'd
Their Goddess, and with her, their dearer Gains to fall,
They draw together a confus'd Multitude,
   And into th' Theater they crowd,
And great *Diana*, great, they loudly call.
   Up into th' Air their Voices flie,
   Some one thing, some another crie,
   And most of them they know not why.
They crie aloud, 'till the Earth ring again,
   Aloud they crie; but all in vain.
Diana down must go; They can no more
Their sinking Idol help, than she could them before.
Down she must go with all her Pomp and Train:

The glorious Gospel-Sun her horned Pride doth stain,
No more to be renew'd, but ever in the Wane;
And Poetry, now grown Divine above must ever reign.

IV.

    A Mon'ment of this Victory
Our *David,* our Sweet Psalmist, rais'd on high,
When he this Giant under foot did tread,
And with Verse, his own Sword, cut off the Monster's Head.
For as a Sling and Heav'n-directed Stone
Laid flat the *Gathite* Champion, who alone
Made Thousands tremble, while he proudly stood
Bidding Defiance to the Hosts of God:
So fell th' infernal Pow'rs before the Face
Of mighty *Herbert,* who upon the Place
    A Temple built, that does outdo
    Both *Solomon's,* and *Herod's* too,
And all the Temples of the Gods by far;
So costly the Materials, and the Workmanship so rare
A Temple built, as God did once ordain
    Without the Saw's harsh Noise
Or the untuneful Hammer's Voice,[2]
But built with sacred Musick's sweetest strain,
Like *Theban* Walls of old, as witty Poets feign.

V.

Hail, heav'nly Bard, to whom great LOVE has giv'n
    (His mighty Kindness to express)
To bear his Three mysterious Offices;
Prophet, and Priest on Earth thou wast, and now a King in
    Heav'n.
        There thou dost reign, and there
    Thy Bus'ness is the same 'twas here,
And thine old Songs thou singest o'er agen:
    The Angels and the Heav'nly Quire
        Gaze on thee, and admire
To hear such Anthems from an earthly Lyre,
Their own Hymns almost equall'd by an human Pen.
    We foolish Poets hope in vain
    Our Works Eternity shall gain:
    But sure those Poems needs must die

Whose Theme is but Mortality.
Thy wiser and more noble Muse
   The best, the only way did chuse
To grow Immortal: For what Chance can wrong,
   What Teeth of Time devour that Song
Which to a Heav'nly Tune is set for glorifi'd Saints to use?
O may some Portion of thy Spirit on me
(Thy poor Admirer) light, whose Breast
By wretched mortal Loves hath been too long
   possest!
When, Oh! when will the joyful Day arise
   That rescu'd from these Vanities,
   These painted Follies I shall be,
If not an inspir'd Poet, yet an holy Priest like thee

Notes

1. Acts 19.24 ff. (author's marginal note).
2. 'I Kings 6.7' (author's marginal note).

—Daniel Baker "On Mr. George Herbert's
Sacred Poems, Called, *The Temple*," *Poems
upon Several Occasions,* 1697, pp. 83–89

SAMUEL TAYLOR COLERIDGE (1818)

I find more substantial comfort now in pious George Herbert's *Temple*, which I used to read to amuse myself with his quaintness, in short, only to laugh at, than in all the poetry since the poems of Milton.

—Samuel Taylor Coleridge, *Lectures and
Notes on Shakespere,* 1818

SAMUEL TAYLOR COLERIDGE (1818)

In the excerpt below, Coleridge compares two of Herbert's poems to works by Renaissance writer Michael Drayton and Christopher Harvey (see selection from Harvey above.) Coleridge, a great admirer of Herbert's style and language, especially in the first poem he references ("The Bosom Sin,") does chide Herbert's second work for using the "most fantastic language [to convey] the most trivial thoughts" (in "Love Unknown.")

Another exquisite master of this species of style where the scholar and the poet supplies the material, but the perfect well-bred gentleman the expressions and the arrangement, is George Herbert. As from the nature of the subject and the too frequent quaintness of the thoughts, his *Temple, or Sacred Poems and Private Ejaculations* are comparatively but little known, I shall extract two poems. The first is a Sonnet, equally admirable for the weight, number and expression of the thoughts, and for the simple dignity of the language (unless indeed a fastidious taste should object to the latter half of the sixth line). The second is a poem of greater length, which I have chosen not only for the present purpose, but likewise as a striking example and illustration of an assertion hazarded in a former page of these sketches: namely that the characteristic fault of our elder poets is the reverse of that which distinguishes too many of our more recent versifiers; the one conveying the most fantastic thoughts in the most correct and natural language; the other in the most fantastic language conveying the most trivial thoughts. The latter is a riddle of words; the former an enigma of thoughts. The one reminds me of an odd passage in Drayton's *Ideas:*

> As other men, so I myself do muse,
> Why in this sort I wrest invention so;
> And why these giddy metaphors I use,
> Leaving the path the greater part do go;
> I will resolve you: I am lunatic!
>   ("Sonnet IX")

The other recalls a still odder passage in the 'Synagogue, or the Shadow of the Temple,' a connected series of poems in imitation of Herbert's *Temple* and in some editions annexed to it:

> O how my mind
>   Is gravell'd!
>   Not a thought,
> That I can find,
>   But's ravell'd
>   All to nought.
> Short ends of threds,
>   And narrow shreds
>   Of lists,
> Knot's snarled ruffs,
>   Loose broken tufts
>   Of twists,

Are my torn meditation's ragged cloathing.
Which, wound and woven, shape a sute for nothing:
One while I think, and then I am in pain
To think how to unthink that thought again.

Immediately after these burlesque passages I cannot proceed to the extracts promised without changing the ludicrous tone of feeling by the interposition of the three following stanzas of Herbert's:

Sweet day, so cool, so calm, so bright,
The bridal of the earth and sky:
The dew shall weep thy fall to-night,
        For thou must die!
Sweet rose, whose hue angry and brave
Bids the rash gazer wipe his eye:
Thy root is ever in its grave,
        And thou must die!
Sweet spring, full of sweet days and rose
A nest where sweets compacted lie:
My musick shows ye have your closes,
        And all must die!
                    ("Virtue")

Lord, with what care hast thou begirt us round!
Parents first season us; then schoolmasters
Deliver us to laws: they send us bound
To rules of reason, holy messengers,
Pulpits and Sundays, sorrow dogging sin,
Afflictions sorted, anguish of all sizes,
Fine nets and stratagems to catch us in,
Bibles laid open, millions of surprizes;
Blessings beforehand, ties of gratefulness,
The sound of glory ringing in our ears:
Without, our shame; within, our consciences;
Angels and grace, eternal hopes and fears!
        Yet all these fences, and their whole array
        One cunning bosom-sin blows quite away. ("The Bosom Sin")

Dear friend, sit down, the tale is long and sad:
And in my faintings, I presume, your love
Will more comply than help.

A Lord I had, And have, of whom some grounds, which may
   improve,
I hold for two lives, and both lives in me.
To him I brought a dish of fruit one day
And in the middle placed my heart. But he
               (I sigh to say)
Lookt on a servant who did know his eye
Better than you know me, or (which is one)
Than I myself. The servant instantly
Quitting the fruit, seiz'd on my heart alone,
And threw it in a font, wherein did fall
A stream of blood, which issued from the side
Of a great rock: I well remember all,
And have good cause: there it was dipt and dy'd,
And washt, and wrung! the very wringing yet
Enforceth tears. *Your heart was foul, I fear.*
Indeed 'tis true. I did and do commit
Many a fault, more than my lease will bear;
Yet still ask'd pardon, and was not deny'd.
But you shall hear. After my heart was well,
 And clean and fair, as I one eventide
               (I sigh to tell)
Walkt by myself abroad, I saw a large
And spacious furnace flaming, and thereon
A boiling caldron, round about whose verge
Was in great letters set AFFLICTION.
The greatness shew'd the owner. So I went
To fetch a sacrifice out of my fold,
Thinking with that which I did thus present,
To warm his love which, I did fear, grew cold.
But as my heart did tender it, the man
Who was to take it from me, slipt his hand,
And threw my heart into the scalding pan;
My heart that brought it (do you understand?)
The offerer's heart. Your *heart was hard, I fear.*
Indeed 'tis true. I found a callous matter
Began to spread and to expatiate there:
But with a richer drug than scalding water
I bath'd it often, ev'n with holy blood,

Which at a board, while many drank bare wine,
A friend did steal into my cup for good,
Ev'n taken inwardly, and most divine
To supple hardnesses. But at the length
Out of the caldron getting, soon I fled
Unto my house, where to repair the strength
Which I had lost, I hasted to my bed;
But when I thought to sleep out all these faults
                    (I sigh to speak)
I found that some had stuff'd the bed with
    thoughts,
I would say *thorns*. Dear, could my heart not break
When with my pleasures ev'n my rest was gone?
Full well I understood who had been there:
For I had given the key to none but one:
It must be he. *Your heart was dull, I fear.*
Indeed a slack and sleepy state of mind
Did oft possess me, so that when I pray'd,
Though my lips went, my heart did stay behind.
But all my scores were by another paid,
Who took the debt upon him. Truly friend,
 For ought I hear, your master shows to you
More favour than you wot of. Mark the end!
The font did only what was old renew:
The caldron suppled what was grown too hard:
The thorns did quicken what was grown too dull:
All did but strive to mend what you had marr'd.
Wherefore be cheer d, and praise him to the full
Each day, each hour, each moment of the week,
Who fain would have you be new, tender, quick!
                    ("Love Unknown")

—Samuel Taylor Coleridge, *Biographia
Literaria*, 1818, ed. George Watson

GEORGE GIFILLAN (1853)

Its poetical merit is of a very rare, lofty, and original order. It is full of that
subtle perception of analogies which is competent only of high poetical

genius. . . Altogether, there are few places on earth nearer Heaven, filled
with a richer and holier light, adorned with chaster and nobler ornaments,
or where our souls can worship with a more entire forgetfulness of self, and
a more thorough realisation of the things unseen and eternal, than in *The
Temple* of George Herbert.

—George Gifillan, *The Poetical Works
of George Herbert*, 1853, pp. xxi–xxvi

ROBERT ARIS WILMOTT "INTRODUCTION" (1854)

In this introduction to a critical edition of Herbert's works, Wilmott
begins by briefly comparing John Milton and Herbert; though to many
students it may seem natural to place the two poets together, as they
both wrote about the church and both lived in the same century,
Wilmott's brief assessment demonstrates the general lack of enthusiasm
most critics have for this comparison, as neither poet is truly like the
other. Wilmott's introduction then begins to suggest some of the ideas
Nichol would write nine years later; he chastises Herbert's style and calls
him "often obscure." Nonetheless, Wilmott richly praises *The Temple*,
labeling it "a Prayer-book in verse," which mirrors Nichol's description of
the work as "Church music crystallized." Wilmott then suggests that the
great power of Herbert is his ability to describe "the central position of
man to the universe." Wilmott writes that Herbert was the first poet who
had the ability to do this, though he sees the idea grow in later authors
and philosophers like Swedish Christian mystic Emanuel Swedenborg.
Students writing on *The Temple* may find this philosophical section particularly useful, as Wilmott provides interesting avenues for comparing
Herbert and more contemporary authors.

Life, it has been said, is a Poem. This is true, probably, of the life of the
human race as a whole, if we could see its beginning and end, as well as its
middle. But it is not true of all lives. It is only a life here and there, which
equals the dignity and aspires to the completeness of a genuine and great
Poem. Most lives are fragmentary, even when they are not foul—they
disappoint, even when they do not disgust—they are volumes without a
preface, an index, or a moral. It is delightful to turn from such apologies for
life to the rare but real lives which God-gifted men, like Milton or Herbert,
have been enabled to spend even on this dark and melancholy foot-breadth
for immortal spirits, called the earth.

We class Milton and Herbert together, for this, among other reasons, that in both, the life and the poems were thoroughly correspondent and commensurate with each other. Milton lived the *Paradise Lost* and the *Paradise Regained,* as well as wrote them. Herbert was, as well as built, *The Temple.* Not only did the intellectual archetype of its structure exist in his mind, but he had been able, in a great measure, to realise it in life, before expressing it in poetry.

We come not to criticise *The Temple,* although the term criticism applied to what is a bosom companion rather than a book may seem cold and out of place. We come, then, we shall rather say, to announce our profound love for the work, and to assign certain reasons for that love. We may first, however, allude to the faults with which it has been justly charged. These are, however, venial, and are those not of the author so much as of his day. He is often quaint, and has not a few conceits, which are rather ingenious than tasteful. Anagrams, acrostics, verbal quibbles, and a hundred other formulae, cold in themselves, although indigenous to the age, and greatly redeemed by the fervour his genius throws into them, abound in *The Temple,* and so far suit the theme, that they remind us of the curious figures and devices which add their Arabesque border to the grandeur of old Abbeys and Cathedrals. It was the wild, crude rhythm of the period, and had Herbert not conformed himself to it, he had either been a far less or a far greater poet than he was. Yet, though bound in chains, he became even in durance an alchymist, and turned his chains into gold.

Herbert has, besides, what may be considered more formidable faults than these. He is often obscure, and his allegorising vein is opened too often, and explored too far; so much so, that had we added a commentary or extended notes on *The Temple,* it would have necessarily filled another volume nearly as large as the present. This the plan of our publication, of course, entirely forbids. We may merely premise these advices to those who would care to understand as well as read the succeeding poem: *1st,* Let them regard it as in many portions a piece of picture-writing; *2dly,* Let them seek the secret of this, partly by a careful study of the book itself, and partly by reading the similar works of Donne, Quarles, Giles Fletcher, and John Bunyan; *3dly,* Let them believe in Herbert, even when they do not understand him; and *4thly,* Let them rejoice that the great proportion of the book is perfectly clear and plain, to Christians by experience, to poets by imaginative sympathy, to all men in general by the power of conscience, the sense of guilt, and that fear of the terrors and that hope of the joys of a future state of being, by which all hearts at times are moved . . .

The Temple, looking at it more narrowly, may be viewed in its devotional, in its poetical, and in its philosophical aspects, which we may figure as its altar, its painted window, and its floor and foundation. First, as a piece of devotion it is a Prayer-book in verse. We find in it all the various parts of prayer. Now like a seraph he casts his crown at God's feet, and covers his face with his wings, in awful adoration. Now he looks up in His face, with the happy gratitude of a child, and murmurs out his thanksgiving. Now he seems David the penitent, although fallen from an inferior height, and into pits not nearly so deep and darksome, confessing his sins and shortcomings to his Heavenly Father. And now he asks, and prays, and besieges heaven for mercy, pardon, peace, grace, and joy, as with "groanings that cannot be uttered." We find in it, too, a perpetual undersong of praise. It is a Psalter, no less than a Prayer-book. And how different its bright sparks of worship going up without effort, without noise, by mere necessity of nature, to heaven, from the majority of hymns which have since appeared! No namby-pambyism, no false unction, no nonsensical raptures, are to be found in them; their very faults and mannerisms serve to attest their sincerity, and to shew that the whole man is reflected in them. Even although the poem had possessed far less poetic merit, its mere devotion, in its depth and truth, would have commended it to Christians, as, next to the Psalms, the finest collection of ardent and holy breathings to be found in the world.

But its poetical merit is of a very rare, lofty, and original order. It is full of that subtle perception of analogies which is competent only to high poetical genius. All things, to Herbert, appear marvellously alike to each other. The differences, small or great, whether they be the interspaces between leaves, or the gulfs between galaxies, shrivel up and disappear. The ALL becomes one vast congeries of mirrors—of similitudes—of duplicates—

Star nods to star, each system has its brother,
And half the universe reflects the other.[1]

This principle, or perception, which is the real spring of all fancy and imagination, was very strong in Herbert's mind, and hence the marvellous richness, freedom, and variety of his images. He hangs upon his *Temple* now flowers and now stars, now blossoms and now full-grown fruit. He gathers glories from all regions of thought—from all gardens of beauty—from all the history, and art, and science then accessible to him,— and he wreathes them in a garland around the bleeding brow of Immanuel. Sometimes his style exhibits a clear massiveness like one of the Temple pillars, sometimes a dim richness like one of the Temple windows; and never is there wanting the Temple music, now wailing melodiously, now moving in brisk, lively, and bird-like measures, and now uttering loud paeans and crashes of victorious sound. It has been truly said of him, that he is "inspired by the Bible, as its vaticinators were inspired by God." It is to him not only the "Book of God, but the God of Books." He has hung and brooded over its pages, like a bird for ever dipping her wing in the sea; he has imbibed its inmost spirit—he has made its divine words "the men of his counsel, and his song in the house of his pilgrimage," till they are in his verse less imitated than reproduced. In this, as in other qualities, such as high imagination, burning zeal, quaint fancy, and deep simplicity of character he resembles that "Child-Angel," John Bunyan, who was proud to be a babe of the Bible, although his genius might have made him without it a gigantic original.

We might have quoted many passages corroborating our impressions of the surpassing artistic merit of George Herbert's poem. But the book, as well as the criticism, is now in the reader's hands, and he is called upon to judge for himself. We may merely recommend to his attention, as especially beautiful and rich, "The Church-Porch," "The Agony," "Redemption," "Easter," "Sin," "Prayer," "Whitsunday," "Affliction," "Humility," "To all Angels and Saints," "Vanity," "Virtue" (which contains the stanza so often quoted, "Sweet Day," &c.), "The British Church," "The Quip," and "Peace." Many more will detain and fascinate him as he goes along,—some by their ingenious oddity, some by their tremulous pathos, some by the peculiar profundity of their devotional spirit; and the rest by the sincerity and truth which burn in every line.

We have spoken of the philosophy of *The Temple*. We do not mean by this, that it contains any elaborately constructed, distinctly defined, or logically defended system, but simply that it abounds in glimpses of philosophic thought of a very profound and searching cast. The singular earnestness of Herbert's temperament was connected with—perhaps we should rather say *created* in him—an eye which penetrated below the surface, and looked right into the secrets of things. In his peculiarly happy and blessed constitution, piety and the philosophic genius were united and reconciled; and from those awful depths of man's mysterious nature, which few have more thoroughly, although incidentally, explored than he, he lifts up, not a howl of despair, nor a curse of misanthropy, nor a cry of mere astonishment, but a hymn of worship. We refer especially to those two striking portions of the poem entitled "Man" and "Providence." The first is a fine comment on the Psalmist's words, "I am fearfully and wonderfully made." Herbert first saw, or at least first expressed in poetry, the central position of man to the universe—the fact that all its various lines find a focus in him—that he is a microcosm to the All, and that every part of man is, in its turn, a little microcosm of him. The germ of some of the abstruse theories propounded by Swedenborg, and since enlarged and illustrated by the author of *The Human Body, Considered in its Relation to Man* (a treatise written with a true Elizabethan richness of style and thought, and which often seems to approach, at least, great abysses of discovery), may be found in Herbert's verses. "Man," Herbert says, "is everything and more." He is "a beast, yet is or should be more." He is "all symmetry—full *of proportions, one limb to another, and all to all the world besides.*"

> Head with foot hath private amity,
> And both with moons and tides.
> His eyes dismount the highest star:
> He is in little all the sphere.
> Herbs gladly cure our flesh, because that they
> Find their acquaintance there.
>
> Each thing is full of duty.
>
> More servants wait on Man,
> Than he'll take notice of: in every path
> He treads down that which doth befriend him,
> When sickness makes him pale and wan.
> Oh, mighty love! Man is one world, and hath
> Another to attend him.

How strikingly do these words bring before us the thought of Man the Mystery! "What a piece of workmanship" verily he is! He is formed as of a thousand lights and shadows. He iscompacted out of all contradictions. While his feet touch the dust, and are of miry clay, his head is of gold, and strikes the Empyrean. Altogether, there are few places on earth nearer Heaven, filled with a richer and holier light, adorned with chaster and nobler ornaments, or where our souls can worship with a more entire forgetfulness of self, and a more thorough realisation of the things unseen and eternal, than in *The Temple* of George Herbert. You say, as you stand breathless below its solemn arches, "This is none other than the house of God, it is the gate of Heaven. How dreadful, yet how dear is this place!"

Notes

1. Adapted from Pope's "Epistle to Burlington", 11. 117-18: 'Grove nods at grove, each Alley has a brother, / And half the platform just reflects the other'. The allusion was identified by Mr Anthony W. Shipps.

—Robert Aris Wilmott, from "Introduction,"
The Works of George Herbert 1854, pp. xxi–xxx

Edwin P. Whipple (1859–68)

In the passage below, Whipple criticizes Herbert for the complex nature of his work, a common objection to the metaphysical style of poetry. When Whipple writes, "Nothing can be more frigid than the conceits in which he clothes the great majority of his pious ejaculations and heavenly ecstasies," he is criticizing some of the poetic conventions that were typically found in the work of metaphysical poets. Whipple's criticisms are common enough in the latter half of the eighteenth century and nineteenth century, and Whipple does find much to admire in Herbert as well, including the "wild flavor and fragrance" of his work and "genuine emotion" of his poems, hampered as they are by the artifice that encumbers them.

His poetry is the *bizarre* expression of a deeply religious and intensely thoughtful nature, sincere at heart, but strange, farfetched, and serenely crotchety in utterance. Nothing can be more frigid than the conceits in which he clothes the great majority of his pious ejaculations and heavenly ecstasies. Yet every reader feels that his fancy, quaint as it often is, is a part of the organism of his character; and that his quaintness, his uncouth metaphors and comparisons, his squalid phraseology, his holy charades and pious riddles, his inspirations crystallized into ingenuities, and his general disposition to represent the divine through the exterior guise of the odd, are vitally connected with that essential beauty and sweetness of soul which give his poems their wild flavor and fragrance. Amateurs in sanctity, and men of fine religious taste, will tell you that genuine emotion can never find an outlet in such an elaborately fantastic form; and the proposition, according, as it does, with the rules of Blair and Kames and Whately, commands your immediate assent; but still you feel that genuine emotion is there, and, if you watch sharply, you will find that Taste, entering holy George Herbert's *Temple,* after a preliminary sniff of imbecile contempt, somehow slinks away abashed after the first verse at the "Church-porch." One of the profoundest utterances of the Elizabethan age, George Herbert's lines on Man.

—Edwin P. Whipple, *The Literature of the*
Age of Elizabeth, 1859–68, pp. 247–48

George Augustus Simcox (1880)

A poet and literary scholar, George Augustus Simcox (1841–1905) is best known for his works incorporating Arthurian themes. Below Simcox theorizes as to the conditions which caused Herbert to compose *The Temple*, which Simcoz characterizes as "full of the author's baffled ambition and his distress."

The Temple is the enigmatical history of a difficult resignation; it is full of the author's baffled ambition and his distress, now at the want of a sphere for his energies, now at the fluctuations of spirit, the ebb and flow of intellectual activity, natural to a temperament as frail as it was eager. There is something a little feverish and disproportioned in his passionate heart-searchings. The facts of the case lie in a nutshell. Herbert was a younger son of a large family; he lost his father early, and his mother, a devout, tender, imperious woman, decided, partly out of piety and partly out of distrust of his power to make his own way in the world, that he should be provided for in the Church. When he was twenty-six he was appointed Public Orator at Cambridge, and hoped to make this position a stepping-stone to employment at court. After eight years his patrons and his mother were dead, and he made up his mind to settle down with a wife on the living of Bemerton, where he died after a short but memorable incumbency of three years. The flower of his poetry seems to belong to the two years of acute crisis which preceded his installation at Bemerton or to the Indian summer of content when he imagined that his failure as a courtier was a prelude to his success in the higher character of a country parson.

—George Augustus Simcox, *English Poets*, 1880, vol. 2, ed. Ward, p. 193

JOHN BROWN
"THE PARSON OF BEMERTON" (1890)

The author of the excerpt below is most likely the British historian John Brown (1830–1922,) a renowned theological scholar and author of an influential biography of John Bunyan, seventeenth-century moralist writer. The journal, *Good Words*, published mostly lighter fare for an evangelical Christian audience.

It is a book to be taken as a friend to be loved, rather than as a performance to be criticised. As a manual of devotion it is as though a seraph covered his face with his wings in rapturous adoration; as a poem it is full of that subtle perception of analogies to be found only in works of genius; while the passage on "Man" shows how the poets in their loftiest moods may sometimes anticipate some of the most wonderful discoveries of science and some of the sublimest speculations of philosophy.

—John Brown, "The Parson of
Bemerton," *Good Words,* 1890, p. 697

❖

ROBERT HERRICK

❖

❖

BIOGRAPHY

❖

Robert Herrick

(1591–1674)

❖

Robert Herrick, cleric and poet, was born in Goldsmith's Row, Cheapside, London, the son of a goldsmith. His father died when Herrick was very young (perhaps by suicide), and Herrick and his siblings were raised by their uncle, the king's jeweler. Herrick graduated from Westminster School in 1607 and began a ten-year apprenticeship in the family business.

Herrick entered St. John's College, Cambridge, in 1613, transferring to Trinity Hall, Cambridge in 1616 to study law. Herrick received a BA in 1617 and an MA in 1620, although he never pursued a legal career. In 1623 he was ordained a deacon and accompanied the Duke of Buckingham on his expedition to Ile de Rhe in 1627 as a military chaplain. Herrick returned to London to begin the life of a literary man-about-town.

Joining the poets and musicians of Ben Jonson's circle, Herrick was a poet of high reputation. In 1629, however, Charles II appointed Herrick to the parish of Dean Prior, Devonshire, in the West Country. Initially Herrick lamented the cessation of his London life and despaired of his churlish congregation. Nevertheless, it was in the quiet of the countryside that Herrick wrote most of his poems. In 1647 Herrick was asked to leave because of his refusal to subscribe to the Solemn League and Covenant, which supported further church reform. Herrick was reinstated by the restored king, Charles II, in 1662. He remained in Devonshire until his death in 1674.

Many of Herrick's poems were included in manuscript commonplace books, including the anthologies *A Description of the King and Queen of Fayres* (1635), *Lachrymae Musarum* (1649), and *Witts Recreation* (1650), which carried sixty-two of Herrick's poems. Herrick himself only published one book of poetry in his lifetime, *Hesperides; or the Works, both Humane and Divine, of Robert Herrick, Esq.* (1648), which included religious verse under the title *Noble Numbers,* dated 1647. The book consisted of some 1,400 poems, varying from elegies, satires, epigrams, marriage songs, ecclesiastical and festival songs, and complimentary verse. Herrick never married, but a number of his poems are addressed to imaginary mistresses. Herrick's *Hebrides* was not reprinted until 1823.

❖

PERSONAL

❖

BARRON FIELD (1810)

Barron Field (1786–1846) was an English-born lawyer and poet who eventually became a prominent judge in Australia. The charming story Field tells about Herrick occurred before he left England for Australia.

Being in Devonshire during the last summer, we took an opportunity of visiting Dean Prior, for the purpose of making some inquiries concerning Herrick, who, from the circumstance of having been vicar of that parish (where he is still talked of as a poet, a wit, and a hater of the county), for twenty years, might be supposed to have left some unrecorded memorials of his existence behind him. We found many persons in the village who could repeat some of his lines. . . . The person, however, who knows more of Herrick than all the rest of the neighbourhood, we found to be a poor woman in the ninety-ninth year of her age, named Dorothy King. She repeated to us, with great exactness, five of his *Noble Numbers,* among which was the beautiful Litany. These she had learned from her mother, who was apprenticed to Herrick's successor in the vicarage. She called them her prayers, which, she said, she was in the habit of putting up in bed, whenever she could not sleep: and she therefore began the Litany at the second stanza,

When I lie within my bed, &c.

Another of her midnight orisons was the poem beginning

Every night thou dost me fright,
And keep mine eyes from sleeping, &c.

She had no idea that these poems had ever been printed, and could not have read them if she had seen them. She is in possession of few traditions as to the person, manners, and habits of life of the poet; but in return, she has a whole budget of anecdotes respecting his ghost; and these she details with a careless but serene gravity, which one would not willingly discompose by any hints at a remote possibility of their not being exactly true. Herrick, she says, was a bachelor, and kept a maid-servant, as his poems, indeed, discover; but she adds, what they do not discover, that he also kept a pet-pig, which he taught to drink out of a tankard. And this important circumstance, together with a tradition that he one day threw his sermon at the congregation, with a curse for their inattention, forms almost the sum total of what we could collect of the poet's life.

—Barron Field, *The Quarterly Review,*
1810, pp. 171–72

William Carew Hazlitt
"Preface" (1869)

Hazlitt is one of the most important nineteenth-century critics of Herrick; he is often credited for having "rediscovered" Herrick's works and is recognized for spurning a revival of interest in the poet in the late Victorian Era. Ironically, Hazlitt was not himself a fan of Herrick's oeuvre, which he calls a "weed-choked garden."

This fine old fellow, this joyous heart, who lived to be eighty-three, in spite of "dull Devonshire" and the bad times, wrote almost as much as Carew, Lovelace, and Suckling united, and how much there is in his weed-choked garden, which is comparable with their best compositions! How little we know of him! How scantily he has been realized to us! Could we but raise up for a summer afternoon the Devonshire which he lived in, and the people with whom he mixed or summon the ghost of faithful Prudence Baldwin, we might be furnished with inspiration to do something better than the bare sketch which follows.

—William Carew Hazlitt, "Preface,"
Hesperides, 1869, vol. 1, p. viii

Justin S. Morrill (1887)

A former congressman and senator from Vermont, Justin Smith Morrill (1810–1898) was most known for his tariff laws and supporter of the federal land-grant university statute, though he was also an author on economic and social issues of interest in his day.

Being ejected by Cromwell from his church living in 1648, he dropped his title of "Reverend" to assume that of "Esquire," and published a volume to which he gave the title of *Hesperides; or, the Works both Humane and Divine, of Robert Herrick, Esq.* Doubtless the "Esquire" was accepted by the public, as well as by himself, as more appropriate than "Reverend" would have been to the character of the lyrics, some part of which he yet seems rather arrogantly to call "Divine."

— Justin S. Morrill, *Self-Consciousness
of Noted Persons,* 1887, p. 90

DONALD G. MITCHELL (1890)

This Robert Herrick was a ponderous, earthy-looking man, with huge double chin, drooping cheeks, a great Roman nose, prominent glassy eyes, that showed around them the red lines begotten of strong potions of Canary, and the whole set upon a massive neck which might have been that of Heliogabalus. It was such a figure as the artist would make typical of a man who loves the grossest pleasures.

—Donald G. Mitchell, *English Lands, Letters,*
and Kings: Elizabeth to Anne, 1890, p. 124

AGNES REPPLIER "ENGLISH LOVE-SONGS" (1891)

Agnes Repplier (1855–1950) was an American author and essayist, noted especially for her wit. Her sprightly style is evidenced below in this brief but interesting passage on Julia, Herrick's muse.

Mr. Gosse, for example, assures us that Julia really walked the earth, and even gives us some details of her mundane pilgrimage; other critics smile, and shake their heads, and doubt. It matters not; she lives and she will continue to live when we who dispute the matter lie voiceless in our graves. The essence of her personality lingers on every page where Herrick sings of her. His verse is heavy with her spicy perfumes, glittering with her many-colored jewels, lustrous with the shimmer of her silken petticoats. Her very shadow, her sighs, distills sweet odors on the air, and draws him after her, faint with their amorous languor. How lavish she is with her charms, this woman who neither thinks nor suffers; who prays, indeed, sometimes, with great serenity, and dips her snowy finger in the font of blessed water, but whose spiritual humors pale before the calm vigor of her earthly nature! How kindly, how tranquil, how unmoved she is; listening with the same slow smile to her lover's fantastic word-play, to the fervid conceits with which he beguiles the summer idleness, and to the frank and sudden passion with which he conjures her, "dearest of thousands," to close his eyes when death shall summon him, to shed some true tears above the sod, to clasp forever the book in which he writes her name! How gently she would have fulfilled these last sad duties had the discriminating fates called her to his bier; how fragrant the sighs she would have wafted in that darkened chamber; how sincere the temperate sorrow for a remediable loss! And then, out into the glowing sunlight, where life is sweet, and the world exults, and the warm blood tingles in our veins, and, underneath the scattered primrose blossoms, the frozen dead lie forgotten in their graves.

—Agnes Repplier, "English Love-Songs,"
Points of View, 1891, p. 33

H.M. Sanders "Robert Herrick" (1896)

H. M. Sanders (fl. 1900) published multiple works on metaphysical writers in the literary journals of his day.

It seems likely that Perilla and her fair companions were actually known to Herrick in London, and were then made the topic of many a gallant verse; and that after he sailed away to the West he continued to write to their memory as though they were actually present; that, in fact, the goddesses he was never weary of worshipping were, to a large extent, abstractions and ideals. And when in the quiet of his little parsonage, or in a sunny Devonshire meadow bright with wild flowers, his fancy coined some musical verse in honour of his ideal love, his memory would glide quickly back and dwell longingly on her prototype of flesh and blood whom he had known and loved in former years; and, cut off from all the noises and all the rivalries of the town, it must have seemed to him that he was thinking of another Robert Herrick who had lived long ago.

—H.M. Sanders, "Robert Herrick,"
The Gentleman's Magazine, 1896, p. 604

Thomas Bailey Aldrich "Introduction" (1900)

Thomas Bailey Aldrich (1836–1907) was an American author and poet most famous for his short story collection *Marjorie Daw and Other People* (1873). He was also the editor of the *Atlantic Monthly* for nearly ten years. In the first selection, Aldrich criticizes a portrait of Herrick, suggesting that the likeness seen in the engraving does not resemble the man Aldrich pictures as the author of Herrick's works. In the second, and longer, piece, Aldrich discusses Herrick's unique position amongst the canon of English poets. He rejects any idea that Herrick was greatly influenced by any of his predecessors or contemporaries; according to Aldrich, neither Shakespeare, Marvell, Herbert, Jonson, nor Fletcher have impressed themselves on Herrick in any measurable way. Aldrich likewise rejects any comparison to subsequent poets, save for William Blake, when he writes, "The structure of Herrick's verse, like that of Blake, is simple to the verge of innocence." Mostly, though, Aldrich emphasizes Herrick's solitary achievement: his poems "bewitch the memory, having once caught it, and insist on saying themselves over and over. Among the poets of England the author of the *Hesperides* remains, and is likely to remain, unique." The quality of Herrick's work that most singles him out from his peers is a "quality of remoteness and nearness," that his work seems both very timely and eminently timeless, at once distancing and entrancing. Aldrich was clearly one of Herrick's most ardent admirers and an important editor of the author, and students will find his analysis useful, especially if comparing Herrick's work to those of his contemporaries.

Whether or not the bovine features in Marshall's engraving are a libel on the poet, it is to be regretted that oblivion has not laid its erasing finger on that singularly unpleasant counterfeit presentment. The aggressive face bestowed upon him by the artist lends an air of veracity to the tradition that the vicar occasionally hurled the manuscript of his sermon at the heads of his drowsy parishioners, accompanying the missive with pregnant remarks. He has the aspect of one meditating assault and battery. To offset the picture there is much indirect testimony to the amiability of the man, aside from the evidence furnished by his own writings. I picture him as a sort of Samuel Pepys, with perhaps less quaintness, and the poetical temperament added. Like the prince of gossips, too, he somehow gets at your affections.

—Thomas Bailey Aldrich, "Introduction,"
Poems of Robert Herrick, 1900, pp. xxvi–xxx

Thomas Bailey Aldrich
"Introduction" (1900)

The details that have come down to us touching Herrick's private life are as meager as if he had been a Marlowe or a Shakespere. But were they as ample as could be desired they would still be unimportant compared with the single fact that in 1648 he gave to the world his *Hesperides*. The environments of the man were accidental and transitory. The significant part of him we have, and that is enduring so long as wit, fancy, and melodious numbers hold a charm for mankind. A fine thing incomparably said instantly becomes familiar, and has henceforth a sort of dateless excellence. Though it may have been said three hundred years ago, it is as modern as yesterday; though it may have been said yesterday, it has the trick of seeming to have been always in our keeping. This quality of remoteness and nearness belongs, in a striking degree, to Herrick's poems. They are as novel to-day as they were on the lips of a choice few of his contemporaries, who, in reading them in their freshness, must surely have been aware here and there of the ageless grace of old idyllic poets dead and gone.

Herrick was the bearer of no heavy message to the world, and such message as he had he was apparently in no hurry to deliver. On this point he somewhere says:

> Let others to the printing-presse run fast;
> Since after death comes glory, I'll not haste.

He had need of his patience, for he was long detained on the road by many of those obstacles that waylay poets on their journeys to the printer. Herrick was nearly sixty years old when he published the *Hesperides*. It was, I repeat, no heavy message, and the bearer was left an unconscionable time to cool his heels in the antechamber. Though his pieces had been set to music by such composers as Lawes, Ramsay, and Laniere, and his court poems had naturally won favor with the Cavalier party, Herrick cut but a small figure at the side of several of his rhyming contemporaries who are now forgotten. It sometimes happens that the light love-song, reaching few or no ears at its first singing, outlasts the seemingly more prosperous ode which, dealing with some passing phase of thought, social or political, gains the instant applause of the multitude. In most cases the timely ode is somehow apt to fade with the circumstance that inspired it, and becomes the yesterday's editorial of literature. Oblivion likes especially to get hold of occasional poems. That makes it hard for feeble poets laureate.

Mr. Henry James once characterized Alphonse Daudet as "a great little novelist." Robert Herrick is a great little poet. The brevity of his poems— for he wrote nothing *de longue haleine*—would place him among the minor singers; his workmanship places him among the masters. The Herricks were not a family of goldsmiths and lapidaries for nothing. The accurate touch of the artificer in jewels and costly metals was one of the gifts transmitted to Robert Herrick. Much of his work is as exquisite and precise as the chasing on a dagger-hilt by Cellini; the line has nearly always that vine-like fluency which seems impromptu, and is never the result of anything but austere labor. The critic who called these carefully wrought poems "wood-notes wild" mistook his vocation. They are full of subtle simplicity. Here we come across a stanza as severely cut as an antique cameo,—the stanza, for instance, in which the poet speaks of his lady-love's "winter face,"—and there a couplet that breaks into unfading daffodils and violets. The art, though invisible, is always there. His amatory songs and catches are such poetry as Orlando would have liked to hang on the boughs in the forest of Arden. None of the work is hastily done, not even that portion of it we could wish had not been done at all. Be the motive grave or gay, it is given that faultlessness of form which distinguishes everything in literature that has survived its own period. There is no such thing as "form" alone; it is only the close-grained material that takes the highest finish. The structure of Herrick's verse, like that of Blake, is simple to the verge of innocence. Such rhythmic intricacies as those of Shelley, Tennyson, and Swinburne he never dreamed of. But his manner has this perfection: it fits his matter as the cup of the acorn fits its meat.

Of passion, in the deeper sense, Herrick has little or none. Here are no "tears from the depth of some divine despair," no probings into the tragic heart of man, no insight that goes much farther than the pathos of a cowslip on a maiden's grave. The tendrils of his verse reach up to the light, and love the warmer side of the garden wall. But the reader who does not detect the seriousness under the lightness misreads Herrick. Nearly all true poets have been wholesome and joyous singers. A pessimistic poet, like the poisonous ivy, is one of nature's sarcasms. In his own bright pastoral way Herrick must always remain unexcelled. His limitations are certainly narrow, but they leave him in the sunshine. Neither in his thought nor in his utterance is there any complexity; both are as pellucid as a woodland pond, content to duplicate the osiers and ferns, and, by chance, the face of a girl straying near its crystal. His is no troubled stream in which large trout are caught. He must be accepted on his own terms.

The greatest poets have, with rare exceptions, been the most indebted to their predecessors or to their contemporaries. It has wittily been remarked that only mediocrity is ever wholly original. Impressionability is one of the conditions of the creative faculty: the sensitive mind is the only mind that invents. What the poet reads, sees, and feels, goes into his blood, and becomes an ingredient of his originality. The color of his thought instinctively blends itself with the color of its affinities. A writer's style, if it have distinction, is the outcome of a hundred styles. Though a generous borrower of the ancients, Herrick appears to have been exceptionally free from the influence of contemporary minds. Here and there in his work are traces of his beloved Ben Jonson, or fleeting impressions of Fletcher, and in one instance a direct infringement on Suckling; but the sum of Herrick's obligations in this sort is inconsiderable. This indifference to other writers of his time, this insularity, was doubtless his loss. The more exalted imagination of Vaughan or Marvell or Herbert might have taught him a deeper note than he sounded in his purely devotional poems. Milton, of course, moved in a sphere apart. Shakspere, whose personality still haunted the clubs and taverns which Herrick frequented on his first going up to London, failed to lay any appreciable spell upon him. That great name, moreover, is a jewel which finds no setting in Herrick's rhyme. His general reticence relative to brother poets is extremely curious when we reflect on his penchant for addressing four-line epics to this or that individual. They were, in the main, obscure individuals, whose identity is scarcely worth establishing. His London life, at two different periods, brought him into contact with many of the celebrities of the day; but his verse has helped to confer immortality on very few of them. That his verse had the secret of conferring immortality was one of his unshaken convictions. Shakspere had not a finer confidence when he wrote:

> Not marble nor the gilded monuments
> Of princes shall outlive this powerful rhyme,

than has Herrick whenever he speaks of his own poetry, and he is not by any means backward in speaking of it. It was the breath of his nostrils. Without his Muse those nineteen years in that dull, secluded Devonshire village would have been unendurable.

His poetry has the value and the defect of that seclusion. In spite, however, of his contracted horizon there is great variety in Herrick's themes. Their scope cannot be stated so happily as he has stated it:

> I sing of brooks, of blossoms, birds and bowers,
> Of April, May, of June, and July-flowers;
> I sing of May-poles, hock-carts, wassails, wakes,
> Of bridegrooms, brides, and of their bridal cakes;
> I write of Youth, of Love, and have access
> By these to sing of cleanly wantonness;
> I sing of dews, of rains, and piece by piece

Of balm, of oil, of spice and ambergris;
I sing of times trans-shifting, and I write
How roses first came red and lilies white;
I write of groves, of twilights, and I sing
The Court of Mab, and of the Fairy King;
I write of Hell; I sing (and ever shall)
Of Heaven, and hope to have it after all.

Never was there so pretty a table of contents! When you open his book the breath of the English rural year fans your cheek; the pages seem to exhale wildwood and meadow smells, as if sprigs of tansy and lavender had been shut up in the volume and forgotten. One has a sense of hawthorn hedges and wide-spreading oaks, of open lead-set lattices half hidden with honeysuckle; and distant voices of the hay-makers, returning home in the rosy afterglow, fall dreamily on one's ear, as sounds should fall when fancy listens. There is no English poet so thoroughly English as Herrick. He painted the country life of his own time as no other has painted it at any time. It is to be remarked that the majority of English poets regarded as national have sought their chief inspiration in almost every land and period excepting their own. Shakspere went to Italy, Denmark, Greece, Egypt, and to many a hitherto unfooted region of the imagination, for plot and character. It was not Whitehall Garden, but the Garden of Eden and the celestial spaces, that lured Milton. It is the "Ode on a Grecian Urn," "The Eve of St. Agnes," and the noble fragment of "Hyperion" that have given Keats his spacious niche in the gallery of England's poets. Shelley's two masterpieces, *Prometheus Unbound* and *The Cenci,* belong respectively to Greece and Italy. Browning's *The Ring and the Book* is Italian; Tennyson wandered to the land of myth for the *Idylls of the King;* and Matthew Arnold's "Sohrab and Rustum"—a narrative poem second in dignity to none produced in the nineteenth century—is a Persian story. But Herrick's "golden apples" sprang from the soil in his own day, and reddened in the mist and sunshine of his native island.

Even the fairy poems, which must be classed by themselves, are not wanting in local flavor. Herrick's fairy world is an immeasurable distance from that of *A Midsummer Night's Dream.* Puck and Titania are of finer breath than Herrick's little folk, who may be said to have Devonshire manners and to live in a miniature England of their own. Like the magician who summons them from nowhere, they are fond of color and perfume and substantial feasts, and indulge in heavy draughts—from the cups of morning-glories. In the tiny sphere they inhabit everything is marvelously adapted to their requirement;

nothing is out of proportion or out of perspective. The elves are a strictly religious people in their winsome way, "part pagan, part papistical"; they have their pardons and indulgences, their psalters and chapels, and

> An apple's core is hung up dried,
> With rattling kernels, which is rung
> To call to morn- and even-song;

and very conveniently,

> Hard by, i' th' shell of half a nut,
> The holy water there is put.

It is all delightfully naive and fanciful, this elfin-world, where the impossible does not strike one as incongruous, and the England of 1648 seems never very far away.

It is only among the apparently unpremeditated lyrical flights of the Elizabethan dramatists that one meets with anything like the lilt and liquid flow of Herrick's songs. While in no degree Shaksperian echoes, there are epithalamia and dirges of his that might properly have fallen from the lips of Posthumus in *Cymbeline*. This delicate epicede would have fitted Imogen:

> Here a solemne fast we keepe
> While all beauty lyes asleepe;
> Husht be all things; *no noyse here*
> But the toning of a teare,
> Or a sigh of such as bring
> *Cowslips for her covering.*

Many of the pieces are purely dramatic in essence; the "Mad Maid's Song," for example. The lyrist may speak in character, like the dramatist. A poet's lyrics may be, as most of Browning's are, just so many *dramatis persona*. "Enter a Song singing" is the stage-direction in a seventeenth-century play whose name escapes me. The sentiment dramatized in a lyric is not necessarily a personal expression. In one of his couplets Herrick neatly denies that his more mercurial utterances are intended presentations of himself:

> To his Book's end this last line he'd have placed—

> Jocund his Muse was, but his Life was chaste.

In point of fact he was a whole group of imaginary lovers in one. Silvia, Anthea, Electra, Perilla, Perenna, and the rest of those lively ladies ending in *a,* were doubtless, for the most part, but airy phantoms dancing—as they should not have danced—through the brain of a sentimental old bachelor who happened to be a vicar of the Church of England. Even with his overplus of heart it would have been quite impossible for him to have had enough to go round had there been so numerous actual demands upon it.

Thus much may be conceded to Herrick's verse: at its best it has wings that carry it nearly as close to heaven's gate as any of Shakspere's larklike interludes. The brevity of the poems and their uniform smoothness sometimes produce the effect of monotony. The crowded richness of the line advises a desultory reading. But one must go back to them again and again. They bewitch the memory, having once caught it, and insist on saying themselves over and over. Among the poets of England the author of the *Hesperides* remains, and is likely to remain, unique. As Shakspere stands alone in his vast domain, so Herrick stands alone in his scanty plot of ground.

Shine, Poet! in thy place, and be content.

—Thomas Bailey Aldrich, "Introduction,"
Poems of Robert Herrick, 1900, pp. xxxviii–1.

❖

GENERAL

❖

EDWARD PHILLIPS (1675)

Edward Phillips (1630–c.1696) was an English author. His work *Theatrum poetarum* (1675), excerpted below, was an accounting of major poets from all time periods and places, with a special emphasis on English poets, and included a preface that many critics contend was written by John Milton, who at one time was Phillips' tutor.

Robert Herric, a writer of poems of much about the same standing and the same rank in fame with the last mentioned (Robert Heath), though not particularly influenced by any nymph or goddess except his *Maid Pru.* That which is chiefly pleasant in these poems, is now and then a pretty flowery and pastoral gale of fancy; a vernal prospect of some hill, cave, rock, or fountain; which but for the interruption of other trivial passages, might have made up none of the worst poetic landscapes.

—Edward Phillips, *Theatrum Poetarum Anglicanorum,* 1675

WILLIAM WINSTANLEY (1687)

William Winstanley (1628?–1698) was a writer and bookseller who penned the important *Lives of the Most Famous English Poets* in 1687. The text includes an account of Herrick, listed below.

Robert Herric one of the Scholars of *Apollo* of the middle Form, yet something above *George Withers,* in a pretty Flowry and Pastoral Gale of Fancy, in a vernal Prospect of some Hill, Cave, Rock, or Fountain; which but for the Interruption of other trivial Passages, might have made up none of the worst Poetick Landskips. Take a view of his Poetry in his Errata to the Reader in these lines.

For these Errata's, Reader thou do'st see,
Blame thou the Printer for them, and not me:
Who gave him forth good Grain, tho he mistook,
And so did sow these Tares throughout my Book.

I account him in Fame much of the same rank, as he was of the same Standing, with one *Robert Heath,* the Author of a Poem, Entituled, *Clarastella,* the ascribed Title of that Celebrated Lady, who is supposed to have been both the Inspirer and chief Subject of them.

—William Winstanley, *The Lives of the Most Famous English Poets,* 1687

ANTHONY Á WOOD (1691–1721)

Anthony á Wood (1632–1695) was an English scholar and important manuscript collector. An antiquarian by training, he published an important study of the history and artifcats of Oxford University in 1669 (reprinted in Latin in 1674.)

———

Robert Heyrick was a Londoner born, but descended from those of his name (which are antient and genteel) in Leicestershire, was elected fellow of Alls. coll. from that of S. John's as it seems, in the year 1628, but took no degree, as I can yet find. Afterwards being patroniz'd by the earl of Exeter, lived near the river Dean-Bourne in Devonshire, where he exercis'd his muse as well in poetry as other learning, and became much beloved by the gentry in those parts for his florid and witty discourse: but being forced to leave that place, he retired to London, where he published

Hesperides: or, Works both humane and divine. Lond. 1648, in a thick oct. with his picture (a shoulder-piece) before it.

His noble Numbers: or, his Pieces. Wherein (among other things) he sings the Birth of Christ, and Sighs for his Saviour's Sufferings on the Cross—printed with *Hesperides.* These two books of poetry made him much admired in the time when they were published, especially by the generous and boon loyalists, among whom he was numbered as a sufferer. Afterwards he had a benefice conferr'd on him (in Devonsh. I think) by the said E. of Essex, and was living in S. Ann's parish in Westminster, after his majesty's restoration. He had a brother or near kinsman named Rich. Heyrick a divine, whom I have elsewhere mention'd.

—Anthony á Wood, *Athenae
Oxonienses*, 1691–1721

JAMES GRANGER (1769–76)

James Granger (1723–1776) was an English clergyman, biographer and important collector of engravings. His *Biographical History of England from Egbert the Great to the Revolution* was an important work of its day.

———

It appears from the effects of her inspiration, that Prue was but indifferently qualified for a tenth muse.

—James Granger, *Biographical History
of England*, 1769–76, vol.3, p. 136

NATHAN DRAKE "ON THE LIFE, WRITINGS, AND GENIUS OF ROBERT HERRICK" (1804)

Drake uses much of the space below to compare Herrick to his contemporary Thomas Carew. In the early nineteenth century, Carew was being considered as one of the harbingers of contemporary verse; Drake argues that "Many of [Herrick's] best effusions have the sweetness, the melody, and elegance of modern compositions." The piece's comparison of two like poets is very useful to any student of either author or of metaphysical poetry in general.

━◯◯◯━ ━◯◯◯━ ━◯◯◯━

One chief cause of the neglect into which the poetry of Herrick has fallen, is its extreme inequality. It would appear he thought it necessary to publish every thing he composed, however trivial, however ridiculous or indecorous. The consequence has been, that productions, which Marlowe or Milton might have owned with pleasure, have been concealed, and nearly buried, in a crude and undigested mass. Had he shewn any taste in selection, I have no doubt the fate of his volume, though reduced two-thirds of its present size, had been widely different. Perhaps there is no collection of poetry in our language, which, in some respects, more nearly resembles the *Carmina* of Catullus. It abounds in Epigrams disgusting and indecent, in satirical delineations of personal defects, in frequent apologies for the levity of his Muse, and repeated declarations of the chastity of his life; it is interspersed, also, with several exquisite pieces of the amatory and descriptive kind, and with numerous addresses to his friends and relations, by whom he appears to have been greatly beloved. The variety of metre he has used in this work is truly astonishing; he has almost exhausted every form of rhymed versification, and in many he moves with singular ease and felicity.

It has been observed by Mr. Headley, that "Waller is too exclusively considered as the first man who brought versification to any thing like its present standard. Carew's pretensions to the same merit are seldom sufficiently either considered or allowed." I may venture, I think, to introduce Herrick to my reader, as having greatly contributed toward this mechanical perfection. Many of his best effusions have the sweetness, the melody, and elegance of modern compositions. He was nearly, if not altogether, contemporary with Carew; for, if the account of Clarendon, who had been intimate with him, be correct, Carew lived fifty years, and as we know that he died in 1639, he must have been born only a year or two anterior to Herrick. It is true Carew's Poems were published earlier, being given to the world shortly after his death, probably in the year 1640 or 1641, for the second edition of his works bears date 1642; but as Herrick's productions were all written before 1648, and many of them twenty, or, perhaps, thirty years previous to this period, it is obvious he could have been no imitator of the friend of Clarendon, but must have been indebted merely to his own exertions and genius, for the grace and polish of his versification. I consider, likewise, the two little Poems, entitled the "Primrose" and the "Inquiry," which were first published in Carew's works, and afterwards appeared among the Poems of Herrick, to have certainly belonged to the latter, and to have been attributed to Carew by the Editor's mistake. In the first place it is not probable that Herrick, who certainly superintended and arranged his own productions, and who must have been familiar with the volume of his ingenious rival, would have republished these pieces as his own, if he had not possessed a prior claim to them; and, secondly, the Poem termed the "Inquiry," by the Editor of Carew, is, in Herrick, addressed to a beloved Mistress, to "Mrs. Eliz. Wheeler," under the name of the lost Shepherdess; and by the nature of its variations from the copy in Carew, bears indubitable marks of being the original from whence those lines were taken; and which, being probably written early, and circulated in manuscript by Herrick's friends, might easily, from a general resemblance of style and manner, be mistaken, by the Editor, for a genuine production of Carew.

If, in point of versification, Herrick may enter into competition with either Carew or Waller, he will be found still more competent to contend with them as to sentiment and imagery. It has been justly observed, that "Carew has the ease, without the pedantry, of Waller;" the remark will apply with equal propriety to Herrick. His amatory poems unite the playful gaiety of Anacreon with the tender sweetness of Catullus, and are altogether devoid of that mythological allusion and cold conceit, which, in the pages of Waller, so frequently disgust the reader. There is a vein also of rich description in the poetry of Herrick, undiscoverable in the productions of the two other poets, and which resembles the best manner of Milton's Minora, and Marlowe's Passionate Shepherd. Nor has he been unsuccessful in imitating the Horatian style and imagery, of which I shall give a specimen, while, at the same time, the morality of another portion of his lyrics breathes an air of the most pleasing melancholy. I hesitate not, therefore, to consider him in the same degree superior to Carew, as Carew most assuredly is to Waller, whose versification, as I have elsewhere observed, has alone embalmed his memory.

—Nathan Drake, "On the Life, Writings and
Genius of Robert Herrick," *Literary Hours*,
1804, vol. 2, pp. 368–71

WILLIAM HAZLITT (1820)

Herrick is a writer who does not answer the expectations I had formed of him. He is in a manner a modern discovery, and so far has the freshness of antiquity about him. He is not trite and thread bare. But neither is he likely to become so. He is a writer of epigrams, not of lyrics. He has point and ingenuity, but I think little of the spirit of love or wine. From his frequent allusion to pearls and rubies, one might take him for a lapidary instead of a poet.

—William Hazlitt, *Lectures on the*
Literature of the Age of Elizabeth, 1820

ROBERT SOUTHEY (1831)

A coarse-minded and beastly writer, whose dunghill, when the few flowers that grew therein had been transplanted, ought never to have been disturbed. Those flowers indeed are beautiful and perennial; but they should have been removed from the filth and ordure in which they are embedded.

—Robert Southey, *Lives of*
Uneducated Poets, 1831, p. 85

RALPH WALDO EMERSON
"BEN JONSON, HERRICK, HERBERT, WOTTON" (1835)

Emerson criticizes Herrick for pushing the boundaries of good taste too far, a criticism that chased Herrick's work throughout the nineteenth century. Emerson laments that Herrick's work utilizes "base and even disgusting themes" for the purpose, as Emerson believes, of selling more books. Emerson does go on to compliment Herrick's musical verse and deft sense of lyric, but it is Emerson's criticism of the author's subject choices that readers will likely find most useful.

A contemporary and friend of Ben Jonson was Robert Herrick, the author of the *Hesperides* and *Noble Numbers,* a genuine English Poet. His verse is exclusively lyric, composed [of] short fugitive compositions upon all topics grave and gay, dainty and coarse, upon the objects of common life. The man of poetic temperament never feels his privilege more proudly than among common and mean objects. The drudge is exalted by the sight of a volcano, an eclipse, or a conflagration but the poet's eye gilds the dullest common or street, his kitchen or hen coop with light and grace. He delights in this victory of genius over custom. He delights to show the muse is not nice or squeamish, but can tread with firm and elastic step in sordid places and take no more pollution then the sun-beam which shines alike on the carrion and the violet. Herrick by the choice often of base and even disgusting themes, has pushed this privelege too far, rather I think out of the very wantonness of poetic power, than as has been said by his biographers, to make his book sell, by feeding the grosser palates of his public.

His talent lies in his mastery of all the strength and lighter graces of the language so that his verse is all music, and, what he writes in the indulgence of the most exquisite fancy is at the same time expressed with as perfect simplicity as the language of conversation.

A beautiful example of the delicacy of his poetic vision is in the little stanza "To Silvia":

> I am holy while I stand
> Circumcrost by thy pure hand
> But when that is gone again
> I like others am profane.

Many of his poems are mere couplets or stanzas of four lines like his "Clothes for Continuance,"

> The garments lasting evermore
> Are works of mercy to the poor
> And neither tettar time or moth
> Shall fray that silk or fret this cloth,

or his definition of Beauty,

> Beauty no other thing is than a beam
> Flashed out between the middle and extreme,

which may serve as a counterpart to Winkelmann's fine criticism upon the antique: "Beauty with the ancients was the tongue on the balance of expression." There is an air of magnanimity in the confidence with which the poet gives us on many grave topics his sense in so little compass as a stanza of two, four, or six lines. It evinces his belief in what I take to be an admitted fact in Criticism, that there may be as unquestionable evidence of wit in a sentence as in a treatise, or that whosoever has written one good sentence has given proof of his ability to write a book. For a good sentence is not merely a proposition grammatically stated but one which contains in itself its own apology, or the reason why it was said. A proposition set down in words is not therefore affirmed. It must affirm itself or no propriety and no vehemence of language will give it evidence.

—Ralph Waldo Emerson, "Ben Jonson,
Herrick, Herbert, Wotton" (1835), *The Early
Lectures of Ralph Waldo Emerson*, 1959,
vol. 1, eds. Whicher, Spiller, pp. 346–49

HENRY HALLAM (1837–39)

Without the exuberant gayety of Suckling, or perhaps the delicacy of Carew, he is sportive, fanciful, and generally of polished language. The faults of his age are sometimes apparent: though he is not often obscure, he runs, more perhaps for the sake of variety than any other cause, into occasional pedantry. He has his conceits and false thoughts; but these are more than redeemed by the numerous very little poems (for those of Herrick are frequently not longer than epigrams), which may be praised without much more qualification than belongs to such poetry.

—Henry Hallam, *Introduction to the
Literature of Europe*, 1837–39, pt. 3, ch. 5

S.W. SINGER (1846)

Best known as a Shakespearean scholar, Samuel Weller Singer (1783–1858) also edited scores of books on other Elizabethan and seventeenth-century literary subjects as well.

As a loyalist and sufferer in the cause, there can be no doubt that Herrick was popular with the Cavalier party, and that his poems were received with the favour they deserved by his contemporaries, for that they were popular must be inferred from the number of them which were set to music by Henry Lawes, Laniere, Wilson, and Ramsay; it is somewhat difficult to account for the seeming neglect which they experienced in after times.

—S.W. Singer, "Biographical Notice,"
Hesperides, 1846, vol. 1, p. xxv

Mary Russell Mitford (1851)

More than any eminent writer of that day, Herrick's collection requires careful sifting; but there is so much fancy, so much delicacy, so much grace, that a good selection would well repay the publisher. Bits there are that are exquisite. . . But his real delight was among flowers and bees, and nymphs and cupids; and certainly these graceful subjects were never handled more gracefully.

—Mary Russell Mitford, *Recollections of
a Literary Life*, 1851, pp. 143–44

David Masson (1858)

David Masson (1822–1907) was a Scottish writer and Historiographer Royal for Scotland. His life of John Milton, excerpted below, was considered his magnum opus.

He was an Anacreon or Catullus in holy orders, whiling away, at the ripe age of forty, the dulness of his Devonshire parsonage in such ditties as these:

Much I know, of time is spent, &c, &c.

. . . And so, in every other poem, he sings or sips his wine, with his arm round a Julia! What eyes, what lips, what a neck! and so on amorously, beyond all clerical limits. Like Anacreon, he is sweet, too, in light sensuous descriptions of physical nature. . . .There was, moreover, a tinge of amiable melancholy in his genius—the melancholy on which the Epicurean philosophy itself rests.

—David Masson, *The Life of John Milton*,
1858, vol. 1, ch. 6

George MacDonald (1868)

It is an especial pleasure to write the name of Robert Herrick amongst the poets of religion, for the very act records that the jolly, careless Anacreon of the church, with his head and heart crowded with pleasures, threw down at length his wine-cup, tore the roses from his head, and knelt in the dust.

—George MacDonald,
England's Antiphon, 1868, p. 163

A. Bronson Alcott (1872)

Amos Bronson Alcott (1799–1888) is best known today as the father of American author Louise May Alcott. In his time, however, Alcott was well-known as an educator and author, for his connections to the Transcendental movement, and for founding a utopian community known as "Fruitlands."

Making due allowance of the time when Herrick's verses were written, his temptation to suit the taste of courtiers and kings, his volumes contain much admirable poetry, tempered with religious devotion. He wrote sweet and virtuous verse, with lines here and there that should not have been written. But he is an antedote to the vice in his lines, and may well have place in the scholar's library with Donne, Daniel, Cowley, Shakespeare, and contemporaries.

—A. Bronson Alcott, *Concord Days*,
1872, p. 136

William Michael Rossetti (1872)

The English author and critic William Michael Rossetti (1829–1919) was brother to writers Dante Gabriel Rossetti and Christina Rossetti. Today Rossetti is best known for his biographical writings.

Many of his compositions are, in the fullest sense of the term, trifles; others are at least exquisite trifles; some are not trifles, and are exquisite. After more than a century of neglect, ensuing upon their first ample popularity, Herrick's writings have for years been kept freshened with a steady current of literary laudation—certainly not unjustified, so far as their finer qualities go, but tending a little to the indiscriminate.

—William Michael Rossetti,
Note to *Humorous Poems*, 1872, p. 98

Edmund Gosse "Robert Herrick" (1875)

Gosse begins the essay below by examining the impact of the English Civil War on the poets of the day. Gosse writes that every active poet of the time was disturbed by the war and the changes in English society and law that occurred after Oliver Cromwell's victory—every poet, that is, save Herrick: "Herrick alone, with imperturbable serenity, continued to pipe out his pastoral ditties, and crown his head with daffodils, when England was torn to pieces with the most momentous struggle for liberty in her annals. To the poetic student he is, therefore, of especial interest, as a genuine specimen of an artist pure and simple. Herrick brought out the *Hesperides* a few months before the King was beheaded, and people were invited to listen to little madrigals upon Julia's stomacher at the singularly inopportune moment when the eyes of the whole nation were bent on the unprecedented phenomenon of the proclamation of an English republic."

To Gosse, this is a very significant fact. The undisturbed nature of Herrick's writing allowed him to flourish as no other poet in his own time. Given his own literary freedom, Herrick followed the school of Ben Jonson, and exists, as a lyricist, according to Gosse, as Jonson's most prominent successor. Gosse sees Jonson's influence in Herrick's poetry about his many mistresses and other women, though, "There is a total want of passion in Herrick's language about women. With all his warmth of fancy and luxurious animalism, he thinks more of the pretty eccentricities of dress than of the charms the garments contain." Gosse labels Herrick's works about his mistresses as "a great deal of nonsense." The exception to this are Herrick's poems to Julia: "We may dismiss Perilla, Silvia, Anthea, and the rest at once, as airy nothings, whom the poet created for the sake of hanging pretty amorous fancies on their names; but Julia is not so ephemeral or so easily disposed of." The *Hesperides* itself is reflective of Herrick's attitude towards the women he writes about: "The book is full of all those pleasant things of spring and summer, full of young love, happy nature, and the joy of mere existence." While many critics thus accuse Herrick of a slightness of subject, Gosse believes that Herrick's fondness for flowers reflects a transition in the nature of English pastoral work: "He was the earliest English poet to see the picturesqueness of homely country life, and all his little landscapes are exquisitely delicate. No one has ever known better than Herrick how to seize, without effort and yet to absolute perfection, the pretty points of modern pastoral life." Gosse suggests that the intimacy of Herrick's pastoral work—he may write of the farm, the manor house, or the country lane, but never of the woods or bluffs behind it—is unique to Herrick.

Gosse's section on Herrick's pastorals is one of the most useful in the essay. He is perhaps a bit more dismissive towards Herrick's religious works, though many critics would contend that he had reason to be so.

About Herrick's religious works, Gosse writes, "they are not inspiriting reading, save where they are least Christian; there is none of the religious passion of Crashaw, burning the weak heart away in a flame of adoration, none of the sweet and sober devotion of Herbert—nothing, indeed, from an ecclesiastical point of view." To Gosse, Herrick's legacy is more enveloped in his pastoral and "lighter" fare, and any student working on those aspects of Herrick's poetry will no doubt find Gosse's writings on them of particular interest.

It is told of Mahommed that when the political economists of the day provoked him by the narrowness of their utilitarian schemes, he was wont to silence them with these words: "If a man has two loaves of bread, let him exchange one for some flowers of the narcissus; for bread only nourishes the body, but to look on the narcissus feeds the soul." Robert Herrick was one of the few who have been content to carry out this precept, and to walk through life with a little bread in the one hand, and in the other a bunch of golden flowers. With an old serving-woman in a tumble-down country parsonage, his life passed merrily among such dreams as Oriental sultans wear themselves out to realise, and his figure stands out in front of the shining ranks of his contemporaries as that around which most vividly of all there flashes the peculiar light of imagination. He may be well contrasted with a man whose native genius was probably exceedingly like his own, but whose life was as brilliant and eventful as Herrick's was retired, namely, Sir John Suckling. The wit, fire, and exuberant imagination that interpenetrated both found scope in the life of one and in the works of the other. Suckling's poems are strangely inadequate to represent his genius and fame; Herrick, on the other hand, may be taken almost as the typical poet, the man who, if not a lyrist, would be nothing—the birdlike creature whose only function was to sing in a cage of trammelling flesh.

There are many features in his career, besides the actual excellence of his verse, which make him an object of peculiar interest. Among the pure poets he occupies the most prominent position in the school that flourished after Ben Jonson and before Milton, and though his life was of immense duration— he was born before Marlowe died, and died after the birth of Addison—his actual period of production covers the comparatively small space occupied by the reign of Charles I. This period was one of great lyrical ability; the drama was declining under Cartwright and Shirley, and all the young generation of poets, brought up at the feet of Jonson and Fletcher, were much more capable of writing songs than plays. Indeed, no one can at this time determine what degree of technical perfection English literature might not have attained if the Royalist lyrists had been allowed to sun themselves unmolested about the fountains of Whitehall, and, untroubled by the grave questions of national welfare, had been able to give their whole attention to the polishing of their verses. In fact, however, it will be noticed that only one of the whole school was undisturbed by the political crisis. The weaker ones, like Lovelace, were completely broken by it; the stronger, like Suckling, threw themselves into public affairs with a zeal and intensity that supplied the place of the artificial excitements of poetry so completely as to put a stop to their writing altogether. Herrick alone, with imperturbable serenity, continued to pipe out his pastoral ditties, and crown his head with daffodils, when England was torn to pieces with the most momentous struggle for liberty in her annals. To the poetic student he is, therefore, of especial interest, as a genuine specimen of an artist pure and simple. Herrick brought out the *Hesperides* a few months before the King was beheaded, and people were invited to listen to little madrigals upon Julia's stomacher at the singularly inopportune moment when the eyes of the whole nation were bent on the unprecedented phenomenon of the proclamation of an English republic. To find a parallel to such unconsciousness we must come down to our own time, and recollect that The-ophile Gautier took occasion of the siege of Paris to revise and republish his *Emaux et Camees*.

Herrick was born in London, in "the golden Cheapside," and bapized on the 23rd of August 1591. His father died in the course of the next year, from a fall from an upper window, which was attributed to suicide. All we can guess about the poet's childhood is to be picked up in one of his own confidential pieces about himself, where he speaks with intense delight of his early life by the river-side, going to bathe in the "summer's sweeter evenings" with crowds of other youths, or gliding with pomp in a barge, with the young ladies of the period, "soft-smooth virgins," up as far as Richmond, Kingston, and Hampton Court. In the same poem he speaks of his "beloved Westminster," from which allusion it has been illogically imagined that he was at school there. The first certain fact in his life is that in 1607 he was apprenticed to his uncle, the rich goldsmith of Wood Street, with whom one may presume that he remained until 1615, when we find him entered as fellow-commoner of St. John's College, Cambridge. His London life, therefore, closed when his age was twenty-four, and his acquaintance with literary life in the metropolis must have come to rapid development within the eight years of his apprenticeship. Speculation in this case is not so vain as usual. If any fact about Herrick be certain, it is that he sat at the feet of Ben Jonson; the poems of rapturous admiration and reverence that abound in the *Hesperides* set this beyond question. In one piece, it will be remembered, he speaks, with passion unusual to him, of the old days when Ben Jonson's plays were brought out at the London theatres, and gives us an important date by describing the unfavourable reception of the *Alchemist,* much as a poet of the Romanticism would have described the reception of *Hernani* for the first time at the Theatre *Francais.* But the *Alchemist* was brought out in 1610, when our poet was nineteen years old, and it was received with great excitement as an innovation. We may well believe that the young apprentice, fired with enthusiasm for the great poet, distinguished himself by the loudness and truculence of his applause, and claimed the privilege of laying his homage afterwards at the author's feet. Nineteen years later exactly the same thing was done by a younger generation, when Carew, Randolph, and Cleaveland made a riot at the damning of the *New Inn,* and then laid their lyric worship at the grand old poet's feet.

Jonson loved to receive such homage, and to pose as the poet of the age; in fact, we cannot be too often reminded that to the intellectual public of that day he took exactly the same regal position among his contemporaries that we now unanimously accord to Shakespeare. Taking for granted that Herrick became a familiar member of Jonson's circle about 1610, we must suppose him to have witnessed in succession the first performances *of Catiline* and of *Bartholomew Fair,* and to have known the poet of the "mountain belly and the rocky face" at the very height of his creative power. More important for us, however, as being far more in unison with the tastes and genius of Herrick, are the masques upon which Jonson was engaged at this time. It is very strange that no writer upon the poetry of that age has noticed what an extraordinary influence the masques of Ben Jonson had upon Herrick. We have seen that he must have become acquainted with that poet in 1610. It is more than remarkable to notice that it was in this year that Jonson produced *Oberon the Fairy Prince,* a beautiful masque that contains the germs of many of Herrick's most fantastic fairy-fancies. *The Masque of Queens,* brought out some months earlier, is full of Herrick-like passages about hags and witches; and we might pursue the parallel much further, did space permit, showing how largely Jonson, on the milder and more lyrical side of his genius, inspired the young enthusiast and pointed out to him the poetic path that he should take.

We cannot with equal certainty say that Herrick was acquainted with any other of the great poets. Shakespeare was setlled at Stratford, and in London only briefly and at distant intervals; he died at the end of Herrick's first year at Cambridge. Herrick writes of Fletcher thirty years later as though he had known him slightly, and speaks of the power of the *Maid's Tragedy* to make "young men swoon," as though he had seen it at the first performance in 1611. He must have known Jonson's jolly friend Bishop Corbet, who was also a lover of fairy-lore, and he may have known Browne, whose poetry Jonson approved of, and who was then studying in the Inner Temple, and beginning to publish *Britannia's Pastorals.* It was probably at this time, and through Ben Jonson, that he became acquainted with Selden, for whose prodigious learning and wit he preserved an extravagant admiration through life. This is as far as we dare to go in speculation. If Herrick, so fond of writing about himself, had found time for a few more words about his contemporaries, we might discover that he had dealings with other interesting men during this period of apprenticeship, but probably his circle was pretty much limited to the personal and intimate friends of Jonson.

In 1615, as we have said, he took up his abode at Cambridge as a fellow-commoner of St. John's, and here and at Trinity Hall he seems to have remained till 1629, when his mother died. How these fourteen years of early manhood were spent it is now impossible to conjecture. That he became Master of Arts in 1620 is not so important an item of history as that he was certainly very poor, and in the habit of making a piteous annual appeal to his rich uncle for ten pounds to buy books with. Fourteen of these appeals exist, written in a florid, excited style, with a good many Latin quotations and old-fashioned references to "Apelles ye painter," in the manner *oiEuphues*. It is amusing to note that he manages to spell his own surname in six different ways, and not one of them that which is now adopted on the authority of the title-page of the *Hesperides.* There can be no doubt that he began writing in London; it is certain that he was known as a poet at Cambridge. One of the few dates in the *Hesperides* in 1627, two years before the exodus into Devonshire, and in "Lacrime" he says that before he went into exile into the loathed west

> He could rehearse
> A lyric verse,
> And speak it with the best.

The *Hesperides,* in its present state, offers no assistance to us in trying to discover what was written early or late, for nothing is more obvious than that the verses were thrown together without the slightest regard to the chronology of their composition. However, on the 2nd of October 1629, he succeeded Potter, Bishop of Carlisle, in the living of Dean Prior, under Dartmoor, in South Devon, and there he remained in quiet retirement until 1648, when he was ejected by the Puritans.

Such is the modest biography of this poet up to the time of the publication of the two books which caused and have retained his great reputation. Fortunately he has himself left copious materials for autobiography in the gossipy pages of his own confidential poems. Glancing down the index to the *Hesperides,* one is constantly struck by such titles as "On Himself," "To His Muse," and "His Farewell to Sack," and one is not disappointed in turning to these to collect an impression of the author's individuality. Indeed, few writers of that age appear more vividly in relief than Herrick; the careful student of his poems learns to know him at last as a familiar friend, and every feature of body and mind stands out clearly before the eye of the imagination. He was physically a somewhat gross person, as far as his portrait will enable one to judge, with great quantities of waving or curling black hair, and a slight black moustache; the eyebrows distinct and well arched, the upper lip short, the nose massive and Roman. In the weighty points of the face, especially in the square and massive under-jaw, there is much of the voluptuous force of the best type among the Roman emperors; and bearing these features well in mind, it becomes easy to understand how it was that Herrick came to write so much that an English gentleman, not to say clergyman, had better have left unsaid. His temperament was scarcely clerical:—

> I fear no earthly powers,
> But care for crowns of flowers;
> And love to have my beard
> With wine and oil besmeared.
> This day I'll drown all sorrow;
> Who knows to live to-morrow?

This was his philosophy, and it is not to be distinguished from that of Anacreon or Horace. One knows not how the old pagan dared to be so outspoken in his dreary Devonshire vicarage, with no wild friends to egg him on or to applaud his fine frenzy.

His Epicureanism was plainly a matter of conviction, and though he wrote *Noble Numbers,* preached sermons, and went through all the perfunctory duties of his office, it is not in these that he lives and has his pleasure, but in half-classical dreams about Favonius and Isis, and in flowery mazes of sweet thoughts about fair, half-imaginary women. It matters little to him what divinity he worships, if he may wind daffodils into the god's bright hair. In one hand he brings a garland of yellow flowers for the amorous head of Bacchus, with the other he decks the osier-cradle of Jesus with roses and Lent-lilies. He has no sense of irreverence in this rococo devotion. It is the attribute, and not the deity he worships. There is an airy frivolity, an easy-going callousness of soul, that makes it impossible for him to feel very deeply.

There is a total want of passion in Herrick's language about women. The nearest approach to it, perhaps, is in the wonderful song "To Anthea," where the lark-like freshness of the ascending melody closely simulates intense emotion. With all his warmth of fancy and luxurious animalism, he thinks more of the pretty eccentricities of dress than of the charms the garments contain. He is enraptured with the way in which the Countess of Carlisle wears a riband of black silk twisted round her arm; he palpitates with pleasure when Mistress Katherine Bradshaw puts a crown of laurel on his head, falling on one knee, we may believe, and clasping his hands as he receives it. He sees his loves through the medium of shoe-strings and pomander bracelets, and is alive, as no poet has been before or since, to the picturesqueness of dress. Everybody knows his exquisite lines about the "tempestuous petticoat," and his poems are full of little touches no less delicate than this.

Only two things make him really serious: one is his desire of poetic fame. Every lyric he writes he considers valuable enough to be left as a special legacy to some prime friend. He is eager to die before the world; to pass away, like Pindar, garlanded, and clasped in the arms of love, while the theatre resounds with plaudits. His thirst for fame is insatiable, and his confidence of gaining it intense. His poesy is "his hope and his pyramides," a living pillar "ne'er to be thrown down by envious Time," and it shall be the honour of great musicians to set his pieces to music when he is dead. When he is dead! That has a saddening sound! Life was meant to last for ever, and it makes him angry to think of death. He rings his head about with roses, clasps Julia to his arms, and will defy death. Yet, if death should come, as he sometimes feels it must, he is not unmindful of what his end should be. No thoughts of a sad funeral or the effrontery of a Christian burial oppress him; he cannot even think of dismal plumes or of a hearse. He will be wound in one white robe, and borne to a quiet garden-corner, where the overblown roses may shower petals on his head, and where, when the first primrose blossoms, Perilla may remember him, and come to weep over his dust:—

Then shall my ghost not walk about, but keep
Still in the cool and silent shades of sleep.

He was never married; he explains over and over again that he values his
liberty far too highly to give it into any woman's hands, and lived in the
country, as it would seem, with no company save that of an excellent old
servant, Prudence Baldwin.

In many sweet and sincere verses he gives us a charming picture of the
quiet life he led in the Devonshire parsonage that he affected to loathe
so much. The village had its rural and semi-pagan customs, that pleased
him thoroughly. He loved to see the brown lads and lovely girls, crowned
with daffodils and daisies, dancing in the summer evenings in a comely
country round; he delighted in the maypole, ribanded and garlanded like
a thyrsus, reminding his florid fancy of Bacchus and the garden god. There
were morris dances at Dean Prior, wakes and quintels; mummers, too, at
Christmas, and quaint revel-lings on Twelfth Night, with wassail bowls
and nut-brown mirth; and we can imagine with what zeal the good old
pagan would encourage these rites against the objections of any roundhead
Puritan who might come down with his newfangled Methodistical notions
to trouble the sylvan quiet of Dean Prior. For Herrick the dignity of
episcopal authorship had no charm, and the thunders of Nonconformity
no terror. Graver minds were at this moment occupied with *Holy Living
and Holy Dying,* and thrilled with the Sermons of Calamy. It is delightful
to think of Herrick, blissfully unconscious of the tumult of tongues and all
the windy war, more occupied with morris dances and barley-breaks than
with prayer-book or psalter. The Revolution must indeed have come upon
him unaware.

Herrick allowed himself to write a great deal of nonsense about his
many mistresses. It was the false Anacreontic spirit of the day; and a worse
offender was in the field, even Abraham Cowley, who, never having had the
courage to speak of love to a single woman, was about to publish, in 1648,
a circumstantial account of his affairs with more than one-and-twenty
mistresses. It is not easy to determine how much of Herrick's gallantry
is as imaginary as this. We may dismiss Perilla, Silvia, Anthea, and the rest
at once, as airy nothings, whom the poet created for the sake of hanging
pretty amorous fancies on their names; but Julia is not so ephemeral or so
easily disposed of. She may well be supposed to have died or passed away
before Herrick left Cambridge. All the poet's commentators seem to have
forgotten how old he was before he retired to that country vicarage where

they rightly enough perceive that the presence of a Julia was impossible. When we recollect that he did not enter holy orders till he was thirty-eight, we may well believe that Julia ruled his youth, and yet admit his distinct statement with regard to his clerical life, that

Jocund his muse was, but his life was chaste.

We have a minute chronicle of Julia's looks and ways in the *Hesperides,* and they bear a remarkable air of truth about them. She is presented to us as a buxom person, with black eyes, a double chin, and a strawberry-cream complexion. Her attire, as described by our milliner-poet, is in strict accordance with the natural tastes of a woman of this physical nature. She delights in rich silks and deep-coloured satins; on one occasion she wears a dark blue petticoat, starred with gold, on other she ravishes her poet-lover by the glitter and vibration of her silks as she takes her stately walks abroad. Her hair, despite her dark eyes, is bright and dewy, and the poet takes a fantastic pleasure in tiring and braiding it. An easy, kindly woman, we picture her ready to submit to the fancies of her lyric lover; pleased to have roses on her head, still more pleased to perfume herself with storax, spikenard, galbanum, and all the other rich gums he loved to smell; dowered with so much refinement of mind as was required to play fairly on the lute, and to govern a wayward poet with tact; not so modest or so sensitive as to resent the grossness of his fancy, yet respectable enough and determined enough to curb his license at times. She bore him one daughter, it seems, to whom he addressed one of his latest poems and one of his tamest.

But it is time to turn from the poet to his work, from Julia to the *Hesperides* that she inspired. They are songs, children of the West, brought forth, if not conceived, in the soft, sweet air of Devonshire. And the poet strikes a keynote with wonderful sureness in the opening couplets of the opening poem:—

I sing of brooks, of blossoms, birds and bowers,
Of April, May, of June and July flowers;
I sing of maypoles, hock-carts, wassails, wakes,
Of bridegrooms, brides, and of their bridal-cakes.

It would not have been easy to describe more correctly what he does sing of. The book is full of all those pleasant things of spring and summer, full of young love, happy nature, and the joy of mere existence. As far as flowers are concerned, the atmosphere is full of them. We are pelted with roses and daffodils from every page, and no one dares enter the sacred precincts without a crown of blossoms on his hair. Herrick's muse might be that Venus of Botticelli who rises, pale and dewy, from a sparkling sea, blown at by the little laughing winds, and showered upon with violets and lilies of no earthly growth. He tells us that for years and years his muse was content to stay at home, or straying from village to village, to pipe to handsome young shepherds and girls of flower-sweet breath, but that at last she became ambitious to try her skill at Court, and so came into print in London. In other words, these little poems circulated widely in manuscript long before they were published. They are not all of the bird and blossom kind, unhappily; the book is fashioned, as we shall presently see, closely upon the model of the *Epigrams* of Martial; and as there the most delicate and jewel-like piece of sentiment rubs shoulders with a coarse and acrid quatrain of satire, so has Herrick shuffled up odes, epithalamia, epigrams, occasional verses and canzonets, in glorious confusion, without the slightest regard to subject, form, or propriety. There are no less than one thousand two hundred and thirty-one distinct poems in the book, many of them, of course, only two lines long. There are too many "epigrams," as he called them, scraps of impersonal satire, in the composition of which he followed Ben Jonson, who had followed Martial. These little couplets and quatrains are generally very gross, very ugly, and very pointless; they have, sometimes, a kind of broad Pantagruelist humour about them which has its merit, but it must be confessed even of these that they greatly spoil the general complexion of the book.

More worthy of attention in every way are the erotic lyrical pieces, which fortunately abound, and which are unrivalled in our literature for their freshness and tender beauty. They are interpenetrated with strong neo-pagan emotion; had they been written a century earlier, they would be called the truest English expression of the passion of the Renaissance. This is, however, what they really are. Late in the day as they made their appearance, they were as truly an expression of the delirious return to the freedom of classical life and enjoyment as the Italian paintings of the fifteenth or the French poetry of the sixteenth century. The tone of the best things in the *Hesperides* is precisely the same as that which permeates the wonderful designs of the *Hypnerotomachia*. In Herrick's poems, as in that mysterious and beautiful romance, the sun shines on a world re-arisen to the duty of pleasure; Bacchus rides through the valleys, with his leopards and his maidens and his ivy-rods; loose-draped nymphs, playing on the lyre, bound about their foreheads with vervain and the cool stalks of parsley, fill the silent woods with their melodies and dances; this poet sings of a land where all the men are young and strong, and all the women lovely, where life is only a dream of sweet delights of the bodily senses. The *Hesperides* is an astounding production when one considers when it was written, and how intensely grave the temper of the age had become. But Herrick hated sobriety and gravity, and distinguished very keenly between the earnestness of art and the austerity of religion. Here he lays down his own canons:—

> In sober mornings, do not thou rehearse
> The holy incantation of a verse;
> But when that men have both well drunk and fed,
> Let my enchantments then be sung or read.
> When laurel spirts in the fire, and when the hearth
> Smiles to itself, and gilds the roof with mirth,
> When up the thyrse is raised, and when the sound
> Of sacred orgies flies around, around,
> When the rose reigns, and locks with ointment
>   shine,
> Let rigid Cato read these lines of mine.

At such moments as these Herrick is inspired above a mortal pitch, and listens to the great lyre of Apollo with the rapture of a prophet. From a very interesting poem, called "The Apparition of his Mistress calling him to Elysium," we quote a few lines that exemplify at the same moment his most ideal condition of fancy and the habitual oddities of his style. This is the landscape of the Hesperides, the golden isles of Herrick's imagination:—

> Here in green meadows sits eternal May,
> Purpling the margents, while perpetual day
> So doubly gilds the air, as that no night
> Can ever rust the enamel of the light.
> Here naked younglings, handsome striplings, run
> Their goals for maidens' kisses, which when done,
> Then unto dancing forth the learned round
> Commixt they meet, with endless roses crowned;
> And here we'll sit on primrose-banks, and see
> Love's chorus led by Cupid.

But although he lived in this ideal scenery, he was not entirely unconscious of what actually lay around him. He was the earliest English poet to see the picturesqueness of homely country life, and all his little landscapes are exquisitely delicate. No one has ever known better than Herrick how to seize, without effort and yet to absolute perfection, the pretty points of modern pastoral life. Of all these poems of his, none surpasses "Corinna's going a-Maying," which has something of Wordsworth's faultless instinct and clear perception. The picture given here of the slim boys and the girls in green gowns going out singing into the corridors of blossoming whitethorn, when the morning sun is radiant in all its "fresh-quilted colours," is ravishing, and can only be compared for its peculiar charm with that other where the maidens are seen at sunset, with silvery naked feet and dishevelled hair crowned with honeysuckle, bearing cowslips home in wicker-baskets. Whoever will cast his eye over the pages of the *Hesperides,* will meet with myriads of original and charming passages of this kind:—

> Like to a solemn sober stream
> Bankt all with lilies, and the cream
> Of sweetest cowslips filling them,

the "'cream of cowslips' being the rich yellow anthers of the water-lilies. Or this, comparing a bride's breath to the faint, sweet odour of the earth:—

> A savour like unto a blessed field,
> When the bedabbled morn
> Washes the golden ears of corn.

Or this, a sketched interior:—

> Yet can thy humble roof maintain a choir
> Of singing crickets by the fire,
> And the brisk mouse may feed herself with crumbs,
> Till that the green-eyed kitling comes.

Nor did the homeliest details of the household escape him. At Dean Prior his clerical establishment consisted of Prudence Baldwin, his ancient maid, of a cock and hen, a goose, a tame lamb, a cat, a spaniel, and a pet pig, learned enough to drink out of a tankard; and not only did the genial vicar divide his loving attention between the various members of this happy family, but he was wont, a little wantonly, one fears, to gad about to wakes and wassailings and to increase his popular reputation by showing off his marvellous learning in old rites and ceremonies. These he has described with loving minuteness, and not these only, but even the little arts of cookery do not escape him. Of all his household poems, not one is more characteristic and complete than the "Bride-cake," which we remember having had recited to us years ago with immense gusto, at the making of a great pound-cake, by a friend since widely known as a charming follower of Herrick's poetic craft:—

> This day, my Julia, thou must make
> For Mistress Bride the wedding-cake:
> Knead but the dough, and it will be
> To paste of almonds turned by thee,
> Or kiss it, thou, but once or twice,
> And for the bride-cake there'll be spice.

There is one very curious omission in all his descriptions of nature, in that his landscapes are without background; he is photographically minute in giving us the features of the brook at our feet, the farmyard and its inmates, the open fireplace and the chimney corner, but there is no trace of anything beyond, and the beautiful distances of Devonshire, the rocky tors, the rugged line of Dartmoor, the glens in the hills—of all these there is not a trace. In this he contrasts curiously with his contemporary William Browne, another Devonshire poet, whose pictures are infinitely vaguer and poorer than Herrick's, but who has more distance, and who succeeds in giving a real notion of Devonian rock and moor, which Herrick never so much as suggests. In short, it may be said that Herrick made for himself an Arcadian world, in the centre of which the ordinary daily life of a country parish went contentedly on, surrounded by an imaginary land of pastoral peace and plenty, such as England can hardly have been then in the eyes of any other mortal, unless in those of the French poet St. Amant, who came over to the court at Whitehall just before the Rebellion broke out, while Herrick was piping at Dean Prior, and who on his return wrote a wonderfully fulsome ode to their serenest majesties Charles and Mary, in which he took precisely the same view of our island as Herrick did:—

> Oui, c'est ce pays bienheureux
> Qu'avec des regards amoureux
> Le reste du monde contemple;
> C'est cette ile fameuse ou tant d'aventuriers
> Et tant de beautes sans exemple
> Joignirent autrefois les myrtes aux lauriers!

St. Amant lived to alter his opinion, and hurl curses at the unconscious Albion; but to Herrick the change came too late, and when the sunshine ceased to warm him, he simply ceased to sing, as we shall see.

The personal epithalamium is a form of verse which had a very brief period of existence in England, and which has long been completely extinct. Its theme and manner gave too much opportunity to lavish adulation on the one hand, and unseemly innuendo on the other, to suit the preciser manners of our more reticent age; but it flourished for the brief period contained between 1600 and 1650, and produced some exquisite masterpieces. The *Epithalamion* and *Prothalamion* of Spenser struck the keynote of a fashion that Drayton, Ben Jonson, and others adorned, and of which Herrick was the last and far from the least ardent votary. His confidential muse was delighted at being asked in to arrange the ceremonies of a nuptial feast, and described the bride and her surroundings with a world of pretty extravagance. Every admirer of Herrick should read the "Nuptial Ode on Sir Clipseby Crew and his Lady." It is admirably fanciful, and put together with consummate skill. It opens with a choral outburst of greeting to the bride:—

> What's that we see from far? the spring of day
> Bloom'd from the east, or fair enjewelled May
>   Blown out of April? or some new
>   Star filled with glory to our view
>   Reaching at Heaven,
>   To add a nobler planet to the seven?

Less and less dazzled, he declares her to be some goddess floating out of Elysium in a cloud of tiffany. She leaves the church treading upon scarlet and amber, and spicing the chafed air with fumes of paradise. Then they watch her coming towards them down the shining street, whose very pavement breathes out spikenard. But who is this that meets her? Hymen, with his fair white feet, and head with marjoram crowned, who lifts his torch, and, behold, by his side the bridegroom stands, flushed and ardent. Then the maids shower them with shamrock and roses, and so the dreamy verses totter under their load of perfumed words, till they close with a benediction over the new-married couple, and a peal of maiden laughter over love and its flower-like mysteries.

Once more, before we turn to more general matters, there is one section of the *Hesperides* that demands a moment's attention—that, namely, devoted to descriptions of Fairyland and its inhabitants. We have seen that it was probably the performance of Ben Jonson's pretty masque of *Oberon* that set Herrick dreaming about that misty land where elves sit eating butterflies' horns round little mushroom tables, or quaff draughts

Of pure seed-pearl of morning dew,
Brought and besweetened in a blue
And pregnant violet.

And with him the poetic literature of Fairyland ended. He was its last
laureate, for the Puritans thought its rites, though so shadowy, superstitious,
and frowned upon their celebration, while the whole temper of the
Restoration, gross and dandified at the same time, was foreign to such pure
play of the imagination. But some of the greatest names of the great period
had entered its sacred bounds and sung its praises. Shakespeare had done it
eternal honour in A *Midsummer-Night's Dream,* and Drayton had written
an elaborate romance, *The Court of Faerie.* Jonson's friend Bishop Corbet
had composed fairy ballads that had much of Herrick's lightness about
them. It was these literary traditions that Herrick carried with him into the
west; it does not seem that he collected any fresh information about the
mushroom world in Devonshire; we read nothing of river-wraiths or pixies
in his poems. He adds, however, a great deal of ingenious fancy to the stores
he received from his elders; and his fairy-poems, all written in octosyllabic
verse, as though forming parts of one projected work, may be read with
great interest as a kind of final compendium of all that the poets of the
seventeenth century imagined about fairies.

Appended to the *Hesperides,* but bearing date one year earlier, is a little
book of poems, similar to these in outward form, but dealing with sacred
subjects. Here our pagan priest is seen, despoiled of his vine-wreath and
his thyrsus, doing penance in a white sheet and with a candle in his hand.
That rubicund visage, with its sly eye and prodigious jowl, looks ludicrously
out of place in the penitential surplice; but he is evidently sincere, though
not very deep, in his repentance, and sings hymns of faultless orthodoxy,
with a loud and lusty voice to the old pagan airs. Yet they are not inspiriting
reading, save where they are least Christian; there is none of the religious
passion of Crashaw, burning the weak heart away in a flame of adoration,
none of the sweet and sober devotion of Herbert— nothing, indeed, from
an ecclesiastical point of view, so good as the best of Vaughan, the Silurist.
Where the *Noble Numbers* are most readable is where they are most secular.
One sees the same spirit here as throughout the worldly poems. In a
charming little "Ode to Jesus" he wishes the Saviour to be crowned with
roses and daffodils, and laid in a neat white osier cradle; in "The Present,"
he will take a rose to Christ and, sticking it in His stomacher, beg for one
mellifluous kiss. The epigrams of the earlier volume are replaced in the

Noble Numbers by a series of couplets, attempting to define the nature of God, of which none equals in neatness this, which is the last:—

> Of all the good things whatsoe'er we do,
> God is the *Arche ana* the *Telos* too.

As might be expected, his religion is as grossly anthropomorphic as it is possible to be. He almost surpasses in indiscretion those mediaeval priests of Picardy who brought such waxen images to the Madonna's shrine as no altar had seen since pagan days; and certain verses on the circumcision are more revolting in their grossness than any of those erotic poems—

> unbaptized rhymes
> Writ in my wild unhallowed times—

for which he so ostentatiously demands absolution.

It is pleasant to turn from these to the three or four pieces that are in every way worthy of his genius. Of these, the tend-erest is the "Thanksgiving," where he is delightfully confidential about his food, thus:—

> Lord, I confess, too, when I dine
> The pulse is Thine,
> And all those other bits that be
> Placed there by Thee,—
> The worts, the purslain, and the mess
> Of water-cress.
> . . .
> Tis Thou that crown'st my glittering hearth
> With guiltless mirth,
> And giv'st me wassail-bowls to drink,
> Spiced to the brink.

And about his house:—

> Like as my parlour, so my hall
> And kitchen's small,
> A little buttery, and therein
> A little bin.

The wild and spirited "Litany" is too well known to be quoted here, but there are two very fine odes in the *Noble Numbers* that are hardly so familiar. One is the "Dirge of Jephthah's Daughter," written in a wonderfully musical and pathetic measure, and full of fine passages, of which this is a fair sample:—

May no wolf howl, or screech-owl stir
A wing about thy sepulchre!
No boisterous winds or storms come hither
　　To starve or wither
Thy soft sweet earth, but, like a spring,
Love keep it ever flourishing.

But beyond question the cleverest and at the same time the most odd poem in the *Noble Numbers* is "The Widows' Tears; or, Dirge of Dorcas," a lyrical chorus supposed to be wailed out by the widows over the death-bed of Tabitha. The bereaved ladies disgrace themselves, unfortunately, by the greediness of their regrets, dwelling on the loss to them of the bread—"ay! and the flesh and the fish"—that Dorcas was wont to give them; but the poem has stanzas of marvellous grace and delicacy, and the metre in which it is written is peculiarly sweet. But truly Herrick's forte did not lie in hymn-writing, nor was he able to refrain from egregious errors of taste, whenever he attempted to reduce his laughing features to a proper clerical gravity. Of all his solecisms, however, none is no monstrous as one almost incredible poem "To God," in which he gravely encourages the Divine Being to read his secular poems, assuring Him that—

Thou, my God, may'st on this impure look,
Yet take no tincture from my sinful book.

For unconscious impiety this rivals the famous passage in which Robert Montgomery exhorted God to "pause and think."

We have now rapidly considered the two volumes on which Herrick claims his place among the best English lyrical poets. Had he written twenty instead of two, he could not have impressed his strong poetic individuality more powerfully on our literature than he has done in the *Hesperides*. It is a storehouse of lovely things, full of tiny beauties of varied kind and workmanship; like a box full of all sorts of jewels—ropes of seed-pearl, opals set in old-fashioned shifting settings, antique gilt trifles sadly tarnished by time; here a ruby, here an amethyst, and there a stray diamond, priceless and luminous, flashing light from all its facets, and dulling the faded jewellery with which it is so promiscuously huddled. What gives a special value to the book is the originality and versatility of the versification. There is nothing too fantastic for the author to attempt, at least; there is one poem written in rhyming triplet, each line having only *two* syllables. There are clear little trills of sudden song, like the lines to the "Lark;" there are chance melodies that seem like mere wantonings of the air upon a wind-harp; there are such harmonious endings as this, "To Music":—

Fall on me like a silent dew,
    Or like those maiden showers
Which by the peep of day do strew
    A baptism o'er the flowers.
        Melt, melt my pains
        With thy soft strains,
    That, having ease me given,
        With full delight
        I leave this light
        And take my flight
          For heaven.

With such poems as these, and with the delicious songs of so many of Herrick's predecessors and compeers before them, it is inexplicable upon what possible grounds the critics of the eighteenth century can have founded their astonishing dogma that the first master of English versification was Edmund Waller, whose poems, appearing some fifteen years after the *Hesperides,* are chiefly remarkable for their stiff and pedantic movement, and the brazen clang, as of stage armour, of the dreary heroic couplets in which they strut. Where Waller is not stilted, he owes his excellence to the very source from which the earlier lyrists took theirs—a study of nature and a free but not licentious use of pure English. But not one of his songs, except "Go, Lovely Rose," is worth the slightest of those delicate warbles that Herrick piped out when the sun shone on him and the flowers were fresh.

It is an interesting speculation to consider from what antique sources Herrick, athirst for the pure springs of pagan beauty, drank the deep draughts of his inspiration. Ben Jonson it was, beyond doubt, who first introduced him to the classics, but his mode of accepting the ideas he found there was wholly his own. In the first place, one must contradict a statement that all the editors of Herrick have repeated, sheep-like, from one another, namely, that Catullus was his great example and model. In all the editions of the *Hesperides* we find the same old blunder: "There is no collection of poetry in our language which more nearly resembles the *Carmina* of Catullus." In reality, it would be difficult to name a lyric poet with whom he has less in common than with the Veronese, whose eagle-flights into the very noonday depths of passion, swifter than Shelley's, as flaming as Sappho's, have no sort of fellowship with the pipings of our gentle and luxurious babbler by the flowery brooks. In one of his poems, "To Live Merrily," where he addresses the various classical poets, and where, by the way, he tries to work himself into a great exaltation about Catullus, he does not even mention the one from whom he really took most of form and colour. No one carefully reading the *Hesperides* can fail to be struck with the extraordinary similarity they bear to the *Epigrams* of Martial; and the parallel will be found to run throughout the writings of the two poets, for good and for bad, the difference being that Herrick is much the more religious pagan of the two, and that he is as much a rural as Martial an urban poet. But in the incessant references to himself and his book, the fondness for gums and spices, the delight in the picturesqueness of private life, the art of making a complete and gemlike poem in the fewest possible lines, the curious mixture of sensitiveness and utter want of sensibility, the trick of writing confidential little poems to all sorts of friends, the tastelessness that mixes up obscene couplets with delicate odes "De Hortis Martialis" or "To Anthea"—in all these and many more qualities one can hardly tell where to look for a literary parallel more complete. As far as I know, Herrick mentions Martial but once, and then very slightly. He was fond of talking about the old poets in his verse, but never with any critical cleverness. The best thing he says about any of them is said of Ovid in a pretty couplet. In a dream he sees Ovid lying at the feet of Corinna, who presses

With ivory wrists his laureat head, and steeps
His eyes in dew of kisses while he sleeps.

How much further Herrick's learning proceeded it is difficult to tell. Doubtless he knew some Greek; he mentions Homer and translates from the spurious Anacreon. The English poets of that age, learned as many of them were, do not seem to have gone much further than Rome for their inspiration. Chapman is, of course, a great exception. But none of them, as all the great French poets of the Renaissance did, went directly to the Anthology, Theocritus and Anacreon. Perhaps Herrick had read the Planudian Anthology; the little piece called "Leander's Obsequies" seems as though it must be a translation of the epigram of Antipater of Thessalonica.

It is curious to reflect that at the very time that the *Hesperides* was printed, Salmasius, soon to be hunted to death by the implacable hatred of Milton, was carrying about with him in his restless wanderings the manuscript of his great discovery, the inestimable Anthology of Constantine Cephalas. One imagines with what sympathetic brotherliness the Vicar of

Dean Prior would have gossiped and glowed over the new storehouse of Greek song. That the French poets of the century before were known to Herrick is to me extremely doubtful. One feels how much there was in such a book as *La Bergerie* of Remy Belleau, in which our poet would have felt the most unfeigned delight, but I find no distinct traces of their style in his; and unless the Parisian editions of the classics influenced him, I cannot think that he brought any honey, poisonous or other, from France. His inspiration was Latin; that of Ronsard and Jodelle essentially Greek. It was the publication of the Anthology in 1531, and of Henri Estienne's *Anacreon* in 1554, that really set the Pleiad in movement, and founded *l'ecole gallo-grecque*. It was rather the translation of Ovid, Lucan, Seneca, and Virgil that gave English Elizabethan poetry the start-word.

To return to Herrick, there is not much more to say. He had sung all the songs he had to sing in 1648, being then fifty-seven years of age. He came up to London when the Puritans ejected him from his living, and seems to have been sprightly enough at first over the pleasant change to London life. Soon, however, bad times came. So many friends were gone; Jonson was dead, and Fletcher; Selden was very old and in disgrace. It was poor work solacing himself with Sir John Denham, and patronising that precocious lad Charles Cotton; and by-and-by the Puritans cut off his fifths, and poor old Herrick is vaguely visible to us in poor lodgings somewhere in Westminster, supported by the charity of relations. In August 1662, some one or other graciously recollected him, and he was sent back in his seventy-second year to that once detested vicarage in "rocky Devonshire," which must now have seemed a kind asylum for his old age.

The latest verses of his which seem to have been preserved are these, carved on the tomb of two of his parishioners in the south aisle of Dean Prior Church—

> No trust to metals nor to marbles, when
> These have their fate and wear away as men;
> Times, titles, trophies may be lost and spent,
> But virtue rears the eternal monument.
> What more than these can tombs or tombstones pay?
> But here's the sunset of a tedious day:
> These two asleep are: I'll but be undress'd
> And so to bed: pray wish us all good rest.

There is something extremely pathetic in the complete obscurity of the poet's last days. In those troublesome times his poetry, after a slight success, passed completely out of all men's minds. The idiotic Winstanley, in his *Lives of the Most Famous English Poets,* written shortly after Herrick's death, says that "but for the interruption of trivial passages, he might have made up none of the worst poetic landscapes." This is the last word spoken, as I think, on Herrick, till Mr. Nichols revived his fame in 1796. All we know of his latest years is summed up in one short extract from the church register of Dean Prior: "Robert Herrick, vicker, was buried ye 15th day of October 1674." By that time a whole new world was formed in poetry. Milton was dead; Wycherley and Dryden were the fashionable poets; Addison and Swift were lately born; next year the *Pilgrim's Progress* was to appear; all things were preparing for that bewigged and bepowdered eighteenth century, with its mob of gentlemen who wrote with ease, its Augustan self-sufficiency, and its horror of nature; and what wonder that no one cared whether Herrick were alive or dead?

—Edmund Gosse, "Robert Herrick," 1875,
Seventeenth Century Studies 1883, pp. 125–56

GEORGE BARNETT SMITH
"ENGLISH FUGITIVE POETS" (1875)

The British literary historian and scholar George Barnett Smith (1841–1909) is best known for his text *Poets and Novelists: A Series of Literary Studies.*

━━ ━━ ━━

Beyond all dispute, the best of the early lyric poets is Robert Herrick, whose verses are flushed with a joyous and tender spirit. He may be styled the Burns of his time, and was imbued with something of the reckless soul of the great north-countryman. . . . Flowers, music, woman, all these had their intense and several charms for him, and, strangely enough for a middle-aged clergyman, he was clearly an amorous and erotic poet

—George Barnett Smith, "English Fugitive
Poets," *Poets and Novelists,* 1875, pp. 381–82

F.T. PALGRAVE "ROBERT HERRICK" (1877)

In the piece below, Palgrave attempts to set Herrick's "place in the sequence of English poets" by examining "his relations to his predecessors and contemporaries." In describing Herrick, Palgrave writes that the author's "subjects are frequently pastoral, with a classical tinge, more or less slight, infused; his language, though not free from exaggeration, is generally free from intellectual conceits and distortion, and is eminent throughout for a youthful *naivete*. Such, also, are qualities of the latter sixteenth century literature." Yet, Palgrave asks, which of Herrick's contemporaries have most influenced him? Palgrave finds many differences between Herrick and his fellow metaphysical poets, suggesting that neither Donne nor any of the other metaphysical writers were a great influence. Indeed, Palgrave spies a world of difference between Herrick's work and the traditional characteristics ascribed to the metaphysics: "Herrick's directness of speech is accompanied by an equally clear and simple presentment of his thought; we have, perhaps, no poet who writes more consistently and earnestly with his eye upon his subject. An allegorical or mystical treatment is alien from him: he handles awkwardly the few traditional fables which he introduces. He is also wholly free from Italianizing tendencies." Palgrave suggests that Herrick consciously set out not to imitate any writer's particular style or oeuvre, an atypical decision for the day. Though this makes Herrick "the last of the Elizabethans . . . the differences between him and them [his fellow poets] are not less marked." Ultimately, Palgrave concludes that Herrick's greatest influences were not fellow metaphysical poets but playwrights and prose authors, and that Ben Jonson was foremost amongst those influences. Palgrave also notes certain Greek and Roman influences on Herrick's work, and students will certainly find his analysis of Herrick's literary influences particularly compelling and illuminating.

Robert Herrick's personal fate is in one point like Shakespeare's. We know or seem to know them both, through their works, with singular intimacy. But with this our knowledge substantially ends. No private letter of Shakespeare, no record of his conversation, no account of the circumstances in which his writings were published, remains: hardly any statement how his greatest contemporaries ranked him. A group of Herrick's youthful letters on business has, indeed, been preserved; of his life and studies, of his reputation during his own time, almost nothing. For whatever facts affectionate diligence could now gather, readers are referred to Mr. Grosart's "Introduction."[1] But if, to supplement the picture, inevitably imperfect, which this gives, we turn to Herrick's own book, we learn little, biographically, except the names of a few friends,—that his general sympathies were with the Royal cause,—and that he wearied in Devonshire for London. So far as is known, he published but this one volume, and that, when not far from his sixtieth year. Some pieces may be traced in earlier collections; some few carry ascertainable dates; the rest lie over a period of near forty years, during a great portion of which we have no distinct account where Herrick lived, or what were his employments. We know that he shone with Ben Jonson and the wits at the nights and suppers of those gods of our glorious early literature: we may fancy him at Beaumanor, or Houghton, with his uncle and cousins, keeping a Leicestershire Christmas in the Manor-house: or, again, in some sweet southern county with Julia and Anthea, Corinna and Dianeme by his side (familiar then by other names now never to be remembered), sitting merry, but with just the sadness of one who hears sweet music, in some meadow among his favourite flowers of spring-time;— there, or "where the rose lingers latest." . . . But "the dream, the fancy," is all that Time has spared us. And if it be curious that his contemporaries should have left so little record of this delightful poet and (as we should infer from the book) genial-hearted man, it is not less so that the single first edition should have satisfied the seventeenth century, and that, before the present, notices of Herrick should be of the rarest occurrence.

The artist's "claim to exist" is, however, always far less to be looked for in his life, than in his art, upon the secret of which the fullest biography can tell us little—as little, perhaps, as criticism can analyse its charm. But there are few of our poets who stand less in need than Herrick of commentaries of this description,—in which too often we find little more than a dull or florid prose version of what the author has given us admirably in verse. Apart from obsolete words or allusions, Herrick is the best commentator upon Herrick. A few lines only need therefore be added, aiming rather to set forth his place in the sequence of English poets, and especially in regard to those near his own time, than to point out in detail beauties which he unveils in his own way, and so most durably and delightfully.

When our Muses, silent or sick for a century and more after Chaucer's death, during the years of war and revolution, reappeared, they brought with them foreign modes of art, ancient and contemporary, within the forms of which they began to set to music the new material which the age supplied. At the very outset, indeed, the moralising philosophy which has characterised the English from the beginning of our national history, appears in the writers of the troubled times lying between the last regnal years of Henry VIII. and the first of his great daughter. But with the happier hopes of Elizabeth's accession, poetry was once more distinctly followed, not only as a means of conveying thought, but as a Fine Art. And hence something constrained and artificial blends with the freshness of the Elizabethan literature. For its great underlying elements it necessarily reverts to those embodied in our own earlier poets, Chaucer above all, to whom, after barely one hundred and fifty years, men looked up as a father of song: but in points of style and treatment, the poets of the sixteenth century lie under a double external influence—that of the poets of Greece and Rome (known either in their own tongues or by translation), and that of the modern literatures which had themselves undergone the same classical impulse. Italy was the source most regarded during the more strictly Elizabethan period; whence its lyrical poetry, and the dramatic in a less degree, are coloured much less by pure and severe classicalism with its closeness to reality, than by the allegorical and elaborate style, fancy, and fact curiously blended, which had been generated in Italy under the peculiar and local circumstances of her pilgrimage in literature and art from the age of Dante onwards. Whilst that influence lasted, such brilliant pictures of actual life, such directness, movement, and simplicity in style, as Chaucer often shows, were not yet again attainable: and although satire, narrative, the poetry of reflection, were meanwhile not wholly unknown, yet they only appear in force at the close of this period. And then also the pressure of political and religious strife, veiled in poetry during the greater part of Elizabeth's actual reign under the forms of pastoral and allegory, again imperiously breaks in upon the gracious but somewhat slender and artificial fashions of England's Helicon: the

Divom numen, sedesque quietae

which, in some degree the Elizabethan poets offer, disappear; until filling the central years of the seventeenth century we reach an age as barren for inspiration of new song as the Wars of the Roses; although the great survivors from earlier years mask this sterility;—masking also the revolution in poetical manner and matter which we can see secretly preparing in the later "Cavalier" poets, but which was not clearly recognized before the time of Dryden's culmination.

In the period here briefly sketched, what is Herrick's portion? His verse is eminent for sweet and gracious fluency; this is a real note of the "Elizabethan" poets. His subjects are frequently pastoral, with a classical tinge, more or less slight, infused; his language, though not free from exaggeration, is generally free from intellectual conceits and distortion, and is eminent throughout for a youthful *naivete*. Such, also, are qualities of the latter sixteenth century literature. But if these characteristics might lead us to call Herrick "the last of the Elizabethans," born out of due time, the differences between him and them are not less marked. Herrick's directness of speech is accompanied by an equally clear and simple presentment of his thought; we have, perhaps, no poet who writes more consistently and earnestly with his eye upon his subject. An allegorical or mystical treatment is alien from him: he handles awkwardly the few traditional fables which he introduces. He is also wholly free from Italianizing tendencies: his classicalism even is that of an English student,—of a schoolboy, indeed, if he be compared with a Jonson or a Milton. Herrick's personal eulogies on his friends and others, further, witness to the extension of the field of poetry after Elizabeth's age;— in which his enthusiastic geniality, his quick and easy transitions of subject, have also little precedent.

If, again, we compare Herrick's book with those of his fellow-poets for a hundred years before, very few are the traces which he gives of imitation, or even of study. During the long interval between Herrick's entrance on his Cambridge and his clerical careers (an interval all but wholly obscure to us), it is natural to suppose that he read, at any rate, his Elizabethan predecessors: yet (beyond those general similarities already noticed) the Editor can find no positive proof of familiarity. Compare Herrick with Marlowe, Greene, Breton, Drayton, or other pretty pastoralists of the *Helicon*—his general and radical unlikeness is what strikes us; whilst he is even more remote from the passionate intensity of Sidney and Shakespeare, the Italian graces of Spenser, the pensive beauty of *Parthenophil,* of *Diella,* of *Fidessa,* of the *Hecatomapathia* and the *Tears of Fancy.*

Nor is Herrick's resemblance nearer to many of the contemporaries who have been often grouped with him. He has little in common with the courtly elegance, the learned polish, which too rarely redeem commonplace and conceits in Carew, Habington, Lovelace, Cowley, or Waller. Herrick has his *concetti* also; but they are in him generally true plays of fancy; he writes throughout far more naturally than these lyrists, who, on the other hand, in their unfrequent successes reach a more complete and classical form of expression. Thus, when Carew speaks of an aged fair one

> When beauty, youth, and all sweets leave her,
> Love may return, but loves never!

Cowley, of his mistress—

> Love in her sunny eyes does basking play,
> Love walks the pleasant mazes of her hair:

or take Lovelace, "To Lucasta," Waller, in his "Go, lovely rose,"—we have a finish and condensation which Herrick hardly attains; a literary quality alien from his "woodnotes wild," which may help us to understand the very small appreciation he met from his age. He had "a pretty pastoral gale of fancy," said Phillips, cursorily dismissing Herrick in his *Theatrum:* not suspecting how inevitably artifice and mannerism, if fashionable for a while, pass into forgetfulness, whilst the simple cry of Nature partakes in her permanence.

Donne and Marvell, stronger men, leave also no mark on our poet. The elaborate thought, the metrical harshness of the first, could find no counterpart in Herrick; whilst Marvell, beyond him in imaginative power, though twisting it too often into contortion and excess, appears to have been little known as a lyrist then:—as, indeed, his great merits have never reached anything like due popular recognition. Yet Marvell's natural description is nearer Herrick's in felicity and insight than any of the poets named above. Nor, again, do we trace anything of Herbert or Vaughan in Herrick's *Noble Numbers,* which, though unfairly judged if held insincere, are obviously far distant from the intense conviction, the depth and inner fervour of his high-toned contemporaries.

It is among the great dramatists of this age that we find the only English influences palpably operative on this singularly original writer. The greatest, in truth, is wholly absent: and it is remarkable that although Herrick may have joined in the wit-contests and genialities of the literary clubs in London soon after Shakespeare's death, and certainly lived in friendship with some who had known him, yet his name is never mentioned in the poetical commemorations of the *Hesperides.* In Herrick, echoes from Fletcher's idyllic pieces in the *Faithful Shepherdess* are faintly traceable; from his songs, "Hear what love can do," and "The lusty Spring," more distinctly. But to Ben Jonson, whom Herrick addresses as his patron saint in song, and ranks on the highest list of his friends, his obligations are much more perceptible. In fact, Jonson's non-dramatic poetry,—the *Epigrams* and *Forest* of 1616, the *Underwoods* of 1641, (he died in 1637),—supply models, generally admirable in point of art, though of very unequal merit in their execution and contents, of the principal forms under which we may range Herrick's *Hesperides.* The graceful love-song, the celebration of feasts and wit, the encomia of friends, the epigram as then understood, are all here represented: even Herrick's vein in natural description is prefigured in the odes to Penshurst and Sir Robert Wroth, of 1616. And it is in the religious pieces of the *Noble Numbers,* for which Jonson afforded the least copious precedents, that, as a rule, Herrick is least successful.

Even if we had not the verses on his own book, in proof that Herrick was no careless singer, but a true artist, working with conscious knowledge of his art, we might have inferred the fact from the choice of Jonson as his model. That great poet, as Clarendon justly remarked, had "judgment to order and govern fancy, rather than excess of fancy: his productions being slow and upon deliberation." No writer could be better fitted for the guidance of one so fancy-free as Herrick; to whom the curb, in the old phrase, was more needful than the spur, and whose invention, more fertile and varied than Jonson's, was ready at once to fill up the moulds of form provided. He does this with a lively facility, contrasting much with the evidence of labour in his master's work. Slowness and deliberation are the last qualities suggested by Herrick. Yet it may be doubted whether the volatile ease, the effortless grace, the wild bird-like fluency with which he

Scatters his loose notes in the waste of air

are not, in truth, the results of exquisite art working in cooperation with the gifts of nature. The various readings which our few remaining manuscripts or printed versions have supplied to Mr. Grosart's "Introduction," attest the minute and curious care with which Herrick polished and strengthened his own work: his airy facility, his seemingly spontaneous melodies, as with Shelley—his counterpart in pure lyrical art within this century—were earned by conscious labour; perfect freedom was begotten of perfect art;— nor, indeed, have excellence and permanence any other parent.

With the error that regards Herrick as a careless singer is closely twined that which ranks him in the school of that master of elegant pettiness who has usurped and abused the name Anacreon; as a mere light-hearted writer of pastorals, a gay and frivolous Renaissance amourist. He has indeed those elements: but with them is joined the seriousness of an age which knew that the light mask of classicalism and bucolic allegory could be worn only as an ornament, and that life held much deeper and further-reaching issues than were visible to the narrow horizons within which Horace or Martial circumscribed the range of their art. Between the most intensely poetical, and so, greatest, among the French poets of this century, and Herrick, are many points of likeness. He too, with Alfred de Musset, might have said

Quoi que nous puissions faire,
Je souffre; il est trop tard; le monde s'est fait vieux.
Une immense espérance a traverse la terre;
Malgré nous vers le ciel il faut lever les yeux.

Indeed, Herrick's deepest debt to ancient literature lies not in the models which he directly imitated, nor in the Anacreontic tone which with singular felicity he has often taken. These are common to many writers with him:—nor will he who cannot learn more from the great ancient world ever rank among poets of high order, or enter the innermost sanctuary of art. But, the power to describe men and things as the poet sees them with simple sincerity, insight, and grace: to paint scenes and imaginations as perfect organic wholes;—carrying with it the gift to clothe each picture, as if by unerring instinct, in fit metrical form, giving to each its own music; beginning without affectation, and rounding off without effort;—the power, in a word, to leave simplicity, sanity, and beauty as the last impressions lingering on our minds, these gifts are at once the true bequest of classicalism, and the reason why (until modern effort equals them) the study of that Hellenic and Latin poetry in which these gifts are eminent above all other literatures yet created, must be essential. And it is success in precisely these excellences which is here claimed for Herrick. He is classical in the great and eternal sense of the phrase: and much more so, probably, than he was himself aware of. No poet in fact is so far from dwelling in a past or foreign world; it is the England, if not of 1648, at least of his youth, in which he lives and moves and loves: his Bucolics shows no trace of Sicily; his Anthea and Julia were no "buckles of the purest gold," nor have anything about them foreign to Middlesex or Devon. Herrick's imagination has no far horizons; like Burns and Crabbe fifty years since, or Barnes (that exquisite and neglected pastoralist of fair Dorset, perfect within his narrower range as Herrick) to-day it is his own native land only which he sees and paints: even the fairy world in which, at whatever inevitable interval, he is second to Shakespeare, is pure English; or rather, his elves live in an elfin county of their own, and are all but severed from humanity. Within that greater circle of Shakespeare, where Oberon and Ariel and their fellows move, aiding or injuring mankind, and reflecting human life in a kind of unconscious parody, Herrick cannot walk: and it may have been due to his good sense and true feeling for art, that here, where resemblance might have seemed probable, he borrows nothing from *Midsummer-Night's Dream* or *Tempest*. If we are moved by the wider range of Byron's or Shelley's sympathies, there is a charm, also, in this sweet insularity of Herrick; a narrowness perhaps, yet carrying with it a healthful reality absent from the vapid and artificial "cosmopolitanism" that did such wrong on Goethe's genius. If he has not the exotic blooms and strange odours which poets who derive from literature show in their conservatories, Herrick has the fresh breeze and thyme-bed fragrance of open moorland, the grace and greenery of English meadows; with Homer and Dante, he too shares the strength and inspiration which come from touch of man's native soil.

What has been here sketched is not planned so much as a criticism in form on Herrick's poetry as an attempt to seize his relations to his predecessors and contemporaries. If we now tentatively inquire what place may be assigned to him in our literature at large, Herrick has no single lyric to show equal in pomp of music, brilliancy of diction, or elevation of sentiment to some which Spenser before, Milton in his own time, Dryden and Gray, Wordsworth and Shelley, since have given us. Nor has he, as already noticed, the peculiar finish and reserve (if the phrase may be allowed) traceable, though rarely, in Ben Jonson and others of the seventeenth century. He does not want passion; yet his passion wants concentration: it is too ready, also, to dwell on externals: imagination with him generally appears clothed in forms of fancy. Among his contemporaries, take Crashaw's "Wishes:" Sir J. Beaumont's elegy on his child "Gervase:" take Bishop King's "Surrender":

> My once-dear Love! Hapless, that I no more
> Must call thee so . . . The rich affection's store
> That fed our hopes, lies now exhaust and spent,
> Like sums of treasure unto bankrupts lent:—
> We that did nothing study but the way
> To love each other, with which thoughts the day
> Rose with delight to us, and with them set,
> Must learn the hateful art, how to forget!
> —Fold back our arms, take home our fruitless
>   loves,
> That must new fortunes try, like turtle doves
> Dislodged from their haunts. We must in tears
> Unwind a love knit up in many years.
> In this one kiss I here surrender thee
> Back to thyself: so thou again art free:—

take eight lines by some old unknown Northern singer:

> When I think on the happy days
>   I spent wi' you, my dearie,
> And now what lands between us lie,
>   How can I be but eerie!

How slow ye move, ye heavy hours,
  As ye were wae and weary!
It was na sae ye glinted by
  When I was wi' my dearie:—

—O! there is an intensity here, a note of passion beyond the deepest of Herrick's. This tone (whether from temperament or circumstance or scheme of art) is wanting to the *Hesperides* and *Noble Numbers:* nor does Herrick's lyre, sweet and varied as it is, own that purple chord, that more inwoven harmony, possessed by poets of greater depth and splendour,—by Shakespeare and Milton often, by Spenser more rarely. But if we put aside these "greater gods" of song, with Sidney,—in the Editor's judgment Herrick's mastery (to use a brief expression), both over Nature and over Art, clearly assigns to him the first place as lyrical poet, in the strict and pure sense of the phrase, among all who flourished during the interval between Henry V and a hundred years since. Single pieces of equal or higher quality we have, indeed, meanwhile received, not only from the master-singers who did not confine themselves to the lyric, but from many poets—some the unknown contributors to our early anthologies, then Jonson, Marvell, Waller, Collins, and others, with whom we reach the beginning of the wider sweep which lyrical poetry has since taken. Yet, looking at the whole work, not at the selected jewels, of this great and noble multitude, Herrick, as lyrical poet strictly, offers us by far the most homogeneous, attractive, and varied treasury. No one else among lyrists, within the period defined, has such unfailing freshness: so much variety within the sphere prescribed to himself; such closeness to nature, whether in description or in feeling; such easy fitness in language: melody so unforced and delightful. His dull pages are much less frequent: he has more lines, in his own phrase, "born of the royal blood": the

  Inflata rore non Achaico verba

are rarer with him: although superficially mannered, nature is so much nearer to him, that far fewer of his pieces have lost vitality and interest through adherence to forms of feeling or fashions of thought now obsolete. A Roman contemporary is described by the younger Pliny in words very appropriate to Herrick: who in fact, if Greek in respect of his method and style, in the contents of his poetry displays the "frankness of nature and vivid sense of life" which criticism assigns as marks of the great Roman poets. *Facit versus, quales Catullus aut Calvus. Quantum illis leporis, dulcedinis, amaritudinis, amoris! Inserit sane, sed data opera, mollibus lenibusque duriusculos quosdam: et hoc, quasi Catullus aut Calvus.* Many pieces have been refused admittance, whether from coarseness of phrase or inferior value: yet these are rarely defective in the lyrical art, which, throughout the writer's work, is so simple and easy as almost to escape notice through its very excellence. In one word, Herrick, in a rare and special sense, is unique.

To these qualities we may, perhaps, ascribe the singular neglect which, so far as we may infer, he met with in his own age, and certainly in the century following. For the men of the Restoration period he was too natural, too purely poetical: he had not the learned polish, the political allusion, the tone of the city, the didactic turn, which were then and onwards demanded from poetry. In the next age, no tradition consecrated his name; whilst writers of a hundred years before were then too remote for familiarity, and not remote enough for reverence. Moving on to our own time, when some justice has at length been conceded to him, Herrick has to meet the great rivalry of the poets who, from Burns and Cowper to Tennyson, have widened and deepened the lyrical sphere, making it at once on the one hand more intensely personal, on the other, more free and picturesque in the range of problems dealt with: whilst at the same time new and richer lyrical forms, harmonies more intricate and seven-fold, have been created by them, as in Hellas during her golden age of song, to embody ideas and emotions unknown or unexpressed under Tudors and Stuarts. To this latter superiority Herrick would, doubtless, have bowed, as he bowed before Ben Jonson's genius. "Rural ditties," and "oaten flute" cannot bear the competition of the full modern orchestra. Yet this author need not fear! That exquisite and lofty pleasure which it is the first and the last aim of all true art to give, must, by its own nature, be lasting also. As the eyesight fluctuates, and gives the advantage to different colours in turn, so to the varying moods of the mind the same beauty does not always seem equally beautiful. Thus from the "purple light" of our later poetry there are hours in which we may look to the daffodil and rose-tints of Herrick's old Arcadia, for refreshment and delight. And the pleasure which he gives is as eminently wholesome as pleasurable. Like the holy river of Virgil, to the souls who drink of him, Herrick offers "securos latices." He is conspicuously free from many of the maladies incident to his art. Here is no overstrain, no spasmodic cry, no wire-drawn analysis or sensational rhetoric, no music without sense, no mere second-hand literary inspiration, no mannered archaism:—above all, no sickly sweetness, no subtle, unhealthy affectation. Throughout his work, whether when it is strong, or in the less worthy portions, sanity, sincerity, simplicity, lucidity, are everywhere the characteristics of Herrick: in these, not in his pretty Pagan masquerade, he shows the note,—the only genuine note,—of Hellenic descent. Hence, through whatever changes and fashions poetry may pass, her true lovers he is likely to "please now, and please for long." His verse, in the words of a poet greater than himself, is of that quality which "adds sunlight to daylight"; which is able to "make the happy happier." He will, it may be hoped, carry to the many Englands across the seas, east and west, pictures of English life exquisite in truth and grace:—to the more fortunate inhabitants (as they must perforce hold themselves!) of the old country, her image, as she was two centuries since, will live in the "golden apples" of the West, offered to us by this sweet singer of Devonshire. We have greater poets, not a few; none more faithful to nature as he saw her, none more perfect in his art:—none, more companionable.

Notes

1. See the Herrick edited by this gentleman, and lately published by Messrs. Chatto and Windus. Looking to the care taken to collect all facts bearing on the poet's life and book, to the critical correctness of the text, and the fulness of annotation, it is not too high praise to say that these volumes for the first time give Herrick a place among books not printed only, but edited.

—F.T. Palgrave, "Robert Herrick," *Macmillan's Magazine*, April 1877, pp. 475–81

EDMUND GOSSE "ROBERT HERRICK" (1880)

In this excerpt Gosse praises Herrick's abilities as a pastoral poet and lyricist, suggesting that he surpasses even Shakespeare and Milton in the latter vein (though not Shelley.) Gosse also labels Herrick a Cavalier poet, a title often given to such authors as Richard Lovelace and Sir John Suckling. Cavalier poetry was the other genre of poetry prominent in Herrick's day and was typified by verse that focused on lighter subjects and exquisitely crafted lines. In contemporary critical circles, it is often seen as a lesser type of writing to metaphysical poetry. Gosse's labeling of Herrick as a Cavalier demonstrates that his work was influenced by writers who worked in both genres; different eras of literary history have placed Herrick into one camp, or both, or neither, as tastes and style dictate.

Among the English pastoral poets, Herrick takes an undisputed precedence, and as a lyrist generally he is scarcely excelled, except by Shelley. No other writer of the seventeenth century approached him in abundance of song, in sustained exercise of the purely musical and intuitive gifts of poetry. Shakspeare, Milton, and perhaps Fletcher, surpassed him in the passion and elevated harmony of their best lyrical pieces, as they easily excelled him in the wider range of their genius and the breadth of their accomplishment. But while these men exercised their art in all its branches, Herrick confined himself very narrowly to one or two, and the unflagging freshness of his inspiration, flowing through a long life in so straitened a channel, enabled him to amass such a wealth of purely lyrical poetry as no other Englishman has produced. His level of performance was very high; he seems to have preserved all that he wrote, and the result is that we possess more than twelve hundred of his little poems, in at least one out of every three of which we may find something charming or characteristic. Of all the Cavalier lyrists Herrick is the only one that followed the bent of his genius undisturbed, and lived a genuine artist's life.

—Edmund Gosse, "Robert Herrick,"
English Poets, 1880, vol. 2, ed. Ward, p. 124

W. Baptiste Scoones (1880)

William Baptiste Scoones (1838 or 1839–1906) was a British author, most known for the text below, but also author of several books on civil service and education.

By a strange irony of fortune the only letters we possess from the genial and glowing pen of the great poet of the *Hesperides* are a series of plaintive notes to his rich uncle, Sir William Herrick; and we may gather from them that this amiable relative's money paid for the piping of some of the most graceful lyrics in the English language.

—W. Baptiste Scoones, *Four Centuries*
of English Letters, 1880, p. 67

John Dennis (1883)

John Dennis's (1825–1911) *Heroes of Literature: A Book for Young Readers* was published under the auspices of the Society for Promoting Christian Knowledge in 1883. Thus when Dennis writes that Herrick "sings well chiefly when he sings of love, but this love is not of the kind which inspires our greatest poets," he is referring to divine inspiration.

— ⁓⁓⁓ — ⁓⁓⁓ — ⁓⁓⁓ —

He sings well chiefly when he sings of love, but this love is not of the kind which inspires our greatest poets. He is enamoured with the accessories of a woman's beauty—the colour of a ribbon, the flaunting of a ringlet, with "a careless shoe-string," or the wave of a petticoat. The charms he sees in his mistress are likened to precious stones, and all the treasures of the lapidary are represented in his verse. There are few traces of tenderness in Herrick and none of passion; it is probable that every pretty girl he saw suggested a pretty fancy. To judge from his own saying, "no man at one time can be wise and love." Herrick was not wise. If we may trust his verses, the poet was perennially in love, chiefly with Julia, "prime of all," but warmly too with Anthea, Lucia, Corinna, and Perilla. Making love is in Herrick's eyes a charming amusement, and the more love-making the more poetry. If Julia prove unkind, he can solace himself with Sappho; and if Sappho be perverse, some other mistress will charm him with her "pretty witchcrafts."

—John Dennis, *Heroes of Literature,*
1883, p. 97

Ernest Rhys "Introduction" (1887)

British writer Ernest Rhys (1859–1946) was also a founding editor of the wildly popular Everyman's Library series of affordable classics of literature.

— ⁓⁓⁓ — ⁓⁓⁓ — ⁓⁓⁓ —

None of our English lyric poets has shown a more perfect sense of words and of their musical efficiency, none has united so exquisitely a classic sense of form to that impulsive tunefulness which we have come to consider as essentially English. In his earlier lyrics Herrick has perhaps more of this impulse, but it served him with the same youthful freshness to the last. It is the way in which Herrick adds to and completes this natural lyrical impulse by the further grace of verse taught by the Latin verse-writers and their English disciples, that makes him so consummate an artist within his range. There is magic in these lyrics, that indefinable quality, born of the spirit, which can alone avail in the end to make poetry live.

—Ernest Rhys, "Introductions," *Hesperides:
Poems by Robert Herrick,* 1887, pp. xxxi–xxxiii

Austin Dobson "In a Copy of the Lyrical Poems of Robert Herrick" (1887)

Henry Austin Dobson (1840–1921) was an English essayist and writer. His biographies of Henry Fielding (1883), Thomas Bewick (1884), Richard Steele (1886), Oliver Goldsmith (1888), and Horace Walpole (1890) are considered his finest achievements. A poet as well, Dobson composed the below piece to Herrick, as many earlier writers had done for Herrick and several of his contemporaries, including George Herbert (see Herbert section of this text.)

Many suns have set and shone,
Many springs have come and gone,
Herrick, since thou sang'st of Wake,
Morris-dance, and Barley-break;
Many men have ceased from care,
Many maidens have been fair,
Since thou sang'st of *Julia's* eyes,
Julia's lawns and tiffanies;
Many things are past—but thou,
Colden-Mouth, art singing now,
Singing clearly as of old,
And thy numbers are of gold.

—Austin Dobson, "In a Copy of the
Lyrical Poems of Robert Herrick,"
Scribner's Magazine, January 1887, p. 66

George Saintsbury (1887)

Divided, in the published form, into two classes: they may be divided, for purposes of poetical criticism, into three. The *Hesperides* (they are dated 1648, and the *Noble Numbers* or sacred poems 1647; but both appeared together) consist in the first place of occasional poems, sometimes amatory, sometimes not; in the second, of personal epigrams. Of this second class no human being who has any faculty of criticism can say any good. They are supposed by tradition to have been composed on parishioners: they may be hoped by charity (which has in this case the support of literary criticism) to be merely literary exercises—bad imitations of Martial, through Ben Jonson. They are nastier than the nastiest work of Swift; they are stupider than the stupidest attempts of Davies of Hereford; they are farther from the author's best than the worst parts of Young's *Odes* are from the best part of the *Night Thoughts*. It is impossible without producing specimens (which God forbid that any one who has a respect for Herrick, for literature, and for decency, should do) to show how bad they are. Let it only be said that if the worst epigram of Martial were stripped of Martial's wit, sense, and literary form, it would be a kind of example of Herrick in this vein. In his two other veins, but for certain tricks of speech, it is almost impossible to recognise him for the same man. The secular vigour of the *Hesperides,* the spiritual vigour of the *Noble Numbers,* has rarely been equalled and never surpassed by any other writer.

—George Saintsbury, *A History of*
Elizabethan Literature, 1887, p. 355

Andrew Lang (1889)

Andrew Lang (1844–1912) was a Scottish man of letters best known for his numerous collections of fairy tales and folk stories. Lang was also an accomplished literary scholar, having published works on Robert Burns and J.G. Lockhart in addition to this numerous studies of mythology and folklore.

Herrick the inexhaustible in dainties; Herrick, that parson-pagan, with the soul of a Greek of the Anthology, and a cure of souls (Heaven help them!) in Devonshire. His Julia is the least mortal of these "daughters of dreams and of stories," whom poets celebrate; she has a certain opulence of flesh and blood, a cheek like a damask rose, and "rich eyes," like Keats' lady; no vaporous Beatrice, she; but a handsome English wench, with

> A cuff neglectful and thereby
> Ribbons to flow confusedly;
> A winning wave, deserving note
> In the tempestuous petticoat.

—Andrew Lang, *Letters*
on Literature, 1889, p. 149

Donald G. Mitchell (1890)

There were those critics and admirers who saw in Herrick an allegiance to the methods of Catullus; others who smacked in his epigrams the verbal felicities of Martial; but surely there is no need, in that fresh spontaneity of the Devon poet, to hunt for classic parallels; nature made him one of her own singers, and by instincts born with him he fashioned words and fancies into jewelled shapes. The "more's the pity" for those gross indelicacies which smirch so many pages; things unreadable, things which should have been unthinkable and unwritable by a clergyman of the Church of England.

—Donald G. Mitchell, *English Lands,*
Letters, and Kings: From Elizabeth to Anne,
1890, p. 125

William Ernest Henley "Herrick" (1890)

The English poet and critic William Ernest Henley (1849–1903) proved an ardent admirer of Herrick's. In the piece below, Henley fancifully labels Herrick "pre-eminently the poet of flowers," later adding that "the flowers are maids to him, and the maids are flowers." A useful account of Herrick's more romantic works, Henley notes that both his poems on flowers and on maids have the same general meaning: "both are lovely and both must die." Henley thus suggests that the best authors to compare Herrick to are Spanish poets, for both their "sincerity and earnestness" and the "inimitable daintiness of surface" that highlights the work of both.

In Herrick the air is fragrant with new-mown hay; there is a morning light upon all things; long shadows streak the grass, and on the eglantine swinging in the hedge the dew lies white and brilliant. Out of the happy distance comes a shrill and silvery sound of whetting scythes; and from the near brook-side rings the laughter of merry maids in circle to make cowslipballs and babble of their bachelors. As you walk you are conscious of 'the grace that morning meadows wear,' and mayhap you meet Amaryllis going home to the farm with an apronful of flowers. Rounded is she and buxom, cool-cheeked and vigorous and trim, smelling of rosemary and thyme, with an appetite for curds and cream and a tongue of 'cleanly wantonness.' For her singer has an eye in his head, and exquisite as are his fancies he dwells in no land of shadows. The more clearly he sees a thing the better he sings it; and provided that he do see it nothing is beneath the caress of his muse. The bays and rosemary that wreath the hall at Yule, the log itself, the Candlemas box, the hock-cart and the maypole, nay,

> See'st thou that cloud as silver clear,
> Plump, soft, and swelling everywhere?
> 'Tis Julia's bed!—

And not only does he listen to the 'decking' of his hen and know what it means: he knows too that the egg she has laid is long and white; so that ere he enclose it in his verse, you can see him take it in his hand, and look at it with a sort of boyish wonder and delight. This freshness of spirit, this charming and innocent curiosity, he carries into all he does. He can turn a sugared compliment with the best, but when Amaryllis passes him by he is yet so eager and unsophisticate that he can note that 'winning wave in the tempestuous petticoat' which has rippled to such good purpose through so many graceful speeches since. So that though Julia and Dianeme and Anthea have passed away, though Corinna herself is merely 'a fable, song, a fleeting shade,' he has saved enough of them from the ravin of Time for us to love and be grateful for eternally. Their gracious ghosts abide in a peculiar nook of the Elysium of Poesy. There 'in their habit as they lived' they dance in round, they fill their laps with flowers, they frolic and junket sweetly, they go for ever maying. Soft winds blow round them, and in their clear young voices they sing the verse of the rare artist who called them from the multitude and set them for ever where they are.

And Amaryllis herself will not, mayhap, be found so fair as those younglings of the year she bears with her in 'wicker ark' or 'lawny continent.' Herrick is pre-eminently the poet of flowers. He alone were capable of bringing back

> Le bouquet d'Ophelie
> De la rive inconnue ou les flots l'ont laisse.

He knows and loves the dear blossoms all. He considers them with tender and shining eyes, he calls them his sweetest fancies and his fondest metaphors. Their idea is inseparable from that of his girls themselves, and it is by the means of the one set of mistresses that he is able so well to understand the other. The flowers are maids to him, and the maids are flowers. In an ecstasy of tender contemplation he turns from those to these, exampling Julia from the rose and pitying the hapless violets as though they were indeed not blooms insensitive but actually 'poor girls neglected.' His pages breathe their clean and innocent perfumes, and are beautiful with the chaste beauty of their colour, just as they carry with them something of the sweetness and simplicity of maidenhood itself. And from both he extracts the same pathetic little moral: both are lovely and both must die. And so, between his virgins that are for love indeed and those that sit silent and delicious in the 'flowery nunnery,' the old singer finds life so good a thing that he dreads to lose it, and not all his piety can remove the passionate regret with which he sees things hastening to their end.

That piety is equally removed from the erotic mysticism of Richard Crashaw and from the adoration, chastened and awful and pure, of Cowper. To find an analogue, you have to cross the borders of English into Spain. In his *Noble Numbers* Herrick shows himself to be a near kinsman of such men as Val-divielso, Ocana, Lope de Ubeda; and there are versicles of his that in their homely mixture of the sacred and the profane, in their reverent familiarity with things divine, their pious and simple gallantry, may well be likened to the graceful and charming romances and villancicos of these strangers. Their spirit is less Protestant than Catholic, and is hardly English at all, so that it is scarce to be wondered at if they have remained unpopular. But their sincerity and earnestness are as far beyond doubt as their grace of line and inimitable daintiness of surface.

—William Ernest Henley,
"Herrick," *Views and Reviews*, 1890

Richard LeGallienne
"Robert Herrick" (1891)

Richard LeGallienne (1866–1947) was an English author and critic. In the piece below, LeGallienne writes that Herrick's most constant theme was "the immortality of his verse: . . . He is constantly giving expression to this comfortable attitude; not even 'The Nipples of Julia's Breast'—each as 'a strawberry, half-drown'd in cream'—or her 'tempestuous petticoat,' are more frequent themes. 'To his Book,' 'To his Muse,' are constantly recurring titles, bearing witness to that more than maternal delight which every devoted artist finds in his work." This provides an interesting contrast to critics such as Ralph Waldo Emerson, who complain of the constant profanity of Herrick's subject matter. Here, LeGallienne argues that the nature of writing itself is a more prominent subject in Herrick's work than lust or pleasure, an interesting concept for students of the poet closely examining the nature of subjectivity in his works.

Not Shakespeare himself had more confidence in the immortality of his verse than Robert Herrick. He was well content to let 'his poetry' be 'his pillar.'

> Behold this living stone
>   I rear for me,
> Ne'er to be thrown
>   Down, envious Time, by thee.
> Pillars let some set up,
>   If so they please:
> Here is my hope
>   And my Pyramides.

He is constantly giving expression to this comfortable attitude; not even 'The Nipples of Julia's Breast'—each as 'a strawberry, half-drown'd in cream'—or her 'tempestuous petticoat,' are more frequent themes. 'To his Book,' 'To his Muse,' are constantly recurring titles, bearing witness to that more than maternal delight which every devoted artist finds in his work. True, that when Charles I. gave him the living of Dean Prior, in Devonshire, he wrote: 'Mr. Robert Herick: his farewell unto Poetrie,' and bade a no less bitter 'Farewell to Sack,' probably at the same time, yet we all know when the poet is sick, how the poet (like another personage) a saint will be; and Herrick loved both sack and poetry too well to really forsake them. No doubt he was far more glad than sorry to be ejected from his living in 1648—on the charge of disloyalty—and be once more free to join his chums in merry London, for it goes without saying that he was hail-fellow with all who loved a song and a glass—and a petticoat. Not that Herrick never wrote what we somewhat absurdly distinguish as serious verse. His poem, 'To his Dying Brother, Master William Herrick,' shows that he knew the tragic as well as the pathetic note of life—though there was probably little of tragic feeling in the comfortable relationship of the two brothers. A poet always thus outsoars his theme:

> Life of my life, take not so soon thy flight,
> But stay the time till we have bade good-night.
> Thou hast both wind and tide with thee; thy way
> As soon despatch'd is by the night as day.
> There's pain in parting, and a kind of hell,
> When once true lovers take their last farewell.

And in regard to pathos, is it not really that tender, tearful quality that has made famous the best known of Herrick's verse—the Horatian sigh for youth going and gone, for the beauty that is so fair, and yet so soon past? His cry is continually 'To the Virgins, to make much of Time,' to the daffodils to

> Stay, stay,
> Until the hasting day
>   Has run
> But to the evensong.

The passing of the glory of the world is continually filling his eyes with tears, which overflow in pearls that drop within his book. There are people—surely they must have lived in a monastery or a vacuum—who are always puzzled that the men who do these exquisite things in poetry should be sensuous, let us say sensual, in their lives; but apart from the many-sidedness of man, it is surely the sensuous man alone who is capable of these rich tearful moments. One must have lived to have lost, and Herrick lived as generously as Solomon, and his poems are a sort of Restoration Ecclesiastes, with less of the whine and a kinder heart. Yet his *Noble Numbers,* or his *Pious Pieces,* though at first they strike one somewhat ludicrously as coming from him, are no mere 'making it right' with the powers above—they are the result of the real religious devotion which was at the bottom of Herrick's, as of every other poet's, heart.

> —Richard LeGallienne, "Robert Herrick"
> (1891), *Retrospective Reviews,* 1896, pp. 1–3

ALGERNON CHARLES SWINBURNE
"ROBERT HERRICK" (1891)

Algernon Charles Swinburne (1837–1909) was a noted Victorian poet and prose author. He is included here as perhaps the most ardent defender of Herrick's work and legacy; of Herrick, Swinburne wrote, "he is and will probably be always the first in rank and station of English song-writers." Swinburne considers Herrick the finest lyric poet ever in the English language, and remarks upon not only the quality of Herrick's poesy but also the quantity of excellent works he composed. Though Swinburne is not immune to observing the common faults Victorian critics ascribed to Herrick—amongst others, Swinburne notes the repetitive nature of Herrick's subject matter—Swinburne still believes that "Herrick at his best [demonstrates] a charm so incomparable and so inimitable that even English poetry can boast of nothing quite like it or worthy to be named after it." Students examining Herrick's critical reception in the nineteenth century will likely find Swinburne at the extreme end amongst those who admired Herrick's work, and will find the text excerpted below useful because of it.

It is singular that the first great age of English lyric poetry should have been also the one great age of English dramatic poetry; but it is hardly less singular that the lyric school should have advanced as steadily as the dramatic school declined from the promise of its dawn. Born with Marlowe, it rose at once with Shakespeare to heights inaccessible before and since and for ever, to sink through bright gradations of glorious decline to its final and beautiful sunset in Shirley; but the lyrical record that begins with the author of *Euphues* and *Eudymion* grows fuller if not brighter through a whole chain of constellations, till it culminates in the crowning star of Herrick. Shakespeare's last song, the exquisite and magnificent overture to *The Two Noble Kinsmen,* is hardly so limpid in its flow, so liquid in its melody, as the two great songs in *Valentinian;* but Herrick, our last poet of that incomparable age or generation, has matched them again and again. As a creative and inventive singer he surpasses all his rivals in quantity of good work; in quality of spontaneous instinct and melodious inspiration he reminds us, by frequent and flawless evidence, who, above all others, must beyond all doubt have been his first master and his first model in lyric poetry—the author of 'The Passionate Shepherd to his Love'.

The last of his line, he is and will probably be always the first in rank and station of English song-writers. We have only to remember how rare it is to find a perfect song, good to read and good to sing, combining the merits of Coleridge and Shelley with the capabilities of Tommy Moore and Haynes Bayly, to appreciate the unique and unapproachable excellence of Herrick. The lyrist who wished to be a butterfly, the lyrist who fled or flew to a lone vale at the hour (whatever hour it may be) 'when stars are weeping', have left behind them such stuff as may be sung, but certainly cannot be read and endured by any one with an ear for verse. The author of the Ode on France and the author of the Ode to the West Wind have left us hardly more than a song apiece which has been found fit for setting to music; and, lovely as they are, the fame of their authors does not mainly depend on the song of Glycine or the song of which Leigh Hunt so justly and so critically said that Beaumont and Fletcher never wrote anything of the kind more lovely. Herrick, of course, lives simply by virtue of his songs; his more ambitious or pretentious lyrics are merely magnified and prolonged and elaborated songs. Elegy or litany, epicede or epithalamium, his work is always a song-writer's; nothing more, but nothing less, than the work of the greatest songwriter—as surely as Shakespeare is the greatest dramatist—ever born of English race. The apparent or external variety of his versification is, I should suppose, incomparable; but by some happy tact or instinct he was too naturally unambitious to attempt, like Jonson, a flight in the wake of Pindar. He knew what he could not do: a rare and invaluable gift. Born a blackbird or a thrush, he did not take himself (or try) to be a nightingale.

It has often been objected that he did mistake himself for a sacred poet; and it cannot be denied that his sacred verse at its worst is as offensive as his secular verse at its worst; nor can it be denied that no severer sentence of condemnation can be passed upon any poet's work. But neither Herbert nor Crashaw could have bettered such a divinely beautiful triplet as this:—

We see Him come, and know Him ours,
Who with His sunshine and His showers
Turns all the patient ground to flowers.

That is worthy of Miss Rossetti herself; and praise of such work can go no higher.

But even such exquisite touches or tones of colour may be too often repeated in fainter shades or more glaring notes of assiduous and facile reiteration. The sturdy student who tackles his Herrick as a schoolboy is expected to tackle his Horace, in a spirit of pertinacious and stolid straightforwardness, will probably find himself before long so nauseated by the incessant inhalation of spices and flowers, condiments and kisses, that if a musk-rat had run over the page it could hardly be less endurable to the physical than it is to the spiritual stomach. The fantastic and the brutal blemishes which deform and deface the loveliness of his incomparable genius are hardly so damaging to his fame as his general monotony of matter and of manner. It was doubtless in order to relieve this saccharine and 'melliso-nant' monotony that he thought fit to intersperse these interminable droppings of natural or artificial perfume with others of the rankest and most intolerable odour; but a diet of alternate sweetmeats and emetics is for the average of eaters and drinkers no less unpalatable than unwholesome. It is useless and thankless to enlarge on such faults or such defects as it would be useless and senseless to ignore. But how to enlarge, to expatiate, to insist on the charm of Herrick at his best—a charm so incomparable and so inimitable that even English poetry can boast of nothing quite like it or worthy to be named after it—the most appreciative reader will be the slowest to affirm or imagine that he can conjecture. This, however, he will hardly fail to remark: that Herrick, like most if not all other lyric poets, is not best known by his best work. If we may judge by frequency of quotation or of reference, the ballad of the ride from Ghent to Aix is a far more popular, more generally admired and accredited specimen of Mr. Browning's work than 'The Last Ride Together', and 'The Lost Leader' than 'The Lost Mistress'. Yet the superiority of the less popular poem is in either case beyond all question or comparison: in depth and in glow in spirit and of harmony, in truth and charm of thought and word, undeniable and indescribable. No two men of genius were ever more unlike than the authors of *Paracelsus* and *Hesperides;* and yet it is as true of Herrick as of Browning that his best is not always his best-known work. Everyone knows the song, 'Gather ye rosebuds while ye may'; few, I fear, by comparison, know the yet sweeter and better song, 'Ye have been fresh and green'. The general monotony of style and motive which fatigues and irritates his too persevering reader is here and there relieved by a change of key which anticipates the note of a later and very different lyric school. The brilliant simplicity and pointed grace of the three stanzas to Œnone ('What conscience, say, is it in thee') recall the lyrists of the Restoration in their cleanlier and happier mood. And in the very fine epigram headed by the words, 'Devotion makes the Deity', he has expressed for once a really high and deep thought in words of really noble and severe propriety. His 'Mad Maid's Song', again, can only be compared with Blake's, which has more of passionate imagination if less of pathetic sincerity.

—Algernon Charles Swinburne,
"Robert Herrick," 1891, *Studies in
Prose and Poetry,* 1894

ALFRED W. POLLARD "HERRICK AND HIS FRIENDS" (1892)

Alfred William Pollard (1859–1944) was a noted English bibliographer and Shakespearean scholar. In the piece below, Pollard examines what is known about Herrick's life through the auspices of his associations with his friends, fellow poets, and patrons. Though the piece directly says little about Herrick's work, it does speak briefly on the influence

of Ben Jonson on Herrick, examines in some useful detail Herrick's rela-
tionships with his patrons, and provides some intriguing commentary
on Herrick's political views. Though generally considered a Royalist,
Pollard qualifies that assessment: "Herrick was a bigoted royalist.
Utterances in favour of the divine right of kings and the duty of implicit
obedience are not hard to find; but they are balanced by epigrams
which show a much more Parliamentary spirit, and it is often difficult
to tell where Herrick is expressing his own sentiments and where he is
simply running into verse some sentence or phrase which happened to
catch his attention." Ultimately, Pollard's piece provides more insight
into Herrick the man than Herrick the author, a useful excursion into the
life and workings of a sixteenth-century poet.

To all but his professed admirers Herrick is chiefly known by a little handful
of lyrics, which appear with great regularity in the anthologies, but bring
with them a very incomplete impression of their author's personality
and life. In the case of Herrick this is no great wonder. The same sensuous
feeling which made him invest his friends with the perfume of Juno or Isis,
sing of their complexions as roses overspread with lawn, compare their lips
to cherries, and praise their silver feet, had also its other side. The unlucky
wights who incurred the poet's wrath were treated in a fashion equally
offensive to good taste and good manners. Nor are these gruesome epigrams
the only apples in the garden of Herrick's *Hesperides* which have affronted the
taste of modern readers. The epigrams indeed, if apples at all, are rather the
dusty apples of the Dead Sea than the pleasant fruit of the Western Isles;
but Herrick's *Epithalamia,* odes whose sustained splendour gives them a
high rank among his poems, because they sing of other marriage-rites than
those of rice and slipper, have also tended to restrict the circle of his readers
in an age which prides itself on its modesty. Hence it has come about that
while the names of the lovely ladies of the poet's imagination,—Julia,
Dianeme, Electra, Perilla—are widely known, those of the men and
women whom Herrick treasured as his friends are all but forgotten, and the
materials for constructing a picture of the society amid which the poet
moved have been neglected and thrown aside.

Like most bachelors Herrick set a high value upon friendship, and in his
sedater middle age, when his poetry had lost something of its fire, he set
himself to construct a poetic temple to commemorate the virtues of the
men and women whom he most loved or honoured. Sometimes instead
of a temple he speaks of a book, sometimes his friends are his "elect," his

"righteous tribe," language which recals the "sealed of the tribe of Ben" of his favourite Jonson. Inclusion among them was clearly reckoned as an honour, and many of the poems in which it is conferred were evidently written in response to solicitation, sportive or earnest as we may choose to think. These friends of his later days are not always very interesting. Many of them are of his relations, Herricks, or some of the innumerable Stones and Soames, well-to-do folk with whom the poet claimed cousinship through his mother, Julia Stone. Some of the outsiders are more to our purpose—John Selden the antiquary, for instance, whose intimacy was no small honour, and Dr. Alabaster, who in his young days had become a convert to Catholicism while serving with Essex in Spain, but whose apocalyptic writings brought him into trouble with the Inquisition, from whose clutches he was glad to find refuge in a return to Protestantism and an English living. Mr. John Crofts, cup-bearer to the King, is another friend who brings with him a distinct sense of reality. Herrick calls him his "faithful friend," and their acquaintance was probably of long standing, for we hear of Crofts as in the King's service a year or two before the poet buried himself in his Devonshire living, and on the other hand all these "Temple" poems impress us as having been written late in Herrick's life. In his younger days Crofts himself may have been a rhymester, for in the State Papers there is a letter from Lord Conway thanking William Weld for some verses, and expressing a hope that the lines may be "strong enough to bind Robert Maule and Jack Crofts" from evermore using some phrase unknown. Mr. Crofts seems to have had worse faults than this of using incorrect phrases, for a year or two later (1634) there is a record of a petition from George, Lord Digby, praying to be released from an imprisonment incurred for assaulting Herrick's friend under very irritating provocation. Jack had passed some insult on a lady under Lord Digby's escort, had apologised, had boasted of the original offence, and when finally brought to book had interspersed remarks such as "Well!" and "What then?" in a manner which made caning seem too good for him. But this is the petitioner's account, and Jack himself might have given a different version.

Others of Herrick's friends seem occasionally to have got themselves into trouble. Dr. John Parry, for instance, Chancellor of the Diocese of Exeter, when first appointed was accused of having oppressed divers people with excommunications for the sake of fees; but we hear of him afterwards as highly recommended by the Deputy-Lieutenants, and his early exactions must have been atoned to the King's satisfaction, since the chancellor was thought worthy to be made a judge-marshal, and to receive the honour of knighthood.

Many of Herrick's poems bear reference, direct or indirect, to the Civil War. He bewailed the separation of the King and Queen, welcomed Charles to the West in verse which sang the "white omens" of his coming, congratulated him on his taking of Leicester in May, 1645, and composed an ode, "To the King upon his welcome to Hampton Court," in which he took all too cheerful a view of the royal prospects. His book is dedicated to Charles II., and it contains also an address "To Prince Charlie upon his coming to Exeter," which probably refers to a visit in 1645. Years before he had sung the Prince's birth in a pretty choral ode, taking note of the star which appeared at noontide when the King his father went to make thanksgiving at St. Paul's Cathedral. Two other incidents in the west-country campaign inspired his muse, the taking and holding of Exeter by Sir John Berkeley, and the gallant victories won in Cornwall by Lord Hopton over very superior numbers. For the rest there is nothing in the *Hesperides* to show that Herrick was a bigoted royalist. Utterances in favour of the divine right of kings and the duty of implicit obedience are not hard to find; but they are balanced by epigrams which show a much more Parliamentary spirit, and it is often difficult to tell where Herrick is expressing his own sentiments and where he is simply running into verse some sentence or phrase which happened to catch his attention.

When the end came, Herrick, like many another country priest, was turned out of his living, shook the dust of Dean Prior off his feet, and returned contentedly to London, there to take his place in a little band of wits who were able to endure the gloom of the Presbyterian rule which then held the city in its grasp. He passed his *Hesperides* and *Noble Numbers* through the press, made friends with young John Hall, then fresh from Cambridge but with a European reputation for cleverness; addressed his "honoured friend" Mr. Charles Cotton, probably the friend of Izaak Walton and translator of Montaigne; overpraised Leonard Willan, a wretched poet and dramatist, and contributed a curious poem to the *Lachrymae Musarum,* in which, under the editorship of Richard Brome, all the wits of the day poured forth their lament for the death of Lord Hastings in 1649. Then Herrick vanishes from our sight, and save that he returned to his living after the Restoration and died there at Dean Prior in 1674 we know no more of him.

The mention of Herrick's "Temple" or "Book" of his heroes has led us to gossip first of the less interesting half of his life which followed on his acceptance of a country living. The nine or ten years which passed between his leaving Cambridge and his retirement to Devonshire were probably the most poetically productive in all his career, and, from the glimpses which his poems give us, were certainly the gayest and most amusing.

He had gone to the University unusually late in life, in 1613 when he was already in his twenty-first year, that is to say, five or six years senior to the average freshman of those days. After his father's suicide (for the fall from a window following immediately on making his will can hardly have been accidental, and was not so regarded at the time) the care of the poet and his brothers had devolved on their uncles Robert and William, and the latter, who was jeweller, goldsmith, and banker to James I., shortly after receiving the honour of knighthood from the King, on September 25, 1607, accepted his nephew as an apprentice for ten years. Herrick's appreciation of material beauty was so keen that the absence from his poems (so far as all memory serves me) of any striking allusions to goldsmiths' work may perhaps be taken as evidence that during his apprenticeship with his uncle he did not make any great progress in the craft. At all events he persuaded Sir William to excuse him the last four years of his time, and betook himself to Cambridge, the poet's University.

Fourteen letters which he wrote to his uncle from his college still survive, all written in a high-flown rhetorical style, sometimes lapsing into blank verse, and with one unvarying theme,—the need of a prompt remittance. His allowance was £40 a year (some £200 present value), probably paid out of the remnant of the £600 odd which came to him from his father's estate. This of itself was no bad "stipend," to use the poet's word, and from the tone of the letters we may guess that it was also supplemented by occasional gifts from his uncle and aunt. But it was apparently not paid regularly; Herrick was frequently in pecuniary straits, and about 1616 he migrated from St. John's to Trinity Hall in order to curtail his expenses, taking his bachelor's degree from the latter college in 1617.

It would be placing too touching a faith in undergraduate nature to attach much importance to the fact that the payments which Herrick requests were mostly to be made through booksellers, and that (save once when he confesses to having "run somewhat deep into my tailor's debt") the need of books or the advancement of his studies are the pretexts mostly given for his requests for speedy payment. But there is no reason to imagine that Herrick's university career was an idle one. His poems show considerable traces of a knowledge and love of the classics. He translates from Virgil that charming passage which describes the meeting of /Eneas with Venus clad as a simple huntress, is full of Horatian reminiscences, borrows a few couplets from Ovid, adapts quite a number of epigrams from Martial, makes so much use of his Catullus that we may guess he knew a fair number of his odes by heart, quotes Cicero, turns a tag or two from Sallust and Tacitus, and had a very extensive acquaintance with Seneca. In Greek he takes a couplet from Hesiod as a motto for his *Noble Numbers,* alludes to Homer, though his reference to Helen at the Scaean Gate is perhaps rather from the *Love Letters* of Aristaenetus than the Iliad, translates some twenty lines of Theocritus into the pretty poem entitled *The Cruel Maid,* knew something of the Planudean Anthology, and knew, loved, translated, and imitated the pseudo-Anacreon.

This brief survey of Herrick's classical studies may suffice to prove that he was no idler, and when he left the university and returned to town he must have been well able to hold his own with the best wits of the day. The well-known poem on "His Age," "dedicated to his peculiar friend, Mr. John Weekes under the name of Posthumus," contains in the printed version some vague reminiscences of their sportive days. In Egerton MS. 2725 at the British Museum one verse of this poem assumes a much more specific form:

> Then the next health to friends of mine
> In oysters and Burgundian wine,
> Hind, Goderiske, Smith,
> And Nansagge, sons of clune and pith,
>   Such who know well
> To board the magic bowl, and spill
> Almighty blood, and can do more
> Than Jove and Chaos them before.

The identity of these heroes is not every easily determined. A friend suggests that Hind may have been John Hind, an Anacreontic poet and friend of Greene, and has found references to a Goderiske (Goodrich) and a Nansagge, of whom, however, only the names are known. Smith, despite the commonness of the name, may almost certainly be identified with James Smith, a poet whose few verses sometimes strike a curiously modern note. Like Herrick he acted at one time as chaplain to a squadron sent to the relief of the Isle of Rhé, and like Herrick also became a Devonshire parson. He was, too, one of the editors and writers of the Anthology known as *Musarum Delicice,* and his colleague in that task, the gallant royalist sailor, Sir John Mennis, was also a friend of Herrick, who addressed a poem to him. John Wicks, or Weekes, the "Posthumus" of Herrick's verses, was another friend of Mennis and Smith, and also a country clergyman. The first poem in the *Musarum Delicice* is addressed "To Parson Weeks; an invitation to London." "One friend?" he is told—

Why thou hast thousands here
Will strive to make thee better cheer.
Ships lately from the islands came
With wines, thou never heard'st their name—
Montefiasco, Frontiniac,
Viatico and that old Sack
Young Herrick took to entertain
The Muses in a sprightly vein—

an invitation which links together the names of all these topers. Weekes, however, so Antony Wood tells us, was a good preacher as well as a merry fellow. His living was in Cornwall, but he added to it a canonry at Bristol. Herrick addresses two other poems to him; one "a paraeneticall or advisive verse," beginning,

Is this a life to break thy sleep,
To rise as soon as day doth peep?
To tire thy patient ox or ass
By noon and let thy good days pass,
Not knowing this, that Jove decrees
Some mirth to adulce man's miseries?

lines which seem to show that Parson Weekes took the cultivation of his glebe somewhat too seriously. In the third poem he is again addressed as Herrick's "peculiar friend," and having apparently come off better than most royalist parsons under the Commonwealth, is exhorted to hospitality:

Since shed or cottage I have none,
I sing the more than thou hast one,
To whose glad threshold and free door
I may a poet come, though poor,
And eat with thee a savoury bit,
Paying but common thanks for it.

If Herrick made some friends among members of his own profession, his love of music probably procured him many more. He addresses poems to William and Henry Lawes, both of whom set verses of his to music; he alludes also to Dr. John Wilson, to Gaulthier, to Laniere, and to Robert Ramsay, in terms of familiarity. The last named, who "set" his version of the dialogue between Horace and Lydia, may have been a Cambridge friend, as he was organist of Trinity College (1628-1634). With another organist, John Parsons

of Westminster Abbey, who died in 1623, Herrick must have been acquainted
very shortly after his return from Cambridge. Evidence of the friendship
remains in two charming little poems addressed to the musician's daughters,
Dorothy and Thomasine:

> If thou ask me, dear, wherefore
> I do write of thee no more,
> I must answer, sweet, thy part
> Less is here than in my heart,

are the lines which have given the elder sister immortality, while the
attractions of the second are for ever celebrated in the couplet,—

> Grow up in beauty, as thou dost begin
> And be of all admired, Thomasine.

Another family into which Herrick's love of music was probably the key
which gained him admission, was that of the Norgates. According to the
Calendars of State Papers, Edward Norgate the elder was in 1611 appointed,
in conjunction with Andrea Bassano, to the office of tuner of the King's
virginals, organs, and other instruments; and six-and-twenty years later
we find him superintending the repair of the organ in the chapel at
Hampton Court. His son, another Edward, was originally a scrivener in
the King's service, and was employed "to write, limn and garnish with gold
and colours" the royal letters to a picturesque list of foreign potentates,
including the Grand Signior, the King of Persia, the Emperor of Russia,
the Great Mogul and other remote princes, such as the Kings of Bantam,
Macassar, Barbary, Siam, Achee, Fez, and Sus. From scrivener he was raised
to be Clerk of the Signet Extraordinary, and thence to be Windsor Herald,
and to fill a variety of small offices of profit. Herrick addresses him as "the
most accomplished gentleman, Master Edward Norgate, Clerk of the
Signet to his Majesty," and remarks that

> For one so rarely tun'd to fit all parts,
> For one to whom espoused are all the arts,
> Long have I sought for, but could never see
> Them all concentered in one man but thee—

a flattering tribute to the universality of Norgate's talents.

We may pass now to some of Herrick's patrons. His relations with the royal
family we have already touched on, so nothing more need be said about them
here. After the King, the Duke of Buckingham, whom he accompanied as

chaplain to the Isle of Rhe, was probably the most influential of the poet's protectors, and Herrick addresses an effusive poem to him, and a prettier one to his sister, Lady Mary Villiers. With the Earl of Westmoreland, himself the author of a volume of verse *(Otia Sacra),* Herrick was probably on rather more intimate terms. He addresses poems also to the Duke of Richmond and Lennox, the Earl of Pembroke (Massinger's patron), Edward Earl of Dorset, Viscount Newark, and also to the Viscount's son, whom he calls *"Ultimus Heroum,* or the most learned and the Right Honourable Henry Marquis of Dorchester." Joseph Hall, Bishop of Exeter (his diocesan), and Williams, Bishop of Lincoln, are the only episcopal recipients of his verses. He bespeaks the favour of the former for his book, while to the latter he addresses a carol and a congratulation on his release from imprisonment, in which he speaks obscurely of some ill-turn which Williams had done him. The list of lesser men of rank, knights and baronets, among Herrick's friends is of about the same length. Sir Simeon Steward, who competed with him in writing fairy poems, is still remembered by literary antiquaries, and Sir John Denham, whom he congratulated on his "prospective poem" *(Cooper's Hill),* is, of course, well known. But Sir Clipsby Crew, Sir Lewis Pemberton, Sir Edward Fish, Sir Thomas Heale, Sir Thomas Southwell, and other worthy magnates of the day, now only survive in Herrick's verse and the indices to County Histories. Sir Clipsby Crew, to whom he addresses five poems (besides two to his lady), was probably the most intimate of these friends, as Herrick speaks of him as "My Crew," "My Clipsby," and after telling him how he and his friends "securely live and eat the cream of meat," quoting Anacreon and Horace the while, bids the "brave knight" come to visit his cell, an invitation which implies familiarity. Yet it is to be feared that with all these good knights Herrick held the Elizabethan relation of poet to patron rather than a purely equal friendship. Various verses to Sir Clipsby Crew, Sir Lewis Pemberton, Mr. Kellan and others, show that Herrick loved to frequent a rich man's table, and that when his own cellar was empty he was not slow to remind his friends that without Bacchus song is impossible. Herrick's ducal patrons probably repaid his compliments in broad pieces, and even a plain commoner, Master Endymion Porter, is commended for his liberality to poets, in that he "not only praised but paid them too."

This Endymion Porter is the last of Herrick's friends with whom we shall concern ourselves, and in many respects the most interesting of them all. Originally in the service of Buckingham, he accompanied the Duke and Prince Charles on their visit to Spain, and passed into the latter's service some time in the year 1624 as a groom of the chamber. He made himself useful to the King in many ways, and as early as May, 1625, was granted a pension of £500 a year for life, and three years later was assigned the invidious office of Collector of Fines to the Star Chamber, "with a moiety of the fines he shall bring in." Porter was as full also of projects as Steele himself, and turned them, it would seem, to much better account. Thus we hear of ventures of his in ships called the *Samaritan* and the *Roebuck*, the latter of which proved so remunerative that the common sailors took £20 apiece as their share. He contracted to drain Somercoates Marsh in Lincolnshire, and complained to the Privy Council when his workmen were interfered with. In 1635 he joined with Lord Conway in petitioning the King for a grant of a kind of inspectorship of silks, for which dues were to be levied and £100 a year paid to the Treasury, the balance passing to the inspectors. Two years later Porter and his son George became deputies in the management of His Majesty's Posts. Then we hear of him as an assistant in the Corporation of Saltmakers of Yarmouth, and a little later he is concerned in the erection of a lighthouse and harbour at Filey, near Flamborough Head. An invention for perfecting bar-iron without the use of Scotch coal was his next venture, and, having apparently obtained a patent for this, he prays the King for a grant of the forest of Exmoor in fee-farm with a tenure in socage and the liberty of disafforestation. Next year (1638) he was given the reversion of the Surveyorship of Petty Customs in the Port of London (Chaucer's old post), and a little later on, with the Marquis of Hamilton, obtained leave from the King to examine all accounts made to his Majesty, and when they found any accountants to have deceived the King, to make what advantage they could, either by compounding with delinquents of that kind or by prosecuting them, the King to have one half the profit, and Porter and the Marquis the other. Many accountants, we are told, came in and offered very considerable compositions, so much more grist to Porter's ever busy mill. These grants and petitions, it must be confessed, shed but a sorry light on the way affairs were managed during the eleven years of Charles's personal government, but Porter knew how to make himself a favourite with the King by purchasing him works of art, conducting negotiations with Rubens and other painters, and many similar services. The State Papers which give us all these details of his business life tell us also some interesting scraps as to his taste in dress and at the table. He orders wine from abroad, and apparently uses his influence to get it in duty free, while a friend gratefully informs him that he has tried the largest soles he ever saw, fried them and pickled them according to Endymion's directions, and found them excellent. A husband who knows much about cookery does not always contribute to the easy digestion of family meals. If Endymion interfered much in this or other respects, he may probably have repented of it, for his wife, Olive, was plainly a little hot-tempered. While Endymion was absent in Spain the letters of husband and wife are full of pretty quarrels and reconciliations. "Her will," he writes once, "must be done, or else there will be but little quiet;" and again,—"I wish no more wrangling till we meet, absence being punishment enough. I beg you not to beat George (their eldest son) so much, unless he be very like me. I will never beat Charles for being like you." But Mrs. Porter could be submissive as well as provoking. Her brother tells her that Endymion is very angry, and she writes that—"She did not think he could have been so cruel to have stayed so long away, and not to forgive that which he knows was spoken in passion. She knows not how to beg his pardon, because she has broken word with him before, but she hopes his good nature will forgive her, and that he will come home." Some day the temptation to piece together these married love-letters, with a sketch of what can be found out as to this interesting man, will become irresistible. Here I must hasten to justify Porter's appearance on the present occasion. Five of Herrick's poems are addressed to him, all in the vein of a poet to a patron with whom he was on familiar terms. One I take to be an answer to a letter of condolence on the death of one of Herrick's own brothers, though it is usually maintained that the death alluded to is that of a brother of Porter himself. The others are all sportive; a letter in praise of a country life, a dialogue in which Herrick and Porter sing in turns the charms of country and court, and two encomiums on Porter's liberality.

> Let there be patrons, patrons like to thee,
> Brave Porter! poets ne'er will wanting be;
> Fabius and Cotta, Lentulus all live
> In thee, thou man of men! who here dost give
> Not only subject-matter for our wit
> But likewise oil of maintenance for it.

And again this quatrain, which calls up an amusing picture:

> When to thy porch I come and ravish'd see
> The state of poets there attending thee,
> Those bards and I all in a chorus sing
> We are thy prophets, Porter, thou our King.

As these verses remind us, Porter was a patron of many other poets besides Herrick, and by them also was duly besung. He was a patron, too (the trait is too delightful to be omitted), of the redoubtable Captain Dover, and in his capacity of Groom of the Bed-chamber, gave that worthy a suit of the King's clothes to lend more grace to the celebration of the Cotswold Games. But here, alas, we must bid farewell to him. There are yet others of Herrick's friends of whom we would fain write, notably a group of charming ladies: Mistress Bridget Lowman, to whom he wrote his "Meadow Verse;" Mrs. Dorothy Kennedy, from whom he parted with so much sorrow; the "most comely and proper Mistress Elizabeth Finch;" "Mrs. Catherine Bradshaw, the lovely, that crowned him with laurels;" and last, but certainly not least, that "Pearl of Putney, the mistress of all singular manners, Mistress Portman." But these, alas, are as mysterious to us as Julia and Dianeme themselves. The gossip that has here been set down has been gleaned, painfully enough, from old records and registers, and even these seemingly inexhaustible treasures will not always yield the information we desire.

—Alfred W. Pollard, "Herrick and
His Friends," *Macmillan's Magazine*,
December 1892, pp. 142–48

George Saintsbury "Introduction" (1893)

In the following piece, Saintsbury roundly criticizes Herrick, flat out declaring that he "had little or no wit," a devastating remark towards a member of the metaphysical school. Like Pollard, Saintsbury compares Herrick to Ben Jonson and to certain Greek and Roman authors, especially Martial; in this instance, however, the comparison is less than favorable. Saintsbury writes that Herrick's epigrams "cannot for a moment be compared in this respect to the epigrammatic work of the two authors who would seem to have suggested them, Martial and Ben Jonson. They are even more destitute of the poisoned wit of the Roman satirist, and the bludgeonly strength which frequently characterizes Ben's performances in this kind. But most of all are they destitute of the literary merit which always distinguishes Martial, and which very commonly distinguishes Jonson." Saintsbury does offer some praise for Herrick: "He is what may be called a common enjoyer, a person who, just as some other persons constantly select the evil, troublesome, and uncomfortable sides of life for their special attention, selects its joyous, pleasing, and gay sides for his special province. Secondly, he is one who is capable of manifold observation; who is not limited to one or two sides of life any more than he is limited to one or two loves." Saintsbury ultimately views Herrick's versatility as a detriment, however: "This combination of genuineness with absence of depth is the key-note of all Herrick's work." Though Saintsbury does praise some of Herrick's work, he maintains that a "lack of depth" remains the hallmark of the poet's poetry.

Saintsbury then examines, in some detail, Herrick's style, a discussion that any individual writing upon Herrick will likely find useful. He writes: "It is prim and it is easy; it is intensely charged with classical reminiscence and even classical quotation, and it is as racy of the soil of England as any style of any English poet; it is extremely artificial, and it has a dewy freshness not easy to parallel elsewhere." This discussion continues for several pages, as Saintsbury attempts to define what he feels are the essential elements of Herrick's poetic styling. He finds the poet's combination of classical and native elements less complex than one may imagine. Ultimately, Saintsbury concludes that Herrick's work, taken as a whole, is idiosyncratic but charming; that while much of it remains inexcusable and likely only appeals to a few, as a whole, Saintsbury concludes that Herrick remains a poetic success story. Despite his many criticisms of the poet's work, in the end, Saintsbury concludes that Herrick "is one of the English poets who deserve most love from lovers of English poetry."

⸺⟋⟍⟍⟋⸺ ⸺⟋⟍⟍⟋⸺ ⸺⟋⟍⟍⟋⸺

Few poets have had, so far as their poetical reputation is concerned, a more curious history than Robert Herrick. He had, at his death, outlived his own generation, but this has sometimes been almost of itself a passport to immortality. Campbell, for instance, and some others found in the fact the securest assurance of continued popularity. But in Herrick's case things went differently. He published very late; and he did not publish at all till the taste for his style was waning. After he published that taste waned still more and more; and it was nearly a century and a half before it revived. Hence it happened that the *Hesperides* occupies, almost alone, the position of a collection of the truest poetry which never had, either in its own day or in any day at all near to its own, any popularity at all. Some two centuries and a quarter after his own birth Herrick met in Hazlitt a critic of the first class, and one who was well disposed to his own style of poetry, who could yet put him by as something newly discovered and hardly worth the discovering. Even a century after the "discovery" his place can hardly be said to be fixed. Part of his work disgusts those who are most prepared to be delighted with other parts of it. Part of the rest finds, in persons quite prepared to appreciate the remainder, critics ill-equipped for its enjoyment. He is described in almost directly contradictory terms by his own admirers. His qualities and his defects by turns attract and repel the very same adherents. Even Mr. Swinburne finds him at times "monotonous" and "nauseating." He less than almost any writer known to me wrote for "Prince Posterity;" and it was left for Prince Posterity almost entirely to do him honour, yet to do it with the uncertain touch which comes from late and literary appreciation . . .

   (Hesperides) contains, counting "Humane'" and Divine poems together, almost exactly fourteen hundred pieces, the longest of them not extending to very many pages, the great majority not consisting of more than a very few lines. The division of the poems into divine and human is common enough: but there is another division in the human poems themselves which must have very often suggested itself to readers, and which has since been carried out in the excellent and elegant edition of Mr. Pollard. This is the separation of a certain class of epigrams which Herrick, either by accident or purposely, included among his non-divine poems, and which are regarded with exceedingly scant affection even by his greatest admirers. The majority of these epigrams consists of brief, excessively foul-mouthed, and for the most part very defectively witty lampoons on persons who are asserted by tradition or guesswork to have been, sometimes at least, parishioners of Dean Prior. They do not as a rule sin very grossly in what is commonly and exclusively called indecency; they cannot for a moment be compared in this respect to the epigrammatic work of the two authors who would seem to have suggested them, Martial and Ben Jonson. They are even more destitute of the poisoned wit of the Roman satirist, and the bludgeonly strength which frequently characterizes Ben's performances in this kind. But most of all are they destitute of the literary merit which always distinguishes Martial, and which very commonly distinguishes Jonson. Herrick's epigrammatic work is incomparably the worst, in a literary point of view, that he has left; and it is, even among the mass of dull, coarse epigram which the late sixteenth and early seventeenth century has left us, exceptionally coarse and dull. It chiefly contents itself with alleging and upbraiding physical weaknesses and defects, common to or exceptional in humanity, in the plainest and foulest terms. It is not much, if at all, above the scribblings on the wall of the lowest kind of schoolboy or popular wit. So astonishingly does it contrast with the main tenor of the work with which it is associated, that some ingenious paradoxers have wondered whether it was not introduced as an intentional foil to the too soft and luscious graces of the rest. It is not necessary to give an opinion on this point. Even elsewhere it

is sufficiently evident that Herrick's taste was not impeccable; he nowhere shows much real wit; and the abusive epigram was a favourite form of his master Ben's. It is probably not needful to look further in order to account for the presence of these loathsome weeds in an otherwise charming, if somewhat "careless-ordered" garden.

On a second, a larger, and a much more respectable division of Herrick's verse, the *Divine Poems,* or *Noble Numbers,* somewhat diverse opinions and many not particularly necessary theories have been uttered. By the admirers of his best productions they have, with a few exceptions, been somewhat disdained; either on that falsest of all grounds, "I must take pleasure in the thing represented before I can take pleasure in the representation," or for other reasons. A collection of poems which contains the "Litany to the Holy Spirit," and "The White Island," to name no others, could not, as it seems to me, be spoken of with anything but respect by any true and catholic lover of poetry. But as a matter of fact we should have to mention much else. What may be called the Divine Epigrams—though they may sometimes stand, for purely poetic worth, in not so very different a relation to the masterpieces as the epigrams of the other division do to the masterpieces there—have at any rate a vast advantage of subject, and an advantage, not so very much less, of form. Herrick had little or no wit: but he had a fair allowance of sententious aphoristic faculty. And many of these pious pieces, even if they attain not to the first two, are splendid verse: "To find God," "The Thanksgiving," "To his Conscience," a score or two more might be instanced. However, the positive or comparative merit of these exercises seems to have employed the critics less than the temper which they may be supposed to express. Were they palinodes, expressions of repentance for earlier license, and attempts to consecrate the hitherto profaned fire? Some would fain think and have us think so. Were they merely professional exercitations, not necessarily the outcome of a deliberate hypocrisy, but "duty work" of a piece with the Sunday sermon, official, not personal, dramatic, not authentic? Some would incline more or less strongly to this hypothesis. Or were they, without being either of these, poetical studies of a not necessarily feigned but somewhat unreal kind, resembling the studies which, beyond all doubt, make up the greater sum of amatory verse? Was Herrick a "Pagan" who simply saw in the religion of his time a suitable subject for verse, likely to be popular and not unlikely to be good, and who, though by no means singing with tongue in cheek, was least of all things singing from or with his heart? None of these theories has wanted defenders.

I have elsewhere expressed my inability to adopt any of these explanations, or even to think that any very elaborate explanation is necessary: and subsequent study of the matter has only confirmed me in this disinclination. I take Herrick to have been not in the least a "Pagan," but very much of a "natural man." Had he been born in the first three centuries or so I do not think he would have become a Christian; I think he would have been quite simply and sincerely contented with whatsoever religion he was educated in. But I think Christianity on more than one of its sides—especially on that side of emotional and almost sensual devotion in which the English agrees with the Roman branch of the Church (though it does not go quite so far), and also in those points of theology which concern the fatherhood of God, the mediatorship of Christ, and so forth—had a strong appeal to Herrick's kindly and fanciful, if not daringly intellectual, soul. I think that his devotion was as sincere, as kindly, though perhaps nearly as little highflying or metaphysical as his more earthly passions. If (which is probable, but by no means certain) he had led a somewhat loose life in his time, I think that the crime of sense never with him became a crime of malice, and that if his repentances in their turn were not the repentances of saints and martyrs they were genuine enough in their way.

This combination of genuineness with absence of depth is the key-note of all Herrick's work; it at once imparts and interprets the peculiar character of the third, the largest, the most famous, and by far the most brilliant division of his poems. It is obvious enough, yet it seems to have escaped or puzzled some, and few have kept it quite so steadily before them as might have been desirable. It is a combination eminently suited to produce a man skilled at catching, and contented to catch, the thoughts, the impressions, the joys, the sorrows of the present minute. Whatever matters, trivial or otherwise, Herrick is meditating he is always *totus in llis*. They do not interfere with each other; and I no more believe that the "Litany" is insincere because it occurs in the same volume with the "Vine," than I believe that Herrick was insincere in his praises of Julia because we find them side by side with raptures about Electra or Dianeme.

Indeed, his numerous actual or pretended loves are hardly more characteristic of, and hardly more beneficial to his verse than the still more numerous subjects of interest of a non-amatory character which he found to sing of. Except the scenery of Devonshire (which he regarded with a Philistinism greater than his century can excuse), and his early troubles for lack of money, whereof he sang not, most of the accidents of life seem to have found in Herrick a sympathetic spectator, sharer, chronicler. Not only his own "girls," but the loves and the weddings (not by any means forgetting the wedding-feasts) of other people, sack in Fleet Street, as well as the hock-cart in the country, funerals not much less than weddings or christenings—all such things attracted the musings and the muse of this singular parson. Nor were his interests limited to occasions of festivity or of sensual pleasure. He was not, as has been said (being a man very much of his age, and not troubled with any excessive originality), gratified with the "warty incivility" of that fringe of Dartmoor towards the South Hams in which his beneficed life was cast. He professed, and very likely felt, a vivid preference for the attractions of the town. Yet not Wordsworth himself, in his very different way, has shown himself more penetrated with appreciation of the joys and beauties of the country than Herrick. It may have been accident, or it may have been intention, that made the later poet, or the later poet's sister, meet the earlier full tilt on the subject of daffodils. But to any impartial judge it is to this day difficult to award the crown—time allowance being given according to the proper rules of such contests—between them. And the daffodils are not alone in having received from Herrick a poetical celebration that in its own way can not be surpassed. Primroses, violets, the very "meads" themselves, owe him to all time a royalty of honour for the magnificent countenance that he has bestowed on them. A contemporary and fellow "son" of his in Ben's family had anticipated him by saying the last word on "Red and White Roses" with a touch of quintessential elegance which even Herrick rarely reached; but Herrick has, on the other hand, the advantage of Carew in a wider range, in a more genuine and unforced inspiration, and in a certain *bonhomie* which is rare in poets. The moderns are, as a rule, wont to deny him the higher extravagances of passion, and the denial may be justified by a sufficient number of documents; but "The Mad Maid's Song," "The Litany," "The White Island," and not a few others are there to show what he could have attained an he would, and what he did sometimes attain when he would. He had two gifts which are in the very rarest instances found together. The one was an original and unique gift of style; the other was a range—low, perhaps, if any one chooses to insist on that point, but wide—of interest which supplied him with the subjects on which he exercised that style. I am not quite sure that there is any English poet who unites these two gifts in quite the same degree except one or two of the very greatest.

The range of Herrick's subjects is wont, I think, to be a little underrated. One or two English critics, followed by such few foreigners as have taken note of him at all, have treated him as a mere "folk-lorist" in verse, busied about old and decaying ceremonies. Hazlitt, in almost the most memorable of his memorable injustices, thought him best as a translator, and rather a lapidary than a poet. Not a few others, while not wholly denying his merits, treat him as an artificial amorist who is sometimes very coarse, and never thoroughly genuine. Now—as I have already endeavoured to make out, and as I hope many readers of this edition who take it as it comes, and are not, as Hazlitt rather strangely says, "dazzled by the motes" of Herrick's poetry, will perceive—he is these things, at least on the good side of them; but he is also something more. He is what may be called a common enjoyer, a person who, just as some other persons constantly select the evil, troublesome, and uncomfortable sides of life for their special attention, selects its joyous, pleasing, and gay sides for his special province. Secondly, he is one who is capable of manifold observation; who is not limited to one or two sides of life any more than he is limited to one or two loves. He describes one of the latter in a delightful poem as

Sappho next, a principal.

The truth is that the girl or the thing which or who happened to be uppermost in his thoughts for the moment was always the "principal" to Herrick. It was sack or it was beer; it was Prue or it was Perilla; it was Sir Clipseby Crewe or no matter what neighbour, or parishioner, or friend; it was King Charles or King Oberon; it was witchcraft or religion; it was the vision of Julia's petticoat or the vision of himself on his deathbed. He might be thinking of his own ill-fortune in being exiled to "this dull Devonshire," or of his good fortune in possessing a competence, of his father, Ben Jonson, or his friend that singular courtier Endymion Porter, who affected in his life and after it the imagination of so many men of letters. He might be meditating unworthy vengeance on any churl or slut in his parish. But he took up all these subjects—so many and so various— with an equal and an almost indescribable zest and relish. Although a good deal in his style is strongly artificial, nothing is more rare in Herrick than the taint of the exercise, nothing more absolutely unknown in him than the mark of the collar. He writes, if not exactly because he must, at any rate because he chooses and feels in the vein. He has the quality which a superannuated school of criticism in another art used to call *gusto*. There is no subject attacked by him that he does not in this way or that touch and transform with the peculiar transfiguration of art, effected partly by his interest in the subject itself, and partly by the idiosyncrasy of his wonderful style.

This style has some of the most singular combinations of quality that can be found anywhere. It is prim and it is easy; it is intensely charged with classical reminiscence and even classical quotation, and it is as racy of the soil of England as any style of any English poet; it is extremely artificial, and it has a dewy freshness not easy to parallel elsewhere. Its most obvious and easily characterized characteristics are, as usual, far from being its best. Herrick's diminutives have attracted, and it is impossible that they should not attract, a great deal of attention. They strongly recall, and may not impossibly have been suggested by, the similar indulgences of the French Pl^iade school, which (though *Zepheria* and a few other things are its chief actual analogues and descendants in Elizabethan English) certainly had some influence on our shores. But to me, at least, they seem to be caricatures by the author of his own genuine spirit—mistaken attempts to emphasize, for the sake of the vulgar, faculties which he could display in a far better and more legitimate manner. "Rubelet," "Compartlement," "Shephardling," always make me think of Bacon's celebrated denunciation of carpet bedding two centuries before it came into fashion. You may oft-times see things as good in tarts. They are all the more unfortunate that what they do emphasize, at least to the taste of the present age, is rather the mechanical and artificial side of Herrick's genius than the natural and poetic.

Yet this latter side is of such rarity and charm as need no garish artificialities to set them off. It reminds us at once in likeness and difference of the most magnificent stanza of Herrick's younger contemporary Marvell:—

My love is of a birth as rare
    As 'tis for object strange and high,
For 'tis begotten of Despair
    Upon Impossibility.

Very different indeed was the actual parentage of Herrick's muse. It was begotten apparently of easy Confidence upon facile Possibility, and its objects were rarely high or strange. But yet it was of a birth as rare as might be found in a month's journey through libraries. It has in the most eminent degree that peculiar quality—a great constituent of style but not to be identified with it, and though never subsisting without it sometimes missing where style is—the quality which can be only called Phrase. There are some, though few, great masters of style who have no very distinct phrase; there are not a few writers cunning in phrase who are too much its servants to be masters of style. But Herrick's phrase though intensely individual was well under his control, and seldom or never got the better of him. In generic character

it was not very different from the other great phrases and styles, even from
some phrases and styles not exactly great, of his day—the day of what may
be called the second Elizabethan period, which comprehends in itself in sub-
varieties the Jacobean and the Caroline. The writers of this stage, under the
general influence of Jonson, aped, to an extent from which their predecessors
were free, classical form in grammar, vocabulary, and order. Mr. Pollard has
specified, more fully I think than any precedent editor, the exact and literal
transcripts in English from Catullus, Martial, Ovid, Horace, Virgil, and the
rest, which Herrick introduces into his verse. I am not sure that there is not
something a little profane in thus betraying to the unlearned the coincidences
and echoes which have always been an additional, perhaps a main, ingredient
in the pleasure with which scholars read the *Hesperides*. But the facts are
indisputable enough, and the classicality thus introduced into English is one
of the main differentia; of the poet's species.

What is less easy to define is the native and individual quality with which
he blends and subdues this almost excessive classicality, so as to make it an
English style of the simplest and the most original, hardly smelling at all of
the lamp or the lexicon. Here we seem to come at once, as with others we
come later and after preliminary analyses, to the ultimate quality of style.
It is comparatively easy to say that the sententious perfection of his phrase,
possessed in lesser degree by persons like Cotton and Sherburne, in equal or
greater by persons like Crashaw and Carew, and exhibited in different material
by others like Herbert and Vaughan, was endemic—that it was the mere trick
of the time, easy then, unattainable afterwards or before. It is tolerably safe
to go a little further, and to assign the influences which produced it to the
sinking but still powerful tide of Elizabethan passion and ardour meeting and
mixed with the rising tide of classical imitation. Whether such a confluence
or conflict would be thought likely to produce such an effect, if we had not
the effect before us, is a question which it is unnecessary to discuss. It must
be sufficient to say here that there is some such idiosyncrasy in Herrick and
(which is extremely interesting) that by the time his book appeared it was an
idiosyncrasy which had somehow or other lost its relish for the public taste.
For those of Herrick's generation who had sunk a little farther—the Cottons,
the Davenants, and so forth—there was still a public. But for Herrick, as far
as we can tell, there was none. It is seldom safe to boast ourselves over our
fathers, but we may here at least be thankful if not boastful.

On the separate divisions of his subjects it is probably not necessary to
say much here. The "folklorist" section has been already glanced at, and
is at this time of day rather in danger of over- than of under-valuation. It

was certainly fortunate that at a critical time we had such a poet as this to record for us the fleeting accidents of an earlier, and as some irreconcilables still think a better, state of society. Another division, that of the fairy poems, seems to me, though charming, less charming than it has seemed to some others. Herrick simply continued Drayton with a less masculine though perhaps a more delicate conception of the fairy theory of their day. Bishop Corbet in his well-known lament has given a version of the same view which, if it is inferior in grace and in strictly poetical expression both to *Nymphidia* and to Herrick's pieces, seems to me to go more to the root of the matter. And in the true envisagement of fairy subjects Scott and Keats, those strangely different and complementary contemporaries, have said the last word. "La Belle Dame sans Merci" sums the matter up once for all on one side, as Scott's various pieces, connected or not with Thomas the Rhymer, do on the other. In what may be called his "various" moods—complimentary, satirical, commemorative and other—Herrick does but example his time in his own inimitable and charming way. We would not lose these pieces, but we do not attach to them any special or extraordinary value. His sacred work has been already discussed, and this again could not be spared; but with one or two famous and already noted exceptions it has been better done by others. The chief attraction of it is the fact of its having been done at all, and having been in these one or two instances done supremely, by the author of the other work which also stands to the name of Herrick, and especially to that of the author of the convivial and amatory poems.

The value of these last seems to me not merely exceptional, but even unique. It is, of course, to a certain extent the value of the whole period; but it is specially presented and differentiated. Donne is a far "greater" poet than Herrick, and moves in a far higher sphere, both of poetry and passion. But he had not Herrick's mastery of expression, and he gave at least some countenance to the theory that his later life had become ashamed of its earlier scenes. Herrick is "smooth and round;" there is nothing that jars with any part of his work in any other part of it. In the very long period which passed between the publication of the *Hesperides* and his death he may have fallen into a different vein of thought or sentiment from that which announces itself even in the *Noble Numbers,* even in the apologetic couplet which closes the *Hesperides* themselves. But we have absolutely no evidence of the fact. He is, if not exactly passionate—I should hold that he sometimes is, and that such pieces as the famous "Bid me to live," and "I dare not ask" have a thrill and a quiver inseparable from sincere passion—eminently simple, and all of a piece. It only remains to examine what this simplicity shows us.

It shows us, as I think, a nature curiously sound and healthy, with no bad blood in it, if with a slight deficiency of some of the nobler spirits which transcend the blood. It has been urged that Herrick has "too many kisses" in him, that he is too luscious. Such a point is impossible to argue, for it is a pure matter of taste. Catullus would not have agreed with these censors: nor do I. But what does seem to me worth noting is that Herrick is entirely free from the chief vice of most amatory poets. It may be the consequence of a defect in sentiment of him, of an insufficient power of feeling

Le regret pensif et confus
D'avoir ete et n'etre plus,

which makes him so destitute of bitterness towards old loves. But of that vice we find nothing at all in him. To Herrick, as to too few poetical lovers, though perhaps to all good lovers, poetical or not, to love once is to love always, however slight and temporary be the bonds. You may add, however wide the range, new loves to the list; but you must never strike out the old.

In the service of Bacchus, as distinguished from that of Venus, Herrick is meretricious rather than absolutely accomplished. His taste seems to me to have been wanting in quality. He anticipated, however, the taste of the next generation in detecting the excellence of Burgundy, and we are still, despite all that has been written on the subject, too uncertain as to what sack really was to appreciate his devotion in that direction. I should conjecture that just as Herrick shows a certain lack of discrimination in his love, so his taste in wine was something promiscuous, and disposed to admit whatsoever, without nastiness or bad after effects, would produce the requisite exaltation.

And these are things infinitely unimportant. The important thing is that we have in Herrick a poet who was able, by the kindness of the Upper Powers, to give a distinct and extraordinary form to his impressions, who was also able, again by the kindness of the Upper Powers, to secure for poetical representation a most unusual number of interesting subjects, and who combined the two gifts in a manner which if not unequalled is equalled by very few persons in poetical history. Indeed, it is not easy to find a poet who is in his own way so *complete* as Herrick. The sole blot of his verse, the dull and dirty epigram section, is rather an excrescence than a fault in grain; his deficiencies, as they have been and may be called, are connected in a singular and intimate manner with his excellences, and his charm is of the very first and greatest. Much of it is quite unaccountable; you may reduce it to its very lowest terms, and the irreducible personal element remains.

Some of it only appeals, no doubt, to certain persons, though I cannot help thinking that this appeal is made to all the more fortunately and happily constituted of the sons of men. A little of Herrick calls for the broom and the dust-pan, but taking him altogether, he is one of the English poets who deserve most love from lovers of English poetry, who have most idiosyncrasy, and with it most charm.

—George Saintsbury, from "Introduction,"
The Poetical Works of Robert Herrick,
vol. 1, 1893, pp. xxv–liii

EDWARD EVERETT HALE, JR.
"INTRODUCTION" (1895)

Edward Everett Hale, Jr. (1863–1932) was son of the famous American author and Unitarian minister and a prominent literary scholar, historian, and author in his time.

Herrick is distinctively a poet from whom to receive pleasure. He is not necessarily to be studied; he is to be enjoyed. Doubtless many who love his verses will be led on by an honorable curiosity to desire to know this and that concerning the man and his work. But the poetic enjoyment is the main thing. Herrick is a very individual poet. He has something about him which lifts him out of the crowd of Jacobean and Caroline lyrists, such as Carew and Suckling, nor do we think of him as on precisely the same level as his predecessors the Elizabethans. His poems have a certain air of distinction. Many of them are trivial enough, doubtless, but they are never quite commonplace.

—Edward Everett Hale, Jr., "Introduction"
to *Selections from the Poetry of
Robert Herrick,* 1895, p. lxiii

FREDERIC IVES CARPENTER
"INTRODUCTION" (1897)

Herrick is indeed the last expression of the pagan Renaissance, prolonged into the quiddities of the metaphysics, the self-reproaches of the mystics and the devotees, and the darkness of Puritanism. Herrick rises to no spiritual heights nor does he sink into spiritual glooms. He is frankly for this world while it lasts, piously content with its good gifts. His naivete is partly art, partly nature, or rather it is nature refined by art; for he is out and out an artist—the most perfect specimen of the minor poet that England has ever known. He is purely a lyrist, and in his own vein he is really unsurpassed, whether in the English lyric or any other.

—Frederic Ives Carpenter, "Introduction"
to *English Lyric Poetry, 1500–1700,*
1897, p. liii

J. HOWARD B. MASTERMAN (1897)

Our own age has awarded the foremost place among Caroline lyrical poets to Robert Herrick, whose verses, after having been unaccountably neglected throughout the eighteenth century, are now represented in all selections of English poetry. . . . "Corinna going a-Maying," perhaps the best known of all Her-rick's country poems, is one of the most perfect studies of idealized village life in the language.

—J. Howard B. Masterman,
The Age of Milton, 1897, pp. 101–05

❖

WORKS

❖

HESPERIDES

Robert Herrick
"The Argument of his Book" (1648)

I sing of *Brooks,* of *Blossomes, Birds,* and *Bowers:*
Of *April, May,* of *June,* and *July*-Flowers.
I sing of *May-poles, Hock-carts, Wassails, Wakes,*
Of *Bride-grooms, Brides,* and of their *Bridall-cakes.*
I write of *Youth,* of *Love,* and have Accesse
By these, to sing of cleanly-*Wantonnesse.*
I sing of *Dewes,* of *Raines,* and piece by piece
Of *Balme,* of *Oyle,* of *Spice,* and *Amber-Greece.*
I sing of *Times trans-shifting;* and I write
How *Roses* first came *Red,* and *Lillies White.*
I write of *Groves,* of *Twilights,* and I sing
The Court of *Mab,* and of the *Fairie-King.*
I write of *Hell;* I sing (and ever shall)
Of Heaven, and hope to have it after all.

—Robert Herrick, "The Argument
of his Book," *Hesperides,* 1648

Unsigned "To Parson Weeks,
an Invitation to London" (1656)

Ships lately from the islands came,
With wines, thou never heard'st by name.
Montefiasco, Frontiniac, Vernaccio, and that old sack
Young Herric took to entertaine
The muses in a sprightly vein.

—Unsigned, "To Parson Weeks,
an Invitation to London,"
Musarum Deliciae, 1656

Unsigned (1658)

An then *Flaccus Horace,*
He was but a sowr-ass,

And good for nothing but *Lyricks*,
There's but One to be found
In all English ground
Writes as well;—who is hight Robert Herick.

—Unsigned, Naps upon Parnassus, 1658

William Carew Hazlitt "Preface" (1869)

In the following passage Hazlitt savages Herrick, suggesting that the writer "published his poems at an age when youth and inexperience could not be urged in extenuation of the blemishes which they presented."

Herrick published his poems at an age when youth and inexperience could not be urged in extenuation of the blemishes which they presented. The author was fifty-seven years old when the *Hesperides* issued from the press, replete with beauties and excellencies, and at the same time abounding in passages of outrageous grossness. The title was perhaps rather apt to mislead, for besides golden apples, this garden assuredly contained many rank tares and poisonous roots. It would scarcely suffice to plead the freedom and breadth of speech customary among all classes and with both sexes at that period. Some share of the blame must, beyond question, be laid to Herrick's voluptuousness of temperament, and not very cleanly ardour of imagination; yet, after all deductions which it is possible to make, what a noble salvage remains! Enough beauty, wit, nay piety, to convert even the prudish to an admiration of the genius which shines transparent through all.

—William Carew Hazlitt, "Preface,"
Hesperides, 1869, vol. 1, p. viii

W.J. Linton (1882)

William J. Linton (1812–1897) was an American art and literature scholar who, unlike Hazlitt in the passage above, greatly admired Herrick's accomplishment in the *Hesperides*.

The *Hesperides* is so rich in jewelry, that the most careless selection can hardly be unsatisfactory. Yet being so rich, there might have been more independent taste. One is led to ask how much of popular favouritism even in literature is, like fashion in clothes, due to dictation of the purveyors.

—W.J. Linton, *Rare Poems of the Sixteenth and Seventeenth Centuries*, 1882, p. 242

Henry Morley "Introduction" (1884)

A prominent scholar of English literature, Henry Morley (1822–1894) was most known for his ten-volume *English Writers* (1864–94). In the passage below Morley provides a somewhat fanciful description of the conditions under which Herrick may have written the *Hesperides*.

In the quiet of his parsonage, the music of his life found utterance in every mood. His whole mind expressed itself, animal and spiritual. In the texture of his book he evidently meant to show the warp and woof of life. He aimed at effects of contrast that belonged to the true nature of man, in whom, as in the world at large, "the strawberry grows underneath the nettle," and side by side with promptings of the flesh, spring up the aspirations of the spirit. Even the dainty fairy pieces written under influence of the same fashion that caused Shakespeare to describe Queen Mab and Drayton to write his Nymphidia, even such pieces of his, written in earlier days, Herrick sprinkled about his volume in fragments. He would not make his nosegay with the flowers of each sort bunched together in so many lumps. There is truth in the close contact of a playful sense of ugliness with the most delicate perception of all forms of beauty. Herrick's "epigrams", on running eyes and rotten teeth, and the like, are such exaggerations as may often have tumbled out spontaneously, in the course of playful talk, and if they pleased him well enough were duly entered in his book. In a healthy mind, this whimsical sense of deformity may be but the other side of a fine sense of beauty.

—Henry Morley, "Introduction," *Hesperides*, 1884, p. 7

George Saintsbury (1895)

That the *Hesperides* is the most typical single book of the class and kind there can be little doubt, though there may be higher and rarer touches in others. Its bulk, its general excellence in its own kind, make it exhibit the combined influences of Donne and Jonson (which, as was pointed out earlier, tell upon, and to some extent account for, this lyrical outburst) better than any other single volume. And long as Herrick had to wait for his public (it must be confessed that, though the times do not seem to have in the least chained the poet's tongue, they did much to block his hearers' ears), there is now not much difference of opinion in general points, however much there may be in particulars, about the poetical value of "The Mad Maid's Song" and "To Daffodils," of the "Night Piece to Julia" and "To the Virgins," of the "Litany" and "The White Island." Yet this book is only the most popular and coherent collection among an immense mass of verse, all informed by the most singular and attractive quality.

—George Saintsbury, *Social England,*
1895, vol. 4, ed. Trail, p. 300

NOBLE NUMBERS

T. Ashe "Robert Herrick" (1883)

Thomas Ashe (1836–1889) was an English Victorian poet. He was also a literary scholar and important editor of the works of Samuel Taylor Coleridge.

Herrick's sacred poems. have often much merit. We cannot doubt their sincerity. But they are mostly strained, and show Herrick ill at ease. They are strangely disfigured with conceits, and the best of them are half secular.

—T. Ashe, "Robert Herrick,"
Temple Bar, May 1883, p. 132

George Saintsbury (1887)

Of the religious poems the already-mentioned "Litany," while much the most familiar, is also far the best. There is nothing in English verse to equal it as an expression of religious fear; while there is also nothing in English verse to equal the "Thanksgiving," also well known, as an expression of religious trust.

—George Saintsbury, A *History of
Elizabethan Literature,* 1887, p. 356

Thomas Bailey Aldrich
"Introduction" (1900)

The religious pieces grouped under the title of *Noble Numbers* distinctly associate themselves with Dean Prior, and have little other interest. Very few of them are "born of the royal blood." They lack the inspiration and magic of his secular poetry, and are frequently so fantastical and grotesque as to stir a suspicion touching the absolute soundness of Herrick's mind at all times. The lines in which the Supreme Being is assured that he may read Herrick's poems without taking any tincture from their sinfulness might have been written in a retreat for the unbalanced.

—Thomas Bailey Aldrich, "Introduction,"
Poems of Robert Herrick, 1900, p. xxv

F. Cornish Warre "Robert Herrick" (1904)

Francis Cornish Warre (1839–1916) was a prominent literary scholar and vice-provost at Eton. Warre begins the essay below by examining Herrick's reception, looking at how his fame has both waxed and waned over the centuries since his death. He concludes: "Herrick is of his own time, one of the poets who continued Elizabethan tradition into the Caroline age and who went out of fashion with the Restoration." This was a shame to Warre, who greatly admired Herrick's pastoral works: "Herrick wrote the most delightful country verse that has ever been written since the *Idyls*, the *Eclogues,* and the Georgics." In these poems Warre spies both a "quality of fullness," which Warre suggests relates to the plethora of ideas and images in Herrick's work, and a fluency of verse. The result is profound: "in freshness and sureness of effect, in choice of words, in colour, form, and rhythm, Herrick is to be placed among the highest poets, quite above the region of Donne or Herbert."

Warre suggests that Herrick's reputation must have surely suffered because of the perceived slightness of range of his subjects. Many critics have accused Herrick's work of being trivial; though Warre agrees that Herrick's subjects tend to be rustic in nature, "The trivial round of quarrelets of pearl, rubies and corals, roses and cherries, cream and lilies comes in all the stylists of the time; but somehow Herrick's cream is whiter and his cherries riper than the others, and the roses and lilies grow in his Devonshire garden, not in the inkstand." Part of Herrick's ability to write so eloquently on seemingly trifling matters is a debt to his great poetic masters, Ben Jonson and the Roman poet Horace. Warre's discussion of Horace's influence on Herrick is perhaps the most interesting part of the text, and any student working on connections between classical poets and seventeenth-century writers should be sure to take note. Warre writes that "Horace was Herrick's model," an important point indeed.

Like Gosse in an earlier selection in this collection, Warre also writes extensively about Herrick's poems to his many mistresses, and also like Gosse, Warre dismisses the depth of feeling in these poems save for the works to Julia. Warre also laments that Herrick is occasionally given over to works that are considered "licentious" in his day, though Warre argues that seventeenth-century poetry tended to be racier than late Victorian social mores would allow. Warre concludes that Herrick's contributions to English poetry have been vastly "underrated," hoping no doubt that his own literary endeavor will help to cure the ill and neglect that Herrick had suffered in the centuries since his death.

The risings and settings of poets on the horizon of fame cannot be calculated. In the long night of the Middle Ages the star of Virgil alone shone undimmed. The great names of antiquity were obscured, some for a time, some for ever, unless the sands of Egypt or the ashes of Herculaneum bring back to light some fragments of the lost treasures. And what the barbarian and Mohammedan cataclysms did on a grand scale has been repeated by the petty neglect of great authors and petty inflation of small authors since the time when the printing press supplied to all classes of writings the prospect of a cheap immortality, and the stream was choked by its own fulness. Shakespeare's fame was obscured for a time; Milton slept on the shelf for a hundred years; Dante had a great reputation, but no readers, in the time when *Pastor Fido* and *L'Adone* were admired. And Johnson, in his *Lives of the Poets,* which canonise Christopher Pitt, Thomas Yalden, and Elijah Fenton, has no place for Herrick. Herrick is of his own time, one of the poets who continued Elizabethan tradition into the Caroline age and who went out of fashion with the Restoration—not that the Restoration had much to do with the change of fashion; if one generation is classical the next shall be romantic or call it what you will; change of fashion has often little to recommend it but the pleasure of change—anyhow, the Elizabethan lyric, of which Herrick was the latest inheritor, gave place to Pindarics and heroics, and Herrick ceased to please; and for a hundred and fifty years no one cared for his memory. 'He was practically forgotten' till Nichols fished him up in the *Gentleman's Magazine*, 1796–7, since[1] which time his reputation has risen with some critics to such a height that there may be danger of its becoming overblown. Yet we doubt whether he is even now commonly estimated at his true value.

We said above that Herrick was of his own time, and that he continued Elizabethan traditions. This may seem a contradiction: but it need not be so. It is easy to under-estimate or to over-estimate the extent of a poet's obligation to the fashion of his day: some lead, some follow a lead, and a poet may be consciously or unconsciously one of a group or a school of innovators or of conservatives, or may by date and temperament belong both to the incoming and the outgoing fashion. Crabbe and Cowper, for instance, whilst undermining the conventions in which they were brought up and levelling the way to be trodden by Wordsworth and the Lakers, who seemed to themselves pioneers—we do not dispute the claim—obeyed the Augustan rule of verse as conscientiously as Gray or Thomson, though they allowed themselves to be 'licentious' in choice of language. No one ever succeeded in defining the terms 'romantic' and 'classical,' which in their day stood to represent the eternal dualism of art which takes new forms as the spirit breathes; and many good poets—as Byron, who maintained the authority of Pope and wrote the *Giaour* were at once Classicists and Romanticists, or neither. There have been moments when a choice had to be made, as when the *Lyrical Ballads* were issued, or when the Preraphaelite brethren attacked established conventions; but for the most part poets write what it is given them to write, without much thought of movements and schools, and little comes of this classifying and docketing of poets and thinkers like specimens in a museum. The 'school' is formed by the imitators, not the inventor, who thinks more of what he has to say than of the dialect in which his followers will repeat it after him. . . .

Herrick, then, owed some of his lyrical mastery to the models of the preceding age. He knew how to play on an instrument the practice of which had been brought to perfection; he used also the exquisiteness of language studied by the framers of conceits, the neatness and quaintness of which George Herbert sets the pattern; but besides this he had his own note and his own methods.

It is sometimes assumed that because Herrick wrote the most delightful country verse that has ever been written since the *Idyls,* the *Eclogues,* and the Georgics, he was just a linnet who sang as the linnets do, 'native woodnotes wild.' So he did; but he was also a finished artist, well read in ancient and modern poetry, a man of letters and a man of the world, one who understood the value of perfection as well as Ben Jonson himself.

The gentleman in Horace who could reel you off two hundred verses at a standing was very proud of his fluency; but fluency is not the same thing as fulness; you may have either without the other. Morris is fluent, Browning full, Byron, Shelley, and Scott are both full and fluent. Fulness is a gift of Nature, but fluency may be acquired; and it is the height of wit to give the appearance of ease to the fruit of effort. Readiness is a convenient quality, but not in any way indispensable, nor even a guarantee of good work. The four qualities or capacities of readiness, freshness, fluency, fulness, are not the same thing, though easily confused. Readiness is rather a thing to wonder at than to admire; it is not even essential to wit, though without it wit may often lose its occasion; it is invaluable to the orator, talker, and letter-writer, not so much to the poet. Freshness is inseparable from all good work, whether produced rapidly or slowly; the smell of the lamp is odious, though you burn perfumed oils, and over-elaboration is as fatal to effort as Sheridan's remark upon easy and hard in reading and writing. We know how Macaulay wrote and rewrote, and was content with two pages a day. We know also that *Alexander's Feast* was written in one evening . . .

To apply this to Herrick. It is no compliment to him to think that he wrote poetry by accident and God's grace, and no disparagement to him if he laboured to attain perfection as other poets have laboured. The appearance of fluency and readiness may be an indication of freshness, not of carelessness; the poet himself would not desire to offer to the Muses that which cost him nothing; his own inclination would rather be to think little of that which came to him easily; he might even take a secret pleasure in counting the cost, known to himself alone, of that which seemed to be so lightly won. If we object to Herrick that he is superficial and immature, we mean that we do not care for his thought and his subjects, not that we comdemn his method; for it is beyond all question that he struck the note which he meant to strike, and with no uncertain finger. His volant touch never failed him when he was poetical, though when he was witty he went sometimes miserably astray.

What his own judgment was he has told us in his 'Request to Julia':

Julia, if I chance to die
Ere I print my poetry,
I must humbly thee desire
To commit it to the fire;
Better 'twere my book were dead,
Than to live not perfected.

In considering the position of a poet among other poets—a barren comparison, but one cannot altogether avoid it—something must be set down on the score of quantity. A poet must bring his sheaves with him; armfuls, not handfuls, or chosen samples of grain more golden than gold, but full measure, running over. The actual bulk of Herrick's work is not great—one small volume contained all that he chose to print; but he has the quality of fulness; there is no poverty of ideas nor any sense that he has said all he had to say within the circle of which he chose to limit himself; the 'monotony of style and motive,' of which Swinburne complains, is only due to that limitation; and if we turn the pages of *Hesperides* to see what poems are to be cherished and set among the masterpieces, we shall find more such there than in the works of poets who wrote twice and three times as much. He is not at his best in long poems; the *Epithalamies* are the best of them; he is, like Schubert and Burns, a singer, and for poems a few stanzas long, faultless in sentiment, diction, and workmanship, he must be put in the very first rank. If we were making an English lyrical Anthology, two or three poems each would be all that we should take from Lovelace, Suckling, Vaughan, Crashaw, Donne, Denham, or the moderns such as Moore, Campbell, Leigh Hunt, Coleridge, or the more modern still, Arnold, Clough, Browning; to find an equal number of indispensable poems we must go to the masters of lyric verse, Shakespeare, Milton, Scott, Wordsworth, Tennyson, and Shelley. But when we come to Herrick, we could not do without the 'Daffodils,' nor all the Julia poems—'Cherry Ripe,' 'Whennas in Silks,' the 'Night-piece,' 'Delight in Disorder,' 'Julia's Churching'— nor 'Corinna's Maying,' Sappho's 'Apron of Flowers,' 'To Blossoms,' 'Gather ye Rosebuds,' 'To Anthea,' the 'Ode for Saint Ben,' the 'Mad Maid,' and more still, till the bunch of flowers would seem almost too big for the garden in which they grew. For these poems have all of them the quality of perfection. They have not the heat and passion of Catullus and Burns, nor the sustained sweetness and strength of Horace, but they bear comparison with Horace better than with any other poet; and where Horace reaches perfection, he is most like Herrick. This is high praise; but in freshness and sureness of effect, in choice of words, in colour, form, and rhythm, Herrick is to be placed among the highest poets, quite above the region of Donne or Herbert; and Mr. Swinburne's praise is not exaggerated when he says of Herrick[2]:—

> As a creative and inventive singer he surpasses all his rivals in
> quantity of good work. In quality of spontaneous inspiration he

reminds us, by frequent and flawless evidence, who above all others must beyond all doubt have been his first master and his first model in lyric poetry—the author of 'The Passionate Shepherd to his Love.'

It is also not to be forgotten, as Mr. Swinburne goes on to say, that Herrick is a song-writer, 'first in rank and station of English song-writers,' one whose songs are 'good to read and good to sing,' musical as well as poetical in intention. In more sustained flights music may give a fresh meaning and power to words, translating them to a new atmosphere, as in Stanford's 'Revenge,' for instance; or the words may be little more than a vehicle for the music, as in Handel's metrical oratorios. When Heine combines with Schumann we have the perfection of song-writing, and the advance of music from Lawes and his contemporaries to the present day has not altered the relation of the song to its setting; the same tunefulness and neatness are still required, and a song must not be burdened with thought, which must always be subordinate to feeling, nor obscure in language. If Herrick asks and solves no riddles for a painful world, this is in part because his thought is musical, not metaphysical.

Why, then, has he not a greater fame, and why is he disparaged by some critics as a trifler? Principally because his range of subjects is small—

I sing of brooks, of blossoms, birds, and bowers,
Of April, May, of June, and July flowers;
I sing of Maypoles, hock-carts, wassails, wakes,
Of bridegrooms, brides, and of their bridal cakes.
I write of Youth, of Love, and have access,
By these, to sing of cleanly wantonness.

Here was his domain—no Urania visited him darkling; he did not sound the depths and climb the heights like the greatest poets; no indignation stings him to write like Juvenal and 'snaky Persius,' His love is no vampire, like Catullus's Lesbia, to lacerate his heart. He could not write sonnets on slaughtered saints or martyred kings, though the 'untuneable times' unstrung his harp, and the tone of his later poems, when he suffered for his opinions, is more serious than his pastoral vein. Nor is there any philosophy in his poetry, except the everyday philosophy of contentment with life and love of beauty; there are no problems or lofty musings and aspirations, no high flights of religion or patriotism. All these abatements detract from his claim to be set among great poets; but a poet he approves himself as truly as any son of Apollo, if you seek what you shall find, and is in his own region unsurpassed. That region is what he has himself defined in the lines just quoted. His country is true England, not Arcadia, and so far more genuine than that of Theocritus and Virgil, if less divinely tuneful; and he paints youth and beauty without description and detail so deliciously that we must go to Shakespeare himself to better him, for no one else can do it, unless it be Tennyson, some of whose creations are perhaps worthy to sit by the side of Julia.

It may be said that his stock-in-trade is small, and that shared with other contemporary poets. The trivial round of quarrelets of pearl, rubies and corals, roses and cherries, cream and lilies comes in all the stylists of the time; but somehow Herrick's cream is whiter and his cherries riper than the others, and the roses and lilies grow in his Devonshire garden, not in the inkstand, where perchance Saint Ben the scholar found some of his. Herrick, to be sure, swore in his 'Farewell to Sack'—

> What's done by me
> Hereafter shall smell of the lamp, not thee.

But we feel sure that his study was not indoors, but under the apple trees in the Rectory orchard.

So well-read and so sensitive a poet could not but have some echoes from other poets. We are reminded not only of Marlowe, but of Shakespeare, of Herbert, and other sixteenth and seventeenth century writers. But Herrick owed most to his beloved 'Ben,' whose full melodiousness emboldened his follower to rise above conceits and niceties and pour himself out in round English words. He comes so near sometimes that one wonders whether it is Herrick or Jonson that is the imitator:

> Give me a look, give me a face
> That makes simplicity a grace;
> Robes loosely flowing, hair as free,
> Such sweet neglect more taketh me
> Than all the adulteries of art;
> They strike my eyes but not my heart:

says one; and the other, as if continuing the thought—

> A sweet disorder in the dress
> Kindles in clothes a wantonness.
> A winning wave, deserving note,

In the tempestuous petticoat;
A careless shoe-string, in whose tie
I see a wild civility:
Do more bewitch me, than when art
Is too precise in every part.

Herrick might have written 'Drink to me only with thine eyes' without departing from his natural manner; and Jonson the verses dedicated to Posthumus. Jonson's bowl is deeper and filled with more generous wine; but Herrick's liquor, too, is *merus Thyonianus.*

Of the ancient poets—and he knew them all—he owes most to Horace. Horace, it is true, was a moralist and philosopher, and Herrick was neither. Like Horace, he has the security of touch, which is the earnest of success, and the workmanlike feeling that will not leave a poem till it is complete and finished. Horace has, beyond other poets, the gift of unity, at least in the shorter odes which we love better than his Pindarics; Herrick has it too, if in a less degree. 'No Luck in Love' is purely Horatian, both in execution and in sentiment:

I do love, I know not what;
Sometimes this and sometimes that:
All conditions I aim at.
But, as luckless, I have yet
Many shrewd disasters met,
To gain her whom I would get.
Therefore, now I'll love no more,
As I've doted heretofore.
He who must be, shall be poor.

The idea and its expression count for more than the personal feeling. Poets have said it a hundred times and not meant it. There is a like unreality of feeling joined with consummate expression in 'Quis multa gracilis,' which so caught the ear of Milton; more, we may be sure, by its manner than its matter. Horace's Phidyle, Pyrrha, Neaera, Glycera, like Tennyson's Adeline, Lilian, Dora, are visions of womanhood and phases of sentiment, not transcripts of passion; and this is partly true of Herrick, as we shall see.

Compare, not with Horace's 'Quo me, Bacche, rapis,' of which he translates the opening words, but with any of his shorter poems, the 'Canticle to Bacchus'—

Whither dost thou hurry me,
Bacchus, being full of thee?
This way, that way; that way, this,
Here and there a fresh love is;
That doth like me, this doth please:
Thus a thousand mistresses
I have now; yet I alone
Having all, enjoy not one.

The following poem, though not specially Horatian, resembles Horace in dignity and the art of saying much in a few lines. It might have been lifted a little higher, and found a place in *Comus;* it might have come as a song in a play of Shakespeare. There is little novelty in thought or diction, nothing to stir the pulses, its echoes of Latin poetry are trite; yet it is perfect—

Music, thou queen of heaven, care-charming spell,
    That strik'st a stillness into hell;
Thou that tam'st tigers, and fierce storms that rise,
    With thy soul-melting lullabies:
Fall down, down, down, from those thy chiming
    spheres,
To charm our souls, as thou enchant'st our ears.

His 'Protestation to Julia' is Horatian, again because the pleasure which it gives us is rather from the expression than the depth of feeling. Once for all let it be said that Herrick is not one of those poets who write with their heart's blood. Without being insincere, Herrick, like other poets, sometimes writes more for the sake of his verse, or for a turn of expression, than because he must sing just so, or break his heart like the nightingale; that is not our jolly Herrick's way. He laughed, and may have wept; but he seldom sighed—

Why dost thou wound and break my heart,
As if we should for ever part?
Hast thou not heard an oath from me,
After a day, or two, or three,
I would come back and live with thee?
Take, if thou dost distrust that vow,
This second protestation now:
Upon thy cheek that spangled tear
Which sits as dew of roses there,

That tear shall scarce be dried before
I'll kiss the threshold of thy door.
Then weep not, sweet, but thus much know,
I'm half returned before I go.

The words may be too strong for the occasion, which is apparently the
same as that of his 'Sailing from Julia;' but the tender feeling is as genuine as
the expression is faultless. We like these better than such direct imitations
of Horace as the poem to Posthumus, or the 'Country Life,' which are as
much dilutions as imitations, and show to disadvantage, inasmuch as the
English language has not the marble smoothness of the Latin, and cannot
be cut to such fineness. In the former, however, he gets clear away from
Horace, and gives us himself—

To thee, and then again, to thee
We'll drink, my Wickes, until we be
        Plump as the cherry,
Though not so fresh, yet full as merry
        As the cricket,
The untamed heifer, or the pricket,
Until our tongues shall tell our ears
We're younger by a score of years.

'His Poetry his Pillar' is inspired by Horace's 'Exegi momumen-tum,'
but is not an imitation. It is not pitched in so high a strain, nor is it so
elaborate; but it is not every poet who could say without fear of envious
laughter—

Pillars let some set up
        If so they please:
        Here is my hope
And my pyramides.

Horace was Herrick's model, so far as he had a model. He knew the Latin poets
so well that echoes of others reach our ear—in particular he was beholden
to Martial, whose terse and neat versification, as well as his unrestrained wit,
attracted him. The Latin poets taught him the value of good workmanship.
We may be sure that Herrick's verse was pruned down, not built up. The rich
substance came first, the shaping and polishing later.

What are we to say of Herrick's mistresses, Anthea, Corinna, Sappho,
Perilla, Lucia, Lalage, Biancha, Myrrha, Silvia, Electra, Dianeme, and

'stately Julia, prime of all'? Are they fancies or realities? Did they live in Devonshire or in London? Did Herrick leave them, or they him? . . .

> . . . all are gone,
> Only Herrick's left alone,
> For to number sorrow by
> Their departures hence, and die.

Did he love them all? and all at once, or singly, or are they but names? There is no external evidence, such as identifies Catullus's Lesbia and Ovid's Corinna, nor any personal certainty, as in the case of the Cynthia whose love was the bane of Propertius. We can only judge from the poems themselves. The dilemma is this: either Herrick wrote these poems in praise of town-bred maidens whom he loved in his early London days, the 'soft, smooth virgins,' with whom he used to glide 'in barge with boughs and rushes beautified' to Richmond and Hampton Court, amongst the swans and the 'pure and silver-wristed Naiades;' or they are addressed to country girls by a middle-aged or elderly country parson, for Herrick was well past thirty-five, the age fixed by Byron as the period of love-making, before he left the 'smoother sphere' and 'most civil government' of London, and migrated to the farmhouses and granges of 'dull Devonshire.'

If we compare 'Discontents in Devon' with another poem on his 'banishment' to the West, we find him saying—

> Justly, too, I must confess,
>   I ne'er invented such
> Ennobled numbers for the press
>   As where I loath'd so much;

which seems to give the *Noble Numbers* to the nineteen years of exile; whilst

> Before I went
> To banishment
>   Into the loathed West,
> I could rehearse
> A lyric verse,
>   And speak it with the best,

would give the poems of the true Herrick note to his earlier life in London. There remains the suggestion that he, too, like Milton, did not care for 'the tangles of Neaera's hair,' and that his many-named love was but a symbol of incarnate virgin youth. But the mere mention of Milton's chaste severity in the same sentence with Herrick's warmth and merrier art disposes of this at once.

If we knew the dates of Herrick's poems, we should know more about his loves. Probably many of his love-poems are youthful fancies, partly real, partly fictitious, the English temperament inspired by classical poetry— poems preserved by him, not as the story of his life, but for their own beauty, for so great an artist must have known the worth of what he wrote. He gave to these visions of beauty, as he would, sweet names from Rome or Greece, whatever suited the line—

> Call me Sappho[3], call me Chloris,
> Call me Lalage, or Doris.

Some of them no doubt belong to his earlier life; but Julia and Anthea are with him to the last. Corinna, the 'sweet slug-abed,' may have gone a-Maying to Kensington or Chelsea, for the poem speaks of streets, and there was whitethorn then within reach of Londoners; as she is named 'for her wit, and the graceful use of it,' she is not an abstraction. 'Smooth Anthea' of the white skin and 'heaven-like crystalline' eyes, smells of the country, for she is invited to go to the wake:

> Come, Anthea, let us two
> Go to feast, as others do.

The Devonshire 'revel' is described with just a touch of contempt. Maybe, in this poem, Anthea' is merely a vocative, not the name of a woman; and, in spite of all its fervour and passionate protesting, we doubt whether 'to Anthea, who may command him anything' is much more than a beautiful piece of music. The relation of a poet to love is not that of a mere lover. He is in love with love itself, not with a woman only, and his inspiration comes from art as well as nature. We have no right to call him insincere because he dramatises. But Anthea is addressed again in a more serious vein, when he couples her name with thoughts of his own death:—

> Now is the time, when all the lights wax dim;
> And, thou, Anthea, must withdraw from him
> Who was thy servant. Dearest, bury me
> Under that holy oak or Gospel tree,
> Where, though thou seest not, thou mayst think
>   upon

Me, when thou yearly go'st procession;
Or, for mine honour, lay me in that tomb
In which thy sacred relics shall have room.
For my embalming, sweetest, there will be
No spices wanting when I'm laid by thee;

and again:—

So three in one small plot of ground shall lie,
Anthea, Herrick, and his poetry.

There is tenderness and friendship in these lines, if no passion. What shall
we say of Sappho?[3] The exquisite poem which begins—

To gather flowers Sappho went,
    And homeward she did bring
Within her lawny continent
    The treasure of the spring,

need not have a personal reference; but Sappho is put by him as 'next' (to
Julia) 'a principal.'

Electra is a more sensuous creation; her rising out of bed brings back
the day a-kindling. Hers is the image of his 'Vision,' and of the 'Semele'
poem; but these lines redeem his innocence and her chaste coldness:

I dare not ask a kiss,
    I dare not beg a smile;
Lest having that, or this,
    I might grow proud the while.
No, no, the utmost share
    Of my desire shall be
Only to kiss that air
    That lately kissed thee.

Myrrha, too, is hard-hearted, and so is Dianeme:

If thou, composed of gentle mould,
    Art so unkind to me,
What dismal stories will be told
    Of those that cruel be?

So the sweet procession goes by, a dream of fair women. They are neither
real nor unreal; they warmed the poet's fancy, but did not possess his

heart. They came across his way, some in youth, some in riper years, when like Herbert he was vowed to the book and the gown in his Devonshire banishment, rustic maids, daughters of yeomen from the upland farms among the sycamores and ashes, who talked the country dialect, wore rough country shoes and stockings, rode to market on Dartmoor ponies, and made butter of clotted cream in a lime-wood bowl. We can imagine the merry Rector living among his simple flock, winning the hearts of young and old and breaking none but his own, not straitlaced enough to please Puritan parishioners whose fathers had been out against Spain in 1588, but welcome in all companies, from the Hoptons and Gren-villes to the freeholders who rode with them to Stratton Down to fight for the King, in those primitive regions where lack of society smoothes distinctions of rank, and the parson has a right of entry everywhere.

But Julia was a lady born, and married in her own condition. Julia alone of all has colour and outline and substance. Though she does not speak, and is only 'briefly' described, she is as real as one of Shakespeare's heroines; and we must go to Shakespeare for her paragon, or to the creators of the most lovely visions of womankind in painting or poetry. Herrick's book is full of Julia from end to end. Her lips are redder than rubies and cherries; 'rubies, corals, scarlets, all' wonder at them. Her teeth are 'quarrelets of pearl.' Her eyes are 'life-begetting,' her breath is 'all the spices of the East,' her voice is 'smooth, sweet, and silvern.' Her raiment becomes part of herself:

> Whenas in silks my Julia goes,
> Then, then, methinks, how sweetly flows
> The liquefaction of her clothes.
> Next, when I cast my eyes and see
> That brave vibration each way free,
> O, how that glittering taketh me!

—a poem which for sweetness and daring is unsurpassed. Only Herrick, again, could have spoken of Julia's azure robe as—

> Erring here, and wandering there,
> Pleased with transgression everywhere;

or, again, for it must be Julia, though she is not named:

> A sweet disorder in the dress
> Kindles in clothes a wantonness;

and the rest of that lovely poem. The riband about her waist is a 'zonulet of love.' Were ever clothes so glorified, unless it were to do honour to Clarissa?

Perhaps all these things have been said before; but Herrick says them as new, and with a directness of feeling which makes them different. He leaves to her the burning of his poetry if he dies before it is printed; he asks her to take in his last breath:

> My fates are ended—when thy Herrick dies,
> Clasp thou his book, then close thou up his eyes.

When he must leave her, he takes his leave in these exquisitely tender lines:

> When that day comes, whose evening says I'm gone
> Into that wat'ry desolation,
> Devoutly to thy closet gods then pray
> That my wing'd ship may meet no Remora.
>   . . .
> Mercy and Truth live with thee! and forbear,
> In my short absence, to unsluice a tear;
> But yet, for Love's sake, let thy lips do this,
> Give my dead picture one engend'ring kiss;
> Work that to life, and let me ever dwell
> In thy remembrance, Julia. So farewell

—lines which would not be out of place in one of Shakespeare's sonnets . . .

It was the custom of that time to circulate poetry in manuscript, and Herrick's poems, like Donne's, were widely read before they were printed. It was thus possible for a writer to have a reputation before he had published a verse; and it was also less easy for him to suppress what had already been seen abroad than never to break privacy at all. The word sent out was not irrevocable, but it was hard to recall. This has been alleged as a reason why Donne's poems were published without expurgation; and if that excuse is accepted, it may serve for Herrick too. His youthful poems were already to some extent published before they were printed, and he had lost the control, of them. He alludes to this in a poem entitled 'To His Books,' in which, with a reminiscence of Horace, he says:

> While thou did'st keep thy candour undefil'd,
> Dearly I lov'd thee as my first-born child;
> But when I saw thee wantonly to roam

From house to house, and never stay at home:
I broke my bonds of love and bade thee go,
Regardless whether well thou sped'st or no.
On with thy fortunes then, whate'er they be:
If good, I'll smile; if bad, I'll sigh for thee.

There is no certainty to be had with regard to the date of any given poem; and the poems as published in the *Hesperides* are without any arrangement whether of date or subject. There are but three dates in Herrick's life—his appointment to the living of Dean Bourn, his ejection, and his return: which poems preceded or followed any of these must be a matter of guess. The *Noble Numbers* are presumably later than the frolicsome ditties addressed to his loves; and the more sober-suited poems, those that talk of monuments, winding-sheets, and funeral odours, have a waft of death in them; but his style was formed early; and though there may be 'a change from Herrick's early poems, with their supreme daintiness and touch of Elizabethan conceit, to his later work, with its almost classical severity,' this criticism, sound though it may be in the main, must not be pressed too closely. Such a theory holds good if we compare the well-known poem on 'His Return to London' with 'Cherry Ripe' or the 'Maids of Honour;' but it is shaken by these lines, certainly among the latest of all, and yet closely resembling his earlier vein:

I will no longer kiss,
    I can no longer stay;
The way of all flesh is
    That I must go this day.
Since longer I can't live,
    My frolic youths, adieu!
My lamp to you I'll give,
    And all my troubles too.

We take it that the content and discontent in Devonshire had more to do with what Herrick wrote, than youth or age, secular or clerical estate. When he was merry, he could be old Anacreon; when he was sad, he thought of his grave, and Julia or Anthea must bury him. The most probable conclusion is that the greater part of Herrick's poetry was written when he was young, that his vein flowed, less freely, but in a more stately manner, in maturer age, and that the *Noble Numbers* were written late.

Lovers of Herrick will always care more for the *Hesperides* than the *Noble Numbers*. They are more fresh and genial, and in that part of his work Herrick has no rival, whereas in this he must be compared at a disadvantage with Herbert, Crashaw, Vaughan, and others. He was a Christian, a clergyman, and a poet, and therefore he wrote sacred verses. Like Herbert, though without Herbert's emotion, in his 'Farewell to Poetry' he exchanged secular poetry for religious, parting from his Muse 'with a kiss of warmth and love.' There is genuine feeling in 'His Prayer for Absolution':

> For these my unbaptised rhymes,
> Writ in my wild unhallow'd times;
> For ev'ry sentence, clause, and word
> That's not inlaid with Thee, my Lord,
> Forgive me, God, and blot each line
> Out of my book that is not Thine.

But this is a higher flight than is common with him; his religion was contemplative, not emotional, his piety aimed at no visions of glory, no blissful union of the soul with its Lord; it was fuller of charity and hope than faith. His faith is thus expressed:

> God is above the sphere of our esteem,
> And is the best known, not defining him.

His description of 'a true Lent' is—

> To fast from strife,
>   From old debate,
>   And hate;
> To circumcise thy life.

He is thankful and merciful; and for Heaven he says—

> I sing and ever shall
> Of Heaven, and hope to have it when I die.

But he also says:

> Weep for the dead, for they have lost their light;
> And weep for me, lost in an endless night;
> Or mourn or make a marble verse for me,
> Who writ for many—*Benedicite*—

a thought as far removed from the spirit of Herbert, Keble, Cowper, or Charles Wesley as it is possible to conceive, but not from that of Falkland or Browne; a spirit in which faith is mingled with doubt, and there is more of resignation than of aspiration, of contemplation than of devotion; neither pagan nor devout, but thankful for life and the lives of others, and content to praise God for the past and present, and leave the future in His hands. This spirit will not raise men to be saints, and Herrick was not a saint, but it is not an unchristian spirit. There are indeed some poems, like the 'Litany to the Holy Spirit,' which speak the language of true devotion; and as Herrick was certainly not a hypocrite, it is reasonable as well as charitable to take him at his best.

We cannot leave our subject without touching on a part of Herrick's work which has much impaired his reputation, and not unjustly: the gross and licentious poems which are found scattered up and down the *Hesperides*. They are not numerous, but we wish them away. Most of them were probably written in his youthful London days, when he was living with the wits, and living as they did, and we do not reckon among them the 'Epithalamies,' which nowhere go beyond the freedom common to such poems and have no taint of licentiousness. Men and women spoke more openly in those days than they do now; and Herrick need not be ashamed to have written—

> To read my book the virgin shy
> May blush while Brutus standeth by;
> But when he's gone, read through what's writ,
> And never stain a cheek for it.

Shakespeare must nowadays be expurgated for the London stage, but Julia saw him acted, and only blushed behind her fan to hear what Imogen, Beatrice, and Rosalind said openly. Not a few are satirical descriptions of his Devonshire neighbours, and can only be explained by a wish to meet Catullus and Martial on their own ground, and their wit does not redeem their scurrility and ugliness. Satire was never more foulmouthed than in Herrick's age, and other poets of the time sin more than Herrick; but they were laymen, and we cannot grant a priest the license of a layman. But when all is said, we accept his own apology:

> Peruse my measures thoroughly, and where
> Your judgement finds a guilty poem, there
> Be you a judge, but not a judge severe.

Though we do not approve, we do not feel called upon to judge him by the rule of 'rigid Cato,' still less to class him with Swift and Sterne. He is as far from the dirtiness of the one as the lubricity of the other, and it is not often that he goes beyond the limit set by himself:

> I write of Youth, of Love, and have access,
> By these, to sing of *cleanly wantonness.*

Leave out a few, and Cato may read Herrick in his sober hours, not only

> When the rose reigns, and locks with ointments shine.

Our conclusion is, that whereas all the world knows Herrick as the author of a few exquisite poems, the amount of his contribution has been commonly underrated; that he is not only a natural singer, but a finished artist and a student of perfection, learned and choice as well as spontaneous; that he is not an immoral writer, though there are blots on his page; and that finally in richness of fancy, fulness of diction, and pure melody of cadence he is worthy to be placed in the highest ring of English poets—

Whose thoughts make rich the blood of the world; and one of his highest merits is that his lovers are never tired of him, but go back to him with fresh pleasure again and again.

Notes

1. A. H. Bullen in Diet, *of Nat. Biography* [Herrick, Robert].
2. Preface to Alfred Pollard's edition, 1898.
3. The first edition and Mr. Pollard's read 'Sappha' here, but 'Sappho' in other places. Herbert Home, xxxvii., in Mr. Earnest Rhys's Preface to his selection.

— F. Cornish Warre, from
"Robert Herrick," *The Edinburgh Review,*
January 1904, pp. 109–27

❖

RICHARD CRASHAW

❖

❖

BIOGRAPHY

❖

RICHARD CRAS

(1612/3–164

❖

Richard Crashaw was born in London, the only s⟨
divine noted for the vigor of his anti-Papist
Charterhouse School and Pembroke College, C⟨
of Peterhouse in 1634 and remained there after
at Cambridge, Crashaw held a minor post at the
may have been ordained. He became interested
community of Little Gidding and was a frequent
Civil War, however, changed Crashaw's life. Both
been influenced by Archbishop Laud and had esp
When the Puritan Parliamentary Commission arri
the chapel of Peterhouse and the church of Little
was time to leave. Subsequently, he seems to have ⟨
Leyden; by 1646, he had converted to Roman Catho
recommendation to the Pope by Queen Henrietta N
he eventually became a minor canon at the Cathed
four months after his appointment.

Crashaw first published poems in 1634, the
Pembroke. The first edition of *Steps to the Temple*
in 1646, with a revised and enlarged edition follow⟨
edition of Crashaw's English sacred poems was pu
the title *Carmen Deo Nostro*.

❖

PERSONAL

❖

Abraham Cowley
"On the Death of Crashaw" (1650)

Famed English poet Abraham Cowley (1618–1667) has sometimes been considered a metaphysical poet by critics. Samuel Johnson, in his *Life of Cowley*, coined the term metaphysical poets when describing the work of John Donne; later, Johnson wrote that Cowley had copied Donne's style. Despite this, though, critics debate whether or not Cowley is truly considered a poet in the metaphysical style.

His faith perhaps in some nice tenets might
Be wrong; his life, I'm sure, was in the right.
And I myself a Catholic will be,
So far at least, great Saint, to pray to thee.
Hail bard triumphant! and some care bestow
On us, the poets militant below!
. . .
And when my Muse soars with so strong a wing,
'Twill learn of things divine, and first of thee, to sing.

> —Abraham Cowley,
> "On the Death of Crashaw," 1650

George Gifillan "The Life and Poetry of Richard Crashaw" (1857)

If Crashaw was not generally popular, and if his detractors malignantly defamed him as a "small poet," a "slip of the times," and as a "peevish, silly seeker, who glided away from his principles in a poetical vein of fancy and an impertinent curiosity," he enjoyed, on the other hand, the praise of some applauded men, and a general "sweet savour" of renown in his day and generation. He is said to have been a universal scholar—versed in the Hebrew, Greek, Latin, Spanish, and Italian languages—to have made the Grecian and Roman poets his study—and to have possessed, besides, the accomplishments of music, drawing, engraving, and painting. In his habits, too, he was temperate to severity; indeed, had he not been so, his poetry would have sunk from a panegyric on God into a bitter, unintentional satire on himself.

> —George Gilfillan, "The Life and Poetry of
> Richard Crashaw," *The Poetical Works of
> Richard Crashaw*, 1857, p. vii.

❖

GENERAL

❖

❖

BIOGRAPHY

❖

RICHARD CRASHAW
(1612/3–1649)

❖

Richard Crashaw was born in London, the only son of William Crashaw, a Puritan divine noted for the vigor of his anti-Papist views. Crashaw attended the Charterhouse School and Pembroke College, Cambridge. He became a Fellow of Peterhouse in 1634 and remained there after receiving an MA in 1638. While at Cambridge, Crashaw held a minor post at the church of Little St Mary's and may have been ordained. He became interested in the quasi-monastic Anglican community of Little Gidding and was a frequent visitor there. The advent of the Civil War, however, changed Crashaw's life. Both Peterhouse and Pembroke had been influenced by Archbishop Laud and had espoused his High Church ideals. When the Puritan Parliamentary Commission arrived in Cambridge, it stripped the chapel of Peterhouse and the church of Little St. Mary's. Crashaw decided it was time to leave. Subsequently, he seems to have spent some time at Oxford and Leyden; by 1646, he had converted to Roman Catholicism and was living in Paris. A recommendation to the Pope by Queen Henrietta Maria sent him to Rome, where he eventually became a minor canon at the Cathedral of Loreto, in 1649. He died four months after his appointment.

Crashaw first published poems in 1634, the year of his graduation from Pembroke. The first edition of *Steps to the Temple* was prepared for publication in 1646, with a revised and enlarged edition following in 1648. In 1652, the final edition of Crashaw's English sacred poems was published posthumously under the title *Carmen Deo Nostro*.

❖

PERSONAL

❖

Abraham Cowley
"On the Death of Crashaw" (1650)

Famed English poet Abraham Cowley (1618–1667) has sometimes been considered a metaphysical poet by critics. Samuel Johnson, in his *Life of Cowley*, coined the term metaphysical poets when describing the work of John Donne; later, Johnson wrote that Cowley had copied Donne's style. Despite this, though, critics debate whether or not Cowley is truly considered a poet in the metaphysical style.

His faith perhaps in some nice tenets might
Be wrong; his life, I'm sure, was in the right.
And I myself a Catholic will be,
So far at least, great Saint, to pray to thee.
Hail bard triumphant! and some care bestow
On us, the poets militant below!
. . .
And when my Muse soars with so strong a wing,
'Twill learn of things divine, and first of thee, to sing.

—Abraham Cowley,
"On the Death of Crashaw," 1650

George Gifillan "The Life and Poetry of Richard Crashaw" (1857)

If Crashaw was not generally popular, and if his detractors malignantly defamed him as a "small poet," a "slip of the times," and as a "peevish, silly seeker, who glided away from his principles in a poetical vein of fancy and an impertinent curiosity," he enjoyed, on the other hand, the praise of some applauded men, and a general "sweet savour" of renown in his day and generation. He is said to have been a universal scholar—versed in the Hebrew, Greek, Latin, Spanish, and Italian languages—to have made the Grecian and Roman poets his study—and to have possessed, besides, the accomplishments of music, drawing, engraving, and painting. In his habits, too, he was temperate to severity; indeed, had he not been so, his poetry would have sunk from a panegyric on God into a bitter, unintentional satire on himself.

—George Gilfillan, "The Life and Poetry of Richard Crashaw," *The Poetical Works of Richard Crashaw*, 1857, p. vii.

❖

GENERAL

❖

UNSIGNED "THE PREFACE
TO THE READER" (1648)

The excerpt below is a prefatory introduction from the early, expanded second edition of Crashaw's work. Though unsigned, it was likely written by someone connected directly to the publisher (as opposed to another man of letters of the day.) The author labels Crashaw "Herbert's second, but equall," a reference to George Herbert, a poet to whom Crashaw is often compared. As is expected for a piece like this, the preface offers brief biographical information as well as unchecked praise of the author; nonetheless, it does provide an interesting and near contemporaneous glimpse into early thought on Crashaw's work and his place in the larger pantheon of the metaphysical poets.

Learned Reader,

The Authors friend, will not usurpe much upon thy eye: This in onely for those, whom the name of our Divine Poet hath not yet siezed into admiration, I dare undertake, that what *Jamblicus (in vita Pythagorai)* affirmeth of his Master, at his Contemplations, these Poems can, *viz.* They shal lift thee Reader, some yards above the ground: and, as in *Pythagoras* Schoole, every temper was first tuned into a height by severall proportions of Musick; and spiritualiz'd for one of his weighty Lectures; So maist thou take a Poem hence, and tune thy soule by it, into a heavenly pitch; and thus refined and borne up upon the wings of meditation. In these Poems thou maist talke freely of God, and of that other state.

Here's *Herbert's* second, but equall, who hath retriv'd Poetry of late, and return'd it up to its Primitive use; Let it bound back to heaven gates, whence it came. Thinke yee, St. *Augustine* would have steyned his graver Learning with a booke of Poetry, had he fancied their dearest end to be the vanity of Love-Sonnets, and Epithalamiums? No, no, he thought with this, our Poet, that every foot in a high-borne verse, might helpe to measure the soule into that better world: *Divine Poetry;* I dare hold it, in position against *Suarez* on the subject, to be the Language of the Angels; it is the Quintessence of Phantasie and discourse center'd in Heaven; 'tis the very Outgoings of the soule; 'tis what alone our Author is able to tell you, and that in his owne verse.

It were prophane but to mention here in the Preface those under-headed Poets, Retainers to seven shares and a halfe; Madrigall fellowes, wholse onely businesse in verse, is to rime a poore six-penny soule, a Subburd sinner into hell;—May such arrogant pretenders to Poetry vanish, with their prodigious issue of tumorous heats and flashes of their adulterate braines, and for ever after, may this our Poet fill up the better roome of man. Oh! when the generall arraignment of Poets shall be, to give an accompt of their higher soules, with what a triumphant brow, shall our divine Poet sit above, and looke downe upon poore *Homer, Virgil, Horace, Claudian?* &c. who had amomgst them the ill lucke to talke out a great part of their gallant Genius, upon Bees, Dung, Froggs, and Gnats, &c. and not as himselfe here, upon Scriptures, divine Graces, Martyrs and Angels.

Reader, we stile his Sacred Poems, *Stepps to the Temple,* and aptly, for in the Temple of God, under his wing, he led his life in St. *Maries* Church neere St. *Peters* Colledge: There he lodged under *Tertullian's* roofe of Angels: There he made his nest more gladly than David's Swallow neere the house of God: where like a primitive Saint, he offered more prayers in the night, then others usually offer in the day; There, he penned these Poems, *Stepps* for happy soules to climbe heaven by.

And those other of his pieces intituled, *The Delights of the Muses,* (though of a more humane mixture) are as sweet as they are innocent.

The praises that follow are but few of many that might be conferr'd on him, hee was excellent in five Languages (besides his Mother tongue) *vid.* Hebrew, Greek, Latine, Italian, Spanish, the two last whereof hee had little helpe in, they were of his owne acquisition.

Amongst his other accomplishments in Accademick (as well pious as harmlesse arts) hee made his skill in Poetry, Musicke, Drawing, Limming, graving, (exercises of his curious invention and sudden fancy) to bee but his subservient recreations for vacant houres, not the grand businesse of his soule.

To the former Qualifications I might adde that which would crowne them all, his rare moderation in diet (almost Lessian temperance) hee never created a Muse out of distempers, nor with our Canary scribblers cast any strange mists of surfets before the Intelectuall beames of his mind or memory, the latter of which, hee was so much a master of, that hee had there under locke and key in readinesse, the richest treasures of the best Greeke and Latine Poets, some of which Authors hee had more at his command by heart, then others that only read their workes, to retaine little, and understand lesse.

Enough Reader, I intend not a volume of praises, larger then his booke, nor need I longer transport thee to thinke over his vast perfections, I will conclude all that I have impartially writ of this Learned young Gent, (now dead to us) as hee himselfe doth, with the last line of his Poem upon Bishop *Andrews* Picture his Sermons

> *Verto paginas.*
> —*Look on his following leaves, and see him breath.*

> —Unsigned, "The Preface to the Reader,"
> *The Delights of the Muses,* 1648

ALEXANDER POPE (1710)

One of the greatest English poets of the first half of the eighteenth century, Alexander Pope (1688–1744) is best know for his mock epic *The Rape of the Lock* and his essays on criticism and translations of Homer.

I take this poet to have writ like a gentleman, that is, at leisure hours, and more to keep out of idleness than to establish a reputation, so that nothing regular or just can be expected from him.

> —Alexander Pope, Letter to H. Cromwell,
> December 17, 1710, *Pope's Works,* vol. 6,
> eds. Courthope, Elwin

NATHAN DRAKE (1798)

Crashawe possessed the requisites of a genuine poet, enthusiasm and sublimity; but he never undertook any grand or original work.

> —Nathan Drake, *Literary Hours,* 1798, no. 28

THOMAS CAMPBELL "RICHARD CRASHAW" (1819)

Crashaw formed his style on the most quaint and conceited school of Italian poetry, that of Marino; and there is a prevalent harshness and strained expression in his verses; but there are also many touches of beauty and solemnity, and the strength of his thoughts sometimes appears even in their distortion.

> —Thomas Campbell, "Richard Crashaw,"
> *Specimens of the British Poets,* 1819, p. 357

WILLIAM HAZLITT
"ON MISCELLANEOUS POEMS" (1820)

Crashaw was a hectic enthusiast in religion and in poetry, and erroneous in both.

> —William Hazlitt, "On Miscellaneous Poems,"
> *Lectures on the Literature of the Age of Elizabeth,*
> 1820, p. 192

SAMUEL TAYLOR COLERIDGE (1836)

These verses were ever present to my mind whilst writing the second part of "Christabel"; if indeed, by some subtle process of the mind, they did not suggest the first thought of the whole poem.

> —Samuel Taylor Coleridge, cited in
> Thomas Allsop, *Letters, Conversations
> and Recollections of S. T. Coleridge,*
> 1836, p. 606

SARA COLERIDGE (1847)

Sara Coledridge (1802–1852) was the daughter of Samuel Taylor Coleridge and a prominent English author and translator. She translated works by Martin Dobrizhoffer as well as medieval French texts, and also authored numerous other works of her own, including *Phantasmion, a Fairy Tale.*

I can only mention to you Quarles, a great favorite with my uncle Southey, and Crashaw, whose sacred poetry I think more truly poetical than any other, except Milton and Dante. I asked Mr. Wordsworth what he thought of it, and whether he did not admire it; to which he responded very warmly. My father, I recollect, admired Crashaw; but then neither Quarles nor Crashaw would be much liked by the modern general reader. They would be thought queer and extravagant.

> —Sara Coleridge, Letter to
> Mrs. Richard Townsend, September 1847,
> *Memoir and Letters,* 1874, pp. 320–21

George Gilfillan "The Life and Poetry of Richard Crashaw" (1857)

In the excerpt below, taken from an introduction written for an edition of Crashaw's poetry, Gilfillan suggests that the dominant influence on and characteristic of Crashaw's work is his religion: "Crashaw was a Catholic; and in saying so, we deem that we have stated at once the source of his poetic weakness and strength." Gilfillan, who was himself firmly a Protestant, believed that Catholicism, or Popery, was "not Christianity," and while Crashaw was "a true Christian poet," he was "considerably perverted by a false and bad form of the religion," a religion Gilfillan equates, at one point, to animalism.

Gilfillan's bias is important to understand in reading his text; fortunately, his bias only colors, and does not negate, his comments about Crashaw's work. Plus, Gilfillan's larger point—that Crashaw's faith impacts how he writes about such topics in his work—has great merit, though anyone studying how Crashaw's faith impacted his work must bear Gilfillan's prejudices in mind. When Gilfillan writes that Crashaw "looks at Popery, not as Dryden does, through the cold medium of the intellect, but through the burning haze of the imagination," he suggests that it is not a weakness on the poet's part, and anyone studying Crashaw's religious influence may very well agree.

Gilfillan argues that the most significant—and at times, negative—influence of Crashaw's Catholic faith on his work is in his imagery itself, where "often you hear the language of earthly instead of celestial love." Gilfillan suggests that Catholic poets are often hampered by utilizing words and images that debase what is being described; at one point, Gilfillan labels Crashaw's poem "The Wounds of our Crucified Lord" as "offensive." This leads Gilfillan into an interesting and useful discussion of the representation of women in Crashaw's work. Little was done prior to the twentieth century in examining how metaphysical poets wrote about women, though mistresses, wives, and lovers were a common enough subject matter in their works. In this aspect, Gilfillan unfavorably compares Crashaw to his contemporary, John Milton: "how different and how far superior is Milton's language in reference to women to that of the Crashaw school! How respectful, dignified, admiring, yet modest and delicate, all Milton's allusions to female beauty! How different from the tone of languishment, the everlasting talk about 'sighs,' and 'kisses,' and 'bosoms,' found in some parts of our poet!" Gilfillan writes that Crashaw seemed "unnerved" by women, and traces this feeling back to Crashaw's Catholic beliefs. Milton's rendition of women is superior, according to Gilfillan, because they become less mysterious by Milton's pen. Still, Gilfillan writes that Crashaw's genius can usually overcome the obstacles of his faith, and that only on occasion is he mired down into the more negative stereotypes about Catholic writers that Gilfillan presents.

Gilfillan also takes time to respond to Crashaw's metaphysical label, and especially Samuel Johnson's description of them as "wits, not poets." Gilfillan argues that Johnson has "confounded wit with perverted ingenuity, and very much under-rated the genius of the men." In defending the metaphysic poets, Gilfillan praises their imaginations and their versatility. Gilfillan does not uniformly praise the metaphysics—like many of his contemporaries, he dislikes their artifice and their conceits—but ultimately concludes that "perhaps *in spite* of their own system, [they] attained a rare grandeur of thought and language." Thus Gilfillan, like many nineteenth-century critics, argues that the inherent beauty of much of what the metaphysics wrote outweighs the numerous flaws of the school itself—flaws that, in Crashaw, Gilfillan believes are exacerbated by the poet's devotion to his Catholic faith.

From the beginning of his being, Crashaw was a Catholic; and in saying so, we deem that we have stated at once the source of his poetic weakness and strength, as well as that of all men of genius similarly situated. Roman Catholicism, in our judgment, is not Christianity; but, by dwelling in its neighbourhood, and trying to mimic its marvellous results, it has imbibed a portion of its spirit, and bears nearly that relation to it which Judaism would have done, had it been contemporaneous with, instead of prior to the Christian scheme. Besides, the admixture of fiction, the amount of ceremony, the quantity to be *supposed,* to be implicitly believed, to be loved without reason, and admitted without proof,—all this renders Popery favourable to the exercise of the poetic imagination; while, on the other hand, the false and useless mystery, the tame subjection it requires of soul and heart and intellect, its "proud limitary spirit," the routine of idle monotonous rite,—stamp a certain vulgarity upon it, against which the wings of lofty genius have to struggle, and often to struggle in vain. In Crashaw, the struggle is generally successful. He looks at Popery, not as Dryden does, through the cold medium of the intellect, but through the burning haze of the imagination. His spirit is generally that of a true Christian poet, although considerably perverted by a false and bad form of the religion. In soaring imagination, in gorgeous language, in ardent enthusiasm, and in ecstasy of lyrical movement, Crashaw very much resembles Shelley, and may be called indeed the Christian Shelley.

His raptures are,
All air and fire.

His verse is pervaded everywhere by that fine madness, characteristic of the higher order of bards.

There can, we think, be little doubt that a great deal of Popish, and not a little of Protestant piety, is animalism inverted and transfigured. The saying of Pope about lust, "through certain strainers well-refined," becoming "gentle love," admits of another application. Desire, thrown into a new channel, becomes devotion—devotion sincere and strong, although assuming a spurious and exaggerated form. Hence in some writers, the same epithets are applied to the Saviour and to God, which in others are used to the objects of earthly tenderness, and we are disgusted with a profusion of "sweet Saviour," "dear lovely Jesus," &c. In the writings of the mystics, in the poems for instance of Madame Guion, you see a temperament of the warmest kind turned into the channel of a high-soaring and rather superstitious piety. Conceive of Anacreon converted, and beginning to sing of celestial love, in the same numbers with which he had previously chanted the praises of women and wine! Nay, we need not make any such supposition. Moore—the modern Anacreon—has written Hebrew melodies, in which you find something of the same lusciousness of tone as in Tom Little's poems; the *nature* coming out irresistibly in both. We are far from questioning the sincerity of these writers, and far from denying that they are better employed when singing of Divine things, than when fanning the flames of earthly passion; but we should ever be ready, while reading their strains, to *subtract* a good deal on account of their temperament. Such writers too frequently become mawkish, and loathsomely sweet, and thus at once repel the tasteful and gratify the profane. Croly says, somewhere, "our religion is a *manly* religion," but we would not refer those who wished a proof of this to the love-sick and sentimental class in question, who seem to prefer Solomon's Song to every other book of the Bible, and without the excuse of oriental day, discover all the languor and voluptuousness of the oriental bosom. There is, too, considerable danger of a reaction on their part—that the fire, after turning up its crest for a season toward heaven, should sink into its old furnace again, and that then their "last state should be worse than the first."

These remarks apply in some measure to Crashaw, although the strength of his genius in a measure counteracts the impression. Yet, often you hear the language of earthly instead of celestial love, and discover a certain swooning, languishing voluptuousness of feeling, as when in his lines on Teresa, he says:

Oh, what delight when she shall stand,
And teach *thy lips Heaven* with her hand,
On which thou now may'st to thy wishes
Heap up thy *consecrated kisses.*
What joy shall seize thy soul when she,
Bending her blessed eyes on thee,
Those second smiles of Heaven, shall dart
Her mild rays through thy *melting* heart.

More offensive are the following lines on "The Wounds of our Crucified Lord:"

O thou, that on this foot hast laid,
Many a kiss, and many a tear.
Now thou shalt have all repaid,
Whatsoe'er thy charges were.
This foot hath got a mouth and lips,
To pay the *sweet sum of thy kisses;*
To pay thy tears, an eye that weeps,
Instead of tears, such gems as this is.

We may remark, in passing, how different and how far superior is Milton's language in reference to women to that of the Crashaw school! How respectful, dignified, admiring, yet modest and delicate, all Milton's allusions to female beauty! How different from the tone of languishment, the everlasting talk about "sighs, " and "kisses," and "bosoms," found in some parts of our poet! Milton seems as much struck with woman's resemblance to, as with her difference from man, and regards her as a fainter stamp of the same Divine image—fainter but more exquisitely finished: her smile that of man, dying away in a dimple of loveliness, the lovelier for the dissolution; her eye his, less, but seeming sometimes larger from the tenderness with which it is filled; her brow his, in minia-desire, and shedding a mild steadfast moonlight on the whole picture and scheme of things;—all this, and much more than all this, to be found in Roman Catholicism, is calculated to please the fancy or delight the taste, or to rouse and rivet the imagination. All this Milton, as well as Crashaw, understood and felt; but he had the intellectual strength and moral hardihood to resist their fascination. He entered the splendid Catholic temple, and he did not refuse his admiration, he bathed his brow in the "dim religious light," he praised the pictures, he was ravished with the music, but he did not remain to worship; he turned away in sorrow and in anger, saying, "It is iniquity, even the solemn meeting: your new moons and your appointed feasts my soul hateth: they are a trouble unto me; I am weary to bear them." Crashaw, on the other hand, seems, without a struggle, to have yielded to the soft seductions of the system, and was soon sighingly but luxuriously lost.

He is a strong man, but no Milton—nay, rather a strong man unnerved by perfumes and lulled with unhealthy opiates—who writes the following lines "in a prayer-book:"

> Am'rous languishments, luminous trances,
>> Sights which are not seen with eyes,
> Spiritual and soul-piercing glances,
>> Whose pure and subtle lightning flies
> Home to the heart, and sets the house on fire,
> And melts it down in sweet desire,
>> Yet doth not stay
> To ask the windows' leave to pass that way.
> Delicious deaths, soft exhalations
> Of soul! dear, and divine annihilations!
>> A thousand unknown rites
>> Of joys, and rarefied delights;
> An hundred thousand loves and graces,
>> And many a mystic thing,
>> Which the divine embraces
> Of th' dear spouse of spirits with them will bring.

If our readers will turn to Shelley, and read his "Lines addressed to the noble and unfortunate Lady Emilia V—." they will find extremes meeting, and that the sceptical Shelley, and the Roman Catholic Crashaw, write, the one of earthly, nay, illicit love, and the other of spiritual communion, in language marvellously similar both in beauty and extravagance. These two poets resembled each other in the weakness that was bound up with their strength. Their fault was an excess of the emotional—a morbid excitability and enthusiasm, which in Shelley, and probably in Crashaw too, sprung from a scrofulous habit and a consumptive tendency. Shelley's conception of love, however, is in general purer and more ideal than that of the other poet.

Crashaw's volume is a small one, and yet small as it is, it contains a good deal of that quaint and tricky conceit, which Johnson has called, by a signal misnomer, "metaphysic." Crashaw, at least, has never mingled metaphysics with his poetry, although here and there he is as fantastic as Donne or Cowley, or any of the class. For instance, he writes thus on the text—"And he answered them nothing:"

> O mighty Nothing! unto thee,
> Nothing, we owe all things that be;
> God spake once when he all things made,
> He saved all when he nothing said.
> The world was made by Nothing then;
> 'Tis made by Nothing now again.

Johnson valued himself on his brief but vigorous account of the "Metaphysical Poets," in his *Life of Cowley*. We think, however, with all deference to his high critical authority, that not only has he used the word "metaphysical" in an arbitrary and inapposite sense, but that he has besides confounded wit with perverted ingenuity, and very much under-rated the genius of the men. He calls them, after Dryden, "wits, not poets," but if wit is almost always held to signify a *sudden perception of analogies more or less recondite,* along with a TENDENCY *to the ludicrous,* then these writers have very little of the quality indeed. They see and shew remote analogies, but the analogies are too remote or too grave to excite any laughable emotion. Coming from far—coming as captives—and coming violently chained together in pairs, they produce rather wonder, tinctured with melancholy, than that vivid delight which creates smiles, if it does not explode into laughter. Sometimes, indeed, the conceits produce a ridiculous effect, but this arises rather from their absurdity than their wit. Who can laugh, however, at such lines as these describing God harmonising the chaos?

> Water and air he for the *Tenor* chose,
> Earth made the *Base*—the *Treble* flame arose.

But apart from their perverted ingenuity, their straining after effect, their profusion of small and often crooked points, and their desire to shew their learning, these writers had undoubtedly high imagination. Cowley, in his poetry and in his prose, has given undeniable evidences of a genius at once versatile, elegant, and powerful—nay, we venture to uphold the great poetical merit of some of the lines Johnson quotes from him to condemn— of the following for example:

His bloody eyes he *hurls* round; his sharp paws
Tear up the ground—then runs he wild about,
Lashing his angry tail, and roaring out;
Beasts creep into their dens, and tremble there.
Trees, though no wind is stirring, shake for fear;
Silence and horror fill the place around,
Echo itself dares scarce repeat the sound.

These are bold metaphors, but they are not conceits. We feel them to rise naturally out of, and exactly to measure the majesty of the theme, not like conceits, to be *arbitrarily embossed* upon the shield of a subject, without any regard to its size, proportions, or general effect. We are happy to find De Quincy coinciding in part with our opinion of Johnson's criticism. Let us hear him speaking with a special reference to Donne: "Dr Johnson inconsiderately calls him and Cowley, &c., metaphysical poets, but rhetorical would have been a more accurate designation. In saying that, however, we revert to the original use of the word rhetoric, as laying the principal stress upon the management of the thoughts, and only a secondary one upon the ornaments of style. Few writers have shewn a more extraordinary compass of powers than Donne, for he combined the last sublimation of dialectical subtlety and address with the most impassioned majesty. Many diamonds compose the very substance of his poem on the Metempsychosis, thoughts and descriptions which have the fervent and gloomy sublimity of Ezekiel or Eschylus, whilst a diamond dust of rhetorical brilliance is strewed over the whole of his occasional verses and his prose. No criticism was ever more unhappy than that of Dr Johnson, which denounces all this artificial display as so much perversion of taste. There cannot be a falser thought than this, for upon that principle a whole class of compositions might be vicious by conforming to its own ideal. The artifice and machinery of rhetoric furnishes in its degree as legitimate a basis for intellectual pleasure as any other—that the pleasure is of an inferior order can no more attaint the idea or model of the composition, than it can impeach the excellence of an epigram that it is not a tragedy. Every species of composition is to be tried by its own laws."

Here it will be noticed that De Quincy takes somewhat different ground from what we would take in reply to Johnson. He seems to think that Johnson principally objected to the *manner* of these writers, and he argues, very justly, that as professed rhetoricians they had a right to use the artifices of rhetoric, and none the less that they wrote in metre;

and he might have maintained, besides, that finding a peculiar mode of writing in fashion, they were quite as justifiable in using it, IF they did not caricature it, as in wearing the bag, sword, and ruffles of their day. But Johnson, besides, denied that these men were poets; he objected to the *matter* as well as the manner of their song; and here we join issue with him, nay, are ready to admit that they were often rhetorically faulty, even by their own standard, if it be granted that they possessed a real and sublime poetic genius. That De Quincy agrees with us in this belief, we are certain, but it was his part to defend them upon another and a lower basis of assault. The most powerful passage in Johnson's account of the Metaphysical Poets is that in which he denies their claims to sublimity. He says with great eloquence—"The sublime was not within their reach—they never attempted that comprehension and expanse of mind, which at once filled the whole mind, and of which the first effect is sudden astonishment, and the second rational admiration. Sublimity is produced by aggregation, and littleness by dispersion. Great thoughts are always general, and consist in positions not limited by exceptions, and in descriptions not descending to minuteness. It is with great propriety that subtlety, which in its original import means exility of particles, is taken, in its metaphorical meaning, for nicety of distinction. Those writers who lay on the watch for novelty could have little hope of greatness; for great things cannot have escaped former observation. Their attempts were always analytic; they broke every image into fragments, and could no more represent, by their slender conceits and laboured particularities, the prospects of nature or the scenes of life, than he who dissects a sunbeam with a prism can exhibit the wide effulgence of a summer's noon."

In these remarks there is much truth as well as splendour; but Dr Johnson seems to forget that with all the elaborate pettiness of much in their writings—Cowley in portions of his "Davideis;" Donne in his "Metempsychosis;" Crashaw in his "Sospetto d'Herode;" Quarles in a few of his "Emblems;" and Herbert in certain parts of his *Temple*, have, perhaps *in spite* of their own system, attained a rare grandeur of thought and language. He might have remembered, too, that in prose Jeremy Taylor and Sir Thomas Browne, who both sinned in over-subtlety and subdivision of thinking, and were "Metaphysical Prose Poets," have both produced passages surpassed by nothing, even in Milton, for sublimity of imagination. He says "Great things cannot have escaped former observation;" but surely, although all men in all ages have seen the sun, the ocean, the earth, and the stars, new aspects of them are often presenting themselves to the poetic eye:

all men in all ages have seen the sun, but did all men from the beginning see him eclipsed at noonday in May 1836? all men have seen the stars, but have all looked through a Rossian telescope at the Moon, Mars, or Saturn? The truth is, Dr Johnson had great sympathy with the broad—the materially sublime and the colossally great; but, from a defect in eyesight and in mind, had little or none with either the beautiful or the subtle, and did not perceive the exquisite effects which a minute use of the knowledge of both these often produces. Of the great passages of Milton he had much admiration, but could not understand such lines as—

> Many a winding bout
> Of linked sweetness long drawn out,—

as what a poet calls it—"a charming embodiment of thin air and sound in something palpable, tangible, malleable;" nor that other wondrous line of "imaginative incarnation"—

> Rose like a steam of rich, distill'd perfumes;

nor would he have, we fear, admired Crashaw's "Music's Duel," which, altogether, we think, is not only his finest effort, but accomplishes with magical ease one of the most difficult of poetic tasks, and seems almost higher than nature. Like an Arabian sorcerer, the soul of the poet leaps back and forward, from the musician to the bird, entering into the very heart, and living in the very voice of each. Let our readers read the whole, and they will agree with us that they have read the most deliciously-true and incredibly-sustained piece of poetry in probably the whole compass of the language.

Just think of this; could Shakspeare have surpassed it?—

> Her supple breast thrills out
> Sharp airs, and *staggers in a warbling doubt*
> Of dallying sweetness, hovers o'er her skill,
> And *folds in wav'd notes with a trembling bill*
> The *pliant series of her slipp'ry song;*
> Then starts she suddenly into a throng
> Of short, thick sobs,

We may close by strongly recommending to our readers the "Sospetto d'Herode," that fine transfusion of Crashaw's—a poem from which Milton, in his "Hymn on the Nativity," has derived a good deal; and by expressing the peculiar satisfaction with which we present the public with a handsome edition of the too little known productions of this exquisite poet.

—George Gilfillan, from "The Life and
Poetry of Richard Crashaw," *Poetical Works
of Richard Crashaw*, 1857, pp. viii–xviii

DAVID MASSON (1858)

Had Milton, before leaving Christ's College, become acquainted with the
younger versifier of Pembroke, and read his "Music's Duel," his "Elegies
on the Death of Mr. Herrys," and such other pieces of verse, original or
translated, as he then had to show, he would have found in them a sensuous
beauty of style and sweetness of rhythm quite to his taste.

. . . On the whole, there was a richer vein of poetical genius in Crashaw
than in Herbert. . . . Apart from the modified intellectual assent expressly
accorded by Donne, by Ferrar, and by others, to some of the Catholic
doctrines which Crashaw seems to have made his spiritual diet, we trace a
more occult effect of the same influence in a rhetorical peculiarity common
to many of the writers of this theological school. We cannot define the
peculiarity better than by saying that it consists in a certain flowing
effeminacy of expression, a certain languid sensualism of fancy, or, to be
still more particular, an almost cloying use of the words, "sweet," "dear," and
their cognates, in reference to all kinds of objects.

—David Masson, *The Life of
John Milton*, 1858, vol. 1, ch. 6

WILLIAM B. TURNBULL
"PRELIMINARY OBSERVATIONS" (1858)

One of Crashaw's more prominent editors, William B. Turnbull (1811–1863)
was a Scottish scholar and author.

As a poet, his works have ever been appreciated by those most qualified
to decide upon their sterling beauties, and have suggested to others (too
frequently without acknowledgment) some of their finest imageries. In every
volume of any pretensions to taste, designed to offer specimens of English
poetry, extracts are to be found; yet, with the exception of being partially,
and by no means accurately, printed in the bulky and inconvenient
collections of Chalmers and Anderson, it is somewhat remarkable that, in

an age when familiarity with our Old English Authors is so eagerly sought, a full reprint should have been deferred till now.

—William B. Turnbull, "Preliminary
Observations," *Complete Works of
Richard Crashaw,* 1858, p. x

D.F. M'Carthy "Crashaw and Shelley" (1858)

The Irish poet Denis Florence M'Carthy or MacCarthy (1817–82) was also a prominent translator and political writer. Below, M'Carthy compares Crashaw to English Romantic poet Percy Bysshe Shelley (1792–1822). Though the two authors are from different eras and belong to different schools of poetry, M'Carthy's brief comparison points out a few similarties he spies in their two bodies of work.

Having said so much on this subject, I fear I cannot point out as much in detail as I would wish, a very striking peculiarity in Crashaw's lyrical poems which seems deserving of special attention. I refer to the extraordinary resemblance both in structure, sentiment, and occasionally in expression, which many passages (that are comparatively less spoiled than others by the prevailing bad taste of Crashaw's time) bear to the lyrics of that first of England's poet-lyrists,—I of course mean Shelley. Strange as it may appear, there are many things in common between them. They both, at great personal sacrifices, and with equal disinterestedness, embraced what they conceived to be the truth. Fortunately, in Crashaw's case, Truth and Faith were synonymous; unhappily with Shelley the Abnegation of Faith seemed to be of more importance than the reception of any tangible or intelligible substitute. Both were persecuted, neglected, and misunderstood; and both terminated their brief lives, at about the same age, on opposite shores of the same beautiful country, whither even at that early period "The Swans of Albion" had begun to resort, there perchance in a moment of peace to sing one immortal death-song, and so die.

—D.F. M'Carthy, "Crashaw and Shelley,"
Notes and Queries, June 5, 1858, p. 419

George L. Craik (1861)

He is perhaps, after Donne, the greatest of these religious poets of the early part of the seventeenth century. He belongs in manner to the same school with Donne and Herrick, and in his lighter pieces he has much of their lyrical sweetness and delicacy; but there is often a force and even occasionally what may be called a grandeur of imagination in his more solemn poetry which Herrick never either reaches or aspires to.

—George L. Craik, *A Compendious*
History of English Literature and
of the English Language, 1861, vol. 2, p. 20

GEORGE MACDONALD
"CRASHAW AND MARVELL" (1868)

In the piece below, MacDonald comments on several of Crashaw's better-known works. MacDonald suggests that Crashaw was highly influenced by his conversion to Roman Catholicism, and compares Crashaw favorably to William Drummond and Percy Bysshe Shelley. MacDonald then briefly comments on "The Weeper," which he suggests is "radiant of delicate fancy." He also notes briefly on several of Crashaw's *Divine Epigrams,* including "Come, See the Place Where the Lord Lay," "Two Went Up Into the Temple to Pray" (which MacDonald labels "perfect,") and "I Am Not Worthy That Thou Shouldst Come Under My Roof." MacDonald also examines Crashaw's famous poem "Easter Day" before concluding with "A Hymn of the Nativity Sung by the Shepherds." Students writing on any of these works may find MacDonald's insights useful in further elucidating these particular texts.

I come now to one of the loveliest of our angel-birds, Richard Crashaw. Indeed he was like a bird in more senses than one; for he belongs to that class of men who seem hardly ever to get foot-hold of this world, but are ever floating in the upper air of it.

What I said of a peculiar Æolian word-music in William Drummond applies with equal truth to Crashaw; while of our own poets, somehow or other, he reminds me of Shelley, in the silvery shine and bell-like melody both of his verse and his imagery; and in one of his poems, *Music's Duel,* the fineness of his phrase reminds me of Keats. But I must not forget that it is only with his sacred, his best poems too, that I am now concerned.

The date of his birth is not known with certainty, but it is judged about 1616, the year of Shakspere's death. He was the son of a Protestant clergyman zealous even to controversy. By a not unnatural reaction Crashaw, by that time, it is said, a popular preacher, when expelled from Oxford in 1644 by the Puritan Parliament because of his refusal to sign their Covenant, became a Roman Catholic. He died about the age of thirty-four, a canon of the Church of Loretto. There is much in his verses of that sentimentalism which, I have already said in speaking of Southwell, is rife in modern Catholic poetry. I will give from Crashaw a specimen of the kind of it. Avoiding a more sacred object, one stanza from a poem of thirty-one, most musical, and full of lovely speech concerning the tears of Mary Magdalen, will suit my purpose.

> Hail, sister springs,
> Parents of silver-footed rills!
> Ever-bubbling things!
> Thawing crystal! Snowy hills,
> Still spending, never spent!—I mean
> Thy fair eyes, sweet Magdalene!

The poem is called *The Weeper,* and is radiant of delicate fancy. But surely such tones are not worthy of fitting moth-like about the holy sorrow of a repentant woman! Fantastically beautiful, they but play with her grief. Sorrow herself would put her shoes off her feet in approaching the weeping Magdalene. They make much of her indeed, but they show her little reverence. There is in them, notwithstanding their fervour of amorous words, a coldness like that which dwells in the ghostly beauty of icicles shining in the moon.

But I almost reproach myself for introducing Crashaw thus. I had to point out the fact, and now having done with it, I could heartily wish I had room to expatiate on his loveliness even in such poems as *The Weeper.*

His Divine *Epigrams* are not the most beautiful, but they are to me the most valuable of his verses, inasmuch as they make us feel afresh the truth which he sets forth anew. In them some of the facts of our Lord's life and teaching look out upon us as from clear windows of the past. As epigrams, too, they are excellent—pointed as a lance.

UPON THE SEPULCHRE OF OUR LORD
Here, where our Lord once laid his head,
Now the grave lies buried.

THE WIDOW'S MITES
Two mites, two drops, yet all her house and land,

Fall from a steady heart, though trembling hand;
The other's wanton wealth foams high and brave:
The other cast away—she only gave.

ON THE PRODIGAL
Tell me, bright boy! tell me, my golden lad!
Whither away so frolic? Why so glad?
What! *all* thy wealth in council? *all* thy state?
Are husks so dear? Troth, 'tis a mighty rate!

I value the following as a lovely parable. Mary is not contented: to
see the place is little comfort. The church itself, with all its memories of
the Lord, the gospel-story, and all theory about him, is but his tomb until
we find himself.

Come, see the place where the Lord lay

SHOW ME HIMSELF, HIMSELF, BRIGHT SIR! OH SHOW
Which way my poor tears to himself may go.
Were it enough to show the place, and say,
"Look, Mary; here see where thy Lord once lay;"
Then could I show these arms of mine, and say,
"Look, Mary; here see where thy Lord once lay."

From one of eight lines, on the Mother Mary looking on her child in
her lap, I take the last two, complete in themselves, and I think best alone.

This new guest to her eyes new laws hath given:
'Twas once *look up,* 'tis now *look down to heaven.*

And there is perhaps his best.

TWO WENT UP INTO THE TEMPLE TO PRAY
Two went to pray? Oh rather say,
One went to brag, the other to pray.
One stands up close, and treads on high,
Where the other dares not lend his eye.
One nearer to God's altar trod;
The other to the altar's God.

This appears to me perfect. Here is the true relation between the forms
and the end of religion. The priesthood, the altar and all its ceremonies,
must vanish from between the sinner and his God. When the priest forgets
his mediation of a servant, his duty of a door-keeper to the temple of truth,

and takes upon him the office of an intercessor, he stands between man and God, and is a Satan, an adversary. Artistically considered, the poem could hardly be improved.

Here is another containing a similar lesson.

I AM NOT WORTHY THAT THOU SHOULDST
COME UNDER MY ROOF
Thy God was making haste into thy roof;
Thy humble faith and fear keeps him aloof.
He'll be thy guest: because he may not be,
He'll come—into thy house? No; into thee.

The following is a world-wide intercession for them that know not what they do. Of those that reject the truth, who can be said ever to have *truly* seen it? A man must be good to see truth. It is a thought suggested by our Lord's words, not an irreverent opposition to the truth of *them*.

BUT NOW THEY HAVE SEEN AND HATED
Seen? and yet *hated thee?* They did not see—
They saw thee not, that saw and hated thee!
No, no; they saw thee not, O Life! O Love!
Who saw aught in thee that their hate could move.

We must not be too ready to quarrel with every oddity: an oddity will sometimes just give the start to an outbreak of song. The strangeness of the following hymn rises almost into grandeur.

EASTER DAY
    Rise, heir of fresh eternity,
      From thy virgin-tomb;
Rise, mighty man of wonders, and thy world with
    thee;
      Thy tomb, the universal East—
        Nature's new womb;
Thy tomb—fair Immortality's perfumed nest.
    Of all the glories make noon gay
      This is the morn;
This rock buds forth the fountain of the streams of
    day;
      In joy's white annals lives this hour,
        When life was born,

No cloud-scowl on his radiant lids, no tempest-
   lower.
     Life, by this light's nativity,
       All creatures have;
Death only by this day's just doom is forced to die.
     Nor is death forced; for, may he lie
       Throned in thy grave,
Death will on this condition be content to die.

When we come, in the writings of one who has revealed masterdom, upon any passage that seems commonplace, or any figure that suggests nothing true, the part of wisdom is to brood over that point; for the probability is that the barrenness lies in us, two factors being necessary for the result of sight— the thing to be seen and the eye to see it. No doubt the expression may be inadequate, but if we can compensate the deficiency by adding more vision, so much the better for us.

In the second stanza there is a strange combination of images: the rock buds; and buds a fountain; the fountain is light. But the images are so much one at the root, that they slide gracefully into each other, and there is no confusion or incongruity: the result is an inclined plane of development.

I now come to the most musical and most graceful, therefore most lyrical, of his poems. I have left out just three stanzas, because of the sentimentalism of which I have spoken: I would have left out more if I could have done so without spoiling the symmetry of the poem. My reader must be friendly enough to one who is so friendly to him, to let his peculiarities pass unquestioned—amongst the rest his conceits, as well as the trifling discord that the shepherds should be called, after the classical fashion—ill agreeing, from its associations, with Christian song—Tityrus and Thyrsis.

A HYMN OF THE NATIVITY SUNG BY THE SHEPHERDS
Chorus: Come, we shepherds, whose blest sight
   Hath met love's noon in nature's night;
   Come, lift we up our loftier song,
   And wake the sun that lies too long.
   To all our world of well-stolen[1] joy
      He slept, and dreamed of no such thing,
   While we found out heaven's fairer eye,
     And kissed the cradle of our king:

Tell him he rises now too late
To show us aught worth looking at.
Tell him we now can show him more
    Than he e'er showed to mortal sight—
Than he himself e'er saw before,
   Which to be seen needs not his light:
Tell him, Tityrus, where thou hast been;
Tell him, Thyrsis, what thou hast seen.

Tityrus: Gloomy night embraced the place
    Where the noble infant lay:
The babe looked up and showed his face:
   In spite of darkness it was day.
It was thy day, sweet, and did rise
Not from the east, but from thy eyes.

Chorus: It was thy day, sweet, &c.

Thyrsis: Winter chid aloud, and sent
    The angry north to wage his wars:
The north forgot his fierce intent,
   And left perfumes instead of scars.
By those sweet eyes' persuasive powers,
Where he meant frosts, he scattered flowers.

Chorus: By those sweet eyes', &c.

Both: We saw thee in thy balmy nest,
    Young dawn of our eternal day;
We saw thine eyes break from the east,
   And chase the trembling shades away.
We saw thee, and we blessed the sight;
We saw thee by thine own sweet light.

Chorus: We saw thee, &c.

Tityrus: "Poor world," said I, "what wilt thou do
    To entertain this starry stranger?
Is this the best thou canst bestow—
   A cold and not too cleanly manger?
Contend, the powers of heaven and earth,
To fit a bed for this huge birth."

Chorus: Contend, the powers, &c.

Thyrsis: "Proud world," said I, "cease your contest,
    And let the mighty babe alone:
The phoenix builds the phoenix' nest—

Love's architecture is his own.
The babe, whose birth embraves this morn,
Made his own bed ere he was born."
Chorus: The babe, whose birth, &c.
Tityrus: I saw the curl'd drops, soft and slow,
    Come hovering o'er the place's head,
Offering their whitest sheets of snow
    To furnish the fair infant's bed:
"Forbear," said I; "be not too bold:
Your fleece is white, but 'tis too cold."
Chorus: "Forbear,   said I, Arc.
Thyrsis: I saw the obsequious seraphim
    Their rosy fleece of fire bestow;
For well they now can spare their wings,
    Since heaven itself lies here below.
"Well done," said I; "but are you sure
Your down, so warm, will pass for pure?"
Chorus: "Well done," said I, &c.

. . .

Full Chorus: Welcome all wonders in one sight!
    Eternity shut in a span!
Summer in winter! day in night!
    Heaven in earth, and God in man!
Great little one, whose all-embracing birth
Lifts earth to heaven, stoops heaven to earth!

. . .

Welcome—though not to those gay flies
    Gilded i' th' beams of earthly kings—
Slippery souls in smiling eyes—
But to poor shepherds, homespun things,
Whose wealth's their flocks, whose wit's to be
Well read in their simplicity.
Yet when young April's husband showers
    Shall bless the fruitful Maia's bed,
We'll bring the firstborn of her flowers
    To kiss thy feet, and crown thy head:
To thee, dear Lamb! whose love must keep
The shepherds while they feed their sheep.
To thee, meek Majesty, soft king

> Of simple graces and sweet loves,
> Each of us his lamb will bring,
> Each his pair of silver doves.
> At last, in fire of thy fair eyes,
> Ourselves become our own best sacrifice.

A splendid line to end with! too good for the preceding one. All temples and altars, all priesthoods and prayers, must vanish in this one and only sacrifice. Exquisite, however, as the poem is, we cannot help wishing it looked less heathenish. Its decorations are certainly meretricious.

Notes

1. How unpleasant conceit can become. The joy of seeing the Saviour was *stolen* because they gained it in the absence of the sun!

—George MacDonald, from
"Crashaw and Marvell," *England's
Antiphon*, 1868, pp. 238–46

ALEXANDER B. GROSART "ESSAY ON THE LIFE AND POETRY OF CRASHAW" (1873)

Grosart's text begins with the author declaring that he will be discussing "Four things . . . in order to give the essentials of Crashaw as a Poet, and to gather his main characteristics: *(a)* Imaginative-sensuousness; *(b)* Subtlety of emotion; (c) Epigrams; *(d)* Translations and (briefly) Latin and Greek Poetry." However, only the first two, the most significant parts of Grosart's study, are included in the excerpt below.

Crashaw's "Imaginative-sensuousness" leads Grosart into a heady and useful examination of Crashaw's literary imagination. Grosart focuses on the root of the word "sensuousness," meaning the five senses, and not the more modern, carnal aspect of what the word "sensuous" or "sensual" might mean. In this respect, Grosart praises Crashaw's "peculiar gift of looking at everything with a full, open, penetrative eye, yet through his imagination; his imagination not being as spectacles (coloured) astride the nose, but as a light of white glory all over his intellect and entire faculties." Grosart declares that Crashaw's important piece "The Weeper" is one of the best places to see Crashaw's poetic imagination in action, and what follows is perhaps the most useful discussion of that poem included in this study, as Grosart uses the poem itself and George MacDonald's criticism of it to launch a substantial examination of the piece, one that any individual studying Crashaw will find eminently suggestive.

Regarding Crashaw's "subtlety of emotions," Grosart proposes that this aspect of the poet is best viewed in his sacred work (several pieces are briefly mentioned throughout this section of the essay.) Grosart writes that Crashaw's "thinking . . . was so emotional as almost always to tremble into feeling." Grosart suggests this represents a rejection of the intellectual aspect of metaphysic poetry that those poets are often chided for; instead, Crashaw embraces the emotional aspects of poetry through his muse, Mary, Mother of God, who Crashaw pays homage to throughout his sacred works. Grosart's indication that Crashaw is particularly inspired by Mary is an interesting counterpoint to Gilfillan's essay above, who criticizes Crashaw's "Popery" and negative representation of women. Grosart's handling of Crashaw's sacred work presents a differing perspective on how Crashaw's faith influenced his poetry, and students working in this area would do well to take note.

⁓⁓⁓　⁓⁓⁓　⁓⁓⁓

Four things appear to me to call for examination, in order to give the essentials of Crashaw as a Poet, and to gather his main characteristics: *(a)* Imaginative-sensuousness; *(b)* Subtlety of emotion; (c) Epigrams; *(d)* Translations and (briefly) Latin and Greek Poetry. I would say a little on each.

(a) Imaginative-sensuousness. Like 'charity' for 'love,' the word 'sensuous' has deteriorated in our day. It is, I fear, more than in sound and root confused with 'sensual,' in its base application. I use it as Milton did, in the well-known passage when he defined Poetry to be 'simple, *sensuous,* and passionate;' and I qualify 'sensuousness' with 'imaginative,' that I may express our Poet's peculiar gift of looking at everything with a full, open, penetrative eye, yet through his imagination; his imagination not being as spectacles (coloured) astride the nose, but as a light of white glory all over his intellect and entire faculties. Only Wordsworth and Shelley, and recently Rossetti and Jean Ingelow, are comparable with him in this. You can scarcely err in opening on any page in your out-look for it. The very first poem, 'The Weeper,' is lustrous with it. For example, what a grand reach of 'imaginative' comprehensiveness have we so early as in the second stanza, where from the swimming eyes of his 'Magdalene' he was, as it were, swept upward to the broad transfigured sky in its wild ever-varying beauty of the glittering silver rain!

> Heauns thy fair eyes be;
>> Heauens of ever-falling starres.
>> 'Tis seed-time still with thee;

> And starres thou sow'st whose haruest dares
> Promise the Earth to counter-shine
> Whateuer makes heaun's forehead fine.

How grandly vague is that 'counter-shine *whatever,*' as it leads upwards to the 'forehead'—superb, awful, Godcrowned—of the 'heauns'! Of the same in kind, but unutterably sweet and dainty also in its exquisiteness, is stanza vii.:

> The deaw no more will weap
> The primrose's pale cheek to deck:
> The deaw no more will sleep
> Nuzzel'd in the lily's neck:
> Much rather would it be thy tear,
> And leaue them both to tremble there.

Wordsworth's vision of the 'flashing daffodils' is not finer than this. A merely realistic Poet (as John Clare or Bloomfield) would never have used the glorious singular, 'thy tear,' with its marvellous suggestiveness of the multitudinous dew regarding itself as outweighed in everything by one 'tear' of such eyes. Every stanza gives a text for commentary; and the rapid, crowding questions and replies of the Tears culminate in the splendid homage to the Saviour in the conclusion, touched with a gentle scorn:

> We goe not to seek
> The darlings of Aurora's bed,
> The rose's modest cheek,
> Nor the violet's humble head,
> Though the feild's eyes too
> Weepers be, Because they want such teares as we.
> Much lesse mean to trace
> The fortune of inferior gemmes,
> Preferr'd to some proud face,
> Or pertch't vpon fear'd diadems:
> *Crown'd heads are toyes. We goe to meet*
> A worthy object, our *Lord's feet.*

'Feet' at highest; mark the humbleness, and the fitness too. Even more truly than of Donne (in Arthur Wilson's 'Elegy') may it be said of Crashaw, here and elsewhere, thou 'Couldst give both life and sense unto a flower,'— faint prelude of Wordsworth's 'meanest flower.'

Dr. Macdonald (in *Antiphon*) is perplexingly unsympathetic, or, if I may dare to say it, wooden, in his criticism on 'The Weeper;' for while he characterises it generally as 'radiant of delicate fancy,' he goes on: 'but surely such tones are not worthy of flitting moth-like about the holy sorrow of a repentant woman! Fantastically beautiful, they but play with her grief. Sorrow herself would put her shoes off her feet in approaching the weeping Magdalene. They make much of her indeed, but they show her little reverence. There is in them, notwithstanding their fervour of amorous words, a coldness, like that which dwells in the ghostly beauty of icicles shining in the moon' (p. 239). Fundamentally blundering is all this: for the Critic ought to have marked how the Poet's 'shoes' are put off his feet in approaching the weeping Magdalene; but that *she* is approached as far-back in the Past or in a Present wherein her tears have been 'wiped away' so that the poem is dedicate not so much to The Weeper as to her Tears, as things of beauty and pricelessness. Mary, 'blessed among women,' is remembered all through; and just as with her Divine Son we must 'sorrow' in the vision of His sorrows, we yet have the remembrance that they are all done, 'finished;' and thus we can expatiate on them not with grief so much as joy. The prolongation of 'The Weeper' is no 'moth-like flitting about the holy sorrow of a repentant woman,' but the never-to-be-satisfied rapture over the evidence of a 'godly sorrow' that has worked to repentance, and in its reward given loveliness and consecration to the tears shed. The moon 'shining on icicles' is the antithesis of the truth. Thus is it throughout, as in the backgrounds of the great Portrait-painters as distinguished from Land-scapists and Sea-scapists and Sky-scapists— Crashaw inevitably works out his thoughts through something he has looked at as transfigured by his imagination, so that you find his most mystical thinking and feeling framed (so to say) with images drawn from Nature. That he did look not at but into Nature, let 'On a foule Morning, being then to take a Journey,' and 'To the Morning; Satisfaction for Sleepe,' bear witness. In these there are penetrative 'looks' that Wordsworth never has surpassed, and a richness almost Shakesperean. Milton must have studied them keenly. There is this characteristic also in the 'sensuousness' of Crashaw, that while the Painter glorifies the ignoble and the coarse (as Hobbima's Asses and red-cloaked Old Women) in introducing it into a scene of Wood, or Wayside, or Sea-shore, his outward images and symbolism are worthy in themselves, and stainless as worthy (passing exceptions only establishing the rule). His epithets are never superfluous, and are, even to surprising nicety, true. Thus he calls Egypt '*white* Egypt' (vol. i. p. 81); and occurring as this does 'In the glorious Epiphanie of ovr Lord God,' we are reminded again how the youthful

Milton must have had this extraordinary composition in his recollection when he composed his immortal Ode.' Similarly we have *'hir'd* mist' (vol. i. p. 84); *'pretious* losse' (ib.); *'fair-ey'd* fallacy of Day' (ib. p. 85); *'black* but faithfull perspectiue of Thee' (ib. p. 86); *'abased* liddes' (ib. p. 88); *'gratious* robbery' (ib. p. 156); 'thirsts of loue' (ib.); *'timerous* light of starres' (ib. p. 172); *'rebellious* eye of Sorrow' (ib. p. 112); and so in hundreds of parallels. Take this from 'To the Name above every Name' (ib. p. 60):

> O come away . . .
> O, see the weary liddes of wakefull Hope—
> Love's eastern windowes—all wide ope
> With curtains drawn,
> To catch the day-break of Thy dawn.
> O, dawn at last, long-lookt-for Day,
> Take thine own wings, and come away.

Comparing Cowley's and Crashaw's 'Hope,' Coleridge thus pronounces on them: 'Crashaw seems in his poems to have given the first ebullience of his imagination, unshapen into form, or much of what we now term sweetness. In the poem Hope, by way of question and answer, his superiority to Cow-ley is self-evident;' and he continues, 'In that on the Name of Jesus, equally so; but his lines on St. Teresa are the finest.' 'Where he does combine richness of thought and diction, nothing can excel, as in the lines you so much admire,

> Since 'tis not to be had at home
> . . .
> She'l to the Moores and martyrdom.[2]

And then as never-to-be-forgotten 'glory' of the Hymn to Teresa, he adds: 'these verses were ever present to my mind whilst writing the second part of Christabel; if indeed, by some subtle process of the mind, they did not suggest the first thought of the whole poem' *(Letters and Conversations,* 1836, i. 196). Coleridge makes another critical remark which it may be worth while to adduce and perhaps qualify. 'Poetry as regards small Poets may be said to be, in a certain sense, conventional in its accidents and in its illustrations. Thus [even] Crashaw uses an image "as sugar melts in tea away;" which although *proper then* and *true now,* was in bad taste at that time equally with the present. In Shakespeare, in Chaucer, there was nothing of this' (as before). The great Critic forgot that 'sugar' and 'tea' were not vulgarised by familiarity when Crashaw wrote, that the wonder and romance of their gift from the East still lay around them, and that their use was select, not common. Thus later I explain Milton's homeliness of allusion, as in the word 'breakfast,' and 'fell to,' and the like; words and places and things that have long been not prosaic simply, but demeaned and for ever unpoetised. I am not at all careful to defend the 'sugar' and 'tea' metaphor; but it, I think, belongs also to his imaginative-sensuousness, whereby orient awfulness almost, magnified and dignified it to him.

Moreover the canon in *Antiphon* is sound: 'When we come, in the writings of one who has revealed masterdom, upon any passage that seems commonplace, or any figure that suggests nothing true, the part of wisdom is to brood over that point; for the probability is that the barrenness lies in us, two factors being necessary for the result of sight—the thing to be seen, and the eye to see it. No doubt the expression may be inadequate; but if we can compensate the deficiency by adding more vision, so much the better for us' (p. 243).

I thank Dr. George Macdonald[3] (in *Antiphon*) for his quaint opening words on our Crashaw, and forgive him, for their sake, his blind reading of "The Weeper." 'I come now to one of the loveliest of our angel-birds, Richard Crashaw. Indeed, he was like a bird in more senses than one; for he belongs to that class of men who seem hardly ever to get foot-hold of this world, but are ever floating in the upper air of it' (p. 238). True, and yet not wholly; or rather, if our Poet ascends to 'the upper air,' and sings there with all the divineness of the skylark, like the skylark his eyes fail not to over-watch the nest among the grain beneath, nor his wings to be folded over it at the shut of eve. Infinitely more, then, is to be found in Crashaw than Pope (in his Letter to his friend Henry Cromwell) found: 'I take this poet to have writ like a gentleman; that is, at leisure hours, and more to keep out of idleness than to establish a reputation: so that nothing regular or just can be expected of him. All that regards design, form, fable (which is the soul of poetry), all that concerns exactness, or consent of parts (which is the body), will probably be wanting; only pretty conceptions, fine metaphors, glittering expressions, and something of a neat cast of verse (which are properly the dress, gems, or loose ornaments of poetry), may be found in these verses.' Nay verily, the form is often exquisite; but 'neat' and 'pretty conceptions' applied to such verse is as 'pretty' applied to Niagara—so full, strong, deep, thought-laden is it. I have no wish to charge plagiarism on Pope from Crashaw, as Peregrine Phillips did (see onward); but neither is the contemptuous as ignorant answer by a metaphor of Hayley to be received. The two minds were essentially different: Pope was talented, and used his talents to the utmost; Crashaw had absolute as unique genius.[4]

(b) Subtlety of emotion. Dr. Donne, in a memorable passage, with daring originality, sings of Mrs. Drury rapturously:

> Her pure and eloquent soul
> Spoke in her cheeks, and so distinctly wrought,
> That one might almost say her body thought.

I have much the same conception of Crashaw's thinking. It was so emotional as almost always to tremble into feeling. Bare intellect, 'pure' (= naked) thought, you rarely come on in his Poems. The thought issues forth from (in old-fashioned phrase) the heart, and its subtlety is something unearthly even to awfulness. Let the reader give hours to the study of the composition, entitled 'In the glorious Epiphanie of ovr Lord God, a Hymn svng as by the three Kings,' and 'In the holy Nativity of ovr Lord God.' Their depth combined with elevation, their grandeur softening into loveliness, their power with pathos, their awe bursting into rapture, their graciousness and lyrical music, their variety and yet unity, will grow in their study. As always, there is a solid substratum of original thought in them; and the thinking, as so often in Crashaw, is surcharged with emotion. If the thought may be likened to fire, the praise, the rapture, the yearning may be likened to flame leaping up from it. Granted that, as in fire and flame, there are coruscations and jets of smoke, yet is the smoke that 'smoak' of which Chudleigh in his 'Elegy for Donne' sings:

> Incense of love's and fancie's *holy smoak;*

or, rather, that 'smoke' which filled the House to the vision of Isaiah (vi. 4). The hymn 'To the admirable Sainte Teresa,' and the 'Apologie' for it, and related 'Flaming Heart,' and 'In the glorious Assvmption of our Blessed Lady,' are of the same type. Take this from the 'Flaming Heart' (vol. i. p. 155):

> Leaue her . . . the flaming heart:
> Leaue her that, and thou shalt leaue her
> Not one loose shaft, but Loue's whole quiver.
> *For in Loue's feild was neuer found*
> *A nobler weapon than a wovnd.*
> Loue's passiues are his actiu'st part,
> The wounded is the wounding heart.
> . . .
> Liue here, great heart; and loue and dy and kill,
> And bleed and wound; and yeild and conquer still.

His homage to the Virgin is put into words that pass the bounds which we Protestants set to the 'blessed among women' in her great renown, and even while a Protestant Crashaw fell into what we must regard as the strange as inexplicable forgetfulness that it is The *Man,* not The Child, who is our ever-living High-Priest 'within the veil,' and that not in His mother's bosom, but on the Throne of sculptured light, is His place. Still, you recognise that the homage to the Virgin-mother is to the Divine Son through her, and through her in fine if also mistaken humility. 'Mary' is the Muse of Crashaw; the Lord Jesus his 'Lord' and hers. I would have the reader spend willing time, in slowly, meditatively reading the whole of our Poet's sacred Verse, to note how the thinking thus thrills into feeling, and feeling into rapture—the rapture of adoration. It is miraculous how he finds words wherewith to utter his most subtle and vanishing emotion. Sometimes there is a daintiness and antique richness of wording that you can scarcely equal out of the highest of our Poets, or only in them. Some of his images from Nature are scarcely found anywhere else. For example, take this very difficult one of ice, in the 'Verse-Letter to the Countess of Denbigh' (vol. i. p. 298, 11. 21–26), 'persuading' her no longer to be the victim of her doubts:

> So, when the Year takes cold, we see
> Poor waters *their own prisoners be;*
> *Fetter'd and lock'd-up fast they lie*
> In a cold self-captivity.
> Th' astonish'd Nymphs their Floud's strange fate
>   deplore,

To find themselves their own severer shoar. Young is striking in his use of the ice-metaphor:

> in Passion's flame
> Hearts melt; but *melt like ice, soon harder froze.*
>   (Night-Thoughts, N. n. 1. 522–3.)

But how strangely original is the earlier Poet in so cunningly working it into the very matter of his persuasion! Our quotation from Young recalls that in the 'Night-Thoughts' there are evident reminiscences of Crashaw: *e.g.*

> Midnight veil'd his face:
> Not such as this, not such as Nature makes;
> A midnight Nature shudder'd to behold;

A midnight new; a dread eclipse, without
Opposing spheres, from her Creator's frown.
                    (Night iv. 11. 246–250.)

So in 'Gilt was Hell's gloom' (N. vn. 1. 1041), and in this portrait of Satan:

Like meteors in a stormy sky, how roll
His baleful eyes!
                    (N. ix. 11. 280–1.)

and

the fiery gulf,
That flaming bound of wrath omnipotent;
                    (Ib. 11. 473–4)

and

Banners streaming as the comet's blaze;
                    (Ib. 1. 323)

and

Which makes a hell of hell,
                    (Ib. 1. 340)

we have the impress and inspiration of our Poet.

How infinitely soft and tender and Shakesperean is the 'Epitaph vpon a yovng Married Covple dead and bvryed together' (with its now restored lines), thus!—

Peace, good Reader, doe not weep;
Peace, the louers are asleep.
They, sweet turtles, folded ly
In the last knott that Loue could ty.
And though they ly as they were dead,
Their pillow stone, their sheetes of lead
(Pillow hard, and sheetes not warm),
Loue made the bed; they'l take no harm:
Let them sleep; let them sleep on,
Till this stormy night be gone,
And the ajternall morrow dawn;
Then . . .
                    (vol. i. pp. 230–1.)

The hush, the tranquil stillness of a church-aisle, within which 'sleep' old recumbent figures, comes over one in reading these most pathetically beautiful words. Of the whole poem, Dodd in his 'Epigrammatists' (as onward) remarks, 'after reading this Epitaph, all others on the same subject must surfer by comparison.' Yet there is much to be admired in the following by Bishop Hall, on Sir Edward and Lady Lewkenor. It is translated from the Latin by the Bishop's descendant and editor, the Rev. Peter Hall (Bp. Hall's Works, 1837–9, xii. 331):

In bonds of love united, man and wife,
Long, yet too short, they spent a happy life;
United still, too soon, however late,
Both man and wife receiv'd the stroke of fate:
And now in glory clad, enraptur'd pair,
The same bright cup, the same sweet draught they
    share.
Thus, first and last, a married couple see,
In life, in death, in immortality.

There is much beauty also in an anonymous epitaph in the 'Festoon' 143, 'On a Man and his Wife:'

Here sleep, whom neither life nor love,
    Nor friendship's strictest tie,
Could in such close embrace as thou,
    Their faithful grave, ally;
Preserve them, each dissolv'd in each,
    For bands of love divine,
For union only more complete,
    Thou faithful grave, than thine.
                    (p. 253.)

His 'Wishes to his (supposed) Mistresse' has things in it vivid and subtle as anything in Shelley at his best; and I affirm this deliberately. His little snatch on 'Easter Day,' with some peculiarities, culminates in a grandeur Milton might bow before. The version of 'Dies Irae' is wonderfully severe and solemn and intense. Roscommon undoubtedly knew it. And so we might go on endlessly. His melody—with exceptional discords—is as the music of a Master, not mere versification. Once read receptively, and the words haunt almost awfully, and, I must again use the word, unearthily. Summarily—as in our claim for Vaughan, as against the preposterous traditional assertions of his indebtedness to Herbert poetically, while really it was for spiritual benefits he was obligated—we cannot for an instant rank George Herbert as a Poet with Crashaw. Their piety is alike, or the 'Priest' of Bemerton is more definite, and clear of the 'fine mist' of mysticism of the recluse of 'Little St. Mary's;' but only very rarely have you in *The Temple* that light of genius which shines as a very Shekinah-glory in the *Steps to the Temple*. These 'Steps' have been spoken of as 'Steps' designed to lead into Herbert's *Temple,* whereas they were 'Steps' to the 'Temple' or Church of the Living God. Crashaw 'sang' sweetly and generously of Herbert (vol. i. pp. 139-140); but the two Poets are profoundly distinct and independent. Clement Barksdale, probably, must bear the blame of foolishly subordinating Crashaw to Herbert, in his Lines in 'Nympha Libethris' (1651):

> HERBERT AND CRASHAW
> When unto Herbert's Temple I ascend
> By Crashaw's Steps, I do resolve to mend
> My lighter verse, and my low notes to raise,
> And in high accent sing my Maker's praise.
> Meanwhile these sacred poems in my sight
> I place, that I may learn to write.

Notes

1. The 'Epiphanie' has some of the grandest things of Crashaw, and things so original in the thought and wording as not easily to be paralleled in other Poets: *e.g. 'Dread* Sweet' (1. 236), and the superb 'Something a *brighter shadow,* Sweet, of thee' (1. 250). The most Crashaw-like of early 'Epiphany' or Christmas Hymns is that of Bishop Jeremy Taylor, from which I take these lines:

> Awake, my soul, and come away!
>   Put on thy best array;
>   Least if thou longer stay,
> Thou lose some minitts of so blest a day,
>   Goe run,
> And bid good-morrow to the sun;
> Welcome his safe return
>   To Capricorn;
> And that great Morne
> Wherein a God was borne,

Whose story none can tell,

But He whose every word's a miracle.

(Our ed. of Bp. Taylor's Poems, pp. 22–3.)

En *Passant,* since our edition of Bishop Taylor's *Poems* was issued we have discovered that a 'Christmas Anthem or Carol by T.P,' which appeared in James Clifford's 'Divine Services and Anthems' (1663), is Bishop Taylor's Hymn. This we learn from *The Musical Times,* Feb. 1st, 1871, in a paper on Clifford's book. Criticising the words as by an unknown T. P.—ignorant that he was really criticising Bp. Jeremy Taylor—the (I suppose) learned Writer thus appreciatively writes of the grand Hymn and these passionate yearning words: 'Who, for instance, could seriously sing in church such stuff as the following Christmas Anthem or Carol, by T. R? which Mr. William Childe (not yet made Doctor) had set to music' Ahem! And so on, in stone-eyed, stone-eared stupidity.—Of modern celebrations I name as worthy of higher recognition than it has received the following 'Hymn to the Week above every Week,' by Thomas II. Gill; Lon., Mudie, 1844 (pp. 24). There is no little of the rich quaint matter and manner of our elder Singers in this fine Poem.

2. Cf. vol. i. p. 143.

3. Like Macaulay in his *History of England* (1st edition), Dr. Macdonald by an oversight speaks of Crashaw as 'expelled from *Oxford,*' instead of Cambridge (cf. our vol. i. p. 32).

4. The Letter of Pope to Mr. Henry Cromwell is in all the editions of his Correspondence. Willmott (as before) also gives it *in extenso.* Of 'The Weeper' Pope says: 'To confirm what I have said, you need but look into his first poem of 'The Weeper,' where the 2d, 4th, 6th, 14th, 21st stanzas are as sublimely dull as the 7th, 8th, 9th, 16th, 17th, 20th, and 23d stanzas of the same copy are soft and pleasing. And if these last want anything, it is an easier and more unaffected expression. The remaining thoughts in that poem might have been spared, being either but repetitions, or very trivial and mean. And by this example one may guess at all the rest to be like this; a mixture offender gentle thoughts and suitable expressions, of forced and inextricable conceits, and of needless fillers-up of the rest,' &c. &c. 'Sweet' is the loftiest epithet Pope uses for Crashaw, and that in the knowledge of the 'Suspicion of Herod.' In 'The Weeper' he passes some of the very finest things. In his 'Abelard and Eloisa' he incorporates felicities from Crashaw's 'Alexias' within inverted commas; but elsewhere is not very careful to mark indebtedness.

—Alexander B. Grosart, from "Essay on
the Life and Poetry of Crashaw," *Complete Works
of Richard Crashaw*, vol. 2, 1873, pp. lxii–lxxv

MAURICE F. EGAN
"THREE CATHOLIC POETS" (1880)

Maurice F. Egan (1852–1924) was an American professor of English and
prominent Catholic author of fiction. In the piece below, Egan discusses
the poem "The Flaming Heart," which he writes "glows with an impetuous devotion which is like the rush of a fiery chariot." Like numerous
other critics in this collection, Egan greatly admires this piece, though
his perspective is enhanced by Crashaw's conversion and the distinctly
Catholic nature of the poem's subject matter. Still, he provides an
enthusiastic description of the poem that should prove useful to any
student writing on the now famous last section of the work.

If Richard Crashaw, a poet who, by reason of his entire devotion to his
faith and his absolute purity, belongs to this group (Southwell, Habington,
Crashaw), had written nothing except the final of "The Flaming Heart,"
he would deserve more fame than at present distinguishes his name.
"The Flaming Heart," marred as it is by those exasperating conceits which
Crashaw never seemed tired of indulging in, is full of the intense fervor which
the subject—"the picture of the seraphical Saint Teresa, as she is usually
expressed with seraphim beside her"—would naturally suggest to a religious
and poetic mind. After what Mr. Simcox very justly calls "an atrocious and
prolonged conceit," *(The English Poets)* this poem beautifully closes:

> O thou undaunted daughter of desires!
> By all thy dower of lights and fires;
> By all the eagle in thee, all the dove;
> By all thy lives and deaths of love;
> By thy large draughts of intellectual day,
> And by thy thirsts of love more large than they;
> By all thy brim-fill'd bowls of fierce desire,
> By thy last morning's draught of liquid fire,
> By the full kingdom of that final kiss
> That seized thy parting soul and sealed thee His;
> By all the heav'n thou hast in him,

(Fair sister of the seraphim!)
By all of him we have in thee,
Leave nothing of myself in me.
Let me so read thy life that I
Unto all life of mine may die.

The mystical fire which lights this poem is a characteristic of all Crashaw's religious verses. "Intellectual day" is a favorite expression of his; "the brim-fill'd bowls of fierce desire" is one of those lowering conceits that occur so jarringly in Habington's poetry and that are intolerably frequent in Crashaw. Born about 1615, he began to write at a time when a poem lacking in quaint conceits was scarcely a poem, and his verse, delicate, tender, original, and singularly fluent in diction, lost much strength from this circumstance and from his habit of diluting a thought or a line until all its force was lost. No poet since his time has been given so greatly to dilution and repetition, except Swinburne. In the famous "Wishes," written to a mythical mistress,

Whoe'er she be,
That not impossible she
That shall command my heart and me,

he plays with one idea, fantastically twisting it and repeating it until the reader grows weary.

In 1646, four years before his death, Richard Crashaw published "Steps to the Temple." Reading it, one may well exclaim, with Cowley:

Poet and saint to thee alone are given,
The two most sacred names in earth and heaven!

It glows with an impetuous devotion which is like the rush of a fiery chariot. It carries the soul upward, although an occasional earthly conceit clogs its ascending rush. And yet it is evident that the devotion of the poet was so genuine that he did not think of his mode of expression. He tore out the words that came nearest to him, in order to build a visible thought. Pope did not hesitate to borrow the finest passages in "Eloise and Abelard" from Crashaw, and there are many lines in Crashaw's poems which unite the perfect finish of Pope to a spontaneity and poetic warmth which the "great classic" never attained.

Crashaw was born in an "intellectual day" tempered by a dim religious light. His father, like Habington's, was an author, a preacher in the Temple Church, London, near which the poet was born. He took his degree at Cambridge. He entered the Anglican Church as a minister. But his views were not orthodox; he was expelled from his living, and soon after he became a Catholic. From his poems it is plain that Crashaw was always a Catholic at heart. He entered the church as one who, having lived in a half-forgotten place in dreams, enters it without surprise. Crashaw went to court, but gained no preferment. The "not impossible she" whose courtly opposites suggested the portrait never "materialized" herself. He became a priest, and died in 1650, canon of Loretto—an office which he obtained, it is said, through the influence of the exiled Queen Henrietta Maria. Crashaw's poems are better known than Habington's, though, with the exception of "Wishes," which, like Herrick's "To Daffodils," is quoted in almost every reader, and the lovely poem beginning,

> Lo! here a little volume but large book,
> > (Fear it not, sweet,
> > It is no hypocrite,)
> Much larger in itself than in its look,

they are read only in odd lines or striking couplets. Crashaw had the softened fire of Southwell with the placid sweetness of Habington. He possessed a wider range than either of them; the fact that he was at his best in paraphrases shows that he did not own the force and power which Habington had in less degree than Southwell, or that his fluency of diction and copiousness of imagery easily led him to ornament the work of others rather than to carve out his own. As he stands, any country—even that which boasts of a Shakspere—may be proud to claim him. For the fame of our three Catholic poets it is unfortunate that they wrote in the great shade of Shakspere; but in the presence of great intellectual giants they are by no means dwarfs. Flawless as men, unique and genuine as poets, they cannot die as long as the world honors goodness and that divine spark which men call poetry. They were Catholic; true alike to their faith and their inspiration; faithful, and, being faithful, pure as poets or men are seldom pure.

—Maurice F. Egan, "Three Catholic Poets,"
Catholic World, October 1880, pp. 138–40

G.A. SIMCOX (1880)

George Augustus Simcox (1841–1905) was a British scholar of classical studies who published editions of works by Juvenal and Demosthenes, among others.

Crashaw is full of diffuseness and repetition; in the "Wishes for his Mistress" he puts in every fantastic way possible the hope that she will not paint; often the variations are so insignificant that he can hardly have read the poem through before sending it to press. . . . He spins the 23rd psalm into three dozen couplets. The Stabat Mater is very far from being the severest of mediaeval hymns, but there is no appropriateness in Crashaw's own title for his paraphrase "A Pathetical descant on the devout Plain Song of the Church," as though he were a pianist performing variations upon a classical air. He extemporises at ease in his rooms at Peterhouse, then the ritualistic college of Cambridge. Like Herbert he was a piece of a courtier, but he did not go to court to seek his fortune, he found nothing there but materials for a sketch of the supposed mistress who never disturbed his pious vigils.

—G.A. Simcox, *English Poets*,
1880, ed. Ward, pp. 195–96

Edmund Gosse
"Richard Crashaw" (1882)

Gosse begins his examination of Crashaw by noting that "his works present the only important contribution to English literature made by a pronounced Catholic, embodying Catholic doctrine, during the whole of the seventeenth century." Gosse initially focuses his piece on the works of men he calls "High Church poets," writers who, during the seventeenth century, combined both theological and political aspects of the day into their works. As Gosse explains: "Their piety was much more articulate and objective than that which had inspired the hymn-writers and various divine songsters of an earlier age; an element of political conviction, of anger and apprehension, gave ardour and tension to their song." Though George Herbert is perhaps best known of these writers, Gosse uses Crashaw as an example of a "typical specimen" of High Church writing. Still, Gosse argues that Crashaw is unique because his work does not imitate the reflective approach of Herbert and his ilk; rather, Crashaw's work is indicative of "the flame-coloured seraph of worship" that belied his Catholic faith. Gosse especially sees this in Crashaw's two famous pieces about St. Teresa, his ode to her and "The Flaming Heart," works Gosse explicates in useful detail.

Gosse then leaves this discussion behind to focus on an extended comparison of Crashaw and the seventeenth-century German Catholic poet Friedrich Spe. Gosse finds that the two have much in common: both were highly influenced by their faith; both were also influenced by the writings of Spanish mystics; both relished writing about some of the gorier details of Catholic martyrhood; and both have an excellent diction and literary imagination. Gosse quickly adds, however, that "The chief distinction between Spe and Crashaw is, in the first place, that Crashaw is by far the greater and more varied of the two as regards poetical gifts, and, secondly, that while Spe was inspired by the national *Volkslied,* and introduced its effects into his song, Crashaw was an adept in every refinement of metrical structure which had been invented by the poet-artists of England, Spain, and Italy." This leads Gosse into a further discussion of Crashaw's Spanish and Italian influences, the latter of which, he speculates, were lacking from Spe's literary education.

Returning to his examination of Crashaw's work, Gosse writes that he, like George MacDonald, dislikes "The Weeper," one of two Crashaw poems (along with "The Flaming Heart") that nineteenth-century critics generally favored. Gosse writes that in "The Weeper," "Every extravagant and inappropriate image is dragged to do service to this small idea." Gosse much prefers Crashaw's more secular work, published in his *Delights of the Muses,* a decidedly unpopular opinion in his day. Here Gosse especially focuses on the poems "Music's Duel" and "Wishes to his Supposed Mistress," and also expends some mental resources examining the origins of these particular poems and their larger place in Crashaw's oeuvre. Students will find Gosse's work on Crashaw's secular poems particularly useful, since they are generally ignored in favor of his sacred verse, but will also surely find his comparisons of Crashaw and Spe and his analysis of Crashaw's continental influences of great importance as well.

No sketch of the English literature of the middle of the seventeenth century can pretend to be complete if it does not tell us something of that serried throng of poets militant who gave in their allegiance to Laud, and became ornaments and then martyrs of the High Church party. Their piety was much more articulate and objective than that which had inspired the hymn-writers and various divine songsters of an earlier age; an element of political conviction, of anger and apprehension, gave ardour and tension to their song. They were conservative and passive, but not oblivious to the tendencies of the time, and the gathering flood of Puritanism forced them, to use an image that they would not themselves have disdained, to climb on to the very altar-step of ritualism, or even in extreme instances to take wing for the mystic heights of Rome itself.

It is from such extreme instances as the latter that we learn to gauge their emotion and their desperation, and it is therefore Crashaw rather than Herbert whom we select for the consideration of a typical specimen of the High Church poets. Nor is it only the hysterical intensity of Crashaw's convictions which marks him out for our present purpose; his position in history, his manhood spent in the last years of the reign of "Thorough," and in the very forefront of the crisis, give him a greater claim upon us than Herbert, who died before Laud succeeded to the Primacy, or Vaughan, who was still a boy when Strafford was executed. There are many other points of view from which Crashaw is of special interest; his works present the only important contribution to English literature made by a pronounced Catholic, embodying Catholic doctrine, during the whole of the seventeenth century, while as a poet, although extremely unequal, he rises, at his best, to a mounting fervour which is quite electrical, and hardly rivalled in its kind before or since . . .

Crashaw's English poems were first published in 1646, soon after his arrival in Paris. He was at that time in his thirty-fourth year, and the volume contains his best and most mature as well as his crudest pieces. It is, indeed, a collection of juvenile and manly verses thrown together with scarcely a hint of arrangement, the uncriticised labour of fifteen years. The title is *Steps to the Temple, Sacred Poems, with other delights of the Muses*. The sacred poems are so styled by his anonymous editor because they are "steps for happy souls to climb heaven by;" the *Delights of the Muses* are entirely secular, and the two divisions of the book, therefore, reverse the order of Herrick's similarly edited *Hesperides* and *Noble Numbers*. The *Steps to the Temple* are distinguished at once from the collection with which it is most natural to compare them, the *Temple* of Herbert, to which their title refers with a characteristic touch of modesty, by the fact that they are not poems of experience, but of ecstasy—not of meditation, but of devotion. Herbert, and with him most of the sacred poets of the age, are autobiographical; they analyse their emotions, they take themselves to task, they record their struggles, their defeats, their consolation.

But if the azure cherubim of introspection are the dominant muses of English sacred verse, the flame-coloured seraph of worship reigns in that of Crashaw. He has made himself familiar with all the amorous phraseology of the Catholic metaphysicians; he has read the passionate canticles of St. John of the Cross, the books of the Carmelite nun, St. Teresa, and all the other rosy and fiery contributions to ecclesiastical literature laid by Spain at the feet of the Pope during the closing decades of the sixteenth century. The virginal courage and ardour of St. Teresa inspire Crashaw with his loveliest and most faultless verses. We need not share nor even sympathise with the sentiment of such lines as these to acknowledge that they belong to the highest order of lyric writing:

Thou art Love's victim, and must die
A death more mystical and high;
Into Love's arms thou shalt let fall
A still-surviving funeral.
His is the dart must make thy death,
Whose stroke will taste thy hallowed breath—
A dart thrice dipped in that rich flame
Which writes thy spouse's radiant name
Upon the roof of heaven, where aye
It shines and with a sovereign ray
Beats bright upon the burning faces
Of souls which in that name's sweet graces
Find everlasting smiles. So rare,
So spiritual, pure, and fair,
Must be the immortal instrument
Upon whose choice point shall be spent
A life so loved; and that there be
Fit executioners for thee,
The fairest first-born sons of fire,
Blest seraphim, shall leave their choir,
And turn Love's soldiers, upon thee
To exercise their archery.

Nor in the poem from which these lines are quoted does this melodious rapture flag during nearly two hundred verses. But such a sustained flight is rare, as in the similar poem of "The Flaming Heart," also addressed to St. Teresa, where, after a long prelude of frigid and tuneless conceits, it is only at the very close that the poet suddenly strikes upon this golden chord of ecstasy:

Let all thy scattered shafts of light, that play
Among the leaves of thy large books of day,
Combined against this breast at once break in,
And take away from me myself and sin;
This gracious robbery shall thy bounty be,

And my best fortunes such fair spoils of me.
O thou undaunted daughter of desires!
   By all thy dower of lights and fires,
   By all the eagle in thee, all the dove,
   By all thy lives and deaths of love.
   By thy large draughts of intellectual day,
And by thy thirsts of love more large than they,
By all thy brim-filled bowls of fierce desire,
By thy last morning's draught of liquid fire,
By the full kingdom of that final kiss
That seized thy parting soul and sealed thee His;
By all the heaven thou hast in Him,
Fair sister of the seraphim!
By all of thine we have in thee—
Leave nothing of myself in me;
Let me so read thy life that I
Unto all life of mine may die.

If Crashaw had left us nothing more than these two fragments, we should be able to distinguish him by them among English poets. He is the solitary representative of the poetry of Catholic psychology which England possessed until our own days; and Germany has one no less unique in Friedrich Spe. I do not know that any critic has compared Spe and Crashaw, but they throw lights upon the genius of one another which may seasonably detain us for a while. The great Catholic poet of Germany during the seventeenth century was born in 1591. Like Crashaw, he was set in motion by the Spanish Mystics; like him, he stood on the verge of a great poetical revolution without being in the least affected by it. To Waller and to Opitz, with their new dry systems of precise prosody, Crashaw and Spe owed nothing; they were purely romantic and emotional in style. Spe was born a Catholic, spent all his life among the Jesuits, and died, worn out with good works and immortalised by an heroic struggle against the system of persecution for witchcraft, in the hospital of Treves in 1635, just when Crashaw was becoming enthralled by the delicious mysteries of Little Gidding. Both of them wrote Jesuit eclogues. In Spe the shepherd winds his five best roses into a garland for the infant Jesus; in Crashaw he entertains the "starry stranger" with conceits about his diamond eyes and the red leaves of his lips. In each poet there is an hysterical delight in blood and in the details of martyrdom, in each a shrill and frantic falsetto that jars on the modern ear, in each a sweetness of diction and purity of fancy that redeem a hundred faults.[1] The poems of Spe, entitled *Trutz-Nachtigal,* were first printed in 1649, the year that Crashaw died.

The chief distinction between Spe and Crashaw is, in the first place, that Crashaw is by far the greater and more varied of the two as regards poetical gifts, and, secondly, that while Spe was inspired by the national *Volkslied,* and introduced its effects into his song, Crashaw was an adept in every refinement of metrical structure which had been invented by the poet-artists of England, Spain, and Italy. The progress of our poetical literature in the seventeenth century will never be thoroughly explained until some competent scholar shall examine the influence of Spanish poetry upon our own. This influence seems to be particularly strong in the case of Donne, and in the next generation in that of Crashaw. I am not sufficiently familiar with Spanish poetry to give an opinion on this subject which is of much value; but as I write I have open before me the works of Gongora, and I find in the general disposition of his *Octavas Sacras* and in the style of his *Canciones* resemblances to the staves introduced to us by Crashaw which can scarcely be accidental.

Mr. Shorthouse reminds me that Ferrar was much in Spain; we know that Crashaw "was excellent in Italian and Spanish," and we are thus led on to consider the more obvious debt which he owed to the contemporary poetry of Italy. One of the largest pieces of work which he undertook was the translation of the first canto of the *Strage degli Innocenti,* or *Massacre of the Innocents,* a famous poem by the Neapolitan Cavaliere Marini, who had died in 1625. Crashaw has thrown a great deal of dignity and fancy into this version, which, however, outdoes the original in ingenious illustration, as the true Marinists, such as Achillini, outdid Marini in their conceited sonnets. Crashaw, in fact, is a genuine Marinist, the happiest specimen which we possess in English, for he preserves a high level of fantastic foppery, and seldom, at his worst, sinks to those crude animal imagings—illustrations from food, for instance—which occasionally make such writers as Habington and Carew not merely ridiculous but repulsive.

In criticising with severity the piece on Mary Magdalene which stands in the forefront of Crashaw's poems, and bears the title of "The Weeper," I have the misfortune to find myself at variance with most of his admirers. I cannot, however, avoid the conviction that the obtrusion of this eccentric piece on the threshold of his shrine has driven away from it many a would-be worshipper. If language be ever liable to abuse in the hands of a clever poet, it is surely outraged here. Every extravagant and inappropriate image is dragged to do service to this small idea—namely, that the Magdalen is for ever weeping. Her eyes, therefore, are sister springs, parents of rills, thawing crystal, hills of snow, heavens of ever-falling stars, eternal breakfasts for brisk cherubs, sweating boughs of balsam, nests of milky doves, a voluntary mint of silver, and Heaven knows how many more incongruous objects, from one to another of which the labouring fancy flits in despair and bewilderment. In this poem all is resigned to ingenuity; we are not moved or softened, we are merely startled, and the irritated reader is at last appeased for the fatigues he has endured by a frank guffaw, when he sees the poet, at his wits' end for a simile, plunge into the abyss of absurdity, and style the eyes of the Magdalen

> Two walking baths, two weeping motions,
> Portable and compendious oceans.

These are the worst lines in Crashaw. They are perhaps the worst in all English poetry, but they must not be omitted here, since they indicate to us the principal danger to which not he only but most of his compeers were liable. It was from the tendency to call a pair of eyes "portable and compendious oceans" that Waller and Dryden, after both of them stumbling on the same stone in their youth, finally delivered us. It is useless to linger with indulgence over the stanzas of a poem like "The Weeper," simply because many of the images are in themselves pretty. The system upon which these juvenile pieces of Crashaw are written is in itself indefensible, and is founded upon what Mr. Matthew Arnold calls an "incurable defect of style."

Crashaw, however, possesses style, or he would not deserve the eminent place he holds among our poets. The ode in praise of Teresa, written while the author was still among the Protestants, and therefore probably about 1642, has already been cited here. It is an exquisite composition, full of real vision, music of the most delicate order, and imagery which, although very profuse and ornate, is always subordinated to the moral meaning and to the progress of the poem. The "Shepherd's Hymn," too, is truly ingenious and graceful, with its pretty pastoral tenderness. "On Mr. G. Herbert's Book sent to a Gentleman" evidently belongs to the St. Teresa period, and contains the same charm. The lyrical epistle persuading the Countess of Denbigh to join the Roman communion contains extraordinary felicities, and seems throbbing with tenderness and passion. We have already drawn attention to the splendid close of "The Flaming Heart." There is perhaps no other of the sacred poems in the volume of 1646 which can be commended in its entirety. Hardly one but contains felicities; the dullest is brightened by such flashes of genius as—

> Lo, how the thirsty lands
> Gasp for the golden showers with long-stretch'd
>   hands!

But the poems are hard, dull, and laborious, the exercises of a saint indeed, but untouched by inspiration, human or divine. We have to return to the incomparable "Hymn to St. Teresa" to remind ourselves of what heights this poet was capable.

There can be very little doubt that Crashaw regarded the second section of his book, the secular *Delights of the Muses,* as far inferior in value and importance to the *Steps to the Temple.* That is not, however, a view in which the modern reader can coincide, and it is rather the ingenuity of his human poems than the passion of his divine which has given him a prominent place among poets. The *Delights* open with the celebrated piece called the "Muse's Duel," paraphrased from the Latin of Strada. As one frequently sees a reference to the "Latin poet Strada," it may be worth while to remark that Famianus Strada was not a poet at all, but a lecturer in the Jesuit colleges. He belonged to Crashaw's own age, having been born in 1572, and dying in the year of the English poet's death, 1649. The piece on the rivalry of the musician and the nightingale was published first at Rome in 1617, in a volume of *Prolusiones* on rhetoric and poetry, and occurs in the sixth lecture of the second course on poetic style. The Jesuit rhetorician has been trying to familiarise his pupils with the style of the great classic poets by reciting to them passages in imitation of Ovid, Lucretius, Lucan, and the rest, and at last he comes to Claudian. This, he says, is an imitation of the style of Claudian, and so he gives us the lines which have become so famous. That a single fragment in a school-book should suddenly take root and blossom in European literature, when all else that its voluminous author wrote and said was promptly forgotten, is very curious, but not unprecedented.

In England the first person who adopted or adapted Strada's exercise was John Ford, in his play of *The Lover's Melancholy,* in 1629. Dr. Grosart found another early version among the Lansdowne MSS., and Ambrose Phillips a century later essayed it. There are numerous references to it in other literatures than ours, and in the present age M. Francois Cop-pee has introduced it with charming effect into his pretty comedy *of Le Luthier de Cremone.* Thus the schoolmaster's task, set as a guide to the manner of Claudian, has achieved, by an odd irony of fortune, a far more general and lasting success than any of the actual verses of that elegant writer. With regard to the comparative merits of Ford's version, which is in blank verse, and of Crashaw's, which is in rhyme, a confident opinion has generally been expressed in favour of the particular poet under consideration at the moment; nor is Lamb himself superior to this amiable partiality. He denies that Crashaw's version "can at all compare for harmony and grace with this blank verse of Ford's." But my own view coincides much rather with that of Mr. Swinburne, who says that "between the two beautiful versions of Strada's pretty fable by Ford and Crashaw, there will always be a diversity of judgment among readers; some must naturally prefer the tender fluency and limpid sweetness of Ford, others the dazzling intricacy and affluence in refinements, the supple and cunning implication, the choiceness and subtlety of Crashaw." Mr. Shorthouse, on the other hand, suggests to me that "Crashaw's poem is surely so much more full and elaborate, that it must be acknowledged to be the more important effort." There can be no doubt that it presents us with the most brilliant and unique attempt which has been made in our language to express the very quality and variety of musical notation in words. It may be added that the only reference made by Crashaw in any part of his writings to any of the dramatists his contemporaries is found in a couplet addressed to Ford:

Thou cheat'st us, Ford, mak'st one seem two by art;
What is *love's sacrifice* but *the broken heart?*

After "Music's Duel," the best-known poem of Crashaw's is his "Wishes to his Supposed Mistress," a piece in forty-two stanzas, which Mr. Palgrave reduced to twenty-one in his *Golden Treasury.* He neglected to mention the "sweet theft," and accordingly most readers know the poem only as he reduced and rearranged it. The act was bold, perhaps, but I think that it was judicious. As Crashaw left it, the poem extends beyond the limits of a lyric, tediously repeats its sentiments and gains neither in force nor charm by its extreme length. In Mr. Palgrave's selection it challenges comparison with the loveliest and most original pieces of the century. It never, I think, rises to the thrilling tenderness which Donne is capable of on similar occasions. Crashaw never pants out a line and a half which leave us faint and throbbing, as if the heart of humanity itself had been revealed to us for a moment; with all his flying colour and lambent flame, Crashaw is not Donne. But the "Wishes" is more than a charming, it is a fascinating poem, the pure dream of the visionary poet, who liked to reflect that he too might marry if he would, and choose a godly bride. He calls upon her—

> Whoe'er she be
> That not impossible She
> That shall command my heart and me;
> Where'er she lie
> Locked up from mortal eye
> In shady leaves of destiny—

to receive the embassy of his wishes, bound to instruct her in that higher beauty of the spirit which his soul demands—

> Something more than
> Taffata or tissue can,
> Or rampant feather, or rich fan.

But what he requires is not spiritual adornment alone; he will have her courteous and accomplished in the world's ways also, the possessor of

> Sydneian showers
> Of sweet discourse, whose powers
> Can crown old Winter's head with flowers;

and finally,

> Life, that dares send
> A challenge to his end,
> And when it comes say, 'Welcome, friend.'
> I wish her store
> Of worth may leave her poor
> Of wishes; and I wish—no more.

The same refined and tender spirit animates the "Epitaph upon Husband and Wife, who died and were buried together." The lovely rambling verses of "To the Morning, in satisfaction for Sleep," are perhaps more in the early manner of Keats than any other English lines. In some of those sacred poems which we have lately been considering, he reminds us no less vividly of Shelley, and there are not a few passages of Crashaw which it would require a very quick ear to distinguish from Mr. Swinburne. We may safely conjecture that the latter poet's "Song in Season" was written in deliberate rivalry of that song of Crashaw's which runs—

> O deliver
> Love his quiver;
> From thine eyes he shoots his arrows,
> Where Apollo
> Cannot follow,
> Feathered with his mother's sparrows.

But perhaps the sweetest and most modern of all Crashaw's secular lyrics is that entitled *Loves Horoscope*. The phraseology of the black art was never used with so sweet and picturesque an ingenuity, and the piece contains some of the most delicately musical cadences to be found in the poetry of the age:

> Thou know'st a face in whose each look
> Beauty lays ope Love's fortune-book,
> On whose fair revolutions wait
> The obsequious motions of Love's fate.
> Ah! my heart! her eyes and she
> Have taught thee new astrology.
> Howe'er Love's native hours were set,
> Whatever starry synod met,
> 'Tis in the mercy of her eye
> If poor Love shall live or die.

It is probable from internal and from external evidence also that all these secular poems belong to Crashaw's early years at Cambridge. The pretty lines "On Two Green Apricocks sent to Cowley by Sir Crashaw" evidently date from 1633; the various elegies and poems of compliment can be traced to years ranging from 1631 to 1634. It is doubtful whether the "Wishes" themselves are at all later than this. Even regarding him as a finished poet ten years before the publication of his book, however, he comes late in the list of seventeenth century lyrists, and has no claims to be considered as an innovator. He owed all the basis of his style, as has been already hinted, to Donne and to Ben Jonson. His originality was one of treatment and technique; he forged a more rapid and brilliant short line than any of his predecessors had done, and for brief intervals and along sudden paths of his own he carried English prosody to a higher refinement, a more glittering felicity, than it had ever achieved. Thus, in spite of his conceits and his romantic colouring, he points the way for Pope, who did not disdain to borrow from him freely.

It is unfortunate that Crashaw is so unequal as to be positively delusive; he baffles analysis by his uncertain hold upon style, and in spite of his charm and his genius is perhaps most interesting to us because of the faults he shares with purely modern poets. It would scarcely be unjust to say that Crashaw was the first real poet who allowed himself to use a splendid phrase when a simple one would have better expressed his meaning; and in an age when all but the best poetry was apt to be obscure, crabbed, and rugged, he introduces a new fault, that of being visionary and diffuse, with a deliberate intention not only, as the others did, to deck Nature out in false ornament, but to represent her actual condition as being something more "starry" and "seraphical" than it really is. His style has hectic beauties that delight us, but evade us also, and colours that fade as promptly as the scarlet and the amber in a sunset sky. We can describe him best in negatives; his is not so warm and real as Herrick, nor so drily intellectual as the other hymnists, nor coldly and respectably virile like Cowley. To use an odd simile of Shelley's, he sells us gin when the other poets offer us legs of mutton, or at all events baskets of bread and vegetables . . .

Too often it is with regret, or with a grudged esteem, that we hail newly-discovered works by standard authors. The best writing generally takes care of itself, and is remembered and preserved, whatever may be lost. The first sprightly running is commonly the best, and editors scarcely earn our thanks by troubling the lees for us. For once we have an exception before us. The pamphlet of newly-discovered poems by Crashaw which Dr. Grosart forwarded to his subscribers in 1888 contains some things which, even in the congested condition of our national literature, are never likely to be obscured again. The British Museum bought from a bookseller, who had picked it up as an odd lot at Sotheby's or Puttick & Simpson's, a MS. volume of Crashaw's poems, indubitably, as would appear, in his own, previously untraced, handwriting. Dr. Grosart gives us an example of the latter in facsimile, selecting the page which contains the well-known epigram on "The Water being made Wine."

We turn at once to the poems which are entirely new. Here is one apparently intended to form the dedication to a gift-volume of the poet's *Steps to the Temple:*

At the ivory tribunal of your hand,
Fair one, these tender leaves do trembling stand,
Knowing 'tis in the doom of your sweet eye
Whether the Muse they clothe shall live or die;

Live she or die to Fame, each leaf you meet
Is her life's wing, or else her winding-sheet.

We could swear this was Crashaw if we picked it up anonymous on Pitcairn's Island. Moreover, something very like the second couplet is to be found already in Love's *Horoscope*: 'Tis in the mercy of her eye If poor Love shall live or die.

It is very pretty. But this, a nameless lyric, is more than pretty; it is exquisite, and in Crashaw's most transcendental manner:

Though now 'tis neither May nor June,
And nightingales are out of tune,
Yet in these leaves, fair One, there lies
(Sworn servant to your sweetest eyes)
A nightingale, who, may she spread
In your white bosom her chaste bed,
Spite of all the maiden snow
Those pure untrodden paths can show,
You straight shall see her wake and rise,
Taking fresh life from your fair eyes,
And with claspt wings proclaim a spring,
Where Love and she shall sit and sing;
For lodged so near your sweetest throat
What nightingale can lose her note?
Nor let her kindred birds complain
Because she breaks the year's old reign;
For let them know she's none of those
Hedge-quiristers whose music owes
Only such strains as serve to keep
Sad shades, and sing dull night asleep.
No, she's a priestess of that grove,
The holy chapel of chaste love,
Your virgin bosom. Then whate'er
Poor laws divide the public year,
Whose revolutions wait upon
The wild turns of the wanton sun,
Be you the Lady of Love's year,
Where your eyes shine his suns appear,
There all the year is Love's long Spring,
    There all the year
Love's nightingales shall sit and sing.

The break in the penultimate verse is a charming addition to the melody, and I am very much mistaken if this lyric does not take its place among the best of Charles I.'s reign.

The remainder of the new poems are religious, and they are not in Crashaw's very finest manner. "To Pontius, Washing his Blood-stained Hands," is a typical example of the monstrous chains of conceits which these most unequal poets were at any moment liable to produce. The face of Pilate was originally a nymph—

> The daughter of a fair and well-famed fountain
> As ever silver-tipped the side of shady mountain,—

(in itself a charming image); this nymph has suffered the fate of Philomela from this new Tereus, the hand of Pilate, and "appears nothing but tears." A paraphrase of Grotius gives us a first version of the well-known verse on the Eucharist:

> The water blushed and started into wine.

We trace the great Crashaw of the fiery surprises but seldom in this long, tame, and somewhat crabbed poem; but he asserts himself in a few such phrases as this:

> Before the infant shrine
> Of my weak feet, the Persian Magi lay,
> And left their mithra for my star;

and this, which well describes the condition of Crashaw's muse:

> A sweet inebriated ecstasy.

The new readings of old poems which the MS. gives are neither, it would seem, very numerous nor very important. "The Weeper" is such a distressing, indeed such a humiliating poem, that we receive a new stanza of it with indifference; we may note one novelty,—this string of preposterous conceits on the tears of the Magdalen must in future close with a conceit that swallows up all the rest:

> Of such fair floods as this
> Heaven the crystal ocean is.

Dr. Grosart takes this opportunity of recording an interesting little discovery. Crashaw's important Latin poem "Bulla" is found to have made its first appearance in a very rare Cambridge volume, the *Crepundia Siliana* of Heynsius, in 1646, two years after the poet's ejection from his

Fellowship. It appeared the same year in the *Delights of the Muses,* with a considerable number of variations of the text. It is a pity that Crashaw did not write "Bulla" in English, for it is full of the characteristics of his style.

Notes

1. As an illustration of almost all these qualities, and as a specimen of Spe's metrical gifts, I give one stanza from the *Trutz-Nachtigai.* Aus der Seiten Lan sich leiten

   Rote Strahlen wie Korall; Aus der Seiten Lan sich leiten
   Weisse Wasser wie Krystal! O du reines, Hubsch und feines
   Bachlein von Korall und Glas, Nit noch weiche, Nit entschleiche,
   O Rubin und Perlengass!

—Edmund Gosse, from "Richard Crashaw,"
1882, *Seventeenth Century Studies,*
vol. 1, 1913, pp. 157–182

George Saintsbury
"Caroline Poetry" (1887)

In the text excerpted below, Saintsbury compares Crashaw to two of his contemporary peers whom he is often critiqued against—Robert Herrick and Thomas Carew. Herrick, Saintsbury writes, is a poet of nature; Carew the gentleman poet; and Crashaw "is religious everywhere." Saintsbury suggests that Crashaw's masterpiece occurs at the end of his work "The Flaming Heart" where, "in a moment, in the twinkling of an eye, without warning of any sort, the metre changes, the poet's inspiration catches fire, and there rushes up into the heaven of poetry this marvellous rocket of song." Saintsbury comments also on the great contrast between the end of the piece and the "colourless" beginning, a contrast that he feels is borne out of the fact that Crashaw likely did not edit his own work. Saintsbury also briefly examines Crashaw's "Wishes to His Unknown Mistress," "A Hymn to Saint Theresa," and "The Weeper" (his comments here can be contrasted with numerous of the other critics who have also discussed this piece, including MacDonald.) Ultimately, Saintsbury suggests that Crashaw's work often produces mixed results: "At his best he is far above singing, at his worst he is below a very childish prattle. But even then he is never coarse, never offensive, not very often actually dull; and everywhere he makes amends by flowers of the divinest poetry." This "divinest" poetry, Saintsbury concludes, is a result of Crashaw's religious devotion, which he calls a "religious fire": "But no Englishman has expressed that fire as he his, and none in his expression of any sentiment, sacred and profane, has dropped such notes of ethereal music." Students writing on any of the specific works Saintsbury mentions, or on the impact of Crashaw's conversion on his works, will no doubt find Saintsbury's text particularly useful.

The third of this great trio of poets (Carew, Herrick and Crashaw), and with them the most remarkable of our whole group, was Richard Crashaw. He completes Carew and Herrick both in his qualities and (if a kind of bull may be permitted) in his defects, after a fashion almost unexampled elsewhere and supremely interesting. Hardly any one of the three could have appeared at any other time, and not one but is distinguished from the others in the most marked way. Herrick, despite his sometimes rather obtrusive learning, is emphatically the natural man. He does not show much sign of the influence of good society, his merits as well as his faults have a singular unpersonal and, if I may so say, *terrcefilian* connotation. Carew is a gentleman before all; but a rather profane gentleman. Crashaw is religious everywhere. Again, Herrick and Carew, despite their strong savour of the fashion of the time, are eminently critics as well as poets. Carew has not let one piece critically unworthy of him pass his censorship: Herrick (if we exclude the filthy and foolish epigrams into which he was led by corrupt following of Ben) has been equally careful. These two bards may have trouble with the censor *morum,*—the *censor literarum* they can brave with perfect confidence. It is otherwise with Crashaw. That he never, as far as can be seen, edited the bulk of his work for press at all matters little or nothing. But there is not in his work the slightest sign of the exercise of any critical faculty before, during, or after production. His masterpiece, one of the most astonishing things in English or any other literature, comes without warning at the end of "The Flaming Heart." For page after page the poet has been poorly playing on some trifling conceits suggested by the picture of Saint Theresa and a seraph. First he thinks the painter ought to have changed the attributes; then he doubts whether a lesser change will not do; and always he treats his subject in a vein of grovelling and grotesque conceit which the boy Dryden in the stage of his elegy on Lord Hastings would have disdained. And then in a moment, in the twinkling of an eye, without warning of any sort, the metre changes, the poet's inspiration catches fire, and there rushes up into the heaven of poetry this marvellous rocket of song:

Live in these conquering leaves: live all the same;
And walk through all tongues one triumphant flame;
Live here, great heart; and love, and die, and kill;
And bleed, and wound, and yield, and conquer still.
Let this immortal life where'er it comes
Walk in a crowd of loves and martyrdoms.
Let mystic deaths wait on't; and wise souls be
The love-slain witnesses of this life of thee.
O sweet incendiary! show here thy art,
Upon this carcase of a hard cold heart;
Let all thy scatter'd shafts of light, that play
Among the leaves of thy large books of day,
Combin'd against this breast at once break in,
And take away from me myself and sin;
This gracious robbery shall thy bounty be
And my best fortunes such fair spoils of me.
O thou undaunted daughter of desires!
By all thy pow'r of lights and fires;
By all the eagle in thee, all the dove;
By all thy lives and deaths of love;
By thy large draughts of intellectual day;
And by thy thirsts of love more large than they;
By all thy brim-fill'd bowls of fierce desire;
By thy last morning's draught of liquid fire;
By the full kingdom of that final kiss
That 'sayed thy parting soul, and seal'd thee his;
By all the heavens thou hast in him,
(Fair sister of the seraphim)
By all of him we have in thee;
Leave nothing of myself in me.
Let me so read thy life, that I
Unto all life of mine may die.

The contrast is perhaps unique as regards the dead colourlessness of the beginning, and the splendid colour of the end. But contrasts like it occur all over Crashaw's work.

Our chief subject . . . is the English poems proper, sacred and profane. In almost all of these there is noticeable an extraordinary inequality, the same in kind, if not in degree, as that on which we have commented in the case of "The Flaming Heart." Crashaw is never quite so great as there; but he is often quite as small. His exasperating lack of self-criticism has sometimes led selectors to make a cento out of his poems— notably in the case of the exceedingly pretty "Wishes to His Unknown Mistress," beginning, "Whoe'er she be, That not impossible she, That shall command my heart and me"—a .poem, let it be added, which excuses this dubious process much less than most, inasmuch as nothing in it is positively bad, though it is rather too long. Here is the opening, preceded by a piece from another poem, "A Hymn to Saint Theresa":

Those rare works, where thou shalt leave writ
Love's noble history, with wit
Taught thee by none but him, while here
They feed our souls, shall clothe thine there.
Each heavenly word by whose hid flame
Our hard hearts shall strike fire, the same
Shall flourish on thy brows and be
Both fire to us and flame to thee:
Whose light shall live bright, in thy face
By glory, in our hearts by grace.
Thou shalt look round about, and see
Thousands of crown'd souls throng to be
Themselves thy crown, sons of thy vows:
The virgin births with which thy spouse
Made fruitful thy fair soul; go now
And with them all about thee, bow
To Him, 'Put on' (He'll say) 'put on,
My rosy love, that thy rich zone,
Sparkling with the sacred flames,
Of thousand souls whose happy names
Heaven heaps upon thy score, thy bright
Life brought them first to kiss the light
That kindled them to stars.' And so
Thou with the Lamb thy Lord shall go,
And whereso'er He sets His white
Steps, walk with Him those ways of light.
Which who in death would live to see
Must learn in life to die like thee."

Whoe'er she be,
That not impossible she,
That shall command my heart and me;

Where'er she lie,
Lock'd up from mortal eye,
In shady leaves of destiny;
Till that ripe birth
Of studied Fate stand forth,
And teach her fair steps to our earth:
Till that divine
Idea take a shrine
Of crystal flesh, through which to shine:
Meet you her, my wishes
Bespeak her to my blisses,
And be ye call'd, my absent kisses.

The first hymn to Saint Theresa, to which "The Flaming Heart" is a kind of appendix, was written when Crashaw was still an Anglican (for which he did not fail, later, to make a characteristic and very pretty, though quite unnecessary, apology). It has no passage quite up to the Invocation—Epiphonema, to give it the technical term—of the later poem. But it is, on the contrary, good almost throughout, and is, for uniform exaltation, far the best of Crashaw's poems. Yet such uniform exaltation must be seldom sought in him. It is in his little bursts, such as that in the stanza beginning, "O mother turtle dove," that his charm consists. Often, as in verse after verse of "The Weeper," it has an unearthly delicacy and witchery which only Blake, in a few snatches, has ever equalled; while at other times the poet seems to invent, in the most casual and unthinking fashion, new metrical effects and new jewelries of diction which the greatest lyric poets since— Coleridge, Shelley, Lord Tennyson, Mr. Swinburne—have rather deliberately imitated than spontaneously recovered. Yet to all this charm there is no small drawback. The very maddest and most methodless of the "Metaphysicals" cannot touch Crashaw in his tasteless use of conceits. When he, in "The Weeper" just above referred to, calls the tears of Magdalene "Wat'ry brothers," and "Simpering sons of those fair eyes," and when, in the most intolerable of all the poet's excesses, the same eyes are called "Two waking baths, two weeping motions, Portable and compendious oceans," which follow our Lord about the hills of Galilee, it is almost difficult to know whether to feel most contempt or indignation for a man who could so write. It is fair to say that there are various readings and omissions in the different editions which affect both these passages. Yet the offence is that Crashaw should ever have written them at all. Amends, however, are sure to be made before the reader has read much farther. Crashaw's longest poems—a version of Marini's *Sospetto d'Herode,* and one of the rather overpraised "Lover and Nightingale" story of Strada—are not his best; the metre in which both are written, though the poet manages it well, lacks the extraordinary charm of his lyric measures. It does not appear that the "Not impossible she" ever made her appearance, and probably for a full half of his short life Crashaw burnt only with religious fire. But no Englishman has expressed that fire as he his, and none in his expression of any sentiment, sacred and profane, has dropped such notes of ethereal music. At his best he is far above singing, at his worst he is below a very childish prattle. But even then he is never coarse, never offensive, not very often actually dull; and everywhere he makes amends by flowers of the divinest poetry.

—George Saintsbury, from "Caroline
Poetry", *History of Elizabethan
Literature,*1887, pp. 364–69

J.R. Tutin "Preface" (1887)

The prolific author and essayist John Ramsden Tutin (1855–1913) was an English editor of Crashaw's and one of his strongest defenders in the nineteenth century.

Crashaw's verse is marked by some of the highest qualities of poetry. He has strong affinities to two of our great nineteenth-century poets; he has the rich imagination and sensuousness of Keats, and the subtlety of thought and exquisite lyrical flow of Shelley. Crashaw is essentially a sacred poet, and, compared with George Herbert, is his superior, judged from the purely poetic standpoint. Herbert is, in a limited degree, a popular poet; Crashaw is not, and has never been so. One of the reasons for this is (probably) the taste for artificial poetry of the school of Waller, Dryden, Pope, &c., during the seventeenth and eighteenth centuries. The fact of his being a Catholic would also deter many readers from studying his works; but, poetical thought now being wider, and religious intolerance almost a thing of the past, it may be hoped that Crashaw will soon receive the recognition which is his due.

—J.R. Tutin, "Preface" to *Poems of
Richard Crashaw,* 1887, p. viii

Sidney Lee (1888)

An English biographer of both Shakespeare and Queen Victoria and a prominent critic, Sir Sidney Lee (1859–1926) was also former assistant editor of the *Dictionary of National Biography*, which still exists as an important reference source.

⁓⁓⁓ ⁓⁓⁓ ⁓⁓⁓

Crashaw's sacred poems breathe a passionate fervour of devotion, which finds its outlet in imagery of a richness seldom surpassed in our language. Diffuseness and intricate conceit, which at times become grotesque, are the defects of Crashaw's poetry. His metrical effects, often magnificent, are very unequal. He has little of the simple tenderness of Herbert, whom he admired, and to whom he acknowledged his indebtedness.

—Sidney Lee, *Dictionary of National Biography*, 1888, vol. 13, pp. 35–36

Francis Turner Palgrave (1889)

In labeling Crashaw a mystic, Palgrave suggests below that he is attempting to connect to the divine through his works (though the addition of the modifier "sensuous" suggests a connection to pleasure and more earthbound delight.) The "Quarles" Palgrave refers to is Francis Quarles (1592–1644), an English poet.

⁓⁓⁓ ⁓⁓⁓ ⁓⁓⁓

Crashaw represents sensuous Mysticism . . . Like Quarles, (though not to the same degree), he quits the ideal point of view, the high Platonic aether. We cannot say of him, as has been said of that "Son of Light," Origen, the great founder of Christian Mysticism, that he "is never betrayed into the imagery of earthly passion used by the monastic writers," and which also marked the style of the Italian Marino, from whose "Herod " Crashaw has left a brilliant paraphrase. Yet this mode of feeling has its place; it also demands and deserves its compartment in a Sacred Anthology. Crashaw's work in poetry, as a whole, is incomplete and irregular; Pope, whilst praising him, was correct in recognizing that he was an amateur rather than an artist. It was the same with Marvell:—neither, one would say, did justice to his fine natural gift. But Crashaw has a charm so unique, an imagination so nimble and subtle, phrases of such sweet and passionate felicity, that readers who. . . . turn to his little book, will find themselves surprised and delighted, in proportion to their sympathetic sense of Poetry, when touched to its rarer and finer issues.

—Francis Turner Palgrave, *The Treasury
of Sacred Song,* 1889, p. 342

J. HOWARD B. MASTERMAN
(1897)

Masterman's view of Crashaw's "extraordinary inequality" reflects the view of many critics, authors, and students today, who find much to praise in the poet's work and often agree with Masterman that, at times, "the music flags, and the moment or inspiration passes, and Crashaw sinks to earth."

Crashaw is remarkable among poets for the extraordinary inequality of his work. It is impossible to open a page of his poems without being rewarded by some charming novelty of metre or language, some sudden turn of expression of melodious cadence of rhythm. But the music flags, and the moment or inspiration passes, and Crashaw sinks to earth, the child of Marini and Gongora, the weaver of trivial conceits and over-elaborate fancies. It is this inequality that has made his poetry less read than it deserves to be. Poets of as widely different schools as Pope, Coleridge, and Shelley—have each acknowledged their indebtedness to him; and Mr. Swinburne has in our own day restored some of his lyrical measures to English verse.

—J. Howard B. Masterman,
The Age of Milton, 1897

FREDERIC IVES CARPENTER
"INTRODUCTION" (1897)

Crashaw is in poetry as in religion an emotional ritualist; a rich and sensuous pathos characterizes his diction and his rhythms, and redeems from tastelessness conceits over-subtle and symbolical, and marked by all the extravagance of the rococo vein.

—Frederic Ives Carpenter, "Introduction,"
English Lyric Poetry, 1500–1700, 1897, p. lix

Francis Thompson "Excursions in Criticism: VI. Crashaw" (1897)

Francis Thompson (1859–1907) was an English poet most known for his work "The Hound of Hell," which coined the phrase "with all deliberate speed." In the excerpt below, which discusses J.R. Tutin's edition of Crashaw's work, Thompson labels Crashaw a poetic innovator, "a turn of the tide in English lyric, though the crest of the tide was not to come till long after, though—like all first innovators—he not only suffered present neglect, but has been overshadowed by those who came a century after him." Thompson views Crashaw as the forerunner of the prominent English poets of the long eighteenth century (he notes Crashaw's influence on Samuel Taylor Coleridge, amongst others.) Though Crashaw's poetry lacks feeling, Thompson admires its diction and imagery, "cleaving like gold-leaf to its object." Thompson then pauses to examine some of Crashaw's more significant pieces. Describing the "Nativity," Thompson writes it "has less deforming conceit than most." "The Weeper," a piece also considered by Macdonald and Saintsbury, amongst others in this collection, contains stanzas that are "the loveliest art in conception and expression." Thompson also remarks briefly on "Wishes to a Supposed Mistress" and concludes his examination with the same piece that Saintsbury labeled Crashaw's masterpiece, "The Flaming Heart," showing this particular poem's resonance to Victorian-era scholars and readers.

—◦◦◦— —◦◦◦— —◦◦◦—

Strange are both the commissions and omissions of this day, in which an uncritical zeal for the poets of the sixteenth and seventeenth centuries has stimulated reprint upon reprint. It seems to be enough for editorial zeal that a poet should have been born in one of those privileged centuries; and he shall find republication. Not alone Campion and other minor lyrists of merit, but even a wielder of frigid conceits like Henry Constable finds his editor—nay, is issued with all the pomp of sumptuous decorative *ensemble*. Yet, while editors search among the dross of these ages for poets to revive, they neglect the gold. Else how comes it that while Henry Vaughan finds reprint, his worthy yokefellow, Crashaw, is passed by? How comes it that Cowley is inaccessible yet to modern readers? Eminent modern poets have singled Crashaw as a man of genius and a source of inspiration. Coleridge declared that Crashaw's "Hymn to St. Teresa" was present to his mind while he was writing the second part of "Christabel"; "if, indeed, by some subtle process of the mind, they did not suggest the first thought of the whole poem." The influence of Crashaw is to be traced in the "Unknown Eros": notably and conspicuously in the "Sponsa Dei."

. . .

Lyric poetry is a very inclusive term. It includes Milton and Herrick, Burns and Shelley, "Tintern Abbey" and "The Grecian Urn," the odes of Coventry Patmore and the songs of Tennyson. But its highest form—that which is to other lyric forms what the epic is to the narrative poem or the ballad—is the form typically represented by the ode. This order of lyric may again be divided into such lyrics as are distinguished by stately structure, and such as are distinguished by ardorous abandonment. In the former kind ardour *may* be present, though under the continual curb of the structure; and this is the highest species of the lyric. In the latter kind the ardour is naked and predominant: it is to the former kind what the flight of the skylark is to the flight of the eagle. The conspicuous first appearance of the former kind in English poetry was the monumental *Epithalamion* of Spenser. Ardour cannot, as a rule, be predicated of Spenser; but *there* is ardour of the most ethereal impulse, equipoised throughout with the most imperial and imperious structure. For the development of the latter kind English poetry had to await the poet of *Prometheus Unbound.* But its first, almost unnoticed and unperfected appearance, was in the work of Richard Crashaw. His age gave the preference to Cowley, in whose odes there is unlimited ostentation of dominating ardour without the reality, the result being mere capricious and unmeaning dislocation of form. Too much of the like is there in Crashaw; but every now and again he ascends into real fervour, such as makes metre and diction plastic to its own shaping spirit of inevitable Tightness. This is the eminent praise of Crashaw, that he marks an epoch, a turn of the tide in English lyric, though the crest of the tide was not to come till long after, though—like all first innovators—he not only suffered present neglect, but has been overshadowed by those who came a century after him.

He is fraught with suggestion—infinite suggestion. More than one poet has drawn much from him, yet much remains to be drawn. But it is not only for poets he exists. Those who read for enjoyment can find in him abundant delight, if they will be content (as they are content with Wordsworth) to grope through his plenteous infelicity. He is no poet of the human and household emotions; he has not pathos, or warm love, or any of the qualities which come home to the natural kindly race of men. But how fecund is his brilliant imagery, rapturous ethereality. He has, at his best, an extraordinary cunning of diction, cleaving like gold-leaf to its object. In such a poem as "The Musician and the Nightingale" (not in this volume included) the marvel of diction becomes even too conscious; in the moment of wondering at the miracle, we feel that the miracle is too researched: it is the feat of an amazing gymnast in words rather than of an unpremeditating angel. Yet this poem is an extraordinary verbal achievement, and there are numerous other examples in which the miracle seems as unconscious as admirable.

For an example of his sacred poems, take the "Nativity," which has less deforming conceit than most. Very different from Milton's great Ode, which followed it, yet it has its own characteristic beauty. The shepherds sing it turn by turn—as thus:

> Gloomy night embraced the place
>> Where the noble Infant lay.
> The Babe looked up and showed His face;
>> In spite of darkness, it was day.
> It was Thy day, Sweet! and did rise,
>> Not from the East, but from Thine eyes.

Here is seen one note of Crashaw—the human and lover-like tenderness which informs his sacred poems, differentiating them from the conventional style of English sacred poetry, with its solemn aloofness from celestial things.

> I saw the curled drops, soft and slow
>> Come hovering o'er the place's head;
> Offering their whitest sheets of snow
>> To furnish the fair Infant's bed:
> Forbear, said I,; be not too bold,
>> Your fleece is white, but 'tis too cold.
> I saw the obsequious Seraphim
>> Their rosy fleece of fire bestow,
> For well they now can spare their wing,
>> Since heaven itself lies here below.
> Well done, said I; but are you sure
>> Your down so warm will pass for pure?

In the second stanza is shown the fire of his fancy; in "The curled drops," &c, the happiness of his diction. In "The Weeper" (a poem on the Magdalen), amid stanzas of the most frigid conceit, are others of the loveliest art in conception and expression:

The dew no more will weep
    The primrose's pale cheek to deck:
The dew no more will sleep
    Nuzzled in the Lily's neck;
Much rather would it be thy tear,
    And leave them both to tremble here.
Not in the Evening's eyes
    When they red with weeping are
For the Sun that dies,
    Sits Sorrow with a face so fair.
Nowhere but here did ever meet
    Sweetness so sad, sadness so sweet.

Two more alien poets could not be conceived than Crashaw and Browning. Yet in the last couplet of these most exquisite stanzas we have a direct coincidence with Browning's line—

Its sad in sweet, its sweet in sad.

In the "Hymn to St. Teresa" are to be found the most beautiful delicacies of language and metre. Listen to this (*apropos* of Teresa's childish attempt to run away and become a martyr among the Moors):

She never undertook to know
What Death with Love should have to do;
Nor has she e'er yet understood
Why to show love she should shed blood;
Yet though she cannot tell you why,
She can love, and she can die.

Among the poems not contained in this volume (J.R. Tutin, *Poems of Richard Crashaw*, 1905), the wonderfully dainty "Wishes to a Supposed Mistress" shows what Crashaw might have been as an amative poet:

Whoe'er she be,
That not impossible She,
That shall command my heart and me;
Where'er she lie,
Shut up from mortal eye
In shady leaves of Destiny.

And so on through a series of unequal but often lovely stanzas. So, too, does "Love's Horoscope." His epitaphs are among the sweetest and most artistic even of that age, so cunning in such kind of verse. For instance, that on a young gentleman:

> Eyes are vocal, tears have tongues,
> And there be words not made with lungs—
> Sententious showers; O let them fall!
> Their cadence is rhetorical!

But, to come back to the peoms contained in Mr. Tutin's book, with what finer example can I end than the close of "The Flaming Heart," Crashaw's second hymn to St. Teresa?—

> Oh, thou undaunted daughter of desires!
> By all thy dower of lights and fires;
> By all the eagle in thee, all the dove;
> By all thy lives and deaths of love;
> By thy large draughts of intellectual day,
> And by thy thirsts of love more large than they;
> By all thy brim-filled bowls of fierce desire,
> By thy last morning's draught of liquid fire;
> By the full kingdom of that final kiss,
> That seized thy parting soul, and sealed thee His;
> By all the Heaven thou hast in Him
> (Fair Sister of the seraphim!)
> By all of Him we have in thee;
> Leave nothing of myself in me.
> Let me so read thy life, that I
> Unto all life of mine may die.

It has all the ardour and brave-soaring transport of the highest lyrical inspiration.

—Francis Thompson, from "Excursions in
Criticism: VI. Crashaw," *The Academy and
Literature*, November 20, 1897, pp. 27–28

FELIX E. SCHELLING "INTRODUCTION" (1899)

In the first half of the excerpt below, Schelling compares Crashaw's lyrics to those of John Donne, the founder of metaphysical poetry. Whereas

Schelling admires Donne's deft writing and intellectual poesy, he finds Crashaw's work denser and more difficult to decipher. After explicating what he feels is a particularly obscure stanza from "Hymn of the Nativity," Schelling observes: "Crashaw is inspired, not by the intellect, which clears and distinguishes objects, but by passion, which blends and confuses them. The language is one mass of involved and tangled figure, in which similarity suggests similarity in objects contemplated and intensely visualized—not in abstractions incapable of visualization." Schelling's observations here are particularly of use to those individuals examining Crashaw's role in the larger pantheon of metaphysical poets or, indeed, for those wondering whether Crashaw is truly a metaphysical writer at all.

In the second half of the excerpt, Schelling compares Crashaw to George Herbert, author of *The Temple* and usually considered the greatest of the sacred poets of the seventeenth century. Schelling finds much in common between the two poets: "Herbert and Crashaw were both good scholars; Herbert knew the world and put it aside as vanity; Crashaw could never have been of the world; his was a nature alien to it." Despite this, though, Schelling finds more warmth in Crashaw's work; and though Schelling praises the self-restraint that Herbert exercises and Crashaw often lacks, "But if Herbert has never fallen into Crashaw's extravagances, he is equally incapable of his inspired, rhapsodic flights." Schelling's essay is of enormous use in looking at the two men whose work perhaps most influenced Crashaw—first Donne, an indirect influence by beginning the metaphysical line of poetry, and Herbert, who was Crashaw's poetic inspiration and mentor.

It is an error to regard the Caroline conceit as wholly referable to Donne's irresponsible use of figure. It is neither so limited and abstract in the range of phenomena chosen for figurative illustration, so unconcerned with the recognition of the outward world, nor so completely referable to the intellectualization of emotion. Let us take a typical passage of Donne:

But, O, alas! so long, so far
    Our bodies why do we forbear?
They are ours, though not we; we are
    The intelligences, they the spheres;
We owe them thanks, because they thus
    Did us to us at first convey,
Yielded their senses' force to us,
    Nor are dross to us but alloy.

On man heaven's influence works not so,
  But that it first imprints the air;
For soul into the soul may flow
Though it to body first repair.[1]

This passage is subtle, almost dialectic. A keen, sinuous, reasoning mind is playing with its powers. Except for the implied personification of the body regarded apart from the soul, the language is free from figure; there is no confusion of thought. There is the distinctively Donnian employment of ideas derived from physical and speculative science: the body is the 'sphere' or superficies which includes within it the soul, a term of the old astro-philosophy; the body is not 'dross' but an 'alloy,' alchemical terms; the 'influence' of heaven is the use of that word in an astrological sense, meaning "the radiation of power from the stars in certain positions or collections affecting human actions and destinies"; and lastly, the phrase "imprints the air" involves an idea of the old philosophy, by which "sensuous perception is explained by effluxes of atoms from the things perceived whereby images are produced ('imprinted') which strike our senses." Donne subtly transfers this purely physical conception to the transference of divine influences.[2] On the other hand, take this, the one flagging stanza of Crashaw's otherwise noble "Hymn of the Nativity." The Virgin is spoken of, and represented with the Child, who is addressed by the poet:

She sings thy tears asleep, and dips
  Her kisses in thy weeping eye;
She spreads the red leaves of thy lips,
  That in their buds yet blushing lie.
She 'gainst those mother diamonds tries
The points of her young eagle's eyes.[3]

This difficult passage may perhaps be thus explained: the Virgin sings to her babe until, falling asleep, his tears cease to flow. "And dips her kisses in thy weeping eye," she kisses lightly his eyes, suffused with tears. Here the lightness of the kiss and the over-brimming fullness of the eyes suggest the hyperbole and the implied metaphor, which likens the kiss to something lightly dipped into a stream. "She spreads the red leaves of thy lips," i.e., kisses the child's lips, which lie lightly apart in infantile sleep, and which are like *rosebuds* in their color and in their childish undevelopment. "Mother diamonds" are the eyes of the Virgin, bright as diamonds and resembling those of the child. "Points" are the rays or beams of the eye, which, according to the old physics, passed, in vision, from one eye to another. Lastly, the eyes of the child are likened to those of a young eagle, and the Virgin tests them against her own as the mother eagle is supposed to test her nestling's eyes against the sun.

Leaving out the figure involved in 'points,' which is Donnian and probably wholly due to the fashion set by him, this passage of Crashaw is inspired, not by the intellect, which clears and distinguishes objects, but by passion, which blends and confuses them. The language is one mass of involved and tangled figure, in which similarity suggests similarity in objects contemplated and intensely visualized—not in abstractions incapable of visualization. Donne fetches his images from the byways of mediaeval science and metaphysic and intellectualizes them in the process. Crashaw derives his imagery from the impetus of his feelings and from an intense visualization of the outer world, which causes him to revel in light, color, motion, and space. He at times confuses his images in a pregnancy of thought that involves a partial obscuration of the thing to be figured. These two methods are at the very poles from each other, and incapable of derivation, the one from the other. But if the difficulties of Donne are largely due to subtlety of thought, and those of Crashaw to impetus of feeling, the figures of the lesser poets may often be referred to a striving after original effect, an ingenious pursuit of similitudes in things repugnant, that amounts to a notorious vice of style. The books are full of illustrations of this false taste, and it is easy to find them in the verse of Quarles, Cartwright, Crashaw, Lovelace, and Davenant; even in Carew, Herbert, and Vaughan. . .

In 1646 appeared *Steps to the Temple,* with a few secular poems under the sub-title, *The Delights of the Muses,* by Richard Crashaw. The *Steps* was so named in modest reference and relation to Herbert's *Temple,* which was Crashaw's immediate inspiration. Crashaw while a student at Cambridge came under influences which, considering the difference in the two ages, are not incomparable to the Oxford or Tractarian Movement of our own century. In the fervent and pious life of Nicholas Ferrar, into whose hands we have already seen the dying Herbert confiding his poetry, Crashaw found much to emulate and admire. Ferrar, notable in science, and a successful man of affairs, forsook the world and formed, with his kinfolk about him, a small religious community at Little Giddings in Huntingdonshire, where he sought to lead a spiritual life in accord with the principles of the Anglican Church. Predisposed as was Crashaw to that intense and sensuous visualization of spiritual emotion which has characterized the saints and fathers of the Roman Church in many ages, in the life of Saint Theresa the poet found his ideal and his hope. His artistic temperament had led him early "to denounce those who disassociate art from religious worship"; the charity and benignity of his temper caused him equally to oppose those who made an attack upon the papacy an article of faith. It is easy to see how this attitude, under the spiritual influence of such men as Herbert, Robert Shelford, and Ferrar, should gradually have led Crashaw, with the help of some added political impetus, over to the old faith. This impetus came in the form of the parliamentary act by which it was provided that all monuments of superstition be removed from the churches and that the fellows of the universities be required to take the oath of the Solemn League and Covenant. On the enforcement of this act against Peterhouse, Crashaw's own college, and the consequent desecration of its beautiful chapel, Crashaw indignantly refused the League and Covenant, and was expelled from his fellowship. Before long he withdrew to Paris, where he met Cowley. Crashaw died in Italy a few years later, a priest of the Church of Rome. The picture of Cowley, the fair-minded, meditative Epicurean, befriending the young enthusiast, when both were in exile, is pleasant to dwell upon.

The relation of Crashaw to Herbert, save for his discipleship, which changed very little Crashaw's distinctive traits, is much that of Herrick and Carew. Herbert and Crashaw were both good scholars; Herbert knew the world and put it aside as vanity; Crashaw could never have been of the world; his was a nature alien to it, and yet there is a greater warmth in Crashaw than in Herbert. Crashaw turns the passions of earth to worship and identifies the spiritual and the material in his devotion; Herbert has the Puritan spirit within him, which is troubled in the contemplation of earthly vanities, and struggles to rise above and beyond them. It is the antithesis of Protestantism and Roman Catholicism, an antithesis which we can understand better if we can bring ourselves to sympathize with each than if we seek to throw ourselves into an attitude of attack or defense of either.

In matter of poetic style, too, despite his quips and conceits, and despite the fact that with him, as with many devotional poets, execution waits upon the thought and often comes limpingly after, Herbert is far more self-restrained, and his poetry of more uniform workmanship and excellence. But if Herbert has never fallen into Crashaw's extravagances, he is equally incapable of his inspired, rhapsodic flights. Herbert felt the beauties of this visible world and has some delicate touches of appreciation, as where he says:

I wish I were a tree
For sure then I should grow
To fruit or shade; at least some bird would trust
Her household to me, and I should be just.[4]

Crashaw knows less of the concrete objects of the world, but is a creature of light and atmosphere, and revels in color and the gorgeousness thereof. Crashaw often rhapsodizes without bridle, and is open at times to grave criticism on the score of taste. It is for these shortcomings that he has been, time out of mind, the stock example of the dreadful things into which the ill-regulated poetical fancy may fall. The "sister baths" and "portable oceans" of *Magdalene are* easily ridiculed, but it is almost as easy, while ridiculing these distortions of fancy, to forget the luminousness and radiance, the uncommon imaginative power and volatility of mind—if I may venture the term—of this devout Shelley of the reign of Charles I.

Notes
1. "The Ecstasy," ed. 1650, p. 43.
2. See Ueberweg's *History of Philosophy,* I, 71.
3. See Felix Schelling, *A Book of Seventeenth Century Lyrics,* 1899, p. 113.
4. Herbert, ed. Grosart, p. 40.

> —Felix E. Schelling, From "Introduction,"
> *A Book of Seventeenth Century Lyrics,*
> 1899, pp. xxx–xxxiii, li–liii

H.C. Beeching "Introduction" (1905)

In the following selection, Beeching briefly examines numerous of Crashaw's works from both *Steps to the Temple* and *Delights of the Muses* (the latter of which, Beeching laments, is far inferior to the former.) Readers will perhaps find it most useful to know which works Beeching discusses below, with a brief addition of what Beeching writes about that piece, when relevant. Readers can then seek out the relevant works they are examining and uncover for themselves what Beeching says about them. The works are: the dedication to the Countess of Denbigh that begins *Steps to the Temple* (Beeching discusses the possible reasons for a second, longer version of this piece having been more recently uncovered); "Hymn to St. Teresa" and "The Flaming Heart" (both of which Beeching greatly admires); "To the Name above every Name"

(Beeching writes, "It is full of good things"); "Charitas Nimia" ("turgid
... and dull"); "In the Holy Nativity of our Lord" (Beeching calls this "the
Christmas poem ... full of happy expressions and ideas"); *Office of the
Holy Crosse*; *Suspicion of Herod* (these last two are translations); "The
Weeper" (Beeching directly addresses Gosse's criticisms of this poem
in the longest section in the text excerpted below); "Wishes to his (supposed) Mistress" (Beeching calls this piece the "best" of Crashaw's secular works); "Music's Duel" ("rather a tour de force than a very successful
or pleasing poem"); "Epitaph on a Young Married Couple;" and lastly
"Love's Horoscope" ("an even finer piece of writing" than the "Epitaph").
Beeching concludes that "Crashaw was certainly wanting in the architectonics of poetry ... [and] certainly he was given to vain repetitions. But
he had imagination and he had passion."

The most interesting feature of *(Steps to the Temple)* . . . is the dedicatory
poem to the Countess of Denbigh "against irresolution in religion" and still
more interesting is the fact that a revised and enlarged version of this exists
in a single copy in the British Museum, bearing the imprint "London," but
with no publisher's name, and with a manuscript note in a contemporary
hand, marking the date of publication as 23 Sext. (*i.e.* August) 1653. It may
have been that Crashaw revised the poem after leaving Paris, and sent his
corrected MS. to the Countess or to Cowley, without sending a copy to his
editor; or it may have been that Car mislaid the revised copy, and recovered
it too late for publication in the volume. But it is idle to conjecture. Turnbull
noted the existence of this second version, but it was not reprinted until Dr
Grosart included it in his private issue (1874). It is in Crashaw's happiest
vein. The suggestion that the lady addressed is sure to come over to the
writer's side by-and-bye, and so is guilty now of the sin of delay, is a sufficiently
subtle weapon in controversy; but how poetically subtle is the expression
Crashaw gives it:

Who grants at last, a great while tried,—
And did his best,—to have denied.

Having assumed that Rome is her destined haven, he chides her
for not emulating the urgency of all natural things, which, as Bacon says,
"move violently to their place." But the climax of the poem is the ironical
suggestion of reasons for man's reluctance to be saved, passing into a
passionate enunciation of the great Christian dogma of the love which
prompted the Incarnation.

All things swear friends to Fair and Good,
Yea suitours; man alone is woo'd,
Tediously woo'd and hardly won,
Only not slow to be undone.
As if the bargain had been driven
So hardly betwixt Earth and Heaven;
Our God would thrive too fast, and be
Too much a gainer by't, should we
Our purchas'd selves too soon bestow.
On Him, who has not lov'd us so.
When love of us called Him to see
If we'd vouchsafe His company,
He left His father's court, and came
Lightly as a lambent flame,
Leaping upon the hills, to be
The humble king of you and me.

I know nothing in devotional poetry finer than this. The best known of the religious poems is the "Hymn to St. Teresa," which has been praised by every critic—by Coleridge amongst the number; and praise can hardly be too high for it. From first to last the inspiration does not flag, but passes with sure success from the tender humour and pathos in which the child's ardour for martyrdom is told, to the ecstatic picture of the mystical martrydom that does await her, followed by the calm bliss of the beatific vision. This poem is succeeded by an Apology for its being written "when the author was among the Protestants," but Protestantism is not referred to in it. Rather it is an apology to Englishmen for praising a Spaniard, and to Spaniards for writing in English. In the second edition (1648), the Apology embraces both the Hymn and a poem called "The Flaming Heart," which was added to that volume and needs more than all the apology that can be made for it. For seventy lines the writer discourses with a pitiful want of taste upon a picture of Saint Teresa, "with a seraphim beside her," to the general effect that the saint is the better seraph of the two. But in the edition of 1652 twenty-four lines are added, which have nothing to do with the picture, but are a passionate invocation of the saint herself. The first eight of these seem to have been written in order to connect the new with the old, but they barely serve their purpose; for the purple passage beginning, "O thou undaunted daughter of desires," is as far superior to them as they are to the old poem. In fact, these glowing verses may well be recognised as the highest achievement of the Muse of religious ecstasy.[1]

The most ambitious of the religious poems, and the one which the poet himself probably ranked highest, for with it he opened his final selection, is the hymn "To the Name above every Name"— an appeal to all the voices of Nature and Art to join with him in the great celebration. It is full of good things. The passages about music are especially beautiful:

> O you, my soul's most certain wings,
>> Complaining pipes and prattling strings;
>>> Bring all the store
> Of sweets you have, and murmur that you have no
>> more.

And a little below wood and stringed instruments are described as

>> Such
> As sigh with supple wind
> Or answer artful touch.

Again how noble is the opening of the final invocation (11. 114–133), and the passage towards the close about the martyrs, beginning, "O that it were as it was wont to be" (1. 190). But with all its merits, the poem cannot, as a whole, be reckoned a success. It is too fluent; there are repetitions both as to sentiments and phrases—*e.g.* the word *nest* occurs no fewer than five times and always as a rhyme; and there is not enough substance in the thought to bear being spun into two hundred and forty verses. Moreover, Crashaw indulges himself now and then in a "conceit" which leaves the modern reader gasping *(e.g.* 11. 132–5). To be successful he needed a subject less vague in definition, and a metre constraining to conciseness. One cannot help wishing that Crashaw had been born a few years earlier, so that at Cambridge he might have formed a friendship with Milton instead of with Cowley. He would have been attracted, we cannot doubt, to "the Lady of Christ's"; and Milton's jealous care that the word, the phrase, the paragraph should be as perfect as choice could make them, would have been invaluable to Crashaw, if he could have learned it. There might also have been some reciprocal influence in matters of temperament which was as sorely needed. But *dis aliter visum,* and we could not have afforded the loss of Cowley's noble elegy on the "Martyr and Saint," even at the price of "Lycidas" purged of its venomous onslaught on the clergy.

"Charitas Nimia" is one of the few religious poems of Crashaw in which no critic could wish for an excision; it is perhaps also the only one that shows any influence of George Herbert. The Hymns upon Christmas and Epiphany, which in form resemble one another, are of curiously different merit. One might have anticipated that such a subject as the visit of the Magi would have set Crashaw's imagination on fire, but it did not do so. The poem is turgid and full of dull "conceits." The Christmas poem, on the contrary, is as full of happy expressions and ideas, such as the line about the snow, the description of courtiers as "slippery souls in smiling eyes," and the stanza on the Mother and Child. Many of the religious poems are elaborate versions of the old Church hymns, best perhaps described in the poet's own phrase as "a descant upon plain song." Nothing could be more unlike the simple directness of the Latin than Crashaw's flamboyant paraphrases; at the same time it must be admitted that he always keeps to his subject and in his wildest excursion never loses the key. The most admired of these has been the "Dies Irae"; the closest version is the *Laudes Sion Salvatorem,* which nevertheless succeeds in breathing poetry into a piece of mediaeval scholasticism; the most elaborate is the *Office of the Holy Crosse.* To show Crashaw's method, it will be sufficient to put one stanza of his by a stanza of the original. The hymn in the Office for the third hour runs:

> *Crucifige* clamitant hora tertiarum:
> Illusus induitur veste purpurarum:
> Caput ejus pungitur corona spinarum:
> Crucem portat humeris ad locum poenarum.

This becomes in Crashaw's rendering:

> The third hour's deafened with the cry
> Of *Crucify Him, crucify.*
> So goes the vote (nor ask them why!)
> 'Live Barabas, and let God die.'
> But there is wit in wrath, and they will try
> A 'Hail' more cruel than their 'crucify.'
> For while in sport He wears a spiteful crown,
> The serious showers along His decent face run sadly
>   down.

The antiphons in the Office deserve particular notice; in the original they are, of course, in prose. Among the translations are included characteristic versions of two Psalms. No one but Crashaw would have rendered "He leadeth me in the paths of righteousness," etc., by

He expounds the weary wonder
Of my giddy steps, and under
Spreads a path, clear as day,
Where no churlish rub says *nay*
To my joy-conducted feet,
Whilst they gladly go to meet
Grace and Peace to learn new lays
Tun'd to my great Shepherd's praise.

The longest of all the translations is the *Suspicion of Herod,* a canto of sixty-six stanzas done, with Crashaw's usual licence, out of the Italian of Marini. As a piece of writing it is excellent, the stanza with its triple rhyme is well managed, and there are not a few passages which for dignity of style recall Milton, who had undoubtedly profited by its perusal. Take, for example, this verse from the speech of Satan:

He has my heaven (what would He more?) whose
    bright
And radiant sceptre this bold hand should bear:
And for the never-fading fields of light,
My fair inheritance, he confines me here
To this dark house of shades, horror, and night,
To draw a long-liv'd death, where all my cheer
    Is the solemnity my sorrow wears
    That mankind's torment waits upon my tears.

Among the religious poems are usually included two about which a word must be added—the amoebean stanzas upon Hope between Crashaw and Cowley, and "The Weeper." Coleridge, referring to the former in a letter to a friend, remarks that "Crashaw's superiority to Cowley is self-evident." I must confess, temerarious as it is to differ from Coleridge on a point of literary criticism, that even though I am at the moment holding a brief for Crashaw the superiority seems to me altogether on the other side. There is undoubtedly great cleverness in the way Cowley's points are taken up one by one and turned against him; but there is nothing in Crashaw's verse that finds a lodging in the memory, as do Cowley's fine lines about the cloud:

Thin empty cloud which th' eye deceives
With shapes that our own fancy gives.
A cloud which gilt and painted now appears
But must drop presently in tears;

or these in the last stanza:

> Brother of Fear, more gaily clad,
> The merrier fool o' th two, yet quite as mad.
> Sire of repentance, child of fond desire
> That blow'st the chymick's and the lover's fire
> Still leading them insensibly on
> With the strong witchcraft of anon.

"The Weeper" is the poem that in most editions opens the *Steps to the Temple,* and it has proved a stumbling block to many would-be worshippers; amongst others, to that very appreciative critic Mr Edmund Gosse, who in an essay included in his *Seventeenth Century Studies* speaks of it as "distressing" and "humiliating" and "a string of preposterous conceits." Undoubtedly it is a poem that requires us at the outset not to be entirely out of sympathy with our author's subject. If we start by calling the theme "a very small" one, we shall inevitably be more and more provoked as the poem draws out its length. But it is the first duty of a critic to renounce prejudice, and one would imagine that in reading the works of a Roman Catholic poet for aesthetic purposes it might be pardonable to abate something from the rigour of our Protestantism. It may be granted that there are stanzas in the poem—most of them added in the second edition—which ought never to have been written, and need not be read; such as the 4th to 6th, 19th to 22nd, 27th, and 29th.[2] But when these nine stanzas have been excised from the thirty-three, there remains a poem which, if its topic be once allowed— it is a rosary of devotion to St Mary Magdalene—should give nothing but delight to the lover of poetry. To begin with, the stanza is admirably fashioned for a "rosary" (by which I mean a string of stanzas the thought in each of which is complete in itself), because it opens with a shortened trochaic[3] line, which emphasises each new beginning, and concludes in a couplet which emphasises the close. The only other poem in English that for a similar contemplative effect can be compared with it, is Rossetti's "Staff and Scrip," but in that case the separate roundness of each stanza is not so completely an advantage, as the poem tells a continuous tale. It will be observed how much variety of rhythm Crashaw obtains within each stanza, without violating the metre, by merely shifting the pause.

> Th' dew no more will weep
> The primrose's pale cheek to deck:
> Th' dew no more will sleep

> Nuzzel'd in the lily's neck;
> Much rather would it be thy tear,
> And leave them both to tremble here
> Not the soft gold which
>> Steals from the amber-weeping tree,
> Makes sorrow half so rich
>> As the drops distill'd from thee,
> Sorrow's best jewels lie in these
> Caskets, of which heaven keeps the keys.
> Not in th' Evening's eyes
>> When they red with weeping are
> For the sun that dies,
>> Sits sorrow with a face so fair,
> Nowhere but here did ever meet
> Sweetness so sad, sadness so sweet.

But, says Mr. Gosse, these are "'preposterous conceits." What is a "conceit?" How does it differ from the legitimate poetical image, the offspring of that imaginative power which illuminates one object by the light reflected on it from another? According to Dr Johnson, the difference is that the latter, though not obvious, is upon its first production acknowledged to be just, whereas, in the case of conceits, "the reader, far from wondering that he missed them, wonders more frequently by what perverseness of industry they were ever found." This distinction, stated in the straightforward commonsense manner of the great eigthteenth-century critic, seems to be a true one, and indeed seems to be the grain of truth at the bottom of the more pretentious distinction between the images of the "fancy" and the "imagination," of which Coleridge, and after him Ruskin, have made so much. Accordingly we may expect to find that, although the greater the poet is, the more natural and satisfying will be the general run of his images, yet even among those of the greatest poets some will strike us by their cleverness rather than their truth, and even in times when the rage for novelty is paramount, some will charm by their truth as much as their novelty. The seventeenth-century writers, coming in the ebb of the great Elizabethan wave, were certainly tempted to depend too much upon ingenuity, too little upon the freshness of natural suggestion; and Cowley's writings afforded Dr Johnson an inexhaustible storehouse of the wrong sort of "wit"; but then Cowley is no less full of metaphors that are as just as they are striking. The lines quoted above are an instance. And so it is with Crashaw. It cannot be denied that when the bright heaven of invention is overcast, he can be beyond measure dull and tedious with his hackneyed conceits of "nests" and "fires" and "eyes," but what ample amends he makes by-and-by whether in single epithets like the *"weary* lids of Hope" or in such splendid images as that in the Description of a Religious House, "still rolling a round sphere of still returning pain." Our modern taste may be jarred by the arrogance of poets who set out with the deliberate intention of saying as many fine things as they can upon Hope or a Saint's tears, instead of "waiting for the spark from heaven to fall"; but for all that we have no right to condemn the result *en bloc:* we must take each several trope upon its merits. Of course it is never the mere intellectual element in the figure that constitutes the poetry, apart from the emotion that has suggested it, or at any rate prompted the search for it, and it is the intellectual element that is predominant in the Caroline poets, but Crashaw's verses do not lack passion. And besides all this, there is the actual writing; and those who refuse to find the conceits other than ingenious, and the passion other than preposterous, cannot be deaf to the exquisite music of the verse.

> There's no need at all
> That the balsam-sweating bough
> So coyly should let fall
> Her med'cinable tears; for now
> Nature hath learnt to extract a dew
> More sovereign and sweet from you.
> Yet let the poor drops weep—
> Weeping is the ease of woe—
> Softly let them creep,
> Sad that they are vanquisht so,
> They, though to others no relief,
> Balsam may be for their own grief.
> Golden though he be,
> Golden Tagus murmurs though;
> Were his way by thee,
> Content and quiet he would go,
> So much more rich would he esteem
> Thy silver, than his golden stream.
> Well does the May, that lies
> Smiling in thy cheeks, confess
> The April in thine eyes;
> Mutual sweetness they express.

No April ere lent kinder showers
Nor May returned more faithful flowers.

To pass now from the *Steps to the Temple* to the "other delights of the Muses," Crashaw's temperament was so eminently devotional that it is not surprising to find but few of his secular pieces of any high merit. The best, and the best known through its inclusion in the *Colden Treasury* (though in a too curtailed form, and from an inferior text) is the "Wishes to his (supposed) Mistress," a poem written in an original and effective metre of three lines of four, six, and eight syllables. It is full of fine thoughts and phrases, some in Crashaw's own superlative manner, as when he speaks of "tresses"

Whose native ray
Can tame the wanton day
Of gems that in their bright shades play.
Each ruby there
Or pearl, that dare appear
Be its own blush, be its own tear;

Others in a direct style of high and simple dignity, that might belong to any of the greater masters; as when he wishes for his mistress

Whate'er delight
Can make day's forehead bright
Or give down to the wings of night.
Days that need borrow
No part of their good morrow
From a fore-spent night of sorrow.
Life that dares send
A challenge to his end,
And when it comes, say, 'Welcome, friend.'

The version of Strada's contest between the lutanist and the nightingale, called "Music's duel," is rather a *tour de force* than a very successful or pleasing poem, inasmuch as vocabulary, though necessary to poetry, is not so necessary as feeling. The reader is amazed more than he is delighted. But an amazing poem it is, and the merit is Crashaw's; for though the story and the plan of the poem are taken from Strada, most of the description of the nightingale's song is Crashaw's own. To even describe the description would task a poet. Mr Swinburne speaks of "its dazzling intricacy and affluence in refinements, its supple and cunning implications, its choiceness and subtlety." But it must be confessed that a part, as often with Crashaw, would have been more than the whole. The "Epitaph on a young Married Couple" is written in the octosyllables that hardly any seventeenth-century poet could handle without some success, and Crashaw is always happy in them.

> Peace, good reader, do not weep.
> Peace, the lovers are asleep.
> They, sweet turtles, folded lie
> In the last knot that love could tie.
> And though they lie as they were dead,
> Their pillow stone, their sheets of lead,
> (Pillow hard, and sheets not warm)
> Love made the bed; they'll take no harm.

"Love's Horoscope," in octosyllabic stanzas, is an even finer piece of writing, curiously perfect in its balanced structure, and the astrological idea is fully worked out, but without over-elaboration. A "song out of the Italian," in a metre copied by Mr Swinburne, equally fantastic in idea, is equally perfect in execution. The decasyllabic poems are not so completely successful, though occasionally they admit of effects in Crashaw's peculiar style, as in the close of "Satisfaction for Sleep":

> Why threatst thou so?
> Why dost thou shake thy leaden sceptre?
> Go Bestow thy poppy upon wakeful
> Woe, Sickness, and Sorrow, whose pale lids ne'er know
> Thy downy finger; dwell upon their eyes,
> Shut in their tears, shut out their miseries.

The history of the development of the heroic couplet is too large a subject to discuss at the end of an Introduction. It happens, however, that Pope in one of his letters to Henry Cromwell has given a criticism upon Crashaw, interesting in itself and for the light it throws upon the eighteenth-century standards of taste. The following extract gives the substance of the criticism

> I take this poet to have writ like a gentleman, that is at leisure hours, and more to keep out of idleness than to establish a reputation; so that nothing regular or just can be expected from

him. All that regards design, form, fable (which is the soul of
poetry), all that concerns exactness, or consent of parts (which is
the body) will probably be wanting; only pretty conceptions, fine
metaphors, glittering expressions, and something of a neat cast of
verse (which are properly the dress, gems, or loose ornaments of
poetry) may be found in these verses. To speak of his numbers
is a little difficult, they are so various and irregular, and mostly
Pindarick: 'tis evident his heroic verse (the best example of
which is his 'Music's Duel') is carelessly made up; but one may
imagine, from what it now is, that had he taken more care, it had
been musical and pleasing enough, not extremely majestic, but
sweet. And the time considered, of his writing, he was (even as
incorrect as he is) none of the worse versificators.[4]

There is justice in some of these strictures. Crashaw was certainly wanting
in the architectonics of poetry, and never attempted an epic or a drama.
As certainly he was given to vain repetitions. But he had imagination
and he had passion, neither of which qualities has a place in Mr Pope's
Anatomy of Poetry. But to speak only of the heroic couplet; let the reader
turn to Crashaw's "Description of a Religious House," and then to Pope's
"Eloisa and Abelard" and say whether he can fail to adjudge the meed to
Crashaw.[5] Pope's couplet, excellent for satiric verse and epigram, is too frail
a vehicle for passion. The recurring caesura in the third foot, often followed
by a conjunction or preposition, and the inevitable epithet in every line
make a thin and artificial instrument which soon disgusts. Crashaw's verses
have far greater variety and far greater robustness, and his epithets, while
perhaps they are over-plentiful, all add something to the conception.

    Another poet who headed the reaction from the school of Pope agrees
with him generally both in his praise and blame of Crashaw. "Crashaw,"
says Coleridge, "seems in his poems to have given the first ebullience
of his imagination, unshapen into form, or much of what we now term
sweetness." He goes on to say that certain verses from the Hymn to St Teresa
(11. 43–64) "were ever present to my mind whilst writing the second part
of Christabel; if, indeed by some subtle process of the mind they did not
suggest the first thought of the whole poem." The student who turns to the
second part of Christabel will be puzzled to trace any direct influence of
Crashaw upon the poem. Coleridge's versification, with its abundance of
extra syllables is jerky by comparison, and suggests hasty workmanship far
more than Crashaw's. But perhaps Coleridge is referring to that portion of

the second part of Christabel which was never written.[6] Coleridge, however, sometimes recalls Crashaw by the richness of his lines, as Shelley does by his smooth and limpid flow; but at his best Crashaw has more radiance than either.

There is a further respect in which Crashaw and Coleridge are alike: they both belong to that body of poets between whose best and worst there seems no recognisable relation. At worst they are both singularly flat and unprofitable and sometimes ludicrous; at best their verse supplies a meaning to the term commonly used of poets, the word "inspiration"; it suggests a theory that the poet is only a medium for supernatural powers to play upon, an Æolian harp for the spirit which blows as it lists; for their best writing seems as far as possible removed from any result that Art alone could compass. Jonson tells us that "a good poet's made as well as born," and in reading Jonson, and indeed in reading his greater disciple Milton, we assent to the theory, for the conscious artist reveals himself in every line. But when we turn to Crashaw we revert to the older theory of the poet as a paradisal creature, "born not made," a "winged and holy being," whose poems are not the work of man, but divine, and though we may readily admit that Prospero would be a more useful member of human society than Ariel, we cannot but regard Ariel with the more wonder for his gift of ethereal music. But besides this inexplicable charm of music, when inspired, Crashaw was gifted with the fervour of a devout enthusiast; and so it comes about that although he has occasionally fine poetry which is not religious, and too often ardent religious verse which is not poetry, yet his most exalted verse is that in which both influences meet. Then the whole man is sublimed and becomes, "all air and fire."

Notes

1. Crashaw's critics usually speak as if the concluding lines of "The Flaming Heart" had formed part of the original poem. Thus Mr Saintsbury: "And then in a moment, in the twinkling of an eye, without warning of any sort, the metre changes, the poet's inspiration catches fire, and there rushes up into the heaven of poetry this marvellous rocket of song" (*Elizabethan Literature*, p. 365).
2. The numeration follows the 1652 edition adopted in J.R. Tutin, *Poems of Richard Crashaw*, 1905.
3. That the effect of the line is meant to be generally trochaic seems certain from the fact that it is so in most of the early stanzas which fix the mould of the metre; also the twelfth stanza opens "There's no need at all," where

otherwise it would have been as simple to write "There is no need at all."
Even in the lines having six syllables, which are the majority, it will be
observed that the dissyllabic words are trochees.

4. Correspondence, Croker and Elwin, vi. 116. The letter contains
also a fairly just criticism of "The Weeper."

5. Pope in this psuedo-Gothic poem borrows a verse from Crashaw's
"Description," which, alas, will not fit its new context:

How happy is the blameless vestal's lot,
The world forgetting, by the world forgot:
Eternal sunshine of the spotless mind!
Each pray'r accepted and each wish resign'd
Labour and rest that equal periods keep,
Obedient slumbers that can wake and weep.
(11. 201-12)

It is plain that if labour and rest keep equal periods, the slumbers must
be such as do *not* wake and weep. But it is easy to sympathise with Pope's
admiration for Crashaw's line. In its own place it is admirable:

A hasty portion of prescribed sleep;
Obedient slumbers, that can wake and weep,
And sing, and sigh, and work, and sleep again;
Still rolling a round sphere of still-returning pain.

6. *Letters, Conversations, and Recollections of Samuel Taylor Coleridge,*
1836. Coleridge repeatedly spoke of the poem as containing 1400 lines, but
the editions know only of less than half this number. See note to Dykes
Compbell's edition, p. 602. Plato, *Ion,* 534

—H.C. Beeching, from "Introduction,"
Poems of Richard Crashaw, ed. Tutin,
1905, pp. xxxvi–lv

HERBERT J.C. GRIERSON
"ENGLISH POETRY" (1906)

Sir Herbert John Clifford Grierson (1866–1960) was a prominent Scottish
literary critic and scholar who is often credited (along with T.S. Eliot)
with reviving interest in the work of Donne and other metaphysical
poets in the early twentieth century. In the excerpt below, Grierson com-

pares Crashaw's work to that of Donne and especially the Italian poet
Giambattista Marino (1569–1625), a popular poet whose works Crashaw
translated.

A more ardent temperament than either Herbert's or Vaughan's, a more
soaring and glowing lyrical genius, belonged to Richard Crashaw (1613-
1649). The son of a Puritan preacher who denounced the Pope as Antichrist,
Crashaw at Cambridge came under the influence of that powerful wave of
reaction of which the Laudian movement was only a symptom. His artistic
temperament felt the charm of church music and architecture, and his ardent
disposition responded, like the Dutch Vondel's, to the Catholic glorification
of love as well as faith, the devotion to Christ and the Virgin of the martyr
and the saint. He read Italian and Spanish, and was infected by the taste for
what one might call the religious confectionery of which Marino's poems
are full. His *Epigrammata Sacra* (1634) elaborate with great cleverness and
point tender and pious conceits. Of his English poems, the secular *Delights of
the Muses* (1648) include experiments in conceit and metrical effect such as
Love's Duel and *Wishes,* and eulogies in the highly abstract style of Donne's,
with less of thought and more of sentiment. But his most characteristic and
individual work is the religious poetry contained in the *Steps to the Temple*
(1646) written before, and the *Carmen Deo Nostro* (1652) published in Paris
after his ardent nature and the failure of Laud's endeavour had driven him to
seek shelter in the bosom of the Roman Church, poems on all the favourite
subjects of Catholic devotion—the Name of Christ, the Virgin, Mary
Magdalene weeping, martyrs, saints, and festivals.

Crashaw's style may have been influenced by Marino as well as Donne.
His conceits are frequently of the physical and luscious character, to
which the Italian tended always, the English poet never. He translated
the first canto of the *Strage degli Innocenti,* frequently intensifying the
imaginative effect, at other times making the conceit more pointed and
witty, occasionally going further in the direction of confectionery even
than Marino. The latter does not describe hell as a "shop of woes," nor say
that the Wise Men went—

Westward to find the world's true Orient

nor would Marino, I think, speak of the Magdalen's tears as flowing upward
to become the cream upon the Milky Way. Marino's early and purer style in
religious poetry is better represented by Drummond's sacred sonnets.

But if Crashaw's taste in conceits is at times worse than Marino's, his lyrical inspiration is stronger, his spiritual ecstasies more ardent. There is more of Vondel than Marino in the atmosphere of his religious poetry. The northern temperament vibrates with a fuller music. His hymn, *On the Glorious Assumption,* is written in the same exalted strain as Vondel's dedication of the *Brieven der Heilige Maeghden,* but Vondel's style is simpler and more masculine. Crashaw's fire is too often coloured—"happy fireworks" is the epithet he applies to his beloved Saint Theresa's writings—but its glow is unmistakable, and occasionally, as in the closing lines *of The Flaming Heart,* it is purified by its own ardour.

—Herbert J.C. Grierson, "English Poetry,"
The First Half of the Seventeenth Century,
1906, pp. 169–71

Chronology

⚜ ⚜ ⚜

1572	John Donne is born.
1584	Donne matriculates at Hart Hall, Oxford University.
1591	Robert Herrick is born.
1592	Donne is admitted to Lincoln's Inn.
1593	George Herbert is born.
1596	Donne sails with Essex in the English expedition to Cadiz.
1597	Donne joins the Azores expedition.
c. 1598	Donne becomes secretary to Sir Thomas Egerton.
1601	Donne marries Ann More, secretly, and is imprisoned by her father, Sir George More, the following year and is dismissed from his post with Egerton.
1605	Herbert attends the Westminster School.
1609	Herbert enters Trinity College, Cambridge.
1610	Donne publishes *Pseudo-Martyr*.
1611	Donne publishes *Ignatius His Conclave* and *The First Anniversarie*.
1612	Donne publishes *The Second Anniversarie*. Herbert publishes two memorial poems, in Latin, on the death of Prince Henry.
c. 1612	Richard Crashaw is born.
1613	Herrick enters St. John's College, Cambridge University; receives a BA in 1617 and an MA in 1620.
1615	Donne is ordained deacon and priest at St. Paul's Cathedral; he is later appointed royal chaplain.
1617	Donne's wife, Ann, dies.
1618	Herbert is appointed reader in rhetoric at Cambridge.
1620	Herbert is elected public orator at Cambridge.

1621   Andrew Marvell is born.

Donne elected dean of St. Paul's Cathedral.

1623   Donne composes *Devotion upon Emergent Occasions.*

Herrick is ordained deacon and priest of the Church of England.

1623–1627 Herrick lives in London, associating with Ben Jonson and other poets.

1631   Donne delivers *Death's Duel,* his last sermon; he dies on March 31.

Crashaw enters Pembroke College, Cambridge; he receives a BA in 1634 and an MA in 1638.

1633   Herbert dies. *The Temple* is published posthumously.

Donne's first collected edition of poems is published.

Marvell matriculated at Trinity College, Cambridge.

1635   Crashaw is ordained as a priest of the Anglican Church.

1638   Vaughn studies at Jesus College, Oxford.

1639   Marvell receives a BA from Cambridge.

c. 1642 Marvell travels to the Netherlands, France, Italy, and Spain.

1643   Crashaw flees from Cambridge before Cromwell's forces; he lives in exile on the Continent.

1645   Crashaw converts to Roman Catholicism.

1646   While in Rome, Crashaw's *Steps to the Temple* and *The Delights of the Muses* are published in London.

1648   Herrick publishes *Hesperides.*

1649   Crashaw dies.

1652   Marvell dedicates "Upon the Hill and Grove at Bill-borow" and "Upon Appleton House" to Thomas, Lord Fairfax.

Crashaw's *Carmen Deo Nostro* is published posthumously in Paris.

1655   Marvell publishes "The First Anniversary of Government under His Highness the Lord Protector."

1657   Marvell is appointed Latin secretary.

1659   Marvell is elected to a seat in Parliament for Hull, a position he holds until 1678.

1660   Marvell works to release John Milton from prison.

1667   Marvell writes "Last Instructions to a Painter" and "Clarindon's House-Warming."

1672   Marvell publishes *The Rehearsal Transpros'd.*

1674   Herrick dies.

1678   Marvell dies.

1681   Marvell's *Miscellaneous Poems* is published.

Index

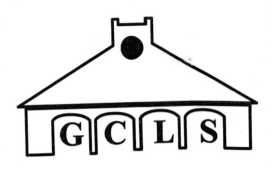

Gloucester County
Library System